B

sociology

Consulting Editor:
Charles H. Page
University of Massachusetts

Alfred A. Knopf   New York

sociology: the study of human interaction

DAVID DRESSLER

California State College, Long Beach

THIS IS A BORZOI BOOK
PUBLISHED BY ALFRED A. KNOPF, INC.

Third Printing

Library of Congress Catalog Card Number: 69-10788

Manufactured in the United States of America.

Designed by Rosemary Wells & Susan Jeffers

PHOTO CREDITS
Marion Bernstein: Part 5
Ceil Coberly: Parts 1 & 7
Diana J. Davies: Title Spread; Parts 3 & 4
Ray Shaw: Parts 2 & 6

Thank you, Joshua Dressler

PREFACE

This text is oriented to two main objectives: to present an academically sound introduction to the study of sociology, and to communicate it in simple English. Obviously, sociological terms must be used in discussing sociology, and these are not invariably part of our common parlance. Except for the necessary use of such special language, however, there would seem to be no intrinsic merit in a fancy word when a plain one is available. Indeed, the excitement of sociology is best communicated in easily comprehended, unadorned English, which conveys a message on any subject more effectively than does highly ornate or turgid phraseology.

I have further sought to facilitate communication by employing some tested pedagogical devices. Persons engaged in teaching will agree, I think, that vivid, effective illustrations illuminate concepts. The student remembers the illustration and relates it to the concept. I have therefore made ample use of examples to illustrate generalizations. Visual aids, we know, are also auxiliaries to the learning process. The cartoons and photographs in this volume are integral parts of the text, reinforcing comprehension of the material, it is hoped.

We identify most readily with things, events, and phenomena already familiar to us. For this reason much illustrative material in the text has to do with home, school, and community situations likely to be within the experience of the student. But since a narrow parochialism is not to be encouraged, other illustrations have to do with human interaction in various parts of the world.

This text probably carries more direct quotations from the works of sociologists, living and dead, than usually appear in introductory volumes. The intention is to introduce students, naturally and casually, to the representative sociologists of the past and present, and in the often felicitous rhythm of their language.

No book, fact or fiction, is ever exclusively the product of the individual whose name is on the title page. Inevitably, he is heavily influenced by other persons with whom he has interacted. In that sense this volume has something in it from all of my former teachers, my past and present professional colleagues, my students, and countless others who have influenced me over the years. I cannot name them all, but I must acknowledge certain persons to whom I am indebted.

My wife, Belle Dressler, read every word of the manuscript, offering apt, hence sometimes acid, commentary. I am truly grateful to her, despite the fact that she did not always become convulsed over what I considered a particularly rib-tickling cartoon.

My colleague, Professor Paul S. Ullman, contributed his thoughts with regard to some of the material in Chapter 2 on the method of sociology, and I owe him sincere thanks.

I am especially indebted to another colleague, Professor George W. Korber, who had a great deal to do with the inception of this book. For years we savored, discussed, and argued sociology, in the course of which he fashioned and refashioned my thinking. Long before I began it, he and I talked about a volume of this sort. He acted as consultant as I wrote it, chewing over every page with me. Every chapter bears the stamp of his thinking, but he contributed most substantially to Chapters 1, 3, 5, 7 through 10, 14, 17, 19, 20, 23. Moreover, a sizable proportion of the cartoons are from his collection, and he selected many of them as effectively illustrating given sociological concepts.

Mr. Clifford Mortimer Crist and, later, Mr. Theodore Caris, both representing the publisher, have been unstintingly helpful and encouraging throughout the lengthy preparation of this volume, and words alone cannot fully express my gratitude.

Professor Charles H. Page has been the perfect editor. Not only has he made penetrating comment on the manuscript, but he has done so with the warmth, consideration, and tact that are so necessary to the morale of any writer. I thank him most sincerely for his generosity and the labor he expended in making this a better book.

It was my good fortune to have Miss Leona Huberman as Manuscript Editor. I have never worked with one who was as knowledgeable, understanding, and patient. I cannot thank her enough for her wisdom and tact, and on occasion, for the preservation of my sanity.

But despite the very substantial and helpful contributions of all concerned, I accept full responsibility for what appears in these pages. I did not always agree with those who were kind enough to criticize my work, and when that was the case I followed my own judgment in preparing the manuscript. For better or worse, I stand by it.

Van Nuys, California   DAVID DRESSLER

CONTENTS

part one
the meaning and method of sociology

1 WHAT IS SOCIOLOGY?

What is sociology? This first chapter attempts to answer this question. Then, having made the point that sociology is a scientific study and that the sociologist employs the scientific method in investigating human interaction, we discuss the point of view from which the scientific method proceeds.

THE TERM "SOCIOLOGY"

Sociology is the scientific study of human interaction. It is also the body of knowledge about human interaction resulting from such study. Let us examine this definition in detail.

Long before there was a study called *sociology,* philosophers, theologians, poets, novelists, and others were intensely interested in human behavior and studied it in their particular ways. They observed that most people generally behave according to certain patterns, but that some depart from these patterns in particular respects under given conditions. They speculated on the reasons for these common patterns and wondered why some individuals deviate from them. They attempted to formulate general principles, or generalizations, concerning the behavior of man as a member of a group. In effect they were describing and interpreting the nature of human nature, a subject that has fascinated thinkers for centuries.

Their generalizations were often highly perceptive but, particularly in earlier centuries, based mainly on logic and common sense, with little supporting evidence of the kind the scientist would demand today. With the development of the scientific method, however, investigations of human behavior took new directions.

It was Auguste Comte (1798–1857) who first applied the term *sociology* to such investigations. Himself a philosopher and the founder of positivism, Comte wanted to see man's understanding of man extended through the scientific (or positive) method of observation, experimentation, and comparison. He advocated that scientific methods be applied to the study of human behavior.

SCIENTIFIC STUDY

What do we mean when we say that sociology is a *scientific study*? To answer that, we must first define *science*. *Science is a collection of knowledge and a deliberate search for additional knowledge through the use of procedures, which we call the scientific method.* Sociology meets this definition. It is a collection of knowledge in a particular field of inquiry and a deliberate search for additional knowledge in that field through the use of the scientific method.

The scientific method enables its practitioner to differentiate between *fact* and *belief*, between *evidence* and *folk theory*. To understand the difference between scientific evidence and folk theory, consider the following examples.

Many years ago in Poland, if a man discovered a white spot under the nail of the little finger of his left hand, he was likely to take this as a warning of his impending death. In Tibet, as a man lies on his deathbed, a lama plucks a hair from his head, so that the soul may escape through the root-hole. In Turkey, a *hoca*, or holy man, wets a dying man's throat with water, because if a soul gets too thirsty as it plods up the hill of eternity, it may sell itself to the Devil for a cool drink. These are examples of the operation of folk theories. *Folk theories are fabricated from beliefs that are accepted on faith.* They may or may not be in accord with fact, but in either case they are accepted without substantiation.

In contrast to belief accepted on faith, *scientific theories are plausible explanations of events that are derived from observed evidence.*

The sociologist is interested in folk theories, for he knows they exert a powerful influence over a great many people. Moreover, what is folk theory today may be established fact tomorrow. For centuries it was a mere folk belief that particular herbs could cure particular diseases. Later, scientists established that those same herbs did have the medicinal value attributed to them. Although the sociologist is interested in folk theories, he does not accept them on faith. He demands evidence, but keeps an open mind and is prepared to accept a theory if it should be verified scientifically.

The sociologist respects truth as an end in itself and in pursuing it stays as objective as possible. How long is a mile? From a subjective viewpoint the answer would be relative to the views of the given individual. To a jet pilot a mile is a very short distance, one he can travel in a few seconds. To an injured man crawling through the desert for help, a mile seems an interminably long distance. But objectively there is little basis for disagreement: a mile is the distance traversed by a ray of light in approximately 0.000005 seconds.

What we perceive depends upon—or, as the scientist would say, is relative to—our own point of view. That point of view, with respect to a given observation, may be largely subjective or largely objective. Probably no observation is entirely one or the other.

In Henry Pratt Fairchild's *Dictionary of Sociology*, a subjective approach is defined as, "An attitude toward a situation in which cultural, group or personal valuations are permitted to affect observation and judgment. . . ."[1] Such subjective evaluations are termed *value judgments.* By that definition, it is almost impossible to arrive at any attitude toward a situation except by the subjective approach, at least in some measure. The individual is reared in his society, is taught manners, morals, other behavior, as well as attitudes toward behavior. He can scarcely assess a situation or object without some reference to cultural and group valuations.

This seems to be acknowledged by inference in the Fairchild dictionary when the objective point of view is defined as, "An attitude toward a situation in which cultural or group evaluations and personal interest or bias are either absent or *so controlled as to reduce their effects to a minimum*."[2] (Emphasis added.)

Realistically considered, every attitude toward a situation

will almost always be partly subjective and partly objective. What we think of as the objective approach is actually one in which a greater degree of objectivity than subjectivity is brought into play. Even the scientist recognizes the practical impossibility of ruling out either subjective or objective judgments altogether in any observation, but he does strive to avoid a purely subjective point of view, for he knows this can create pitfalls to understanding. Judgments based mostly on the subjective approach are founded more on unverified belief than on verifiable data. In the approach that is more objective than subjective, cultural or group valuations and personal interest or bias are controlled so as to reduce their effect to a minimum. This control permits the observer to reach conclusions on the strength of largely objective examination and scientific verification.

Although fact can be ascertained principally through the objective viewpoint, subjective judgments are nevertheless of real significance in human interaction. They sustain man in the stands he takes on many issues vital to him. For example, they help determine whom he will love, how he will rear his children, whether he will fight for his country.

In the final analysis, the sociologist himself makes a value judgment that is partly subjective when he concludes, on what he considers good evidence, that the scientific method is superior to folk theory as a means of accumulating knowledge. Cultural and personal valuations are reflected in this judgment.

And the very term *superior* has subjective connotation. How can we prove superiority or inferiority? Only in terms of standards generally used and accepted in our particular society. We tend to consider coffee superior to tea as a beverage for adults at mealtime. A Briton might rate tea superior. Which is "better," coffee or tea? An individual can determine this only to his own satisfaction, and his decision will be influenced by the standards of his society.

At best, then, the sociologist hopes to discipline himself to reduce subjectivity to a minimum in the course of his studies. He maintains as much scientific detachment as he can. As a sociologist, he is reluctant to apply such labels as *good, bad, right,* and *wrong* to phenomena. When he considers the monogamous or polygamous pattern of family, he does not characterize it as good or bad. He pursues truth, and generally leaves it to others to place what moral valuations they deem appropriate on what he advances as truth.

This search for truth does not mean that having found what seem to be the facts on a given subject the sociologist is necessarily content to let the matter rest. Sometimes he applies his knowledge professionally toward the solution of practical problems. Sociologists sit on city planning commissions; they participate in human relations programs designed to reduce discrimination against minority groups; they engage in many other pursuits where their specialized training is put to practical use.

And despite the scientific detachment the sociologist tries to maintain in his professional pursuits, he holds many personal, subjective convictions in private life. He considers certain individuals good and others evil. He thinks of some behavior as moral, some as immoral. He fights for causes in which he believes.

HUMAN INTERACTION

Our definition of sociology goes on to say that it is the scientific study of *human interaction*. What is human interaction? What it is and how it manifests itself are the subject matter of this entire volume, but you will need a preliminary statement on what the sociologist means when he uses the term.

Human interaction is the process that occurs whenever human beings respond to the actions of other human beings. A girl accepts a boy's invitation to a dance. Boy and girl are interacting. Two men get into a heated argument. They are interacting. Police and pickets clash during a sidewalk demonstration. Police and pickets are interacting.

Human interaction is not limited to face-to-face contact. It occurs as you read this textbook. The author is telling you something; you grasp his meaning; interaction has taken place. You laugh at the sallies of the comedian on your television screen. That is interaction. A man in a prison cell is writing an answer to his wife's letter. The professor explains a theory, indicating he will test the class on it at examination time, and many students put pen to paper. A motorist approaching an intersection extends her hand, whereupon the driver behind her steps on the brake pedal of his car, anticipating that she is about to slow down or stop. Each of these instances represents *interactive behavior*, which occurs whenever human beings stimulate and respond to one another. *Any communication of meaning*, by speech, writing, gesture, or other medium, is human interaction. It occurs whenever human beings are influenced in any way by the communicative actions of other human beings.

Returning to our definition, sociology is the scientific study of human interaction and is also *the body of knowledge about human interaction*. The study yields the knowledge. Both the scientific study of human interaction and the product of that study make up what we call sociology.

LOGIC & THE SCIENTIFIC METHOD

Sociologists use the scientific method in their investigations. Logic plays an important role in this method. Logic is concerned with the connection between one event and another. Logical thinking is not easy. Reasoning that seems logical may not be logical upon closer analysis.

Look at the following statements. Each contains at least one logical fallacy.

1. All people on relief are chiselers. I knew a woman who claimed her husband deserted her and their children. Actually, he was living at home and working. She received forty-seven dollars a week in public assistance for more than a year before they caught up with her.

2. Sorry, sir! The shirts we sell are carefully inspected at the factory before shipment. Only those perfect in workmanship are offered at retail. This shirt you are returning couldn't have had the buttons off when we sold it to you.

3. It must be all right to do sixty miles an hour in Centerville. I saw a car doing at least that, right down Main Street. And there was a police car, half a block behind it, doing better than that, so it must be legal.

4. NOW! New-formula HAIR CONTROL, with secret Factor CD added! Girls go for men who use our new HAIR CONTROL. Look at poor Jim. He never had a date. Then he bought a bottle of HAIR CONTROL, applied it, and the very next day asked Jane to go to the Candlelight Dinner with him. She accepted! You, too, can make girls swoon! Use new-formula HAIR CONTROL!

5. Wasn't that terrible about Harry? He committed suicide last night! All because that awful Professor Gates gave him an F on his poly sci test. Went right home and hanged himself!

6. A man who would grab the last seat on the bus when there's an old lady trying to get it is no good! Mean through and through!

We will return to these items later. First, let us understand a little more about logic.

Logic is a system of thinking we use for understanding and responding to events that occur in our world. As we indicated, the use of logic helps us find the connection between one event and another.

You are about to cross the street. Just then you see a car speeding down the lane closest to you. You do not step off the curb. Why? Because you understand the logical connection between one event and another. Event 1: speeding car. Event 2: a hypothetical person stepping directly into the path of the car. You know that almost certainly when two events are connected this way, in this sequence, death or injury results. You are thinking systematically. You understand *events that occur in a regular manner.*

That is what the scientist seeks to understand. His logic is an extension of this sort of thinking. *Scientists search for knowledge about relationships among events.*

Ascertaining such relationships may not be a simple matter. Suppose a recently appointed college librarian notes that the reading room is jammed with students on a given day. It was never the case before, in her limited experience. She reflects, "This is the week before final examinations. All students, everywhere, crowd into their college libraries for last-minute study before finals."

Does the fact that the reading room is filled to capacity on this particular day establish the truth of the librarian's conclusion? No. She reached it on the strength of but one observation. That is not enough to establish that the event occurs with regularity.

Suppose she now decides to study the phenomenon further. She keeps careful records of hourly and daily use of the reading room for ten years. Each semester, beginning the week before final examinations, the room is jammed. Has she now proven her thesis that all students in all colleges study in their school libraries at this point in every semester? No, again. The evidence does indicate that many students of this particular college react alike to the given circumstances. But it does not prove that all students of the college do so. There may be exceptions. Perhaps some are so confident that they are well prepared for the examinations that they do not come to the library for last-minute review during this period. Others may own the books they need; they may be studying at home. A small minority may be so discouraged over their performance in classes all term that they feel certain no amount of study at this juncture will improve their position. They have given up, will do no more studying.

Let us say that the librarian realizes all this and, qualifying her original assumption, now concludes, "All college students use their college libraries, beginning about a week prior to the onset of final examinations, provided they believe they need and can profit from this preparation."

The statement still needs qualification. She has not established that the pattern of library use in this college is duplicated in all other colleges. The conclusion cannot be assumed to hold for all such institutions. Furthermore, she has not taken account of the probability that a number of students of any given college find it convenient to use a noncollege library for study. There are other possibilities. It is not reasonable, then, to conclude, without any qualification, that all students in all colleges flock to their college libraries every semester the week before final examinations begin. Observation of a large number of college libraries would be required before it could be established whether regularities in the one institution are characteristic of college libraries as a whole.

Like anyone else studying situations involving the behavior of human beings, the sociologist finds he must constantly qualify and refine his conclusions. He should not assert, for instance, that all societies prohibit the slaying of newborn babies with deformities. Rather, he says, "*Most* of the societies *that have been studied to date* have *some* rules or laws prohibiting the killing of newborn babies with deformities." It is almost impossible to make an assertion about human beings that will apply always and to all. Not all mothers love their newborn babies at first glimpse. All individuals do not strike back when struck, nor do all turn the other cheek. Not all persons react the same way to the same stimulus. Moreover, a given individual may react differently at different times to a particular stimulus. He may smile the first time a man swings a fist at him, believing it is done in jest. The next time, he may do some fist swinging himself.

We return now to the series of statements made at the beginning of this section. They are examples of logical pitfalls in reasoning about human behavior.

Some of the more common hazards to clear thinking in sociology are the following:

1. *Concluding that what is characteristic of a few cases is necessarily characteristic of the entire class of cases.* That is the obvious fallacy in statement 1. The assumption was that all people receiving public assistance are "chiselers." Because one—or several—out of thousands of relief recipients is a "chiseler" does not reasonably lead to the conclusion they all are. The same fallacy is illustrated in Figure 1.1. The professor apparently assumes that only students have cars of recent model, whereas no instructor is as fortunate. Because some cars owned by students are of recent model does not mean they all are. Because some professors' cars are dilapidated does not necessarily mean that every car owned by a professor is about to fall apart.

2. *Concluding that what is characteristic of a class of cases is necessarily characteristic of each individual case.* Here, instead of assuming that what is true of one case must be true of the entire class of cases, the reasoning is that what is true of the class must be true of every unit within the class. Most of the shirts sold in the hypothetical retail store (statement 2) may be perfect in workmanship, but it does not reasonably follow that the one particular shirt could not have been imperfect.

Research into the behavior of people reveals many individual exceptions to general conclusions. Alfred Charles Kinsey's study of sexual behavior[3] led to the general conclusion that in our present-day culture girls of about college age indulge in some petting with boys. The young man in Figure 1.2 is in effect saying that something may be generally true of a class, but that this does not mean it is invariably true of every member of that class.

3. *Drawing conclusions on incompletely understood evidence.* The individual in statement 3, quoted as saying he saw a car going sixty miles an hour on a city street, followed by a

Figure 1.1
Jumping
to Conclusions
Dahl, in the Boston
Herald.

*"What's that student's car doing
in the faculty parking space?"*

police car that was going even faster, arrived at a conclusion on evidence he probably did not fully understand. The police car may very well have been pursuing the other car because the driver was exceeding the speed limit.

4. *Concluding that when one event follows another, the second is necessarily caused by the first.* The advertisement for Hair Control argues that since Jim never had a date before he used Hair Control, and since he had Hair Control in his hair when he asked Jane for a date and she accepted, her acceptance must be due to Jim's use of Hair Control.

Such reasoning is sometimes referred to as the *post hoc, ergo propter hoc* fallacy. (The Latin words mean: After this, therefore because of this.) In 1956, Detroit had a newspaper strike lasting several weeks. A local minister was quoted in a magazine as declaring, "Some of the laggards in my congregation awake on Sunday morning, grope blindly for the Sunday paper and, unable to find it, decide that the only other profitable Sunday morning activity is a visit to the church."[4] Since church attendance rose after the strike began, he inferred that the first event—the strike—caused the second event—increased church attendance. This may have been correct reasoning in whole, in part, or not at all. Better weather might have brought more of his parishioners out. The minister may have been delivering unusually fine sermons just preceding the strike. These and a great many other factors may have played a part.

Figure 1.2
Exception to Kinsey's Rule

Charles Prostone (ed.). *A Cartoon Guide to the Kinsey Report*. New York: Avon Publications, Inc.

"According to Kinsey she pets but according to me she doesn't."

5. *The single factor fallacy.* In statement 5, the F that Harry received in political science may have upset him deeply, but it is doubtful that the one factor—an F in political science —caused him to take his own life. As a rule, social behavior such as this is the result of many factors.

Why are you reading this book? Your first answer may be, "Because it is required." But consider. Another reason is that you want a higher education. You want a good grade. And your parents probably would be unhappy if you failed a course. And the college where you are enrolled perhaps required that you take an introductory sociology course. We could continue almost indefinitely. For example, you are reading this text because your prehistoric ancestors labored and developed an alphabet, because Gutenberg and others perfected the art of printing, because you learned to read, and so on. Social behavior can seldom be explained entirely on the basis of one factor.

Consider Figure 1.3. The boy wants his father to identify the one factor that will explain his poor grades. Almost cer-

Figure 1.3
Is It Either-Or?

From the book *Oops, Wrong Party!* by Syd Hoff. Copyright, 1951, by Syd Hoff. Reproduced by permission of E. P. Dutton & Co., Inc.

*"What do you think the trouble with me is, Dad—
heredity or environment?"*

tainly there were many, both hereditary and environmental, that contributed in some measure to his unhappy situation.

6. *The black-or-white fallacy.* In the final statement, the man on the bus who appropriated a seat ahead of the elderly lady was characterized as mean through and through. We have a tendency to classify people and things in rigid categories. Individuals are, by this line of reasoning, out-and-out rascals or models of virtue. They are brilliant or feeble-minded, well informed or ignorant. The fact is that behavior does not conform to the black-or-white, either-or pattern. Human beings are part good, part bad, by whatever definition one uses. Sometimes they are generous, sometimes selfish; and exactly what is meant by these words depends upon how the particular observer defines them. Moreover, the kindly philanthropist may be a taskmaster at the factory; a gangster who will cruelly torture his victim may be gentle and loving with his family. People are many things at the same time and at different times.

Behavior needs to be thought of as on a *continuum.* Here we introduce a word very important in sociological thinking. *A continuum is the logical relationship that prevails among things that vary from one another in degree only.* Midgets and giants vary in the degree of their respective heights. In this sense, *height* is a continuum. If we measured ten thousand men, we would find that they ranged in height from perhaps three to almost eight feet. Suppose we raise the question, "Are Americans cowardly?" Whatever our subjective concept of cowardly behavior may be, the answer is best expressed in terms of a continuum. The degree of cowardice among Americans will vary from one individual to another. Some will show behavior we tend to define as courage under all but the most perilous conditions. At the other extreme will be those who cut and run at the slightest danger. In-between will be a great many individuals who manifest varying degrees of what we would think of as cowardice and courage. And taking one individual alone, he may be courageous in a certain situation one time and cowardly when confronted by essentially the same circumstances another time. His behavior over a period of time will be on a continuum with respect to these circumstances in question.

The concept of the continuum is portrayed in Figure 1.4. At least one man does not want to settle for either of Patrick Henry's two alternatives, liberty or death. He would like to find a reasonable in-between position to take.

We can minimize the hazards of black-and-white thinking if we bear in mind the continuum, the subtle shadings of gray between the whites and the blacks.

THE RELATIVITY OF TRUTH

This brings us to an important point of view held by the sociologist as a scientist. *Whenever human action is concerned, all truth is relative.* You may question this statement. Is not something either true or false? Do not facts speak for themselves? The answer to both questions is "no." We all have our value judgments, a subject we talked about earlier. Consequently, it is virtually impossible to observe phenomena from a completely objective viewpoint. What we call facts are based upon observations and standards of judgment previously learned. These standards are called *frames of reference.* What is a fact to John may not be one to Mary because she sees and judges from a different frame of reference.

When is a man too old to do productive intellectual work? A youth of twenty might say that the compulsory retirement age ought to be sixty, or perhaps sixty-five. A man of sixty-five might feel otherwise.

A good way to get an understanding of the relativity of

Figure 1.4
What's in Between
From *Saturday Review*, July 10, 1965. Reproduced by permission of Mrs. Burr Shafer.

"About this 'Liberty or Death' business, Mr. Henry. Isn't there some reasonable position in between?"

truth is to consider the matter of *distance*. Astronomers use the light-year as a unit of measurement. It is the distance a ray of light, moving at approximately 186,000 miles per second, will travel in one year. From the astronomer's frame of reference this is a relatively short distance. He knows that errors of a few light-years are bound to creep into his calculations when he attempts to determine the distance between the earth and certain stars a thousand or more light-years away. He can only approximate complete accuracy (absolute truth), and he acknowledges that his measurements are only relatively accurate. But astronomers do not consider an inaccuracy of several light-years a serious matter. From their particular viewpoint, or frame of reference, a light-year, which is about 6 trillion miles, is a short distance.

Going to the other extreme, scientists studying filterable viruses use the millimicron as a unit of length. A millimicron is 1/25 millionth of an inch. Such minute distances can be gauged with an instrument called an electron microscope, which has such great magnifying power that it makes the surface of the most highly polished plate of steel look like an aerial view of the Rocky Mountains.

You may believe that this millimicron represents a very short distance. However, the scientist who uses it as a unit of measurement thinks otherwise. A few millimicrons one way or the other frequently enable him to determine the kind of virus with which he is dealing. Since diseases caused by viruses now appear to be responsible for a great deal of human suffering and death, this type of knowledge may ultimately help solve some serious problems. Viewed in this frame of reference, a millimicron is not a short distance—any more than a light-year is a long distance from the point of view of the astronomer. Each is an appropriate unit for measuring distance in terms of the needs of the respective sciences.

Turning to sociology, suppose we ask an acquaintance to jot down a few simple, obvious truths about himself and the world in which he lives. He responds, "I am writing with a pencil. It is a hot day. I am a young man. I am a frank, moral person. As an American, I have the right to enjoy life, liberty, and the pursuit of happiness."

Are these indeed obvious truths?

"I am writing with a pencil." What is a pencil? To most of us it is a writing instrument. To a nursery school child it may be a club for pounding his classmate. The pencil is defined in the frame of reference in which each of us has learned to view and judge its functional value. Its utility is relative to our respective backgrounds of learning experience. Since each of us sees the pencil in a somewhat different frame of reference, it is impossible to use the term to transmit truth with absolute precision.

"It is a hot day." A visitor from Haiti might consider it cool.

Our informant tells us he is a young man. What does the word "young" mean? The person making the statement evidently considers himself young in comparison to other men he knows. If he is twenty, he may view himself as young against a man of fifty, whom he may consider old. The person who is fifty might not accept that judgment, calling himself young in comparison to people the age of his father. Someone wisely remarked that an elderly person is anyone ten years older than oneself.

The "young man" states as obvious truth that he is frank. If frankness is taken to mean "saying exactly what one thinks," it is questionable whether, in given situations, he knows or can express in words exactly what he thinks. Moreover, to speak with complete and undeviating frankness calls for great intestinal fortitude. It is easy for him to tell a friend she looks lovely if he thinks she does. He will have little difficulty acknowledging he enjoyed someone's company if he in fact did. But will he tell his hostess he was terribly bored at her party? Or that the steak she served was tough? Will he inform an instructor that he thinks his lectures are bumbling and superficial? Will he tell the boy sitting beside him in class that he believes his shoulder-length hair makes him look ridiculous? We all learn to be only relatively frank. The degree of frankness any of us can achieve is relative to, or depends upon, our own definition of frankness and the circumstances confronting us at the particular moment.

Our informant asserted he is a moral person. Exactly what does *moral* mean to him? Would you define the word as he does? Some people in our society consider dancing and drinking immoral; others do not. And morality is defined differently according to the society. Our young man who says he is a moral person may consider it immoral for a male and female to live together and have sexual intercourse unless they are married. In Polynesian society, when anthropologist Margaret Mead studied it, marriage was not considered an essential in such arrangements.

Now let us consider the statement, "As an American I have the right to enjoy life, liberty, and the pursuit of happiness." All these words have variable definitions, depending upon the frame of reference in which they are judged. A Japanese scholar attempted to interpret the words "life, liberty, and the pursuit of happiness" so they could be understood by his countrymen. He finally wrote that the words mean "license to commit lustful pleasure."[5]

We have considered the relativity of meaning of only a few words in our language, but the generalization that truth is a relative matter applies to all of the propositions ever expressed by human beings. Each is subject to flexible interpretation, each is defined in terms of a particular frame of reference. Every object and every event that we observe has meaning that can be understood and explained only in terms of other related events and objects.

Sociologists generally believe it is futile to search for final and ultimate truth. That does not mean it is futile to try to learn anything about human beings in interaction. There are general regularities of human behavior that can be studied and explained in an approximate manner. Sociologists hope to increase the accuracy of observations about human interaction and to amplify the degree of truth in their conclusions.

What can studying sociology do for you? If you expect direct and absolute answers to perplexing questions about yourself, your family, or your community, you will probably be disappointed in what sociology has to offer. It will not tell you specifically what sort of person you should marry, nor will it give you exact rules for getting along with people. It will not enable you to discover the "best" religion, the "worst" transgression, or the "greatest" value in life. Sociology has no ready solution for many of the problems you may face from time to time.

But although the solution of personal problems may not be found in sociological literature, the study of sociology can give you a better understanding of human behavior generally, and through this you may be able to work out your own solutions. The literature of sociology sheds light on how people behave, how they may be expected to behave under given conditions, how they came to think, feel, and believe as they do.

Suppose you learn that persons with certain traits have a greater statistical chance of contracting a successful marriage than those who do not possess those traits. This may help you decide whether you want to marry a particular person in whom you are romantically interested. If you are made aware that Negroes have the same range of intelligence as whites, this may resolve the question you may have in your mind as to whether Negroes, as a group, are intellectually inferior to whites as a group.

Sociology is by no means the only study that makes it possible for you to understand and explain human behavior, but it plays its part. Your studies should help you decide what to believe about various kinds of behavior. Do you think persons over sixty can continue to perform satisfactorily in the labor market? Some evidence supports that proposition. Do you think that the monogamous form of family life is an outcome of entrenched custom rather than of an inborn biological need to limit one's affections to only one spouse? The belief that monogamy might be an entrenched custom finds some verification in studies of family systems in various areas of the world. Do you believe members of African nations can transform their economy and modify their behavior patterns through an understanding and use of contemporary technological methods such as are employed in Europe and America? Evidence suggests that an affirmative answer would be justified.

Just as the study of sociology can sustain certain beliefs about human behavior, it can also dispel other beliefs that are not in accord with fact as it is understood at the time. Are Italians more emotional by nature than Swedes? Are Eastern Europeans biologically inferior to Western Europeans? Is breakup of marriage more prevalent among Protestants than among Catholics? These commonly held beliefs can be shown to be contrary to evidence. At least they have been unproven by scientific research to date.

Summing up, then—the study of sociology will probably not offer ready solutions to many of your immediate personal problems, but it can direct your attention to all of the reasonably scientific data about human interaction. It can disabuse your mind on conclusions concerning behavior based on sheer guess or folk theory and unsubstantiated by scientific evidence. It can discipline you to observe phenomena with some objectivity, and this can be beneficial in many ways with regard to all your study and observations as you go through life. It can enable you to make scientific evaluations of observed data. In these and other respects, an understanding of sociology can be of service to you. Given sufficient objectivity and a scientific viewpoint, you should then be better able to solve some of your individual problems, to understand the problems of other people, and to play your part in the solution of problems in society.

· NOTES

1. Henry Pratt Fairchild (ed.), *Dictionary of Sociology* (New York: Philosophical Library, 1944), p. 13.
2. *Ibid.*
3. Alfred Charles Kinsey, Wardell B. Pomeroy, and Clyde E. Martin, *Sexual Behavior in the Human Male* (Philadelphia: W. B. Saunders, 1948). Also, Alfred Charles Kinsey *et al.*, *Sexual Behavior in the Human Female* (Philadelphia: W. B. Saunders, 1953).
4. *Time*, LXVII, 1 (January 2, 1956), 30.
5. Clyde Kluckhohn, *Mirror for Man* (New York: McGraw-Hill, 1949), p. 154.

BAIN, READ. "The Scientist and His Values." *Social Forces*, XXXI (December 1952), 106–109.
The author addresses himself to the question: Can and should a social scientist separate his personal values from his scientific pursuits?

CHASE, STUART. *Guides to Straight Thinking*. New York: Harper & Row, 1956.
A clear, often diverting discussion of common fallacies in thinking, and how to avoid such pitfalls.

CHASE, STUART, with EDMUND DE S. BRUNNER. *The Proper Study of Mankind*. New York: Harper & Row, 1956.
A lively statement on what the social sciences have contributed and can contribute further to the solution of human problems.

DAVIS, KINGSLEY. *Human Society*. New York: Macmillan, 1949, Chapter 1, "The Study of Society."
Expounds the sociological point of view and the value of sociology as a social science.

2 THE METHOD OF SOCIOLOGY

Now we examine more carefully the sociologist's use of the scientific method in the investigation of human interaction.

Having read that sociology is a *scientific study* and that the sociologist uses the *scientific method* of investigation, you may still wonder whether sociology is a *science,* in the sense that chemistry and physics are sciences. Our answer to this question is in the affirmative.

Some would raise objections to this answer. They would say sociologists have not yet developed measuring devices as efficient as those employed in the physical sciences, and have therefore not been able to reduce their findings to very precise quantitative terms. Consequently, sociology has not been brought to the state where it can properly be called a science. Sociologists themselves agree that because chemistry and physics evolved long before sociology, the physical scientists have had more time to perfect their methods of investigation and to add to their respective bodies of knowledge. But those same sociologists are likely to insist that sociology is a science nevertheless. How so?

The chemist or physicist is a *physical scientist;* the sociologist is a *social scientist.* But these designations refer only to their respective areas of investigation and particular bodies of data. Both are scientists, making use of the *scientific approach* and the *scientific method.* Leslie White, an anthropologist, contributes some highly stimulating thinking on this subject. The word *science*, he says, should be thought of as a verb. An investigator *sciences*. He ". . . deals with experience according to certain assumptions and with certain techniques." Psychology is what psychologists do, according to this conception. This, White declares, is just as valid a definition as that psychology is the study of mind, or of behavior. The basic assumptions that the psychologist uses are also those of the chemist or biologist. "We must . . . view science as a way of behaving, as a way of interpreting reality, rather than as an entity in itself, as a segment of that reality."[1]

Applying White's thinking, sociologists are scientists. They engage in sciencing.

However, we need not think of *science* as being exclusively a verb. It may also be a noun. The sociologist *sciences*, but the product of his sciencing is a body of knowledge we call sociology, a *social science*.

What is this use of the scientific method? We referred to it briefly in Chapter 1. We now examine it at greater length.

The scientific method includes the utilization of *concepts*, *theory*, and *research*. These are inextricably bound together, but for purposes of analysis we will discuss each separately.

CONCEPTS

You see an elderly man running down the street to catch a bus, puffing painfully as he reaches the corner. In order to perceive this, you had to make use of *concepts*. *Man* is a concept. *Elderly, running, street, bus, puffing, pain, corner,* are concepts. So is *running to catch a bus,* and *reaching the corner.*

We make use of hundreds of concepts every day. *A concept is a general unit of meaning. It is a generalized idea incorporating an entire class of persons, objects, or processes that are presumably related to one another.* Your concept of *man* derives from your observation of men, your interaction with them, your study of them, your analysis, and finally your generalization concerning what a man always is.

We said a concept is a generalized idea incorporating an entire class of persons, objects, or processes that are *presumably* related to one another. A particular concept, as held by a given individual, may not be entirely in accord with the facts as interpreted by most others. Suppose you conceptualize *newborn infant* as a toothless human being. Most newborn infants do fit that conception, but there are exceptions. Some babies already have teeth when they come into the world. Or consider Figure 2.1. Presumably the servicemen conceive of the natives in their immediate environment as naïve, in contrast to their own sophistication.

Concepts, then, are subject to continuous reexamination in the light of all available evidence. The closer they are to being true generalizations, the closer they come to being scientific.

Sociological concepts are generalizations concerning human interaction incorporating an entire class of persons, objects, or processes that are presumably related to one another. The concept of *cooperation* describes a type of behavior that regularly takes place when all the members of a group interact in a certain way.

We think in terms of concepts. They are products of observation and experience, are perceived through the mental processes, and are expressed in language. When we say *kulak*, we are putting into words the concept of a well-to-do farmer in Russia who profits from the labor of peasants. When we say white-collar worker, we are using language to express a concept that concerns a certain class of employee.

Concepts are *learned*. In Figure 2.2, the child supposedly cannot conceptualize a *corner* because, the cartoonist would have us understand, it has always lived in a rounded igloo, has never seen a sharp angle, hence is unable to visualize a corner mentally.

Sociologists deal with many of the same concepts that are held by human beings generally. They are, additionally, concerned with concepts within the province of the student of human interaction—for instance, the concepts of *culture* and *society*, which we will examine in the next chapter.

THEORY

Concepts are essential to theory formation, but they are not theories in themselves. *Adult, male, family, middle class, wage earner, depression, unemployment, desertion* are concepts; each may bear a relation to the others in certain contexts. But their mere array side by side does not constitute a theory. However, we could use them to formulate one, as for example:

Figure 2.1
Faulty Concept

"Dis is gonna be like taking candy
from a baby, eh, boys?"

(1) Members of the middle class tend to accept and conform to middle-class values. (2) Deviations from these values are most likely to occur when the individuals concerned are under severe stress. (3) A highly regarded middle-class value is that adult male heads of families should live with and support their dependents. (4) Economic depressions that produce long-time unemployment make it impossible for some middle-class heads of family to support their dependents. (5) This creates great stress, since they themselves accept the middle-class dictum concerning their obligations. (6) We may therefore expect that in periods of economic depression some husbands and fathers will resort to behavior they ordinarily would avoid—they will desert their families in order to escape what they believe is the disapproval and contempt of associates whose values they respect. (7) As a consequence we may expect a rise in family desertions among middle-class male adults in times of severe economic depression.

Just as we could not theorize without concepts, so we could not accumulate knowledge in sociology without theories. They are attempts to formulate principles of behavior whereby we may enhance our understanding of human interaction.

A theory is a generalization based on observation and analysis, intended to explain the relationship between events.

Figure 2.2
No Concept

"Little Jack Horner sat in a corner, eating . . .
What's a corner?"

Adapting this to our field of inquiry, we may say that *a sociological theory is a generalization based on observation and analysis, intended to explain the relationships between events occurring in human interaction.*

Sociological theory not only leads to understanding of immediate present events, conditions, and other phenomena; it additionally improves our ability to predict human interaction generally, with respect to the given subject. Thus, we may theorize from immediate observation and analysis that in a group of people who are on the verge of starvation because there is a shortage of available food, individuals will to a greater or less extent abandon traditional ideas about approved behavior and fight each other for what food is available. This theory, if proven sound, will enhance our ability to predict what will occur *whenever* a group of people are on the verge of starvation because of a shortage of available food.

This example suggests that theories vary according to how efficient and comprehensive they are as aids in predicting the relationship between events. We theorized, above, that behavior of individual members of the group would change "to a greater or less extent." This indicates that not every member is expected to depart in the same degree from traditional modes of behavior. It is desirable, therefore, to classify theories on the basis of the predictability factor.

Scientific theory is educated and well-reasoned conjecture based on available facts. However, the unavailability of all of the pertinent facts at a given time places some theories in the category of hypothesis. *Hypotheses are tentative explanations of the relationship between events.* They are in the nature of "hunches," still to be fully proven, as for instance when our hypothesis is that hungry mice will eventually learn to run a maze to the point where food awaits them.

Some theories are referred to as laws. *Laws are invariable explanations of the relationship between events.* An example is the so-called law of gravity. Gravitational pull seems to be present only and always when certain factors are present.* Sociologists have discovered no laws of human interaction. Can you think of one? What law of courtship makes it certain, without any exception, that marriage will follow? When the white man introduces his advanced technology into a more primitive African society, what law states precisely what the effect will invariably be upon family life in that society?

The hypothetical hunch and the supposedly invariable law are connected by a continuum of predictability. Although no sociological theory is law, it does contribute to our understanding of human interaction, and for this reason it is necessary for us to inquire into how a theory is constructed.

1. *A proposition is advanced. A proposition, in this context, is an assumed relation between one factor and one or more others.* Here is an example from sociological literature: ". . . the occurrence of aggressive behavior always presupposes the existence of frustration and, contrariwise, . . . the existence of frustration always leads to some form of aggression."[2]

2. *Data on the subject are accumulated.* The sociologist may collect his own or rely wholly or partly on what already exists bearing on his problem. Either way, in our example, a logical procedure would be to observe persons who are frustrated in their attempts to achieve a desired goal.

3. *The data so secured are classified and analyzed.*

4. *The original proposition is tested against the data and is confirmed, rejected, or modified.*

5. *A generalization, or theory, is formulated* concerning the problem under investigation.

To illustrate with the frustration-aggression proposition referred to above, every element in it would have to be so clearly and precisely defined that the investigator knows exactly what

---

* Actually, we cannot ever be sure that even this is a law. Any so-called law may require revision or total repudiation on the basis of later evidence.

he is dealing with. Moreover, another investigator, wishing to repeat the test, must be enabled to do so by the fact that the definitions are so clearly stated they have the same meaning to him as to the original investigator. In our frustration-aggression investigation it would be essential to define such terms as *occurrence, frustration,* and *aggression.*

The original investigator seeking to test his proposition would next seek data in research reports that concern his problem. We know, as a matter of fact, that he would learn from such reports that many, but not all, persons react to frustration by some form of aggression. Further, that aggression, when present, takes several characteristic forms.

From these data we would conclude that the proposition is not to be entirely rejected. Neither has it been completely confirmed. Rather, it seems generally valid, but subject to modification.

We emerge finally with a *generalization,* or *theory,* which may be stated as follows: *

When an individual seeking to achieve a certain goal finds an external barrier standing between him and that goal, he normally attempts to (1) remove the barrier, (2) bypass it, or (3) otherwise master it. Failing in this, he is frustrated. In that condition, he may take some action that is not to be classified as aggression: He may flee from, rather than attack, the barrier. (Example: failing to gain admittance to a crowded theater, he leaves.)

But instead of taking flight, the frustrated individual may indulge in some other characteristic form of aggressive behavior. He may assault the invulnerable barrier. (He kicks the door that will not open.) He may displace his aggression, directing it, not at the barrier, but at a more vulnerable, although innocent, object. (Failing to get into the crowded theater, he shoves others in the lobby aside and rudely shoulders his way out.) He may revert to an earlier mode of behavior that is ill-adapted to removal of the present barrier. (He stamps his foot or bursts into tears or has a temper tantrum when he fails to open a door.)

Ideally, any theory would include the following characteristics:

* Based largely on Bernard Berelson and Gary A. Steiner, *Human Behavior, An Inventory of Scientific Findings* (New York: Harcourt, Brace & World, 1964), pp. 266–271.

1. *The concepts employed are defined with painstaking exactitude.* (In our illustration, as already pointed out, occurrence, frustration, and aggression must be defined. So must goal, barrier, displaced aggression, and others.)

2. *The propositions are consistent with each other.* ("The occurrence of aggressive behavior always presupposes the existence of frustration." If we hope to prove this, we must expect the proposition to be consistent with its corollary, that "the existence of frustration always leads to some form of aggression.")

3. *The final generalization, or theory, is an outcome of careful observation, facilitated by efficient measuring devices.* (In our example, observations, facilitated by measuring devices, corroborated the propositions.)

4. *The theory can be verified by other investigators.* (This is true of the studies contributing to the frustration-aggression generalization.)

5. *The theory is tentative.* No theory is ever final. It is always subject to modification and even repudiation, if and when further evidence is discovered.

RESEARCH

Research is not separate and distinct from theory, but complementary to it. The function of theory is to stimulate research, and the function of research is to test and improve theory.

Research is scientific inquiry undertaken under controlled conditions in which careful observations are made in order to determine the relation between one factor and one or more other factors.

Sociological research is scientific inquiry into social phenomena undertaken under controlled conditions in which careful observations are made for the purpose of determining the relation between one factor and one or more other factors.

These factors are called variables. *A variable is a trait or characteristic that can vary in magnitude in different individual cases.* When research is concerned with the relationship between two variables, one is called *dependent*, the other *independent*. The independent variable may influence the dependent variable. An independent variable such as noise, for instance, may influence a dependent variable, the efficiency with which a student studies. More than one independent variable may affect a dependent variable. For example, if the latter were the number of persons matriculated in institutions of higher learning, independent variables that could affect this dependent variable might include the geographical location of colleges and universities vis-à-vis centers of population, the employment index, the proportion of the total population between the ages of eighteen and twenty-five, and whether the nation is at war or enjoying peace.

We often solve an everyday problem by a rough equivalent of the scientific method of research. Suppose Mr. Smith, having planted a new lawn, wishes to find out which of several commercial fertilizers will make the grass grow best. How can he solve the problem?

He could conduct a survey of his neighbors' experience in the matter. Or he might get, from one neighbor or several, a full history of his or their attempts to find the most efficient fertilizer. In either case, he is on safe ground, for his neighbors' yards have the same kind of soil that he has, and they probably would have experimented with the same fertilizers. However, let us say Mr. Smith decides to solve his problem by using another method. He will conduct an experiment that will enable him to find out for himself which fertilizer is most efficient.

He buys samples of commercial fertilizers and spreads them on separate plots of ground on his lawn. He leaves one plot unfertilized. It is his *control* plot, against which he will measure the efficiency of the several fertilizers applied to the other plots. He makes sure that all the plots are the same size and get the same amounts of water and sunshine. Thus each fertilizer has a fair and equal chance. In due time, Smith examines the growth of grass on each plot. He compares the growth on the control plot with that on plots to which the several fertilizers were applied. He compares the growth on each fertilized plot with the growth on each of the other fertilized plots. He increases the accuracy of his observations by measurement—he weighs the grass clippings from each plot on a calibrated scale. Now he can decide which fertilizer is his best buy.

In this simple experiment Mr. Smith applied the scientific method to his research. He began with a *question:* Which fertilizer is best? He set up an *experimental plan,* called a *design,* to help him find the answer to his question. He applied some degree of *scientific control,* making certain each plot of ground received an equal amount of water and sunshine so that differences in grass growth could be attributed only to differences in the quality of the fertilizers. He used careful *observation,* comparing the fertilizers' performance in stimulating grass growth. If he had any lingering doubts about his findings, he could have repeated the test, in order to *verify findings.* All this accomplished, he was in a position to advance a generalization—that one way to solve the particular problem would be to proceed as he did, and that, under such circumstances, the particular fertilizer in question should prove most efficient in stimulating grass growth.

The evidence disclosed by the procedure Smith followed should have been more convincing than the claims of any fertilizer salesman. He followed the same scientific procedure that is employed to reveal knowledge about things as close to us as the cells in our bodies, as remote from us as the stars and planets.

To be sure, scientific investigations involve more complicated and refined procedures than Mr. Smith used, but the basic approach is similar: Scientific method is applied to problems that presumably can be solved by research; a proposed solution is formulated; it is tested; the testing either verifies the proposed solution or establishes that it was not a solution in fact, in which case another proposed solution is advanced and tested. This second solution may solve the problem or indicate that still another hypothesis must be devised and tested. Finally, a solution is found, or it is determined that none is possible by pursuing the particular line of reasoning. A solution could be expressed as a generalization, presumably applying to all identical circumstances.

The procedure should include the following steps:

1 · *A question is raised.* It is sometimes expressed in the affirmative, as a *proposition.* Smith asked: Which fertilizer is best? He could have begun with a proposition: Fertilizer B is more efficient than fertilizers A, C, D, or E.
2 · *A test plan is designed*—to try to get an answer to the question or to establish whether the proposition is valid.
3 · *Measuring devices may be employed*—to increase the accuracy of observation.
4 · *Observations are made*—to obtain the knowledge necessary to answer the question.

5 · *The test may be repeated*—to ascertain whether the knowledge obtained from the original set of observations was correct. This last step is called *replication*. Its purpose is to validate the findings.

6 · *The findings are evaluated.*

7 · *Conclusions are drawn*—in the form of a generalization presumably applying to all identical circumstances.

Mr. Smith used common sense in comparing the fertilizers, but his procedures, as far as they went, did not differ from those that would be employed in scientific research. However, a scientist, having obtained an answer to the question, would go farther than those who are content with the findings of common sense. The demands of common sense were satisfied when a solution was found to the practical problem of determining which fertilizer grows grass best. The scientist accepts the factual evidence that one fertilizer is more effective than the others, but he wonders *why*. He wants additional knowledge that will enable him to *explain* the facts he has observed. He wants to know whether the most effective fertilizer contains a higher proportion of calcium than the others. Or whether it contains more nitrogen. Are the differences in growth-stimulating power due to some deficiency or efficiency in the soil where the tests were made? Would similar results occur if the different fertilizers were applied to garden vegetables rather than to lawn grass? Answers to these questions may be revealed by repeated use of scientific investigative procedures.

The scientist is like Hercules, who tried to destroy Hydra, a gigantic monster with nine heads. According to the legend, whenever Hercules lopped off one head, two new ones popped up in its place. With the scientist, answers to a question suggest new questions. The quest for knowledge is constantly regenerated.

METHODS OF RESEARCH

There are three basic methods, or designs, of sociological research: the *experiment*, the *sample survey*, and the *case study*.*

* In the ensuing discussion of research methods the author relies principally on the analysis in Berelson and Steiner, *op. cit.*, pp. 19–27.

In the experimental method a variable is manipulated or controlled by the researcher, and systematic observation or measurement of the result is made. Suppose we want to study the effect of alcoholic intake on motor and mental coordination. Alcoholic intake is the independent variable, motor and mental coordination the dependent variables. We might select a hundred experienced typists and take samples of their output when they have had no alcoholic beverage. This gives us a measure of their efficiency in producing typed copy. We will find a certain percentage of error.

We now administer a fixed amount of an alcoholic drink to those same typists and measure the efficiency of their production under these conditions. We increase the dosage and again make measurements. Eventually we find a pattern. Alcoholic intake regularly results in increased typing errors. The greater the intake, the greater the number of errors, until finally the typists are totally unable to operate.

The experiment called for *the active intervention of the investigator* (he administered the alcohol) with regard to the phenomenon under investigation (the mental-motor coordination of typists). *Observation and measurements* showed the effects produced by the intervention.

It could not be taken for granted that a given intake of alcohol would produce exactly the same results under other, dissimilar circumstances; for instance, if handwritten copy instead of typed copy were studied. However, the findings are significant and have carry-over implications. They suggest that alcohol intake does impair mental-motor coordination in certain predictable ways and to a predictable degree. This further suggests that if we tested fliers or machinists, we would get somewhat similar results.

The experimental method has its limitations in sociological research, valuable as it is on the whole. There are limits beyond which the experimenter must not go in his intervention. For example, he would not subject people to live gunfire in order to study the phenomenon of panic. However, less drastic intervention is possible and has proven effective in research of this kind.

What may be termed the classical approach to the experiment involves an *experimental group*, which is compared with a *control group*, to determine whether and to what extent the independent variable affects the dependent variable. An example is a study by the California Department of Corrections[3] to determine whether prisoners might safely be paroled earlier than they would normally be, provided they receive intensive supervision and treatment by competent parole agents upon release. There were several stages and variations in the study, but we describe only one.

TWO GROUPS ARE MATCHED · The department utilized a Base Expectancy Score table, devised by its sociologists, which assigns weights to a number of factors that, according to experience, are predictive of success or failure on parole. Factors included, but were not limited to, the number of prior arrests and convictions, educational attainments of the subject, and marital status. The table made it possible to score releasees according to the statistical chance each had of adjusting satisfactorily to life outside the institution. The department set up two matched groups of inmates, each containing the same number of individuals with respectively about the same chance of succeeding or failing on parole, according to their Base Expectancy Scores. Success was defined as nonrepetition of seriously antisocial behavior.

ONE GROUP IS GIVEN EXPERIMENTAL INTERVENTION · The inmates in one group were paroled earlier than they normally would be. They were placed under the supervision of parole agents with caseloads much lower than the average for the agency. This enabled the agents to give each parolee considerable time and attention. Collectively, these parolees represented the *experimental group*.

THE SECOND GROUP IS NOT GIVEN EXPERIMENTAL INTERVENTION · It was also released ahead of schedule, but assigned to agents carrying caseloads about three times the size of experimental loads. This second group of parolees constituted the *control group* against which the performance of the experimental group would be measured.

It was assumed that the parolees in the two groups had an equal statistical chance of succeeding on parole at the time they left the institution. It was further assumed they would all receive supervision and treatment by equally competent parole agents. Admittedly, this was a somewhat dubious assumption, since measuring competence of this sort is an exceedingly difficult task. However, the department believed that reasonably scientific criteria were employed to accomplish this end.

If it is accepted that the parolees in one group were pretty evenly matched with those in the other and that their parole agents were of about equal competence, then we would expect to find, after a period of supervision and treatment, significant differences in the performance of the two groups. The parolees in the experimental group should revert to serious misconduct in lesser proportion than those in the control group. If that should prove the case, it would be logical to conclude that intensive supervision and treatment played a part in reducing misconduct among parolees released from California's state prisons, under the indicated conditions, during this particular period. Although there were some negative findings and some that were not fully understood, it may be asserted that on the whole the hypothesis of the study—that prisoners might safely be paroled ahead of normal schedule if the indicated treatment were to follow—was supported by the findings. The parolees of the experimental group did become involved in serious misconduct less frequently than did those in the control group.

THE SAMPLE SURVEY

Another research design is the sample survey, consisting of two separate elements, the *sample* and the *survey.*

The investigator plans to study a certain group, referred to as a *population.* Perhaps it is middle-class American housewives, college students, or voters. Since he cannot study all of the individuals in that population, he selects a statistically valid sample of it. There are several reliable procedures for accomplishing this. The sample must enable the investigator to draw conclusions about the entire population under study. It must be truly representative of the total group.

Suppose the research worker was interested in the food preferences of teen-agers residing in Cleveland, Ohio. He would want a representative sample of Cleveland teen-agers. The sample would be a small version of the teen-age population as to age, sex, ethnic background, educational attainment, and other features pertinent to the problem under investigation. Unless the sample does amount to a reduced version of the teen-age population of Cleveland, the researcher cannot assume that what is true of the sample is true of the larger group.

Having selected his sample, the investigator proceeds to survey it. He collects data by one or more standard procedures. He might have questionnaires completed by the young people, their parents, or both. He might conduct personal interviews instead of, or as supplementary to, the questionnaires. He would collect information on what percentage of individuals in the sample ate vegetables, meats, fruits, eggs during the preceding week. Or the teen-agers could be asked to list foods they most enjoy, in the order of preference. If the study called for it, the research worker would analyze the relation between given variables. Are food habits of children of Italian descent different from those of children of Russian parentage? In what ways and to what degree? Are certain foods in greater demand in one season of the year than in another? Do proportionately more Cleveland children whose parents were reared in the New England states like seafood better than do children whose parents were born and reared in Cleveland?

The sample survey is an efficient design in which the phenomena under investigation can be observed and measured with great accuracy. We could establish quite exactly what proportion of eighth graders in a particular city can spell certain words, provided our sample conformed to the population of eighth graders in that city with respect to the significant factors. But the method is more limited where highly elusive phenomena are to be studied. If we wished to determine what percentage of college students at a given institution cheat on examinations, the data derived through the sample survey would raise some questions. If we asked students whether they cheated, we would probably not receive a wholly frank report. If we kept students under very close observation while they were taking a test, we still could not be certain we had detected every instance of cheating. There are ways of increasing the efficiency of observations under such circumstances, but getting the true facts would be difficult at best. A sample survey on cheating would be subject to greater error than one on spelling ability.

The *case study* design is especially useful when the objective is to study a single *unit* in considerable depth. The unit may be a person or a group. The group might be a gang, employees of an industrial plant, residents of a neighborhood, or perhaps hospital patients. The investigator sets out to learn as much as possible about the behavior of the unit. Whereas the sample survey focuses on a select few characteristics of the behavior of individuals, the case study focuses on the total behavior of the unit.

An example of the method is found in *Burlesque as a Cultural Phenomenon*,[4] a doctoral dissertation by a student of sociology. Part of the research concerned the life organization of performers in this branch of show business. The investigator interviewed burlesque performers at length, separately and in groups. Sometimes they were encouraged to talk "open end," spontaneously; at other times they were asked to reply to questions put by the interviewer. Additionally, certain entertainers were requested to write autobiographical statements. The same method was used in securing material from patrons of burlesque theaters, and producers and directors of the shows.

Thus, in each instance, the investigator had a first-person statement covering such matters as the subject's childhood, education, family relations, associations, sex and marital history, attitudes on a number of subjects including but not restricted to burlesque. The first-person documentation represents the "own story" technique of case-history writing.

The case studies were then analyzed and incorporated into the larger study. Part of the larger study made use of the experimental method; part, the sample-survey method. The document as a whole was an attempt at assessing burlesque as a cultural phenomenon, its function in the society, and its meaning to patrons, performers, and the city in which it operates.

Case material may be reported in the third rather than first person, as in Frederic M. Thrasher's *The Gang, A Study of 1,313 Gangs in Chicago*,[5] published in 1927. Acting in the role of what is called a *participant observer*, Thrasher associated with gang youths, observing them under a great variety of circumstances and over a long enough period of time to make certain that he had thoroughly covered the entire range of their activities and of their reactions to these activities. As a participant observer, he became more than a casual outsider to the young men. He gained their confidence, broke down their reserve. Thrasher's study shed a great deal of light on the function and structure of youth gangs of that period, and also broke ground for many subsequent studies in that area of investigation.

The case study method has the advantage of permitting exploration in depth into causal factors explaining behavior. A limitation lies in that the findings and conclusions are based on a relatively small number of social units (gangs, cities, etc.). It cannot invariably be assumed, therefore, that the generalizations derived are applicable to other, similar units, or to the total population of the category under scrutiny. However, if we build up a large number of comparable case studies, and they all yield similar findings, this would tend to corroborate and support the derived generalizations as applicable to the entire category.

THE NATURE OF EVIDENCE

The validity of research findings is dependent upon the soundness of the evidence. What is evidence? How does the investigator know he has come upon it? Although these questions cannot be answered satisfactorily in a few words, certain criteria of scientific evidence can be stated without much danger of oversimplification.

1. *Scientific evidence comes from a competent source.* Should a child of five report that a man lying in the street is dead, the information would not of course be as trustworthy, in and of itself, as would a statement from a physician who made that diagnosis after examining the body.

2. *Under constant conditions the same thing is seen by different people.* Two medical research workers discovered the spirochete of syphilis in the spinal fluid of a patient suffering with general paresis, a dread mental disease with accompanying physical effects. They deduced that when the spirochete got into the spinal fluid, it eventually attacked the brain, producing the symptoms noted in general paresis.

When spinal fluid of the patient was drawn off and observed under a powerful microscope, every research scientist saw the same thing—the spirochete.

3. *Observations can be repeated and thus confirmed.* Every time the spinal fluid of a person suffering with general paresis is examined under the same conditions as in the original discovery, the spirochete of syphilis is observed. This confirms its presence in the spinal fluid of paretics. It also strongly indicates that syphilis of the central nervous system is the most direct causal factor in the development of general paresis.

4. *Scientific evidence provides a basis for predicting the repeated occurrence of an event with some degree of accuracy.* After repeated observations establish that no one suffering with general paresis fails to have syphilis of the central nervous system, it is possible to predict that (1) a person exhibiting the outward symptoms of general paresis will have the spirochete in his spinal fluid, and (2) a person with the spirochete in the spinal fluid will develop general paresis unless the disease is checked well in advance.

THE COMPLEMENTARY NATURE OF THEORY & RESEARCH

Theory formation and research are two procedures in what is actually a single method of sociological inquiry and analysis. We have already said that theory and research are not independent of, but are complementary to, each other. *The common purpose in the use of sociological theory and research is to explain observed phenomena through generalizations that express uniformities in human interaction.* If they are sound they have predictive value, enabling us to foresee what is likely to be the consequence of given causal factors.

We shall be studying uniformities in human interaction throughout this volume. We shall also be reminded of the relations among concept, theory, and research.

· *NOTES*

1. Leslie A. White, *The Science of Culture* (New York: Farrar, Straus and Cudahy, 1949), pp. 1–6.
2. John Dollard *et al.*, *Frustration and Aggression* (New Haven: Yale University Press, 1939), p. 1.
3. Joan Havel and Elaine Sulka, *Research Report No. 3, Special Intensive Parole Unit, Phase Three* (Sacramento: Department of Corrections, State of California, March 1962), mimeo.
4. David Dressler, *Burlesque as a Cultural Phenomenon* (Ph.D. dissertation, New York University, 1937).
5. Frederic M. Thrasher, *The Gang, A Study of 1,313 Gangs in Chicago* (Chicago: University of Chicago Press, 1927).

· SUGGESTIONS FOR FURTHER READING

BERELSON, BERNARD, and GARY A. STEINER. *Human Behavior, An Inventory of Scientific Findings.* New York: Harcourt, Brace & World, 1964, Chapter 2, "Methods of Inquiry."
A useful, easily understood statement on methods of investigation in the behavioral sciences.

HUFF, DARRELL. *How to Lie With Statistics.* New York: Norton, 1954.
An entertaining, but sound, treatment of the many pitfalls in statistical procedures and the interpretation of statistics.

HUXLEY, T. H. "We Are All Scientists," in Shapley, Harlow, Samuel Rapport, and Helen Wright (eds.). *A Treasury of Science.* 5th ed., rev. New York: Harper & Row, 1963, pp. 14–20.
A clear, succinct statement, showing how we use scientific procedures in our daily lives.

KIRK, RUSSELL. "Is Social Science Scientific?" *The New York Times Magazine,* June 25, 1961, pp. 11, 15, 16, 18.
A professor examines sociology (mainly), and decides it is not really a social science.

MERTON, ROBERT K. "The Canons of the Anti-Sociologist," *The New York Times Magazine,* July 16, 1961, pp. 14, 19–21.
A sociologist responds heatedly to Russell Kirk's thesis that sociology is not a social science.

SHAW, CLIFFORD R. *The Jack Roller, A Delinquent Boy's Own Story.* Chicago: University of Chicago Press, 1930.
An early, still impressive, example of the case study method of research.

STEPHAN, FREDERICK F. "Sampling." *American Journal of Sociology,* LV (January 1950), 371–375.
Observations on the sampling technique in research.

THRASHER, FREDERIC M. *The Gang, A Study of 1,313 Gangs in Chicago.* Chicago: University of Chicago Press, 1927.
Old, but still an excellent example of the participant observer approach in sociological research.

YOUNG, PAULINE V. *Scientific Social Surveys and Research.* Englewood Cliffs, N. J.: Prentice-Hall, 1966.
A guide to methods of collecting, classifying, and interpreting social data.

part two
culture and society

3 TWO BASIC CONCEPTS: CULTURE & SOCIETY

We shall now examine two very basic concepts in sociology: *culture* and *society*. They are so fundamental to an understanding of human interaction that we discuss them at considerable length.

A PRELIMINARY DEFINITION OF CULTURE

What does the sociologist mean when he uses the word *culture*? First, let us understand what he does not mean. In everyday conversation, the term culture has a variety of meanings, none precisely synonymous with the sociological definition. We say a man is "cultured," meaning "refined." He speaks courteously, shows consideration for others, has no vulgar, offensive habits. He enjoys vintage wines and beautiful sunsets.

"Culture" also means the special kind of refinement suggested in the Gilbert and Sullivan operetta *Patience*: "If you're anxious for to shine in the high aesthetic line as a man of culture rare." A man "of culture rare" has high aesthetic interests, a sophisticated understanding of the arts and humanities, a keen appreciation of beauty and truth in literature and painting. He is the "highbrow" lampooned by author A. P. Herbert as "the kind of person who looks at a sausage and thinks of Picasso."

We also say a man is "cultured" when we mean he is knowledgeable about a wide range of subjects, has a penetrating view of the world based on this knowledge.

Also, a person may be considered "cultured" simply because he or she is a lady or gentleman coming from a long line of ladies and gentlemen who have inherited incomes, do not work, and spend their time in fashionable salons and watering places. "A gentleman," Confucius is supposed to have said, "never contends in anything he does—except perhaps in archery."

A person may be called "cultured" merely because he observes the rules of etiquette—as, for example, when he follows the rule of allowing a lady to precede him into an elevator.

Finally, we sometimes use the term "culture" in general parlance to indicate group perfection. We may say that the French are "cultured," have achieved a very high level of perfection in the arts and sciences, and have contributed much to philosophy and the theory of government.

The sociologist finds places for all these conceptions in his understanding of *culture*, but collectively they still do not represent everything he has in mind according to his definition of *culture*. Both "refined" and "unrefined" people are products of the culture he studies. So are the musical styles of Bizet, Bach, Dizzy Gillespie, and Thelonius Monk, none of which, from the sociologist's viewpoint, is "better" or more "aesthetic" than another. From this viewpoint, grand opera, burlesque, rules of etiquette, liberal-arts education, conspicuous consumption, and poverty are all aspects of culture. So are archery, salons and saloons, religion and atheism, sin and salvation, murder and law enforcement, pride in country and prejudice in evaluating other countries. Science is part of culture, as are technology, the idea of building a destructive weapon, skill in threading a needle. Some Africans fear sorcery; this fear is part of culture. So, too, are the Frenchman's interest in superb cookery, the Roman Catholic's belief in the infallibility of the Pope, the Israeli's conviction that he owns Jerusalem, the Arab's conviction that he was ousted from his legitimate ownership of Jerusalem. All these are phenomena of culture. And culture is more than the sum of these parts.

From the sociological point of view, *culture consists of the skills, beliefs, and knowledges that are commonly shared by a number of people and transmitted to their children.* Through a culture we learn to communicate with each other, to behave and think in certain ways.

Culture is a social heritage, transmitted by one generation to another. *It is shared.* The individual receives and shares it as a member of a group. Language is an example; a person completely out of touch with people and their culture could not learn language. It is transmitted only in the process of social interaction.

A PRELIMINARY DEFINITION OF SOCIETY

A society consists of all the people who share a distinct and continuing way of life (that is, a culture) and think of themselves as one united people. A society may be a small rural community or a great city, a region or an entire nation. The determining factor is that the individuals concerned share the culture and think of themselves as united by common interests.

Society is the breeding ground of culture. Here we learn the skills and gain the knowledge of a given way of life. Here, for example, we learn to safeguard children against health hazards, to marry according to specified rules.

Human societies are also systems of social relationships. In the main, these relationships are determined by the culture. Human beings achieve unity and integration through that culture, for its members learn and acquire the cultural heritage, including what is expected of them under given conditions.

As a *system* of social relationships, *society* serves to fashion those relationships into a functioning whole. The outcome is that we engage in human interaction in characteristic ways that are approved by the consensus of the members of the society and are calculated to promote group solidarity and mutual welfare. We educate our children, prepare them for parenthood, teach them ethical codes. We do not steal from others, nor do we kill deliberately except in the conduct of a war. We write books, paint pictures, play baseball, elect legislators, pay wages, collect wages.

The anthropologist Ralph Linton listed the universal characteristics of society:

1 · Society, rather than the individual, is ". . . the significant unit in our species struggle for survival." Except by accident, as in the case of the fictional Robinson Crusoe, all human beings ". . . live as members of organized groups and have their fate inextricably bound up with that of the group to which they belong." They cannot survive the hazards of infancy, nor can they satisfy their adult needs, without the aid and cooperation of others.

2 · Societies ordinarily persist far beyond the life span of any one of their members.

3 · Societies are functional, operative units. Although made up of individuals, societies function as entities in themselves. "The interests of each of their component members are subordinated to those of the entire group."

4 · In every society ". . . the activities necessary to the survival of the whole are divided and apportioned to the various members."[1]

With these preliminary definitions of *culture* and *society*, we now turn to a closer examination of each.

A MORE OBJECTIVE VIEW OF CULTURE

If we were flying at great speed high in the air, but did not look outside the airplane, we would have the impression that we were standing still. This is because there would be no fixed point, such as a tree or a building, and no moving objects, such as other aircraft, against which to gauge our velocity. Similarly, it is difficult for us to evaluate our culture and society if we have no models with which to compare them. Under such circumstances we are likely to take our own culture and society for granted and to believe that those phenomena we observe within them are natural and normal ways of believing, thinking, and doing.

One way to overcome this cultural myopia and to comprehend the meaning of culture and society generally is to look at our ways through the eyes of an outsider. Below is part of a recorded interview by the author and a colleague (Dr. George W. Korber) with a young Iranian who came to the United States to pursue his studies. Before coming to the United

States he had gleaned impressions of our society and culture through seeing American movies. Moreover, at the time of the interview he had been in this country some two years. Although he still recalled his earlier reactions to our ways, he was no longer speaking exclusively from first impressions and was not altogether an outsider. Nevertheless, to some extent his commentary allows us to view our culture through the eyes of a stranger.

QUESTION: What impressed you most when you first arrived in this country? Do you remember?

ANSWER: When I got to New York, I was impressed with all the white shirts. The houses did not impress me at all. They looked like shacks to me. I didn't know you had wooden houses. We have brick and stone houses in Iran. A wood house is a shack. Someone who is very poor lives in a wooden house.

. . . Moving west, the most amazing thing I saw was the advertising. The big signs impressed me. I didn't know what they were.

The food on the train was very different. I just ate chicken salad because I knew what that was. I didn't know anything else. Then they told me what hamburger is, so I ate hamburger, too.

[He arrives in California, enters a university.]

I knew English. We studied it in high school. I went to the movies in Iran, too, and that helps a lot.

One day a lady came to me and said she was giving a party for foreign students. She said I should come and bring a friend. I said, "All right, I come. I have a friend, his name is Guerrero."

She said, "Oh, no! Not Mexicans!"

QUESTION: You encountered prejudices that were new to you? Did you come over with prejudices of any kind?

ANSWER: Oh, yes. When I came here I was very prejudiced. I was trying to glorify—maybe you call it ethnocentric—I was trying to glorify everything Persian. I would make fun of American ways. I made fun of the jazz, which as a matter of fact I like very much now. I made fun of how loud people are and how loud they play records.

QUESTION: The voices of the people in this country, are they usually pitched higher and louder than in Iran?

ANSWER: No. In Iran we usually talk very loud. We shout at each other. Yours is a different kind of loudness. I explain it this way: When two people converse with each other here, they are free and informal, which is lack of respect in Iran. In Iran, when two Persians are talking, they talk very loud. . . . But it is respectful talk.

QUESTION: Would our way of talking be considered discourteous?

ANSWER: Very discourteous. One thing which seems unusual is smiling all the time. You smile all the time. We don't.

QUESTION: How did you interpret a smile when you came here?

ANSWER: I thought it was a fake. Everyone who smiles all the time is kind of queer. What is wrong with them?

QUESTION: If, when you first came to New York, you had asked directions of someone and he turned around and smiled at you, how would you have interpreted it? Would you have considered it stupid, silly, queer, impolite—what?

ANSWER: Well, no. *I* wouldn't. Because now I have seen the movies, and I know that you people are like this. But in Iran, that would be different. The person who smiles is sort of loose and giggly.

QUESTION: Do you tell funny stories in Iran?

ANSWER: Yes.

QUESTION: Do people smile at funny stories?

ANSWER: Yes. They ha-ha then. It's all right to smile at funny stories.

QUESTION: Then there has to be a definite occasion for a smile?

ANSWER: That's it. You know, I still have trouble with smiling. My wife, she's American, introduces me to somebody. Afterwards she says, "Well, can't you smile when you talk?" I just can't.

QUESTION: What else did you find strange here?

ANSWER: Lipstick on little girls. Ten or twelve years old. The only ones who put lipstick on their face in Iran were married girls.

QUESTION: Does this have some moral connotation?

ANSWER: It has a moral connotation, yes. If an unmarried girl has lipstick on, she is a loose girl.

Another thing that bothered me. I used to go to a sorority with some other boys, and they always talked about sex. Girls and boys talking so freely about things like that. I thought it was silly.

QUESTION: Can you analyze a little more why you were sort of perturbed by the freedom, in a mixed group, of discussion involving sex?

ANSWER: I can't tell exactly. From what I had heard about college boys and girls I took it for granted it was their custom. But it bothered me because so much of the talking was with girls, you see. We talked about sex with boys in Iran. . . . But in Iran we never talk in front of the girls. . . . You just never mention sex in front of a girl, what you call a good girl.

QUESTION: What else about relations between the sexes?

ANSWER: American girls, I found very, very aggressive.

QUESTION: What was your first date here?

ANSWER: It was with an American girl who lived in Persia until she was about ten.

She said, "Where are you going to take me?"

I said, "I don't know any place. Why don't you take me some-place?"

She said all right. She lives in Beverly Hills. I went over there and we just went for a walk. She said, "The next time you take me out you will have to pick out a place. It is a custom here."

I said, "Do you like movies?"

She said, "No, I hate movies."

When I called her next week, she said, "Where are you going to take me?"

I didn't have any place picked out, so when she asked me, I said, "I won't tell you. It's confidential. A surprise."

When I got there, she was all dressed in a formal. I didn't know what to tell her. We got on a bus. I didn't know which bus or which direction it was going. She said, "Where are you going?"

I said, "Well, to tell the truth, I don't know."

She said, "You are all alike, you Persian men! This is a cheap, mean thing to do to a girl! What do you think I am?"

I said, "If you shout any more, I am going to get out of this bus."

"Who is shouting?" she shouted.

I pulled the cord and got out. . . . I was furious. Of course, it was my fault, but she should have shut up. After all, I thought, she was half-Persian. She should know that she shouldn't talk to a man like that.

QUESTION: You mean that a girl in Persia would never shout at a man? She should show respect for him?

ANSWER: Yes. Not in public, anyhow. She might shout her head off at home, but not in public.

QUESTION: Did you go out with other girls after that, girls who had no Persian background?

ANSWER: There was this other girl, she picked me up. That's what I mean about being aggressive. I was sitting in front of the library at school. All of a sudden, she said, "Hello!"

I said, "Hello."

She said, "Do you mind if I sit down next to you?"

What could I say? I said no, I didn't mind.

She said, "Do you like dentistry?" Imagine that for opening a conversation!

I said, "Well, I have a brother, he is going to be a dentist."

She said, "Well, that's good! I'm in dentistry school. Do you mind if I read this book to you? That's the only way I can study."

She sat down and started reading to me—for two or three hours. I just had to sit there. She would read and read and read, then say, "Now! Do you see?" And she would explain. And I would nod and pretend that I understood.

Then she said, "You were very nice and I think you deserve a date."

This was custom. I was shocked, but it was custom. I said, "OK, but I have no car."

"Well," she said, "I have a car. Have you decided where to go?"

I thought it was starting all over again, but I told her I didn't know any place, so she said, "All right. We will go to a drive-in movie."

She came for me and we went to the movie. We sat there a while. . . . Finally she said, "I thought you Persians were supposed to be very aggressive people, from what I read."

I didn't understand what she was driving at. . . .

She said, "Would you like to hold my hand?"

So I held her hand. Then she put her head on my shoulder. Then she said, "Well, haven't you ever kissed a girl?"

I said yes.

She said, "Well, why don't you kiss me?"

I kissed her. It went on and on and no one looked at the show. We were just kissing each other, what you call necking.

Afterward she said, "Do you have a landlady where you live?"

I said yes.

She said, "Why don't you just come to my apartment for a little while? I don't have a landlady."

So we went.

Three or four times we had dates. She got me all involved. And then one day she said, "I found another boy friend. Is that all right with you?" I said it was.

QUESTION: Were you shocked by this whole thing?

ANSWER: In a way. In a way, I was expecting it, too, you see. There we go again. Back to the movies. I learned so much about your customs from the movies. . . .

QUESTION: Did it shock you to discover that men were not always boss here?

ANSWER: It did then. It doesn't now. I'll tell you something else. I dated girls, and whenever I took them home, the parents were never there to come down and greet me. I never could sit down and talk with the parents. Except with this girl I married. Probably one reason I had for marrying her was I could see her father and mother. They came down and talked. The rest of the girls, I had just seen to the door. Or if I came in, the parents went into another room.

QUESTION: Here we sometimes consider that very nice. We say that's keeping out of children's hair, not interfering with them.

ANSWER: It had the opposite reaction in me. I wasn't pleased. If a person has parents, they should let themselves be seen. To me, when I took a girl home, I thought to myself, "When am I going to see her dad? Why doesn't she show me?" There seemed to be always a backing away, which I thought was a reflection on me. I thought, "They don't like me around or something."

QUESTION: When you arrived here, did you think American girls were as beautiful as those in Persia?

ANSWER: Much more beautiful. The Western standard has come to Persia. Our girls are trying to do like your girls. They are trying to pick up your ways, and it's a very clumsy imitation. Sometimes, though, it seems to go the other way. A boy friend of mine said, "Look. It seems like Americans are catching up lately." He showed me a picture of Marilyn Monroe. The buxom kind of girl. They are considered the beautiful kind in Iran, when you're not trying to be like Americans, with long thin legs, all legs.

QUESTION: What are some concepts, say such as *honor,* which differ in definition as between Iran and here?

ANSWER: For instance: It's not illegal for a married man to commit adultery, but the woman concerned is the responsible one. If a married man has intercourse with another woman, his wife can never sue him for divorce.

About honesty, it's about like here. To steal is dishonest, like stealing food. But since we are a very poor people. . . . Over there, every policeman is known to be dishonest. They brag about it. They say, "Well I am a policeman, so I have a nice on-the-side income." The policeman's taking graft isn't dishonorable or sinful. It's just illegal. . . .

A man may have any number of wives. There is a possibility when my wife and I go back to Iran that I might take another wife. There is nothing in my way legally. . . . A woman, though, can't have more than one husband.

Things change, though. My parents were monogamous, and they make fun of anybody who has more than two wives. There is a tendency toward more and more families being monogamous. I think it is the surge of Western ideas.

QUESTION: Did you notice any great difference between the countries in their recreational interests?

ANSWER: Well, we don't have any professional sports at all.

QUESTION: How do you look upon a professional football game today?

ANSWER: I think it's ridiculous. There is nothing for me to look for. It's not my school, not my town, they are doing it for money. We have amateur sports, like soccer. It's all for sport. . . .

QUESTION: What did you think of our treatment of parents and the older generation?

ANSWER: I considered the treatment of the old people backward. In our country, the older you are, the more status you have. I see lots of old men here, very lonely, walking around in the parks. They don't show you that in the movies.

QUESTION: Were you prejudiced against Christians at all?

ANSWER: I don't know if it's prejudice. I was born to think of them as not clean.

Certain things I still haven't got used to. The girls. They all look alike. Mass production. The same hairdo, all of them. Same clothes, and they all change styles when the fashion changes. In my country, styles don't change fast. They don't all wear one hairdo. Here, you see one, you've seen them all. . . .

Another thing. Here, people are always busy. There, everybody has time. This business efficiency you have here—ho! A businessman will say he has to end a conversation because he has to meet an appointment or catch a bus! That would be very offensive in Iran. You are very time-conscious. For what?

Here, you have professionals entertain you. Theaters. Ball games. You even go to the Rotary Club and you have professional singers there. It's so artificial! Can't you entertain yourselves?

And your conversation! Always the weather! It's shocking! We never talk about it. You'll even write, "It's raining now. It wasn't raining yesterday. It's going to rain tomorrow." Weather predictions! You say, "Fine weather!" just to say "How are you?"

You talk so much at the table, too. With us, there is some talk, but too much talk isn't nice.

We don't compliment as much about the food as you do here. You overcompliment. I can't compliment the food unless it's really wonderful. But Americans can be artificial about this. "The gravy is simply *divine!*"

You compliment about everything. . . . In Iran, if a woman asked another, "How do you like my dress?" and she didn't like the dress, she'd say so, and it wouldn't be considered bad taste. Here, a girl will be wearing something that looks terrible. Her friends will say, "My! What a gorgeous costume!" Oh, well! That's America!

This young man's impressions were colored by his Iranian culture. He envisioned the people of the United States living in shacks. We were loose and giggly and smiled for no good reason. American girls were aggressive; boys were rude—they discussed sex in mixed company. There were other, adverse criticisms—of our treatment of older people, our reliance on professional sports and entertainment, our "business efficiency," our time-consciousness. Our conception of what constituted dishonorable conduct did not entirely agree with views held in Iran.

The Iranian student ridiculed certain of our modes of behavior; they were inappropriate and improper because, in Iran, responses to the particular situations would have been different, and Iran's patterns of response were taken to be natural.

But inasmuch as he had already been influenced by our culture to some extent by the time he was interviewed, having spent almost two years among us, he was not as critical as he might otherwise have been. Moreover, the American movies he saw while still in Iran served as shock absorbers. He was prepared to consider American girls more beautiful than Persian girls. And he married a girl born and reared in the United States.

Something else is noteworthy. He mentioned changes that had occurred, within his time, in the Persian way of life. Women no longer wore veils in public. Iranian men were to some extent abandoning the practice of taking many wives. ("I think it is the surge of Western ideas.") Persian girls had taken to imitating Western standards of dress.

CHARACTERISTICS OF CULTURE

If we are startled by some of the Iranian's impressions of life in the United States, it is because we, too, find it well nigh impossible to view the culture into which we were born with complete objectivity. The way we respond to given stimuli seems just natural. Yet very little of social behavior is natural in the sense in which the biological functioning of the human organism is natural. *Every behavior pattern in human society is influenced by culture.* The Russian is not born with a biological need for borscht or the German with a natural preference for Limburger cheese. It is not out of biological necessity that we take showers, shave, drive automobiles, and dance to jazz. These behaviors are culturally, not biologically, transmitted. To be sure, our biological make-up is such that when we have not eaten for a number of hours, we feel physical discomfort, but what we select as food to satisfy our hunger is culturally determined. Mate selection has a biological base in that sex characteristics are hereditary, but a particular culture accounts for the way that males who wish to be approved in their society establish a relationship with a female according to a prescribed marriage ritual. Marriage and family behavior patterns are largely culturally determined.

How does this selection of cultural behavior come about? To understand this we must consider the nature and characteristics of culture at greater length.

1. *Only man has culture.* The contemporary sociologist Kingsley Davis writes:

If there is any single factor explaining man's uniqueness, it is this: He and he alone, has culture. From this all other differences flow. . . . Culture is therefore a profound possession that ramifies throughout human life and accounts for all of man's truly unique qualities. It adds an extra dimension to existence and makes human what would otherwise be merely animal.[2]

2. *Culture exists in the minds of individual human beings who have learned it in their past associations with other human beings and who use it to guide their own continuing interaction with other human beings.*

Are we saying that culture has only a mental dimension, that there is no material culture, such as bridges, buildings, and apple pie? Not all sociologists would agree with this view. Some reason that culture consists of both ideas and things, nonmaterial and material phenomena, the ideas yielding the things. We decide we need airplanes and think our way through to building one. As some sociologists would theorize, the *idea* that we need planes and the skill in building them represents the nonmaterial aspect of culture, whereas the plane itself is one item in a vast array of *artifacts* that make up our material culture.

Other sociologists, the author among them, reject the conception of a material culture separate from the nonmaterial. They say culture consists only of ideas, of mental phenomena. These ideas take on meaning for the group when they have been *internalized* by the individual members, which is to say, when these ideas have become part of our culture. If we accept this theoretical point of view, we agree that it is impossible to distinguish between material and nonmaterial culture. A battleship is not material culture but *materiel,* derived from ideas, cultural values, skills, beliefs, and knowledge commonly accepted by a number of people and transmitted to their children.

As a beginning student in sociology, you are under no obligation to adopt one position or the other as to whether there is only nonmaterial culture or both material and nonmaterial. The disparate theories are presented here because both have currency among sociologists.

3. *Human cultures vary considerably, one from the other.* In our culture, for instance, the "eternal triangle" is a serious problem. Not so with the individuals in Figure 3.1. Their particular cultural background does not permit them to see it as such. Our culture prescribes that a man shall not have more than one living wife at a time. The Iranian student came from a culture where a man may have many. We bury our dead in a recumbent position, usually underground. The Jivaro of Peru and Ecuador seat the dead person on a bench, head in hands, and inter him beneath the floor of his home, which is then abandoned. In Tibet the deceased is chopped up and tossed to the vultures.

4. *But although different in some respects, cultures resemble one another to a considerable extent.* In Iran, the United States, England, and China, people marry, raise children, protect themselves against the elements, maintain religious beliefs, use speech to communicate with each other. And the cultures of these nations are similar in many other respects.

5. *Once a culture has been learned and accepted, it tends to persist.* The Iranian student was reluctant to surrender judgments reflecting his own culture, even after he discovered they had little transfer value and in fact might lead to erroneous conclusions about our way of life. He still believed that one should be reserved in complimenting others on their cooking or their dress. Aside from tradition and love of ceremony there is no reason why students and faculty should wrap themselves up in voluminous cap and gown for graduation rituals. We have learned and accepted something that is part of our culture, and while change is not impossible, resistance to it exists at present.

6. *All cultures are gradually and continuously being changed, even though human beings tend to resist these changes.* Iran's culture has changed since our informant was a small boy. Until about 1850, membership in a labor union

Figure 3.1
Cultural Variation

From the book *What's Funny About That?* by the Editors of *This Week*. Copyright, 1954, by E. P. Dutton & Co., Inc. Reproduced by permission of the publishers.

*"I don't understand it.
Why didn't he marry both of them?"*

for the purpose of attempting to raise wages was considered a criminal conspiracy by numerous courts in this country. As late as 1934, a New England textile trade journal, *Fibre and Fabric*, took notice of a clash between strikers and troops in the streets of Rhode Island, observing, "A few hundred funerals will have a quieting influence." But today, laws sustain labor's right to negotiate with management and even to strike except under certain conditions. The battles that take place between management and labor are usually fought over the conference table.

We examine cultural change and cultural persistence at greater length in later chapters.

7. *In the process of changing a culture, members of a society often borrow from other cultures.* Iranians borrowed one of our means of communication, the cinema. Their women borrowed a product of our technology, sheer stockings. California vineyards have largely duplicated the growing conditions and technology of European countries and are producing wines formerly procurable only abroad. Nearly every nation of the world has contributed its unique dishes to the United States, so that what we once considered exotic foods have become part of our daily diet—for instance, spaghetti, kippers, enchiladas, shish kebab. When Louis Pasteur developed an effective treatment for rabies, our own country adopted it.

It is probably impossible to find a culture unalloyed by borrowings. A political orator cries, "I pledge myself to preserve the American way of life!" Precisely what is that way?

The answer must be that there is no 100 percent American way of life, entirely untouched by cultural influences from abroad. Much of our common law is a transplant from England, which in turn borrowed from Roman law and other sources. Some of our techniques of scientific investigation come from Germany. Our country is compounded of people from diversified backgrounds who contributed items of their culture to this land. Our culture is a blend. It is not unusual to find a United States native, born of a German mother and a Danish father, celebrating the Irish St. Patrick's Day by drinking Scotch whiskey. He smokes certain leaves, a practice that originated with American Indians; he eats Chinese food; and he dances to a rhythm partially borrowed from Africa, Spain, and what was Bohemia.

8. *Different individuals of the same society may behave differently in response to a given situation, even though all have internalized certain elements of the same culture.* The girls the Iranian student dated exemplify this. One of them expected him to decide where to take her. Another made her own suggestions as to how to spend an evening together. Most girls he dated did not introduce him to her parents. The girl he dated and subsequently married had parents who made themselves visible and accessible when he called.

One reason for the variegation of behavior among individuals of the same society when they respond to a particular situation is that *the immediate social environment and what is learned in it are never quite the same for any two persons.* This was illustrated several years ago when newscaster Edward R. Murrow brought a number of people before the cameras in his television broadcast "Who Speaks for the South?" All were residents of Georgia, yet they expressed radically different views regarding integration of public schools. One man said he would gladly die fighting integration. A woman gave it as sound Christian doctrine that all men must be treated alike and as brothers, while another woman believed she had it directly from the Bible that Negroes and whites were not meant to mix. One Negro spoke out for complete integration, another indicated he would be satisfied with "separate but equal" public school facilities.

To a degree, culture is transmitted in a personalized way. Individuals with somewhat disparate views transmit them to the young. And young people assimilate these ideas in a personal manner, the same idea taking on different meanings for different individuals.

Another reason for this variability of response is that *a given culture is composed of many subcultures*. We live in a complex society. Our culture is not homogeneous. There are regional and occupational subcultures, as well as those based on language differences, economic circumstances, and other factors. Wealthy United States families dwell in a subculture dissimilar in certain respects from that of families residing in tenements on "the other side of the tracks." Catholic, Protestant, and Jew—and the criminal and the law-abiding—are influenced by both their common overall culture and their subcultures. The physician, the narcotics addict, the prostitute, and the policeman have their subcultures while responding to the common culture of the society.

Subcultures may be distinguished from the dominant culture and from other subcultures by such characteristics as language, attire, diet, mannerisms. Occupational subcultures affect the behavior of those who follow a particular line of work. The miner and the banker will behave differently in certain respects. The very language of an occupational group may be incomprehensible to the uninitiated. To the speculator, a *curb broker* is a certain kind of Wall Street businessman; to the journalist he is someone who predicts the outcome of sports events. When the geographer speaks of an *oasis* he is thinking of a fertile spot in an otherwise barren desert, whereas the physician uses the word to designate a piece of healthy tissue surrounded by diseased tissue.

Just as one may be influenced by both the dominant culture and the subculture, one may participate in and be affected by several subcultures at one time. A street-gang youth may be influenced by his peer group and also by social workers attempting to channel his interests and energies into socially approved undertakings.

9. *No person can escape entirely from his culture.* If our Iranian student continues to live in the United States, he will accept an increasing number of cultural patterns of the society. His personal culture will consist of a blend of Persian and American ways of life. Not even the hermit, living alone in a cave, really escapes his culture. He is connected with it in many ways. He thinks in its language. He retains behavior fashioned by and in the very cultural group he now seeks to

abandon. He continues to experience the culturally derived emotions of remorse, fear, elation, perhaps even loneliness. He thinks certain abstractions common to the culture in which he was reared—health, reason, piety, honesty. He has learned that rain will make him wet, that fire burns, and that some animals are dangerous. As a hermit, he will utilize some of the ideas he gained in the environment he has deserted: how to use matches, an axe, a rifle. Perhaps he has learned to fish, to pray, to kill rattlesnakes. In short, he cannot leave his culture behind; he must take it with him into the cave and carry it in his own mind as long as he lives.

FUNCTIONS OF CULTURE

One way of coming to grips with the concept *culture* is to think of it in terms of its functions. What does culture do for us?

1. *It enables us to communicate with others through a language that we have learned and that we share in common.* If we did not all understand the language, it would be impossible for a chemist to explain a formula to students, for a minister to preach his faith to parishioners, or for a poet to convey his feelings and ideas in a poem.

2. *It makes it possible to anticipate how others in our society are likely to respond to our actions.* We are aware that they learned, as we did, to accept and expect certain standards of behavior. We can be confident that if we wear a raincoat in a thunderstorm, members of our society will not be shocked, but if we allow a three-year-old to chew tobacco, they will be.

3. *Culture gives us standards for distinguishing between what is considered right and wrong, beautiful and ugly, reasonable and unreasonable, tragic and humorous, safe and dangerous.* When a thief steals, he knows that members of his society view his behavior as wrong. A girl reared in the United States knows she would be considered macabre if, like the Sara tribeswoman in Africa, she grossly enlarged her lips. When a man accidentally steps on someone's foot, it is unlikely that he will get a clout on the head in return. He has learned that this would be deemed an unreasonable overreaction.

4. *Culture provides methods for training children to behave in ways generally considered appropriate in the society.* We

teach our children what we were taught. We instruct them, formally and by example, to respect parents, obey laws, get an education, support dependents. We teach them to show compassion for the poor and the sick. Thus we perpetuate our culture by transmitting it to our young.

5. *Culture provides the knowledge and skill necessary for meeting sustenance needs.* From the cultural accumulation we gain knowledge and skill needed in order to provide for ourselves and our families. We learn to be farmers, doctors, lawyers, teachers, aviators, plumbers, and actors.

6. *Culture enables us to identify with—that is, include ourselves in the same category with—other people of similar background and to think in terms of the social "we" in addition to the personal "I."* We come to classify ourselves as one of many human beings and, as the case may be, as Italians, Americans, Spaniards, or Iranians. We in the United States think of ourselves as eaters of some flesh but not of the human variety; we think of ourselves as members of a society in which monogamy is the approved family pattern; we regard ourselves as citizens whose public officials govern by our consent.

CULTURE: FROM GENERAL TO PARTICULAR

Another way to improve our understanding of culture is to analyze it from the general to the particular. What are the components of culture? A contemporary sociologist, Richard T. LaPiere,[3] subdivides human culture into three interdependent systems:

1 · *The ideological system—that part of culture consisting of the ideas, beliefs, values, and ways of reasoning that human beings learn to accept in defining what is desirable and undesirable.* LaPiere calls the ideological system the "mental component" of the social system; it serves as a foundation for human thinking activities. Our ideas about the supernatural, democracy, justice, liberty, loyalty, honesty, beauty, the value of education or science are derived partly from the ideological system of the culture, as we have internalized it.

2 · *The technological system—consisting of the skills, crafts, and arts that enable human beings to produce material goods derived from the natural environment.* Our ability to cook a

meal, drive an automobile, and mine coal constitutes part of the technological component of our culture as we have learned it.

3 · *The organizational system—comprising all the learning that makes it possible for human beings effectively to coordinate their behavior with the actions of others.* The ability to enact a particular role—to behave as a son or daughter, a parent, a discussion leader, a voter—constitutes part of the organizational component of the culture we have internalized. When a number of people are in the process of interacting with one another, they constitute an organized social group.

The three systems—ideological, technological, and organizational—are interdependent and reinforce each other.

Ralph Linton writes of a Gilbert Islander who settled on Hiva Oa in the Marquesas group, taking a native wife and becoming a fisherman. The natives' canoes were personal property and were moored at an unguarded point along the shore. Earlier group controls over behavior had broken down, and canoe "borrowing" was common. An owner might find his property several days later, abandoned in some neighboring cove.

As part of the *ideological* system, canoes were deemed essential to the economy of the Marquesans. The fishing craft needed to be safeguarded against appropriation by other than the owners. However, the islanders had found no certain way of accomplishing this.

The system of group controls prevalent in former days having become ineffective by the time the Gilbert Islander joined the community, he took steps to change the *technological* system. He devised a new kind of outrigger for his craft, its great advantage being that it was detachable. When he returned from a fishing trip, he simply unlashed the float and crosspieces that comprised the outrigger and carried it up to his dwelling. His canoe was safe; it could not be operated minus the outrigger.

The *organizational* system took care of the rest. Other islanders, realizing the advantage in having a detachable outrigger, set about manufacturing their own. Linton reports, "The invention . . . spread like wildfire. By the time of my visit the [old] type of outrigger had gone out of use so completely that there was said to be only one canoe which still had it left in the group and this was on the most remote island."[4]

Ideological, technological, and organizational systems, as they existed in the minds of individuals, were thus linked together. In effect, the islanders expressed the idea: "We must protect our canoes." The recent arrival offered technological advice: "Here is how I am doing it." The others organized: "We will do the same and protect our economy."

THE RELATIVITY OF CULTURE

In some Eskimo groups, when a man becomes too old to hunt, appropriate ceremonies are performed, and he is walled up or cast into the sea to die. Is this way of thinking and acting right or wrong?

An individual's answer will depend upon the culture he has learned to accept. The sociologist puts it this way: *Standards of right and wrong, good and bad, are relative to the culture in which they appear.* What is "right" in one society may be "wrong" in another. Infanticide, approved under specified conditions in some groups, is criminal in others. Premarital chastity is demanded in one society, prohibited in a second, of no consequence one way or another in a third. Novelist Samuel Butler spoke a sound sociology when he declared, "Morality is the custom of one's country and the current feeling of one's peers. Cannibalism is moral in a cannibal country."

The American sociologist Robert Bierstedt writes:

> . . . it is not only difficult but, in the present state of our knowledge, apparently impossible to find a universal taboo, that is, the prohibition of a single act in all circumstances at all times in all societies. As far as our knowledge goes, the norms are always relative to a particular culture and a particular set of circumstances. They are never absolute.[5]

What is "right" or "wrong," then, depends upon what people have come to accept as such. In this sense, culture can make anything right or wrong for the members of the particular society.

To argue that there are no universally applicable moral absolutes does not imply that there are no standards of right and wrong, moral and immoral, for the people who have learned a particular culture. Such standards do exist. Although we know of no moral absolute applicable and accepted in all societies, standards of conduct do exist in every society, and they are powerful influences because they are so generally acceptable.

Ideas and behavior are defined as right or wrong according to the efficiency with which they can be integrated into the culture generally. The late Clyde Kluckhohn, an American anthropologist, wrote: ". . . the appropriateness of any positive or negative custom must be evaluated with regard to how this habit fits with other group habits."[6] If it is alien or antagonistic to other, established cultural habits, it will probably be considered bad or immoral or impractical or unwise. Morality comes to mean moral for *us*.

While recognizing the relativity of cultural patterns, the sociologist does not undervalue the influence of moral concepts upon those who share a common culture. He must take cultural relativity into account in studying human interaction, but this does not mean that he holds that people should adopt no positions whatever on moral issues. First, this would be impossible, for no individual is completely uninfluenced by the ideas and standards of others in his society. Second, these standards, by definition, do serve the people of the society. When most of its members agree that a particular moral standard is conducive to their well being, then it is, for they have tested it by experience and concluded it is serviceable.

Individuals want to survive, and they want their group to survive. Their standards of behavior are expressions of this aspiration. If there is any justification for speaking of a universal moral absolute, it may be in this connection. So far as we know, it seems to be the consensus of every society that it is wrong and immoral to act in such a way as to threaten the continued existence of the group. However, what is considered threatening will still be relative to the particular culture.

A FURTHER EXAMINATION OF SOCIETY

As we did in the case of *culture*, let us examine the concept of *society* in greater detail.

1. *Society is more than the sum total of its individual parts, that is to say, its members.* If we studied each member of a society individually, we would not get a true or a whole picture of the society. Society consists of more than the people who

comprise it, for it has a structure and a continuity. Men are born into it, they die, are replaced, and the society continues to exist and to maintain its characteristics as a society.

2. *For a society to survive, certain basic functional needs must be fulfilled.**

Social order must be secured. This is accomplished by customs, rules of behavior, laws, a system of authority that applies sanctions to violators of the normative code.

There must be provision for fulfillment of basic subsistence needs of members of the society and for replenishment of the material apparatus used to meet such needs. Our agricultural and industrial systems fulfill these functions.

The population must be renewed as members die off. Consequently some activities must be organized for reproduction and care of offspring. Our marriage and family system, which prescribes rules for procreation and the maintenance of children, serves this purpose.

Children must be inducted into the culture of the society and trained in its value systems and skills. Parents and others teach them to talk, read, and write. They are instructed in the morality of the group. They are educated and trained in skills whereby they may eventually become comparatively independent adults.

There must be some system of ritual actions in which the ultimate value system is periodically reaffirmed. We celebrate Washington's and Lincoln's birthdays, have school children salute the flag. We make awards for bravery, honesty, leadership.

There are other functional needs of a society; there are needs, for instance, for recreational outlets and for the expansion of knowledge. However, the five functional needs that have just been discussed represent the most basic of all.

3. *The culture of a society includes a system of ultimate values that meets with the consensus of members of the society.* The members consider these values as primary and essential. In our own society we may safely assert that there is consensus on the right of citizens to formulate government policy either directly or by representation. Among followers of

* What follows is based on and paraphrased from Logan Wilson and Wilson L. Kolb, *Sociological Analysis, An Introductory Text and Case Book* (New York: Harcourt, Brace & World, 1949), pp. 513–514.

the religion of Islam, submission to the will of God is an ultimate value. Joe E. Pierce, an American anthropologist, reports of the villagers of Demirciler, Turkey:

> The villagers do not make a distinction . . . between the religious and the secular. Islam is a way of life and is the dominant factor in the making of any decision, no matter how slight, in the mind of the villager. . . .
>
> The religion is basically fatalistic in that no one can really go against the Will of Allah, but it is considerably more than that. The true Moslem not only resigns himself to the inevitable Will of God, but attempts to be of significant help in putting this plan into operation.[7]

Thus, the true Moslem, according to the consensus of Moslems in Turkey, considers it an ultimate value to live every hour as Allah has ordained he shall live. It is essential that he resign himself to God's will.

4. *A society also has a system of intermediate values that implements the values considered ultimate.* In our legal theory the United States Constitution is an instrument, intermediate in character, for guaranteeing the ultimate values of the society. The Constitution confers no rights upon us; it merely states those rights that preexisted, before we drafted a constitution; and those rights represent ultimate values. Among those specified in the Constitution is government by representatives of the people for the benefit of the people.

The Koran, so important to the Turkish villager in Pierce's report, is the bible of Islam, expressing its ultimate values. The five pillars of Islam are intermediate values implementing the basic teachings of the Koran. They provide for prayer five times daily, confessing belief in Allah as the one and only true God and in Mohammed as His Prophet, giving of alms to the poor, fasting during the sacred month of Ramadan, sacrificing a lamb on a specified occasion and giving some of the meat to the poor, and making a pilgrimage to Mecca or having someone make it in one's stead.[8]

· NOTES

1. Ralph Linton, *The Cultural Background of Personality* (New York: Appleton-Century-Crofts, 1945), pp. 15–19.
2. Kingsley Davis, *Human Society* (New York: Macmillan, 1949), p. 3.

3. Richard T. LaPiere, *Sociology* (New York: McGraw-Hill, 1946).
4. From: *The Study of Man* by Ralph Linton, pp. 313–315. Copyright 1936 by D. Appleton Century Company, Inc. This and following quotes are reprinted by permission of Appleton-Century-Crofts.
5. Robert Bierstedt, *The Social Order, An Introduction to Sociology,* 2nd ed. (New York: McGraw-Hill, 1963), p. 164.
6. Clyde Kluckhohn, *Mirror for Man* (New York: McGraw-Hill, 1949), p. 41.
7. Joe E. Pierce, *Life in a Turkish Village* (New York: Holt, Rinehart and Winston, 1964), p. 87.
8. *Ibid.,* pp. 87–88.

· SUGGESTIONS FOR FURTHER READING

BENEDICT, RUTH. *Patterns of Culture.* Boston: Houghton Mifflin, 1934.
An anthropological treatment of the similarities and differences in cultures.

HART, C. W. M., and ARNOLD R. PILLING. *The Tiwi of North Australia.* New York: Holt, Rinehart and Winston, 1965.
A study of a society in which the currency is women, and men compete for prestige and influence through their control over members of the female sex.

HAYS, H. R. *From Ape to Angel.* New York: Knopf, 1958.
An enjoyable history of anthropology written for laymen, which should be helpful because sociology owes so much to anthropology for the development of the concepts of "culture" and "society."

KLUCKHOHN, CLYDE, and WILLIAM H. KELLEY. "The Concept of Culture," in Ralph Linton (ed.), *The Science of Man in the World Crisis.* New York: Columbia University Press, 1945, pp. 78–106.
A conversation among anthropologists, who explore the concept of culture.

LEWIS, OSCAR. *The Children of Sanchez, Autobiography of a Mexican Family.* New York: Random House, 1961.
An anthropologist presents an extremely interesting picture of the culture of a Mexico City slum.

LINTON, RALPH. *The Study of Man.* New York: Appleton-Century-Crofts, 1936, Chapter 5, "The Background of Culture," Chapter 6, "The Distinctive Aspects of Culture," and Chapter 7, "Society."
An excellent explanation, by a distinguished anthropologist, of the meaning of "culture" and "society."

4 CULTURAL VALUES & ATTITUDES

When we discussed the subjective approach (Chapter 1), we said that subjective evaluations, termed *value judgments,* have great significance in group life. Later (Chapter 3) we made the point that culture can make anything right or wrong, depending upon people's value judgments. In this and following chapters, we begin to study these value judgments at closer range, to investigate their origins, force, and perpetuation.

Would you like to make it your career to perform the functions of a stool pigeon? Do you prefer boiled earthworms to roast pork? As the minister delivers his sermon, would you turn on your portable radio in church to catch the baseball game?

Why not? Because your behavior is influenced by values and attitudes acquired in the society.

A value is an individual's socially acquired judgment of the degree to which a particular stimulus is desirable or undesirable. An attitude is an individual's learned inclination to respond to a specific stimulus in a particular way. The inclination is dependent on the individual's values.

Take the term *stool pigeon.* If it makes you think of a type of person who is repugnant to you, then this stimulus has a negative *value* for you, and your *attitude* would likely be one that, among other things, consisted of an inclination not to become a stool pigeon. If in your judgment listening to a baseball game in church is undesirable because it would shock people, then that value may produce an attitude that stops you from listening, much as you would like to know what the Giants are doing in the second inning.

In other words, *values* produce *inclinations to respond to specific stimuli*. Values and attitudes are associated in human interaction and facilitate such interaction.

Values and attitudes are not concrete entities but refer to an idea or concept. Although we cannot see a value or an attitude, we can infer it by observing its influence. Perhaps you are convinced that God is good, all-powerful, and is to be worshiped. Your neighbor cannot see this value judgment of yours, but it gives you the inclination, or attitude, to act in a certain way, and your neighbor can infer the value judgment when he sees you attend church regularly and follow the precepts of your religion in daily life.

But verbal statements and observed reactions will not always and necessarily reflect underlying values and attitudes accurately. "Who can say with any certainty," writes Richard T. LaPiere, ". . . that the man who goes off to war is doing so because he feels loyalty to his country, as he may say that he does, or that he is going because he fears social disapproval if he does not go?"[1]

Sociologists and social psychologists have devised techniques for measuring what are assumed to be attitudes, but it would seem they are really measuring inferences they make from the verbal statements or observed actions of their subjects. A person may say his attitude is one of opposition to cheating on examinations, yet he may not be opposed to the practice at all. A research investigator may not detect a student who is cheating on examinations. This does not incontrovertibly establish that the student holds an attitude against cheating, or that he is not cheating at the time, or that he would not cheat under other conditions.*

Aside from this hazard, the measurement of attitudes is further complicated by the fact that what the researcher gets from a respondent is, as a rule, *merely* an expression of liking or disliking, favoring or disfavoring something. The respondent says he likes (or dislikes) professional boxing. He says he

* What follows is based on Robert M. MacIver and Charles H. Page, *Society: An Introductory Analysis* (New York: Rinehart, 1949), pp. 29–30.

favors (or disfavors) the abolition of professional boxing. This does tell us something, after we have analyzed the responses of a number of individuals, but left out of account is the *intensity* of the attitudes exhibited. That is extremely difficult to measure with anything like mathematical precision. Suppose John, Mary, and Ted take the attitude that professional boxing ought to be outlawed. How deeply does each feel regarding the matter? John may feel very strongly about it, Mary less so, Ted even less than Mary. But if, unable to measure the difference in intensity in mathematical terms, we tally the responses to show three "votes" for outlawing professional boxing, we are assigning to each response an identical weight. This is somewhat misleading.

Another problem of attitude measurement is that a given object or phenomenon does not have precisely the same significance for all who exhibit attitudes toward it. Bob may view war as an undertaking in which neither side ever wins. Charles may consider it an effective procedure for settling disputes between nations. David may believe war is a useful device for keeping world population and means of subsistence in balance. Now, suppose we asked each of these individuals: "Do you believe we ought to go to war with Zambodia?" Each would react in terms of his personal conception of *war*. Thus, the identical question, raised with each respondent, would not yield strictly comparable results, for each person concerned has an attitude qualitatively different from that of the other respondents.

Despite the present difficulty in measuring attitudes, however, the techniques devised are valuable contributions to the study of human behavior; they are constantly being improved; and in applying them, behavioral scientists are learning to make increasingly accurate inferences about values and attitudes.

FOUR CATEGORIES OF VALUES & ATTITUDES

Values and attitudes may be classified into four categories:

1. *Those learned from nonhuman sources.* If an infant is bitten by a dog he may develop an inclination to flee when he sees one thereafter. Such a tendency to behave, based upon

experience from a nonhuman source, is of only incidental interest to the sociologist.

2. *Those learned from human sources but kept private and concealed from others.* Suppose a married woman wants very much to have a male acquaintance become romantically interested in her, but bows to convention and other practical considerations and gives no outward sign of her feelings. Her acquaintance will not know about her inclinations under these circumstances.

While undisclosed values and attitudes are of great interest to sociologists, few have confidence in their ability to bring them out into the open where they can be studied. If you asked a group of married women, "Have you ever felt you would like to engage in extramarital romance?" what answers would you get? Some would say "No!" and mean it. Some would say "Yes!" and mean it. Others would be evasive or downright untruthful. And some would say what they believe to be true, but which would actually not be, because they do not fully understand their own behavioral tendencies.

3. *Those learned while associating with human beings— disclosed in interacting with some, concealed in interacting with others.* A wife may tell her best friend that her husband is easily seduced by flattery, yet keep that observation from her husband. A man may enjoy telling risqué stories and regale friends with them at parties, but be extraordinarily discreet when the minister comes to tea.

Social scientists are interested in values and attitudes on this level and have achieved a limited success in gaining an understanding of such personality tendencies.

4. *Those learned from other human beings and openly revealed in any interactive situation that brings them to the surface.* These are attributes that are generally required or preferred within the society when one is in the presence of other people. Most of us will see our guests to the door when they leave. We generally postpone eating until grace has been said in a home where this custom prevails.

Categories 2, 3, and 4, can correctly be designated *cultural* values and attitudes. They are cultural in that they are acquired and shared in common with cultural groups. They provide individuals with bases for deciding how to act. They enable us to predict what others will do in a given situation. Cultural values and attitudes have social sources and consequences. Considered in terms of their social significance, they tend either to unite or to separate us from one another, or, as some sociologists express it, they are *associative* or *dissociative* in their effect on human social relations.

CONSISTENT & CONFLICTING VALUES & ATTITUDES

Values and attitudes within a given group tend to become standardized. People generally take over the approved values and attitudes of those about them. In our society most of us do not kick our neighbor's dog, nor do we eat dogs. The Iranian mentioned in the preceding chapter married a girl born in the United States. He did not consider adding another wife to his household, for this would be regarded with disapproval in this country and would subject him to legal sanctions. However, he tells us, "There is a possibility when my wife and I go back to Iran, that I might take another wife." There it would be approved and legal behavior.

Complete uniformity of values and attitudes does not exist in a society, and its members neither expect nor want absolute standardization. The Iranian said men in his country may have any number of wives. His own parents are monogamous and "make fun of anybody who has more than two wives." Among candidates for the United States Presidency in 1964, Lyndon B. Johnson, a Democrat, received over 42 million votes; Republican Barry M. Goldwater, over 27 million; candidates representing the Socialist Labor Party and the Socialist Worker Party polled, respectively, some 21,000 and 11,000 votes. We must assume that values and attitudes played a part in the selection of candidates by voting citizens, and it is obvious that they were by no means unanimous in their choice. Our value system, in fact, favors a certain amount of individuality in such issues.

Dissimilar and even conflicting values and attitudes are certain to prevail wherever men dwell together in considerable numbers. How does this come about?

The words *value* and *attitude* are always associated with desirability or undesirability, whether applied to the usefulness of an axe handle, the aesthetic appeal of a Van Gogh painting, or the propriety of wearing bathing trunks to a formal dinner. Disparate and conflicting values and attitudes develop when individuals or groups find it necessary to choose between courses of action that they anticipate will lead to almost equally desirable or equally undesirable consequences.

Sometimes it is an individual who finds himself in conflict over what is desirable. A man would like to remain sober but is tempted to get drunk. (Such a pull in two directions is called *ambivalence*.) Sometimes it is a group that must choose between two opposite courses of action. That would be the case if representatives of a small nation, desiring independence but being threatened by a great power, gave that power some economic concession in order not to be invaded.

Disparate and conflicting values and attitudes that are generally shared by and characteristic of large segments of a society must be construed as part of its culture. Such internal contradictions, we have suggested, are in keeping with the fact that members of a society will tolerate, expect, and in some instances even want something less than total standardization. Consider our own society in the United States:

We want to be considered honest but sometimes seek to gain advantage by other than honest means.

We express moral indignation over a scandal luridly reported in a newspaper, although we received some vicarious satisfaction from reading it.

Most people would assert that playing a good game of golf is less noble than saving a human life, but the professional golfer may gain greater recognition and financial reward than the man who saves a life.

On the whole, we respect people who work hard and disapprove of idlers; nevertheless, many of us are attracted to the seductive lines of Don Marquis' *The Almost Perfect State:*

> A MOTTO FOR YOUR WALL
> ALAS!
> THE HOURS WE WASTE
> IN WORK
> AND SIMILAR
> INCONSEQUENCE!
> FRIENDS,
> I BEG YOU
> DO NOT SHIRK
> YOUR DAILY
> TASK
> OF INDOLENCE![2]

THE FORMATION & PERPETUATION
OF VALUES & ATTITUDES

We arrive at our values in two ways: *on the basis of intimate, first-hand knowledge and experience* and *on the strength of general notions derived from limited knowledge and experience.*

Suppose a brother with whom you were reared were coming to visit you, and you were telling a friend what sort of person he is. You might say, "Al's kind of a bashful fellow, but after he gets to know you better he opens up. He really likes to be with people, after the ice is broken." You go on, describing other characteristics of his as you understand them.

Al arrives. Your evaluation of him might have been somewhat different from the one your friend will now make, but for the most part Al's manner and conduct will confirm your judgments. This grows out of the fact that the values and attitudes you formed about him were *based on intimate, first-hand knowledge and experience over a long period of time.*

Now assume that Pat Riley, a native of Ireland, is coming to visit you. You have never had contact with him, and your knowledge of any Irishman is limited to the few you met casually for brief periods of time. Suppose a friend asks, "What kind of a fellow is this Riley?" Let us say you reply, "I don't know him personally, but he's Irish, so I wouldn't be surprised if he has red hair. He's probably very jolly, and likes his beer and whiskey. I'll have to get up early on Sunday to drive him to church. He'll be Catholic, so he'll want to attend Mass."

But then Pat arrives, and his hair is black, he proves a somber chap, and is a teetotaler. As for Sunday Mass, he is not interested. He is Jewish, not Catholic.

The values and attitudes you formed about him were based upon general notions derived from limited knowledge and experience. You had what sociologists call *categorical,* or *stereotyped,* values and attitudes about Irishmen in general, and you applied them to this particular Irishman.

Put another way, when we know someone personally and well, and consider him "one of us," we tend to evaluate him as an individual, although he "belongs" in our group. We see that in particular respects he has his own individuality. But when we do not know a person well and do not consider him "one of us," we have a tendency to place him in a class, or category, of people, not recognizing what individuality he may have as a member of that category. Since we know little about those who make up the category, it is likely that we will have an unrealistic notion of what the individual in question is like. He is "one of them," and we are somewhat uncertain as to what "they" are like. Al, mentioned above, is a brother. We know a great deal about him and are able to individualize him. We know in what ways he resembles certain other people with whom we are familiar, but we also know how he differs from them. We do not know Pat Riley, hence cannot individualize him, not having had the opportunity to observe his distinctive characteristics. We put him in the category of Irishmen as we understand (or misunderstand) that category, evaluating Pat on the strength of assumed similarities among all members of this category.

Values and attitudes based on intimate, first-hand knowledge tend in time to become fixed. We will not readily believe rumors that respected friends acted dishonorably. We do believe an unfavorable report about a man we know well and consider capable of villainy. We either like or dislike people we know intimately. Correspondingly, we are inclined to be attracted to or repelled by them on the basis of what we know about them as individuals.

Categorical or stereotyped values and attitudes may be as durable as those based on intimate first-hand knowledge. Or they may not. Many people hold to their stereotyped conceptions of Mexicans, Italians, Frenchmen, and Latin Americans for years, even for life. On the other hand, a great many change their judgments when they have had sufficient contact to be able to reevaluate a situation, person, or class of persons.

The sociologist is interested in values and attitudes regardless of their origins. They must be taken into account in the study of human interaction. We shall be discussing them, directly and inferentially, throughout this volume. However, in the rest of this chapter we confine ourselves to further consideration of *stereotyped* values and attitudes.

STEREOTYPES

In considering people, things, situations, or subjects he knows on a limited basis only, an individual resorts to generalizations. A native American may think of the French as a nation of winebibbers, or the English as a people without a sense of humor, or Italians as all highly emotional. The clever verse writer, Ogden Nash, plays on this tendency to generalize when he tells us that

> A girl who is bespectacled
> Don't even get her nectacled.[3]

Assertedly, "the good die young," surely a severe judgment on our older folk. "Money will buy anything," civil servants lack ambition, and all American Indians are tall—according to some reports and beliefs.

Each of these beliefs and assertions is a generalization, and each is false in that it ascribes characteristics to an entire class of people, things, or phenomena without taking into account the many variations within the class. Some girls who wear glasses do not attract men romantically, some attract them to a modest degree, and some are besieged by eager, romantically inclined men. Some civil servants lack ambition, some are mildly eager to gain promotion, and some so eager for advancement that they go far beyond the call of duty in perfecting their skills and serving the public. Some American Indians are tall by our standards, some are of average height, some are short.

The generalizations cited above are constructed from limited contacts with the persons, things, situations, and subjects involved. They serve as substitutes for real understanding that might emerge from continued contacts. They are stereotypes, which are oversimplified generalizations about persons, situations, things, or subjects. They are incorporated into the culture, transmitted, in some instances, from one generation to another. They may be complimentary or the reverse, but *they are always distortions of fact to some degree.*

On the other hand, stereotypes about groups and categories of people often have some basis in historical or contemporary facts. For instance, consider the stereotype: "Negroes are great athletes." Some of our most capable athletes have been Negro, but it does not follow that all Negroes are great athletes. Again: "Jews are political radicals." By no means is this true of all Jews, but a number of Jews have played prominent roles in European and in United States left-wing movements. An important reason, in fact, why stereotypes are difficult to change is that they often contain an element of truth.

Figure 4.1
The Dumb
Athlete Stereotype
Drawing by F. Kliban; ©
1963 The New Yorker
Magazine, Inc.

"Look! Jim has the ball!
See him run! Run, Jim, run!"

Gifted cartoonists furnish some of the most dramatic illustrations of common stereotypes. They exploit those already in existence and have at times contributed to the formation of others. The artist who drew the scene in Figure 4.1, for instance, presents the common stereotype of the school athlete as a stupid, practically illiterate fellow, in this case one who talks in language like that in some first-grade readers. In Figure 4.2, the artist presents a stereotype of women drivers, who are supposedly very poor drivers indeed. In Figure 4.3, we have a stereotype of college professors, supposedly so absent-minded they forgot to attend a scheduled meeting to protest against jokes about absent-minded college professors.

A stereotype may emerge out of what people say, write, draw, paint—anything that communicates meaning. George Bernard Shaw was a master of the delusive stereotype. In *The Crime of Imprisonment* he wrote: "The vast majority of our city populations are inured to imprisonment from their childhood. The school is a prison. The office and factory are prisons. The home is a prison."[4] Anyone accepting these statements as true for the majority of cases accepts a stereotyped idea.

Stereotypes may be positive or negative in value, depending upon whether the characteristics attributed are considered desirable or undesirable. "Grasping bankers," "cunning politicians," and "smart Jews" are examples of negative stereotypes. In the positive category are "decent citizens," "the motherly

Figure 4.2
The Woman Driver
Stereotype

Reprinted by permission of Charles Rodrigues, from Ralph Shikes (ed.), *Cartoon Annual*, New York: Ace Books, 1953, p. 63.

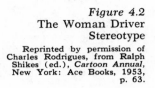

"Will you look at how close that maniac is driving ahead of me!"

type of woman," and "the kind of fellow who can hold his liquor." We label people. If we approve of a man who uses his mind for independent, creative thinking, we may call him an "intellectual," and describe him favorably, using a positive stereotype. If we disapprove, we perhaps apply the derogative label of "egghead," describing him unfavorably, using a negative stereotype.

So effective may stereotypes be that they are constantly brought into play during political campaigns. When Adlai Stevenson was running for President of the United States, his adversaries ridiculed him and his followers as eggheads. This brought from Mr. Stevenson the cry, "Eggheads of the world, arise! You have nothing to lose but your yolks!"

Whether positive or negative in value, stereotypes do not provide realistic grounds for assessing the attributes of any particular person, thing, situation, or subject. Do you believe you can pick a brilliant child out of a crowd of children on the basis of his appearance? Exposure to stereotyped cartoons, movies, television shows, and written or verbal opinions brings some people to think they can. They perhaps visualize the highly intelligent young person as puny, with a massive forehead, and wearing spectacles. Another stereotyped notion is that such children lack athletic prowess. Actually, studies of gifted children reveal that on the average they are slightly taller than other children their age, their foreheads are about the same in conformation as foreheads of most children, and they are not especially prone to deficient eyesight. Further-

Figure 4.3
The Absent-Minded
Professor Stereotype
© Punch. Reproduced
by permission.

*A mass meeting of absent-minded professors
has been called to protest against jokes about them in the comic papers.*

more, they are at least as good at athletic sports as their less intelligent peers. You would not do very well, then, attempting to pick brilliant children out of a crowd on the basis of stereotyped notions, for some resemble the stereotype, some do not, and some of the less brilliant children resemble the stereotype of the brilliant youngster.

Paul Secord conducted a study that revealed the existence of certain standardized attitudes. A series of ten photographs of Negroes was shown to a number of subjects. The individuals depicted were scaled so that they ranged widely in appearance from those with markedly Negroid to those with markedly Caucasian physical features. The subjects were asked to rate the photographs according to whether the individuals in them possessed any of fifteen specified attributes, such as "lazy," "stupid," "dishonest," and "superstitious"— attributes that commonly constitute part of the stereotype of the American Negro. Moreover, the photographs were identified as those of Negroes.

Interestingly, there was no difference in the degree of personality stereotyping by the subjects. The mere fact that a photograph was identified as that of a Negro apparently was sufficient to evoke the judgment that the person possessed all of the attributes commonly ascribed to Negroes. There was no decrease in stereotyping as the photographed person's appearance proceeded from the most Negroid physical features to the most Caucasian.[5]

Whether positive or negative in value, stereotypes facilitate standardization of attitudes in a culture. If most of us accept the belief that the white man has a "natural" right to bring "civilization" to jungle "savages," then we are likely to adopt the attitude that white colonization of these "backward" lands is no more than "the white man's burden." If most of us believe that the only "true" democracy in the world is to be found in the United States and that "true democracy" is a perfect form of government, then we are likely to adopt the attitude that our government must be defended against encroachment by any other political ideology.

Whether positive or negative in value, stereotyped attitudes provide individuals with bases, however unrealistic, for anticipating the behavior of other individuals and for adjusting their own conduct accordingly. Sometimes a stereotyped attitude is so strongly positive or negative in value that it amounts to what is called *prejudice* in ordinary conversation. Actually, all stereotypes are prejudices, whether much or little emotion is invested in them. A dictionary defines prejudice as "a judgment or opinion formed without due examination of the facts or reasons that are essential to a just and impartial determination." All stereotypes fit that description. When a stereotype has a great deal of positive or negative value for an individual, he feels rather strongly about it, and his *learned inclination to respond* to the particular stimulus may result in a very vigorous response, based on a bias formed "without due examination of the facts."

Stereotyped attitudes not only provide bases for anticipating the behavior of others and adjusting to it, but also are frequently influential in creating behavior. Group stereotypes often influence the behavior of members of groups so stereotyped. Thus, some "hippies," aware that they are stereotyped as individuals who are unconventionally garbed and who experiment with psychedelic drugs, begin to live up to the stereotype. The juvenile delinquent is generally stereotyped as tough-spoken, quick with his fists, and unchivalrous toward girls. A youngster who is officially or informally labeled a delinquent in his community may begin to fulfill this conception of the delinquent even if he did not do so previously. One stereotype of Japanese-American youths is that they are outstanding scholastically. This may account in part for the exceptionally high achievement in school of many of these young people. Perhaps they exert extra effort to live up to stereotypical attitudes and expectations.

Particularly in past decades, doctors were stereotyped as selflessly dedicated to their patients, willing to minister to them even without charging fees, and prepared to answer a call any time of the day or night. Undoubtedly many physicians did fit the stereotype, and very likely many did not. But who can say how many of those who did not fit it by inclination conformed to it by force of social pressure?

Stereotypes, as well as judgments founded on evidence, make up the value system of a society. The values of a society form a system of social norms. Norms operate as social control.

· *NOTES*

1. Richard T. LaPiere, *Sociology* (New York: McGraw-Hill, 1946), p. 272.
2. Don Marquis, *The Almost Perfect State* (New York: Doubleday, Page, 1927), p. 13.
3. From "Lines Written to Console those Ladies Distressed by the Lines 'Men Seldom Make Passes, Etc.'" from *Hard Lines* by Ogden Nash. Copyright 1931 by Ogden Nash, reprinted with permission of Little, Brown and Company.
4. George Bernard Shaw, *The Crime of Imprisonment* (New York: Philosophical Library, 1946), p. 18.
5. Paul F. Secord, "Stereotyping and Favorableness in the Perception of Negro Faces," *Journal of Abnormal and Social Psychology*, LXIX (November 1959), 309–314.

· *SUGGESTIONS FOR FURTHER READING*

BAIN, READ. "Our Schizoid Culture." *Sociology and Social Research*, XIX (January 1935), 255–276.
A sociological classic, this article deals with the irrational, contradictory, and conflicting behavior that characterizes United States culture.

BLUMER, HERBERT. "Attitudes and the Social Act." *Social Problems*, III (October 1955), 59–65.
The author has some doubts as to whether attitudes direct and control behavior.

KLUCKHOHN, CLYDE. "Have There Been Discernible Shifts in American Values During the Past Generation?" in Elting E. Morrison (ed.), *The American Style: Essays in Value and Performance*. New York: Harper & Row, 1958, pp. 145–217.
An anthropologist discusses those current value changes that are documented by some empirical data.

KLUCKHOHN, RICHARD (ed.). *Culture and Behavior: Collected Essays of Clyde Kluckhohn*. New York: Free Press, 1962.
Kluckhohn discusses and clarifies the function and meaning of cultural values.

MINER, HORACE. "Nacirema Culture." *American Anthropologist,* LVIII (June 1956), 503–507.

An amusing description of the sometimes quaint, sometimes odd cultural values of a contemporary society, Nacirema (spell it backward).

NEWMAN, EDWIN S. (ed.). *The Hate Reader.* Dobbs Ferry, N. Y.: Oceana, 1964, pp. 59–61.

A spectacular example of stereotyped thinking on the part of a radio orator, who attacks "aliens, Communists, crackpots, . . . Socialists, termites, and traitors," to wit, Jews, Negroes, and sundry others.

VANDER ZANDEN, JAMES W. *American Minority Relations.* New York: Ronald Press, 1966, pp. 79–88.

A concise discussion of the nature of stereotypes and their role in producing antipathy toward minority groups.

WILLIAMS, ROBIN M., JR. *American Society.* 2nd ed. New York: Knopf, 1960, Chapter II, "Values and Beliefs in American Society."

An inventory of prevalent values and beliefs in American society.

5 THE NORMATIVE SYSTEM OF SOCIETY

The authority of culture in the regulation of human behavior resides in the norms, which collectively comprise the normative system of society. We deal with the normative system in this and the next chapter.

THE BINDING & BLINDING POWER OF CULTURE

The temperature is 98 degrees, the humidity almost the same. Dr. Hubert Grimm, Professor of Sociology, arises limp and enervated. He shaves, an operation he loathes, then carefully parts and combs his hair. The shirt he puts on makes him hotter. The collar he buttons increases his discomfort, and when he knots a tie about his neck, his body temperature goes up even higher. He would not think of going into town except in the trousers he now steps into. As the final act of self-torture he dons a jacket. Thus inappropriately attired against the heat he comes to breakfast.

He greets his wife in accustomed manner, seats himself at his usual place at the table, and reaches for his coffee cup without looking, knowing just where it will be. He eats his grapefruit with a narrow-pointed spoon, stirs his coffee with a rounder one.

Meantime, reading his mail, which is neatly stacked in its usual place, he opens a letter from a neighboring householder, informing him in blunt, discourteous language that unless Dr.

Grimm makes immediate financial settlement for grievous damage inflicted on the person of said neighbor, a court action will be instituted forthwith. The correspondent reminds Grimm of his "gross negligence" in failing to keep his sidewalk free of snow and ice the previous December. The writer concludes with the declaration that Grimm is a curse to the community and an unprincipled scoundrel who is probably a fugitive from justice already, if truth were known.

This letter opened with the salutation "Dear Professor Grimm." It closes with "Yours truly" above the irate writer's signature. He does not hold Grimm dear to him and does not feel he is truly Grimm's, but the irony here apparently did not occur to the author of the letter, nor does it now enter Grimm's consciousness.

Breakfast over, Dr. Grimm puts on a hat, which only increases his irritability, kisses his wife good-bye, because this is a ritual of long standing, and gets into the Buick he could not afford but that he bought because it is a middle-class status symbol in his community.

Driving to school, he stays within the speed limit, stops at red lights, gives pedestrians the right of way. He enters his classroom, makes some preliminary remarks, then involves the students in discussion, carefully refraining from expressing personal opinions himself, lest they amount to indoctrination.

On his way home Grimm stops at the barbershop. He does not believe he needs a haircut, but two weeks have elapsed since the last one, and he knows that people he respects and whose respect he wants to preserve follow the convention of twice-monthly trips to the barbershop.

His hair trimmed, he tips the barber, shoeshine boy, and checkroom attendant. Each says, "Thank you!" but does not mean it, since he considers the tip obligatory. Dr. Grimm responds with, "You're welcome!" and does not mean it, for he considers the business of tipping absurd.

He is to speak at a dinner tonight, on "The Power of Culture." He dislikes such affairs, for several reasons. Mass feedings annoy him; the small talk will bore him; and he feels imposed upon, realizing he was invited because he is a local figure in the community, and local figures are not paid for speaking. Dr. Grimm will attend out of a sense of duty—a professor is expected to make "a contribution to the community."

He grunts into his tuxedo that evening and goes to make his contribution. He makes small talk to left and right, in the course of which he gently ridicules academicians in general and sociologists in particular, because he knows this will bring a conspiratorial, appreciative chuckle. Actually, he has the utmost respect for academicians, and sociologists are to him the most venturesome and praiseworthy of the breed.

After dessert the chairman taps for silence and introduces a sweet-faced, generously upholstered lady who will provide a musical interlude while waiters clear the tables. Her rendition of "On the Road to Mandalay" is excruciating. Guests shift in their seats, exchange glances and mutter, but when the lady throws her arms out in the final notes of her song, they applaud generously.

The chairman rises, thanks the lady effusively, and congratulates the city on having such a talented thrush. Now the professor is introduced. He is credited with talents and accomplishments he little dreamed he possessed. He arises to speak, fully aware that after a heavy dinner his listeners want to be entertained, not enlightened. He knows they will sit through his remarks, not because they want to, but because it is the custom of the organization to have a speaker and to sit respectfully through his address.

Grimm assures his audience he is delighted to have the honor and privilege of speaking before it. He delivers his talk and sits down to applause that would have been accorded him, at least in some measure, no matter what he said. The chairman assures him the group has rarely listened to a more inspiring address. He thanks Grimm profusely.

Wearily, Dr. Grimm drives home. His wife informs him that she received a call from Mrs. Smathers, reporting that the professor's talk was simply magnificent. "She says you're an iconoclast," Mrs. Grimm says. "What's that?"

"Oh," Grimms says modestly, "an iconoclast is a sort of idol smasher, a person who defies tradition."

"Oh?" Mrs. Grimm seems a bit worried. "I hope you didn't. . . ."

"Well," Grimm says, smiling as he removes his jacket, "I don't know that I'm *really* an iconoclast, but, ahem! I flatter myself I'm not altogether hidebound by tradition either, heh, heh!"

. . .

Actually, our imaginary Professor Grimm is as hidebound by custom and tradition as are most people with whom he comes in contact. He is not entirely bound by rules of behavior, but like all those with whom he interacts, he pays those rules considerable respect. He bowed to his culture, to the accepted and expected ways of doing things, during the day just ending. What impels him to wear a jacket in the hottest weather? Why does he make sure to use the proper silverware at table? Why does he appear at a public dinner when he would rather remain home? Why does he submit to so many activities in a predictable manner? What is this power the culture exerts over him?

Dr. Grimm behaves as he has learned to behave in the process of associating with other human beings. He has acquired many of the values and attitudes common to his culture. He has learned to enact responses that are generally in accord with what is expected. When he accepted these modes of behavior as desirable, appropriate, or at least expedient, he showed that he had internalized the culture of his society.

Charles Horton Cooley, a major figure in American sociology, defined *conformity* as *the endeavor to maintain a standard set by a group.* (This is exemplified in Figure 5.1.) Each member of the group has in him what may be regarded as a strain toward conformity, that is, toward voluntary imitation of prevalent modes of action. Note the word *voluntary.* This distinguishes the behavior from involuntary imitation, which is practically mechanical. As Cooley explained, when we speak the English language, this is not conformity, for we have practically no choice in the matter if we want to get along in our society. But we might choose to conform to particular pronunciations used by those with whom we wish to associate. For instance, a New Englander, whose pronunciation is like that of others in the region, may, upon taking up residence in the West, choose to adopt Western pronunciation.

In an earlier chapter the internalization of culture was explained as the means by which an individual is socialized and becomes a social being. Socialization perpetuates the culture. Through it the individual acquires what some call conscience. The essayist Montaigne wrote: "The laws of conscience, which we pretend to be derived from nature, proceed from custom." This was a sage observation. Established customs of the culture comprise a sort of internal governor en-

Figure 5.1
The Strain Toward
Conformity
Grin and Bear It by George
Lichty courtesy Publishers-Hall
Syndicate.

"Why do we spend money we haven't got—
on things we don't want—
just to impress people
we can't stand the sight of?!"

abling the individual to satisfy his adjustive needs, to predict
the behavior of others, and to keep his behavior "in step" with
theirs. In effect the person has developed what may be termed
a social conscience. It enabled Professor Grimm to satisfy his
adjustive needs reasonably well—he slept as long as he
needed, earned an honest livelihood, kept as cool or as warm
as need-versus-custom permitted. His social conscience warned
him how people were likely to behave if he followed certain
inclinations—to dress sensibly instead of conventionally, to
decline a dinner instead of accepting it. He "got in step."

In his as in all cases, culture functioned to regulate behavior. This regulation is a phenomenon of great meaning in the
study of sociology. Whereas philosophers, novelists, and painters often stress the uniqueness of individuals, the sociologist
focuses his attention mainly on the regularity of men's behavior. He attempts to discover principles explaining the relation of the individual to the social order as a whole. Why do
the members of the society, for the most part, behave in certain predictable, regular ways? Why do most people conform
to most of the customs of the group most of the time? What
is this process by which we become *culture bound,* rarely free

of the influence of that culture? Why are we apt to become *culture blind,* so accustomed to our ways that we consider them the only "right" ways? What, in short, is this social force that brings us to behave in an approved manner? The sociologist refers to this force as *social control.*

SOCIAL CONTROL

Social control is the force that encourages the individual to behave in an approved manner, as this is culturally defined. Stated another way, it is the force that inhibits the individual from following his immediate inclination when he realizes that to do so would lead to unfavorable responses from members of the society.

When you drive a car you generally behave in an approved manner. You obey traffic signals, stopping at red lights even when you are in a hurry. You pull aside and stop to give an ambulance the right of way. This illustrates the phenomenon of social control. You will have acted under inner control. No external or physical force prevented your violating the law. You knew what was expected of you. You realized what might happen if you failed to come up to expectation—you might cause an accident, or a traffic officer might appear and give you a ticket. You gave the ambulance the right of way because you had an idea of the consequences of not doing so. In this sense, *social control is an internalized control.*

Consider the lady in Figure 5.2. She is oblivious of what her husband has in mind. On the very verge of flicking the towel, he desists, of his own accord. He knows that following his own inclinations will lead to an unfavorable response from his spouse.

Since social control must be internalized in order to function effectively, it has the meaning usually associated with *self-control.* However, usually it is a self-control based upon recognition of the social consequences of certain behavior. Spanking a child is not a manifestation of social control. Social control is exemplified in the child who refrains from behaving a certain way because he knows that otherwise he may be spanked.

True, social control will not always be sufficiently influential to prevent individuals from following their inclinations. Despite possible consequences, for instance, we may some-

Figure 5.2
Social Control

Reprinted from *You've Got Me—And How!* Edited by Lawrence Lariar, published by Dodd, Mead & Company and George Wolfe.

times picnic on grounds posted against trespassing. In such cases, our desire to do so will have outweighed fear of the consequences. But most of us, even if frustrated by doing so, follow required and preferred standards of behavior most of the time, because we realize it would ultimately cost more than it is worth to follow certain inclinations. We accept social control because we are afraid we might be subjected to social disapproval, economic reprisal, or physical punishment if we did not. Social control thus becomes an effective force in maintaining conformity among individuals of every human group, whether a family, a gang of pickpockets, monks in a monastery, or a squad of soldiers surrounded by a hostile force. Even the individual members of a group of "hippies," who like to think of themselves as nonconformists, conform in many ways to the requirements of their society. Moreover, they tend to conform strictly to the expectations of "hippies" as a group.

Although there is a strong negative force, such as fear or apprehension, in regulating behavior, social control has a positive aspect as well. One reason why we fear ridicule, contempt, censure, punishment, or loss of face is because we have learned to place great positive value on social approval, on security and physical well-being. The negative force of fear derives from, and accompanies, the positive force, the desire for social approval and well-being. Moreover, we conform to custom, to our society's code of behavior, because we have learned to believe in it, to accept it as right.

SOCIAL NORMS

Social control is operative through the norms of society. We have already discussed cultural values and the attitudes that correspond with them. Now let us turn our attention to how these values and attitudes are translated into behavior.

The members of every society express their values through a system of social norms. These norms guide individual members into behavior they "ought to" enact. Without social norms there is no society.

A social norm defines the behavior that a number of people ordinarily expect or require of others and regularly enact themselves in response to particular situations. The behavior defined by social norms may be considered important or trivial, but it is always accompanied by an element of "ought to" or "must."

Professor Grimm knew that he "ought to" tip his barber, but he would not have been severely penalized if he had not. He was well aware that he "must" drive his car as prescribed by law and that he would have been subject to an uncomfortable penalty had he failed to observe the law, for law requires certain behavior.

Social norms both prescribe and proscribe behavior. Prescribed behavior is expressed affirmatively. We *must* protect infants against physical and psychological hazards. Proscribed behavior is expressed in the negative. We *must not* steal.

Some norms apply to an entire society, others only to certain groups within the society. In our country, every one of us "must" refrain from incest, but only certain of us are required to register for military conscription.

Certain standards of conduct always apply to given people at a particular time and place. All strictly Orthodox Jews in the United States are expected by their fellow religionists to refrain from labor of any kind from sundown on Friday to sundown Saturday. Every sworn witness in a court proceeding is expected to testify truthfully.

The socially defined positions that people hold in a society are factors in determining whether and to what degree a given norm shall be applicable. Norms are selectively and differentially applied. The professors on the same campus with Grimm would believe he ought to be a member of the American Association of University Professors. They would not expect the parking-lot attendant to join the organization. In fact that functionary would be ineligible for membership. In Larten, a town in Ghana, all male teachers wear long stockings, white shirts, and blue shorts. This is their official costume, selected for them by the government. It is their right to wear it by virtue of their important social position. Headmasters wear similar costumes, except that their shorts are white instead of blue.[1]

Factors contributing to the selective and differential application of standards of behavior include, among many others, sex, age, occupation, marital status, and physical and mental capacity. We call upon only males for combat duty in wartime. We require young people below a specified age to attend school, exempting those who are older. We fully expect the business man to sell only those items that will bring him a reasonable financial profit, but we believe a doctor should sometime give his time without fee, when a patient needing his services cannot afford to pay for them. We approve certain courting behavior of the single person, but we do not approve when that behavior is enacted by a married individual. A civilian, provided he is physically able, is required by law, when he comes upon one person assaulting another, to do all he can to force the assailant to stop. A physically handicapped individual who could not reasonably be expected to perform a like function is not held to the rule. A legally sane defendant is held to account for his crimes, while a legally insane person is not.

In Burma, persons holding the socially defined position of Buddhist monk are expected, in pursuance of their occupation, to beg daily for their food.

With a begging bowl slung over the shoulder, they are to wait, eyes downcast, looking neither at the householder nor at the food, and then shuffle off wordlessly to the next house. They are to eat the contents of the begging bowl without regard. The villagers tell the tale of the Buddha, who, on finding a leper's thumb in his begging bowl, ate it without flinching.[2]

Social norms are also selectively and differentially applied according to subcultural groupings. In one, a daughter would consider herself disgraced if she did not have an extravagant and formal introduction to "society," in the ceremony known as making a debut. In another subcultural group, the daughter neither expects nor is expected to "come out" through such a ceremony. In Mexican American families an adolescent boy is expected to act as guardian and protector of his sisters, both younger and older, and of his younger brothers.[3] Adolescent boys of German parents living in the United States are not expected to act in this role vis-à-vis their sisters and brothers.

What is expected or required behavior will also vary with time in the same society. A century ago the deportment of females was very much more rigidly controlled than now. Writing about life in the United States in the mid-nineteenth century, Meade Minnegerode asserted:

In general, custom forbade a lady to make inquiries concerning a gentleman's health unless he were ill or very aged; all slang words were detestable from the lips of ladies, and they must never say snooze, pants, gent, seedy, rich for amusing, or "polking" for dancing the polka.[4]

These rules of conduct do not hold today. A woman may feel free to inquire as to a gentleman's health, whether he be young or old, sick or well. And if she uses slang with reasonable discretion, she will not be censured.

Before African natives of Zambia felt the impact of the urbanization and industrialization that followed the coming of the white man, marriages were arranged by kindred. Later, with many girls working in the towns, there were increased opportunities for them to meet men, without supervision by kin. It became accepted, in the towns, that choice of a mate would be based on love, congeniality, and sexual attraction rather than by arrangement among the kinfolk.[5]

Although the culture exerts a powerful influence upon the behavior of individual members of a society, they often have choices they may make. Much of social behavior is not regulated by social norms. This is particularly the case in large, complex societies, where a wide variety of permissive activities are open to the members. Although Professor Grimm was mildly irritated by some of the gentler compulsions of life in his community, he knew that in a great many matters he could behave as he chose without evoking criticism from those in a position to observe, or learn of, such behavior. It was entirely optional whether he would live in an apartment or a private house. He could decide to buy a lawnmower or not, to subscribe to one newspaper or another. He was accorded the right to espouse a religious faith or to remain unaffiliated. He could eat haddock or striped bass for lunch. If he wanted a hobby, his associates would be equally receptive to his engaging in gardening, book collecting, fishing, or rock hunting.

It should be borne in mind, however, that although a great many kinds of behavior are tolerated in a particular time and place, wherever a choice of response is open to a participant in a cultural group, it is expected that that choice will be made only from among the possible responses that are socially acceptable. Dr. Grimm could have selected psychology as his field of study rather than sociology, but he could not with impunity have chosen the vocation of burglary.

The collective social norms make up the *normative order*, or *normative system*, of society. Every human society has a normative system, comprised of an interrelated complex of social norms, functioning to guide the behavior of its members.

Norms for sexual behavior are related to those concerning courtship, marriage, procreation, and family life. Standards of dress are related to standards for sexual behavior, as well as to standards applying, among a great many other things, to work, recreation, getting married, and graduating from college. Norms of society are organized into a system that, despite some seeming or actual contradictions, is harmonious for the most part and consistent with a society's conception of morality, practicality, and other desired ends.

The normative system of each human society will have some similarity to all other human societies. For example, all have some regulations for contracting the relationship we call marriage. The rules may differ among societies, but all have rules on the subject.

And while similarities exist, there are also differences in normative systems, each containing distinctive and perhaps unique features. The Iranian student mentioned in Chapter 3 pointed up some of the differences between our social norms and those in his native land. He ridiculed what he considered our overeffusiveness. Apparently we smile more freely than Iranians would consider appropriate, and smiling has a somewhat different meaning in the two countries. Our norms permit girls to be more "aggressive" than they are expected to be in Iran.

It should be understood that, highly influential as the normative system of society is in regulating behavior, it still does not operate as certainly and invariably as does a "law" of physical science.

American sociologists Robert M. MacIver and Charles H. Page point this out when they say that unlike the "laws" of the physical world, the rules of behavior that sustain society ". . . can be disobeyed and they can be changed. They lack the inexorable character of natural laws." Furthermore, MacIver and Page emphasize, social codes differ from natural "laws" in that they carry with them a sense of obligation.

They are addressed to the feelings and to the reason of those they govern. And they constantly run counter to the inclinations of many individuals. [They] reveal the solidarity of the group, but the solidarity is never complete. For the self-centered or *like* interest of individuals is always running counter to the general or *common* interest. And the interest of the small group, such as the family or the club, often runs counter to some demands of the larger group, such as the community or class. The social norms of conduct are often too restrictive for the self-seeking. On the other hand, many of the regulations are framed in the interest of dominant groups or classes and are resisted by other groups. The prescriptions of the social codes are never equally accepted or equally obeyed.[6]

But whatever the degree of resistance to them, social codes represent obligations where behavior is concerned. What accounts for the general tendency of individuals to adhere to the behavior codes of the society? Negative sanctions—the penalty attached to the violation of codes—could not of themselves accomplish this. "No social order could long endure," say MacIver and Page, "if it depended merely on the sanctions of the codes. Unless the codes were more deeply rooted in the group over whom they hold sway they would soon prove unavailing."[7]

But they *are* deeply rooted. Individuals adhere to the behavior codes of society through indoctrination, habituation, the desire for group identification, and the recognition of the utility of the codes.

Codes are *indoctrinated* when ways of thinking, believing,

and behaving are inculcated in individuals, early in life, in the process of socialization. Children are taught by parents and others to accept the customs and codes of the society as right. They grow up believing in them. They have internalized them.

You probably learned to accept and approve the proposition that if you disagree with another person's point of view, you might discuss or argue it with him, but you must not spit in his face in token of your opposition. Indoctrinated as you are, you follow the approved mode of behavior; it seems proper and right.

For untold generations, the Navajo farmer lived in a domed structure, called a hogan, made of wood and plastered with mud. He constructed the hogan for himself and his family, and he taught his children to do the same when they left the family home. Members of the tribe who have not deserted their traditional culture continue to live in hogans. They do not question why. They were indoctrinated into the custom; they accept it.

Social codes are also adhered to through *habituation*.

Closely allied to and supporting indoctrination is habituation. While indoctrination imposes opinions and beliefs by the direct method of communication and instruction, habituation is a process in which people *unconsciously* adapt their ways and thoughts to the social conditions under which they live. . . . What is familiar often comes to appear as both inevitable and good; what is unfamiliar often seems alien or evil.[8]

You probably unconsciously accept the idea that you should be governed by elected representatives who will express your will in their votes and acts. Very likely, you do not want to be ruled by a dictator. You are habituated to a democratic form of government.

Contemporary city dwellers of Japan follow a custom called *o-hirome*—advertisement—when they move into a neighborhood. The entire household, or just the wife, goes from house to house, leaving a name-card and a small gift—perhaps a towel, a bar of soap, or a few boxes of matches. The newcomer introduces himself, tells where he lives, says he may have to call upon his neighbor in the future for assistance in some matter, and asks his kind indulgence. Now he is a member of the group of neighbors.[9] He takes for granted that this is the proper way to become a neighbor. He is habituated to the custom. He would probably look with some disfavor on another newcomer in the neighborhood who did not follow the custom.

A third reason why we conform to the normative system of society is that *we seek group identification.* By behaving as those around us do, we are expressing the idea that we belong to and feel ourselves part of the group. Do you send Christmas cards to your friends? If so, you thereby identify yourself with them and with all persons who follow the custom. Perhaps you raise the flag outside your home on Flag Day. This also is a gesture of identification, in this case with others who consider themselves loyal to the United States.

A fourth reason why we follow customary ways is that *we comprehend their utility.* You are driving along a one-way, two-lane road, when it suddenly begins to narrow to one lane. You slow down in order to permit the car to your right to get in ahead of you. Why? Because you realize that this is a useful custom, beneficial to all concerned. If no one yielded the right of way there would soon be a traffic jam that would affect all motorists at that point.

We are distinguishing, then, between behavior based solely on the desire to avoid social sanctions and behavior we want to adopt for other or additional reasons.

The members of a medical or legal association do not conform to their respective codes merely because otherwise they would lose their right to practice. . . . Nor do people generally obey the legal codes *just* because they are afraid of the policeman. People conform to a social code also because they think it right to do so, or because they have become habituated to it so that obedience is the line of least resistance, or because they wish to stand well with their fellows, or because it serves their interests, or for other reasons. The *motives* of the individual are always manifold and mixed and hard to disentangle.[10]

THE FUNCTIONS OF SOCIAL NORMS

The coercive force of norms serves positive and constructive purposes.

1. *Social norms make it possible for the human organism to survive.* The newborn infant does not enter the world with full equipment and capacity to respond appropriately to every-

thing it will encounter in its environment. It would not survive without social norms that influence adults to take care of it.

2. *Social norms are the means by which society is maintained and the needs of its members are fulfilled.* Unrestrained, our biological needs and inclinations would encourage or, perhaps, guarantee anarchy. When norms control behavior, individual participants in a culture are constrained to fulfill societal needs, sometimes at the expense of their organic drives. Our culture demands that every newborn infant have a personal and family identity, hence we do not tolerate indiscriminate procreation of children. We require marriage before procreation and also registration of births by personal and family names. We also require adherence to a sociolegal system of rules setting forth the rights and obligations of parents and the duties and privileges of their children.

3. *Social norms make it possible for much of individual behavior to become automatic, greatly reducing the number of personal decisions to be made.* In the process of internalizing the norms of his society, an individual learns countless time-tested procedures for the maintenance of life, health, comfort, the proprieties. Once learned, they can be applied automatically in appropriate situations. You do not reflect, each time you wish to greet a friend, whether to extend your right or left hand. When driving a car, you no longer stop to consider whether to stay in the right or left traffic artery. These procedures were decided for you and you are habituated to them.

Without norms, MacIver and Page assert, ". . . the burden of decision would be intolerable and the vagaries of conduct utterly distracting."[11] And Cooley has this to say:

The standards which conformity presses upon the individual are often elaborate and valuable products of cumulative thought and experience, and whatever imperfection they may have they are, as a whole, an indispensable foundation for life; it is inconceivable that any one should dispense with them. If I imitate the dress, the manners, the household arrangements of other people, I save so much mental energy for other purposes.[12]

We would not want all our procedures predetermined for us, but a great deal of time and energy are conserved when the more routine behaviors we will be needing become automatic, leaving us free to that extent to decide on a number of other matters calling for individual thought and choice. By accepting and following a cultural pattern, Cooley says, we get "the selected and systematized outcome of the past."[13]

The strain for conformity, then, is frequently accompanied by no real feeling of strain. The coercion is not felt, in such instances, because the person is fully accustomed to responding to it. A man who does not want to contribute to charity may feel under coercion when a persistent canvasser presses him for a donation. However, if he is someone who fully internalized his culture's standard concerning donating to charities, he does not feel under duress, for he genuinely would like to contribute and will do so to the extent he considers within his means.

RESISTANCE TO NORMATIVE CONTROLS

Up to now we have emphasized the authority of the norms in regulating behavior. However, we did suggest that to some extent every individual at some time offers some resistance to the coercion implicit or explicit in social norms. This resistance is not always evident to other people, for there is a difference between *ideal norms of behavior* and *action responses*.

An ideal norm of behavior consists of what people say should be done in responding to a situation; action response is what they actually do when confronted by the situation. Ideal norms, then, are standards or guidelines for behavior in specific situations. And what people say they will do may be inconsistent with what they actually do in responding to specific situations. The work of Alfred E. Kinsey and his associates makes it clear that, ideally, many Americans consider it desirable that young people postpone sexual intercourse until after marriage. But approximately 90 percent of the men and 60 percent of the women in Kinsey's sample said they had engaged in premarital sexual intercourse. This reflects considerable divergence between what people in the United States admit doing and what they consider desirable.

Why does the action response of some people run contrary to the ideal norm for the behavior concerned?

1. First, let us point out that *no individual is an absolute and total nonconformist, refusing to behave in accord with any of the norms of his society.* Consider the late Joe Gould, who called himself the last of the bohemians.* A Harvard graduate, class of 1911, he chose to live in Greenwich Village, the bohemian center of New York City in his time. He held no paying job for almost half a century, cadging money, liquor, food, and cast-off clothing. He slept on park benches and in subway stations. He told his associates he subsisted on "air, self-esteem, cigarette butts, cowboy coffee, fried-egg sandwiches, and ketchup." He carried on as promiscuous a sex life as his disreputable appearance and unwashed condition permitted.

He insisted he wanted to own nothing at all. "If Mr. Chrysler tried to make me a present of the Chrysler Building," he told a reporter, "I'd damn near break my neck fleeing from him. I wouldn't own it; it'd own me."

Gould insisted he was devoting his life to writing *An Oral History of Our Time,* a book that would contain reports on what he had personally seen and heard. "What we used to think was history," he said, "all that chitty-chat about Caesar, Napoleon, treaties, inventions, big battles, is only formal history and largely false. I'll put down the informal history of the shirt-sleeved multitude—what they had to say about their jobs, love affairs, vittles, sprees, scrapes, and sorrows." Part of his *Oral History,* he claimed, contained remarks scribbled on the walls of public washrooms. Other chapters would carry essays on such subjects as the flophouse flea, spaghetti, the zipper as a symbol of the decay of civilization, remorse, false teeth, and the jury system.

Supposedly in pursuit of data, and also because he enjoyed it, he consorted with drunks, narcotics addicts, brothel keepers, prostitutes, artists, novelists, poets, bums, and free-love advocates.

He was indeed an extreme nonconformist in numerous respects, and yet his action responses demonstrated that in many other ways he abided by the norms of his society. Rag-

* Part of the Joe Gould story comes from Gould himself, whom the author knew; part comes from the author's conversations with journalist Joseph Mitchell and from the latter's book *McSorley's Wonderful Saloon* (New York: Duell, Sloan and Pearce, 1943), pp. 68–75, 85, 86.

gedy and eccentric as was his garb, he did wear some kind of clothing in public—he did not stroll the streets in the nude. He spoke a conventional American language, heavily laced with equally conventional slang. Although he subsisted on handouts, he was not known to steal, and if he ever assaulted a human being, no such charge was ever laid against him. He often went hungry, but did not eat human flesh. He derided many of the customs of more conventional people, yet he ceremoniously kissed the hand of handsome women when they met; and while living through two world wars in which the United States was a combatant, he did not offer his services to an enemy nation. In much of his behavior, he followed the standards of the social norms. And indeed, it is difficult to conceive of a human being long surviving in any society if he totally rejects all of its norms and acts or fails to act accordingly.

In Figure 5.3, the bedraggled man arriving home is obviously considered nonconformist by the lady we presume to be his wife. We may assume the cartoonist wanted us to get certain inferences about this scene—that the husband did indeed violate the norms of the neighborhood by arriving home more than slightly the worse for wear and alcoholic intake, and that his wife is unhappy about this evidence of his nonconformity. But in other respects he definitely conforms. He lives in a neat house similar to others in the area. He is a family man, with a wife and at least one child. He keeps his lawn up to the standard set by his neighbors. He has a television set. He reads the newspaper and brings it home with him. And rumpled though they be, he does wear conventional suit, shirt, tie, hat, and shoes.

2. *Some people see themselves as conformists on the whole; they choose to carry out the dictates of a particular norm most of the time; but under pressures they violate that norm.* A man may be a courageous comrade-in-arms throughout most engagements in a battle zone, but panic and desert his fellows when the stress of bombardment, coupled with fatigue, destroy his self-discipline and morale for the time being. A professor may fully subscribe to the principle of academic freedom and time and again stand staunchly with his colleagues against invasion of this freedom, yet on one occasion, faced by the possibility of punitive action, capitulate to forces opposed to the principle he holds dear.

Figure 5.3
Only Slightly
Nonconformist
Drawing by Robt. Day;
Copr. © 1953 The New
Yorker Magazine, Inc.

*"Why do you always have to be different
from everybody else?"*

3. *Some people violate the norms generally applicable in
their society out of loyalty to the behavior standards of a subcultural group of which they are members.* For example, take
the "hippies" (or hipsters). As pointed out earlier, much of
their behavior runs counter to the norms of the society of
which they are a part. Viewed from this point of reference,
they are nonconformists. In another frame of reference, however, they can be viewed only as very strict conformists indeed
—to the norms of their own subcultural group. In their dress,
speech, housing, recreational interests, sexual morality, and in
many other respects, their very nonconformity to societal
standards represents real conformity to the standards of the
subcultural group. This is visually suggested in Figure 5.4.
The man knows he and the girl are conforming to their standard of unconventionality to an extreme degree.

4. *Some nonconformity occurs when organic drives are in
conflict with social regulation.* All human beings have biological urges, some of which the norms inhibit in the interest of
group welfare. The norms allow for behavior to satisfy sexual
appetites, but set limits beyond which other activities are not
culturally tolerated. In our society, there are norms for behavior calculated to allay hunger, but they do not provide for
doing so under any and all circumstances. Theft of food, for
example, is disapproved. These are injunctions of the culture,
but some individuals are unable or unwilling to curb their
biological inclinations in favor of conformity to social norms.

Figure 5.4
Slavish Nonconformity
Reprinted from *Saturday Review*, February 2, 1966, by permission of John Ruge and the publisher.

"We're becoming slaves to unconventionality!"

5. *Some individuals, for a variety of reasons, either have not internalized certain norms of the culture that most other members of the society have assimilated and accepted, or have rejected them after internalizing them. Therefore they feel no great compulsion to conform.* The heroin user, for example, usually knows such use violates norms accepted by most other members of the society, but he either has not internalized those norms or has rejected them after internalizing them. Dance musicians furnish another example of rejection of conventional norms. The serious jazz artist voluntarily isolates himself from "squares." Sociologist Howard S. Becker, himself formerly a professional musician, writes that in that subculture, the term "square" refers to ". . . the kind of person who is the opposite of all the musician is, or should be, and a way of thinking, feeling, and behaving . . . which is the opposite of that valued by musicians." All nonmusicians are "squares," outsiders. The musician sees himself as having an artistic gift that sets him apart from all other people. "Possessing this gift, he should be free from control by outsiders who lack it. The gift is something which cannot be acquired through

education; the outsider, therefore, can never become a member of the group."[14]

And the musician who adopts this view feels justified in not conforming to norms he considers inappropriate to a person of his artistic attainments. He believes he has a right to his pattern of sexual behavior, for instance, whether it runs counter to "square" conventions or not. In general, he tends to admire behavior that flouts conventional norms. In the musician subculture the highly individualistic, devil-may-care person is admired, as a "character." One member of a band told Becker: "You know, the biggest heroes in the music business are the biggest characters. The crazier a guy acts, the greater he is, the more everybody likes him." Another musician told about the time when a band had finished playing a dance and got into its bus for the ride back to the city. The bus would not start, no matter what was tried. Suddenly, one man said, "Let's set it on fire!" They did. "What an experience!" said the musician who was telling the story. "The car burning up and all these guys standing around hollering and clapping their hands. It was really something."[15] It was indeed, but "squares" would very likely have considered it something worthy not of admiration but of stern disapproval.

6. *Nonconformity to a given social norm may be the result of adhering to another, also approved, norm.* A man "ought not" take unnecessary chances of becoming crippled or losing his life, but he is rated a courageous fellow when he succeeds in climbing a towering mountain peak despite the physical hazards involved. In 1965, during this nation's involvement in the war in Vietnam, a youth of twenty-two set himself afire in front of the United Nations building in New York City, proclaiming he was doing so as a protest against "war, all war." Although suicide is proscribed under our normative system, we also value the person who upholds his convictions against all odds. The young man, who claimed to be a pacifist, violated one social norm while conforming to another.

Sometimes, what may be conceived of as nonconformity derives from the fact that norms are arrayed at different levels of generalization and are applicable in different contexts within the same society. This helps account for some of the seeming norm conflict. Thus, children learn to "tell the truth." At the same time they learn that to be truthful under all circumstances is "bad." It is "good" for a child to admit he was responsible for a baseball crashing through a neighbor's window. It is "bad" if, when Grandma asks how he likes the cake she baked for him, he tells her it tastes awful—even if it does. We learn to "handle" seemingly conflictive norms, at least to a degree. And actually, there is, in examples like those just mentioned, less conflict than might appear to be the case.

7. *Some individuals have internalized parts of two or more different cultures and are thus oriented to conflicting cultural values. Cultural hybrids, they conform only partially to the normative system of any one culture.* As an example of one such individual in the United States we might cite a person who has one white parent and one Negro parent. Sociologist Robert E. Park applied the term "marginal man" to him, asserting he "lives in two worlds, in both of which he is more or less of a stranger."[16]

Persons not born of intermarriages may also become marginal men. This frequently occurs when a person from one culture settles among individuals from another culture. To some extent, Puerto Rican migrants to the United States fall in this category. They retain some of their earlier values, give up others in favor of those of the society where they now find themselves. They often strive to hold on to certain earlier values even though these values conflict with the values of the new society. During this transition period, following their immigration to the new society, some of their old habits are being discarded while new ones are not yet formed.

8. *Nonconformity may be a consequence of norm confusion.* The individual cannot fail to recognize that there are contradictions between one value and another in the same society. He is expected to support law and order and to do his part in combating crime. At the same time he will be regarded with some hostility and contempt if he informs police that his good friend committed a crime, for members of his society hold loyalty to friends a virtue. "Honesty is the best policy," but "caveat emptor" ("Let the buyer beware").

It is not always clear under what conditions a given norm applies. A man may vehemently declare that juvenile delinquents should be handled with severity. But then suppose his son gets into trouble with the law, and the same man pleads for gentler treatment of his child. If the son is confused by what appear to be contradictory norms, it would not be surprising.

Certain norms are behavior standards in theory but in practice are so often violated as to lead to confusion in the mind of the person who would like to conform. He may not understand how inflexibly or under precisely what conditions the standard is to be followed. Children are taught to be honest, but may become confused when they discover that their parents claimed income tax deductions for expenses they did not actually incur.

Having touched on reasons behind nonconformity, let us again emphasize that not all such deviation from social norms is regarded with equal disapproval. Moreover, some nonconformity carries with it a certain prestige. We look upon it as a mark of laudable individuality. Daniel Bell, a sociologist, writes:

The curious fact . . . is that no one in the United States defends conformity. Everyone is against it, and probably everyone always was. Thirty-five years ago, you could easily rattle any middle-class American by charging him with being a "Babbitt." Today you can do so by accusing him of conformity.[17]

Whether or not it is entirely a fact that no one in the United States defends *conformity*, it can scarcely be questioned that some *nonconformity* is defended. We may not admire hippies, but we do tend to respect the painter who lives in poverty and squalor in order to express his creativity without being dependent upon what the world will think of his art.

CONFORMITY BEHAVIOR AS A CONTINUUM

The choice open to an individual who is confronted by a given situation is not one of either absolute conformity or absolute nonconformity. A number of years ago, Floyd H. Allport, an American psychologist, conducted an interesting experiment that suggests there are alternatives between these two extremes. Conformity measurements actually fall along a continuum, he found.[18]

He studied motorists' observance of traffic rules. His premise was "The question of to what extent, or how well, one obeys the traffic rule can be determined only by interpreting what one actually does in the traffic situation." If the existence of a traffic rule opens the way to only two kinds of behavior, conformity and nonconformity, a motorist will either stop before a traffic sign signaling a full halt, or he will not stop. Allport stationed observers in two large cities, to note to what degree autoists actually conformed to the law in traffic.

The purpose of a traffic signal is to assure safety in driving. In Allport's experiment, stopping completely before a red signal light or a street stop sign would be the maximum degree of fulfillment of the purpose of the signal. Slowing down considerably but not stopping represented a lesser degree of fulfillment of that purpose. Slowing down only slightly was the third and still smaller measure of fulfillment, while going ahead without change of speed represented entire disregard for the signal and no fulfillment whatever of the purpose of the safety device.

The records of actual motorist performance in traffic were charted by the observers. Conformity, it appeared, was not an all-or-nothing matter. It ran along the scale of a continuum. Some drivers were scrupulously careful to obey the law; some disregarded it entirely; and between the two extremes were motorists who showed varying degrees of conformity.

Deviation from a norm on a particular occasion need not signify that the person who deviates is rejecting the values inherent in the rule of behavior in question. The motorist probably understands and agrees that ordinances enacted in the interest of safety are sound and useful. Occasionally, however, he makes his own rule, covering a specific traffic situation of the moment. Values furnish only a general guide to action. The individual does not always conceive of them as useful in deciding on courses of action in concrete situations. In such situations, says sociologist Howard S. Becker, ". . . people develop specific rules more closely tied to the realities of everyday life." Values still provide the major premises from which specific rules are deduced. After considering the various values to which they subscribe, people ". . . select one or more of them as relevant to their difficulties and deduce from it a specific rule. The rule, framed to be consistent with the value, states with relative precision which actions are approved and which forbidden, the situations to which the rule is applicable, and the sanctions attached to breaking it."[19] Sometimes individuals hazard punishment by breaking a rule or law of their society, applying instead their own rule of behavior for the specific situation.

THE FUNCTIONAL NATURE OF
NONCONFORMITY

The mere fact that a person fails to conform in certain respects to the normative system does not in itself mean that such nonconformity is devoid of social utility, either to the individual or to the society. In our culture, the man who goes about barefoot and bare-chested—who will not eat conventional foods, who subsists on raw vegetables only, who massages his body with snow, eats kelp, and stands on his head ten minutes a day—a man like this is considered highly eccentric, a nonconformist. But he may believe his regimen contributes to good health and longevity—and perhaps it does. But whether it does or not, if he firmly believes it does and that it will continue to bring health and long life, his nonconformist pattern serves his purpose. It functions in a positive fashion for him.

The "rebel" who advocates doing away with certain deeply rooted procedures in a society may eventually prove to have guided most of its members to a better way of life as they define it.

Great artists have refused to live in the strait jacket of conformity, and possibly this has allowed their creativity its fullest expression. From Jesus to Gandhi to Socrates to Van Gogh, some of the world's most extreme nonconformists have produced ideas, deeds, and creative works that the world in time came to revere, to respect, and to hope to emulate in some measure.

Consider certain elements of our contemporary culture that are direct and indirect outcomes of nonconformity. The individuals in the following descriptions who deviated from norms played a part in producing cultural changes that are generally considered of social utility.

Lucy Stone, Victoria Woodhull, and others rebelled against the then current conception that women were naturally inferior to men, intellectually and physically. By this conception, women should play a role in society secondary to men. The suffragettes refused to abide by this dictum and set into motion the Woman's Rights movement. Seventy-two years later, they had secured the franchise for women, via the Nineteenth Amendment to the Constitution, effective 1920. They also won greater equality with men in other respects. They were accepted in the labor market. Wives' rights to property approximated that of their husbands. Mothers became fully equal to fathers, under law, with respect to rights and obligations in connection with the rearing of children.

When Mrs. Elizabeth Smith Miller designed a special costume for herself, she was not protesting against male domination, but against the norms of her society, which required that women appear in public tightly constricted by corsets and swathed from neck to ankles in yards and yards of cloth. Mrs. Miller, who liked to take long walks, decided she would defy the norms, be comfortable although not proper. She made a walking costume consisting of a bodice and full long trousers reaching to the ankles. Over this she wore a short skirt that went a little below the knee. Today, we might think of this as a jacket, a pair of slacks, and a short skirt partly covering the trousers.

Mrs. Miller's innovation was observed by a temperance reformer, Mrs. Amelia Jenks Bloomer, who was charmed by it and proceeded to copy it. When she took a walk in the costume along the streets of Seneca Falls, New York, the people were scandalized. The outfit was highly publicized and became known as a "Bloomer" costume. "Bloomerism" soon symbolized a revolt against masculine-influenced styles for women. Bloomerism did not, of itself, bring about the subsequent revolution in female styles, but, coupled with the ideas of other rebels, finally made it possible for women to emerge from their cumbersome clothing cocoons and to don more comfortable, functional garb.

Nonconformists such as Margaret Sanger and Mary Ware Dennett flew in the face of the proprieties in order to further the birth-control movement in the United States. Nonconformists advocated a less puritanical, more scientific attitude toward sex and in time went far in winning the society over to their views. Artificial insemination of married women who would otherwise remain childless was made possible, only a few decades ago, when some doctors became willing to ignore existing values on the subject in their practice. There is still some legal and religious opposition to artificial insemination, but the trend is toward increased acceptance.

Every "new school" of painting or sculpture or music represents a departure from established norms of an older school. The New Deal shocked many in the United States by pushing through federal aid to the states for unemployment relief during the Great Depression. When President Franklin D. Roosevelt followed with the Social Security program, cries went up that this was "creeping socialism" and that Social Security payments would bankrupt the nation. Today we accept Social Security, the National Labor Relations Act, minimum-wage and maximum-hours laws, and other New Deal measures as vital to the economy and well-being of the nation. Succeeding administrations have amended the laws, in most instances increasing benefits under them.

A certain amount of nonconformity, then, can be functional in a society.

· NOTES

1. David Brokensha, *Social Change at Larteh, Ghana* (Oxford: Clarendon Press, 1966), p. 242.
2. Manning Nash, *The Golden Road to Modernity, Village Life in Contemporary Burma* (New York: Wiley, 1965), p. 137.
3. Celia S. Heller, *Mexican American Youth: Forgotten Youth at the Crossroads* (New York: Random House, 1966), p. 35.
4. Meade Minnegerode, *The Fabulous Forties* (New York: Putnam, 1924), p. 82.
5. Hortense Powdermaker, *Copper Town: Changing Africa, The Human Situation on the Rhodesian Copperbelt* (New York: Colophon Books, 1962), pp. 151–152.
6. Robert M. MacIver and Charles H. Page, *Society: An Introductory Analysis* (New York: Rinehart, 1949), p. 138. Copyright 1937 by Robert M. MacIver; 1949 by Robert M. MacIver and Charles H. Page. This and all following quotations are reprinted by permission of Holt, Rinehart and Winston, Inc., Publishers, New York.
7. *Ibid.,* p. 142.
8. *Ibid.,* p. 145.
9. Ronald P. Dore, *City Life in Japan, A Study of a Tokyo Ward* (Berkeley: University of California Press, 1958), p. 256.
10. MacIver and Page, *op.cit.,* p. 139.
11. *Ibid.,* p. 207.
12. Charles Horton Cooley, *Human Nature and the Social Order,* rev. ed. (New York: Schocken, 1964), pp. 296–297.
13. *Ibid.,* p. 297.
14. Howard S. Becker, *Outsiders, Studies in the Sociology of Deviance* (New York: Free Press, 1963), pp. 85–86.
15. *Ibid.,* p. 87.
16. Robert E. Park, "Human Migration and the Marginal Man," *American Journal of Sociology,* XXXIII (May 1928), 881–893.
17. Daniel Bell, *The End of Ideology,* 2nd rev. ed. (New York: Collier Books, 1962), pp. 35–36.

18. Floyd H. Allport, "The J-Curve Hypothesis of Conforming Behavior," *Journal of Social Psychology*, V (May 1934), 141–183.
19. Becker, *op. cit.*, p. 131.

· *SUGGESTIONS FOR FURTHER READING*

BECKER, HOWARD S. *Outsiders, Studies in the Sociology of Deviance.* New York: Free Press, 1963, Chapter 5, "The Culture of a Deviant Group."
A study of the dance musician as a nonconformist.

BROWN, PAULA. "Changes in Ojibwa Social Control." *American Anthropologist*, LIV (January 1954), 57–70.
A description of the problem of social control, which resulted from the loss of traditional controls in this society and the absence of effective substitutes for them.

CHASE, STUART. "On Being Culture Bound." *Antioch Review*, IX September 1949), 293–306.
A highly readable analysis of the binding power of culture. The author shows how thinking in terms of one's own culture may make it difficult to understand people from other cultures.

DAVIS, KINGSLEY. *Human Society.* New York: Macmillan, 1949, Chapter III, "Norms."
The concept of "norms" is explained, and how norms function in society is discussed.

HARPER, ROBERT A. "Is Conformity a General or a Specific Behavior Trait?" *American Sociological Review*, XII (February 1947), 82–86.
A study of World War II conscientious objectors as a nonconformist group.

LANDIS, PAUL H. *Social Control.* Philadelphia: Lippincott, 1956.
A well written textbook on social control.

PIERCE, JOE E. *Life in a Turkish Village.* New York: Holt, Rinehart and Winston, 1964.
An anthropological account of the highly traditionalized culture of a contemporary Turkish village.

WILLIAMS, ROBIN M., JR. *American Society.* 2nd ed. New York: Knopf, 1960, Chapter 10, "Institutional Variation and the Evasion of Normative Patterns."
Deals with norm evasion in our society, and what produces it.

6 FOLKWAYS, MORES, & LAW

We now embark upon an analysis of social norms by categories: *folkways, mores,* and *law*. We also deal briefly with *systems* of norms referred to in sociology as *institutions*.

Although all social norms have the effect of regulating behavior, they are not all enforced with equal stringency. On the basis of the degree of conformity expected, they may be categorized into *folkways, mores,* and *law*.

FOLKWAYS & MORES

William Graham Sumner (1840–1910), a Yale professor, introduced the terms *folkways* and *mores* into the vocabulary of sociology in his book *Folkways*. He defined folkways as *behavioral standards*. Some folkways represent behavior that is *expected*—what we should or should not enact. Other folkways represent behavior that is *demanded*—what we must or must not enact. This second type of folkways he called the mores. In other words, all mores are folkways but not all folkways are mores.

However, it is unrealistic to attempt clear-cut distinctions between folkways and mores. As sociologists Robert M. MacIver and Charles H. Page put it: ". . . we should not think of the mores as something different from the folkways. They *are* the folkways, in their capacity as instruments of control. They express the group standards, the group sense of what is fitting, right, and conducive to well being."[1] Viewed this way, *folkways are standards and practices within a given society, representing expected and required ways of thinking, feeling, and behaving under specified conditions, and enforced by informal or formal means, as the case may be.*

Let us examine the folkways in some detail:

1. *As a general rule, folkways come into a society without planning on the part of its members.* We may presume that initially people make various responses to a particular situation; eventually, however, they conclude that one type of response is more applicable to that situation than another; they become habituated to what appears the more appropriate response; and thus that behavior becomes accepted, fixed in custom. It is now the right way to behave in that situation, and being right, it is either expected or required of participants in the culture.

2. *Folkways enter the culture when most members of the group to whom they apply have come to accept them as customary and appropriate.*

The use of cosmetics is an example. In the 1800s a woman in the United States who valued her reputation was unlikely to use facial cosmetics, or if she did she applied them so artfully as not to advertise her duplicity in presenting a face not entirely her own. She bowed to the then current verdict that artificial beautification was "bad." But at least as early as 1919, cosmetics had become more respectable, four manufacturers having been encouraged to advertise their wares in *Ladies Home Journal.* Three of them merely listed a product by name, very discreetly. The fourth, bolder than the rest, publicized the alleged qualities of the rouge offered for sale. Even here, the advertising copy reflected the still current value judgment that artificial beautification was a bit questionable, for readers were advised that the rouge was "imperceptible if properly applied."

That attitudes concerning artificial beautification were changing was attested by the advent of "beauty parlors," which frankly advertised that their "facials" retarded wrinkles and sagging chins. They also offered to pluck eyebrows and "touch up" hair. Despite such daring pioneer efforts, beauty treatments remained for a time of such dubious repute that in 1917 only two operators paid income tax on a "beauty culture" business. By 1927, however, beauty culture had gained much greater acceptance. Some 18,000 firms and individuals paid taxes on profits from beauty shops and products.

Today artificial beautification is no secret. Beauty shops are openly patronized. Women freely admit that the color of their lips is due partly to lipstick. They acknowledge that their eyelashes are artificially colored and shaped or even that they are wearing false eyelashes. The mass media loudly advertise not only rouge and lipstick but deodorants, depilatories, razors for women, "skin softeners," and "hair tints." Obviously, the artificial beautification of the United States female has entered the folkways.

3. *Since many folkways are introduced into the culture without planning, their sources are likely to be obscure.* Who can prove how the custom of clapping hands to show appreciation originated? Why do men's shirts have buttons on the right, buttonholes on the left?

4. *Folkways are transmitted informally,* by word of mouth, by example in behavior, through the mass media, and in other ways. A child is told, or learns from observation, that it is not considered good manners to interrupt when someone is speaking. Since he also learns to want to be considered well-mannered, he adjusts his behavior to the requirements of the situation.

5. *In the main, folkways are informally enforced.* Since they are customary behaviors, members of society are not disposed to call them into question. Should an individual do so, it is resented. Retaliatory measures may be invoked, the offender becoming the subject of gossip, ridicule, contempt, or perhaps economic reprisal. He may be censured or ostracized by his peers.

Early in the century a famous European novelist arrived in this country, accompanied by his common-law wife, to fulfill a series of lecture engagements. This flouting of then vigorously supported folkways was so deeply resented by an articulate and influential segment of society that a boycott was organized against the allegedly immoral practitioner of "free love." As a result, almost all his speaking engagements were canceled.

Informal means of showing displeasure over violation of folkways can be as punitive and damaging to the self-esteem, social standing, and career of the nonconformist as a sentence pronounced by a judge. The unkempt man in Figure 6.1 is

Figure 6.1
Informal Enforcement

Reprinted with permission of Donald Reilly and the publisher from *The Saturday Evening Post* © 1963, The Curtis Publishing Co.

"All your friends and neighbors are pitching in on a 'spruce up' campaign, and we'd like you to do your bit by moving."

being notified, quite informally, that he has seriously displeased his neighbors and that they have imposed an informal "sentence" upon him.

6. *Although folkways are expected or required behavior, some are more arbitrary than others.* There is no doubt that you are expected to tip the hotel bellman who carries your bag, but the householder is not as obligated to give the postal carrier a Christmas gift. It would be considered a serious, perhaps even a hazardous, violation of a behavior norm in some United States communities for a Negro to sit down next to a white person in a restaurant. On the other hand, although it would be unusual and subject to some criticism, a white man may choose to play in an otherwise all-Negro jazz band.

7. *Folkways are comparatively durable.* Folkways are customs, and customs tend to persist. Literally, "folkways" means "way of the folk."

8. *Although folkways tend to be durable, they sometimes do disappear from a culture.* Men in this country no longer wear hats made of beaver fur. Hashimah Roose, a Malayan woman, writes that until quite recently family tradition and custom forbade the education of daughters. The reason generally advanced ". . . was that such an education would be of no use to them other than to enable them to write love letters or arrange for trysts with young men leading to possible elopement." Beginning some three or four decades ago, however, Malaya

underwent great social change in a comparatively brief period of time. Ideas from abroad entered the culture. The role of women was reexamined, and some inhabitants urged that female children be educated. More conservative natives retorted with a proverb: "It is better to let your children die than allow traditions and customs to lapse." But in time, resistance to the idea of educating females diminished.

As a precaution, girls were at first not allowed to go to school on their own. They were escorted or chaperoned by old men . . . to and from their schools. This practice was eventually allowed to lapse. . . . Nowadays girls are allowed to go to school either on foot, by bus or car or even by cycle. . . . Twenty years ago a girl cycling to school was unheard of![2]

9. *The regulatory function of folkways determines much of individual behavior.* In effect, the folkways encourage and discourage certain activities. This results in pressure on individuals to conform. We may assume that the folkways of the particular business organization depicted in Figure 6.2 influenced employees' manner of dress.

The student from Iran, whom we quoted elsewhere, had something to say about courtship and marriage customs in his native land:

QUESTION: Would you generalize and say all American girls are like the "loose" one you described, the one who introduced herself to you and suggested you date her?
ANSWER: Not today. Not *loose*. Not all of them. But always there *are* girls who come around you and talk to you. I understand now that doesn't necessarily make her a loose girl. Not the way custom is here. But in Persia this is not the custom.
QUESTION: Was it conceivable to you at the time that you might fall in love with a girl you met this way?
ANSWER: I don't know what "falling in love" means. People don't have any courtship in Persia. So if I say I fell in love with a Persian wife, it doesn't mean the same thing as it does here. Here, I think, people usually date, they go on courtship, and then they say they "fell in love." Falling in love came later on. That has no connotation for us. The parents fix a marriage, and the couple loves each other or not.

10. *Folkways make it possible for an individual to achieve a feeling of identification with other members of a group.* In

Figure 6.2
Business Folkway
Drawing by R. Taylor;
© 1963 The New Yorker
Magazine, Inc.

*"Gentlemen, I want you to meet Mr. Fannin,
who has just joined our staff."*

conforming to its norms he gains that feeling. He is "in." The Catholic who attends to the requirements of his faith is enabled thereby to feel he "belongs" with other Catholics. The man who salutes when the United States flag passes on parade identifies himself with patriotic United States citizens.

11. When we said that folkways make it possible for an individual to achieve a feeling of identification with other members of a group, this was not to suggest that he responds solely to the customary patterns of behavior generally followed by members of the entire society. *The individual responds not only to the generally accepted folkways of his society, but also to those of the subcultural groups with which he identifies himself.*

The youth gang member responds to many of the same folkways that most members of his society do, concerning family, courtship, perhaps religious practices. He also responds to the more specialized customs of the street gang subculture, as this excerpt from a tape recording reveals. The speaker is a nineteen-year-old boy:

When I was twelve, thirteen, we used to think it was smart to walk past a newsstand and when the guy turned his back we'd snatch a bunch of papers. . . . We just did it to be ornery. You did just what the others did.

Now, a guy don't have to be a good fighter to belong to our gang. . . . I don't even care if he's a sissy, so long as he minds his own business. If trouble starts, he don't have to be a Joe Louis, but he sure as hell can't run off. I myself, I like to go out with a guy that isn't going to run from it . . . because if it's your fight, you don't want to chicken out.[3]

This same boy observed the folkways that were more generally accepted: he paid for purchases in the department store; courted a girl along conventional lines. Some years after the tape recording he married a young lady, in a civil ceremony; supported his wife, and a daughter when she was born, to the best of his capacity.

Another example of response to the folkways of a subcultural group is the protocol of a certain business establishment in Dover, Delaware:

Dover clings to many old customs which are based not on law but on habit and long tradition. . . .

Newcomers can easily violate some cherished old Dover custom unwittingly. When William K. Paton came down [to Dover] from New Jersey to serve as president of the rich, venerable, and conservative Farmers Bank of the State of Delaware, he knew, of course, that twice a year he must be host to his directors at a dinner. Eager that everything should go off well, he had planned to serve particularly large and juicy steaks and had taken steps to obtain some. Vice-President Gordon Willis, who had been in Dover two years . . . set him straight. Since 1807, Willis explained, the president of the Farmers Bank had served his directors Delaware diamond-back terrapin and pheasant at the January meeting. At the July meeting the gentlemen must be fed Lewes lobster and guinea hen.[4]

AN EXPANSION OF SUMNER'S ANALYSIS

Sumner's analysis of folkways and mores suggests a dual classification—behavior that is expected and behavior that is required. It may be helpful to think in terms of three levels of cultural expectation instead of two: *required, preferred,* and *permitted* behavior. We should conceive of them as lying on a continuum.

Let us apply this classification to actual behavior. When you were six years old, your parents may have required you to brush your teeth at least once a day, although they preferred that you use the toothbrush twice daily, and would have permitted you to brush your teeth after every meal if you so desired. One college instructor requires that students write extensive notes as he lectures, another prefers that they do, and a third permits students to decide for themselves whether or not they will take notes, the instructor not caring one way or another what the decision may be. You can see that the areas between these levels on the continuum blend almost imperceptibly into one another. A strongly preferred standard of behavior, for instance, is practically a required standard, as it is impossible to draw sharp, distinct lines separating one level from another.

Keeping this continuum in mind, we can amplify the meaning and consider other applications of the three concepts, required, preferred, and permitted behavior.

Required standards of behavior are modes of conduct rigidly demanded of individuals in responding to particular situations. At the turn of the century, most people in England and the United States considered it a fact that sex had nothing to do with mental disturbances. It was therefore accepted as fact that a doctor could have no legitimate motive for inquiring into the sex life of a patient. The folkways forebade open discussion of the subject, and those who did not conform were treated accordingly. In 1910, the very mention of sex in relation to Freud's theories caused the chairman of a Hamburg meeting of physicians to bang his fist and shout, "This is not a topic for discussion at a scientific meeting; it is a matter for the police!"

Preferred standards of behavior are modes of conduct generally accepted and expected but not rigidly demanded of individuals in responding to particular situations. We consider it appropriate that a person place a napkin in his lap at the dinner table; we expect he will do so; but we will not censure him severely or invoke a penalty against him should he fail to come up to our expectation in this respect.

Permitted standards of behavior are modes of conduct available to the individual which he may or may not pursue, as he sees fit, without incurring censure or penalty. Nowadays, in the United States, a man may choose to wear a hat out of doors, or he may choose to go bareheaded. Either way, no penalty will attach to the behavior.

Even by this three-part classification of norms it must be acknowledged that it is not always possible to say definitely that a given mode of conduct is required, preferred, or permitted. Between about 1925 and the present there have been various shades of intepretation as to whether skirts were the only acceptable garb for girls. Were they required, expected, or permitted? Today, the wearing of slacks, shorts, and other forms of trousers by females is defined by a few as a serious violation of required behavior. It is regarded by others as merely a rude or brazen revolt against standards of preferred behavior, and by still others as behavior that is permitted, at the option of the individual concerned, the behavior being interpreted as having no moral connotation.

LAW

The third major class of social norms is law. It may be, and often is, based on values inherent in the folkways, but it is more than custom. *Law consists of legislatively enacted or otherwise formally drafted and proclaimed rules of behavior, supported by organized government, which establishes sanctions, or negative penalties, for violations.* Although all societies have folkways, not all have laws. A very small, loosely organized band of people may function without formal law, behavior being regulated by custom. However, law does exist in most contemporary societies.

MacIver and Page delineate the difference between law and custom. Law, they write,

. . . derives from various sources, including custom, but it becomes law when the state, which means in the last resort the courts, is prepared to enforce it as a rule binding on citizens and residents within its jurisdiction. . . . The distinctive nature of the legal code in modern society is seen in its coercive and inclusive character as enforced by . . . the state.[5]

Law, then, is a code upheld by the state. How is it different from custom?

Whereas law is often *made,* and is always applied, by the definite power of the state, custom is a group procedure that has gradually emerged, without express enactment, without any constituted authority to declare it, to apply it, to safeguard it. Custom is sustained by common acceptance. . . . Customs are the most spontaneous of all social rules and often the most compelling. But they are sanctioned not like law, by organized coercive authority, but by a wide variety of informal social pressures.[6]

Why is there law in addition to custom? Why cannot custom alone guide behavior?

1. *The state cannot allow private persons to undertake settlement of certain types of disputes among themselves.* In societies lacking a formally organized central government, disputants often settle their differences unilaterally, one retaliating against the other for the wrong presumably done him. This retaliation may take the form of physical violence, the seizure of property, or other direct action by one party to the dispute against the other. When a state is formed, those who govern cannot countenance such private justice. The state must be supreme over any individual; public order must be maintained; disputes of a certain order must therefore be submitted to designated tribunals for adjudication according to law.

2. *Custom is comparatively static (although less and less so in complex, modern societies). Laws can be enacted and repealed with relative ease to serve new needs stemming from social change.* For many years, when custom alone prevailed, a venereally diseased person in this country could decide for himself whether he would seek medical treatment. He might infect a succession of other individuals through physical contact, since custom, not law, defined such behavior as reprehensible.

When public health departments came into being, their personnel launched educational programs, alerting residents to the symptoms of syphilis and gonorrhea and to the need for early identification and treatment of infected persons. These campaigns had considerable effect, but not enough to furnish maximum protection. It became obvious that a great many people, suspecting or knowing they were carriers of venereal disease, fell back on custom and considered it their right to decide how to behave under the circumstances. In other words, custom was not changing with sufficient rapidity to meet current needs.

As a consequence, local, state, and federal laws were enacted, setting forth under what conditions it was mandatory upon an individual to seek medical diagnosis. Laws further required that an infected person take treatment, either from a private physician or in a free public clinic or hospital. It became obligatory upon doctors who discovered venereal disease in a patient to inform public health authorities. These authorities, in turn, were empowered to quarantine venereally diseased persons in an infectious stage, even against their will. All these steps were accomplished, with some success, in a comparatively short period of time, by the enactment of laws.

3. *Most customs are ignored at times by individual members of a society. Where, by definition within the society, such nonconformity is to be strictly prohibited, laws have the advantage over custom of (1) universal applicability and (2) coercive authority.* A law applies to all persons in a given class, whether this class be the entire nation or a special group. No policeman is supposed to deprive any person in the United States of his constitutional right to due process of law. Here the law applies to a class of persons—policemen. Every individual inside our boundaries is forbidden by law to commit burglary and robbery. Here we are guided by statutes that apply to all persons within the United States.

All children under a specified age must attend school. All aliens resident in this country must report their addresses annually. These are laws applying to special classes of people, but to all within the class without exception.

4. *Custom often defines approved and disapproved behavior imprecisely. Law is usually more precise.* The Small family purchases a home in a neatly kept residential neighborhood whose residents take pride in keeping their houses and lawns in excellent condition. The Smalls show little interest in this cultural value esteemed by their neighbors. They do not weed their lawn, but allow their grass to grow ragged. The weeds go to seed, are carried by the wind to neighboring lawns, whose owners must work all the harder to preserve the appearance of their yards.

This is contrary to established custom and residents are resentful of the Smalls, but just what shall they do to rectify the situation? Custom provides no exact rule for determining when grass has grown too tall; how often weeds shall be pulled; what to do about a family such as the Smalls when they offend neighborhood custom. They could be ostracized, and this might accomplish the desired end. But it might not. In the final analysis, the Smalls own their property—that is law—and only custom suggests how they shall treat it. If they are willing to withstand neighbors' informal sanctions, they need not conform with custom.

But suppose the Smalls are even more careless about their housekeeping. Suppose they set out open garbage receptacles in front of their house every Monday, dropping into it their daily accretion of refuse, from that day until Friday, when the weekly garbage collection takes place. The daily accumulation sets up a stench between collections, and moreover draws insects and constitutes a health hazard.

This, too, is a violation of customary norms in the community. Other residents resent the unsightly display in front of the Small home, and furthermore are indignant over the health hazards to which they have become exposed. But in this case, there is no need to examine custom in order to define whether and how badly the Smalls have breached it. Nor is there the necessity to deduce remedies. The community is protected by a city ordinance that very precisely sets forth that (1) no garbage receptacle shall be placed on the sidewalk except on Friday morning, collection day; (2) when so placed, it shall be covered. The ordinance provides penalties for violation, and these, too, are so specific in the wording that the Smalls will surely understand what penalty they may suffer for nonconformity. The neighbors, then, have a clear course of action laid out for them. They complain to the authorities, who warn the Smalls, who either conform or eventually suffer legal sanctions for repeated nonconformity.

In some situations, then, law serves as supplement and support to custom. And it has the advantage of specificity—it spells out what is required. Further, every law provides enforcement authority and procedure, concerning which custom is ordinarily more vague.

5. *But although it has certain advantages, law is not equally effective in all areas of human endeavor.*

Laws that are in conflict with strong emotions and impulses are sometimes ineffective. It is questionable whether a law can materially affect how people feel about their religion or pattern of family life. These are so firmly fixed by custom, so much a part of the emotional life of the individual, that a statute intended to bring about radical change would almost certainly fail of its purpose as envisaged by the drafters.

Law can effectively regulate overt behavior. It is less effective in regulating the ideas and feelings that generate particular behavior. A statute may effectively restrain fathers from strangling their adolescent offspring. It will not prevent their wanting to do so on occasion.

Fortunately, laws are generally in harmony with the society's system of folkways and in fact tend to stem from this system. Our laws providing free education of children are in harmony with the general view that it should be possible for all of our people to get a reasonably good education. But what if a statute seriously conflicts with the norms of behavior approved by the great majority of a population? *When a law is in direct and significant conflict with the folkways, the law may suffer from unenforcement.* The Eighteenth (Prohibition) Amendment to the Constitution was steered through Congress by an organized minority. On the eve of January 17, 1920, when the law would become effective, the Anti-Saloon League issued a statement declaring: "At one minute past twelve tomorrow morning a new nation will be born. Tonight John Barleycorn makes his last will and testament." And yet, six months later, Chicago's courts were clogged with between 500 and 600 cases awaiting trial for violations of the Prohibition law. In the first year of Prohibition the people of a "dry" United States consumed, according to government estimates, some 200 million gallons of hard liquor, 684 million gallons of malt liquor, and 118 million gallons of wine. The income of professional bootleggers was assessed at 4 billion dollars, making bootlegging the nation's largest industry. By 1930, ten years after John Barleycorn presumably was interred, federal officials estimated that in Chicago alone over 10,000 speakeasies were operating. By 1932, 500 Prohibition agents had been killed. Custom had defeated law.

A hundred years ago we amended the Constitution to give Negro residents all of the rights and obligations guaranteed to whites. Today, despite further enactments intended to strengthen the enforcement arm of government in protecting the rights of Negroes, it is still a fact that the folkways of the majority are in direct and significant conflict with the law of the land, and the law is often abused as custom prevails over statute.

In our definition of law we said it was legislatively enacted or otherwise drafted and proclaimed. Having discussed enacted law, we now turn to that class that is otherwise drafted and proclaimed. This refers to so-called customary law. In the United States and elsewhere customary law is expressed in a body of *common law*. Common law emerges in the course of adjudication of cases in criminal and civil courts, at both trial and appeal levels. It comes much closer to reflecting the folkways than does statutory law, for *common law is custom as defined by the courts*. It is not created by courts. It is found by them, according to the legal theory.

How is common law found? An issue comes before a judge, who discovers it cannot be decided on the basis of existing legislated enactment, either because no law covers the precise legal point at issue or because an existing law covering the subject is ambiguous on the particular point and may be interpreted several ways.

Suppose you tossed a firecracker into the street near a marketplace, just for fun; somebody kicked it away; somebody else kicked it toward another person, who picked it up and tossed it wildly in an entirely different direction, where it exploded in the face of an unsuspecting bystander. Suppose the bystander lost an eye as a result. You certainly did not expect that result when you tossed the firecracker; you meant no harm to anyone; you did not directly harm anyone. But someone lost an eye because you initiated the chain of events. Could you be held liable?

Yes. Exactly such a case was before a British court in 1773. Since no statute covered this precise situation, the judge explored such questions as: How have people in this society *customarily* treated a chain of events like this? What does the public conscience suggest as a fair solution for the question before the court?

After examining what he understood to be customary ways of regarding such matters, the judge "found," and announced it as a common law principle, that there was such a thing as "liability without fault." Liability could be placed upon the person who initiated the chain of events that resulted in the injury. This principle holds in England. Since we adopted much of that country's common law, it holds here as well.

This case, *Scott v. Shepherd,* typifies the process by which customary, or common, law emerges. In the absence of formal legal guides, the judge examines into the customs of his society, searching for a standard that will be consistent with the general pattern of legislated law as well as with the unwritten folkways. He finds the standard. He does not make a law on the subject, he only identifies a custom as applicable to the issue under examination. Theoretically, the principle involved already existed, manifested in the folkways of the people.

Not all folkways are of equal importance in a society. Those considered most compelling constitute organized clusters centered around major human needs. These clusters are *social institutions,* the most basic of which are the family, religion, government, the educational system, and the economic system. We discuss social institutions at length later in this volume, but notice must be taken of them here, too. Preliminarily, let us say that *a social institution is a system of interrelated folkways and laws organized around a given function of society.* It is through the system of social institutions that norms are translated into action.

Because we generally think of an institution as a thing, such as a bank building or a hospital, the sociological concept of *social institution* may seem confusing. It may help if one thinks of the verb, "to institute." We institute procedures. When we institute a procedure for delivering mail, we institutionalize mail delivery, which is to say we establish a regular, standardized procedure for delivering mail. In its way, it is an established, organized mode of performing a function in society that meets certain human needs.

Now apply this. Before there were formal laws in the modern sense, human beings engaged in courtship, sexual relations, cohabitation, and procreation. In time, folkways and, finally, laws developed around these activities. There evolved a system of interrelated, interdependent, permissive, expected, and required behavior, organized around the concept of *family.* The family was *institutionalized.* The various kinds of behavior permitted, expected, and required of members of the society in connection with family were brought into comparative harmony. Folkways and laws regarding dating, courting, mating, founding a family, and functioning as a family formed a unified whole. *The institution of family* consists of a reasonably consistent system of behavior standards deemed highly important and beneficial to all members of the society.

In the same manner a system of interrelated folkways and laws becomes organized around other functions of society. The economic system is regulated. Standards for the conduct of government are formulated. And so on. Such social institutions are comparatively durable. At the same time, they go through change, a matter discussed in the next chapter.

· *NOTES*

1. Robert M. MacIver and Charles H. Page, *Society: An Introductory Analysis* (New York: Rinehart, 1949), pp. 19–20.
2. Hashimah Roose, "Changes in the Position of Malay Women," in Barbara E. Ward (ed.), *Women in the New Asia* (Paris: United Nations Educational, Scientific and Cultural Organization, 1963), pp. 287–294.
3. Anonymous, "Gang Boy," in David Dressler (ed.), *Readings in Criminology and Penology* (New York: Columbia University Press, 1964), pp. 148–163.
4. Harold H. Martin, "The Cities of America: Dover, Delaware," *Saturday Evening Post*, CCXXII, 8 (August 20, 1949), 80.
5. MacIver and Page, *op. cit.*, pp. 175–176.
6. *Ibid.*, p. 176.

· *SUGGESTIONS FOR FURTHER READING*

ANONYMOUS. "Gang Boy," in David Dressler (ed.), *Readings in Criminology and Penology*. New York: Columbia University Press, 1964, pp. 148–163.
A participant in a youth gang subculture graphically depicts its mores.

HOEBEL, E. ADAMSON. *The Law of Primitive Man*. Cambridge, Mass.: Harvard University Press, 1954.
Anthropological observations on the sources and functions of law in primitive societies.

MATTHEWS, DONALD R. "The Folkways of the United States Senate: Conformity to Group Norms and Legislative Effectiveness." *American Political Science Review*, LIII (December 1959), 1064–89.
An intriguing report on the unwritten, generally accepted, informally enforced norms that influence the behavior of members of the United States Senate.

ROOSE, HASHIMAH. "Changes in the Position of Malay Women," in Barbara E. Ward (ed.), *Women in the New Asia*. Paris: UNESCO, 1963, pp. 287–294.
A very interesting account of the changing folkways of contemporary Malay women.

SUMNER, W. G. *Folkways*. Boston: Ginn, 1906.
This is the earliest systematic formulation of the concepts of folkways, mores, and institutions. See especially Chapters 1 and 2.

7 CULTURAL CONTINUITY & CHANGE

Culture tends to persist, yet it gradually and continuously changes. In this chapter we study both processes—cultural persistence (or continuity) and cultural change. Why do we cling to values, attitudes, skills? What are some of the immediate as well as long-range effects of cultural conservatism? What processes are discernible in cultural change? What conditions facilitate it? What are some of the consequences of cultural change upon the living patterns of people?

Place a check in the approprite column below, indicating whether the statement is true or false.

		TRUE	FALSE
1 ·	The blood of a white person is chemically different from the blood of a Negro.	....	....
2 ·	A check is worthless if dated on a Sunday or a legal holiday.	....	....
3 ·	If the sun shines while it is raining, it will rain tomorrow, too.	....	....
4 ·	Persons affiliated with one of the three major religious denominations in the United States are less prone to crime than the nonaffiliated.	....	....
5 ·	Divorced women in the United States remarry in lesser proportion than do widowed women.	....	....

	TRUE	FALSE

6 · Sharks will not attack human beings unless they smell blood. ....

7 · The United States never lost a war. ....

8 · When squirrels store unusually large quantities of food, a hard winter is ahead. ....

9 · No one can be induced to do things under hypnosis that he would not do when not under its influence. ....

10 · If liquor and oysters are consumed together, they will make you ill. ....

How many items did you check as true?

So far as we know at present, every one of the statements is false. Yet a great many people, maintaining beliefs passed on to them, hold one or another to be true. We tend to hold on to our cultural patterns of behavior. We are going to discuss this phenomenon of cultural persistence, or continuity, but you must always bear in mind that it is solely for purposes of analysis. In all societies, so far as we are able to ascertain, cultural continuity and cultural change are evident at one and the same time. They are two processes that go on with regard to one phenomenon: culture. When participants in a culture hold on to certain ways of life, this is *cultural continuity*, which affects the prospect of *cultural change* with regard to those ways. When *cultural change* occurs, this means *cultural continuity* has been affected to that particular extent.

In order to examine each in some detail, we will discuss cultural continuity and cultural change separately. However, you will note that at times this becomes impossible, since the two processes not only are evident at one and the same time but, from a realistic viewpoint, are interactive, one with the other.

CULTURAL CONTINUITY

Centuries ago, while medical pioneers were announcing scientific, empirically based evidence on causes of disease, some cultural groups, at the very same time and place, continued to believe with St. Augustine that "All diseases of Christians are to be ascribed to demons." These demons literally leapt into the bodies of human beings and made them physically or mentally ill. Gregory the Great told of a nun who had eaten some lettuce without first making the sign of the cross. As a result, a devil jumped onto the lettuce and was swallowed. A holy man, by proper and potent ceremonial, ordered the devil to come forth. It did, whining, "How am I to blame? I was sitting on the lettuce, and this woman, not having made the sign of the cross, ate me along with it."

In our own time, some people persist in believing that the number 13 is "unlucky." Most of us would agree this belief is no more than a superstition. So influential is it, however, that officials of Johns Hopkins Hospital felt obliged to take it into account. In 1963, when adding four surgery suites to the twelve already in use, they skipped 13, numbering the new units 14 through 17. A spokesman was quoted in the press as explaining, "A patient is anxiety ridden already by thoughts of undergoing surgery, and the knowledge that he is scheduled for No. 13 might produce unnecessary fears if he is the least bit superstitious."[1]

These items are examples of *cultural continuity*, also referred to as *cultural persistence* and *cultural conservatism*. As used here, *cultural continuity is the tendency to continue using the "tried and tested" procedures transmitted to us from the culture of the past*. Once behavioral patterns are learned, we tend to transform them into psychological habits, to follow them without wondering why. They have taken on the aspect and support of folkways and mores.

The imaginary cultural conservative in Figure 7.1 illustrates this. We may assume that, following tradition, he refused to take cover during a rain. When a contemporary uses a sort of umbrella made of leaves and branches, the conservative falls back on tradition to explain his disapproval and finds what he considers good reasons for doing so.

H. Ian Hogbin, of the Department of Anthropology, University of Sydney, Australia, discusses the opposition of inhabitants of the primitive sections of Melanesia to regulations designed to prevent the spread of infectious diseases. At the root of this opposition, he says, are contradictory theories concerning causes of illness, as subscribed to by the Melanesians on the one hand and scientifically oriented people on the other. The natives are convinced that sickness is brought about by supernatural forces set in motion either by sorcerers or by spirits. Therefore certain ceremonies, rather than public health

Figure 7.1
Cultural Conservatism
From *Saturday Review*, July
16, 1955. Reproduced by
permission of Mrs.
Burr Shafer.

*"I don't like it.
It's against nature."*

measures, are required to counteract the evil magic or win
back the approval of the spirits.

For instance, Hogbin tells us, the traditional-minded Wogeo
bury their dead in a shallow grave beneath the floor of the
house. The stench becomes nauseating, but the occupants are
convinced this is the acceptable way of showing respect and
affection for the deceased. Patrol officers banned the practice,
ordering residents of each hamlet to set aside a plot of ground
as a cemetery.

The islanders carried out the command, and when I reached them
every settlement had its enclosure. This was protected from the
ravages of the domestic pigs by a stout fence, and the individual
graves inside . . . were all neatly bordered with shells or blocks of
white coral. But they were without exception fakes. Only once had
a body actually been placed in a burial ground. This incident occurred when a man died during the course of a visit by a government official. Later, after the officer [departed], the relatives
exhumed the corpse and reinterred it in the more usual place.[2]

Despite resistance to change in some aspects of their culture, the Wogeo have undergone change in others. And this
is true, to one degree or another, in all societies.

This may be illustrated by reference to the so-called emerging, or developing, nations of Africa and other parts of the
world. They have undergone great technological and other
change in recent decades; at the same time much of their
older ways of thinking and behaving persist. When, for exam-

ple, anthropologist Hortense Powdermaker reported on it in 1962, the population of the Copperbelt, in what was then Northern Rhodesia (now Zambia) was mostly African, from approximately 70 Bantu tribes; only a minority was European. The Africans came from their small, homogeneous tribal villages in Northern Rhodesia and Nyasland to the town, where they worked the copper mines. They brought with them their tribal culture, in many respects vastly different from the culture they encountered in town, which was essentially oriented to the technological and social world of the white Europeans. Driving in the township one evening, Professor Powdermaker observed the old and the new—cultural persistence along with cultural change:

. . . I saw the mine shafts and derricks starkly silhouetted against the sky. . . . The smelter belched forth its smoke. I passed a meeting of the African Mine Workers' Union in the movie amphitheatre of the Welfare Hall, and a rehearsal, with the drums beating, of a tribal dance to be held the forthcoming Sunday afternoon, within earshot of the showing of slides of Noah's life by a missionary to a small congregation.

. . . Men who participated in a tribal dance on Sunday afternoon might be dancing on Saturday night to jazz music at the Welfare Hall. Witchcraft-thinking did not prevent people from using the services of the clinic and hospital. They listened to modern songs and to current news and stories over the radio, and used their traditional proverbs and folk tales to make a point in colloquial conversation.[3]

The Amish people in our country furnish an excellent case study of the coexistence of cultural persistence and cultural change. Of a sect originally led by the Swiss preacher, Jacob Ammon, the first Amish migrated to the United States some 250 years ago, settled on the land, and made it prosper. They built a figurative stockade around themselves to exclude outside influences, so they might live according to their accustomed ways. Today, wherever the Amish make their home, it is a "culture island," inhabited by people who think, speak, and act much as did their ancestors two and a half centuries before. They are Americans, yet distinctly different from other Americans.

It is against their religious beliefs to use any mechanized objects. For this reason they work their farms with equipment considered primitive by most American farmers. They do not ride in automobiles, trains, or planes, using only horse and buggy. Their homes are equipped with no plumbing, telephones, or electricity.

Children are taught the Amish tongue, a dialect preserved as a consequence of the isolation of the sect. It is alloyed with a sort of mongrelized English. When the children enter public school (briefly and only because the law commands it), they must relearn the English language to some degree. This author once heard an Amish child, living in Lancaster, Pennsylvania, say: "Am furhuddled. When the little dot comes, the story's all, ain't?" (This meant: "I am confused. When you come to the period, that means the sentence is ended—right?")

The Amish call themselves "plain" people and dress accordingly. Their clothing is simple and equipped with hooks and eyes rather than buttons. (Buttons suggest military uniforms, and the Amish are noncombatants.) Ties and belts are considered worldly and frivolous, hence men do not wear them. Women wear full, long skirts of discreet shades, a black or gray Amish bonnet, and usually carry a cape or shawl over their shoulders. A girl who drifts into the "outside world" and takes to wearing lipstick or a flowered dress is said to have "gone gay," a serious indictment among Amish folk.

Families live modestly, like their ancestors, doing without telephone, radio, TV, tractor, can opener, iceless refrigerator, power lawnmower.

This is orthodox Amish society, encrusted with tradition, bound by customs often at odds with those of neighboring non-Amish people.

And yet, despite all that parents do to teach children to maintain this culture, the solid island that is the Amish world is eroding. Inevitably, young folk come into contact with "outside" ideas and modes of behaving. Occasionally a son shocks his parents, leaves home to get a college education. He even travels to the campus by train. A daughter "goes gay" in dress. A few children leave the family farm, remain permanently in the outside world. Their elders grieve.

The above illustrates several points: *Counterforces of cultural change and cultural continuity are found in all human societies.* And although resistance to change may be greater with regard to one value or another, although some individuals are readier to accept particular changes than are others, and although some groups are more receptive than others to given kinds of change, the fact remains that human individuals and groups tend to resist cultural change.

Cultural traits tend to be durable. Why? Why do people continue to follow customary modes of behavior? Partly because they seem necessary for the perpetuation of the society and culture. Children in our country are taught to read, write, and make mathematical computations. Eskimo youngsters learn to hunt seal. In most societies, young people generally understand the relation between certain values they acquired in their groups and the cultural provisions for satisfaction of those values. Growing up, they become increasingly certain that the culture will enable them to solve their problems, satisfy their needs, and live contentedly among others. Therefore, the existing culture is viewed as desirable and "right." Thus, one vital reason for cultural conservatism is that since culture makes it possible for people to solve their problems and satisfy their needs, they feel it must be continued.

FOUR LEVELS OF CULTURAL CONSERVATISM

But why do people continue certain modes of behavior after they no longer serve a useful purpose, whereas a change would provide more reasonable and practical means of achieving desired ends? To understand this, let us examine what may be thought of as four levels of conservatism applying to certain aspects of culture having no clearly evident functions.

1. *Change is sometimes resisted because it is easier to follow cultural paths already well established and learned than to learn and adapt to new modes of behavior.* Following established patterns of behavior conserves physical and mental energy. We in the United States persist in spelling by inconsistent rules. Why is it lau*gh* and not laf? Why amb*ition* and not ambishun? Why *right* and not rite? Anthropologist Clyde Kluckhohn observed that it would be just as logical to go to the extreme of spelling *fish* g-h-i-t-i. The *gh* would be pronounced as in lau*gh,* the *iti* as in amb*ition.*[4] Spelling could be learned more readily and in less time if we adopted a systematic and phonetic form, yet when proposals along this line have been advanced, they have met with little enthusiasm.

Another illustration of the fact that it is sometimes easier to follow established paths than to adapt to new modes of behavior is this: When the automotive era dawned in this country, the first Packard car body delivered to the manufacturers had a whipstock, for horses, on the dashboard.[5]

2. *There is sometimes vigorous opposition to proposed changes, exerted by special interest groups.* They believe such changes would affect them adversely. Therefore they want to preserve the status quo.

When research scientists presented evidence that cigarette smoking is an important cause of cancer, the tobacco industry fought the inference that the findings justified launching an educational campaign to discourage the sale and consumption of cigarettes.

Unions have used featherbedding to keep men employed in the face of new processes and inventions that threatened to displace them. Thus a theater operator may be required to employ a full crew of scene shifters when the production involves no scene changes whatever.

3. *There exist generally accepted beliefs that proposed changes constitute a threat to the basic values of an entire society.* In these instances the culture provides a rationale for resisting change, and resistance is not limited to special groups within the society. Approximately a century ago, two physicians, William Morton of the United States and James Y. Simpson of Scotland, advocated the use of anesthesia to alleviate pain in surgery and childbirth. Strong objections were raised. One clergyman cried, "Chloroform is a decoy of Satan, apparently offering itself to bless women; but in the end it will harden society and rob God of the deep, earnest cries which arise in trouble for help." Genesis 3:6 was cited as authority for opposition to use of anesthesia: ". . . in sorrow thou shalt bring forth children." Interestingly, Simpson cited the Bible to justify the use of anesthesia, pointing out that God caused deep sleep to fall on Adam before removing the rib used in the creation of Eve. (Genesis 2:21.) However, the use of anesthesia was strongly opposed for many years after the initial demonstrations.

4. *Anything that stands in marked opposition to the cultural values of the given society may be thought of as to some extent "unnatural" and hence undesirable.* William Graham Sumner employed the term *ethnocentrism* to connote this attitude. Ethnocentrism is a powerful force for cultural continuity.

We are born into a culture, and in the main it is the only one accessible to us as we grow up. We accept its ways and judgments because they were there when we first became aware of the world about us and we were exposed to no alternative cultures. As a consequence, we have a tendency to evaluate other cultures, later on, by the degree to which they resemble or differ from our own. Those that are markedly different seem strange and unusual to us, perhaps ridiculous or dangerous. We are *ethnocentric.*

Ethnocentrism is the tendency to judge other cultures by one's own. This is beautifully illustrated in the following folktale of the Ozark territory:

One time there was several families come from back East somewheres, and homesteaded on the other side of Blytheville, Arkansas. It was pretty near fifty miles south of the Missouri line. They went around saying, "You got to show me!" and bragging how Missouri is the garden spot of all creation. Most of them was poor ignorant people, not much better than Yankees if the truth was knowed.

After while the country got more settled up, and then a gang of government surveyors come out to put up stone markers. The homesteaders didn't pay no attention at first, but when they seen where the state line was marked they set up a terrible holler. The damn fools says they don't want to live in Arkansas, because the Arkansas climate ain't healthy, and the people in Arkansas can't read nor write. Also they says Arkansas is full of bears and panthers and copperhead snakes, so it ain't safe for civilized folks to stay there over night even. The surveyors tried to explain how the whole bunch had been a-living in Arkansas all this time, but it wasn't no use. Them people was so dumb they couldn't get it through their head.[6]

Here you get two-way ethnocentrism. The man presumably relating the tale displays contempt for the homesteaders from Missouri. They were "poor ignorant people." They were "not much better than Yankees," another group of people compared unfavorably with Arkansans. The people from Missouri, on their part, considered their home state "the garden spot of all creation." They did not know they were living in Arkansas, and when told they were, they had all sorts of unflattering things to say about it. The Arkansan was ethnocentric about Arkansas. The Missourians were ethnocentric about Missouri.

In Figure 7.2 the cartoonist, perhaps unwittingly, pictured

Figure 7.2
Piratical Ethnocentrism
Drawing by Kraus; Copr. © 1957
The New Yorker Magazine, Inc.

"It's a grand old flag."

what can be thought of as ethnocentrism. Even pirates, as a group, can be proud of being pirates and consider the skull-and-crossbones emblem "a grand old flag."

Human beings tend to classify themselves in terms of in-groups and out-groups, concepts we shall discuss in more detail in Chapter 11. An in-group includes all the people about whom an individual is thinking when he uses the word "we." When the individual says "they," he is thinking of outsiders, people who do not "belong." They are of the out-group. When Sumner employed the word *ethnocentrism*, it was to denote the tendency on the part of people to use in-group values and standards in evaluating out-groups.

We enhance our own importance when we use ethnocentric measuring sticks; they are elastic and stretch our own importance while shrinking that of others. In-group and out-group contrasts, used in this way, convince us that our food is tastier, our women more beautiful, our art esthetically more pleasing, our men more courageous, our buildings more impressive, and our behavior more virtuous than "theirs." And "they" may be the neighbors across the street or all the people in the world who do not have United States citizenship. Ethnocentric attitudes often have to do with race, nationality, religion, and the family, but it is not limited to these. A person may be ethnocentric about his lodge, club, fraternity, profession, indeed anything with regard to which he judges other cultural and subcultural groups by his own, concluding, to his personal gratification, that his is superior.

Ethnocentrism was once defined as the belief that the "axis of the world runs through my home town." Residents of neighborhoods and cities develop strong in-group feelings. The native of Joplin, Missouri, is likely to say New York City is a nice place to visit, but he wouldn't want to live anywhere except in Joplin. Popular songs, a fertile field for in-group feeling, boast of that wonderful town, Chicago, and claim that away down yonder, New Orleans is a veritable garden of Eden.

Ethnocentrism extends beyond neighborhoods and cities; it is very often regional. The "dear old Southland" has been proclaimed a region beyond compare. A tall tale has it that the soil of Kansas is so fertile that there was a farmer once whose yield was so great that he had to stack all the wheat he could outdoors, then store the rest of his crop in the barn.

National ethnocentrism is common, of course. It is usually called patriotism when expressed by residents of "our" country, and chauvinism or jingoism when expressed by people of "other" countries. An outstanding example is the speech delivered before a Rotary Club a number of years ago. Part of it went:

My friends, we've been asleep as a nation! But we are waking up. We always have waked up in time. We've been in just as bad holes as any of the nations of Europe, but there is always this difference, we always wake in time. . . . That's a characteristic of us Anglo-Saxons. Babylonia went into a hole—and stayed there. Rome went down—and never came up. Greece—swept away. Spain went down and we don't see her getting out. But we somehow do and always will![7]

Racial ethnocentrism was expressed by Adolf Hitler when he called Germans members of the "master race."

One negative effect of ethnocentrism is to make it difficult for people to see either themselves or others objectively. This in turn limits opportunities for intercultural relations.

A positive effect is cultural stability. Ethnocentrism encourages fealty and conformity, discourages interpenetration by other cultural groups, justifies and perpetuates the status quo. In this sense, ethnocentrism contributes to the survival of a culture. When the members of a society accept their way of doing things as good, when they feel comfortable living that way, then they want to preserve what they have.

OGBURN'S THEORY OF CULTURAL LAG

The maintenance of old customs and traditions creates no difficulties for members of a society so long as they are consistent with other aspects of the culture. But in a rapidly changing society, such as ours, people seem more receptive to alterations in some phases of their culture than in others. As a result, the component parts tend to get out of functional alignment. The late William F. Ogburn, a well-known American sociologist, had this tendency in mind when he introduced the concept of *cultural lag*. In our own discussion, to follow, we employ it, but in a somewhat different sense than Ogburn did.

In recent years our ability to maintain peace with people of neighboring societies has lagged far behind our ability to wage war. The only way we seem able to avert a war that no one wants is to build more and bigger weapons than our prospective enemies, thus instilling fear in them. They in turn use the same tactics on us. It has been aptly observed that we have a hydrogen bomb technology and a bow-and-arrow ideology.

The concept of cultural lag, while subject to considerable criticism on some scores, is logically useful in improving our understanding of cultural strain and tension in our society. The following examples reflect the tendency of one phase of our culture to lag behind another:

Our willingness to appropriate money for school buildings generally lags several years behind the need for them in rapidly growing communities.

Highway-building programs have lagged far behind the need, based on the number and speed of vehicles owned by people in the United States.

We have many scientific contrivances and techniques for crime detection and apprehension that are not used in the majority of police jurisdictions.

In some parts of the country farmers allow the soil to become depleted, despite available scientific knowledge of how to maintain soil fertility.

Our ability to prevent venereal disease has forged ahead of our willingness to educate young people in the use of preventive techniques.

Ogburn attempted to define the phenomenon of cultural lag: *"A cultural lag occurs when one of two parts of culture which are correlated changes before or in greater degree than the other part does, thereby causing less adjustment between the two parts than existed previously."*[8] (Emphasis added.)

One reason why lags accumulate is the rapidity and volume of technological change. Ogburn offered as an example the lag in adjusting to nuclear fission. The atomic bomb was produced in two and one-half years, but in the ten years that followed we had developed no defense against it. We had made no effective adjustment, Ogburn pointed out, in the dispersion of urban populations, or in controlling atomic energy, or in agreeing to ban the atomic bomb.

As he saw it, cultural lags are one characteristic of the process of social evolution that occurs in a closely integrated society in periods of rapid change. But some events, he suggested, tend to result in a crumbling of cultural lags. He cited political revolutions as an example. Reports on the revolutionary movement in China in the 1950s, he pointed out, indicated that many lags—which concerned the family, rural life, and Confucianism—were overthrown by the revolution. Women were less in bondage. Feudalism was destroyed.

Wars tend to result in a decline in the pile of accumulated lags within a society. A consequence of World War II was that a greater proportion of women than previously gave up housekeeping for paid employment outside the home. They tended to remain in the labor market after hostilities ceased. Negroes remaining in civilian life were drawn into Northern cities in increasing numbers, to engage in defense work.

CULTURAL CHANGE

In 1924 in Muncie, Indiana, a town which was studied by Robert S. and Helen M. Lynd (they called it Middletown), a Bible class teacher concluded a lesson on the Creation with the question, "And now, children, is there any of these animals that God created that man could have got along without?"

"The horse!" said one boy. The class agreed.[9]

The "horse culture" of earlier generations had all but disappeared by 1924. Where 2 million horse-drawn carriages were manufactured in the United States in 1909, only 10,000 were constructed in 1923. Years ago, a man had to be a jack-of-all-trades. He would make a set of harness, repair a buggy wheel, whittle an axe handle, tap shoes, manufacture bullets, build his home. Today, even the farmer does not need to own a harness and is likely to purchase his axe handle and shoes ready-made. When his car stalls, he calls the Automobile Club or a garage. His bullets come neatly packaged from a sporting goods store. His home is built by professional construction men. Mr. American is no longer a jack-of-all-trades. Specialists do things for him.

His wife's grandmother could spin, dye, weave, make soap, churn butter. Mrs. American has also surrendered many of her functions to specialists. She buys her clothes ready-made, shops at the supermarket for soaps, butter, and canned goods. Prior to 1920, she was not even entitled to vote. Since then, aided by changing folkways, she has been freed of many domestic chores and works in factories and offices, engages in politics, holds political office, practices medicine, accounting, and law. She even engages in professional baseball and wrestling.

We are more outspoken about sexual behavior than we were a few decades ago. At the turn of the century, Mrs. Burton Kingsland advised, in *Ladies Home Journal*, that it was highly improper for a young man to place his arm around a girl on the way home from an "entertainment." Counseling a young lady how to put such a miscreant in his place, Mrs. Kingsland suggested he be told, "Don't you think it is rather cowardly for a man to act toward a girl as you are doing when she has trusted him and is in a measure powerless to resist such familiarity?"[10]

A bachelor writes to a contemporary "heart and home" columnist that he knows a sweet, demure girl whom he loves and would marry. He has another, who is "uninhibited, gay." She "comes up to my room." He asks, "How shall I discourage this girl?" The columnist replies: "Which girl?"[11]

Most recently, it seems to be a hippie philosophy that sexual cohabitation, whether relatively permanent or fleeting, may properly be based upon a feeling of companionship alone and not upon the intention to marry, in the conventional sense, or to found families. These views represent cultural change in a society where cultural continuity on the subject still persists and has strong adherents.

Cultural change is the modification or discontinuance of existing "tried and tested" procedures transmitted to us from the culture of the past, as well as the introduction of new procedures. Man is always learning, yearning, competing, retreating, cooperating, combating. Culture is never static. How does change come about? Sociologists have advanced numerous answers to the question, but in the final analysis it must be acknowledged that causes of cultural change have not been satisfactorily identified. However, it is possible to make observations that shed some light on cultural change:

1. *When members of a society are confronted by customs that differ from those they learned to accept, they adopt some of the new customs, reject others, and follow modified versions of still others.*

At one time, most women in our country did not smoke cigarettes, and many were shocked when they learned that a few feminine "rebels" did use tobacco products. Nowadays, millions of women smoke. They *adopted* the new custom.

A few decades ago, nudist groups were organized in the United States. Advocates of nudism argued that going about unclothed was healthy and led to a reduction of sexual tensions. Nevertheless, the great majority of United States men and women declined to follow the nudists. They *rejected* a new custom.

Among the black Africans of the then Northern Rhodesia studied by Hortense Powdermaker, it had been traditional that marriages were arranged by kinfolk. Marriage payments were made, and continuing gifts were given to the in-laws in lieu of traditional services. Later, new values, and custom based upon them, emerged among those Africans who had left their villages for the industrialized Copperbelt. Borrowing from the Western value system, it became customary to marry on the basis of love, congeniality, and sexual attraction. This weakened the traditional system of arrangement of marriages by kindred. But marriage payments and continuing gifts to in-laws persisted, even in the marriages based on choice.[12] Thus, these people followed a *modified* version of a new marriage custom made available to them.

The fact that a people adopt some new customs, reject others, and follow modified versions of still others demonstrates the process of selection. What determines which customs will be accepted in whole or in part and which will be rejected within a society? This is also incompletely understood, but quite obviously people do not adopt at random every change available to them.

2. *New customs are likely to be more readily adopted if they represent what is viewed as socially desirable and useful and if they do not clash with preexistent and still-valued customs.* Changes having to do with artifacts such as tools are an example. They are considered desirable and useful in a society. Suppose a steel axe were introduced into a tribal group that had heretofore been using one made of stone. The fact that axes, in general, were already accepted in the society would facilitate acceptance of a steel axe to replace one of stone.

Hogbin points out that tools tend to be judged according to one standard—their utility. "Everyone, regardless of his previous experience, agrees that a steel axe is better for cutting down trees than a stone axe."* Tools are impersonal. They make no counter demands on the user. "He can experiment with them and, if he tires of them, throw them away."

Certain social customs having no connection with the use of tools are judged by other standards than mere efficiency and utility, however. Hogbin goes on: "If natives have believed for generations that polygamy is right, a missionary who thinks it is wrong faces a hard task in bringing them round to his point of view." Disengagement from such social practices is more difficult than disengagement from the use of a tool.[13]

3. Whatever they may accept in the way of new customs, *people do not completely abandon their traditional culture.* Significant elements of the old will remain in the modernized society. Again, we have cultural continuity along with cultural change. This is exemplified by the behavior of some people in South Africa. The lure of money and what it will buy has brought many natives to leave their rural villages and take work in the towns, which are under the influence of white people. Although town life becomes an indispensable means of earning wages, many Africans avoid what they consider the

* Actually, this does not always hold. Some people persist in the belief that something they have always used must be the most efficient.

contamination of the urban way of life, at least to an extent. They select certain aspects of the newly available culture, reject others, and follow modified versions of still others.

The Xhosa take employment in East London, South Africa. Some of them have accepted a good deal of the white man's culture—these people are referred to as the School people. Others resist change—these are the Red Xhosa. School people attend the Christian church, send their children to school, and adopt certain European customs. The Red Xhosa wear their traditional red blanket, rub their bodies with ochre, and remain devoted to a rural way of life.

Both the School people and the Red Xhosa earn wages in East London, for they could not subsist otherwise under the changed economy. But whereas School people spend money on the Western-style clothes and recreation that may be found in town, the Red people accumulate what surplus money they have, hoping someday to build a homestead in the rural area, to stock it with cattle and sheep, and to make this their true home.

Since the Red people hope their stay in town is but a temporary expedient until they set up their rural homestead, they, more than School people, hold on to traditional customs while in town. So far as feasible, they associate only with Red Xhosa. They meet to chat and to drink beer when the day's work is done, the sharing of beer being the traditional expression of hospitality and friendship. When a Red person is ill, all the "home" people visit him. When one Red Xhosa commits an offense against another, the matter, if at all possible, is dealt with according to the traditional way; this is preferred to bringing it before a town magistrate. The disputants appear before a meeting of "home" people, similar to one that would take place in their villages. A sanction of ostracism is imposed on the individual adjudged guilty.[14]

Thus both School and Red Xhosa accept certain aspects of white town culture, but their choices are not identical. Each group accepts what its members consider is not opposed to their values. Each group rejects some aspects of the newly available culture, these being viewed as in conflict with the values of the members.

Clearly, although the School people accept more elements of white culture than do the Red Xhosa, neither group completely abandons its traditional way of life.

4. *Changes in culture are always superimposed on existing culture,* somewhat as each new deposit of lava from a volcano is affected by the contours of previous deposits.

Note the youngsters in Figure 7.3. They are desert Arabs. They adopted a game new to them—baseball. They superimposed it upon their existing culture. Part of that existing culture is represented by their mode of dress.

5. *Change is relative.* We do not have a *changed* but a *changing* culture, strictly speaking. We do not stop behaving one way on a Monday and begin behaving altogether differently on a Tuesday. Cultural changes *emerge*—gradually, but incessantly. Accordingly, we find a coexistence of old and new customs in one society. In the United States:

WE HAVE	AS WELL AS
Classical music	Jazz
Train transportation	Plane transportation
Handwriting	Typewriting
Realism in art	Nonobjective art
Cigarette smoking	Research findings that cigarette smoking is a contributing cause of cancer
Continued disenfranchisement of Negroes in some areas	Enfranchisement of Negroes in those same areas
Hand sewing	Machine sewing
Belief in the essentiality of premarital chastity	Belief in premarital sexual experimentation
Superstitious beliefs	Scientific findings
The concept of legal insanity	The conflicting concept of medical insanity
Imperialistic ideology	The idea of national self-determination
Isolationism	One-world-ism
Integrated public education	Segregated public education

This coexistence of the old and the new is an individual as well as a group phenomenon. To some extent all of us follow traditional and newly acquired customs at one time or another.

Ni Ni Gyi, the wife of a Burmese scientist, has contributed an autobiographical document that sheds light on this phenomenon.[15] Educated in Rangoon and in the United States, Ni Ni Gyi holds the B.A. degree and is a leading figure in Rangoon social life. She is not typical of the majority of Burmese, who are farm dwellers, for she is of the middle class, a city dweller, and the daughter of a former government official. She is more representative of the literate, urbanized, comparatively well-to-do segment of Burmese society.

Ni Ni Gyi has internalized much of the older culture of her land, a culture going back centuries. She has also adopted new customs, many of which became available to her over a span of time that, in historical perspective, is quite brief. Between the years when her grandparents were alive and the present day, Burma was ruled by native kings, by the British, and by the Japanese. When the Japanese were repelled, Burma was again occupied by the British. Finally it became independent. It has, therefore, had contact with people from several quite different societies.

Figure 7.3
Existing and Superimposed Culture
Dmitri Kessel, *Life* Magazine © Time Inc.

The household in which Ni Ni Gyi was reared included her grandmother, father, mother, sisters, an aunt, and a cousin. The grandmother, as the oldest member of the family, was its recognized head. Ni Ni Gyi's father would do nothing without the approval and consent of the grandmother. The family system was strictly upheld.

. . . absolute respect and obedience were shown all along the line. Even the children had to obey the next in line, according to their ages. The deep-seated belief is that one is to show respect for people even if they are one day older than you are.

That was some years ago. But:

The attitude is somewhat changed now; the trend is toward more rational obedience, and relations between my mother and ourselves are on a more informal plane. . . . now, if my mother makes a certain decision, we are able to explain things to her and even disagree with her and she takes it in the best light.

Ni Ni Gyi's mother had some formal education, but not beyond "the middle grade," since "it was strongly felt that a full education was only for a man." By the time Ni Ni Gyi was of school age, she was able to get a higher education, and this brought upon her only mild criticism.

The marriages of Ni Ni Gyi's grandparents and parents were arranged for them, in accordance with established custom. However, her father and mother told her they would leave the choice of a mate to her, subject to their approval.

Ni Ni Gyi, as we can see, has accepted a number of new customs. But she retains some older patterns. She has the traditional faith in Buddhism. She respects the *raya-ko-su*, a ceremony in which offerings are made to nine gods in the hope that they will keep evil spirits away from the household. She never leaves on a journey on what are considered the "bad" days of the month on the Burmese calendar. Moreover, she buys property only on "good" days.

6. *Some changes introduced into a culture are at the time deemed necessary for human survival. Others are accepted in order to satisfy socially acquired needs not essential for survival.*

Suppose you are lost in the woods. You must eat to survive. Driven by hunger, you discover that insect larvae and wood grubs are nutritious and will sustain life. This knowledge would enable you to survive.

Finding a place to sleep would be easy. You could simply lie down on the ground. But let us say you make yourself a comfortable bed out of sapling boughs. It is not necessary to your survival, but it would satisfy a socially acquired need.

A hunting people who have depleted their supply of game animals will perish unless they move to another location or find other means of sustaining life in the old environment. Anthropological research provides numerous examples of people who have shifted from one kind of technology to another; from hunting, for example, to fishing or reindeer herding. The people of our own South have had to change from the plantation system based on a cotton economy to one of diversified crops and increased industrialization.

There is impressive evidence that Mother Nature is not as bountiful as depicted by some poets. She might more realistically be described as a niggardly old hag who yields up her treasures only when compelled. Man's struggle for existence has necessitated continuous change, constant adjustment to the geographical and biological environment.

And yet most of the changes taking place in our contemporary society are not imperative for survival. As individuals, we often accept change to satisfy, not survival needs, but acquired needs, for recreation, convenience, and the like. We adopt new ways in order to please associates or perhaps to keep up with the Joneses. But then, changes that were initially accepted for the amusement or convenience of a few individuals may become culturally defined as a necessity for the many (although still not essential for survival). In this category one thinks of automobiles, radios, and television sets.

7. *Some cultural change originally meets neither a survival need nor an acquired need of a people. Cultural change may be forced upon a people.* Where the white man penetrates and exploits underdeveloped countries, he usually brings or develops rules and laws that are new to the native population. He has forbidden private vengeance as a means of settling disputes. He has made it compulsory to observe new ways of disposing of the dead. Tribal life has been weakened through the superimposition of outside authority. Missionaries have proselytized natives, attacked the ideological foundations of tribal authority by inducting tribesmen into the Christian fold. But the point is

that even social change forced upon a people may eventually be accepted by them; customs they began following out of compulsion sometimes come to be followed from choice. Christianized Africans, for instance, may fight those who seek to exterminate Christianity. American Indians, forced to attend English-speaking schools, often *want* their children to attend.

8. *Crisis tends to produce or accelerate cultural change.* In wartime, we developed in a relatively short time new armaments, airplanes, guided missiles, "nerve gas," the atomic bomb. We accepted women in defense plants when there was a manpower shortage. When epidemic disease scourges a society, the crisis tends to produce a concerted effort to discover preventives and treatment methods, whether these are based on scientific investigation or magic. Once accepted, changes generated in time of crisis tend to persist.

9. *Culture change is cumulative in its total effect.* Much is added, little lost. Figuratively, the growth of culture is like the growth of a tree, continuously expanding in total size as long as it lives, while losing its leaves and even some of its limbs from time to time. Each change adds to the total inventory of items from which future cultural innovations may be assembled.

10. Furthermore, *whenever a change is incorporated into the culture and becomes defined as a social necessity, new needs emerge, generating the desire for still further changes to complement or supplement the original change.* Think what happened after television entered our culture. At first it was distinctly a luxury, enjoyed by the few. Then, by social definition, it became a virtual necessity. Now we have color and black-and-white television transmission; educational television programs and entertainment programs; closed-circuit television for business and industrial uses; the principle of television applied in crime detection, such as viewing posts in banks and prisons.

THE PROCESSES OF CULTURAL CHANGE

Anthropologists and sociologists have sought clues to the processes involved in cultural change. Their thinking may be summarized as follows: Cultural change is introduced through four processes: (1) borrowing from other cultures; (2) invention; (3) discovery; and (4) discontinuance of old cultural patterns.

CULTURAL BORROWING · *Cultural borrowing consists of adopting into a society a technique, practice, idea, or artifact of another society.*

Cultural borrowing (the anthropologist sometimes uses the term *cultural diffusion*) contributes much to changes in contemporary cultures. Because it is difficult to trace all that is part of our culture back to its source, we often assume we are its fountainhead, the originators of everything from cigarettes to the doctrine of democracy. This encourages ethnocentrism. The fact is that few cultural groups can point to anything that they and they alone originated. Intercultural give-and-take is the rule, not the exception.

Ralph Linton illustrated this in an article titled, "One Hundred Per Cent American," which appeared in the *American Mercury*.[16] He describes a man, proud of his American cultural heritage, awaking one morning. He wears pajamas, which are East Indian in origin, lies on a bed patterned after those first used in either Persia or Asia Minor. His sheet is made of cotton, first processed for domestic use in India; his blanket comes from the wool of an animal native to Asia Minor. He glances at his clock, a medieval European invention.

In his bathroom, generally considered this country's contribution to the world's culture, the glass is something that originated in ancient Egypt, the tile is a product first manufactured in the Near East. The porcelain is Chinese in origin. The bathtub and toilet are slightly modified copies of Roman originals. The one purely American contribution—in other rooms, of course, as well as the bathroom—is the steam radiator.

Our 100 percent American washes with soap, invented by the ancient Gauls. He shaves, "a masochistic rite" first developed by the heathen priests of ancient Egypt and Sumer. His razor is of steel, an iron-carbon alloy developed either in India or Turkestan.

The clothes he puts on are patterned after the skin garments of ancient nomads of the Asian steppes. He fastens them with buttons whose prototypes appeared in Europe at the close of the Stone Age. His shoes derive from Egypt and Greece. His tie is a vestigial survival of shoulder shawls worn by seventeenth century Croats.

Everything on the breakfast table comes from foreign cultural sources—the dishes, knives, forks, spoons. Coffee was first made from an Abyssinian plant discovered by the Arabs. Sugar first came from India, the melon from Persia, the cereal from grain domesticated in the Near East.

After breakfast, our 100 percent American leaves for his office on an English-invented train. He lights up a cigarette (native to Mexico) or a cigar (native to Brazil). He reads the paper, "imprinted in characters invented by the ancient Semites by a process invented in Germany upon a material invented in China."

And, Linton winds up, "As he scans the latest editorial pointing out the dire results to our institutions of accepting foreign ideas, he will not fail to thank a Hebrew God in an Indo-European language that he is one hundred percent (decimal system invented by the Greeks) American (from Americus Vespucci, Italian geographer)."

Another anthropologist, T. T. Waterman, listed contributions made by the Chinese to the "civilization" we know. They include tea, porcelain, gunpowder, silk, rice, parasols and umbrellas, spectacles, pepper, the printing press, the mariner's compass, asbestos, paper money, watertight compartments in ships, the fingerprint system of identification, kites. He also listed cultural items borrowed from American Indian societies: maize, tobacco, the potato, sweet potato, hammocks, quinine, toboggans, snowshoes, the tepee (original of the Sibley tent), cocaine, vanilla, chocolate, peanuts. Waterman concludes, "The American Indians and the Chinese, two people we rarely think of as civilized at all, have apparently made a full contribution to human culture. The American Indian has, in fact, made more numerous *original* contributions than the classical Greeks made."[17]

In Figure 7.4 we see an example of cultural diffusion. The woman, who lives in the sheikdom of Kuwait, is carrying a sewing machine. The first such invention on record was made by an Englishman, Thomas Saint, in 1790. In the following century, a French tailor, Berthelmy Thimonnier, and the Americans, Walter Hunt, Elias Howe, and Isaac M. Singer produced their own machines. Thus, at least three nations are represented in the development of the machine the lady in the photograph is carrying on her head.

Do you, like so many others, believe jazz is an American in-

Figure 7.4
Cultural Diffusion
Photo J. P. Charbonnier—*Realites.*

novation? Its roots lie in Africa, Spain, and other lands. American jazz has itself been diffused throughout much of the world.

An example of cultural borrowing is furnished by Clifford Geertz, in *Peddlers and Princes, Social Change and Economic Modernization in Two Indonesian Towns.*[18] Modern Western symbols are favored as trademarks for garments manufactured (via borrowed technology) in Modjokuto, which is in

Java, Indonesia. The trademarks, also borrowed, are applied to goods of an entirely different sort from those bearing their name in the country of origin. For instance, the Javanese sell Ford socks, General Motors shirts, and Frigidaire underpants.

We pointed out earlier that selective acceptance of cultural changes occurs. We now apply this to add that *human beings tend to be highly selective in the process of cultural borrowing.* They generally borrow only those items that seem to fit or to have immediate value in terms of their own cultural frame of reference. They are usually more reluctant to borrow ideological than technological items. The tractor was adopted as a farm implement in Soviet Russia, but a democratic form of government has not been accepted there.

Although in this analysis we differentiate between *borrowing* and *invention,* the first can almost never be entirely separated from the second. When technique, practice, or idea has been borrowed by members of a society, it usually must be modified to fit their culture. Invention is closely involved with cultural borrowing.

INVENTION · *Invention consists of putting existing elements of culture together in a different manner, either for the purpose of doing old jobs more effectively or to fulfill new purposes.* The inventor does not create anything basically new. He finds new ways of combining known techniques and ideas. Preexisting products of the culture are synthesized in different ways, permitting human beings more effectively to satisfy one or another of their acquired needs. This is the basic principle of all inventions.

The automobile was dependent upon antecedent inventions, from the prehistoric wheel to the modern internal combustion engine. The 1895 model combined the water jacket (invented 1833), differential gear (1840), pneumatic rubber tires (1845 and 1883), and many other items.

Obviously, an invention is not necessarily the work of just one individual. S. C. Gilfillan, a student of the sociology of invention, illustrates: "A steamship like the *Leviathan* resembles the *Clermont* no more than she does the *Flying Dutchman* or a quinquireme." Every principle that was in the *Clermont* might be found aboard the *Leviathan,* too, "but her 60,000 tons are built up on inventions—other, countless, millions of inventions. She has ears beneath the water, wherewith to hear the signals of the sea, when the fog lies over, and she has varied instruments as well to pierce the fog, hearing and making heard." The stockless anchor she carries is an invention, as are the machines that forged the links of her chain cables. Other inventions are the typewriters aboard, the elevators connecting her decks, the antifouling paint on her keel, the tools that fashioned the great ship. The steel that made her possible is one of the great modern inventions,

. . . and necessary for that steel were all the instruments, processes and sciences involved, from finding the iron's ore in Lorraine, to devising the giant's thumb and finger, that pinched her plates together with one-inch rivets, and left the surface smooth. . . . So we might progress from her keel up to the wireless antenna, and find represented in her, or involved ashore, so many inventions that their very descriptions would load the ship. . . . Few of these inventions were represented in the *Clermont*. The *Leviathan*'s real inventors were half of all the fathers of devices or improvements who have lived since time began. . . . Why then is there that ridiculous common report . . . that Fulton invented the steamship of today, or any steamboat?[19]

Invention is not limited to the technological phase of culture. Such cultural elements as our Social Security laws, the Constitution of the United States, and the juvenile court system represent syntheses of many ideas introduced previously into European and American thinking.

Ogburn stressed the importance of the cultural inventory as a source of continuing change. He noted that in many instances two or more individuals simultaneously but quite independently invented the same devices the same year. Among them: photography (Daguerre, Niepce, and Talbot, 1839), the balloon (Montgolfier and Ritten-Hopkins, 1783), centrifugal pump (Appold, Gwynne, and Bessemer, 1850), phonograph (Edison and Cros, 1877), electromagnetic clock (Wheatstone and Bain, 1845), and color photography (Cros and Du-Hauron, 1869).[20] It seems reasonable, then, that had Thomas Alva Edison or Sir Charles Wheatstone never lived, the inventions credited to them might have developed within a short time nevertheless, since other persons with about the same degree of motivation and ingenuity had access to the same inventory of cultural items.

In discussing *innovations*, a term with essentially the same meaning as inventions, Ogburn and Nimkoff assert that these depend upon (1) mental ability, (2) demand, and (3) existing knowledge.[21] Given the required intellectual capacity to understand the need for some innovation in order to solve a problem, there must still be a demand by members of the society for a solution of the problem. And along with demand, there needs to be knowledge on how to devise the innovation and to use it in furthering solution of the problem.

One other consideration might be added. It is only part true that "Necessity is the mother of invention," that is, that "demand," as defined by Ogburn and Nimkoff, leads to invention. It is at least equally a fact that "Acceptance of an invention is the mother of necessity," and, as has been indicated, acceptance resides in the culture. In a very real sense, therefore, it is culture, internalized in imaginative human minds, that is the real mother of invention. Notwithstanding our urgent, immediate need for defensive mechanisms to counteract the devastating potential of this century's nuclear fission bombs, such devices cannot be invented until and unless the cultural base makes their invention possible, that is, until the participants in the culture of the society accept the idea that invention of a counter force to neutralize the bomb is an urgent necessity.

DISCOVERY · *Discovery consists of finding previously unknown facts*. This differs from the process of invention, which, we said, utilizes old knowledge in a different and synthetic way. However, inventions often make new discoveries possible. Invention of the microscope made possible discovery of microorganisms.

And, obversely, new discoveries lead to inventions. Wilhelm Konrad Roentgen's discovery of X-rays led to the subsequent invention of devices of great current value in medical diagnosis and therapy.

Ralph Linton interestingly underlines the difference between invention and discovery. When, he says, a small child pulls a cat's tail and gets scratched, the child has made a *discovery*. The observed fact that cats will scratch when their tails are yanked is an addition to his store of knowledge. Now, armed with this fact, suppose the youngster gets an idea: He pulls the cat's tail when someone else is holding it, and, as he had anticipated, *that* individual gets scratched. That is in the nature of an *invention*. The child put together knowledge previously acquired to achieve a particular end—getting the cat to scratch the other individual. And, Linton adds, "If the child is then spanked, he will have another discovery to his credit."[22]

If the scene in Figure 7.5 represents the first occurrence of its kind, the individuals concerned would have hit upon an important discovery: Water douses fire.

DISCONTINUANCE OF CULTURAL PATTERNS · *Discontinuance of cultural patterns involves the loss of old ideas, skills, and arts as they are superseded and supplanted by new items of culture.*

There is a difference between arts and skills that have completely disappeared in a culture and those that are in the process of disappearing. We have altogether lost the art of embalming as the ancient Egyptians practiced it. The medieval process of armor fabrication constitutes another example of a skill that is no longer part of our present cultural inventory. But the skill used in driving a team of horses, highly prized some years ago, is only in the process of fading into obscurity; eventually, of course, it may completely disappear.

CONSEQUENCES OF CULTURAL CHANGE

When human beings change any aspect of their way of life, they usually realize some immediate satisfaction of the needs that initially induced them to change. In the long run, however, *acceptance of cultural change also leads to unanticipated consequences that may be viewed as either desirable or undesirable.* According to Ogburn, "the invention of the automobile has had more influence on society than the combined exploits of Napoleon, Genghis Khan, and Julius Caesar."[23] And yet this influence was largely unanticipated. The first cars were novelties, intended for the amusement of their owners. This effect was anticipated and was generally considered desirable. But among consequences not foreseen (and also now generally regarded as desirable) are the following:

Automobiles have made it possible for urban workers to live much farther from their places of employment, thus contributing to—although not, of course, causing—the extensive development of suburbs.

Figure 7.5
Discovery
Drawing by Weber; © 1964 The
New Yorker Magazine, Inc.

"Hey! This wet stuff puts out that hot stuff!"

The "little red schoolhouse" of rural America has practically disappeared because buses can collect children from farming regions and deliver them to central consolidated schools that approximate city schools in size and facilities.

Industries that extract and process metals, oil, rubber, paint, and textiles have undergone tremendous expansion as a consequence of the general acceptance of the automobile. Millions of people gain their livelihood from the production or use of cars, with occupational differences ranging from rubber-plantation workers to traffic court judges.

Among the consequences not anticipated and generally considered undesirable are:

Professional criminals have improved their *modus operandi,* including escape techniques, through the use of cars.

The automobile has affected the health of people in a number of ways. About 1,500,00 persons annually suffer temporary or permanent disabilities due to motor vehicle accidents. There is reason to believe that smog, produced partly by pollutants expelled from moving automobiles, contributes to the development of respiratory diseases, including possibly cancer.

Still other consequences of our use of automobiles are viewed as desirable by some people, undesirable by others:

The use of cars to enhance prestige is important to many people in our society. If possession of a Continental evokes admiration or envy from neighbors and associates, it may give the owner a feeling of relative importance.

Automobiles are extensively used by young people in dating activities. For some, the car may be a motorized boudoir, for others a means of escape from parental scrutiny. For most, it is a means of becoming acquainted with persons of the opposite sex.

The list might be expanded almost indefinitely. The general acceptance and use of automobiles currently influences the life of practically every American. It has induced change in every phase of our relations with one another, including our religious, educational, and economic behavior. A similar multiplicity of consequences emerged from acceptance of other cultural products, such as the telephone, radio, television, refrigerator, and power washing machine.

Evidence suggests that culture may be expanded indefinitely. Conceivably, human beings, through bringing about cultural change, can satisfy most needs presently motivating them and solve the great majority of problems currently plaguing them.

At the same time, we reiterate: Each change incorporated into the culture will be followed by unanticipated consequences and problems, thus continuously generating the interminable process of cultural change.

Moreover, cultural change does not move steadily in the direction that cultural or subcultural groups would define as increasingly beneficial.

One example is reported by Professor W. F. Cottrell.[24] A small community formed on the western desert of the United States during the time when steam engines began pulling trains toward the Pacific Coast. These engines required servicing every 200 miles, and the subsistence of people living in the desert town was dependent almost entirely upon this technological need.

Then the diesel engine was invented, and transcontinental trains were pulled by the new rather than by the old type of locomotive. The diesel did not require servicing at intermediate points across the desert. Practically overnight, the townsmen lost their means of livelihood. The economy of the town collapsed. Where, earlier, residents of the desert community were enthusiastic about the railroad industry, they now attacked it as an example of big-business heartlessness. Where they had been proud of their independence and ability to provide for themselves, they now asked for government aid.

The diesel engine represented "progress" to the railroad owners. It meant economic frustration and a huge step backward for the dwellers of that desert community.

We have now examined some aspects of culture and society. We turn, in the next section, to a study of the individual as a member of society and participant in its culture.

· NOTES

1. AP dispatch, datelined Baltimore, Md., in *Omaha World-Herald,* August 15, 1963, p. 10.
2. H. Ian Hogbin, *Social Change* (London: Watts, 1958), pp. 105–107.
3. Hortense Powdermaker, *Copper Town: Changing Africa, The Human Situation on the Rhodesian Copperbelt* (New York: Colophon Books, 1962), p. 7.
4. Clyde Kluckhohn, *Mirror for Man* (New York: Whittlesey House, 1949), p. 149.
5. Robert S. Lynd and Helen M. Lynd, *Middletown* (New York: Harcourt, Brace & World, Harvest Book, 1956), p. 489n.
6. Collected by Vance Randolph, *The Talking Turtle and Other Ozark Folk Tales* (New York: Columbia University Press, 1957), p. 36.
7. Lynd and Lynd, *op. cit.,* p. 228n.
8. William F. Ogburn, "Cultural Lag as Theory," *Sociology and Social Research,* XLI (January-February 1957), 167–174.
9. Lynd and Lynd, *op. cit.,* p. 251.
10. E. S. Turner, *A History of Courtship* (New York: Dutton, 1955), pp. 194–195.
11. Reported in *Time,* LXIX, 3 (January 1, 1957), 70.
12. Powdermaker, *op. cit.,* p. 152.
13. Hogbin, *op. cit.,* pp. 64–65.
14. Lucy Mair, *New Nations* (Chicago: University of Chicago Press, 1963), pp. 152–155.
15. Ni Ni Gyi, "Patterns of Social Change in a Burmese Family," in Barbara E. Ward (ed.), *Women in the New Asia* (Paris: United Nations Educational, Scientific and Cultural Organization, 1963), pp. 138–148.
16. Ralph Linton, "One Hundred Per Cent American," *American Mercury,* XL (April 1937), 427–429.
17. T. T. Waterman, "The Great World Theater," in *Essays in Anthropology Presented to A. L. Kroeber* (Berkeley: University of California Press, 1936), p. 421.

18. Clifford Geertz, *Peddlers and Princes, Social Change and Economic Modernization in Two Indonesian Towns* (Chicago: University of Chicago Press, 1963), p. 64n.
19. S. C. Gilfillan, "Who Invented It?" *Scientific Monthly*, XXV (December 1927), 529–534.
20. William F. Ogburn, *Social Change* (New York: Viking, 1938), pp. 90–102.
21. William F. Ogburn and M. F. Nimkoff, *Sociology*, 2nd ed. (Boston: Houghton Mifflin, 1950), Chap. 25.
22. Ralph Linton, *The Study of Man* (New York: Appleton-Century-Crofts, 1936), p. 306.
23. William F. Ogburn, *Machines and Tomorrow's World*, Public Affairs Pamphlet No. 5 (New York: Public Affairs Committee, 1938), p. 3.
24. W. F. Cottrell, "Death by Dieselization," *American Sociological Review*, XVI (June 1951), 358–365.

· SUGGESTIONS FOR FURTHER READING

ADORNO, T. W., ELSE FRENKEL-BRUNSWIK, DANIEL J. LEVINSON, and R. NEVITT SANFORD. *The Authoritarian Personality.* New York: Harper & Row, 1951, Part I, Chapters 4–8.
Difficult reading in spots, but worth it. Highly respected research in which ethnocentrism is measured according to a specially designed scale. The relation of ethnocentrism to personality factors is also explored.
BOTKIN, B. A. (ed.). *A Treasury of American Folklore.* New York: Crown, 1944, pp. 276–317.
A series of ethnocentric boastings about country, state, and locality, loaded with hyperbole and in effect proclaiming "my place is the world's greatest."
GILFILLAN, S. C. *Sociology of Invention.* Chicago: Follett Publishing, 1935.
One of the best statements on society as the generating force, as well as the effect, of invention.
LINTON, RALPH. *The Study of Man.* New York: Appleton-Century-Crofts, 1936, Chapter 18, "Discovery and Invention," Chapter 19, "Diffusion," and Chapter 20, "Integration."
These chapters explore the phenomena of discovery, invention, cultural borrowing, and diffusion of inventions, and their integration into the borrowing societies.
MACK, RAYMOND W. *Transforming America, Patterns of Social Change.* New York: Random House, 1967.
Assesses major social trends in the United States and their implications for Americans. Worth reading in its entirety at this point, although some chapters relate to subjects covered farther along in the present text.
MEAD, MARGARET. *Cultural Patterns and Technical Change.* New York: Mentor Books, 1955.

An inquiry into the impact of modern technology on five traditional societies. The author is a well-known anthropologist.

MOORE, W. F., and M. M. TUMIN. "Some Social Functions of Ignorance." *American Sociological Review,* XIV (December 1949), 787–795.

Presents some of the effects of ethnocentric thinking upon a society. Such thinking tends to reduce or prevent criticism, thereby strengthening the status quo.

OGBURN, WILLIAM F. "Cultural Lag as Theory." *Sociology and Social Research,* XLI (January-February 1957), 167–174.

A discussion of cultural lag, by the foremost theorist of social change.

PAULMORE, ERDMAN B. "Ethnophaulisms and Ethnocentrism." *American Journal of Sociology,* LXVII (January 1962), 442–445.

An examination of the derogatory racial and ethnic nicknames in the Dictionary of American Slang. *These "ethnophaulisms" support ethnocentrism and discriminatory practices.*

POWDERMAKER, HORTENSE. *Copper Town: Changing Africa.* New York: Harper & Row, 1962.

An anthropologist, who writes as skillfully as a professional journalist, presents a sound and fascinating account of social change on the Rhodesian Copperbelt.

STOUFFER, SAMUEL A. *Communism, Conformity and Civil Liberties.* New York: Doubleday, 1955.

Among other things, this volume points out the characteristics of people who are likely to be ethnocentric. It also presents a "tolerance" scale for measuring attitudes toward nonconformists.

part three
the individual in society

8 WHAT IS HUMAN BEHAVIOR?

Having discussed in some detail culture and society, we begin a discussion of the individual in society. In this and in succeeding chapters, we turn our attention to how the individual comes to share, internalize, and enact the culture of his society. We will examine heredity and environment as sources of human behavior, communication as a feature of human behavior, and the manner in which man learns social behavior in his environment.

A human being is an organism. That is, the human being has life. What is life? Even the biologist cannot fully explain that, but whatever it is, creatures other than human beings also have it. Dogs, horses, whales, worms, crows, gnats—all are living organisms. Because they have this vital force we call life and because, also, they are not human, the question then is: What makes the human organism human?

BIOLOGICAL & SOCIAL SOURCES OF HUMAN BEHAVIOR

The human being is a product of two basic forces: biological and social.

Biological influence is transmitted by heredity, through human reproduction. *Heredity is the transmission of certain characteristics from parents to offspring.* Color of eyes is an example.

Social forces operate through the environment. *Environment may be defined as all of the external conditions and circumstances that surround an organism at a given time.* When you are in class, your environment includes, among other items, the air you breathe, the classroom and its furnishings, fellow students, and the instructor.

Biologically, man is human in that, through heredity transmitted in the process of reproduction, he differs significantly from nonhuman organisms. Human beings stand and walk in an erect position, whereas most animals do not. Human beings have manual dexterity, which is increased by the fact that their thumbs "oppose" their fingers; this is not characteristic of nonhuman animals. Human beings have a particular kind of vocal equipment.

But these distinctions do not exist between human beings and animals in all instances. A bear walks upright at times. Anthropoid apes can approximate human beings in manual dexterity. Parrots can mimic human speech.

What makes man a human being, biologically, is the physical and mental equipment that is different in marked respects from that of a nonhuman creature. His particular biological equipment gives him the potential for human behavior. The walking bear still does not behave like a man. The anthropoid ape may peel a banana, but cannot repair watches or paint pictures. The parrot might scream, "What's your I.Q., Buster?" but it cannot comprehend the meaning of *Intelligence Quotient.*

Obviously, human behavior includes much more than the behavior of a newborn infant, although the latter is a human being *biologically.* The individual is born with the potentiality to behave as human beings behave. Utilizing this inherited capacity, an infant learns through his social environment to behave like a human being.

Biologically, you were born a human *being.* But, for the most part, you had to develop human *behavior.* You had to become aware of people and things, to gain a conception of who *you* were. You learned fears, affections, and feelings for your parents, playmates, and others. You acquired a sense of humor. You took on judgments of good and bad, ugly and beautiful. You began to understand and react to certain highly abstract concepts such as *honesty, truth, fairness, courage, danger, security.* You attained notions about life, death, deity, war, peace, the races of man. These did not come to you biologically, by inheritance. You learned them in your society.

Now you are not only able to breathe, burp, and focus your eyes, but capable of frying an egg, laughing at a joke, reading a book, fighting for a principle, making a living, falling in love. You are a human being, engaged in human behavior all of the time.

THE BIOLOGICAL BASIS OF HUMAN BEHAVIOR

How is man biologically separate and distinct from all other living creatures? What biological characteristic is common among all human beings and unique to them? What differentiates human from nonhuman organisms?

Ancient peoples had a simple answer to the last question. They were not animals, but special creatures born to conduct themselves in certain ways, quite different from the ways of animals. Dogs bred indiscriminately, but human beings selected their sexual and marital partners according to prevailing customs. Men made tools to cut down trees; beavers used their teeth for the same purpose. Human beings fabricated clothing to cover their bodies, while monkeys neither wove nor wore garments.

But ancient belief notwithstanding, we know today that human beings *are* animals and in many ways behave as other types of animal. And we have learned from anthropology and other studies that what a person, in his own community, may assume to be the way all mankind was born to behave is only one of many ways. Most human beings wear clothes, but some do not. All human beings have customs prescribing acceptable sexual and marital partners, but customs vary widely from one cultural group to another. All human beings live in societies that construct weapons, but they might be crude stone axes, rocket-propelled missiles, or a great many things between these extremes. Wherein, then, lies the uniqueness of the human being?

IS HIS ABILITY TO LEARN FROM EXPERIENCE UNIQUE? · No. A human baby learns not to touch live coals, but so do baby monkeys, rabbits, elephants. The pig in Figure 8.1 learned to tip a sprinkling can in order to provide water for a bath. A hungry

Figure 8.1
Learning by Doing
Joe Schershel, *Life* Magazine © Time Inc.

rat may be placed in a box containing a lever that is connected to an automatic magazine. When the lever is pressed, food pellets are delivered. The rat will run about aimlessly and restlessly at first. Then he happens to press the bar; a food pellet follows; he eats it. Soon he repeats the performance, gets another pellet. Before very long the rat is so conditioned that he presses the bar continuously. He has learned from past experience how to get fed under these circumstances.

DOES MAN ALONE HAVE THE ABILITY TO ENGAGE IN COOPERATIVE ENTERPRISES? · Again, no. Human beings hunt game in parties, but coyotes and wolves also often work together to get food. Human beings organize business enterprises. Ants organize to gather their particular kind of wealth.

ARE HUMAN BEINGS THE ONLY LIVING CREATURES CAPABLE OF CONSTRUCTING TOOLS? · Not at all. Chimpanzees, under laboratory observation, fitted one piece of bamboo into another so that with the elongated pole they could obtain food otherwise beyond their reach.

DO ONLY HUMAN BEINGS HAVE THE ABILITY TO COMMUNICATE WITH, AND RESPOND TO COMMUNICATION FROM, OTHERS OF THEIR KIND? · Nonhuman creatures can, too. Many use signals to warn of impending danger. The pronghorn antelope has a rump patch of long white hairs that expands into a chrysanthemum-shaped disc when the animal is alarmed. The disc opens and shuts rapidly, catching the light and sending warning flashes like those of a heliograph. A herd of antelope grazing far away, receiving the signal, will scamper off.

However, we approach a real distinction between human and nonhuman behavior when we consider man's abilities in communication. Human beings can communicate with, and respond to communication from, others of their kind to a much greater extent than can nonhuman creatures. They have the capacity to use a complicated language system. They have speech, and *speech is the monopoly of man,* the talking animal. This is implied in Figure 8.2. However much like a nonhuman animal the wrestler in the corner may appear, the other fighter's representative will accept him as human if he proves he is a talking animal.

The biological basis for human behavior, and the criterion that distinguishes it from the behavior of other animals, is potential ability to learn to communicate through the medium of language. The chimpanzee can learn by trial and error to construct a tool enabling him to extend his reach, but he cannot tell the next generation of young chimps how to do it. He cannot write a textbook: *How to Construct a Pole for Reaching and Pulling Down Bananas.* Every chimpanzee laboriously follows the same process as his predecessor in learning to construct what the human being considers a simple tool.

The ability to use some form of language is an essential requirement for learning other modes of human behavior. An individual who lacks ability to understand and respond to instructions from others cannot learn to repair a watch, drive a car, or solve a mathematical problem.

THE ENVIRONMENTAL BASIS OF HUMAN BEHAVIOR

Communication also involves an environment; there are other people with whom to communicate. Here we again approach a fundamental distinction between the behavior of man

Figure 8.2
Human?

Drawing by Richard
Decker; © 1934, 1962
The New Yorker
Magazine, Inc.

"My man don't wrestle till we hear it talk."

and of other forms of life. All living creatures, including human beings, have behavior patterns that are determined partly by heredity, but only man develops social patterns of behavior as well, which are fixed by culture. Every spring the wild geese wing their way north in V-shaped flocks, a pattern made possible by their inherited ability to fly. When a squadron of Air Force pilots flies its planes in a similar formation, however, the pilots' pattern of behavior has both a biological and a cultural base. Geese and men are biologically capable of moving in social groups, but the manner in which man moves, the individuals with whom he associates, and the "rules" of such association are culturally determined. And *only* man's movements and behavior are culturally determined, as we shall see.

The behavior pattern of geese—or of other nonhuman creatures—is based on what may be termed *biosocial* forces. Sociologist Kingsley Davis writes:

In the nonhuman world every social system meets its basic needs primarily through mechanisms determined by heredity. The social responses of each individual spring from an inherited tendency to react in a fixed manner to stimuli provided by other members of the group. . . . Since the perpetuation of the social system is accomplished through the transmission of the genes, any change in the social order must come primarily from a change in the germ plasm.[1]

Among human beings, on the other hand, a change in the germ plasm is not a prerequisite for a change in behavior or in the social order. The behavior pattern of man is based on biological, social, and cultural influences. Thus, where non-human animals are subject to biosocial forces in this respect, a man's behavior pattern is an outcome of what we may call *bio-socio-cultural* forces, awkward as the term is. The element of culture has been added. Quoting Davis again: "Culture has been built onto and has fundamentally modified a previously existing bio-social system."[2] And the existence of a culture implies a social environment in which the individual with the inherited potentiality to behave is motivated to learn to behave in a human way.

Are you à "born leader"? Is Willie Mays a "born" athlete? Was Professor Albert Einstein a "born" mathematician? Are the Chinese "naturally" passive and unemotional? Are Italians "naturally" passionate and fiery-tempered? Are women "naturally" more docile and gentle than men?

The answer to all these questions is "no." The words "born" and "naturally," used this way in common parlance, imply that the attributes mentioned are biologically inherited. Not so. Evidence indicates that leadership techniques, athletic prowess, and mathematical thinking are learned after birth. A Chinese child, reared in an Italian social environment, will probably learn to behave as an Italian child is expected to behave; an Italian child, reared in a Chinese social environment, will very likely learn to behave as a Chinese child is expected to behave. Cultural rather than biological heritage is the significant factor determining the difference between the conduct of Italian and Chinese people. As to whether women are born with the tendency to be more gentle than men, the evidence is that they have this tendency only in cultural environments in which they learn that they are expected to be more gentle than men.

Most of the human behavior we may think of as "just natural" to mankind, something with which human beings are born, does not occur because man is biologically so equipped that he must behave this way. It is an outgrowth of learning from others, of social pressures that indicate, in effect, "This is how to behave." Nothing in your biological inheritance makes it inevitable that you must love your mother. You *learned* to love her, if you did, in the course of your relations with her and with other people who expected that "normally" a child will love his parents.

Biological heritage makes the learning of social behavior possible; the social heritage, or culture, determines what behavior will be learned. Every human being, within the limits of his capacity, learns that his behavior is controlled and directed by his relations with other people. In that sense his *behavior is socially transmitted.* Biological transmission is restricted to the parent-child relationship, that is, it passes only from parents to offspring. Social transmission is not as limited. It occurs as we interact with a great many people, most of them not part of the immediate family.

NATURE OR NURTURE?

Which, then, is more influential in establishing patterns of human behavior, heredity or environment? In the past, one class of thinkers has insisted that human beings behave as they do because they were born to do so. It is their "nature" so to behave. A mother protects her child from danger at the risk of her own life, the argument runs, because it is her maternal nature to behave in this way. Another class of thinkers has been equally emphatic in saying that human behavior is largely the product of external forces. People are "nurtured" by their environment. From it they learn to behave the way they do. By this reasoning, a mother protects her child even at the risk of her own life because she has learned in her environment that she should do so.

The nature-nurture issue became the subject of heated academic controversy as the twentieth century opened. Each side —nature, nurture—tended toward an all-or-nothing position. This attitude was greatly revised in the course of time. Today, while such discussion still plays a part in academic debate, it is not as a rule in terms of nature versus nurture. Scientists do not insist that a choice must be made in favor of heredity *or* environment. Rather, it is generally accepted that the sources of human behavior are to be found in heredity *and* environment. They are interdependent, not mutually exclusive. We are all influenced by both nature and nurture. In discussing human behavior, we must think of them as two aspects of one phenomenon. Charles H. Cooley put it this way: "When our individual life begins, the two elements of history, the hereditary and the social, merge in the new whole and cease to exist as separable forces. . . . Heredity and environment . . . are, in fact, abstractions; the real thing is a total organic process."[3]

When the football player intercepts a forward pass, is he using nature or nurture? He is using a combination of both. He inherited a capacity to see, run, jump. This was biological: "nature." He became interested in developing these capacities to their fullest in order to catch the ball, as a means of bringing a certain kind of honor to his school. This was social: "nurture." When he plays football, a total organic process is in play —nature, nurture, and a human organism motivated to use nature and nurture this particular way.

Since neither heredity nor environment can be excluded from consideration when human behavior is under study, it is meaningless to ask which is more important in determining behavior. There is no answer. Which is more important in propelling a car, the motor or the fuel? Which is more vital to the process of fertilization, the sperm cells or the ova?

THE COMMUNICATION OF MEANING

We asked: What are the sources of human behavior? What is unique about man in this respect? In answer we pointed out that only the human animal is biologically capable of communicating with others of its kind through the medium of a language system that includes speech.

We also pointed out that all social behavior is learned in interaction with people. Now we turn our attention to one way in which learning occurs—through *symbolic communication*.

As used in the behavioral sciences, a symbol is something that "stands for" or represents another thing. It may be verbal or nonverbal. Verbal symbols are expressed by speech or writing. Nonverbal symbols are expressed by gestures, visual images, and sounds not produced by the human voice but conveying meaning to human beings. *A symbol is any verbal or nonverbal expression intended to represent something and used to transmit meaning from sender to receiver.* Symbols employed in communication, considered collectively, are called *language*.

VERBAL SYMBOLS

We noted that verbal symbols are expressed by speech or writing. *Speech is a verbal action used to transmit meaning.*

Everything we shall say about speech is equally applicable to the written word, since it is "frozen speech," to borrow a term from Richard T. LaPiere and Paul R. Farnsworth. It is speech committed to written form.

Think what can be accomplished through the use of words in speech. We teach children how to behave under given circumstances, to add and subtract, read and write, solve problems, sing songs, salute flags. Words are used in establishing laws, declaring a law violated, meting out a penalty for the violation. Words are employed to convey the idea a war is coming, has been declared, is over. Politicians create enthusiasm or distaste for themselves by utilizing words, which, of course, are interlarded with more or less appropriate gestures. Evangelists bring worshipers to religious ecstasy by words. Children make their parents proud by words spoken from a school platform. Parents communicate the idea of security, insecurity, fear, love, hate, admiration, respect—all through words.

SPEECH IS ENTIRELY SOCIAL; IT IS LEARNED IN SOCIETY · No combination of sounds "naturally" means anything or the same thing to all peoples on earth. You may react negatively to the work *stink*. It could not elicit the same reaction from someone unfamiliar with our speech. The word *bloody,* used in a certain context, has a meaning in England that it does not have here.

SPEECH IS CONTINUOUSLY IN PROCESS OF CHANGE · We do not go to *talkies* any longer. And if you do not know what a *hokey-pokey man* is, perhaps your grandfather does not understand newer words like *hi-fi* and *frug*. There was a time when *getting stoned* meant becoming intoxicated. More recently it took on the meaning of getting "high" on drugs. When one *took a trip* a few years ago, he went to Europe or to Evanston, Illinois. The term still means the same thing, but today it has an additional, specialized meaning for initiates. To *take a trip* is to have an "experience" with a psychedelic drug, such as LSD.

No matter how a dictionary defines a word or how precisely we use the vocabulary at our command, some misunderstanding cannot be avoided. A certain amount of unintentionally misleading communication takes place in society. Such words as *patriotism, communism, charity, sociology, religion, fairness* convey many meanings. The Burmese people learned a bitter lesson in this regard. When the Japanese took over Burma during World War II, the natives welcomed them. They came to hate them, however, and one reason was a difference of interpretation of certain terms. Burmese have no word in their language for "hello!" or "good-bye!" As a rule, they say "How are you?" only when a person looks ill. When one Burmese meets another on the street, he generally greets him with: "Have you eaten yet?" or he might ask: "Where are you going?" or: "Where do you come from?" These questions, merely affable greetings, were called out to the Japanese invaders, just as we might say, "Hello!" or "How are you?" The Japanese interpreted them as demands for military information, and responded by slapping and otherwise abusing villagers who only wanted to offer a conventional greeting.[4]

NONVERBAL SYMBOLS

Nonverbal symbols, it will be recalled, include *gestures, visual images,* and *sounds not produced by the human voice but conveying meaning to human beings.*

Gesture consists of nonverbal behavior used to convey meaning—a wink, grimace, smile, kick, nod. Gestures are not as precise as speech in conveying meaning. Nevertheless, we do use gestures to communicate, and this is possible because so many of them are shared symbols in a given culture. In Figure 8.3, one boy understands what the other is "saying." We see what social psychologist George Herbert Mead called "the conversation of gestures." Each youth will decide how to behave in terms of what the other is beginning to do. The lad on the right may take a defensive attitude, go on the offensive, make conciliatory gestures, or run away. Thus, in this particular set of circumstances, the gestures are symbols of action not yet taken. And they influence action that will be taken.

As with speech and the written word, gestures do not have universal meaning. There is no one "natural" way to express pleasure or grief. The gesture of welcome varies widely. One Polynesian greets another by stroking his own face with the other's hand. Among the Burmese, a person greets another by smelling his cheeks. If you were raised in a certain Eskimo tribe, you would greet a stranger by licking your hands, running them over your face, then over the stranger's face.

Like gestures, *visual images* convey meaning that might be interpreted differently by different people. Most would probably agree that the man in Figure 8.4 loves his children. Some

Figure 8.3
Gestural Language
Photograph by Homer Page.

might use the words "is proud of" instead of "loves." Perhaps others would say the expression on the man's face has no bearing on the children but relates to someone he sees who is not in the picture.

Some *sounds not produced by the human voice* are used by human beings for the purpose of communication. When you hear thunder, the sound is neither made by the human voice nor initiated by human beings; no human being is trying to communicate meaning to you thereby, even though the thunder has meaning for you. Hence the sound of thunder does not represent human communication. But when a telegrapher presses a key that relays a sound across the continent, he is conveying meaning to another human being. *Communication is a reciprocal process,* and thunder lacks this element. You cannot communicate a message to the natural forces producing thunder. But the telegrapher receiving a message from another telegrapher can respond.

These, then, are the symbolic behaviors by which we communicate with one another. We communicate through language.

And what is the function of language, or symbolic communication? What part does it play in the development of *human* behavior?

LANGUAGE & HUMAN BEHAVIOR

The broad functions of language in the development of human behavior may be stated as follows:

Figure 8.4
What Message Does This Visual Image Convey to You?

1. *Language makes thinking possible,* and if we could not think we could not understand, nor could we assimilate the culture of our society.

Perhaps it is difficult for you to accept the idea that we must have language in order to be able to think. If so, try to think of something without using words or nonverbal gestures. Think of a horse. In your "mind's eye" you "see" the animal. When you recognize it, it means *horse*. The concept *horse* is perceived in terms of a word that stands for something.

Think of an idea: happiness. Perhaps you envisage dancing children, or a man and a woman in love, or a soldier returning home from war. But you could not translate this imagined behavior into the idea of *happiness* without understanding and using the word *happiness* or *happy*. You might *say* to yourself: "That's a picture of happiness" or "He certainly is happy."

You cannot think without using words. You cannot think about thinking, except in words. Which may be why Joyce O. Hertzler, an American sociologist who has contributed to our knowledge of the social function of language, says, ". . . brains think with words."[5]

2. We have already said that *language employed in communication is always a social phenomenon,* an instrument of communication between and among people. Communication possesses no separate existence apart from a social situation. It is never altogether an individual act. It requires a *sender,* a *receiver,* and a *message.* Thus language is *shared behavior.* If you shout, "Happy birthday!" from a mountain top, with no one else within earshot, you are not communicating, for although you speak a message intelligible in your society, you send it only into the air. There is no receiver. If, upon encountering a friend, you repeat the same message, you are communicating, for you send a message that is received.

3. *Language is the means by which human experience is recorded,* making possible the readier transmission of ideas concerning human behavior. Language is the basis of individual and group memory. A scientist describes in writing how he performed an experiment and what results he got. Another experimenter adds a report on the same subject, carrying the project a little farther. Still other scientists contribute their experiences concerning the subject under investigation. In time, all scientists and other interested persons have at their disposal the "group memory" recorded by the investigators.

4. *As the memory agent of man, language is the principal means by which culture is accumulated, shared, and transmitted from generation to generation.* We pointed out that nonhuman animals cannot accumulate what they learn for transmission to other nonhuman animals of a later generation. Their learning, says Hertzler, ". . . remains static from one generation to the next. Through the recording function of language, however, man is able to live simultaneously in the past, present, and future. Human beings utilize knowledge and respond to activities dating back thousand of years."[6] It is, Hertzler continues, by means of its own language ". . . that *the society indoctrinates the individual with its 'history' and its basic operational principles and rules.*"[7]

Language, then, makes possible the sharing of experience, despite time and spatial differences, so that the individual is enabled to become a recipient of the culture. And to say that the culture of society is transmitted through symbolic communication is to make clear that language is the primary instrument in the socialization of the individual.

5. *Language symbols reflect attitudes. To the extent that they convey these attitudes, they enable us to adjust our behavior to ideas, things, and other human beings.* A mother says, "Now, Jimmy!" and Jimmy stops doing something he knows is disapproved. In Figure 8.5, Herbert knows that father does not fully trust him in the particular circumstances. The symbol conveys an attitude. Herbert gets the message.

6. *Language is a means through which we exercise social control.* Imagine Charles, a fraternity man, on a campus. He believes a recently matriculated student, Sol, would make a fine addition to the local chapter. He so informs his fraternity brothers, who greet the comment with a sudden, chilly silence. Then one member says, "Oh, I really don't believe he's, ah, our kind of fellow, you know? Nice guy and all that, but well, uh, I guess you didn't know, did you? He's Jewish. Now, I've got nothing against Jews . . ." Charles, who proposed Sol as a possible pledge, looks around. Everyone else in the room, by word and gesture, makes clear that some of his best friends are Jews, but—. And everyone makes clear that, naturally, had Charles been aware that Sol was Jewish, he would not have proposed him. Charles' fraternity brothers almost seem to be "saying," by nonverbal gestural language, that perhaps it was a mistake to have inducted *him* into the fraternity. He

Figure 8.5
Reflection of an Attitude
Reprinted with permission from The *Saturday Evening Post* © 1956 The Curtis Publishing Company.

"I'm afraid Father doesn't trust you, Herbert."

is not sure, at that moment, whether he still "belongs."

He may inform his "brothers" that indeed he did not know Sol was Jewish. He might say he did know, but that he would like him considered for membership nevertheless. Either way, he would to some extent have been influenced by his associates, and the social control involved was introduced through the use of language.

If action speaks louder than words, as some say, it may also be asserted that words and gestures spur and inhibit action.

LEARNING SOCIAL BEHAVIOR

Several terms are employed in the behavioral sciences to designate what is essentially the same phenomenon. We speak of *the development of personality, the process of socialization,* and *internalization of culture*. All of these terms refer to *the learning of social behavior*.

What do we mean by the word *learning*? According to many psychologists, *learning is a change in the nature or strength of a response to a stimulus*. An oft-used example is the stimulus-response experiment of Ivan Petrovich Pavlov,[8] a Russian physiologist. Pavlov harnessed a dog so he could be fed while his accumulation of saliva was measured. When the animal ate, saliva flowed automatically, a normal physiological response to food in the mouth. At the outset of the experiment, food was the original *stimulus* and salivation the initial *response* to food. Now, through the active intervention of the experimenter, a bell was rung just before food was delivered to the dog. At first, this produced no increase in saliva. Intervention continued. The bell rang each time just before food was delivered. Finally, the ringing of the bell, by itself, produced salivation. The bell had become a *conditioned stimulus* that produced a *conditioned response*. The conditioned response, salivation, was produced regularly in a number of trials, even when the ringing was not accompanied or followed by food. The dog showed a change in the nature and strength of a response to a stimulus.

With human beings, *a learning experience takes place when an individual, seeking satisfaction of a need, finds a way of obtaining this satisfaction by modifying his behavior. Every experience that changes a person's subsequent behavior is a learning experience.* Learning occurs through any of four kinds of activity: *responding to communication, following human example, using trial and error,* and *thinking.*

Suppose you want to learn to operate a portable tape recorder and, as a first step, you want to understand the recording procedure. Probably the soundest way to go about it would be to read the instruction booklet. When you do, and follow the instructions given there, you are responding to communication, in this instance, written communication. You might have learned the same procedure by watching someone else do it, in which case you would be learning by imitation, that is, by following human example. In the absence of either opportunity, you could use trial and error. You might try to plug the jack of the microphone cable into an outlet on the machine. If it did not fit, you would try another outlet and eventually succeed. By the same hit-miss process you would learn to set the machine's speed and to perform other necessary operations in order to record. Thinking, the fourth way of learning, is involved in all the others, but you conceivably could learn to use your recorder effectively if you did nothing but think through the problem involved, without receiving any other help. However, in connection with such a complex mechanism, it is unlikely that you could succeed with this method alone. But you might think your way into and through at least several steps without responding to communication, without imitating, or without experimenting with trial and error. For instance, say you surmised that because the cable jack is red and only one of the outlets on the machine is ringed in red, it must be where to plug it in. In that event, provided you were correct, your process of thought was essentially a mental substitute for trial-and-error experimentation.

The learning process begins soon after birth and is directly related to, and part of, the culture into which the baby is born and in which he will live. With this statement we approach the part that learning plays in socialization of the individual.

As soon as an infant is born he begins to become a little different than he was. He is learning social behavior. He encounters stimuli, reacts to them, and learns.

Initially the newborn baby is apparently unaware of any connection between a stimulus and a response. Perhaps his hand happens to touch a lighted electric bulb; the heat brings screams of pain from him. But he is unaware that the heated bulb was the stimulus provoking the screaming response. In time, however, he will become aware of the regularity in the sequence: lighted bulb; hand touches; pain. Thereafter, he will not respond by touching when he is exposed to the stimulus of the lighted bulb.

He becomes increasingly aware of other regularities of sequence: He cries when he has hunger pangs; mother brings food. Crying begins to have a purpose. It becomes a device, learned by trial and error, to evoke responses from others.

Mother so often satisfies the baby's needs that her very presence begins to please him. By a chain of associations he has acquired a new need, to have his mother near him. Her presence brings satisfaction of needs; her presence pleases him because she satisfies his needs; mother's presence in itself becomes a need.

The process by which old needs are directed into new channels and become connected with new needs has been called *association* by psychologists. The baby will go through a life-long process of shifting associations of this sort.

The baby's need for mother's presence is transformed into a need for her approval. He happens to make a facial contortion. It has no meaning to him, but mother cries, "Look! Baby is smiling at me!" She pats and caresses him, which gives baby pleasant sensations. By chance, he grimaces the same way another time. Once more mother responds warmly. Eventually, as this continues, baby perceives a regularity. Whenever he grimaces, his mother responds in a way that gives him pleasurable sensations. Now he will use the "smile" to evoke her approving response.

Baby also learns his first words by trial and error. He babbles, but the sounds mean nothing to him. Sooner or later he emits a particular combination of sounds that you might hear as "Ooooah, wahw!" but which his mother or father hear as "ma-ma." They gurgle approvingly, caress him. Gradually he will learn to say, "Ooooah, wahw!" or "ma-ma" so as to get the response he wants. At first "ma-ma" means nothing in particular; then perhaps it means anyone and everyone; finally it becomes the symbol for one particular person.

The infant gradually learns to use other symbols to elicit desired responses. Eventually he becomes aware that these sounds can be used two ways. They will evoke responses *from* others, and with them he can respond *to* others. *This is the foundation of thinking behavior.*

His increasing ability to use symbols speeds up the entire process of learning. For instance, a child can learn not to stick his hand into a flame if he has a painful trial-and-error experience of this kind. But if he is able to understand and respond to symbols, he may avoid the experience altogether. Mama will tell him that fire is hot and will hurt him. He will learn that way.

The child also becomes aware he can gain satisfaction of needs by following the example of others. He discovers that such emulation will bring a desired response. He may sweep the floor "just like mama" or "cut" the grass with a toy mower, "like daddy." He is not likely to smoke cigarettes at that age, like mama or daddy, unless they encourage such imitation.

As he grows a little older and broadens his contacts, the child will follow the example of persons outside his immediate family as a means of gaining satisfaction of his needs. He will try to throw a ball the way his playmate does or to walk with a swagger like the older boy he admires.

At some point, the youngster realizes that adults are selective in responding to his behavior. They reward him for some actions, punish him for others. Mother becomes intolerant when he screams for food. Having acquired a need for her approval, he must gradually find new ways to behave that will bring him both food and approval. In the same way he learns how to dress himself, and to have "manners" at table. He is guided, corrected, and directed through a long succession of learning experiences. Each adds something to the cumulative storehouse (more accurately, the *personality*) that will eventually prepare him to function as a full-fledged member of his society.

The process of learning social behavior does not come to a halt when an individual is accepted as an adult by other adults. It continues. All of us continuously learn new ways of behavior. In our earliest years we learned *general* modes of social behavior that distinguished us from nonhuman creatures. Later we acquired *specific* modes of social behavior, enabling us to conduct ourselves as students, parents, citizens, clergymen, salesmen, bricklayers, doctors, grandparents.

INDIVIDUAL VARIATIONS IN LEARNING

If all human beings learn to behave by the same general processes, why is it that two people reared in apparently similar social environments may differ considerably from one another? Why will two brothers of the same family so behave that one goes to the governor's chair, the other to the electric chair?

A number of factors contribute to these variations in individual behavior:

1. *No two persons are biologically identical.** Some are more sensitive to pain than others, some more capable of learning, and so on.

2. *The social environment is never quite the same for any two individuals.* This is true even within the same household. Sam Smith is born when his father is twenty-three years old. Sam's brother Harry is born when Mr. Smith is thirty-three. When Sam is ten years old, his father is earning a modest income, able to provide his family with few luxuries. On the other hand, Mr. Smith is still physically fit, able to engage in vigorous sports with Sam and to enjoy many of the same

* However, monozygotic ("identical") twins are biologically very similar.

things his older son does. Moreover, he has few responsibilities on the job that prevent his being home early in the evening, in time to see and play with the younger boy, Harry.

When Harry is ten, his father is forty-three. He is an executive now, with a fine income. The family owns a comfortable home. Mr. Smith provides many luxuries for Harry that he could not offer Sam at the same age. But now Mr. Smith tires in late afternoon. He is no longer in the pink of condition physically. Playing baseball fatigues him. At forty-three, he does not enjoy the same things his ten-year-old Harry does. He does not engage in vigorous sports with him. And his added office responsibilities keep him away from home many nights. Moreover, these office burdens make him tense and irritable when he is home.

The same father is not quite the same man ten years later. The treatment one son receives is different from what his brother received at a given age. Smith's expectations concerning the behavior of children were not the same when Harry was born as when Sam was born. In many ways, quite aside from these and other inevitable changes in the family's living pattern, Mr. Smith does not provide an identical social environment for his two sons.

3. *The total impact of learning is never the same for any two individuals.* Most of us learn somewhat the same general patterns of behavior that others in our society do, but in varying sequence and combinations.

Consider two girls, Norma and Molly, whose histories are known to the author. They were reared in a small town in a rural area. The mother—we will call her Mrs. Jones—was noted for her fine baking and needlework, which won her many prizes at county fairs. As soon as Norma, the first child, was old enough, her mother began teaching her to sew and bake.

Molly was born seven years after Norma. When she was a toddler, her older sister was receiving high praise from adults. Her needlework was proudly displayed before guests. At dinner it was pointed out that she prepared the particularly savory main dish or the tasty sponge cake. When Mrs. Jones' club met at her house, Norma proudly sat with the ladies, doing needlework along with them, accepting their bountiful praise. Soon, like her mother, she was winning prizes at county fairs.

Meanwhile, Molly, wanting to be praised like her sister,

asked her mother to teach her to bake and sew, too. She became as expert as Norma had been at that age, but now the older girl was of course more proficient. Molly's work suffered by comparison.

Relatives and other visitors to the home, without meaning to be unkind, made it clear to Molly that, in their judgment, she would never come up to Norma in baking a pie or sewing a blouse. Molly was hurt, unhappy.

Her father perceived this. A rugged, outdoor type, he casually invited Molly to come fishing with him. She became a proficient fly caster. He took her camping, taught her to hunt, swim, and ride. She became "Daddy's girl" to members of the family and to acquaintances. She lost interest in sewing, cooking, housework. At eleven, she took a prize in horsemanship, at twelve won a medal for marksmanship with a rifle. Now she was receiving greater recognition for her particular skills than Norma had gained for hers.

The two girls now showed marked differences in behavior pattern. If Norma got her dress dirty, she cried. Not Molly. Norma spent her time indoors. Molly went outdoors as soon as she came home from school. Norma was always crisply dressed and fastidiously clean. Molly loved nothing better than to go about in sloppy dungarees, smelling of last week's fishing expedition, her face smeared with dirt and sweat from her violent exercise.

By the time Norma was twenty and Molly thirteen, it was the younger girl who was getting most attention. It was only to be expected that Norma, at her age, should be a fine cook and seamstress. But Molly was viewed as spectacular, a child of thirteen and already a champion shooter, rider, huntress.

They are both married now. Norma is a confirmed housewife, delighted to handle all household chores herself, and noted for her superlative cookery. Molly takes care of her home in slapdash fashion, hurries out to play golf, ride, or teach *her* daughter to fish.

Norma and Molly were reared in the same family, but the total impact of learning, within that family, was not the same for each girl.

OBSTACLES TO LEARNING

What we said about the learning process requires some qualification. It does not invariably apply to all people to the same degree. Possible reasons for this include the following:

1. *Some individuals are born without the necessary capacity to learn social behavior.* They cannot acquire the ability to behave as human beings, no matter what the social environment. In this category would be the idiot, unable to feed or clothe himself or control his body functions.

2. *Some people, born with the necessary capacity to learn social behavior, become isolated from most other individuals and are limited in the degree to which they have an opportunity to learn the social behavior approved in the society.* An excellent illustration is found in a report by Kingsley Davis on this kind of person, who is called a *social isolate*.[9]

Anna was born in the United States, out of wedlock. Anna's mother, rather than face the wrath of her father, with whom she lived, secreted the child in a second-floor attic-like room on the family farm. Anna was five and one-half months old at the time. She received only what care was required to keep her alive, was fed mostly on milk, was given no training that a growing child ordinarily receives, no friendly attention. Her clothing and bedding were filthy.

Anna was discovered and removed from the home when she was nearly six years old. She was emaciated, did not walk or talk, was apathetic, indifferent to people about her. She did not ". . . do anything that showed intelligence," Davis reports.

But she responded to the careful treatment she received after her release from the farm, and within two years could walk, understand simple commands, feed herself, and keep herself fairly neat. She remembered people and showed an awareness of their presence. But she still did not speak and in many ways was not normal for her age.

She was transferred to a private home for retarded children, where she made a little more progress. However, the head of the establishment reported that the girl walked about aimlessly, made periodic rhythmic motions of her hands, guttural and sucking noises at intervals, regarded her hands as if seeing them for the first time. It was impossible to hold her attention for more than a few seconds at a time, and she still spoke not at all.

Some two years after this, Anna could bounce and catch a ball, her toilet habits were firmly established, she played with other children, and she could dress herself except for fastening her clothes.

And finally she began to develop speech. She called attendants by name and expressed her wants in a limited number of complete sentences. A report from the school concluded she was feebleminded.

Before Anna died, which was when she was only ten and a half, she had become a more humanized child than she was when first discovered. Robert M. MacIver and Charles H. Page point out that her case ". . . illustrates once again that human nature develops in man only when he is social man, only when he is one of many men sharing a common life."[10]

LEARNING & SOCIALIZATION

As has been explicit throughout much of this volume, we not only learn the content of our culture, but also come to accept its standards of social behavior and to want or at least be willing to enact most of the behavior that is expected of us. This process, we have indicated, is sometimes referred to as *socialization*, sometimes as *internalization of culture*.

1. *Internalization of culture is a consequence of both formal and informal transmission.* Formal transmission is through direct instruction and education, as in schools, churches, and other establishments having educational functions of one sort or another. The primary and most influential source of formal education, however, is the family. Here, in his most impressionable years, the child is taught the cultural values of his society, and much of the teaching is by direct methods of instruction. He learns the foundation of the language, the folkways of the society, certain skills he will need. At his age he tends to accept cultural values unquestioningly.

Formal instruction also takes place in play groups and later in occupational and other groups.

Culture is transmitted informally through the same media, but the method of transmission is not as direct. The individual observes the patterns of thought and behavior of people with whom he comes into contact. He learns without formal tutoring, often without being conscious that he is learning. If his parents dig out cantaloupe balls with a spoon, he eats his cantaloupe that way. If they address each other courteously, he will address people courteously, barring a counterinfluence through other associations. When he is of an age for play outside the home, the child picks up ways of behaving that are transmitted informally and frequently without specific intent. If his playmates enact the idea that boys climb trees and play baseball but do not cook indoors or knit, no formal instruction may be necessary to cue him to similar behavior. Given an example like that in Figure 8.6, a youngster may quite informally learn to gain satisfaction of his needs by certain psychological devices.

And when he is an adult, the individual still learns informally. Depending upon his associations, he finds out, without formal instruction, that a man drinks whiskey or does not; uses profanity to relieve tensions in certain circumstances or does not. He learns that members of the opposite sex are to be feared, revered, respected, cuddled, coddled, wheedled, blarneyed, or dominated as the case and given circumstance indicate. By informal precept he can learn what to eat, what cause to espouse, what profession to follow, what sort of person to marry, how to be a good spouse, what to expect of children, what proportion of one's income to bank, and whether to be buried, cremated, or have his body turned over to a medical school when he dies.

2. *Internalization of culture tends to be cumulative.* The individual relates one learning experience to another. A child of two will pick up another youngster's toy in the park and toddle off with it. His mother, aware that he does not yet understand such moral concepts as honesty and stealing, disengages him from the toy as gently as possible. But the experience is painful for the child.

Now this same youngster, growing older, learns through repeated incidents that when he takes a toy unfamiliar to him, he has an unpleasant experience. Eventually, as he reaches for one that does not belong to him, a mere frown or shake of the head from an adult may suffice. He desists, although he still does not think of his proposed act as stealing. But already the cumulative effect of socialization is in evidence.

Gradually he reaches the age where he can understand and learn what private property means. He no longer appropriates a toy that does not belong to him. His self-control is exercised out of a desire not to be punished, because he wants the approval of others, or because he now fully accepts the concept of private property.

Finally he no longer needs to be externally controlled as much as before. There has been further socialization on this

Figure 8.6
Informal Learning
Reprinted with permission
from *The Ladies Home
Journal*, © 1964 The Curtis
Publishing Company.

*"I learned a magic word.
It's 'insecure.'"*

matter of private property, and social control operates.

3. *Internalization of culture is continuous.* A child has greater need for socialization than an adult, but the internalization of culture does not cease when he becomes an adult. There is always something more to learn about the society, what it offers and what it expects.

Internalization of culture is continuous in another sense, a time sense over the generations. Society is perpetuated through internalization of culture. By this means its members transmit their culture to the next generation. The child renews within himself the culture of his ancestors.

4. *No individual internalizes the total culture of a society.* It is impossible in our own society, for instance, for one person to internalize all the ways of creating works of art, using mechanical contrivances, interpreting the American language, responding to threats of physical violence, selling at a profit, detecting deceit, making cocktails—and so on practically ad infinitum.

5. *Although the expected result of internalization of culture is conformity to the requirements of the culture, some deviation from what is considered proper behavior and thinking is allowed in all societies.* You will very likely want to conform

to the basic laws of the United States and to most customary ways of behaving. But you may choose to be an atheist in a predominantly religious community or a Democrat in an overwhelmingly Republican town; and while you might lose some prestige thereby, you will probably still be accepted as an employee and even as a friend by many people.

You will recall that at the beginning of this chapter we made the point that the process of learning social behavior in effect is the same phenomenon as the development of personality. In the next chapter we deal with the development of personality in another way.

· NOTES

1. Kingsley Davis, *Human Society* (New York: Macmillan, 1949), p. 31.
2. *Ibid.*, p. 32.
3. Charles H. Cooley, *Human Nature and the Social Order* (New York: Scribner, 1902), p. 15.
4. Manning Nash, *The Golden Road to Modernity, Village Life in Contemporary Burma* (New York: Wiley, 1965), p. 6.
5. Joyce O. Hertzler, *A Sociology of Language* (New York: Random House, 1965), pp. 42–43.
6. *Ibid.*, p. 51.
7. *Ibid.*, p. 399.
8. I. P. Pavlov, *Conditioned Reflexes* (Oxford: Oxford University Press, 1927).
9. Kingsley Davis, "Extreme Social Isolation of a Child," *American Journal of Sociology*, XLV (January 1940), 554–565; and Kingsley Davis, "Final Note on a Case of Extreme Isolation," *American Journal of Sociology*, LII (March 1947), 432–437.
10. Robert M. MacIver and Charles H. Page, *Society: An Introductory Analysis* (New York: Rinehart, 1949), p. 45.

· SUGGESTIONS FOR FURTHER READING

BROWN, CLAUDE. *Manchild in the Promised Land.* New York: Macmillan, 1965.
In this powerful autobiography, a Negro youth reared in Harlem gives an unforgettable account of how he internalized that distinctive subculture.
GOODMAN, PAUL. *Growing Up Absurd.* New York: Random House, 1960.
A highly critical appraisal of the consequences of being socialized in our own contemporary society.
HALL, EDWARD T. *The Silent Language.* New York: Doubleday, 1959.

Spoken language is only one means of communication, this anthropologist points out. People "talk" to each other without using words. Hall presents a theory of examining culture as a complex of message systems.

HERTZLER, JOYCE O. *A Sociology of Language.* New York: Random House, 1965.

This is a sociological analysis of the function of language in human societies. Recommended reading are Chapter 3, "The Major General Functions of Language," and Chapter 4, "Language as a Social Phenomenon and Social Agency."

LINTON, RALPH. *The Cultural Background of Personality.* New York: Appleton-Century-Crofts, 1945.

The noted anthropologist discusses the effects of culture and social structure on human personality.

MONTAGU, ASHLEY. *Human Heredity.* New York: New American Library, 1960.

Montagu always writes provocatively and well. In this volume, he explores the dynamic interplay between heredity and environment in producing the human personality.

SINGH, J. A. L., and R. M. ZING. *Wolf Children and Feral Men.* New York: Harper & Row, 1939.

A case-documented discussion of social isolates.

9 THE SELF, PERSONALITY, CULTURE, & SOCIETY

Having examined the sources of human behavior and the process of learning to enact social behavior, we now discuss the enactor, he who has learned to behave as he does. He thinks of himself as a human *self*. What is the self? How does a person arrive at his understanding of who he is, what he is?

This *person*, with a conception of *self*, has a *personality*. What is personality? How is it formed? What is the relation between personality on the one hand and culture and society on the other? These are the questions pursued in this chapter.

THE SELF

Which is the *real* person in Figure 9.1? The one you see, holding a toothbrush in his hand? The one reflected from the mirror? Neither? Both?

For that matter, who are you? A student? A son or a daughter? A Christian, Jew, Moslem? An honest person? A hothead? A good-natured Joe? Someone who follows the Golden Rule? Which is the real *you*?

To answer that, you probably pick out some characteristic that describes the real you (as you understand yourself) in the particular situation. Thinking of your relation to the school you attend, you say you are a student. As a member of a family you are a son or a daughter.

A factory worker mutters, as the foreman passes, "I'm a

Figure 9.1
Which Is the Real "Me"?
Reprinted with permission of the *Los Angeles Times*.

"What worries me is—that could be the 'REAL' me—"

fellow who minds his own business. I wish other people would do the same."

"I bad girl!" sobs a three-year-old. "Mama spank me 'cause I breaked a cup."

The factory worker is not *just* a fellow who minds his own business. The little girl is not *just* "bad." These are random, transitory impressions of self.

THE MEANING OF SELF

What, then, is this self? *The self consists of all ideas and feelings the individual associates with the words "I," "me," "my," and "mine"* (if English is his language).

Does everyone have such ideas and feelings? Yes, except possibly an individual so mentally deteriorated he no longer is aware that he exists. Every human being has a conception of himself. He can tell you something about who he is. He distinguishes between the "me," the one central self that is *he,* and all other individuals. He feels the need to find and define his self. A person becomes confused and disturbed if he loses this conception, as in the case of someone suffering with amnesia. If he cannot define "me," he is unhappy and upset, urgently seeks to rediscover his identity.

A conception of self is essential to the individual's understanding of other people in his environment and of his relation to them. Only when he comprehends who and what he is can he behave as a social being.

How does one gain a conception of "I," "me," "my," "mine"? *A conception of self derives from social interaction and is essential for continued social interaction and enactment of culture.* The individual learns to comprehend his self as he interacts with others. Given that comprehension, he can further interact, with greater effectiveness, coming closer to what members of his society expect of him. He cannot say who he is except in relation to people about him. In arriving at a conception of self every person sees himself in relation to others.

Do you find it hard to accept this? Then, once more, think of *yourself* for a moment. Who are you? A husband or a wife? You cannot be one or the other except in relation to someone else—a spouse. A leader? You cannot be a leader without followers. A daughter? Only in relation to your parents. It is impossible to be a social being except in a context of other social beings.

LIFE BEFORE WE KNEW OURSELVES

Let us go back a few years to the time when a child was a newborn baby. It was a very important creature to its parents, but in plain fact an unprepossessing sight. It was a clawless, toothless, furless, and completely helpless little parasite that would have perished within a few hours had it not been provided with constant care and attention. It was neither grateful nor ungrateful for the services so essential to its survival. It could not reason, had no feeling of self-pity, no sense of right and wrong, no plans for tomorrow. It was not aware there was a tomorrow. In fact, it was not even aware that it had a body or a mind. It was no more than a living organism potentially capable of becoming a self, but not one yet.

A few weeks later, it was a little more aware of things. Perhaps its hand caught its eye and it momentarily and fleetingly focused attention on it. The baby did not know it was a hand or that it was part of its own body, for it still had no understanding of *hand* or *itself.*

Gradually it learned that the hand helped satisfy vaguely sensed wants. The infant could poke all sorts of interesting objects into its mouth with that hand. A little later the baby discovered that its hand, foot, body, and vocal cords were controlled by one force, the child itself. It could slap out, kick, roll over, yell. It felt pain when the objects attached to it were slapped, pinched, or perhaps punctured by a doctor's needle. Eventually all this led to a beginning awareness of its physical body as a separate and distinct entity.

During the early months it also learned there were other moving objects around it and that they were useful in satisfying needs and relieving tensions. The baby began to anticipate the appearance of these objects. It did not recognize them as human and similar to itself, since it did not know what "human" meant and had no realization it was a human being. It knew its mother first as a moving object that occasionally appeared and did something to relieve its unpleasant sensations.

Even during those early months, it was constantly collecting impressions of experiences that were painful or pleasant. When something occurred repeatedly and affected it with regularity, it was capable of drawing conclusions that helped it avoid future pain and gain future satisfaction. It learned to distinguish between moving and stationary objects, between strangers and familiar people. Eventually it became vaguely aware that other people were necessary.

Necessary to whom? Without deliberately trying to answer that question, the baby began to be aware of itself as a particular being whose needs were satisfied by other human beings. While the entire process may never be completely understood and explained, students of human behavior agree that awareness of self has its source in the recognition of the need for services provided by others.

In due time the child learns to talk, to communicate with people, a phenomenon we touched upon earlier. Now it has an important tool. Language helps the individual gain a consciousness of self. Joyce O. Hertzler writes:

This . . . is exemplified when the child learns his own name and comes to use it regarding himself in distinction to others, thereby accentuating his separate identity and independent existence. In addition to awareness of and response to his name, his sense of self-other identity is also reflected in his use of such pronouns as "you" or "me," such phrases as " 'I' am 'Jimmy,' " " 'you' are 'Tommy.' "[1]

But the child's awareness of self is by no means fully formed at this stage. How does awareness grow and develop? For one answer we turn to Charles Horton Cooley.

COOLEY'S THEORY OF THE SOCIAL SELF

The process of gaining awareness of self, we have seen, begins in infancy. The self develops out of social experience, as the child has communicative contacts with others. In *Human Nature and the Social Order*, published in 1902, Cooley advanced the theory that *we learn to see and judge ourselves as we imagine others see and judge us.*

Cooley coined the expression, "the looking-glass self." He compared other people to a mirror. We gaze into it, note how others respond to us, and as a result of their reactions we develop feelings about ourselves. That is, we gain a conception of self by reflection. We use these reflections from the "mirror" as a basis for knowing and evaluating ourselves. The individual is largely what he understands his friends, acquaintances, and others with whom he interacts think he is. As a student you evaluate yourself partly in terms of the impressions you believe you are making on your instructors and other students. As a son or a daughter, you are in part what you think your parents consider you to be. If you keep secrets from them, you see yourself as the kind of son or daughter you believe your parents would judge you to be if they knew the hidden facts. Your total impression of yourself is a composite of all the impressions you think you have made on other people and of all the evaluations you imagine they have made of your behavior.

You are probably of an age when you still rely heavily on others for a reflection of your self. If you were to give a talk before your speech class, how would you decide whether you are satisfied with your performance? Doubtless largely in terms of how you believe the instructor and your classmates evaluated it. Self-feeling derives from perceiving or imagining how other people see and evaluate us.

If, in speech class, you felt keenly that you were not, in the opinion of the others, performing satisfactorily, you might try to change their view of you by improving your performance, improvement being defined in your mind according to their standards. You are not entirely passive in accepting and acquiring the attitudes other people hold toward you. Because you are dependent upon the attitudes of others for the satisfaction of your wants, you examine and reexamine yourself vis-à-vis those attitudes. You attempt to change other people's attitudes toward you at times. You want their evaluation and your self-image to agree, and to do so to your satisfaction.

But, you may object, surely some people maintain a self-image that does not correspond with what they know to be the judgment of most persons who know them? And yet they do not attempt to get those people to change their opinions? Yes. Some individuals consider themselves more important, for instance, than others credit them with being. The English poet-essayist Matthew Arnold was believed by many of his contemporaries to have a highly exalted notion of his worth, so much so that when he died an acquaintance remarked: "Poor Matthew! He won't like God!" We say people with an exaggerated conception of their importance in society have "superiority feelings."

In contrast to the person with superiority feelings is the individual who regards himself as much less worthy than he actually is in the eyes of his fellowmen. When that genius in the arts, Leonardo da Vinci, lay dying, the king paid him a visit. The artist pulled himself to a sitting position in deference to royalty and cried that he had offended God and man in that he had not labored as tirelessly and fruitfully as he should have. With particular regard to his artistic achievements, da Vinci suffered from what we call "inferiority feelings."

Considering the existence of people with superiority and inferiority feelings, we cannot assert that *all* individuals gain *all* of their conception of self from what they consider to be the evaluation of others. Some individuals do over- or underestimate themselves vis-à-vis what they conceive to be the valuations of other persons.

There is another source of distortion in gazing into the mirror for a perception of the looking-glass self. A person may deceive himself, finding it pleasant to see himself a certain way and not precisely as others see him. He does this unwittingly, for it is easy as well as pleasant to accept at times the flattering verdict of a distorted mirror. He chooses to look no farther. "The living skeleton" from the circus sideshow may prefer to view himself in a convex mirror that makes him appear stouter than he actually is. Figure 9.2 shows another possible use of the distorting mirror.

Going a step farther, mirrors are at times deliberately constructed by persons who hope to further their own ends thereby, the glass reflecting grossly distorted images. A man of great wealth and power may be so surrounded by sycophants and self-seekers that he is scarcely aware what the rest of the world thinks of him. Those who fawn on him run down a curtain between him and others outside their little coterie. He may develop a distorted conception of himself, not only at marked variance with the judgment of the world at large, but also of the sycophants, who outwardly praise him but privately ridicule or condemn him. He may lose the faculty of critically evaluating himself because his ability at self-analysis is rarely put to the test. He sees himself as certain others *pretend* they see him.

There is another possibility. Some individuals, looking into the mirror, understanding the valuation people place upon them and not liking it, deliberately try to impress others with the idea that the valuation is unrealistic, even though they themselves feel it is not. Here the person concerned is not arriving at a different conception of himself from that held by others. He is merely camouflaging what he believes *is* his self, trying thereby to make himself more acceptable to others. We shall have more to say on this when we discuss the work of Erving Goffman.

For the present, let us understand that sometimes an individual does formulate a less than realistic appraisal of self. With these qualifications, Cooley's conception of the looking-glass self seems basically valid.

Cooley made other important observations on the subject. *An individual's idea of himself*, he said, *comes much more from what he imagined people thought of him when he was a child than from what he imagines they think of him now.*

Figure 9.2
"Mirror, Mirror
on the Wall . . ."
© Medical Economics, Inc.

Early impressions, Cooley felt, are more durable than those
of later life. If a child learned to see himself as his doting
mother saw him, he might continue to have that impression
later in life, even if most other people he met did not agree he
had the great gifts credited to him by his adoring parent. Conversely, if people rejected an individual when he was a child,
he might regard himself as an unnecessary nuisance the rest
of his life, even though most of his associates liked and respected him.

Although Cooley pointed to the relative strength of early
impressions, he also emphasized that a person's conception of
himself undergoes virtually continuous change. Constantly
interacting with others, reflections of their judgments may
bring him to alter his behavior and his conception of self.
Seeking approval yet incurring disapproval, he changes his
behavior in certain ways, looks in the mirror again. The conception of self is adjusted on the strength of the altered reflection.

But, Cooley further postulated, although conception of self
undergoes much change over the years, people tend to become
resistant to change and, as they grow older, tenacious in cling-
ing to already established evaluations of themselves. They
reach a point where they seem to think, "I am what I am.
There is no need to change my evaluation of myself. If others
agree with it, I respect their judgment. If they don't, I re-
pudiate their judgment and will find other associates who
will like and accept me for what I am."

From your own point of view, the acid test of Cooley's
theory of the social self is whether it rings true in terms of

your personal experience. Have you ever felt embarrassed after saying the wrong thing to the wrong person at the wrong time? Would you feel humiliated if you found yourself in a situation similar to that of the young lady in Figure 9.3? If Cooley's theory is realistic, you will answer affirmatively, since you think you would have made an adverse impression on people on the occasion in question. Cooley would say that your self-feeling derives from imagining how other people are judging you. That is the essence of his theory of the social self.

MEAD'S THEORY OF THE SOCIAL SELF

George Herbert Mead, a contemporary of Cooley, contributed his own theory of the social self. He agreed with Cooley that the self is a social product, formed out of the judgments of other poeple. As the individual, developing from infancy to adulthood, interacts with particular people—parents, playmates, teachers, others—he learns to interpret their facial expressions and other gestures. He understands when they are pleased, displeased, approving or disapproving of certain ideas or behavior. Thus he can adopt the attitude of those others with regard to his own ideas and behavior. In effect he says, "What I am doing is good or bad—they would say." He can anticipate the responses of others to his behavior. And he can assess himself, as a person, in terms of the definitions of other people. In this manner the individual learns to anticipate what others expect of him and to control and evaluate his own actions accordingly.

But note that originally he anticipates what *particular* others, such as his mother and father, expect of him. He assumes the role of those persons in his own mind and evaluates and controls his behavior accordingly.

If you have seen children at play, you know that they do assume the roles of others, both in their minds and in actual behavior. A three-year-old, "playing house," becomes Mama and treats her doll the way she believes she herself is treated by her mother. She praises it for keeping its dress clean, scolds it for not coming when Mama calls, spanks it for wetting the bed. In assuming attitudes toward the doll that duplicate those her mother adopts toward her, the child shows

Figure 9.3
Is There a Looking-Glass Self?
Reprinted with permission from Richard Bibler, *Little Man on Campus*, Stanford, Calif.: Stanford University Press, 1952.

"Oh, come now, Miss Swerf! That's the reason we start you out on these little one-minute speeches, so you won't be nervous."

she has internalized the attitudes of a particular other person, her mother.

But every person interacts with a great many people in the course of time. He takes the attitude of diverse individuals with regard to respective situations. Those people do not invariably agree in their evaluations of ideas or of particular kinds of behavior. How, then, does a person form a conception of his own self, the sort of person he is, out of these disparate judgments? He cannot become a different self for different people at one and the same time.

Mead's answer was that the individual proceeds from the particular to the general. As he develops, he internalizes "the role of the generalized other." In his thinking he consolidates all of the particular "others" into one generalized "other," representing a sort of consensus within the group or society. *The individual adjusts his conception of self to what he conceives is the conception within his organized society with regard to him.*

As we grow into adulthood, we tend to forget the generalized other and to believe that the standards we have learned to use in testing our own performance are entirely our own creations; but, as we have shown, this is not the case. You may assert, "I have always been a moral person." That is not so. You were not born with the morals you accept today. In fact you were not born with *any* morals. Morality is socially defined, and morals must be learned.

We become what in our society is called moral human beings as we respond appropriately to what we anticipate others expect of us, and we control and evaluate our behavior accordingly. We observe what other people consider moral behavior, and when we assume the role of the generalized other, we reflect the judgments about morality of that generalized other. We assess our own conduct and our own self by these judgments.

Placing Mead's theory alongside Cooley's, we may say we become equipped with two "mirrors." Particularly in the earlier years we are greatly dependent upon the *external* "looking-glass" for a reflection of ourselves. In time, however, we become equipped with a *built-in* "mirror," and thereby are increasingly independent of the external "looking-glass" of others.

Mead's theory further suggests that each person looks at the self from two different viewpoints:

There are *situational impressions* of self. These ideas come from an awareness of ourselves in the immediate situation in which we are participating. Probably you have had an experience in which you became intensely aware of yourself. Let us imagine that, entering a classroom a bit late, you slipped and went sprawling across the floor in a most undignified fashion. The instructor stopped talking and stared at you. Some students burst into laughter. You arose, flushed and terribly embarrassed. You had a feeling of overwhelming self-consciousness. That feeling was a situational impression of yourself, an outgrowth of the immediate situation. The self you see in this way changes often, with varying circumstances.

There are *general impressions* of self. These develop gradually, in the process of anticipating what others expect of us. They are relatively durable, yet seldom completely inflexible. The self we see from this viewpoint provides us with more lasting standards for evaluating our actions. We come eventually to say, "I am thrifty and careful with my money." Or "I am a very hot-tempered person." Or "I am a person who holds honor above financial gain."

Sometimes general impressions of self are inconsistent with one another, as in the statement: "My employees think I am a penny-pinching miser, but my wife thinks I am quite generous with her allowance."

Returning to the unfortunate Miss Swerf in Figure 9.3, we can contrast the situational with the general impression of self. Miss Swerf is suffering from a temporary loss of self-composure, to put it mildly. Her humiliation is a situational impression of herself, based on what she imagines other people are thinking. But although her situational impression is adverse, her general impression of self will probably remain intact. If, before the horrible event, she thought of herself as a good student, or as a friendly, well-liked person, chances are she will cling to these impressions despite many embarrassing incidents.

Now let us consider a contrasting episode that actually happened on a campus. A young man was completing his graduate work at a university, at the same time teaching in a nearby college. One day he was caught cheating on an examination at the university and was suspended for a year. Several days later his body was discovered in his room, a suicide note beside it, expressing bitter remorse and self-condemnation.

We never know all the forces that motivate a person to take his own life, but apparently one reason this young man committed suicide was that he could not reconcile his actual behavior with the general impression he had of himself. It seems plausible he conceived himself to be an honest person. Then, as a university student, he engaged in the very behavior he condemned as a college instructor. His general impression of self was altogether inconsistent with his dishonest behavior. In the looking-glass that had once reflected a complimentary image he suddenly saw a monster. He denounced and destroyed himself.

Miss Swerf was embarrassed only by her *situational* impression of self. The young instructor took his life when in his judgment his *general* impression no longer could be sustained. In the first instance, a transitory, relatively unimportant assault was made on the self. In the second, a basic, hard-hitting attack took place on a durable, long-standing conception of self.

GOFFMAN'S THEORY OF THE SOCIAL SELF

Cooley and Mead theorized on the conception of self one gains by reflection from others. Erving Goffman, a professor of sociology at the University of California, theorizing more recently, contributed a stimulating appraisal of the part the individual plays in *projecting to others* a conception of his self that he hopes they will accept. Goffman deals with the individual as he conveys an impression of himself to others in order that he may achieve certain objectives.

In the *Presentation of Self in Everyday Life*,[2] published in 1959, he uses as analogy an actor on the stage who consciously and to some extent unconsciously projects across the footlights a person with certain characteristics, interest, and objectives. The performer may possess some of the characteristics he portrays; others he merely enacts; they are not part of his self. Much the same thing occurs in everyday social intercourse, says Goffman. The individual is the actor. He presents himself before an audience—other people. The place where this occurs is his stage. He enacts a role before the audience and hopes it is convincing.

When, Goffman writes, *the individual presents himself before others, he consciously and unconsciously guides and controls the impressions they will form of him.* To use an illustration of our own, let us say a man who wants to be governor of his state attends a meeting of influential citizens who will decide whether they will support his candidacy, financially and otherwise. He hopes that by his manner, speech, and background of past activities he will be able to project to the group an impression of himself favorable to his cause. *In presenting himself before others, an individual tries to persuade others to accept a definition of the situation suitable to his aims.* The gubernatorial candidate will influence the definition of the situation that the others come to formulate "by expressing himself in such a way as to give them the kind of impression that will lead them to act voluntarily in accordance with his own plan."[3]

His listeners, for their part, will study the candidate, evaluate his strong and weak points, attempt to determine whether he would make the sort of governor they want to see elected. When an individual enters the presence of others, they ordinarily want to gain some information about him or to use information about him which they already have, in order that they may define the situation.

Using the analogy of the actor, Goffman speaks of the individual as putting on a "performance." Our gubernatorial aspirant does that. And like the actor, some of the impressions he conveys to others are realistic; they represent his "real" self. Other impressions are not realistic. They are products of mere stage-acting. The candidate may lead his audience to infer that he is antilabor, when he is not. He may project the impression of a man who is making a great personal and financial sacrifice in seeking public office, when in fact he hopes to enrich himself at the expense of an unsuspecting citizenry.

Chances are, then, that some of the impressions of himself that our politically ambitious man conveys are deliberately concocted and projected, whether realistic or not. But chances are also very good that certain impressions are conveyed unwittingly. A gleam of the eye, a smile, a smirk, involuntarily project impressions upon his audience, whether those impressions are valid or not as indicators of the "real" candidate.

Goffman asks whether a "performer" himself believes in the impression of reality he tries to convey to others. His answer in effect is that, to some degree, some do and some do not. At one extreme stands the enactor who is entirely taken in by his own act. "When his audience is also convinced . . . about the show he puts on . . . then for the moment at least, only the sociologist or the socially disgruntled will have any doubts about the 'realness' of what is presented."[4]

At the other extreme, we have the individual who is not taken in at all by the performance he puts on. The boy in Figure 9.4 knows he is not a person who gets his good grades by cheating. He deliberately dissembles, for a reason, and may "take in" his schoolmates, but he does not deceive himself.

Goffman calls the deliberate, conscious dissembler "cynical," but he points out that not every cynical performer dissembles out of self-interest. A doctor, knowing a patient is in the terminal stage of cancer, may untruthfully tell him he has a nonmalignant tumor, if he believes this is in the patient's best interest. A mother, talking to her child just before he goes into surgery, may act calm, relaxed, even gay, although in-

Figure 9.4
Presentation of Self
Copyright 1965 Jules Feiffer.

wardly she feels anguish and fear. She does this in order to allay the child's fears. She may deliberately misinform the child that he is merely going to get some medicine, when she knows he is going to be cut open. She is "cynical" only in that she is consciously dissembling.

Summing up, Goffman would not quarrel with the proposition that we gain impressions of self by reflection from others. He adds that we are not helpless in the situation, that we can do something to convey particular impressions of ourselves to other people.

PERSONALITY, CULTURE, & SOCIETY

The individual who gains and conveys impression of self is invested with certain personality traits. Let us now consider the human personality in culture and society.

An imaginary Henry Hayes is a college student, ambitious to earn his letter in football. He has spent most of the season on the bench. Now, in a crucial moment of a game with the school's archrival, the coach calls, "Hayes! Go on out there! You know what to do!" Hayes will carry the ball in the next play. He has mastered a tricky maneuver upon which the coach is now banking.

Hayes knows the rules of the game. He knows how to cooperate with his teammates and how to avoid injury when tackled. He has a modest amount of general skill and a special talent for executing one specific field operation. In less than a minute he may be the hero or the dunce of his school. As he sprints onto the field, firmly resolved to be the former, his self, personality, culture, and society are all involved.

Hayes is acutely aware of himself. He knows he is momentarily the center of attention. He is sensitive to the impression he may be making upon others. He sees himself as he imagines his coach, teammates, opponents, officials, and spectators see him. This is his situational impression of himself. He also has a general impression of himself as a football player. It is based on the skill and confidence he has acquired in learning to play the game. In these circumstances, all the impressions of self that Hayes holds, considered together, help make up his personality at the moment—his football personality. That is, of course, only a tiny fraction of his total personality.

Because of our conception of self, which is based partly on the fact we anticipate what others expect of us, we develop a readiness to act in given ways in given circumstances. *All of the readiness to behave, the tendencies to act, which an individual acquires in the process of interacting with other people, constitute his total personality.* Hayes is about to demonstrate one facet of his personality—his readiness to behave in a football game, a readiness he acquired while interacting with other football players.

In trotting out onto the field Hayes also carries with him a small segment of his culture. All the players share a common knowledge of the rules of the game, the special language of football, the particular skills necessary, and the value of good sportsmanship. The culture of football, among the players and officials, consists of the common denominator of learning about how to play the game. In the more general sense, as we said in an earlier chapter, culture consists of the skills, beliefs, and knowledges that are commonly shared and accepted by a number of people and transmitted to their children.

The relationship between culture and personality should be evident. *In a general sense an individual's culture is represented by that part of his personality which he shares in common with others. His personality is predominantly that par-*

ticular part of the culture of his society which he has acquired through learning, resulting in his readiness to behave in certain ways. The culture an individual has internalized and his personality are not exactly and entirely the same thing, but they are very closely related.

Returning to Hayes. He carries his football personality and culture onto the field. In the game, society occurs. Society, we have said, is a process of interaction among people.

Personality, we are now prepared to say, *consists of all of a person's learned preparations to behave. Society occurs when personality and culture are transformed into interaction.*

This is an oversimplification of the relationship among the self, personality, culture, and society. If you find it difficult to grasp at first, it may be because the self, personality, society, and culture are abstract concepts. When you see a man bow his head in prayer, you do not actually and literally *see* a facet of his personality, his learned preparation to behave that way. You "read into" what he is doing, infer something about his personality. You see an *individual,* not his *self.* Your ideas regarding his self are drawn from observation of his behavior.

In the same sense, although you do not actually *see* a tangible something called culture, or society, these can be studied and evaluated through observation of people as they *enact* their culture in *a* society.

BIOGENIC, PSYCHOGENIC, & SOCIOGENIC FACTORS IN PERSONALITY

Biogenic, psychogenic, and *sociogenic* factors are involved in personality. They function as an integrated, interactive complex. If a healthy unity of personality is to be achieved, societal demands must not exceed the individual's biogenic and psychogenic ability to respond appropriately. Imagine someone whose biogenic and psychogenic sexual drives are beyond his power to control. He cannot adjust to the demands of his society. Imagine a man who wants to gain acceptance in his community, which entails in part his support of himself and family without outside help. Suppose his intellectual, physiological, or anatomical make-up is such that he cannot earn enough to supply these needs?

Although these factors function as an integrated, interactive complex, we will discuss each separately.

Let us first bring our human infant into the world. What is his biogenic personality? What is he born with that will play a part in developing his learned preparations to behave?

1. *Instincts.* Is the newborn baby equipped at birth with instincts?

An instinct is an unlearned, unvarying, biologically determined behavior pattern common to all members of a species and invariably elicited whenever a given condition exists. We know that nonhuman forms of life have instincts. These patterns of behavior are not learned. All members of the species will manifest those patterns each and every time certain conditions exist. For example, a female gray goose will retrieve her eggs in a particular way when they are removed from the nest. She will do it that way every time they are removed. And every female gray goose will retrieve her eggs that way every time they are removed from the nest.

Does the human being have instincts functionally equivalent to those of other animals? Until about the 1920s many students of behavior answered affirmatively. Psychologists issued lists of so-called human instincts. None of these listings was the result of scientific observation and investigation. Each was the product of casual observation and presumably logical inference.

The sociologist Cooley challenged the psychologists who believed they found instincts in man. As early as 1902, he was saying that human children gave no evidence of possessing them. His conclusion was based on fairly careful observation.

In 1911, anthropologist Franz Boas published *The Mind of Primitive Man,* in which he stated that after examining all known and various ways in which people lived in primitive societies, he found no universal patterns among them. A human instinct would by definition have to be universal in the species.

Today no reputable scientist holds that men are born with instincts. We must conclude, therefore, that instincts do not influence the formation of human personality, since humans do not have instincts.

2. *Reflexes.* What about these? Do they influence personality formation?

A reflex is a simple, automatic, biologically determined re-

sponse to a stimulus, common to all members of a species. It is present at birth of the organism, is untaught, unlearned, and in many cases quite unmodifiable. Human beings do come into the world equipped with reflexes.

The basic difference between an instinct and a reflex is this: An instinct is a more or less complex *pattern* of behavior, whereas a reflex is a simple, single muscular movement. The female gray goose's instinctual retrieving of her eggs, you will agree, is a fairly complex *pattern* of behavior. It involves numerous and different but integrated and related movements. A reflex is much simpler behavior. In the human, it is exemplified by the jerk of the knee when tapped or by muscle contraction around the pupil of the eye when a sharp light is focused on it. The motions are automatic, in response to specific stimuli.

Reflex action can sometimes be modified by a process termed *conditioning*. Say you love dill pickles. You salivate when you merely smell them, even though you know you are not going to eat one at the time. Your reflex salivation is conditioned. You may even become further conditioned so that just thinking about dill pickles under given circumstances will cause your saliva to flow.

3. *Physiological-anatomical structure.* Can the physiological and anatomical structure of the human organism influence the formation of personality? Yes.

Physiologists have established that the *endocrine glands,* tiny organs located in several different parts of the body, do affect behavior. They secrete small amounts of chemical substances, called *hormones,* into the blood stream. Hormones affect various body organs, resulting in general emotional "sets," or predispositions. These predispositions may alter behavior, since they affect the individual's alertness, spontaneity, reaction time, speed of movement.

Hormones are necessary to normal functioning. One of them, adrenalin, mobilizes the body for increased effort. A man spies a friend turning the corner ahead of him. His mind informs him he will have to hurry if he is to catch up with his friend. His body secretes more adrenalin upon that "signal." The man is ready to break into a trot.

Sometimes the glands send an abnormally high amount of adrenalin into the blood stream, temporarily or for prolonged periods. This oversecretion renders an individual restive, anxious, without his knowing why he feels this way. He may become angry, overaggressive, "spoiling for a fight." An abnormally low production of adrenalin makes the individual feel lethargic. His body is not mobilized for very much action.

Clearly, then, the physiological action of the glands bears a functional relation to the learned preparation to behave that an individual acquires in the process of interacting with other people. But man is not completely at the mercy of his glandular system. Within limits, the effect of secretions upon behavior and personality can be modified, by psychological and other means. A man who has developed lethargic habits may force himself into greater activity by telling himself he must do so. A person who feels generally hostile can master his emotional set by rigid self-discipline. These are psychological devices for modifying or nullifying physiological drives. Environmental forces accomplish similar results. The phlegmatic man, knowing he will lose his job, which he needs badly, if he continues his lackadaisical efforts, mobilizes himself for stepped-up performance. The quick-to-anger individual, realizing he will get into trouble if he punches the traffic officer in the nose, controls himself and refrains from doing what he would like to do. In both examples, social control has operated to modify learned preparations to behave.

Certain investigators have held that the inherited anatomical structure of the human being affects his personality. The size and shape of the body, the muscle and bone structure, supposedly create in the individual at least a predisposition to develop a certain temperament, which in turn is conducive to particular kinds of behavior. Some physiologists and anthropologists have held, for instance, that people with long, thin, attenuated bodies tend to be gloomy and misanthropic, while those with rounder and plumper bodies are inclined to be genial, friendly folk.

Is this so? Can anatomical structure influence the development of an individual's personality? Probably not in the sense that the biological-anatomical structure, of itself, has that influence. Rather, people of certain body types are more likely than those of other types to be affected by given environmental phenomena. A person with an athletic build may be appreciated by his peers for his ability to run fast, swim long distances, or play basketball. Such approval perhaps reinforces his interest in athletic sports. Or his brawny build may indirectly lead to his becoming something of a bully, if, for instance, his adolescent peers learn to depend upon him to establish the supremacy of their gang or club by beating up nonmembers in the neighborhood.

The obese man may simply never develop an interest in ballet dancing. The puny man may learn to behave as puny men had better behave if they want to remain healthy—he will not become involved in a fist fight with more muscular specimens of manhood.

These examples suggest that the social situation exerts greater influence over the formation of personality than does anatomical structure of the organism as such. A better way to put it might be that potentially there is a reciprocal relation between anatomical structure and environment with regard to personality formation. An obese man eats because he is fat and his body "needs" a lot of food, and he is fat because he eats a lot. Given his anatomical-physiological body structure, he feels hungry often, eats a good deal and frequently, gains weight because his body takes on weight readily.

There are social and psychological variables to be considered, too, in connection with anatomical structure. The woman who meets the society's definition of great beauty will likely be treated differently than less fortunately endowed women. She will react and interact accordingly. A "he-man" who appeals to women may learn to behave as he believes the female of the species expects "he-men" to behave.

4. *Intelligence.* Does intelligence influence the formation of human personality? We believe it does, even though we are not entirely certain what intelligence is or how it is best defined. One useful definition is that *intelligence is the individual's inherited capacity to learn from experience.* But precisely what is intelligence, biologically? We know it is a product of the efficient functioning of the brain, particularly of the large frontal lobes, called the *cerebrum.* We conjecture that this functioning is related to the chemical composition of the brain cells and that these cells permit impulses to travel through the brain, transmitting meaning. The chemical composition of the brain cells, we infer, differs among individuals, so that impulses transmitting meaning travel at different rates of speed in different brains.

As we are somewhat in the dark concerning the biological basis of intelligence, so too are we uncertain regarding the exact psychological meaning of intelligence. Is it a *general* ability to respond effectively in new situations? That is, if Bill responds at a very high level of efficiency when learning the mechanism of a car, will he be equally effective in learning to spell, to make chemical analyses, to do geometry? Or is intelligence a number of *specific,* separate abilities for different kinds of behavior, such as composing music, using words, building mechanical contrivances, thinking in abstractions? We are not quite sure, but probably there is something we may term *general* intelligence, or *general* ability. Additionally, it seems, certain abilities are *special,* based upon a particular kind of intellect. In this category probably lie such special aptitudes as the ability to compose music at the interpretive level and to understand and work with highly complicated machinery.

With the advent early in this century of the Binet-Simon and, later, other intelligence tests, psychologists believed they had an instrument for measuring what they conceived of as "general intelligence," an across-the-board ability to operate at a given level of efficiency in responding to new situations, expressed as an intelligence quotient, I.Q. Later, some skepticism arose. Did the tests really measure native ability? All of it? Only that? Since the majority of tests involved communicating with the subject in the English language, were foreign-born subjects at a disadvantage? Since test items often involved concepts in our particular culture, was the foreigner again at a disadvantage? Did his score represent a true measure of his native intelligence? Might he not interpret the test administrator's words differently than native-born subjects would? If so, were we then measuring not innate intelligence exclusively, but to some extent the degree to which an individual had assimilated the culture of the society in which he found himself?

Although there is still some unresolved doubt whether tests separate intelligence from cultural determinants of how native intelligence will be applied, we may make the following generalizations:

a. *Intelligence potential is biologically determined.* We inherit it.*

b. *Intelligence tests do not measure native intelligence ex-*

---

* Inherited intelligence potential may be impaired, however, by the time an infant is delivered: if a parent suffered from one of several diseases when the child was conceived; if the fetus was injured while in embryo; or if the infant received certain kinds of injuries in the course of delivery.

clusively. Evidence suggests that what an individual has or has not learned in his culture will affect his test score to some extent. No test, it is commonly believed today, measures "pure" intelligence. If the tests measured intelligence to the exclusion of anything else, we would expect a person's I.Q. to remain the same throughout life, since it is presumably an indicator of *intellectual capacity,* not of *acquired knowledge.* A number of studies have demonstrated, however, that a change of milieu may be followed by an upward or downward swing in I.Q. This suggests that the sociocultural factor has not been entirely eliminated from test results.

c. *With the types of exceptions noted, the I.Q. score tends to be stable, particularly at the upper and lower extremes.* Highly intelligent children retain their high intelligence quotients and dull children their low, although a bright child may not fulfill his potential in actual behavior and a dull one may be trained to utilize his capacities to the fullest. No treatment to date has been effective in elevating the I.Q. of severely retarded individuals to any appreciable extent.

PSYCHOGENIC FACTORS

Psychogenic factors of personality are those traits an individual possesses, largely acquired in society, that influence his mental-emotional inclinations to behave. Fear of the dark is such a trait. So is the need some individuals feel to love all humankind, or to "reform" people. These felt needs predispose but do not necessarily destine the person to behave in the expected fashion, given the appropriate stimuli.

How do we develop our mental-emotional make-up? Scientists know even less about this than they do about intelligence.

Charles H. Cooley spoke of "sentiments that constitute human nature," traits he believed would be found in practically all human beings everywhere in the world. He derived this hypothesis from the seeming fact that when a person, influenced by his own culture, considers an individual from a radically different culture, he usually understands the latter's emotions and motives. Observing the individual from the disparate culture, he understands when he is feeling the emotions of love, hate, or fear under particular conditions. He comprehends when the individual is about to attack or embrace another person.

And yet, Cooley reflected, these emotions and motives are not fixed, as a biological instinct would be, so that a given stimulus invariably elicits a specified instinctive response. Cooley's *sentiments* were highly changeable. A particular stimulus might elicit hatred upon one presentation, love when presented another time. Emotions and motives, Cooley knew, were brought into play under a wide variety of social situations. Why, then, were these sentiments universally recognized?

Because, he suggested, practically all human beings had certain experiences in common, resulting in universal similarities in behavior along particular lines. All people possessed "human-ness," so to speak, however this might be expressed in a specific culture. Particular sentiments were encouraged or discouraged, to a greater or less degree, according to the culture, but all were phenomena of every society.

This was speculative, of course, and Cooley offered few clues to just how experience brought forth particular sentiments. He did point, for instance, to the alleged fact that fondling a baby (experience) stimulated a feeling of love (sentiment) in the person doing the fondling. But this is indeed speculative.

No theories advanced by sociologists concerning psychogenic features of human personality have had the impact of those propounded by a Viennese physician, Dr. Sigmund Freud. Freud advanced his theories during the last quarter of the nineteenth century and well into the first half of the twentieth. "The father of psychoanalysis" was a therapist, primarily interested in the mentally abnormal persons whom he treated; these persons were primarily neurotics. Seeking to understand the neurotic personality, Freud arrived at a line of reasoning now known the world over under the name of psychoanalysis. Although Freud's thinking involved psychological much more than sociological concepts, the heart of his theory implicitly if not explicitly posits that environmental factors are inextricably bound up with the psychological in the formation and expression of individual personality.

Like Cooley, Freud postulated that all humans possess certain traits in common. He analyzed these differently at various stages in his thinking, finally identifying three basic elements of personality, all of which must be brought into reasonable balance if the individual is to remain in good mental-emotional health. These elements he termed the *id,* the *ego,* and the *superego.*

The id, following Freud, *is the great reservoir of untamed biological-psychological drives underlying all human behavior.* The id operates unconsciously for the most part; the person is unaware of its function in producing within him certain drives to behave in given ways.

The ego is the conscious facet of personality, which the individual seeks to develop and control. He is aware of it and attempts to mold it to suit his needs.

The superego is the force of conscience, of self-criticism, within the unconscious of the individual. It is the "censor" component of human personality, reflecting what the person has learned through social experience in his particular culture. It makes him aware of his society's morality, its demands upon him for conformity.

The id provides the individual with the basis for seeking to fulfill a given need. The superego may inform him that satisfying that need will bring him into disfavor. The ego mediates between id and superego, attempting to effect a compromise between naked biological-psychological needs and the demands of society.

Freud's formulations, scientifically verifiable or not, have had such widespread influence that it is worthwhile illustrating them.

Charles lusts for power and the money that will make it possible for him to gain that power—to manipulate and control people. He has an opportunity to wreck a sound corporation by illegal means, such as spreading false rumors about its financial condition. If he brings the corporation crashing into bankruptcy, he can buy it for a pittance, operate it as the giant, sound corporation it was and would have been but for his machinations. As head of the great firm he will make the fortune and achieve the power he so very urgently wants.

The powerful urge to wreck the corporation, rebuild it, and thus gain great power over people reflects the operation of Charles' id. The operation of his superego alerts him to the fact that if he follows his urge, distasteful consequences will ensue for him. He will be regarded by people important to him as a pirate of industry. He may be convicted for disseminating false reports about the company. Social disgrace would follow.

Thus Charles is caught between two desires, to satisfy his

lust for power and to retain his freedom, social standing, and the respect of significant others. His ego mediates the internal battle. It will help Charles use his conscious mind to weigh the alternatives, so that he may decide which course of action to pursue.

Although Freudian theory evolved out of observation of persons in mental distress, Freud and his disciples have expressed the conviction that psychoanalytic thinking sheds light on the behavior of people in good mental health as well. For example, they would point out, there is the Freudian conception of *mental conflict*. We all experience it briefly or over extended periods, intensely or moderately, in a wide variety of situations.

You want to sleep a little longer; you also want to get to school on time. The conflict is not very violent. You arise.

Dan realizes he is an alcoholic. He must have a drink in order to feel at ease, but if he has one he cannot control the urge to take more, until he has lost control of his senses. Alcohol has reduced him to such anguish, made him feel so unworthy, so guilty, that he desperately wants to quit drinking. He knows if he continues he will die or have a mental collapse. Every hour, every day, for many months now, he has been torn between the two consuming drives—to take a drink and not to take a drink. For the alcoholic, such conflict is of overwhelming intensity. And it has been boiling in Dan's conscious mind for a long time. His physical and mental stamina are near the breaking point. Very soon now he will be forced into an irrevocable decision. He will cut himself off absolutely and permanently from all alcoholic beverages, regaining his mental stability and peace of mind. Or he will yield once too often to the alternative compulsion, open one more bottle, and die or wind up in a hospital for the insane.

Mental conflict, then, can exert a potent effect on the personality. In the process of resolving his conflict, an individual may *repress* unacceptable thoughts and feelings into his *unconscious*. The unconscious, as viewed by the psychoanalyst, is a repository of feelings, thoughts, and tendencies to behave that have been submerged as undesirable, socially disapproved, and perhaps sinful. This material accumulates in the unconscious as the individual matures and develops his personality. He is no longer conscious of the repressed material. His conscious mind has forgotten it. But it remains "alive," pushes toward the conscious level, according to psychoanalytic theory.

Tim is eight. His father, a stern, unbending martinet, has given the boy a severe whipping for alleged misconduct. Tim goes to his room, hating his father. "I wish he were dead!" he mutters. "Then there would be just Mummy and me!" Immediately he is shocked by what he has been thinking, overcome with feelings of guilt. It is "bad" to want your father to die! Tim rids himself of this horrendous thought by repressing it into his unconscious mind. Before long he has forgotten he ever had such a notion. He has submerged the attitude into his subconscious and left it there as he continues to grow and develop into manhood.

But repressed ideas and impulses (Freud also called them *complexes*) do not become extinct when submerged. These elements of the personality need to be expressed. They may rise to the conscious level at some time. A little boy who has repressed his feelings of hostility for his father may on a particular occasion have those feelings reach the conscious level again. They may find expression in words, as when he explodes angrily against his father. They may be expressed in deeds, such as punching or kicking at his father.

Very frequently, according to psychoanalysts, repressed material finds expression, not in direct but in roundabout, symbolic manner, thus outwitting the internal "censor." The lady in Figure 9.5 believes the man is expressing his hostility toward her symbolically, by what Freudians term a *substitute response*.

The psychoanalyst argues that *all behavior, even the seemingly absurd or incomprehensible, is meaningful, an expression of individual personality*. To Freud, even slips of the tongue were significant. They were inadvertences, ambiguous verbalizations of thoughts and feelings escaping from the unconscious. A British clergyman is said to have remarked, upon concluding a marriage ceremony, "And now, it is kisstomary to cuss the bride." About such slips Freud wrote that the suppressed tendency obtains expression against the speaker's will. Applying this, we may reason that the minister meant to say, "It is customary to kiss the bride," instead of which he said, slightly camouflaging it, what he truly felt but hoped he had suppressed, that the bride should be "cussed," not kissed.

Many sociologists have serious reservations as to the scientific validity of psychoanalysis. They would not agree with Freud that personality is fully developed and becomes fixed

Figure 9.5
A Substitute
Response?
Drawing by Lorenz;
© 1964 The New
Yorker Magazine, Inc.

"The ball, I presume, is me."

during the childhood years. Certainly Cooley and Mead would not accept this. (And even some of those psychologists who generally follow Freud—Karen Horney and H. S. Sullivan among them—tend to depart from his theory on this score.) This so-called *genetic* theory of personality formation is at variance with the sociologist's observation that personality consists of *all* of the individual's preparations to behave. They would say he learned these in the course of accumulating feelings, thoughts, and experiences—in his society, in interaction with people, *from birth to adulthood.*

SOCIOGENIC FACTORS

It is almost unnecessary to underscore again the part that social factors play in the development of individual personality. The human being about to be born is dependent upon the social environment long before he draws breath. His parents were reared in that environment and he was conceived in it. He was born into a society in which behavior norms were already established. They influenced his parents' conception of how to treat him. Others with whom he eventually interacted were similarly responsive to societal norms. His own learned preparations to behave developed within this environment. His personality was *mainly* fashioned by social forces.

We so implied in defining personality as a person's *learned* preparations to behave. Man's inherited biological equipment determines the upper limits of his *capacity* to learn; psychogenic factors impede or advance *the degree to which he utilizes* this capacity; but what he learns is learned in social interaction, in a social setting.

· *NOTES*

1. Joyce O. Hertzler, *A Sociology of Language* (New York: Random House, 1965), pp. 395–396.
2. Erving Goffman, *The Presentation of Self in Everyday Life* (New York: Anchor Books, 1959).
3. *Ibid.,* pp. 3–4.
4. *Ibid.,* p. 17.

· *SUGGESTIONS FOR FURTHER READING*

BANDURA, ALBERT, and RICHARD H. WALTERS. *Social Learning and Personality Development.* New York: Holt, Rinehart and Winston, 1963.
Personality development is discussed from the viewpoint of behaviorist learning theory.

COOLEY, CHARLES H. *Human Nature and the Social Order.* New York: Scribner, 1902.
A classic, this book discusses human nature and the socialization of the individual. The concept of "the looking-glass self" is treated. See especially Chapters 5 and 6.

ERIKSON, ERIK H. *Childhood and Society.* New York: Norton, 1950.
Erikson is anthropologically and psychoanalytically oriented. He discusses the relationship between culture and personality.

FREUD, SIGMUND. *A General Introduction to Psychoanalysis.* New York: Horace Liveright, 1920.
The "father of psychoanalysis" examines personality formation (and sometimes disintegration) in a lively and highly readable style.

GOFFMAN, ERVING. *The Presentation of Self in Everyday Life.* New York: Anchor Books, 1959.
In this highly original book, the author sets out to "consider the way in which the individual in ordinary work situations presents himself and his activity to others, the ways in which he guides and controls the impression they form of him . . ."

LINTON, RALPH. *The Study of Man.* New York: Appleton-Century-Crofts, 1936, Chapter 26, "Culture and Personality."
The author discusses the close relationship that exists and the interaction that takes place between the human personality and the culture of the society in which an individual belongs. Personality affects culture, culture affects personality.

MEAD, GEORGE HERBERT. *Mind, Self and Society.* Chicago: University of Chicago Press, 1934.
An analysis of symbolic interaction and of the structure and process of the self. Difficult reading.

10 SOCIAL ADJUSTMENT, MALADJUSTMENT, & DEVIANCE

We have been discussing the process of learning social behavior, how the individual gains a conception of self, and how development of personality comes about. We now turn to the investigation of how the learned social behavior of an individual, his conception of self, and his personality affect his social adjustment. In this connection we also examine maladjustment and social deviance.

A CASE STUDY

Thomas Stephens (the name is fictitious) was an only child, deeply loved by his parents, who nevertheless acknowledged he was "Daddy's boy," since he was so closely attached to his father. As a toddler, Tommy followed Mr. Stephens about the house, romped with him, hugged and kissed him constantly. Mrs. Stephens did not mind the partiality her son exhibited, considering it natural and healthy that a boy prefer a man's company to a woman's.

During his preschool years (when this author first became acquainted with the family), Tom was a happy child and not at all difficult. His sunny disposition endeared him to relatives and neighbors. When he entered elementary school, he became an outstanding pupil. His grades were top rank, he read voraciously, engaged in athletic sports, and was accepted as a leader by his many playmates. People who knew him classed him as a wholesome, well-balanced youngster.

This opinion did not change when Tom entered high school,

where he again stood out, scholastically and as a highly attractive personality. He played baseball for the school, at the same time maintaining a near-A average in his classwork.

Throughout, he maintained his close relations with his father until one day, out of a clear sky so far as he was concerned, his parents informed him they were getting a divorce. He took the news in stunned silence and declined the opportunity to discuss the matter further in ensuing days. When his parents tried to explain, he simply nodded and walked away.

Tom remained with his mother after the divorce, but their relations were strained. He was as courteous and obedient as ever, but reserved and withdrawn. When he came home from school he went directly to his room, remaining there until dinner time. After dinner, he went back to his room and closed the door.

At school, his friends and teachers noticed a similar change in his demeanor and behavior. He lost interest in sports and other extra-curricular activity. His grades slumped. He avoided his former associates and spent recess in a corner of the school cafeteria, alone.

Mrs. Stephens had expected Tom to be shocked for a time, after the divorce was granted, but when his seeming lethargy continued for months, she became alarmed and attempted to reason with him, to explain that a divorce did not necessarily mean that either parent was less responsible or respectable than before. She tried to get through to the boy, to show him he was loved, to get him to demonstrate affection for her. He not only did not meet her demonstrations of love with an equivalent feeling, but showed very little feeling of any kind. He had erected an invisible barrier between himself and his mother, and she could not break through.

Mr. Stephens, who visited regularly, was aware of the situation and did what he could to mend matters, but he, too, was rebuffed. Tom retreated into himself when anybody at all made overtures to him.

Then, almost imperceptibly, another change occurred. Tom began to emerge from his self-imposed isolation, to relate to people again. But now he related in a highly emotional, even violent manner. He cried easily, threatened to commit suicide, blamed his mother for breaking up the home, and at the same time called his father a "failure," "no father at all," and a person who was irresponsible, who had no regard for his son. He exploded in rages, threatened to leave home, and finally did, after stealing money from his mother's purse.

Mrs. Stephens telephoned her former husband, who dropped everything to go in search of his son. He found him in a cheap hotel and asked him to return to his mother. The boy turned on his father, angrily accused him of being a bully, a skirt-chaser, a man without any human feelings, who had only pretended to love his son in the past. Tom did finally consent to return home, however.

He remained there and also continued in school, but now he was so surly, rude, and bitter that he was a problem in and out of class. He went out of his way to challenge the authority of teachers. He courted fights in the school yard. His former friends were now entirely alienated from him, and when he engaged in a fist fight with one, he was conducted to the vice-principal's office, where he was severely rebuked for his rebellious attitude and conduct. Tom retorted insolently and vituperatively. He absented himself from classes after that and wound up in Children's Court. Both of his parents appeared in his behalf, and he was returned to the custody of his mother.

In the next several months both of Tom's parents reasoned with him, jointly and separately. They told him that a man and wife could be responsible and respectable, yet find themselves incompatible, one with the other. They tried to convince him that he had developed a warped, unrealistic view of his parents, both of whom continued to love him dearly. They insisted that neither was a monster, neither was unfeeling, and that it was time he "grew up," understood himself, his parents, and the situation much better.

Very gradually, his rages diminished; he became less pugnacious, verbally and physically. He came to accept his parents' version of himself and themselves. He began to respond to them, and to others, in a positive, outgoing manner again. He accepted his parents' love and gave them his love. His interest in school was revived. He formed friendships once more.

By the time he entered his senior year at high school he was again looked upon by those who knew him as a well-adjusted, friendly, normal individual.

What had happened over the years? Originally, Tom was what we ordinarily consider a normal person. He was reasonably well *adjusted*. After his parents were divorced, he became *unadjusted*, disinterested in other people, in school, and in sports. Still later he was *maladjusted*, raging at people, thinking of suicide, attacking erstwhile friends. The people he abused considered him abnormal in particular respects. Some disliked or resented him. Gradually, he regained an interest in the world about him. He listened to his parents. He looked into the "mirror" they furnished him, saw his "self," and did not like what he saw. He gradually changed. When that change began, he was on the road to becoming *adjusted* once more.

ADJUSTMENT TO REALITY

What is meant when we say someone is *adjusted*? What is *adjustment*? In our particular frame of reference we are speaking of *social adjustment*—that is, the adjustment of the individual to his social surroundings. Basically, human adjustment consists of facing and accepting reality.

And what is reality? Again in our frame of reference, there are three kinds of reality, personal, social, and objective.

1. *Personal reality consists of ideas and opinions an individual holds about himself and other people.* Suppose Mr. Gerber believes his wife is unfaithful. He checks her movements and is convinced his suspicions are well founded. As he defines the situation, his wife *is* unfaithful. This is his personal reality.

2. *Social reality consists of ideas and opinions people generally apply in judging others.* Friends of Mr. and Mrs. Gerber believe she is entirely innocent of wrongdoing and that her husband is judging her unfairly. This is part of the social reality of the situation.

3. *Objective reality consists of the observable, verifiable facts about a social situation.* The objective reality about social situations may never be known unless some of the persons involved deliberately seek the truth through careful observation and verification. Let us assume a private detective follows Mrs. Gerber for months and never discovers her in a compromising situation. Her husband's suspicions that she visited a certain address regularly are confirmed, but the detective finds an innocent reason for these calls. Mr. Gerber knows that a man living in that building was in love with Mrs. Gerber before she was married. But the investigator is positive she does not visit him. She is calling on a woman friend who happens to live in the same building. This is the objective reality of the situation.

Mr. Gerber's friends may tell him he is wrong to suspect his wife. He may get a report from the detective indicating the same. Despite the *social reality* (the opinions of his friends) and the *objective reality* (the verified facts), Gerber may yet remain unconvinced. If so, his *personal reality* regarding the situation remains unchanged.

Objective reality, then, will not necessarily be accepted and made part of personal reality. Nor will it invariably become part of social reality. If we believe something strongly enough, it is "truth" to us, and factual evidence to the contrary will not shake our conviction.

If Mr. Gerber's personal reality were in agreement with the social and objective reality of the situation, he would be socially adjusted apropos this matter. But insofar as social adjustment is concerned, objective reality is not the significant factor. *Regardless of objective reality, social adjustment is a product of the balance between personal and social reality.* Thus, assuming Mrs. Gerber is in no way guilty of the behavior in question, but that both her husband and other people believe she is, then he is socially adjusted in connection with that particular situation. When an individual's sense of personal reality corresponds closely with social reality, as defined by his associates, he tends to be well adjusted to his social environment. And whenever an individual's associates become aware that he refuses to accept reality as they define it, they will begin to consider him maladjusted.

Social adjustment takes place when the individual, facing the social reality of his situation, achieves some measure of harmony in satisfying personal needs while fulfilling the expectations of others.

LEVELS OF SOCIAL ADJUSTMENT

Let us apply the terms *adjusted, unadjusted,* and *maladjusted* to the case of Thomas Stephens again. When he accepted the fact that his divorced parents were respectable, responsible individuals who loved him; when he acknowledged to himself that his evaluation of the situation had been unrealistic; when he organized his behavior around the reality of his situation (in terms of what he was expected to do about it, how he expected to behave)—when he did all these things, he was *adjusting.* People around him considered his behavior appropriate. At the same time, Tom was not acting as he did solely in order to please his parents and others with whom he came in contact. He was satisfying his own needs as well—to be accepted, to love and be loved, to do well at school. The adjustment brought his needs and his society's expectations into better agreement.

An individual's needs will not necessarily be in conflict

with the expectations of members of his society. Where there is relatively little disparity, adjustment is made more readily. For instance, Tom and his associates may be in complete accord that he ought to go on to college, graduate, work hard thereafter, and "get ahead," so he might live comfortably, engage in worthy civic and social endeavors, and "become a credit to his community." In this sense, his associates think of him as a well-adjusted individual.

But some people's needs run counter to the expectation of others. They tend to become socially *unadjusted*. If Tom did not accept the judgment of others—if, believing he ought to quit school and not continue into college, he remained at his studies nevertheless, against his wishes and better judgment—he might still not become so unhappy or rebellious as to find himself in serious conflict with members of his society. He might be only *unadjusted*, meaning *not adjusted* to the situation. He might before long become *adjusted*, accepting the verdict in his society as to the behavior he should follow.

On the other hand, he may not adjust. Suppose he quits school, leaves home, goes from unskilled job to unskilled job, is discharged time and again for incompetence. Suppose, resentful and hostile to the authority of his society, he says, "All right! If that's how they feel about it, I'll just show them I can be a success, my own way." Assume he goes on a rampage of robberies, in the course of which he pistol-whips several of his victims. We can scarcely continue to consider him merely unadjusted. He is *maladjusted*. His needs are far out of balance with the expectations of members of his society.

Pulling together what we have said to this point: A comparatively adjusted person is one whose behavior satisfies both his needs and the expectations of others. An unadjusted person might be thought of as one whose needs are not yet satisfied but whose search for satisfaction has not led him seriously to violate the expectations of others. A maladjusted person is one who satisfies his needs in such manner as seriously to violate the expectations of others.

But the differences are more in degree than in kind. Perfect adjustment is virtually impossible. All of us are somewhat unadjusted and sometimes maladjusted.

A person deemed maladjusted need not invariably and for all time be the object of disapproval or the source of tension in his society. There are positive consequences of maladjustment in many cases. Until many American Negroes became seriously maladjusted, refusing any longer to accept their supposed inequality with whites, they had little chance of gaining those privileges of citizenship guaranteed them by the Constitution. When their maladjustment became extreme, to the point where they refused to wait any longer for full citizenship, they erupted. This brought both hostile and friendly responses, as well as tangible gains toward full acceptance. It is practically axiomatic that by the time the American Negro is generally defined as a full-fledged citizen, with all of the rights, privileges, and obligations accorded him by the Constitution, he will by the same token be deemed well adjusted. This will be an outcome of the fact that he will have satisfied his personal needs reasonably well, and members of his society, white and black, will have accepted the fact that Negroes and Caucasians are social and legal equals. Thus, the Negro's personal reality will be in harmony with the newer definition of the social reality.

Social reformers are often considered maladjusted in their society, since in some measure they are convinced the status quo must be changed. In their time, the suffragettes were considered maladjusted, since they demanded "women's rights" and the consensus in the society was that women already had the rights to which they were properly entitled, and those "rights" they were demanding were not theirs and should not be. We would not take the same position today, inasmuch as most of us now accept the concept that women and men are civil and social equals, and that this is as we want it. We have redefined social reality.

We are emphasizing that personal adjustment, unadjustment, and maladjustment are *socially defined*. Suppose a man kills his infant daughter? Is he maladjusted? That depends upon the social definition of the situation. If he lived in the United States and committed the act there, we would certainly say he is maladjusted. If he lived in a society in which infanticide is sanctioned under certain conditions, members of that society would most likely not adjudge him maladjusted if the prescribed conditions were present when he killed his daughter.

What about the baby killer himself? Would he consider himself adjusted to his social reality? The man in the United States would very likely deem himself maladjusted. The man in the other society would probably consider himself adjusted.

We have learned that the individual gains a conception of himself by reflection of the judgments of other people who share his culture. The United States resident will almost certainly be aware that he is *considered* maladjusted. The other man will almost certainly know he is *considered* adjusted. Most likely, the former concurs in the adverse judgment of other members of his society, at least to the extent of feeling some guilt over what he has done. He has failed to achieve harmony between the satisfaction of his personal needs and the expectations of others, and he knows it.

It is conceivable, of course, that our American is entirely unaware that he has been defined as maladjusted. In that event, he could remain quite content with himself, confident that he is well adjusted. Despite *his* judgment in the matter, however, others in the society would continue to believe he is maladjusted. A personal feeling of maladjustment always derives from the reflected judgments of others. But an individual who is unaware of this assessment may think of himself as socially adjusted. Sometimes we say such persons have "escaped" from the reality of the social situation.

May an individual be defined as maladjusted by members of one group but not by those of another, within the same society? This is quite possible. A banker who took to the picket lines to denounce capitalism would probably be adjudged maladjusted in banking circles. His fellow pickets might think of him as an individual who finally "saw the light," who followed his social conscience. Where they are concerned, he would be well adjusted to social reality.

LEARNING TO ADJUST

How do we proceed to adjust to reality? *Adjustment is a process learned through association with other people.* Consider an imaginary Mr. Black. He has a powerful urge to control and dominate people. To satisfy this need he attempts to exercise dictatorial leadership in a club to which he belongs. He is contemptuous of any opinion contrary to his own. He rudely orders people about. He refuses to follow the suggestion of any member concerning anything having to do with club activities.

His fellow members do not intend to be treated this way, and their demeanor and behavior show it. They resent him and are hostile to any proposal coming from him.

This infuriates him, but although he has no intention of giving in to others, he changes his approach to them, outwardly, when the members convene. Mr. Black no longer tries to take over complete command the moment he enters the room. He sits down, listens to what others say, does not immediately fire back a counterargument.

Mr. Black has already made some adjustment to social reality. But he is not thereby satisfying that urgent need to dominate others. And he is dissembling. His attitude of seeming willingness to listen to others is a sham. But having brought himself to listen instead of talking incessantly, he discovers some pleasure in such conversation. Gradually, he comes around to the view that many of the ideas advanced by fellow members are sensible and acceptable to him. As time goes on, he no longer insists on having his own way, without exception. He offers advice, but accepts it, too. He wins some arguments, loses others. His needs have altered. The desire to dominate club members has been supplanted by a need for acceptance by and cooperation with them. His behavior now satisfies both his needs and the expectations within this particular group. He has *learned* to accomplish both these ends in the process of associating with group members.

This is the essence of the problem of human adjustment. Each man wants to satisfy his personal needs, at the same time conforming, within reason, to the expectations of others.

RESPONSES TO PROBLEMS OF ADJUSTMENT

Mary wants to meet the right man, become a good wife and mother. She attains her goal. Members of her society fully approve, for such behavior is within the expected standards of conduct.

Jim has an impelling need to be a big-league baseball pitcher. No one in his society would disapprove should he make the big league, but he lacks the talent.

Pete aspires to become a big-time confidence man. Members of his society disapprove and will do everything possible to prevent his entering his projected career in crime.

Mary can make an easy adjustment to social reality in satisfying her needs. Jim and Pete, although for different reasons, will find it not so easy. They may be frustrated. *When an in-*

dividual realizes his needs are blocked from satisfaction, he is said to be frustrated.

How do people adjust to frustrating social situations? We can analyze possible types of responses according to how they relate to social reality.

1. One response to frustration is *aggression,* which is *hostility directed against others.* A young man sees a baseball bat lying on the front lawn of a private residence. Yielding to temptation, he decides to steal it. As he picks it up, a boy runs out of the house, snatches the bat away from him, collars him, and says he is going to get the police. The frustrated would-be bat snatcher shoves his captor violently, breaks the hold, and runs away. He has reacted *aggressively* to social reality.

Aggression need not be physical. At a department store sale, a woman reaches for the last remaining yellow blouse on the counter. Another shopper brushes past her and snatches the garment herself. The loser of this battle of the blouse tells the winner, in crisp and pungent language, exactly what she thinks of her. She has employed a mental-verbal form of aggression.

In Figure 10.1, Barbara apparently aggresses against both her husband and her mother-in-law by nonphysical means.

2. Another common adjustment to frustration is *compensation,* which is *the substitution of a new need, which can be satisfied, for an old one, which cannot.* Robert is most desirous of fame as an actor, but all he can get after years of trying is a succession of bit parts, which bring him no recognition whatever. He decides he can be just as happy writing novels. At this he is highly successful. He finds his new way of life satisfying; he has adjusted to frustration by compensating for it.

In Figure 10.2, the bald man, unable to satisfy a need to have hair on his head, compensates by substituting a new need, for a bushy, eye-provoking mustache to distract attention from his baldness.

3. Adjustment sometimes takes the form of *escape, a retreat from a frustrating condition, in a real or figurative sense.* Above all else, Paul, an advertising executive, would like to become president of the company where he is employed. He creates many advertising ideas that are highly profitable for the firm, but time after time, Paul is passed over for promotion. At last, frustrated and brooding, he begins drinking heavily,

Figure 10.1
Non-Physical Aggression
Reprinted with permission
of Cissie Peltz and
Today's Health.

"And, Barbara, it might help
if you refer to Tom's mother as a
'senior citizen,' and not an 'old bag.'"

seeking solace in alcohol. He has adjusted to his frustrating
situation by *escaping,* figuratively speaking.

4. Still another reaction to frustration is *rationalization,*
which consists of *finding a socially acceptable reason for one's
inability to achieve a socially sanctioned objective.* Rationalization is not the sort of excuse that one does not himself believe.
The individual offering a rationalization actually believes it.

Maria applies for a secretarial job, is given a dictation and
typing test, informed (truthfully) that she lacks the requisite
speed and accuracy. Later, she tells her parents she was not
hired because the office manager quite obviously was prejudiced against her as a person of Italian extraction. She is offering one form of rationalization, provided she really believes
she qualified for the post but was rejected solely because of
prejudice against girls of Italian extraction.

5. Another possible response to the problem of adjustment
is *dissociation, a process in which inconsistent values are kept
in separate "mental compartments" so that the individual is
not constantly made aware of the inconsistency in his needs.*

Elmer is a salesman, on the road weeks at a time. He dearly
loves his wife back home; despite this fact he has several brief
romantic interludes with women he has met in his travels. He
tells himself he is not *really* unfaithful to his spouse. "This is
altogether separate," he reflects. "It has nothing to do with
my marital life. It's just one of those things."

Figure 10.2
Compensation

Reprinted with permission of Katherine Mace and the publisher from *The Saturday Evening Post* © 1957 The Curtis Publishing Company.

"Some wild theory about it taking people's attention away from his baldness."

He is confronted with needs that many people would deem contradictory in our culture—to have sexual intercourse only with his wife and to satisfy sexual urges by extramarital relations while on the road. If he satisfies the first need, he frustrates the second, and vice versa. In our hypothetical case, Elmer resolves his adjustive problem by *dissociating*. Having two mutually exclusive standards of behavior, he has learned to follow one at a time. At home, he is a loving husband, devoting his sexual attention exclusively to his wife. On the road, he indulges in extramarital relations. He compartmentalizes these separate activities—the second "has nothing to do with my marital life." This compartmentalization of his contradictory behavior insulates one kind from the other.

In Figure 10.3, the woman speaking seems able to dissociate certain inconsistent values. She wants to lose weight but also wants a sundae, which is fattening. She sees no inconsistency between the need to diet and her desire for the sundae.

6. Finally, one may adjust to a frustrating situation by accepting it. In the sense meant here, *acceptance consists of realizing the existence of a frustrating situation or condition and matching one's behavior to it as far as possible.*

Ida is blinded by an explosion. For a time she refuses to believe she will not regain her sight. She is angered when doctors inform her she is permanently blind. She declines jobs suited to people with her handicap. But at last she faces facts, accepts her condition and its implications, and begins reorganizing her life accordingly. She is now making what others judge to

Figure 10.3
Dissociation

Reprinted by permission of Reamer Keller and Adcox Associates, Inc.

"I just discovered the most wonderful diet.
Let's go in and have a sundae while I tell you about it!"

be a desirable social adjustment. She has *accepted* her social reality.

All of us, at least at times, use these six ways of adjusting to social reality. No one uses one way exclusively. And a person may employ more than one in a particular situation. For instance, Elmer, who *dissociated* his marital from his extra-marital sexual life, employed *rationalization* to arrive at his dissociation.

Fortunately, most of us sooner or later accept frustrating situations we can do nothing about. A man acknowledges to himself he is not the great creative writer he once thought he was; he gives up starving in a garret and becomes a book sales-man. A one-time ravishing beauty accepts the fact, later in life, that she no longer is a *femme fatale*. She settles down to the satisfying if less self-centered life of wife and mother.

Why must we accept *social* reality? Is it not possible that one's *personal* reality offers more for the individual and per-haps society as well? That is a matter of values, of definition. And every age, every culture, every society has its rebels who refuse to bow to the verdict of the many on how to behave. They insist they have a standard that, if accepted and followed, would benefit all concerned.

The "hippies" furnish a current example of this. Their phi-losophy is not always clear and often must be inferred from their behavior. Different groups hold conflicting views on particular matters. But a common thread runs through all the groups: The argument is that there is no need to conform to the norms of the society, that indeed such conformity is to be eschewed as "bad." The hippies disregard certain aspects of social reality in favor of their personal reality. They disaffiliate themselves from the larger society in greater or less degree. They dress to please themselves, not others. They seek satisfaction and self-discovery through the use of psychedelic drugs, in defiance of convention and law. Their "love-ins" are the hippies' answer to a world where international and national tensions run high, where strife is a common occurrence.

Who can say whether the hippies will fade from the social scene as have other unconventional groups before them? Who can affirm with certainty that the personal reality of the hippies will never come into balance with social reality? The hippies might become more conventional, or others in their society might become more receptive to the thinking and behavior of hippies. The fact is that in the past many a rebel has produced an idea, ideal, or thing that has, by definition of the members of the society, benefited it, although originally there was strong opposition to it. However, when the rebel and most members of society see things differently, so long as the rebel's personal reality is far removed from the social reality of his environment, the people in that environment will tend to consider him maladjusted. If he converts them to his point of view, or they convert him to theirs, then personal and social reality come into balance, and social adjustment is realized.

GENERAL FACTORS IN ADJUSTMENT

Most of us are motivated to adjust to social reality, although some of us rebel. What influences determine whether and how we adjust?

Three general factors play a part in human adjustment: (1) personality, (2) the individual's definition of the situation, and (3) the social definition of appropriate behavior in this kind of situation.

Consider the part played by *personality*. Has a given individual perhaps acquired a strong aversion for snakes? Or does he like them? What are his acquired needs, and how intense are they in given circumstances? For instance, does he have a need to appear nonchalant in the face of danger? Or does he perhaps like to play the part of a defenseless person who must be protected by others? The part of the individual's personality that is involved in determining his reaction consists of his past learning as it pertains to the given situation.

Suppose a classroom instructor in your school brought a snake into the room and turned it loose. You might chuckle appreciatively as it slithered in your direction. The girl alongside you might become hysterical. Your personality and hers are involved here.

Another general factor in adjustment would be the *individual definition of the situation.* In the hypothetical illustration just cited, is the snake harmless, in your opinion? Would the instructor actually turn a dangerous reptile loose in class? Has he manifested homicidal tendencies in the past? A person's definition of the situation is the way in which he sees and relates himself to immediate conditions. In our illustration, you might conclude this is a harmless experiment and sit quietly, observing developments. Another student, assuming any instructor who brings a live snake into class must be insane, might dive through a window.

The *social definition* of the appropriate behavior in a given kind of situation will affect the individual's adjustment, too. Does the instructor who loosed the snake consider his conduct appropriate, and will he reprimand you if you bolt from the room? Will other students ridicule you? The social definition of appropriate behavior in this kind of situation consists of what other people expect of us. Comprehending the definition may prevent your following your immediate inclinations, since you realize that to do so would lead to unfavorable responses from your associates.

Of course, the social definition may play little or no part in what you do. The probable anger of the teacher and the ridicule that your friends would cast upon you may not be enough to compensate for your terror. If you define the situation as dangerous, you may be up and out of there in a trice, regardless of what people will think.

IS ADJUSTMENT AN INDIVIDUAL OR SOCIETAL MATTER?

A discussion of social adjustment would be incomplete without some reference to views held by several influential writers, who say that it is not the individual who should need to adjust to the demands of the society, but that the society should change in order better to meet the needs of the individual. Put another way, the argument is that where there is an absence of adjustment between man and his society, it is the society, not the individual, which is maladjusted, or "sick." Probably the most widely read expounder of this thesis is Erich Fromm, a German, trained in psychoanalysis, who has written extensively on what he considers the social maladies of our time. Fundamentally, he writes as a humanist and moralist, not as a social scientist.

Fromm uses the term *mental health* to mean much the same as the sociologist's *social adjustment*. Mental health, he writes, cannot properly be defined in terms of the adjustment of the individual to his society. Rather:

> . . . *it must be defined in terms of the adjustment of society to the needs of man*, of its role in furthering or hindering the development of mental health. Whether or not the individual is healthy, is primarily not an individual matter, but depends on the structure of his society. A healthy society furthers man's capacity to love his fellow men, to work creatively, to develop his reason and objectivity, to have a sense of self which is based on the experience of his own productive powers.[1]

An unhealthy society, Fromm states, renders it difficult or impossible for man to fulfill these basic needs. All men are born with these needs, he says, and it is our society that lacks sanity when it fails, as it does, to provide for them. The Western world has created societies in which man is a pawn rather than the reason for the existence of society. We have created great wealth and at the same time have ". . . managed to kill off millions of our population in an arrangement which we call 'war.' " We live in an economic system ". . . in which a particularly good crop is often an economic disaster, and we restrict some of our agricultural productivity in order to 'stabilize the market,' although there are millions of people who do not have the very things we restrict, and who need them badly." We have reduced working hours and have more free time as a result, but "We do not know how to use the newly gained free time; we try to kill the time we have saved, and are glad when another day is over."[2]

Fromm points out that the very societies (the United States included) that have the greatest prosperity are the same societies that have the highest rates of suicide and alcoholism. Can it be, he wonders, that our society, while emphasizing the value of great wealth, satisfies our mutual needs but leaves us with a feeling of intense boredom? Are suicide and alcoholism ". . . pathological ways of escape from this boredom?"[3] Can it be that modern civilization fails to satisfy the profound needs of man? Fromm emphatically answers in the affirmative. Man does not live by bread alone; he has other, more profound needs, and ". . . a sane society is that which corresponds to the needs of man."[4]

What ails our society, Fromm holds, is its emergence into "the new capitalism," which has tended to isolate the individual (who wants to feel he belongs) and has brought about the withdrawal of older social supports (thus reducing man's emotional security).

There was the technological revolution, which has brought an impersonal automation. Concentration of capital has been accompanied by the separation of ownership and control. The number of independent, self-employed entrepreneurs has declined, and there has been a consequent increase in the number of employees of great corporations. Employees, not things, are manipulated these days. And "the miracle of production," which has made increasing consumption the vital principle of the economy, has brought with it an entire new industry, devoted to creating the desire to consume.

What kind of men, then, does the "new capitalism" type of society require?

It needs men who cooperate smoothly in large groups; who want to consume more and more, and whose tastes are standardized and can be easily influenced and anticipated.

It needs men who feel free and independent, not subject to any authority, or principle, or conscience—yet willing to be commanded, to do what is expected, to fit into the social machine without friction.[5]

That is Fromm's "sick" society. "We do not choose our problems," he writes, "we do not choose our products; we are pushed, we are forced—by what? By a system which has no purpose and goal transcending it, and which makes man its appendix."[6]

If, then, society is sick, society must be changed, so that man's mental health may improve.

Although much of Fromm's indictment of our society is generally conceded to be true, his thesis suffers from several shortcomings. He has not proved that all men are born with certain needs that are basically the same. His description of the characteristics of a healthy society is very general and loose. Finally, he has not provided reasonably scientific criteria for diagnosing societies. From his own rather vague description of the healthy society, it is apparent that he is maintaining there has never actually been one that is "perfect," one that is entirely healthy. How can we gain knowledge of the "perfect" society in the absence of any model?

SOCIAL DEVIANCE

A maladjusted person is one who satisfies his needs in such manner as seriously to violate the expectations of others. There is a distinction between such *social maladjustment* and what the sociologist terms *social deviance*, or *deviant behavior*.

If you visited a hospital for the mentally ill, you would discover that the patients behave a good deal like other people you know. They read, talk, joke, play checkers, dance, watch television. But you would also be likely to encounter a patient sitting crouched in a corner, his head bent far forward, almost buried between his knees. An attendant would perhaps inform you that he had been in this condition for several years, that he sits like that all day, uttering not a word. No one seems to "get through" to him. If you spoke to him, he would not reply, as if he did not hear you. He does not eat unless carried to the table, pushed into a chair. An attendant must place the food in the patient's mouth.

He is carried to bed, sleeps on rubber sheets because he does not bother to get up nights. The morning shift cleans up his bed and carries him to the shower. Then he does the only thing he ever does by himself. He gets over into the corner and assumes the rigid, trance-like position in which you found him.

As you gaze at him, perhaps you think, "Thank heavens I'm not like him!" But shocking as it may be, the fact is you *are* somewhat like the patient, in one respect. Every once in a while you, too, lose contact with social reality. Do you doubt this? Then, imagine you have had a most distressing day, which began when you awoke with a throbbing headache. At school, you overlooked several questions on a quiz, and of course you could easily have answered them. A date you were eagerly anticipating was suddenly canceled. "Everything" went wrong.

Now, here it is evening, and you decide to go for a stroll. You think back to the dismal events of the past few hours. You pass a friend, who cries, "Hello!" You are so preoccupied with your thoughts that you neither see nor hear him.

Most of us behave in this way on occasion. Momentarily, we are concentrating so intensely on other matters that the stimuli of the immediate situation are excluded from consideration. We lose contact with social reality for the moment.

In other words, your behavior under such circumstances differs from the patient's *only in degree*. His loss of contact, in the situation described, is more intense and persistent than yours. Yours would be only mildly deviant behavior.

What does the term *deviant* mean in this connection? Obviously, your behavior is quite different from the mental patient's. If both are to be deemed deviant in some ways or degrees, then the term itself needs to be defined more precisely.

The concept *deviant* can be properly understood only in relation to another concept: *norms*. Put most obviously, deviant behavior is behavior that deviates. Deviates from what? From some social norm.

None of us is entirely normal, at all times, in all respects, since our behavior very frequently deviates from the "normal," which in essence means "most typical." At the present time a college student is deviant, in the sense that his behavior is oriented toward attaining a higher level of education than is "the norm" for the country at large.

At one time or another each of us has deviated from behavior norms in a degree that would lead our associates to consider us deviant, were the facts known. When Austin Porterfield questioned university students in Texas, every one of the 437 male and female respondents admitted having engaged in delinquent behavior serious enough to have justified court action had it been observed, or had observers decided to instigate court action.[7] (Of course, although each such act would be considered deviant, we must not assume that the actors were characteristically given to deviant behavior. None of the individuals concerned habitually committed delinquent acts.

The most typical behavior of the 437 persons was nondeviant.)

How can *both* an unusually high level of educational attainment and delinquent behavior be considered deviant? They can be—relative to the normal and typical. And here we find a characteristic of social deviance that distinguishes it from social maladjustment. We *may* deviate in a direction *approved* by those about us. The maladjusted person is so defined because he behaves in a disapproved manner.

Thus, we would define not only the behavior of the criminal, the prostitute, and the feebleminded person as deviant, but also that of the champion swimmer, the straight A college student, and the great writer. The term *deviant behavior* refers not to judgments that this is "good" and that "bad" but to actions that differ markedly from social norms.

We are now ready for a definition: *Deviant behavior is behavior that varies significantly, in direction or degree, from the social norm for that behavior.*

We may contrast it with social maladjustment as follows: Social maladjustment produces behavior that is always regarded with disapproval within a society, while social deviance is behavior that may or may not meet with social disapproval. It is different from the norm, not necessarily in conflict with it. Two factors, we noted, are involved in the definition of deviant behavior, the *direction* and the *degree* of nonconformity. To understand what we mean by *direction*, consider the distinction between the scientist and the arsonist. The first is respected, appreciated, rewarded, for the direction of his behavior. The second is regarded with disfavor, fear, perhaps horror. He is not appreciated. He is punished.

Degree may be exemplified by the case of a small child who thoughtlessly tramples over a flower bed. If the homeowner speaks sharply to the youngster, that would not seriously violate our norms for behavior under the given circumstances. We would not call that man deviant in this respect. But if, in response to such mild provocation, he flew into a rage and beat the child severely, we would feel his behavior differed from the norm to such a degree that he must be considered a social deviant *in this particular situation.*

It is most important to note how we qualified that statement. We said the man would be considered a social deviant in *the particular situation.* It is essential to understand that an individual may be deviant with regard to one kind of behavior and not another, or in response to a given stimulus on one occasion and not on another when the same stimulus is presented. Therefore we should not categorize a *person* as a social deviant —in other words, we should not say that there is a social-deviant type—since that suggests he is always nonconformist, in all ways. We can only say that his *behavior* is deviant in specific situations and that on those occasions, only with respect to those situations, he is a social deviant. The artist Vincent Van Gogh was deviant in his superb ability at painting. His behavior was also deviant when he cut off his ear. He was not deviant with regard to certain other behavior. He ate the food of his countrymen (when he could afford it). He wore the clothes customary in his society. In other words he behaved as those interacting with him would expect, in a manner of which they approved.

When may we properly speak of behavior as deviant? What degree of deviation is required?

How often do you bathe? How often should people bathe?

How many hours do you sleep daily? How many hours do you think people should spend sleeping?

How rapidly do you read? About how many words a minute do you think an adult should be able to read?

What is the caloric content of the food you consume each day? About how many calories should people consume daily?

If you answered those questions, and had many other people do the same, you would find varying responses to every one. A large number of these responses would be clustered fairly close together, representing the majority of all answers. But the rest would extend outward from the center of a continuum until you had very few at the extremes. The large middle cluster would constitute a *central tendency*, and in each case could logically be construed to reflect the norms.

But an individual might deviate somewhat from the central tendency and still be considered "normal" with regard to the particular behavior. Take bathing. Probably most people you queried would say they bathe daily. That, then, would be the central tendency. Some would report they bathe once every two days. A very small number would bathe perhaps five times a day; another few would indicate they bathe once every two months. Where do we draw the line and say, "Here is where deviant bathing behavior begins"? It would be difficult to establish, since the figures shade outward gradually, away from the central tendency. But there can be little argument that those who bathe five times a day, or once every two months, differ enough from commonplace tendencies to justify our considering their behavior deviant. They do not even approximate the norm of their associates.

TOLERATION OF DEVIANT BEHAVIOR

We said that deviant behavior is not invariably regarded with disapproval. Let us now consider this point further. Ask yourself these questions regarding behavior generally considered in our society to be serious infractions of social expectations.

1 · Should a woman divorce an otherwise desirable husband who was sexually unfaithful to her?
2 · Should a man generally known as a responsible citizen be sent to prison after committing one robbery?
3 · Should a pacifist who refuses to bear arms for his country in wartime be imprisoned at hard labor?
4 · Should an individual convicted of selling narcotics to juveniles be given a life sentence?
5 · Should a person who insists "I am God" be confined in a mental hospital?

If you tabulated the responses of several thousand people to these questions, you would find considerable agreement but not unanimity. Some respondents would be inclined to favor a life sentence for the narcotics peddler; others would not. You might believe the deceived wife should divorce her husband, while another person would comment, "Let her forget it and continue living with him." Still another would perhaps remark, "It would depend upon other factors I don't know enough about."

Central tendencies would appear in the tabulation. Stated another way, *norms of tolerance* for deviant behavior would be revealed. *Just as there are norms regulating behavior, so there are norms of tolerance for nonconformist behavior.* We allow minors to "talk back" to adults (but only up to a point). We condemn and punish murder very severely in most cases, but tend to deal more leniently with women who kill husbands or lovers who have "deceived" them. The minister in Figure

Figure 10.4
Tolerance Norm
Drawing by B. Tobey; Copr. © 1957
The New Yorker Magazine, Inc.

*"It behooves us to be forgiving and understanding
and tolerant toward all of God's children,
and that includes the summer people."*

10.4 is suggesting that good Christians should tolerate even the deviant behavior of summer-resort visitors, since they, too, are "God's children."

Culture changes, and so do norms of tolerance, which change with the times. A dramatic example in this country is the shift in attitudes with regard to homosexual behavior. Less than fifty years ago overt homosexuals were jailed, subjected to abuse, contempt, ridicule, and social disgrace. The very mention of the word "homosexual" was proscribed in polite society, and no "respectable" newspaper or magazine used it. When the novel *The Well of Loneliness* appeared in the late 1920s, it was attacked because it dealt—albeit in subtle, unsensational, and sincere fashion—with female homosexuality. The book was banned in some cities. Booksellers were jailed for selling it, and the publisher was convicted for placing it on the market. (The convictions were later reversed on appeal.)

Homosexual behavior is contrary to established norms today, but a more tolerant attitude has gradually emerged. The word "homosexual" appears in print, and the practice of homosexuality is openly discussed. In 1963, *Harper's Magazine* published "New York's 'Middle-class' Homosexuals,"[8] an article dealing nonjudgmentally with the subject. At least two magazines explicitly addressed to homosexuals appear on newsstands. Illinois law provides that homosexual relations between consenting adults shall not be considered illegal. Obviously, although homosexual behavior is still adjudged deviant in our contemporary society, norms of tolerance with regard to it have changed markedly since the turn of the century.

CLASSIFYING DEVIANT BEHAVIOR

Deviant behavior may be classified in several ways.

1. *We may distinguish between individuals who choose to enact deviant behavior and those who do so as a consequence of factors over which they have no control.* Suppose a truck driver is unemployed although jobs are available in his line. It may be that he chooses to loaf and to allow others to support him. Or he may be searching for work but unable to find it because his prospective employers know he occasionally lapses into unconsciousness, which would create a dangerous situation in traffic. In either event he would be considered deviant in some respect. But there is a very real difference between those who have ability and lack ambition and those who have ambition but lack ability.

In actual practice this distinction is sometimes difficult to establish. Psychiatrists find it hard, and at times impossible, to separate malingerers (who feign illness in order to escape responsibilities) from patients who are unemployable as a consequence of emotional maladjustment beyond their control. As behavioral scientists, of course, we do not blame malingerers any more than we do feebleminded persons for their deviant behavior, but we do contend that some people are more responsible than others for the fact that they do behave deviantly.

2. *Deviant behavior may be classified according to whether people tend to approve or disapprove of such deviance.* The accomplishments of men like Thomas Alva Edison and Charles Proteus Steinmetz deviated considerably from norms of expected achievement, but in a direction generally considered desirable and appropriate. Deviant behavior defined as inappropriate was exemplified by the conduct of a criminal such as Al Capone.

Again it must be pointed out that cultural change may bring a change in definition of certain behavior. What was defined as appropriate in one historical period might be considered inappropriate in another. Copernicus and Galileo, who pioneered in science three centuries ago, were considered heretical by many of their contemporaries. We honor them today.

3. *Deviant behavior may be classified according to whether it is individual-centered or manifested through group activity.* In comparing the conduct of two types of deviants—inmates of prisons and patients in mental hospitals—observers have often noted this difference: Prisoners are generally group conscious, engaging in continuing interaction, while mental patients are often secluded and alone in their deviant behavior. But this is only a general tendency, for mental patients sometimes do cooperate with others, and prisoners occasionally operate as "lone wolves," separating themselves from the inmate population so far as possible.

It should be borne in mind that deviant behavior manifested through group interaction may be normal within that particular group. When a half-dozen or more individuals get together periodically to smoke marijuana, their behavior, deviant in the eyes of the law and most of the people in our society, may not be deviant so far as they themselves define it. On the other hand, persons who smoke marijuana in groups may accept the definition of the larger society, feel guilty about their "unusual" behavior, and accept the verdict that they are deviant in this respect.

The same comment applies to other forms of deviant behavior, as for example juvenile delinquency. Individual members of a group of boys engaged in stealing hubcaps may regard their behavior as normal. But some individuals may not. Sociologist Albert K. Cohen, author of *Delinquent Boys: The Culture of the Gang,* maintains that the delinquent believes in the legitimacy of official norms, even when he repudiates them in conversation with his peers. The repudiation is more apparent than real, according to Cohen; the delinquent actually has a secret, repressed, perhaps not fully recognized desire for what he openly rejects:

May we assume that when the delinquent seeks to obtain unequivocal status by repudiating, once and for all, the norms of the college-boy culture, these norms really undergo total extinction? Or do they, perhaps, linger on, underground, as it were, repressed, unacknowledged, but an ever-present threat to the adjustment which has been achieved at no small cost? There is much evidence from clinical psychology that moral norms, once effectively internalized, are not lightly thrust aside or extinguished.[9]

G. M. Sykes and David Matza agree with Cohen, although they believe the delinquent's acceptance of the legitimacy of official norms is often quite conscious rather than repressed. They write in the *American Sociological Review*: "The juvenile delinquent frequently recognizes *both* the legitimacy of the dominant social order and its moral rightness."[10]

DEVIANT BEHAVIOR & CONTRADICTORY NORMS

Much deviant conduct in our society can be traced to confused and contradictory norms prevalent among different subcultural groups. It may be quite normal for the Anderson family to engage in noisy parties on weekends, but the Browns, in the next housing tract, regard such conduct as scandalous. The industrial manager may not understand why his workers do not increase their production when he offers them a piece-work bonus for speeding up on the job. It seems normal to him that their efforts should be proportionate to the amount they can earn. He fails to understand that production quotas are often determined by informal agreements among workers and not entirely by the economic motivation of individuals.

People of different age groups also tend to follow conflicting norms. Middle-aged Americans frequently express the opinion that young people are "going to the dogs." The youngsters, for their part, may regard members of the older generation as "squares" or may use some other colloquialism equivalent to yesteryear's "old fogey." This seems to be an ever-recurring theme in what we sometimes think of as the war between old and new generations. Summarizing research on the subject, Bernard Berelson and Gary A. Steiner point out that although the most conspicuous factor in the development of a person's social values appears to be his home and family life, children tend to grow away from the original parental influence as they grow a little older—at least in some measure, and in the degree to which they come into contact with news ways of life. At such time, the authors assert, the more important the subject of an opinion, attitude, or belief, the more likely young people are to go along with their peers rather than their parents.[11]

Conflict between the generations also emerges when youngsters copy norms of behavior considered appropriate for adults but not for juveniles. A man may smoke cigars but when his ten-year-old son uses him as model and does the same, his father is not likely to consider such behavior at all appropriate.

Some norms are to be observed under certain circumstances and not others—a seeming contradiction that may cause confusion, particularly among young people. Thus, children are taught both to be truthful and to lie. They are told they must tell the truth about a great many things, such as where they have been, where they are going, and whether they brushed their teeth. On the other hand, they learn that when Auntie asks if the cake she sent was good, they must lie, tell her it was, if in fact it was not. They learn that when mother says so, they must inform a caller at the door that mother is not home, when in fact she is.

A child learns that the norm for truthfulness regarding a particular subject is flexible enough to permit him to lie regarding that same subject. He must give his true age to visitors and teachers, but, with the active connivance of parents, some children are allowed to claim to be younger than they in fact are when they board a bus or buy a ticket to the movies.

Conflict exists between American norms stressing "success" and norms that render achievement of that "success" impossible for some individuals. Thus, children learn to want a college education, leading to a career that will bring them wealth and a nice home with a garage for a nice car in a nice part of town. Some young people achieve these goals. Some cannot, since other norms in the society that apply to them preclude the possibility that they will get to college, prepare for a career, amass some wealth, and live comfortably as "successful" persons. The Negro child, in certain parts of the country, is in this category, as is the child of the tenant farmer and the child of the itinerant field laborer.

The American sociologist Robert K. Merton has advanced what has become an influential set of postulates concerning this matter. A characteristic of our culture, he writes in *Social Theory and Social Structure*, is our emphasis on the amassing of wealth as something to be highly desired. Every individual in the society hopes to achieve this kind of "success." But values concerning the legal means of realizing this goal deny "success" to some members of the society, notably those of low economic status. This brings some of the people concerned to seek and achieve legitimate ends by illegitimate means. They gain "success" by violating certain behavior norms. They steal, for instance.[12] "It is only," Merton writes, "when a system of cultural values extols, virtually above all else, certain *common* success-goals for the population at large while the social structure rigorously restricts or completely closes access to approved modes of reaching these goals *for a considerable part of the same population*, that deviant behavior occurs on a large scale."[13]

Contradictory norms exist not only in a society. They may also exist in the mind of one individual. A father may be less disturbed when a son becomes involved in a sexual venture with a neighbor's daughter than he would be if his daughter became similarly involved with a neighbor's son. The father here tends to follow contradictory norms when judging the behavior of young people.

ALIENATION

Deviant behavior sometimes takes the form of *alienation*, a phenomenon that has interested sociologists for many years. We introduce the subject here with an excerpt from the novel *Invisible Man* by Ralph Ellison. The protagonist, a Negro, speaks:

I am an invisible man. No, I am not a spook like those who haunted Edgar Allen Poe; nor am I one of your Hollywood-movie ectoplasms. I am a man of substance, of flesh and bone, fiber and liquids—and I might even be said to possess a mind. I am invisible, understand, simply because people refuse to see me. Like the bodiless heads you see sometimes in circus sideshows, it is as though I have been surrounded by mirrors of hard, distorting glass. When they approach me they see only my surroundings, themselves, or figments of their imagination—indeed, everything and anything except me.

. . . I am not complaining . . . It is sometimes advantageous to be unseen, although it is most often rather wearing on the nerves. Then too, you're constantly being bumped against by those of poor vision. Or again, you often doubt if you really exist. . . . It's when you feel like this that, out of resentment, you begin to bump people back. And, let me confess, you feel that way most of the time. You ache with the need to convince yourself that you do exist in the real world, that you're part of all the sound and anguish, and you strike out with your fists, you curse and you swear to make them recognize you. And, alas, it's seldom successful.[14]

Sociologists would say that Ellison's protagonist is *alienated*. This term has been given somewhat different connotations by various scholars, hence we had better indicate how we use it here. *Alienation is a feeling of dissociation from society.* The feeling may or may not result in overt behavior. If it does, the behavior may or may not be considered deviant to the point of serious social maladjustment. But to a greater or less degree, *alienation involves the separating of the individual from society, either physically or psychologically.*

Alienation seems to be especially a phenomenon of complex and highly organized societies, in which depersonalization has progressed to a high degree, replacing intimate face-to-face relationships. In the tremendous industrial complexes of our society, for example, the individual workman has become, for the most part, a cog in a huge machine. He does not control decisions concerning that machine, may never have met those who do, and may be known to them only as a payroll number. Similarly, we elect our government officials, but our control over them is indirect and remote at most; the personal contact between citizen and official, characteristic during this country's earlier years, is no more. In many ways, today's citizen has been depersonalized, in some instances even to the extreme degree represented by the "invisible man" portrayed by Ellison. He may develop a feeling of powerlessness, become alienated from his society out of frustration.

Or, and this may be part of the same feeling of powerlessness, he may become alienated when he concludes that life in his society is meaningless. Thus, in *The Road Back*, German born novelist Erich Maria Remarque writes of a group of soldiers returning home from World War I after Germany's defeat. They had fought for the Fatherland with a patriotism as intense and genuine as the patriotism the enemy felt for the Allied cause. They were convinced that they had braved death for noble principles, for idealism, for the welfare of the world. Defeat was all the more bitter, therefore, since it signified that the cause of justice and humanitarianism had not prevailed.

Now they were back home, and they found a nation they had not discerned before. There was no idealism, no love of country, no brotherhood of man. The civilian world, they suddenly discovered, was cynical, grasping, self-seeking, vicious. The soldiers had been deceived. Their dead had died in vain. There were no values in society worth fighting and dying for. Why had they failed to realize this when they marched to the battle-field?

And now, Remarque's principal character stands before a class of youngsters he is teaching and reflects:

Here I stand before you, one of the hundreds of thousands of bankrupt men in whom the war destroyed every belief and almost every strength. . . . What should I teach you? Should I tell you that in twenty years you will be dried-up and crippled, maimed in your freest impulses, all pressed mercilessly into the selfsame mould? Should I tell you that all learning, all culture, all science, is nothing but hideous mockery?[15]

Since those prophetic words, man has been at war again and again, and we are currently witnessing the alienation (some call it disaffiliation) of some of the young people of our land. The "hippies" may be used as an example again. They insist they feel identified only with other "hippies" and that they distrust the older generation, which has brought the world to its present sorry state.

ANOMIE

Some writers consider alienation a more severe form of what sociologists term *anomie*. Admittedly, anomie is very difficult to define clearly, perhaps because it is a somewhat confused concept to begin with.

Anomie has been defined by some as synonymous with *normlessness*. This is misleading, since no one is completely normless. A better characterization is Robert M. MacIver's, for whom it ". . . signifies the state of mind of one who has been pulled up from his moral roots . . . who has no longer any sense of continuity, of folk, of obligation. The anomic man has become spiritually sterile, responsive only to himself, re-sponsible to no one."[16]

When an individual "falls into anomie," he loses his sense of belonging to the group. He rejects its norms and for a time at least finds few if any substitute norms by which he will be guided. He is, so to speak, adrift on the sea, in a ship without a rudder. To be sure, as has been pointed out, he has not totally abandoned the norms of his society, but he feels *removed*, with little sense of identification with others.

Anomie is not synonymous with mere lawlessness, although

the anomic person may violate the law in given cases. Gangster Al Capone was lawless in many ways, but scarcely anomic. He did reject many norms of the society, but substituted for them a clearly defined code of the racketeer in organized crime. This included concepts such as hostility toward police, contempt for law and order, intimidation of the law-abiding in order to gain one's ends, the murder of competitor gangsters and disloyal henchmen. By contrast, an anomic person has lost his sense of belonging in one group and has not yet found a feeling of identification with another, if he ever will.

Individuals who survived Nazi concentration camps have testified they were in a state that sociologists might define as extreme anomie. Upon admission to the camp, they maintained their customary values, including a feeling of close indentification with fellow sufferers. They treated each other compassionately, cooperated to outwit guards, did not steal from each other. Gradually, however, some changed. Driven by privation, ill health, torture, and the threat of extermination, they violated norms they regarded highly upon admission. Some stole from fellow inmates; some informed on prisoners who had violated regulations; some sought special privileges by collaborating with their captors in one way or another.

These defectors withdrew from fellow prisoners, not so much physically as spiritually and psychically. They knew they no longer belonged in that world. But they had no other world to join. They had undergone a personality deterioration, abandoning norms to which they formerly subscribed, while being activated by no consistent, comprehensive, or consciously recognized and accepted system of substitute norms. No longer compassionate toward their fellow inmates, they did not hate them either. They simply had *no* feeling to speak of, for or about them. Their present behavior was neither "good" nor "bad"; it was simply survival behavior. It just *was*.

The feelings of these individuals were no more positive toward the guards with whom they now may have been collaborating. They felt no loyalty or affection for them. Nor did they feel great hatred for them. They *did not feel*, except superficially; their senses were deadened; they lived for the day, in a state of anomie.

To put it allegorically, the anomic individual has lost his past, foresees no future, and lives only in his immediate present, which is virtually nowhere.

We made clear that although it is appropriate enough to speak of *social deviance*, we ought not to refer to anyone as a *social deviant*, since that would suggest he is deviant at all times, in connection with all norms of his society. We pointed out that no one is entirely normless and deviant in this sense. Now, however, we must qualify this slightly.

Some individuals manifest deviant behavior in one or more respects and do so fairly consistently and persistently. They conform to some or many of the norms of the society, but at the same time habitually deviate from others.

Feebleminded individuals are an example. Their thinking and learning behavior remain markedly at variance with the norms.

The mentally ill, suffering from psychoses, will behave in characteristic fashion, outside established norms, so long as they suffer from the disease. About 50 percent, however, will recover or have a remission of illness and return to a normal way of behaving.

Persons who engage in what the law defines as sexual deviation may continue in this form of behavior indefinitely. On the other hand, some will seek treatment, benefit from it, and thereafter follow a pattern of sexual behavior that is generally acceptable.

· *NOTES*

1. Erich Fromm, *The Sane Society* (New York: Holt, Rinehart and Winston, 1955), p. 72.
2. *Ibid.*, pp. 3–6.
3. *Ibid.*, pp. 10–11.
4. *Ibid.*, p. 20.
5. *Ibid.*, p. 102.
6. *Ibid.*, p. 87.
7. Austin L. Porterfield, *Youth in Trouble* (Austin, Texas: Potishman Foundation, 1946), pp. 38ff.
8. William J. Helmer, "New York's 'Middle-class' Homosexuals," *Harper's*, CCXXVI, 1354 (March 1963), 85–92.
9. Albert K. Cohen, *Delinquent Boys: The Culture of the Gang* (New York: Free Press, 1955), p. 129.
10. G. M. Sykes and David Matza, "Techniques of Neutralization: A Theory of Delinquency," *American Sociological Review*, XXII (December 1957), 665.
11. Bernard Berelson and Gary A. Steiner, *Human Behavior, An*

Inventory of Scientific Findings (New York: Harcourt, Brace & World, 1964), pp. 564–566.

12. Robert K. Merton, *Social Theory and Social Structure* (New York: Free Press, 1957), pp. 161–194.
13. *Ibid.,* p. 146.
14. Ralph Ellison, *Invisible Man* (New York: Random House, 1952), p. 3.
15. Erich Maria Remarque, *The Road Back* (Boston: Little, Brown, 1931), pp. 252–253.
16. Robert M. MacIver, *The Ramparts We Guard* (New York: Macmillan, 1950), p. 84.

· SUGGESTIONS FOR FURTHER READING

BECKER, HOWARD S. (ed.). *The Other Side: Perspectives on Deviance.* New York: Free Press, 1964. Paperback Edition 1967.
The entire volume is worth reading. Especially relevant to this chapter are "Good People and Dirty Work," pp. 23–35; "On the Politics and Sociology of Stupidity in Our Society," pp. 37–49; and "Thieves, Convicts, and the Inmate Culture," pp. 225–45. (Pages refer to paperback edition.)

CAMUS, ALBERT. *The Stranger.* New York: Knopf, 1946. Vintage Books, 1954.
This novella, by the Nobel Prize winner, was originally published in this country in 1946. It has the outward form of a crime story, but reveals the mind of the uncommitted, disengaged person whom we call "alienated" today.

CLOWARD, RICHARD A. "Illegitimate Means, Anomie, and Deviant Behavior." *American Sociological Review,* XXIV (April 1959), 164–176.
Other theories of anomie focus on variations in the availability of legitimate means to achieve approved cultural goals. In this article, Cloward considers differentials in access to approved goals by both legitimate and illegitimate means.

COSER, LEWIS A. "Some Functions of Deviant Behavior and Normative Flexibility." *American Journal of Sociology,* LXVIII (September 1962), 172–181.
Social deviance should not be viewed as inevitably negative in character, says Coser. It has positive functions, too.

FROMM, ERIC. *The Sane Society.* New York: Holt, Rinehart and Winston, 1955.
A lively discussion of personal adjustment and the consequences for the individual personality of certain aspects of life in our contemporary society.

HELMER, WILLIAM J. "New York's 'Middle-class' Homosexuals." *Harper's Magazine,* CCVI (March 1963), 85–92.
This article furnishes insights into the life of the respected middle-class man, who may have a wife and children, but who leads the secretive existence of a homosexual. An unsual glimpse of this kind of social deviance.

KLAPP, ORRIN E. "The Folk Hero." *Journal of American Folklore,* LXII (January 1949), 17–25.

———. "Hero Worship in America." *American Sociological Review,* XIV (February 1949), 53–62.

These two interesting articles should be read together. The first discusses individuals who have deviated in a positive direction, toward super-fulfillment of cultural norms. The second considers the admirers of such "heroes."

MERTON, ROBERT K. "Social Structure and Anomie." *American Sociological Review,* III (October 1938), 672–682.

A now famous statement on "socially derived sin," and the fact that some social structures exert pressure upon some individuals so that they engage in nonconformist behavior.

SEEMAN, MELVIN. "On the Meaning of Alienation." *American Sociological Review,* XXIV (December 1959), 783–791.

The writer examines alternative meanings of the term "alienation," as employed in sociology.

part four
group
behavior

11 SOCIAL GROUPS

We used the term *group* many times in the preceding pages, and since it is a word in common usage, did so without giving it a sociological definition. We will now define and discuss "group" as a sociological concept. We will consider how social groups form, their significance in society, their principal characteristics. We shall also distinguish between groups and other collections of human beings.

AGGREGATIONS, CATEGORIES, & GROUPS

The sociologist is concerned with the behavior of individuals, but his emphasis is on individuals as interacting members of groups. It is the concept of *group*, therefore, toward which thinking in sociology converges.

What is *a group*? To answer that, we must first distinguish between it and other collections of individuals that many sociologists designate as *aggregations* and *categories*.

An aggregation is any number of people who happen to be in close physical proximity to one another at a given time.

A category consists of any number of persons who have some particular attributes in common.

A group exists when a sense of relatedness is shared by a number of individuals as a consequence of their interacting or having interacted with one another.

Three persons seated on a sidewalk bench waiting for a bus are not necessarily a group. They may merely comprise an aggregation. Fifty people with an attribute in common, such as faith in God, may be a category rather than a group. The members of a family probably are a group, since the individual members think of themselves as being related by kinship. They are involved in a social relationship with each other.

Imagine a suburban railroad station. Every morning some thirty people board the 8:15 bound for the city. They are not by that fact a group. They have not developed the web of acquaintanceship that would bind them together. This collection of individuals constitutes an aggregation.

So long as they wait for the train to arrive, board it, and proceed to their destination without interacting with each other in any way, they remain an aggregation. But let us now suppose that Jenny Murphy and Peter Sandusky, two of the commuters, happen to sit next to each other on the train. Jenny has a crucifix hanging from a chain around her neck. Peter wears a Knights of Columbus pin in his lapel. Jenny assumes Peter is Catholic. Peter presumes Jenny is Catholic. Whatever the facts, Jenny and Peter are not a group. They lack a sense of relatedness as a consequence of interacting or having interacted with each other. True, there has been *some* interaction. We defined the latter as the process that occurs whenever human beings respond to the actions of other human beings, and Mr. Sandusky's lapel button communicates a certain meaning to Miss Murphy, just as the crucifix she wears communicates meaning to him. Since any communication of meaning represents interaction in these circumstances, a limited sort of human interaction has taken place. But it has not resulted in *a shared sense of relatedness* between the two travelers. Assuming they are indeed Catholic, they belong in one social category, having an attribute in common, but that is about all we can say up to this point.

Now suppose that on this particular day the train grinds to a stop and remains stalled. The passengers become fidgety, squirm in their seats, look out the window to see what is holding things up. A conductor coming through informs them that a car developed a hotbox and the train will remain stationary for approximately an hour. Passengers groan, express unflattering opinions of the railroad line. Giving vent to their feelings, they converse with one another, sharing the same problem and irritation. Jenny sighs, "Oh, dear! I'll never make it to work in time!" Peter mutters, "This is the worst commuter line in the country!"

Interaction has begun for these two. A rudimentary feeling of relatedness has been established. Jenny and Peter continue to converse. A chance remark reveals they both attended the same parochial school. By the time the train falters into the city terminal, Peter and Jenny feel they know each other. He says he hopes he will see her on the train again. She replies she hopes so, too.

In ensuing weeks, the two greet each other on the train platform. By unspoken agreement they sit together on the train. Conversation is easy and pleasant now. They like each other.

One morning, Jenny does not board the 8:15. Next day, when they meet, Peter says he worried about her. Was she ill the day before? Definitely, a feeling of *group* has developed between them.

The concepts *aggregation, category,* and *group* are also exemplified when, on a very hot New York day, a million people disport themselves on the beach at Coney Island. Together, they comprise an aggregation. Of the million, perhaps a hundred are Moslems. They are a category. Under one beach umbrella, four people are having a picnic. They are a group.

But the classifications are not mutually exclusive. Suppose it is four Moslems who are having the picnic under the umbrella. They represent both a category and a group. Suppose three friends are playing in the surf, two of them Negro, one white. The three are a group. The two Negroes are of one category.

Classifications of people are not mutually exclusive, we have seen. And the character of a number of people together may change. Suppose an aggregation, consisting of three women, happens to be walking on the same street at the same time, going their independent ways, interacting not at all, feeling no sense of relatedness. Suddenly, a man appears, perched on the ledge of a window twenty stories high, threatening to jump. The women might immediately be galvanized into a *group*, excitedly crying to each other to watch out, that the man might plummet to the sidewalk. They would possibly form a plan of action, one running to telephone the police, another to summon a minister, while a third stands watch, out of the potential danger zone. Thus the individuals who made up the *aggregation* become members of a *group*.

And just as an aggregation of individuals may metamorphose into a group, so a group may go through change, cease being a group. Suppose an imaginary Cole University has a spectacularly successful football team. The members practice together, eat together, study together, and attend many of the same classes together. When they get out on the field to meet a rival team, they work together like a perfectly meshed machine. They have a tremendous *esprit de corps*, think of themselves as a team, and virtually consider themselves brothers. They represent a solidly united group.

Now they are about to graduate. Each has won a letter and has been awarded a miniature gold football, commemorating the team's garnering the intercollegiate football championship. Before commencement day, the members of this group get together for dinner and an evening of conviviality. It is a sentimental occasion, and the teammates vow never to lose contact with each other. They form a club, which is to meet once a year.

Several years in succession the club convenes for dinner, drinks, and reminiscence. The members write, telephone, and sometimes visit each other between annual meetings. They still constitute a group.

But the members are separated by distance. They have been developing their individual interests. They marry, have children, become engrossed in professional and civic activities. Attendance at the annual get-togethers becomes smaller each year. The merriment at the meetings is a little forced. Finally, by unvoiced but common consent, one year there is no call to a meeting. And there never is again. The men who were once so closely identified completely lose touch with one another. The feeling of relatedness is gone. The group no longer exists.

But the former members still constitute a category, since they have certain attributes in common. They are all Americans, males, and they speak the same language. They are alumni of Cole University, former members of its football team, holders of a major letter, and winners of gold football trophies.

BECOMING A GROUP MEMBER

When does an individual become a member of a group? A clue lies in this tape-recorded colloquy between a street-gang youth and the author.

Q: Are you a member of the gang that hangs out on West Street?

A: Oh, yeah!

Q: How does a fellow get to be a member?

A: A fellow wants to hang out with us, he belongs. Anybody from our part of town can belong. Now, there's no offense in a guy's being from a different side of town. Some of them fellows come over to our side and we get along fine with them. But they wouldn't really be part of our gang, because you can't always depend on what they'll do. You meet a guy and ask, "Where are you from?" The other guy says, "I'm from the north side." Another guy says the south side. Them are more or less the gangs—the side of town you come from.

Q: Any guy, so long as he's from your side of town, can become a member? Just by hanging around?

A: Not just by hanging around, exactly.

Q. Well, how do you know who is and who isn't a member?

A: It's like this. I couldn't tell you how many is in our gang because it don't work that way. Today we might have ten, next week twenty guys at one time. Still in all, if you was to ask me if a certain guy belongs with us, I could pretty well tell you. We didn't vote him in. He just got in. But he kind of knows he's one of the regulars, and the rest of the guys know it, too.

Q: What makes a regular?

A: Well, even from our side of town, there's some guys don't get in with us. He's got to be our kind, a good sport. I wouldn't want to be with a guy, if he seen a fight, he'd walk away from it. . . . Lots of times you find guys, when a fight starts, they're just gonna haul tail and be gone. Them kind, I don't want around.

Q: Suppose a fellow stands up and fights. Is that the only thing you look for?

A: There's other things. Our fellows are the ones you more or less have dealings with. If there's a party or something, you'd rather mention it to them than somebody else. If your guys are gonna fight a gang from the other side of town, you'd rather tell certain buddies about it, invite them in, because you know they ain't chicken. They ain't like these fellows that all the time would rather stay home and toast marshmallows. You go with the regulars.

As suggested in this statement, two criteria determine whether an individual is a member of a group. First: *Does he have a feeling of identification with it?* In the case of the gang boy, that means that he thinks of himself as a member of the group. He says, "I'm one of them." The second criterion is: *Is the individual accepted by others who think of themselves as members of the group?* In our illustration, the other members of the gang must say of our informant, "He is one of us." Our young man meets both tests of membership in his group. He considers himself a member, and others in the gang accept him as one. An individual is a member of a group when he identifies himself with it in his own mind and when the other members accept him as part of the group.

If the individual thinks he belongs, but most members of a group reject him and deny he is of the group, then he is not a member. For a time, a hunchbacked, dwarf-like boy with short, crooked legs traveled around with the street gang mentioned above. He was physically unable to participate in street fights along with the other boys. Since he could not run fast, he was not permitted to accompany the gang on its stealing expeditions. He was taken along to the house parties the youths attended, but here he was often the butt of cruel ridicule from his associates. Despite all this, he proudly informed others in the neighborhood that he was a full-fledged member of the gang. And he believed it. However, when the gang youth whom the author recorded was asked whether the hunchbacked lad was a member of the gang, the answer was, "Nah! We just keep him around for laughs. We don't none of us consider him one of us." Although the boy *identified* himself as a member of the gang, he was not *accepted* as such by the individuals comprising the group. Therefore, according to our criteria, he was not a member of that group.

In Figure 11.1 there is no evidence of *identification* or *acceptance*. Neither the man nor the woman appears to feel identified with the other as part of a group of two. Neither of the individuals seems to accept the other as "belonging."

In Figure 11.2, every indication is that there is both *identification* and *acceptance*. These men are shown in a combat zone during the Korean War. They have a common purpose and share a common danger. They feel identified with the unit as a whole. Each is accepted by the others as a fellow fighting man. Each will support the other against the enemy.

VOLUNTARY & INVOLUNTARY GROUPS

Becoming a group member is not always a voluntary matter, based upon a person's desire to join and the members' acceptance of him as one of the group. Social groups are of two types, according to whether membership is gained at the will of the individual or without regard to voluntary choice. Sociologists distinguish between *voluntary social groups* and *involuntary social groups*. As used in this context, an involuntary social group does not have precisely the meaning it may have in ordinary parlance.

A voluntary group is one in which individuals gain membership by their own choice. You are not forced to join a Y.M.C.A., nor are you commanded to affiliate with Hoo Hoo, International, an organization of some 10,000 members. If you are a member, it is by choice, not by compulsion. You have an *achieved status*, a concept we discuss in a later chapter.

An involuntary group is one in which individuals become members as a result of external social forces rather than through their own personal choices. They have an *ascribed status,* also to be discussed later.

You did not decide to be classed as a female or a male, as the case may be; by a definition arrived at in your society you are grouped with one or the other classification. You are a legal "infant" or an adult, as the law specifies. You are Caucasian, Negro, or Oriental, through no personal decision.

Sex, age, and racial background are *biologically determined,* although *socially defined.* We say, "This is a male child of Caucasian ancestry." "Male," "child," and "Caucasian" are the social definitions of the biological facts. Other characteristics are both *socially determined* and *socially defined.* You are

Figure 11.2
Identification and Acceptance
U.S. Army photo by Al Chang.

identified with a particular language group, although you did not deliberately make up your mind to speak that tongue. Your parents and others with whom you associated spoke it; you learned it from them. By and large, you are considered a Christian, Jew, or Moslem, because your parents are so classed.

On any given day, each of us is a member of a number of voluntary and involuntary groups. Your father might be classified in many ways—as male, a son, middle-aged, Caucasian, Canadian by birth—all involuntary groups. He may be a minister, a scoutmaster, lodge member, part-time teacher, author, member of the Literary Guild, a Republican, and a member of the board of education. These would constitute his voluntary group memberships.

The line between voluntary and involuntary membership is quite distinct with regard to certain groupings, indistinct where others are concerned. Your decision to join a club may be entirely voluntary. Your being a member of your particular racial group was entirely involuntary. But there is a "gray" area, a shading, between voluntary and involuntary groupings, in which the degree of voluntarism is difficult to ascertain. A wealthy corporation director may accept membership on the board of directors of a social agency, despite his reluctance to invest the time in it. He does so partly because he wants to serve the community, but also because it is expected of him and he would be subjected to criticism by people who are important to him if he did not accept the post. Is he a voluntary or an involuntary member?

Our membership in groups changes, even daily. Your father would remain in a group classified as male, and he would retain membership in the racial classification to which he belongs. But he might lose his parents and no longer be anyone's son. He might attain membership in the grandfather group, drop his book-club membership, switch from Republican to Democratic ranks, affiliate himself with the categories of painters, baseball fans, and stamp collectors while giving up membership in his professional category, whatever that might have been.

Certain of your involuntary group memberships may change in time. You will decide for yourself if you want to switch your religious affiliation. You may elect to become a married rather than a single person. Years from now, it is possible you will leave the ranks of one profession and enter another.

Another way of viewing membership of collectivities is according to *in-group* and *out-group* feelings—concepts we mentioned briefly earlier. The term *in-group* seems to have been employed originally by William Graham Sumner, in *Folkways*, published in 1907. *Out-group* came into use in sociology somewhat later.

An in-group is a social unit with which an individual feels identified, to which he feels he belongs, and from which he expects recognition and loyalty. It is his subjective attitude that produces these feelings. He considers that he and the members of the group have something in common. These are "my people." He thinks of them as "we." "We" are Baptists, or students at Middletown High School, or members of the Ku Klux Klan, or the Jones family.

An out-group is a social unit with which an individual does not feel identified, to which he does not feel he belongs, and from which he does not expect loyalty or much recognition. Where his in-group is "we," he thinks of the out-group as "they." "Those others" are not his "people." "They" are Unitarians and he is not. "They" attend a rival high school. "They" are Negroes, not Klansmen. "They" are Smiths, whereas he is a Jones.

A sympathetic bond of some sort exists among in-group members. And they feel there is a difference between them on the one hand and members of what they consider an out-group on the other.

Figure 11.3 illustrates both in- and out-group attitudes. The speaker in effect is saying, "*We* have something in common. *We* don't have to pay income taxes. *Those others*, supposedly more fortunate than we, do have to pay." The "we," "they" feeling may be low-keyed, devoid of any real antagonism, bespeaking only a consciousness of kind on one hand, a consciousness of difference on the other. Thus, Big Billy Broonzy, composer of authentic blues, remarks:

Of course we know that it ain't just Negroes that play and sing the blues because there's some hillbillies and cowboys that sing the blues, too. They sing it their way and we sing our way, we know and love our way and they know and love their way.[1]

But frequently the out-group attitude amounts to more than merely a feeling that "they" are different. "They" are regarded

Figure 11.3
In-Group, Out-Group
Reprinted with permission of the *Los Angeles Times*.

"*This is a lovely time of the year—
they're all paying taxes!*"

with downright hostility. Thus, we are informed that the boy in Figure 11.4, who lives in Milford, Delaware, is one of several youngsters who were encouraged by adults to carry placards like the one shown, to indicate how residents reacted to the then just promulgated Supreme Court decision ordering de-segregation of public schools. The boy in the photograph might have scarcely understood the "we" and the "they" of the demon-stration, but the adults apparently not only sensed what they considered a difference between "us" and "them," but felt very bitterly about it.

An individual is a member of many in-groups in a society of any considerable size and complexity. Take the late Presi-dent John F. Kennedy. We may reasonably assume that his in-groups included, among others, the Kennedy family, the Catholic Church, the Democratic party, the government of the United States, the coteries of Hollywoodians whose company he enjoyed, the world-wide collectivity of persons of Irish eth-nicity. He felt himself identified with Harvard graduates, elected public officials, professional and amateur politicians, intellectuals, and highly talented artists, writers, and scientists.

In-group and out-group attitudes are comparatively fluid. The individual loses his sense of identification with some groups, identifies himself with others with which he was not

Figure 11.4
"We" and "They"
George Skadding, *Life* Magazine © Time Inc.

identified in the past. A man may maintain a durable in-group attitude toward his family, abandon allegiance to his church, become a member of the American Federation of Musicians. With respect to out-groups, he may go through life with a strong bias against "those Catholics." He may develop a feeling of warmth for, and of belonging with, the Quakers and their Society of Friends, whereas he formerly considered them odd, not at all like "our people." This same person, who for years was proud to be a member of the Union League Club, may decide to withdraw from it, no longer feeling identified with "those chaps," who are said to sit for hours in armchairs, decrying any change or suggested change in the culture.

In-group, out-group relationships frequently overlap. In a society such as ours, it is inevitable that we will belong to so many groups that there will be considerable overlap in our in-group, out-group relationships. George and Harry are in-group-related in the Benevolent, Protective Order of Elks. However, George, who owns a retail establishment, considers Harry of the out-group in that frame of reference, since Harry is a union official, actively engaged in trying to organize George's employees.

SOCIAL DISTANCE

Still another way of analyzing groups is by using the concept *social distance. Social distance is the degree of closeness or acceptance felt by a member of one group for members of particular other groups.* This might be measured by some sort of social attitudes test, or it might be roughly inferred from observation. The distance involved is *social,* not geographical. The social distance between a young man in New York and his mother in Los Angeles may be much less than the distance between him and his employers in New York City.

Social distance is sometimes expressed in folk sayings: "The rich own the land and the poor own the water." "He always takes off his hat when he mentions his own name." "Where were you raised—in a barn?" "You don't know enough to pound sand in a rathole."

SOME CHARACTERISTICS
OF GROUPS

No classification of human groupings satisfies all sociologists. No systematization has been precise and comprehensive enough to account for every conceivable collection of human beings. Nevertheless, we attempt a systematization here, as a means of isolating certain features of groups so that we may analyze them. Groups may be roughly differentiated according to such characteristics as size, range of interests, duration of interests, degree of organization, degree and quality of intimacy among members.

SIZE

Considering our definition, we know that two Boy Scouts hiking together comprise a group. So do fifty athletes representing the Soviet Union at the Olympics. All the residents of a village coalesce into a group when they work together piling up sandbags to stem a river flood that threatens to inundate the inhabitants. When delegates to the United Nations, representing countries from all parts of the globe, debate an international crisis, they are a group, despite differences of opinion among them, since they share a sense of relatedness as a consequence of their interaction.

The size of a group is relative to its function. Nine players make a baseball team but not a football team. A million soldiers may launch an attack against an invading army, but we would not expect Mr. and Mrs. Smith to invite even a thousand guests for dinner next Sunday. In general, the size of a group is functionally related to its objectives.

RANGE OF INTERESTS

Groups vary according to the range of interests of the members, acting as a group. Some are concerned with a narrow range, as in the case of a glee club, whose members meet to sing together for their own pleasure or for the entertainment of others. A depiction of groups, each limited in range of interests, is found in Figure 11.5.

By contrast, a family group is concerned with a wide variety of interests, including the rearing of children, establishment of economic security, perpetuation of affectional ties, gaining acceptance in the community, maintenance of physical and mental health of the members, and a great many others.

DURATION OF INTERESTS

Groups vary according to the duration of interests that hold the members together. A dozen individuals, with no particular

LINTERLANDX©1966, LOS ANGELES TIMES

"*That's the group protesting.*
We're the counter protest.
The group protesting against
both groups is over there!"

Figure 11.5
Specialist Groups
Reprinted with permission of the *Los Angeles Times*.

interest in one another, are walking along a street when two cars collide and burst into flame. The twelve pedestrians rush to the flaming vehicle, extricate the autoists from their inferno, administer first aid, summon fire equipment and an ambulance. When all that needs to be done is done, the pedestrians go their separate ways. They were not a group prior to the accident; became one shortly thereafter; remained one for the duration of the emergency; ceased being a group when it was over. The total life of this group was perhaps no more than an hour.

A dozen youngsters form a social club, meet regularly, hold dances and other functions. The club may last a year, perhaps two or three. Eventually, it disbands, as members lose interest, go their separate ways. The social club remained a group longer than did the pedestrians helping the motorists involved in the accident.

Local businessmen establish a Better Business Bureau to further ethical, legal practices among all merchants in the city. This group will probably remain in existence for many years. Its membership will change from time to time, but the BBB will remain an entity for an indefinite period.

Groups, then, exist for a short time, to accomplish short-term objectives, or may be relatively permanent, serving long-range needs of the members.

And interests of a continuing group may change in nature. Some labor unions, once interested exclusively in negotiating wages and hours, have become interested in fringe benefits for members, the civil rights struggle, and the War on Poverty. The Society for the Prevention of Cruelty to Animals originally was concerned only with protecting nonhuman creatures. It was a number of years before members of the society developed an interest in protecting human beings, which they continued to do until the establishment of the first Society for the Prevention of Cruelty to Children. Both the Democratic and the Republican parties have dropped some interests and taken on others in the course of years.

DEGREE OF ORGANIZATION

Groups vary in degree of organization, from the relatively unorganized to the highly complex. A crowd of Dodger fans watching their team play a rival constitutes a group, although it is comparatively unorganized. There are no officers, no formal regulations prescribing behavior, no commitments to each other among members outside of cheering their team.

In contrast, a huge corporation is highly organized. Its lines of authority are clearly charted, from the board of directors at the top of the hierarchy to the administrative officers, to subordinate supervisory personnel, to bottom-echelon employees.

Organization of groups may be viewed as either *informal* or *formal*. Informal organization is characterized by a relatively loose structure. There is no constitution prescribing rules of operation. There are no officially designated officers. Interaction among members is comparatively unstructured. The community at large generally does not charge it with specific functions. Thus, a half-dozen men who spend one week of each year on a fishing trip comprise a group that is informally organized.

A formally organized group has a definite structure. It has a constitution or other recognized prescription for operation. Officers are selected by a specified procedure, and each official has his delineated authority and functions. Such a group may have one or more buildings as a base of operations; they may have office furnishings, plant equipment, raw materials to be processed, a sales force, a system for distribution of goods, and the like. The larger community usually has certain expectations regarding the functions and procedures of the members of the organization. A department store is formally organized. So is a military establishment.

Both formal and informal organization may be found within one group. Thus, the military establishment has its fixed, formalized lines of organization: enlisted men under the authority of noncommissioned officers, who are responsible to the commissioned officers. At the same time, little cliques develop, several enlisted men perhaps regularly going to town together, or playing cards in barracks. A small coterie of commissioned officers may associate with each other; their families may socialize at informal get-togethers.

DEGREE & QUALITY OF INTIMACY
AMONG GROUP MEMBERS

Groups vary according to the degree and quality of intimacy that exists among the members. Sociologists often classify them according to whether they are *primary* or *secondary* groups.

PRIMARY GROUPS · Saul Alinsky, a gifted community organizer, told *Harper's* editor Marion K. Sanders that his professional activities brought him into contact with the Capone gang in Chicago. Here, he said, he learned the "terrific importance" of personal relationships.

Nitti [a gangster] once explained to me why from time to time they were hiring out-of-town killers. It's one thing, he said, to go up to a guy you don't know. You've been told he'll be wearing a dark gray hat and coat, and so forth. You walk up to him in a crowd and put the gun up against his belly and you let him have a couple and fade off. That's doing a job. But if the killer knows the other guy, when he puts it up against his belly he suddenly looks up and sees his face, he knows his wife, he's taken his kids to the ball game, he knows that if he pulls that trigger there's going to be a widow, kids without a father, there'll be tears, there'll be a funeral—then it becomes murder. It isn't a job anymore, and he's going to hesitate, and maybe not even do it. That was the reason they used out-of-town killers.

This is what sociologists call a "primary relationship." They spend lecture after lecture and all kinds of assigned reading explaining it. Professor Nitti taught me the whole thing in five minutes.[2]

Mr. Alinsky would rather be called almost anything but a sociologist, but he has a sound sociological point of view, and in the above comment has caught the subtleties and the essence of the concept *primary group*. Charles Horton Cooley first used the term in a sociological frame of reference, conceiving of it as *two or more people in intimate and relatively durable personal relationship*.

Robert M. MacIver and Charles H. Page emphasize the significance of the primary group as the nucleus of all social organization, the "simplest, the first, the most universal of all forms of association," in which a relatively small number of persons meet face-to-face "for companionship, mutual aid, the discussion of some question that concerns them all, or the discovery and execution of some public policy."[3]

The family is a primary group, the relationships of its members being intimate, relatively durable, and highly personal. Normally it is a source of mutual love and affection (as well as of strong feelings of rivalry, conflict, and sometimes hatred). Here a child learns the language, is socialized, taught to behave in a manner that is approved in society. The members influence each other deeply. They feel very closely related.

A young man and woman in love, or a closely knit colony of artists, may be a primary group. And primary groups exist in the most complex social systems, such as a factory. Relations between workers and managers are impersonal for the most part, but a plant foreman may establish close and meaningful ties with a worker under his supervision. Two secretaries may become very close friends.

The primary group, according to MacIver and Page,

. . . is the group through which . . . we first give creative expression to our social impulses. It is the breeding ground of our mores, the nurse of our loyalties. It is the first and generally remains the chief focus of our social satisfactions. In these respects the face-to-face group is *primary* in our lives.[4]

It is not merely the fact of face-to-face relationships that make for a primary group, however. It has other distinctive qualities. The members come together freely, of their own volition, often spontaneously. They share information, experiences, feelings. They cooperate in many ways. One yields to the collectivity when this will further the central interest.

Every individual is a member of a variety of primary groups, at one time and at different times. You are a member of a family group. At some time you may also have a primary relationship with a few students, with members of a club or of a work group or of an athletic team. When you fall in love, you establish a primary relationship. When you marry and have children, you become part of still another primary group.

The establishment and maintenance of primary groups is facilitated by a number of factors, among them:

1. *Physical proximity.* If intimacy is to develop and continue, the individuals concerned must have fairly close contact, and physical separation in space is something of an impediment. "Absence makes the heart grow fonder" does not apply to the primary group.

But not every face-to-face collectivity is a primary group. A policeman informing a pedestrian he is about to be cited for jaywalking stands face-to-face with the unhappy violator, but the two scarcely are engaged in a primary-group relationship. The intimacy, the warmth, the feeling of relatedness are not present.

2. *Limited size.* A face-to-face group, practically by definition, is composed of relatively few members. In Mark Twain's novel, Tom Sawyer, Huck Finn, and Jim made a very intimate group with like interests, one easy to convene and activate. Several hundred individuals could not as readily become closely allied in feeling and action. Limited size of the group, like physical proximity, facilitates primary-group formation.

3. *Shared values and norms.* Although complete agreement among members is not essential to the existence of a primary group, a fair degree of consistency among them with respect to significant values and behavior norms encourages feelings of closeness. One can scarcely imagine a primary group made up of ten boys who adhere strictly to conventional behavior norms because they accept them, and ten others who reject those norms and engage in thefts, assaults, and other socially disapproved behavior.

4. *Interaction.* We have learned that two people, in close physical proximity, may represent an aggregation rather than a group, as when they sit side by side in a streetcar, total

strangers, disinterested in each other, with no interaction between them. The two are also a category—of streetcar passengers. They may share certain values and adhere to common norms, but they will not take on the aspect of a group unless there is interaction between them. And even then they will not constitute a primary group unless the interaction is more than casual and of some duration. For the two riders to constitute a primary group, they must have engaged in enough interaction of a sort that results in feelings of close, personal relationship.

5. *Equality among members*. A club or play group has its leaders, either in connection with a given project or most projects, but this does not imply that inequality exists among members *as members*. In an authoritarian group, consisting of guards and the prisoners they supervise, leadership, in the person of the guards, is established by fiat of those in power. Inequality does exist, and partly as a consequence of this the collectivity is not likely to constitute a primary group.

On the other hand, in a social club, leaders are usually selected by the members, formally or informally. Leadership is accepted voluntarily. The group is democratically oriented; the members choose their leaders; all members have an equal voice in discussion; all are listened to with the respect and consideration that, in the opinion of the group, their comments deserve. Such a collection of individuals, given other necessary elements, may maintain primary-group relations.

But democratic procedures and complete equality among members is not an absolute essential to the existence of a primary group. The children do not decide by vote whether they will accept their parents as family heads. Particularly in the years before adolesence, they accept instruction and rules of behavior on the authority of their father and mother. Yet the family remains a primary group. Of course, too absolute a parental dictatorship has broken up many families. In that case, the primary group no longer exists. With the sense of unity and intimacy impaired or destroyed, the children may rebel or leave home.

6. *Stable membership*. Primary-group relationships are enhanced when membership remains stable. The easy flow of members into and out of the group has a tendency to encourage instability. Men who have served in the armed forces have testified to the effect of fluid membership upon the solidarity

of the group. A small contingent, in training at a camp, living in close quarters, working and spending leisure time together, normally develops a group feeling. Individuals exercise the GI's traditional privilege of griping about the food, the top sergeant, and the commissioned officers. They lay plans for outwitting the "enemy," in this case those in authority over them.

Perhaps the contingent is then shipped to a battle zone. The feeling of closeness is further developed as the servicemen fight a common enemy, this time not their own officers. Inevitably, several are killed. Others are wounded and transferred to hospitals. Replacements arrive. They have not shared the weeks of training and live combat with the "oldtimers." They are "outsiders." The "old bunch" has not admitted them to first-class citizenship in the group. Not until they have shared experiences with the veterans, worked to achieve common objectives, fought for their own lives and the lives of their fellows, will they become members in anything more than a nominal sense.

On the basis of personal observations, Edward A. Shils writes that, on the whole, replacements in a military unit:

. . . seemed to feel inferior *vis-à-vis* the established primary group into which they are not yet accepted and which had a dual source of prestige in their eyes—both as combat veterans and as an established primary group sharing intimacies and "knowing the ropes."[5]

7. *Duration of the group relationship.* Stable membership per se does not guarantee the development of primary-group feeling. The duration of the group will play an important part.

A dozen people are on a conducted tour of an art museum. If they were not a primary group at the outset, they will not be one at the termination of the tour. The group has had too short a life to permit the development of intimacy. It will disband. Intimacy is developed through the frequency and intensity of associations. Within limits, these are relative to the length of time a group of individuals remain together.

SECONDARY GROUPS · Although our strongest emotional ties are with primary groups, it goes without saying that we are also associated with a great number of secondary groups in the course of a lifetime. The term *secondary groups* was not coined by Cooley, but it represents a projection from his thinking on the subject of groups.

A secondary group is one in which the relationship among the members is relatively impersonal. You have a primary-group relationship with your immediate family and a secondary group relationship with the newsboy who delivers your daily paper.

MacIver and Page delineate the essence of secondary-group relationships by contrasting them with those in primary groups:

> In primary group life our relations with the others are always, to some extent, *personal.* Here we *feel* sympathy or antipathy, we often love or hate. In any event we face our fellows as total human beings and with them we *directly* co-operate and directly conflict. These sympathetic or "sentimental" relationships may be distinguished from those that are characteristic of the larger and more formally organized groups. The relations within which people confront one another in such specialized group roles as buyers and sellers, voters and candidates, officials and citizens, teachers and students, practitioners and clients, are *secondary*, involving categoric or "rational" attitudes.[6]

The authors go on to state that the fundamental basis for the distinction between primary and secondary relationships is the quality of the attitudes involved in the social relationship. Mere physical proximity does not make a group a primary group. "Thus even the relation of prostitute to client is usually of the secondary type, for whatever the degree of physical intimacy the attitudes of both parties in the relationship tend to be categoric, devoid of the sentiment characteristic of primary bonds."[7]

In any relationships, the character of the group may change, from primary to secondary, or the reverse. It is just possible that you and the boy who delivers your newspapers may meet under circumstances where a close friendship results. A secondary group thereby becomes a primary group.

Suppose you and a schoolmate are a primary group. You both graduate, go to live in different cities. You correspond for a while, see each other occasionally, but gradually your friendship cools, even though there is no hostility between you. You simply mean less to each other than formerly. A primary group has become a secondary group. What we are saying is that a secondary group may become a primary group, and a primary group may become a secondary group, as the quality of the relationship among members undergoes change.

An important distinction between the two types of groups exists in their respective functions. *The maintenance of primary relationships is in itself one of the major objectives of the members of primary groups, whereas secondary-group relationships more often serve as the means of achieving other ends.* A man says, "I can't stand this job, but it's the best I can get, and I'm going to hold onto it, so I can support the people I love—my wife and children." In effect he is asserting that what he does to earn a living is secondary to his determination to maintain his *primary*-group relations with his family.

A salesman says, "In this business you have to get along with a lot of people you don't like." He is suggesting that he builds *secondary* relationships, not as an end in itself, but as a means of achieving a different objective—a satisfactory income.

PRIMARY AND SECONDARY GROUPS AS EXTREMES ON A CONTINUUM · Although for purposes of analysis we have discussed primary and secondary groups separately, they are not mutually exclusive types of groups. A more exact analytical description would be that primary and secondary groups represent opposite extremes on the same continuum.

"Ham" radio operators are in frequent communication over the air, discussing electronics problems or merely chatting. They follow informal rules of broadcasting, for the benefit of all operators. They relay messages from station to station in order to help out in emergencies. But although "hams" cooperate in many ways, they meet face-to-face only infrequently, and their conversations over the air waves are casual for the most part. Their acquaintance with one another is transitory, and many lose interest in their hobby after a few years. They no longer communicate with other shortwave operators. Should one of them go off the air for any reason, others who "worked" him might not even notice it and, if they did, would not be likely to grieve.

Compare "hams" with members of Alcoholics Anonymous, an organization for alcoholics who want to stop drinking and who believe the best way to accomplish this is to associate with like-minded alcoholics, who help one another maintain sobriety. Members of Alcoholics Anonymous are fiercely loyal to each other. They feel responsible for one another, stand ready at any time of day or night to rush out to help one of their kind who fears the compulsion to drink is about to overcome him again. Members meet face-to-face at regular sessions of Alcoholics Anonymous. They visit each other's homes, discuss their common problem. Many a courtship begins at an AA meeting, alcoholic wedding alcoholic quite frequently. If a member of a particular AA group fails to show up at meetings, his absence is noted, and the others worry about him, hope he has not succumbed to the bottle. They consider other persons "on the program" necessary to their own continued sobriety and well-being.

"Ham" operators, considered collectively, may be thought of as a secondary group, members of local chapters of Alcoholics Anonymous as a primary group. In between on the continuum are groupings not so clearly definable. A bowling club may be less a secondary group than the collectivity of "hams" and not quite a primary group, like Alcoholics Anonymous. A Veterans of Foreign Wars post may be close to being a primary group, yet not quite one. A number of newspaper reporters who work the same stories but for different papers may be a secondary group, yet have some of the characteristics of primary groups.

GROUPS VIEWED ACCORDING TO INDIVIDUAL DEFINITION · *The same interactive social unit may be a primary group for one member, a secondary group for another.* To Hazel, her sorority is a primary group, in which she finds satisfaction of many needs. She has a deep personal involvement in it. For her it is a home away from home, and she thinks of every sorority member as a sister. She accepts, happily or otherwise, the adverse comments of her "sisters" concerning her manner of dressing or her behavior on a double date. After all, they are deeply interested in promoting her welfare, as she sees it. She accepts the fact that, according to protocol, she is to attend the dances sponsored by one fraternity, not those conducted by another. She is loyal to her sorority sisters and expects reciprocal loyalty from them. She assures herself that so long as she lives she will maintain intimate relationships with these wonderful girls.

Mae, a member of the same sorority, has a secondary group relationship with its members. Associating with her "sisters" is pleasant but comparatively unimportant to her. She joined because, at the time, she understood that membership brought prestige, and she wanted prestige. She thought it would be "nice" to "belong," and she still thinks so, but she now has many interests outside the sorority. Moreover, she has come to consider some of its rituals silly and its social viewpoint snobbish. As she increasingly engages in activities having nothing to do with sorority life, her relations with her "sisters" become casual, and she even feels indifferent toward them. She may not take criticism from sorority members seriously, since she does not always accept their judgments. She considers her behavior is her own business and not theirs. She does not agree that she is her "sister's" keeper, and she assuredly does not want a member of the sorority to feel responsible for her own actions. She looks upon these girls in about the way she might look upon any others with whom she might happen to share quarters. She has no intention of continuing social relations with sorority sisters after she has graduated.

Thus, in terms of personal definition, the particular sorority is a primary group for Hazel, a secondary group for Mae.

IS THE PRIMARY GROUP DECLINING IN INFLUENCE?

Some sociologists hold that the people of the United States have moved from a society characterized largely by primary-group relationships toward one predominantly made up of secondary-group relationships. They believe this change has been one of many resulting from the shift from a rural to an urban way of life. In the small villages and farming communities of a century ago, everyone knew everyone else, quite intimately. Now, the argument goes, the general store and its cracker barrel are gone. A city dweller cannot become well acquainted with and personally attached to all the people with whom he interacts. How well do you know the man who delivers your milk? If you live in an apartment house, how familiar are you with your neighbors? You interact with them, to be sure, but generally you do not depend upon them to any great extent, nor do you hold yourself very responsible for their behavior.

Perhaps you know the supermarket check-out clerk by name, but chances are you do not even recognize the faces of the salespeople who wait on you in department stores. There seems to be an increasing acceptance of the social attitude that "I am not my brother's keeper, nor is he mine, and furthermore, he'd better keep his nose out of my business."

Other sociologists do not agree that we have moved away from primary-group relationships to any great extent. They point to studies that seem to bear evidence that when people are isolated from or otherwise deprived of contact with one primary group, they tend to find another. Perhaps the general store has merely been superseded by the fraternal lodge. The search for lost primary groups may partially explain why some juveniles join street gangs, some housewives spend their afternoons in bridge clubs, some men stay up until dawn about the gaming tables. The many men and women who drift into Lonely Hearts clubs would seem to be trying to find primary-group relationships, too.

In the long run, sociologists may find that their attempts to establish distinctions between primary and secondary groups lead into theoretical blind alleys. If we use only Cooley's criterion of the intimacy of the relationships among the members as a basis for distinguishing the two types of groups, we can demonstrate differences in degree between them. Difficulties arise, however, when we attempt to apply other criteria at the same time, as indeed we have done in this chapter. Some sociologists claim that primary groups tend to be small, secondary groups larger. Some contend primary groups are durable, secondary groups temporary. Some say primary groups are characterized by informal relationships, while secondary groups are more formal in nature. And yet it is easy to find comparatively small, durable, and informal secondary groups. Logically, therefore, we must conclude that no one of these criteria—size, durability, and the like—is invariably found in conjunction with the others, nor are the criteria that supposedly distinguish primary from secondary groups exclusive with the respective groups.

· NOTES

1. William Broonzy, as told to Yannick Bruynoghe, *Big Bill Blues, William Broonzy's Story* (London: Cassell, 1955), p. 3.
2. Quoted by permission of the author from "The Professional Radical," Part I, by Saul Alinsky, *Harper's Magazine* (June 1965), pp. 37–47.

3. Robert M. MacIver and Charles H. Page, *Society: An Introductory Analysis* (New York: Rinehart, 1949), pp. 218–219.
4. *Ibid.,* p. 219.
5. Edward A. Shils, "Primary Groups in the American Army," in Robert K. Merton and Paul F. Lazarsfeld (eds.), *Continuities in Social Research* (New York: Free Press, 1950), pp. 16–39.
6. MacIver and Page, *op. cit.,* pp. 220–221.
7. *Ibid.,* p. 221.

· SUGGESTIONS FOR FURTHER READING

BURMA, JOHN H. "Student Attitudes towards and Participation in Voluntary Organizations." *Sociology and Social Research,* XXXII (November 1947), 625–629.
The question posed in this article is whether scholastically better students or poorer students are more likely to be members and officers of voluntary organizations on campus.

COOLEY, CHARLES H. *Social Organization.* New York: Scribner, 1909, Part I.
Cooley introduces the concept of primary groups.

DOTSON, FLOYD. "Patterns of Voluntary Association Among Urban Working Class Families." *American Sociological Review,* XVI (October 1951), 687–693.
This is a study of the participation of urban, working-class families in voluntary groups.

FARIS, ELLSWORTH. "The Primary Group: Essence and Accident." *American Journal of Sociology,* XXVIII (July 1932), 41–50.
A critique of the then current criteria for identifying primary groups. Faris, a pioneer American sociologist, qualifies Cooley's primary-group concept. Faris says that the essence of such a group is not face-to-face association or certain other criteria, but the functional and emotional character of the relationship involved.

GROSS, EDWARD. "Some Functional Consequences of Primary Groups in Formal Work Organizations." *American Journal of Sociology,* XVIII (August 1953), 368–373.
A description of the ways in which primary groups may support the objectives of secondary groups in formal work organizations.

MARSHALL, S. L. A. *Men Under Fire.* New York: Morrow, 1947.
The meaning and importance of the group as a social unit is illustrated in this study of American combat soldiers in World War II. The principal variable determining how well a man would fight was the degree to which he was integrated into his combat unit. Men who would not shoot to save themselves would, when well integrated into the unit, shoot to save their comrades.

MAYER, MILTON. *They Thought They Were Free, The Germans 1933–45.* Chicago: University of Chicago Press, 1955.
In their own words, ten German Nazis who lived through World War II express a clear-cut in-group, out-group feeling. Jews, for instance, are "out." Nazis are "in." The ten men ac-

cepted Nazism, says Mayer, *"with a whoop and a holler. . . .*
They wanted it; they got it; and they liked it."

SHILS, EDWARD A., and MORRIS JANOWITZ. "Cohesion and Disintegration in the Wehrmacht in World War II." *Public Opinion
Quarterly*, XII (Summer 1948), 280–315.
*Why did the German Army continue fighting so stubbornly when
they knew all was lost? According to this study, the German
soldier's primary group was the most important source of this
determination to continue fighting.*

WRIGHT, CHARLES R., and HERBERT H. HYMAN. "Voluntary Association Memberships of American Adults: Evidence from National
Sample Surveys." *American Sociological Review*, XXIII (June
1958), 284–294.
*Are we a nation of "joiners"? This study shows that participation
in voluntary organizations varies considerably, depending upon
ethnicity, socioeconomic status, occupation, and residence.*

12 SMALL GROUPS & LARGE ORGANIZATIONS

In this chapter we examine the social organization of small groups and large organizations, and the relationships among the members.

SMALL GROUPS

When Emil was fourteen he joined the Spartans, a social club consisting of a dozen members who engaged in outdoor sports on weekends. After each session, Emil returned home to his parents, brothers, and sisters. He finished high school and college, was drafted into the Army, and sent overseas during the war in Vietnam. Here he became one of almost half a million fighting men in that theater of operations. At the same time, he formed a close personal relationship with three soldiers in his unit, who thought of themselves as "buddies," a clique of men who fought shoulder to shoulder, ate and drank together, and felt a deep regard for one another. After completing his tour of duty and being honorably discharged, Emil became a member of a national peace movement, the object of which was to organize opposition to this nation's further involvement in Vietnam. He was placed on a committee that was to report on ways and means of raising funds for a series of television spot announcements urging viewers to join the cause.

· · ·

In his lifetime, Emil would be a member of a great many large and small social groupings. Some of those mentioned above are what sociologists call *small groups*. Bernard Berelson and Gary A. Steiner define a small group as:

. . . an aggregate of people, from two up to an unspecified but not too large number, who associate together in face-to-face relations over an extended period of time, who differentiate themselves in some regard from others around them, who are mutually aware of their membership in the group, and whose personal relations are taken as an end in itself.[1]

The same sociologists identify several types of small groups:

1 · The autonomous group of close friends who come together out of free choice for voluntary association. The Spartans, the club that Emil joined, exemplifies this type.
2 · The institutionalized small group, such as the family, of which Emil was a member.
3 · The small group within a larger organization, as represented by Emil's clique of "buddies" in the Army.
4 · The problem-solving group, as in the case of the committee he was on, which had a task to perform.

Taken as a whole, Berelson and Steiner add, these categories come down to two broad types, those with specific tasks to perform and those, like the family, with more diffuse purposes.[2] The committee of the peace organization to which Emil belonged was of the first variety, with the specific task of raising funds. The Spartans social club more likely is classifiable as a group with more diffuse purposes—recreation, friendship, interstimulation.

Although small groups differ in structure and functions, they all contain certain elements:

1 · The membership is fairly small.
2 · Personal relations are close and face-to-face.
3 · The members have common values and share common contacts.
4 · The group tends to be durable, remaining a group for days, months, or years. However, a small group might last for only a number of hours of a single day. It would belong in the small-group category if it contained the other elements common to small groups.

5 · Members have a feeling of identification with the group, some loyalty for it and its objectives.

6 · Group membership is determined by reciprocal acceptance of individuals.

7 · Members see the group as a distinct entity and differentiate it from other groups.

8 · The group is perceived by the members as having certain goals.

Small groups have been studied extensively by psychologists and sociologists. Among their many findings, the following observations and propositions are of special interest:

1. A stable membership is important to the morale of the small group. The less change in membership, the higher the morale is likely to be. Harold D. Lasswell and Abraham Kaplan have remarked that a tightly knit group is difficult to enter; its members identify closely with one another, less so with nonmembers. The more difficult it is to penetrate the group, the more value attaches to membership, and the more intense the adherence to group standards and values.[3]

Take a very "exclusive" club of men who have been carefully screened before being admitted to membership. All come from "the best families," have graduated from elite schools, possess wealth, conduct themselves accordingly. So long as the original membership remains stable, with very few additions because eligibility requirements are stiff, the group is united, high in morale. Its members may feel like those in Figure 12.1. But suppose, as old-timers pass away, the bars are lowered, and new members are admitted under less stringent eligibility requirements. Younger than their predecessors, they bring new ideas and values with them. The old-timers may huff and puff that the club has come to a sorry pass, that "anybody" can get in now, even whippersnappers with newfangled, "radical" notions. "In *our* day," they reflect, "fellows like that simply wouldn't have been admitted." Morale deteriorates, for it is likely that now there is not one tightly knit group but two relatively hostile groups.

2. The small group influences the behavior of its members, not only with regard to what is expected inside the group, but also with respect to norms of behavior outside it. An example was an informally organized group of a dozen men, known to the author, who met weekly in a country club in a small and

Figure 12.1
Small Group : High Morale
Drawing by Lorenz; © 1960 The
New Yorker Magazine, Inc.

"I may be a philosopher, George, but I say,
if we didn't belong on top, we wouldn't be on top."

exclusive community. As a group, they confined their activities
to card playing and the socializing that goes with it. At their
get-togethers, each member followed the ritualistic behavior
expected—he took his turn buying drinks; he held to the ante
for bets; he did not drop out of the game, whether winning or
losing, until the stipulated time agreed upon in advance by all
the members. These were the norms for the group, as a club
of card players.

Although the members of the group did not associate with
each other very closely outside the country club, they influenced each other nevertheless. They played golf—it was a
"gentleman's sport" and something to talk about during card
games. They invited only Christians to their homes—a folkway
of the group. They voted the same ticket politically—in this
town the majority of the residents were upper middle class,
and they voted solidly Republican, as a patriotic duty. One
member told the author, "Between me and you, Jim [a Democratic candidate] would make the better mayor, but I won't
vote for him. The others [his fellow card players] would know,
and what's the use of getting in that kind of bind? Anyhow,
what's the difference? One politician or another?"

3. Authoritarian leadership, in some small groups within
the framework of our "democratic" culture, does not appear
to be as effective as democratic leadership in maintaining

group morale and accomplishing the aims of the collectivity. When people associate by free choice, on the basis of equality, they tend to share their values and to come to like one another. Authoritarian methods, on the other hand, when carried to extremes for a continuous period, may result in dissension, dislike among the members, and eventual dissolution of the group. Under democratic leadership, as contrasted with authoritarian, the members of a small group tend to be more effective in expressing and maintaining views independent of the leader's. Their productivity on a given task is likely to be greater.

But this is qualified by the fact that persons who themselves are authoritarian personalities have been found to accept strong, directive leadership. They have a tendency to rate the authoritarian leader as "better" than his more democratic counterpart. By contrast, those persons who prefer to associate on the basis of equality among all the group members are likely to accept authoritarian leadership only if circumstances make this necessary.

The authoritarian personality has been the subject of a number of studies, particularly since world attention became focused on the Hitler regime in Nazi Germany. Although the evidence is not as complete and solid as it might be, there is indication from case studies that children whose parents were severe disciplinarians, given to harsh punishments and to placing exaggerated emphasis on morality and unquestioning obedience, tend to develop authoritarian personalities. Other studies have found that certain traits supposedly indicative of authoritarianism tend to occur in combination. These traits include a great concern with authority; deference to superiors; little personal regard for others; general hostility, destructiveness, and cynicism; a tendency to manipulate and exploit others and to expect others to manipulate and exploit them. These traits also include conventionality and conformity, a high degree of self-righteousness and moral indignation, and a tendency to attribute evil intentions and actions to members of certain groups, especially minorities, where the authoritarian is not himself a minority-group member. According to the studies, authoritarian personalities also tend to show, in combination with the traits already mentioned, inflexible thinking of the "black-and-white" variety, superstition, bigotry, intolerance, and an exaggerated concern with sex.

Studies also show that many people, including Americans, want, expect, and even demand tight, rigid authoritarian leadership in all of their social relationships. Whether authoritarian or democratic leadership is more effective seems to depend, in many cases, on the personality attributes of the followers, at least in part.

FORMAL ORGANIZATIONS

Small groups are not highly organized. We now turn our attention to the highly organized type of group. We call it a *formal organization*.

General Motors Corporation is an example of a formal organization. It is said to be the biggest industrial organization in the world. Its estimated worth is between 12 and 13 billion dollars. Its plants and offices circle the globe, directly and indirectly contribute to the employment income of some 600,000 people, roughly the population of Pittsburgh, Pennsylvania. Additionally, thousands of automobile salesmen, directly employed by franchised dealers, gain a livelihood by selling General Motors products.

The firm uses unskilled and skilled laborers, foremen, subexecutives, executives, administrators, and policy makers, organized into a clearly established chain of command. It maintains relations with some 750,000 stockholders, 27,000 suppliers, 20,000 wholesalers, and 200,000 retailers.[4] In 1964, it produced 3,956,637 passenger cars in its United States plants.[5]

WHAT IS FORMAL ORGANIZATION?

General Motors could not operate without formal organization. A large, complex, and heterogeneous society such as ours has need for a great many formal organizations. There were, for instance, approximately 4.6 million business concerns in the United States at the beginning of 1960,[6] and business firms by no means comprise the sum total of all formally organized groups.

Formal organization develops when a number of individuals construct a social unit to further their common objective or objectives. A property owners' league would be an example. It would probably be organized by a group of individuals who own real estate in the community. They would have certain common objectives: maintenance of low property tax rates, preventing public expenditures likely to bring about an increase in the tax rate, and so forth. Their activities would be relative to these objectives. To carry on these activities, they would need some sort of policy guideline, such as a constitution and bylaws. They would choose officers, perhaps engage a paid executive director.

All formal organizations have certain attributes:

1. *Formal structure.* By definition, such organizations have a formal structure, deliberately arrived at and officially enunciated. As we have said, the hypothetical property owners' league would have a constitution and a body of officers. Relations among members, between members and officers, and between officers and the paid executive director would be established formally. The organization's objectives and program for effectuating them would be expressed in formal terms, at least to a degree.

2. *Relative permanence.* When people go to the trouble to set up a formal organization, they generally expect to maintain it for some time, perhaps indefinitely. They establish it in order to achieve some goal. This takes time.

Suppose the property owners' league set up a subsidiary, a Citizens Committee Against Proposition X, prior to an election. This would require organization and capitalization. The committee would be in existence for some weeks or months, but its founders would not plan to maintain it after it had served its purpose, the defeat of Proposition X on election day.

On the other hand, the property owners' league itself would continue to operate after the election, as long as it had an interested membership and perceived goals. This might be for several years or even for decades.

3. *A hierarchy of authority.* Formal organizations require leadership, an authority vested in certain individuals to make decisions and take action under given conditions. This leadership is arranged in a chain of command, with a line of authority running from one to another. Thus, our imaginary property owners' league might have a board of directors, which selects officers and appoints an executive committee. The board, on recommendation of the executive committee, would establish policy. A paid executive director would administer the policy, under the board and officers. He might have an

assistant responsible directly to him. A clerical staff would be responsible to the assistant executive director.

4. *A program.* A formal organization is made up of members who want to carry forward a certain program, whether it is a reduction in property taxes, raising funds for charity, or mobilizing a scientific attack on heart disease.

5. *Some degree of complexity.* Formal organization implies systematization, which means there will be a more complex structure than is involved in the direct relation of one person to one other person, each on the same level of authority and having the same functions. The structure need not be extremely complex. The property owners' group would require a relatively uncomplicated system of relationships in order to carry on its work. By contrast, General Motors requires a very complex set of relationships among those concerned with the corporation's objectives.

FORMAL ORGANIZATIONS AS ASSOCIATIONS

As our definition would imply, formal organizations are *associations,* which is to say, groups of individuals working together for a common purpose or to pursue similar ends. Sociologists refer to *voluntary associations,* meaning *formally organized social units comprised of members who belong by choice.*

Strictly interpreted, when a man and woman marry, they form a voluntary association, since of their own volition they are entering into a relationship, with specific outcomes in mind. They mean to cohabit, to share a social life, perhaps to procreate. However, for some members, the family is not a voluntary association. A child born to the man and woman who got married did not deliberately undertake to become part of that association. It came into the world a member of a family *group,* but it took no conscious part in the construction of that social unit. But as the child continues in the family group, by imperceptible degrees that group ". . . is transformed for him also, as he grows up, into an association of, often intense, but limited interest. Eventually he will normally leave it to establish a new family."[7] When he weds, he forms an association.

The state, too, is an association, established to serve, but also to exert control over, individuals under its jurisdiction.

Whether we can call it a *voluntary* association is open to question, for every resident automatically comes under its control simply by living within its boundaries.

The family, then, is a voluntary association, at least for the contracting parties to a marriage. The state is an association, although it is not voluntary in the sense in which this term is used here. But most associations are not subject to the qualifications just expressed. Man, a social animal, seeks likeminded men and forms a great variety of associations, some to make profits, some to promote health, religion, hobbies, or other objectives. In 1955, some 55 percent of people in this country belonged to one or more voluntary organizations, according to a survey by the National Opinion Research Center. In 1959, there were some 8,716 national associations in the country.[8] In 1960, we had 18,117,000 members of national and international unions with headquarters in the United States, representing 23.4 percent of the total labor force.[9]

The World Almanac for 1966 requires 15 1/2 pages of fine print to list the better known associations in the nation. Included are the American Legion, the Associated Press, Actors Equity Association, the American Bankers Association, and the National Association of Manufacturers. Doctors had their associations, lawyers, judges, and teachers, theirs. Among more highly specialized organizations were those for professional magicians, bottlers of carbonated waters, and chiefs of police. Also listed was a National Association of Babysitter Registries, that is, an association of associations.

Associations are by no means restricted to occupational groupings. Witness an American Contract Bridge Association, an Auto License Plate Collectors Association, and the Button Society of America, not to mention the Society for the Preservation and Encouragement of Barber Shop Quartet Singing in America.

Associations are formed to further the aims of *their* members. Inevitably, groups with divergent, even hostile interests, enter the field. Labor and management organizations have different objectives, in part. Associations for furthering sales at retail meet with some opposition from organizations promoting consumer interests. The National Association for the Advancement of Colored People opposes the aims of the White Citizens Council. The Black Muslims attack the orientation of the National Urban League. "Hate groups" campaign to "protect" what they call "100 percent Americanism" against what they call "Communism." They champion the "cause" of white Protestants against Negroes, of Catholics and Protestants against Jews, of "patriotic Americans" against mental health programs.

The question is not whether you will become affiliated with an association in the course of your life—it is inconceivable, in our society, that you can avoid it. But some people join more readily than others. Participation in voluntary associations seems to be greater among persons who:

1 · Live in urban rather than rural territory.
2 · Are in the prime of life.
3 · Are married and have children.
4 · Are "moving up in life," socially and economically.
5 · Have already achieved high socioeconomic status.
6 · Have residential stability.
7 · Are at least fairly well educated.[10]

LARGE-SCALE ORGANIZATIONS

An association is an organization, and an organization is an association, but there are great differences in the number of people involved in them, and we now direct our attention to the *large-scale organization*, a notable phenomenon in our society. Robert M. MacIver and Charles H. Page comment regarding the emergence of large-scale organizations:

Where life is relatively simple, as in a primitive community or in a frontier settlement, or where . . . the area of effective communication is small, the face-to-face group suffices for most purposes. But where society expands, another kind of association becomes necessary, the large-scale organization with its impersonal . . . relationships and its specialization of functions.[11]

Thus we have great corporations, international cartels, labor unions, national political parties. These and others reflect the fact that:

Interests become differentiated. The service of experts is required. Techniques are elaborated, and the average member has neither the time nor the energy nor the skill to attend to them. The new range of interest demands a complex organization. It is no longer localized and no longer controllable by the local group. The members are too numerous and too scattered to conduct their business through the face-to-face relationships. Specially selected persons must act on behalf of the whole . . . and the executive or controlling groups become distinct from the mass of the members.[12]

The immensity of some organizations has already been indicated in the General Motors illustration. We might expand upon this. The AT&T has assets of over 20 billion dollars. It has 2 million stockholders.[13] A study by the Federal Trade Commission, 1947–1949, showed 113 corporations with assets in excess of 100 million dollars. These 113 corporations held 46 percent of the total assets of all the manufacturing firms in the country. Corporation income tax returns in a fairly recent compilation showed 525,000 active nonfinancial corporations reporting a total of 413 billion dollars of assets.[14] Some corporations take in more revenue per year than the largest state:

If you rank the big corporations and governments according to revenue, you have eight corporations after the Federal government before you get to the first state, California; then another five before arriving at New York State and New York City; and ten more before Pennsylvania. Out of fifty-five organizations with a billion or more annual revenue (1958), only nine are official government units.[15]

LARGE-SCALE ORGANIZATIONS & BUREAUCRACY

Large-scale organizations become bureaucracies. *Bureaucracy is an hierarchical arrangement within an organization based upon a line of authority and a division of work predicated upon this arrangement.*

Figure 12.2 might be thought of as a representation of a proposed bureaucracy. The man talking—we assume he is a diplomat, perhaps at the United Nations—plans to set up a twelve-nation conference, the function of which will be to establish a nine-power treaty organization, to be governed by a five-nation steering committee. This committee "will be dominated by you and me." Here we have the division of work and the hierarchical line of authority of our definition of bureaucracy.

Most of us work for bureaucratic organizations—only 15 percent of residents of the United States are self-employed.

Figure 12.2
Bureaucracy in the
Making

Drawing by Peter Arno; Copr.
© 1955 The New Yorker
Magazine, Inc.

*"Basically, what I have in mind is a twelve-nation
conference for the purpose of setting up
a nine-power treaty organization governed
by a five-nation steering committee,
which in turn will be dominated by you and me."*

All of us consume the products of bureaucracies and are subject to rules they impose on us. In 1965, there were 2,527,941 paid civilian employees of the federal government, a very large-scale bureaucracy.[16] In 1964, 9,502,000 persons were working for some branch of government—municipal, county, state, or federal. Some 17,303,000 were engaged in manufacturing, 3,976,000 in transportation and public utilities operations, 635,000 in mining.[17] These individuals, and others unlisted, worked for bureaucratic organizations.

Although the word "bureaucracy" has taken on an unpleasant connotation in common parlance, the fact is that without it we could not operate government, manufacture goods, provide services, build a sound economy. The U. S. Department of Health, Education, and Welfare is a bureaucracy, and could not serve the public welfare if it were not. The question is not whether we should countenance bureaucracy—we have no alternative. More pertinent is the question as to how we can make bureaucracy work for us most efficiently.

CHARACTERISTICS OF BUREAUCRACY · First we must understand the characteristics of bureaucracies. The German sociologist, Max Weber, outlined the "ideal type," which, in context, was not synonymous with "the best conceivable type." Weber, who was attempting to delineate the "pure" form of bureaucracy, that is, the most characteristic elements of all bureaucracies, found the following:[18]

1. *Division of labor.* The regular activities of the organization are allocated to given individuals. A clear-cut division of labor is thus established. Such a system makes it possible to hire specialists for respective posts, holding them responsible for the effective performance of their assigned tasks. In a manufacturing concern, for instance, an administrator is selected on the assumption he can and will administer effectively. That is all he is to do. A plant foreman is a specialist in his line and will be held responsible for performing his duties in a competent manner. An oiler is an oiler, a machinist a machinist—both are specialists, who will be expected to serve the concern in that capacity.

2. *Hierarchy of authority.* Typically, the organization has a chain of command, each official responsible to an official above him until the top of the hierarchy is reached. Each official in authority is responsible for the work of his subordinates. It is the duty of those subordinates to comply with instructions from a supervisor. Each official has only that authority specifically vested in him. Its scope and limits are clearly outlined.

In the U. S. Army, the noncommissioned officer is responsible to his superiors, not only for his own acts but also for those of the enlisted men under him. The commissioned officers have a hierarchy of their own within the overall hierarchy. The general tells the colonel he wants the troops in top shape for a parade on Memorial Day. The colonel so instructs the lieutenant colonel, who passes the word down to the major, who orders the company captains to have their lieutenants see to it that the sergeants make certain the enlisted men are properly drilled for the occasion, spotlessly uniformed, properly armed, and ready in good time to begin the march down Main Street.

3. *Rules governing behavior of potential incumbents.* The operations of the bureaucratic organization are governed by a set of abstract rules presumably consistent with the major

objectives of the unit. They define the functions and appropriate procedures of persons holding given posts. They also specify the relationships that shall exist among the functionaries. Note, these rules do not specify that Mr. John Jones shall do thus and so, but rather that *whoever* holds position X shall do thus and so. In this sense, the rules are abstract, applying to any person who now or in the future holds the particular position.

The existence of these rules serves two ends: They are a basis for predicting the behavior of individuals in the organization—if a regulation provides that the incumbent in the Executive A position shall report all tardy employees, it may be expected he will do so. Rules also facilitate continuity of operation. Since they apply to the post and not the particular incumbent, it makes little or no difference who holds a position or for how long. Regardless of changes in personnel, whoever is the incumbent of the Executive A position at a given time immediately picks up from his predecessor and performs the duties called for.

4. *Impersonality*. The bureaucrat is expected to perform his functions in an impersonal manner. He is required to treat customers, clients or subordinates, as the case may be, impersonally. Not that he must be aloof. He must be impersonal in that he is *impartial* in dealing with persons connected directly or indirectly with the organization he represents. He is not to allow personal considerations to sway his decisions. Personally, he may like Jones better than Smith, but he cannot favor one over the other in enforcement of rules. Impersonality, whatever difficulties it promotes, provides equitable treatment of all concerned. In this respect, bureaucracy can further "democratic" administration of large-scale organizations.

5. *Technically competent functionaries*. The bureaucratic assumption is that posts will be filled by individuals who possess the technical competence appropriate to those positions. Applicants are not supposed to be selected for jobs because they voted a certain way, or have distinguished parents, or know "the boss." Selection is to be on merit. It is reasoned that merit appointments are more likely to yield efficient employees.

6. *Career provision*. Employees are appointed on the basis of presumed competence, not on extraneous factors. They

must please their immediate superiors, not the stockholders or citizens in general. If they perform effectively in the judgment of the immediate superior, they may expect continuance of employment, perhaps promotion, and in either event a career with the organization, barring unforeseen circumstances.

The foregoing paraphrase of Weber's formulations concerning the "ideal" bureaucracy would presumably apply to private and public organizations alike.

FUNCTIONS OF BUREAUCRACY · The sociologist S. N. Eisenstadt remarks that almost all classical works dealing with bureaucracy have raised the same question, ". . . whether bureaucracy is master or servant, an independent body or a tool, and, if a tool, whose interest it can be made to serve."[19] Let us consider this question. What do we expect members of a bureaucracy to do? The characteristics of bureaucracy, just discussed, provide something of an answer. Bureaucracy is meant to further the objectives of the organization. It should be the servant, not the master, of that organization. It is a tool for attainment of organizational aims. Division of labor, specialization of functions, equitable administration of rules, coordination and synchronization of activities—these are for the purpose of providing efficient operation. They are not in principle ends in themselves, but designed for the benefit of those who own, control, or are served by the organization.

Take the corporation. Its stockholders expect the bureaucracy to work in their favor. They want it to produce more and better goods, at competitive prices, so that the corporation may make a profit and pay good dividends to the stockholders.

Take the private citizen of a democracy in his relations with his government. He wants the bureaucracy inside that government to serve him, to further his welfare. He does not want it to become his master. He believes the official who issues motor vehicle licenses has a job because citizens need someone to issue licenses to them. He does not believe that officials should rule the private citizen, but that private citizens should ultimately decide, through their elected representatives, what public officials shall pass on what matters in the interest of the public welfare. The citizen expects the government bureaucracy to serve the public welfare at all times and to bring about social change, when that seems indicated, for the continued welfare of the people.

Thus we may say that, at least in theory, bureaucracies are established in the expectation they will contribute to the survival and efficient operations of social units. We also expect them to play a part in bringing about desirable social change. If they meet these criteria, they are functional. If they do not, they are dysfunctional.

BUREAUCRACY & SOCIAL CHANGE

We have just heard the theory. What are the facts? To what extent is bureaucracy, viewed broadly and in the whole, fulfilling our expectations? A general answer would be: to the extent that it contributes to the survival and efficient operations of the social units concerned, and to the degree that it furthers social change when this seems desirable in the interest of those social units.

Since culture is continuously changing, the efficiency of a bureaucracy will in part be relative to the degree to which its members keep in step with these changes or help bring about the changes. Suppose a plant continued manufacturing wire recorders long after the more efficient tape recorder was perfected. It would become an inefficient organization, unwilling to keep up with technological change, unable to serve us effectively.

Peter M. Blau, an American sociologist, has done a great deal to focus attention on the function of bureaucracy in modern societies like our own. He emphasizes the *dynamic* quality of bureaucracy. It can and does change in response to changing conditions and constraints.

Bureaucracy may be viewed both as a product of social change and as an agency for furthering it. Let us consider an organization manufacturing farm implements at the turn of the century. The bureaucracy within it was established in order that the company might produce horse-drawn equipment, mostly of wood. Then technological changes made motors and high-grade steel available. The company reorganized its bureaucracy and the functional relationships involved, so as to manufacture farm equipment powered by motor rather than by horse. The reorganized bureaucracy and its manufactures were products of social change.

Now farmers could own implements each of which could do the work of many men. Agricultural method was revolutionized. The economy was affected. Farm hands were in less demand. Owners of small farms could not afford the expensive equipment, could not produce a crop at competitive prices. Consolidation of small farms into huge spreads resulted. The bureaucracy that was influenced by social change, that capitalized on it to produce new, more profit-making machinery, had done its part in bringing about social change.

Blau discusses bureaucracy as *an instrument of innovation*.[20] In the large, complex societies of today, he says, bureaucratic machinery is needed to implement new social policies. Consider inventions, ". . . which are sometimes viewed as spontaneous sources of social change." Take the atomic bomb. To be sure, Blau says, Enrico Fermi and other scientists had some brilliant ideas without which the bomb would not have been invented. But these ideas alone do not account for the bomb. "A complicated bureaucratic organization had to be set up both to produce atomic bombs and to furnish scientists with laboratories where they could work together on improvements and new developments."

Not all social change in modern society is bureaucratically instituted, Blau agrees. New customs do arise without the mediation of bureaucracy. "But deliberate introduction of a social innovation on a large scale, whether it involves the production of a new weapon or the enforcement of a new law, depends on bureaucratic methods of administration."

The dynamic of bureaucracy is exemplified in this nation's military establishment. Once, men went into action on horseback, firing small arms and waving sabers. Somewhere in the hierarchy of this vast bureaucracy a decision was ultimately made, in tune with technological developments. Soldiers would be unhorsed; they would take the field in armored tanks.

Before World War I, men fought on the ground and at sea. Today they also fight in the air. The weaponry of past generations would be museum pieces today. With changing technologies, our armed forces bureaucracy has provided greater firepower, easier troop mobility, electronic devices such as radar. Particularly since World War II, officers have been trained to control men less by force of authority and domination, more by psychological manipulation. Psychological warfare has become an important part of the armament of the nation. Air-to-air missiles have replaced earlier weapons for fighting aloft.

And this military bureaucracy, which responded to social

change, facilitates it as well. With increased troop mobility, wider arenas of battle became possible. With the fantastically destructive power of nuclear fission bombs, there has been a lessened emphasis among nations on the application of violence, greater emphasis on deterrence of physical violence. Fear of "the bomb" has produced diplomatic efforts to avert a war that could exterminate the human race.

But although many bureaucratic organizations, responding to social change, function effectively as a consequence, the fact remains that some do not. They do not respond to changed conditions, do not work effectively. And some that do on the whole are dysfunctional in certain respects, that is, are characterized by abnormal, impaired, or incomplete functioning. What contributes to this dysfunction?

1. We point out again that people tend to resist change. Career men in civil service sometime exhibit this trait. What was good enough a decade ago must be good enough today. The man with an idea for doing it a new way is looked upon with suspicion. Why upset things? It worked up to now, didn't it?

2. Since rules are drafted to facilitate efficient operation, bureaucrats are encouraged to abide by them and to see that their subordinates do the same. An effective bureaucracy, Robert K. Merton has noted,[21] demands reliable responses and strict devotion to regulations among members of the organization. This devotion to the rules sometimes ". . . leads to their transformation into absolutes; they are no longer conceived of as relative to a given set of purposes." In other words, they no longer are a means to an end, as intended, but ends in themselves. It must be done this way because it must be done this way, not because doing it this way will accomplish such and such a purpose.

An attitude such as this impedes adaptation to change within an organization. It also fails to take into account that general rules are drawn up to serve anticipated conditions only. Drafters of the rules cannot anticipate every conceivable eventuality. In given circumstances, circumvention of rules will serve the organization best, provide a warranted exception to the rules. To hold otherwise defeats the overriding aims of any code of rules. Quoting Merton again: "Thus the very elements which conduce toward efficiency in general produce inefficiency in specific instances."

To support his argument, Merton makes use of an article by Charles Hunt Page, "Bureaucracy's Other Face," a discussion of bureaucracy in the U. S. Navy. Navy rules prescribe the correct way to write a letter, greet fellow personnel, load weapons, bury the dead, report infractions of rules, pack one's clothing for travel. Learning these techniques represents the formal side of learning Navy procedure, but it also, Merton points out, represents ". . . a process which all too frequently sanctifies for the learners the methods themselves, induces a non-logical 'pride of craft.'" (Thus, a salute must be perfect in form, because that is *how* to salute. The fact that the salute is a certain kind of greeting and mark of respect becomes secondary to its style.)

Sanctification of procedures creates the hazard that they will be employed beyond the point of effectiveness. "Red tape" as an end in itself is dysfunctional.

3. A by-product of sanctification of rules may be the stifling of personal initiative, where it might serve the organization better than blind fealty to regulation. A college youth took a summer job as assistant recreation director on a school playground. He was instructed to wear white slacks and a certain type of cap, which must be red. Those were the rules. He complied, but after several days work, during which he found himself almost blinded by the sun, he purchased a white cap, with a longer bill than the officially approved headgear. It had the advantage of shading the eyes better than the approved cap. Moreover, the bill was made of a transparent material that filtered out glare, much as sunglasses do. When the young man came to work wearing the new cap, his supervisor asked why he was not officially garbed. The boy explained—he could work more effectively this way. It was safer for the children as well as for the staff to be able to see what was going on. He could avoid accidents, watch a ball sail through the air, get children out of its path in time. And so on. The playground director shook his head. "We don't wear white caps," he said. "We wear red caps. And we don't wear transparent visors."

Another aspect of this problem relates to *unwillingness* of a bureaucrat to take the initiative and make a decision that is within his authority to render. This is most likely in an official who has subordinates under him and superiors over him. Suppose a subordinate comes to him and asks whether he may have the day off tomorrow. Instead of saying yes or no, which would be his prerogative, the subexecutive "passes the buck" on up. If he made the decision, he reflects, it might be one his superior would not agree with. If his superior makes it, the man subordinate to him is absolved of responsibility.

"BUREAUCRACY'S OTHER FACE"

We have indicated that bureaucracy is a feature of formal organizations, particularly large-scale organizations. We have said that its representatives are to deal with clients and employees impersonally. And the very atmosphere of very large organizations is depersonalizing to an extent. Despite this, informal organization does exist inside large-scale organizations, in the form of networks of personal relations among given employees.

A top executive learns that an employee in the factory who had been with the company a long time is upset because his wife requires surgery and he cannot afford the specialist he would like. The executive provides the funds, as a gift from the company.

Three stenographers form a clique. They have lunch regularly, occasionally spend an evening in town together.

Staff from middle management forms a bowling team, which plays against a team of blue-collar employees. They "rib" each other during play and sometimes on the job, although there is no question that the management group gives orders that the blue-collar group must carry out, in the plant.

Charles H. Page has contributed an analysis of the informality possible in the formal organization.[22] He refers to it as "bureaucracy's other face," using the Navy as one example to make his points. This bureaucracy is, of course, formally organized to a marked degree. Its informal arrangements are not quite as visible. There are rules, groupings and sanctioned systems of procedure, just as for the formal Navy structure. These informal ways of behaving are not codified in any book of rules, despite which they are understood and accepted by those to whom they apply. "They are generated and maintained with a degree of spontaneity always lacking in the activities which make up the formal structure." Although not officially recognized and approved, they are clearly and semi-permanently established, Page writes. They "are just as 'real' and just as compelling on the membership as the elements of the official structure."

This informal structure is semisecret. It resists exposure, since it serves the very significant role of providing "a channel of circumvention" of the formally prescribed rules and methods of procedure. For instance, there is an informal procedure for by-passing several echelons of command and communicating with an officer higher up, despite the prohibition of such procedure set by formal regulations.

Anyone who has served in the armed forces is familiar with this "other face" of bureaucracy. The rule books do not so provide, but it is within the folkways for enlisted men to "liberate" a roast chicken or a ham for the benefit of one's self and cronies. It is informal but standard operating procedure for enlisted men to cooperate in outwitting a commissioned officer or keeping him in the dark regarding some breach of regulations. In the higher ranks, it is informally understood that at social functions officers of given rank will dance at least once with the wives of associates.

Civilian life also reflects "bureaucracy's other face," in factories, offices, and on campuses. The formal arrangement of a college or university, for instance, calls for certain relationships between faculty and administration on the one hand, faculty and student body on the other. Formal rules set the time span of a class session. The grading system is subject to certain regulations. Conditions for awarding degrees are set forth in specific detail. This, and much more, is part of the formal arrangement of the college and university bureaucracy. But there are also unwritten, informal arrangements. An instructor may show a special interest in a bright student, but a student should not "make a play" for such attention, else he brooks criticism from both faculty and the student body. A faculty member must not pass along gossip to a student, whether it is about other students or faculty. One instructor must not visit another's class without invitation. In the student subculture, it is generally understood that although those who cheat on examinations have a competitive edge over honest students, the latter will not inform on the cheaters.

Informal structure representing "bureaucracy's other face" is by no means simply a negative factor, an instrumentality for circumventing bureaucratic rules and thus defeating certain aims of the bureaucracy. It often functions positively, serving the official ends of the bureaucracy in the final result. Wars cannot be fought effectively, universities cannot be run adequately, and business corporations will not be operated at maximum efficiency without the positive contributions of "bureaucracy's other face." There have been occasions on battlefronts when a group of men, ignoring or evading orders from above, have fought an engagement by their own rules, in violation of official orders, and have accomplished their mission successfully, whereas they might well have failed had they followed orders. A few faculty members, acting on their own, have instituted a change of one sort or another on campus, in disregard of official rules, and the *fait accompli* has ultimately been accepted as sound by all concerned and used as a guide for the future. If no employee could ever get to the president of a corporation except the first vice-president, the president might well fail to receive information or a suggestion vital to the accomplishment of the bureaucracy's objectives.

To sum up, bureaucracy has both formal and informal aspects. Formal bureaucracy is a phenomenon of large-scale organizations and complex societies especially. We could scarcely get along without some bureaucracy. Our need for goods, services, and governance would be inadequately served without bureaucracy. But bureaucracy is intended to be the tool and not the master of those who establish it.

Bureaucracy has a dynamic, but it may be static at times, or partly so at a given time. It impedes social change, facilitates it, is affected by social change. It increases efficiency of operations, may decrease it if established rules become ends in themselves rather than means to an end.

We are committed to some form of bureaucracy, for the complexity of society demands it.

· *NOTES*

1. Bernard Berelson and Gary A. Steiner, *Human Behavior, An Inventory of Scientific Findings* (New York: Harcourt, Brace & World, 1964), pp. 325–326.
2. *Ibid.*, p. 326.
3. Harold D. Lasswell and Abraham Kaplan, *Power and Society: A Framework for Political Inquiry* (New Haven: Yale University Press, 1950), p. 35.
4. David T. Bazelon, *The Paper Economy* (New York: Vintage Books, 1965), p. 197.

5. *The World Almanac, 1966* (New York: Newspaper Enterprise Assn., 1966), p. 792.
6. Bazelon, *op. cit.*, p. 195.
7. Robert M. MacIver and Charles H. Page, *Society: An Introductory Analysis* (New York: Rinehart, 1949), p. 13.
8. Murray Gendell and Hans L. Zetterberg (eds.), *A Sociological Almanac for the United States*, 2nd. ed. (New York: Scribner, 1964), p. 57.
9. *Ibid.*, p. 59.
10. Berelson and Steiner, *op. cit.*, p. 379.
11. MacIver and Page, *op. cit.*, p. 230.
12. *Ibid.*
13. Bazelon, *op. cit.*, p. 187.
14. *Ibid.*, p. 194.
15. *Ibid.*, pp. 194–195.
16. *The World Almanac, 1966, op. cit.*, pp. 476–477.
17. *Ibid.*, p. 791.
18. H. H. Gerth and C. Wright Mills (eds. and trans.), *From Max Weber: Essays in Sociology* (New York: Oxford University Press, 1946), pp. 196–244.
19. S. N. Eisenstadt, *Essays on Comparative Institutions* (New York: Wiley, 1965), p. 179.
20. Peter M. Blau, *Bureaucracy in Modern Society* (New York: Random House, 1956), pp. 90–91.
21. Robert K. Merton, "Bureaucratic Structure and Personality," *Social Forces*, XVIII (May 1940), 561–568.
22. Charles H. Page, "Bureaucracy's Other Face," *Social Forces*, XXV (October 1946), 88–94.

· SUGGESTIONS FOR FURTHER READING

BLAU, PETER M. *Bureaucracy in Modern Society.* New York: Random House, 1956.
A well-written analysis of the structure and dynamics of bureaucracy.

BLAU, PETER M., and W. RICHARD SCOTT. *Formal Organizations.* San Francisco: Chandler, 1962.
This is a good sourcebook, summarizing and evaluating much of the research and theory on the structure and functioning of complex organizations.

GERTH, H. H., and C. WRIGHT MILLS (eds. and trans.). *From Max Weber: Essays in Sociology.* New York: Oxford University Press, 1946.
This volume carries Weber's classic essay on bureaucracy as an "ideal type" of social system. It also contains related items on power, authority, and discipline.

HARE, PAUL. *Handbook of Small Group Research.* New York: Free Press, 1961.

This is a good reference volume, which reviews the literature from 1900 to 1959 on small groups.

HOMANS, GEORGE C. *The Human Group.* New York: Harcourt, Brace & World, 1950.
Worth reading; attention is especially directed to Chapter 16, "The Job of the Leader."

MILLER, GEORGE A. "Professionals in Bureaucracy: Alienation Among Industrial Scientists and Engineers." *American Sociological Review,* XXXII (October 1967), 755–768.
A study of the relationship between alienation from work and two factors of bureaucratic organization—the degree of organizational control and the professional incentives available. The subjects are scientists and engineers employed in a large aerospace company.

MOORE, WILBERT. *The Conduct of the Corporation.* New York: Random House, 1962.
A sprightly treatment of the nature of the modern corporation.

PAGE, CHARLES H. "Bureaucracy's Other Face." *Social Forces,* XXV (October 1946), 88–94.
This article (discussed in the chapter) deals with the informal organization of activities and the interactions inside the formal structure of bureaucracy.

WHYTE, WILLIAM FOOTE. *Street Corner Society: The Social Structure of an Italian Slum.* Chicago: University of Chicago Press, 1943.
The street corner gangs in this study represent a form of small group.

ROETHLISBERGER, FRITZ J., and WILLIAM J. DICKSON. *Management and the Worker.* Cambridge, Mass.: Harvard University Press, 1939, especially Parts IV and V.
An important study of informal organization inside large-scale, formal organization.

13 MASS SOCIETY

Here we deal with the concept of *mass society* and discuss certain phenomena typical of such a society—crowds, audiences, mass communication, fads, and fashion.

THE MASS

First, what is the *mass* in "mass society"? It has several sociological usages, but as employed in our particular frame of reference in this chapter, *the mass consists of a large number of people, each separately and independently exposed to a common social stimulus, each responding to it independently, sometimes with little or no communication with others exposed to that stimulus.* An example would be several million persons reading and reacting to a syndicated columnist in their respective newspapers. Another would be a million people following election returns over radio.

Let us proceed to an analysis of mass, as we employ that concept in discussing mass society.*

1. *The mass is an unorganized, spontaneous grouping, with little or no social interaction among the members.* Independently, 10,000 people read and respond to an editorial in the

* This analysis is in the main a paraphrase of Herbert Blumer, "The Mass, the Public, and Public Opinion," in Alfred McClung Lee (ed.), *New Outline of Principles of Sociology* (New York: Barnes & Noble, 1946), pp. 185–193.

Wall Street Journal. Each does so of his own volition, interacting not at all with the 9,999 other readers. It is a one-to-one communication process: message to receiver #1, response to message; message to receiver #2, response to message; and so on.

2. *Whenever members of the mass react as individuals to given stimuli, they are enacting mass behavior.* All 10,000 readers of the *Wall Street Journal* editorial behave the same way in one respect—they read the editorial.

3. *With few exceptions, members of the mass are not in physical proximity to one another while responding to a given communication.* Some of those who read the *Wall Street Journal* editorial would have been in New York, some in Boston, some in Detroit. Even where several thousand might have been in the same city, they do not necessarily have social contact with one another.

4. *Membership in the mass is nonrestricted.* Persons from all walks of life, all levels of prestige, all religious faiths may participate in receiving and responding to the communication. Anyone who has the price may buy a book or a magazine. The rich and the poor, male and female, Caucasian and Oriental, may follow radio or television reports of an astronaut's flight into outer space.

5. *Members of the mass are anonymous.* One is not likely to know whether or which others are receiving and responding to the communication.

6. *Members of the mass behave in terms of their individual needs.* A million persons read an advertisement extolling Soothing Shaving Cream. Mr. Harper decides it is what he needs for his tough beard. Mr. Snodgrass decides he will stay with Formula ZX49, the shaving cream he has been using. Tommy, age 10, who also read the ad, has no decision to make. He does not shave, has no immediate need for shaving cream.

7. *Since they are unorganized and are behaving to meet individual needs, members of the mass do not act as a united group.* A half-million individuals hear a radio orator declare that Jews are subhuman creatures and should be deported or shot. Many listeners are shocked, disgusted, or infuriated. These are *individual* reactions. Some may telephone the radio station, protesting the use of the airwaves for such a purpose. Again, each does so individually. It is unlikely that the listeners who objected to the speech will intercommunicate. Lack-

ing organization, they will not march on the station in a body, and if they write letters of complaint to the Federal Communications Commission, this will be as individuals, not as a cohesive group.

8. *Although mass behavior is not united, the individual lines of behavior may converge, in which case the influence of the mass may be considerable.* Suppose fifty of the half-million radio listeners who heard the anti-Semitic speaker decide to write to newspapers, expressing their indignation. Suppose the fifty, learning of each other through publication of their letters, get together, form the spearhead of a drive to recruit others of like mind, build an organization of such strength and power that it will convince the federal government that regulations must be drafted that will redefine the rules of radio broadcasting so that inflammatory speeches are prohibited in future. If the organization succeeds, the uniting of individual behavior by members of the mass has resulted in an action of potentially momentous consequences, whether these are good or evil according to the definitions of persons in the society.

However, be it noted, at the point where organization developed, mass behavior terminated:

> When mass behavior becomes organized, as into a movement, it ceases to be mass behavior and becomes societal in nature. Its whole nature changes in acquiring a structure, a program, a defining culture, traditions, prescribed rules . . . a we-consciousness.[1]

MASS SOCIETY

As in the case of the mass, the phrase *mass society* has been used variously in sociology. The particular usage employed here refers to *that kind of society in which mass behavior plays an important part.* The number of individuals in the society is not the most important criterion, however. What delineates a mass society is the type of relationship that exists between the individual and the social system.

A mass society is a social system characterized by relative anonymity and psychological isolation of the individual, and by comparative impersonality of existing relationships.

Ours is a mass society. Think of yourself reading a recently published novel. It stirs you deeply, makes you laugh, cry.

You are tremendously affected by it. It may even influence the course of your life in some way. Some 50,000 other people may read the same book at about the same time. Some do, some do not respond to it as you did. Now note that you purchased the volume in a comparatively *impersonal* exchange with a bookseller. You read it in *anonymity,* for few if any of the others who read it were aware of your existence. They did not know you by name, did not know you were reading the novel. At the very most, you interacted with a select few of your acquaintances in sharing your feelings about the book. You were *psychologically isolated* from most other readers.

We said that in mass behavior the number of persons is not the criterion most essential to the definition of *mass society,* and now you should understand why. Up to the beginning of the twentieth century, China had a vast population, but comparatively little mass behavior, in the sense in which we are using the term. Relations among the people were closer and more personal than they would be in a complex, highly industrialized society such as our own. Anonymity and psychological isolation were uncommon. What the Chinese farmer did was known to and evaluated by other farmers in his vicinity. They cared a great deal how he behaved in relation to them. They were guided by common behavior norms. Just about everything the farmer did was important to his fellow farmers.

Now contrast the situation in old, traditional China with your own today. You also have neighbors and they know and evaluate you. They expect you to be law-abiding and not to outrage their conception of common decency. But in our mass society, contrary to the situation in old China, some depersonalization has set in. Millions of people have never heard of you and care not at all how you behave with respect to any particular matter. They are not concerned about whether you go to college or not. You may drive a car or roller-skate to school, and they will neither know nor react. The department-store clerk who sells you a typewriter ribbon does not know you, and, looking at the relationship from your viewpoint, to you she is a nameless functionary. You are not interested in her background, and she is interested in you only to the extent of consummating the sale agreeably.

In the course of any day you interact closely with acquaintances, but also with numerous individuals who conceive of you as a customer, a passenger, a statistic, a sales prospect, a voter, a utilities consumer, a movie patron, a library user, but not to any extent as a person—as someone with an individuality, whose behavior is of more than transitory interest except in the most theoretical sense. What we are emphasizing is that *the number of people* does not determine the existence of a mass society. *The relation between the individual and the social system* does.

THE EMERGENCE OF MASS SOCIETY

Mass society evolved gradually. The trend began centuries ago. Factors contributing to the trend include:

1. *Industrial and commercial revolutions,* leading to technologies and to industrial and commercial undertakings of increasing complexity.

2. *Great population shifts within a society,* occasioned by the developments just mentioned. Laborers move to locations where employment is available. To cite one example: As the industrialization of England progressed, feudal society decayed. Agricultural laborers left the land, traveled to the cities, seeking employment in factories. Urban population burgeoned. A closely integrated, highly personal form of group life is possible among farmers, difficult among city residents.

3. *Geographical mobility.* This was facilitated by improved means of transportation, which further increased the movement from rural to urban areas.

4. *Invention of mass media.* These provided a means of communicating with vast audiences of widely dispersed people.

5. *Changes in, the decline of, or total disappearance of customary ways of behaving* that formerly served as a bulwark supporting the value system of medieval European society. Church influence declined. Family life underwent change. The Industrial Revolution

. . . weakened the integrating effect of certain institutions by forcing people to segmentalize their lives to a certain extent. The conjugal family no longer provides economic occupations, the primary source of recreation, education for the young. There are now specialized institutions where one works, plays, goes to school, etc., and each of these is distinct from the family. This segmentalization . . . has further broken up the integrated community in which people once lived in a high degree of mutual interaction with one another.[2]

CONDITIONS OF MASS SOCIETY

Social and social psychological conditions closely associated with mass society include: *

1. *Functional interdependence.* Industrialization, mercantilism, and the development of a complex technology have rendered individuals in a society increasingly dependent upon others, but this is not a dependence leading to closer association and a higher degree of social interaction. The reverse is rather the case. Each of us is dependent upon millions of persons whom we will never identify, who are geographically far removed, with whom we will have no contact, even by correspondence.

You depend upon this textbook for certain viewpoints and knowledge. Therefore, you were and are dependent upon all of the following: an author; a publisher; an editor; a copy-editor; a proofreader; a paper manufacturer; a bookbinder; a glue manufacturer; an ink manufacturer; manufacturers of a wide variety of printing machinery; architects and construction workers who erect buildings where manufacturers house printing equipment and offices; water, electricity, and other utilities suppliers; a type designer; a type manufacturer; a designer to engineer the book's layout, spacing, captioning, art work; an artist to design the book's dust jacket; a writer to prepare the dust jacket's "blurb," informing you what is inside the volume; an advertising staff; a promotion staff; a sales staff; a bookkeeping staff; a distribution facility; retail outlets; retail sales employees; retail management; retail maintenance staff.

This is only a partial list, but it suggests the great number of people needed if a book is to reach the consumer's hands. How many of these persons do you know by name? How many have you communicated with in any fashion?

Consider functional interdependence from another perspective. In 1966, the International Association of Machinists

* The basic framework of the analysis that follows is from Kurt Lang and Gladys Engel Lang, *Collective Dynamics* (New York: Crowell, 1961), pp. 364–365.

called a strike against a number of major airlines. Untold thousands were affected because of their dependence upon the airlines for one thing or another. For instance:

Thousands of passengers were stranded en route when the machinists walked out. Other thousands had their bookings canceled before they could take off.

Some 66,000 airline employees, idled by the strike, lost 1.6 million dollars a day in wages.

The officers and stockholders of the airline corporations took a revenue loss of 7 million dollars every day of the strike.

Restaurants, newsstands, bars, and souvenir shops in airports lost thousands of patrons.

Airmail deliveries were disrupted. The struck lines had been carrying 70 percent of the nation's air mail.

Air-freight schedules were disrupted. The lines in question had been carrying 73 percent of the country's air freight.

New York City lost an estimated 500,000 dollars a day in tourist trade, retail sales, and entertainment spending. Miami Beach hotels, very dependent on packaged air tours for the summer trade, laid off employees as occupancy shrank as much as 25 percent below normal. Motels and hotels in certain parts of the United States lost the trade of would-be vacationers, business travelers, and stopover passengers.

Federal government employees became involved in arbitrating the dispute.

Reporters for all the news media were assigned to various locales to cover developments.

Baggage porters at airline terminals lost tips.

Cab drivers lost riders.

With several exceptions, these were "bad" outcomes of functional interdependence. There were "good" ones, too. The strikers won better wages, fringe benefits, and improved working conditions. Passengers stranded in a city because they could not make an airline connection spent money in that locality. Bars, restaurants, hotels, movies, newsstands, cabs profited from the strike. Men who could not fly to negotiate business in person did so by wire, adding to the income of Western Union. Telephone companies also benefited from long-distance calls made to transact business, notify people that the caller would not arrive on schedule, and for other emergency reasons. The airlines lost revenue, but railroads and long-distance buses were jammed with passengers who had to get somewhere somehow.

2. *Accelerated social change.* Technological and scientific developments create conditions conducive to change in other aspects of the culture, some of it sudden. An invention may create unemployment for a time. Automation in the United States has rendered a proportion of our population unemployable unless it is retrained to new skills. Other technological developments have at times reduced unemployment. The tempo of social change tends to accelerate with technological and scientific developments, these changes having both positive and negative connotations for the society. Rapid and extensive changes in a culture often produce at least a temporary instability in the behavior of the mass.

3. *Exclusion of the mass from meaningful participation in certain aspects of the culture.* Many of the durable values of rural life cannot be successfully transplanted to industrialized mass society. The intimate social ties of rural dwellers do not flourish in cities. The individual in mass society is not as important a factor in educating children, or directly influencing public affairs, as were his progenitors. He has less to say about government, international relations, than did his colonial ancestors.

When we said that rural values cannot be successfully transplanted to industrialized mass society, we were not suggesting that mass society exists only in urban areas. The inhabitants of all sectors of our nation are component units of our mass society. Both rural and urban life are affected by the emergence of mass society. What was implied in the reference to transplanted rural values was that whereas, when this republic was in its infancy, a man could move from the country to the city, bring his values with him, and hold on to them in his new environment, this is no longer possible to the same extent. And it was the rural-type values that yielded the maximum in close personal relations. It is the more contemporary, city-type value system that is geared to mass society, and that system tends to be a force for depersonalization. Even those who reside in rural areas are to an extent unsuccessful in preserving what we think of as rural life-ways. They, too, as members of mass society, are anonymous when they react to a television commercial, impersonal figures when they send in the boxtop in response to the commercial.

Arnold M. Rose expressed the pervasive consequences of the evolution of folk society into mass society:

Consensus between people on values and ways of behavior hardly exists any longer because tradition and closely knit social structures have been weakened. People have increasingly become mentally isolated from each other, and they are confused by and suspicious of the forces that seem to control them.[3]

Despite these negative features of mass society, something can be said on the positive side. The relative anonymity of the individual in mass society, the comparatively impersonal quality of relationships, do have a tendency to diminish the strength of pressures for conformity. If you do not know your neighbor very well, you are not very familiar with his habits and somewhat disinterested in them. In mass society, individuals can have greater freedom of thought and action than in a more highly integrated society characterized by very close relationships. Anonymity, if it does nothing else, provides the individual with greater scope for his thinking and behaving, at least in that there are fewer pressures from others to conform to a common set of values. When he is less subject to community pressures, more choices of behavior are available to him, more selectivity is possible. He may attend church on Sunday, or go fishing, or attend a burlesque show. He may get around in an automobile or a bicycle, and no one will much care. He may vote Democratic or Republican, Socialist or Prohibition Party, so long as he maintains his relative anonymity, and can do so without feeling the pressure of potentially censuring or approving neighbors.

MASS POLITICS

A number of scholars* have observed that the conditions of mass society encourage the emergence of *mass politics*, which sociologist William Kornhauser defines in this manner: "Mass politics occurs when large numbers of people engage in polit-

* Among them, William Kornhauser, in *The Politics of Mass Society* (New York: Free Press, 1959); Hannah Arendt, in *The Origins of Totalitarianism* (New York: Harcourt, Brace & World, 1954); Erich Fromm, in *Escape from Freedom* (New York: Rinehart, 1945); and Robert A. Nisbet, in *The Quest for Community* (New York: Oxford University Press, 1953).

ical activity outside of the procedures and rules instituted by a society to govern political action."[4] Theoreticians generally agree that mass society is particularly vulnerable to the kind of political leadership that is destructive of liberal democratic institutions. The extreme case of the resulting political orientation is totalitarianism, such as fascism or communism, but less extreme examples are also antidemocratic in that they represent political activity outside of the procedures and rules instituted in the society to govern political action; hence they contravene the constitutional order.

Kornhauser points out that there are "elites" and "nonelites" in any society. Elites are a relatively small category of individuals who claim the right to, and are charged with, responsibility for framing and sustaining the fundamental values of the society within their areas of competence. Nonelites are those who are expected to be, and by and large are, responsive to the leadership of the elites. But as mass society develops, relations between elites and nonelites undergo change. This is a consequence of the fact that mass society, as we learned, is characterized by impersonality. The individual is an anonymous unit among a great many others. The mass is said to be "masslike, shapeless, structureless, undifferentiated."[5] Primary group relationships tend to deteriorate in mass society. Ties to family, social class, ethnic identity, and the local community lose some of their significance. A feeling of detachment, even of alienation in many cases, sets in as people become less identified and affiliated with distinctive social groups in and through which they formerly derived a feeling of security. Kornhauser and others conclude that persons who lack or lose the security that comes of association with these groups become available for mobilization by "counterelites," who seek to supplant existing elites.

In this, counterelites have an advantage, for existing elites become rather remote figures as large-scale, bureaucratic organizations increasingly dominate the society. Nonelites are no longer as willing as formerly to accept their leadership and decisions. Because, on the one hand, the population's participation in direct and meaningful societal activities is diminished, and, on the other, the elites have lost some of their authority and ability to lead, control of the values and political aspirations of citizens becomes difficult to achieve. The mass, cut adrift from sustaining group ties, less influenced now by values

framed by elites, is in a figurative void, and likely to be responsive to counterelites, who seek to assume power and to become
the society's new elites. In a comparatively liberal democratic
society, fascism and communism may offer the alienated, unorganized masses substitute loyalties for those they have
abandoned.

Kornhauser further traces the vulnerability of mass societies
to antidemocratic forces; he attributes it to the decline of what
he terms "intermediate relations." All but the simplest societies,
he asserts, are characterized by three levels of social relations.
The first level consists of highly personal or primary relations,
notably the family. The third level contains relations that include the entire population, notably the state. The second level
is comprised of all the intermediate relations, notably the local
community, voluntary associations, and the occupational
groupings. These constitute links between the individual and
his primary relations, on the one hand, and the state and other
national relations, on the other.

In mass society, the intermediate relations tend to become
weak. Members of the society are interconnected largely
through their common ties to national centers of communication and organization. Primary groups become isolated from
the larger society and become unable, by themselves, effectively to provide a basis for participation in that society.

To illustrate: Consider a relatively simple society, which has
not developed the complex, large-scale organizational structure of mass society. A primary group such as the family can
expect to participate directly and meaningfully in various
aspects of community life, on the strength of intermediate relations, in part. Families belong to religious and political associations that must be given consideration. Individuals are
members of unions and other voluntary associations that play
a part in shaping policies and decisions in the society.

By contrast, in mass society, although intermediate social
relations of some sort continue to exist, the primary group,
such as the family, becomes relatively isolated even from these.
Representative government, where it exists, becomes remote;
it cannot be easily manipulated by a family, an individual, or
an intermediate association. Religious organizations become
hierarchical bureaucracies. Unions and other large-scale voluntary associations are likewise directed by a comparatively
impersonal bureaucracy. Where, then, does the mass look for

meaningful, or seemingly meaningful, participation in shaping its social life? To mass politics, according to theoreticians, a type of politics that seems to offer what has been lost. The mass is thus a population available to leaders of mass politics.

Kornhauser observes that, for instance, totalitarian regimes are set up by counterelites who have successfully mobilized the available population and installed themselves as the new elites. This is facilitated when the erstwhile leaders lack the will and capacity effectively to mobilize the mass to support them. Furthermore, the ruling elites are in competition among themselves in many respects; they have maintained their leadership in the past only by establishing a balance of power, which can be upset. Moreover, the old elites are restrained by their value commitments, which they framed. They have a vital stake in preserving the status quo, hence they oppose change. Kornhauser writes:

> Thus it is that popular mobilization generally is the work of counter-elites, since they are not inhibited by commitments to the social order, nor by constraints resulting from participation in a balance of power. These counter-elites are pushed towards making allies among the masses, since this is the only way to gain total power in mass society. . . .
>
> A rising totalitarian movement finds its prey not only in an exposed mass but also in an exposed elite. The penetration of an existing elite by a successful totalitarian movement (as the Nazis penetrated the Weimar government) is *prima facie* evidence of its accessibility.[6]

Authoritarian-minded, mass-oriented counterelites—that is, those who offer the people substitute values for those they have given up—may capture political power. It is for this reason that freedom is precarious in mass society.

When the takeover is by totalitarian-minded counterelites, *mass society* is transformed into *totalitarian society,* as Kornhauser views it. He points out, however, that both types are abstractions, and that no large-scale society is purely one or the other. But once the new elites establish totalitarianism, they become inaccessible to the available population in order to sustain a system of relatively total control from above.

The elite is inaccessible in that elite elements are selected and fixed . . . by virtue of a monopoly over the means of coercion and persuasion in the hands of those at the apex of the structure. The population is available in that its members lack all those independent social formations that could serve as a basis of resistance to the elite. Instead, the population is mobilized by the elite through multiple organizations taken over or created for that purpose.[7]

Mass politics, whether of the totalitarian stripe or not, involves direct communication between the leaders and citizens, without strong intervening organizations. Mass societies facilitate the rise of a charismatic leader, who gets directly to the people, face-to-face as well as through use of the mass media (which we discuss farther along in this chapter). The leader or leaders may eventually seize control of the communication media and set up a propaganda machine in order to continue in power.

An example of a man engaged in mass politics was Huey Long, whose history included the governorship of Louisiana and membership in the United States Senate during the thirties. Cutting through bureaucratic governmental structures, he appealed directly to the people, posing as a simple, untutored man, sprung from the common people and speaking their language, who had only their best interests at heart. Once a New Dealer, he broke with the leadership of that party to play on the fears and insecurities of the Depression-victimized citizenry. Attacking the Roosevelt administration in colorful language, he indicated what he would do if the people followed his leadership and made him head of the government. He would make "every man a king," sharing the nation's abundant wealth equally. Denouncing President Franklin D. Roosevelt in Congress, he declared: "While millions have starved and gone naked, while babies have cried and died for milk, while people have begged for meat and bread, Mr. Roosevelt's administration sails merrily along, plowing under and destroying things to eat and wear. . . . Is this government? It looks more like St. Vitus dance."

Although Senator Kenneth McKellar of Tennessee remarked of Long that "I don't believe he could get the Lord's Prayer endorsed in this body," Huey Long's speeches, even when delivered before the Senators, were not meant primarily for them. He was addressing himself to the people; his words, he well knew, would be disseminated among them through the mass media.

And the people flocked to his support, despite the fact that, as time passed, it appeared evident that he favored either an out-and-out dictatorship or something very close to it. The important proviso, of course, was that he hold the top position. He formed a Share our Wealth organization. If he gained control of the federal bureaucracy, he promised, he would distribute wealth liberally to all the citizens of the land. He would accomplish this through a scheme that was devious, never quite clear, and certainly impractical. But upon superficial examination it sounded highly attractive, and a great many people followed his instructions, delivered over radio and by means of thousands of mailings, to form local Share our Wealth clubs. Anybody must be allowed to join, he adjured his audiences. There must be no dues. This must be a "poor man's movement." By 1935, over seven and a half million people had joined a Share our Wealth club, forming a large nucleus opposed to New Deal policies and supporting Huey Long's political aspirations. It did little good that New Dealers proclaimed the Share our Wealth movement a deception, one which, if it were implemented, could only bankrupt the national economy and create chaos. General Hugh Johnson, a New Deal bureaucrat, knew why the government was failing to sway Long's followers. "Who," he asked, "is going to tell any man he ought not to have five thousand dollars a year? The fact is that nobody is answering Huey in language anybody can understand. He is getting away with it without a contest."

He almost did. But he was assassinated in 1935, and his movement dwindled and finally collapsed.

Most of the theoretical statements given above are based on Kornhauser's thinking. Other sociologists would agree with it, but some do not. One of the latter is Joseph R. Gusfield, who holds that mass society is less vulnerable to extremist mass politics than has been asserted. In fact, he writes, there must be some cultural cohesion in mass society, else democratic-type politics could not be sustained. Conditions of mass societies provide support to democratic political norms, according to Gusfield. Mass communications strengthen rather than weaken the ties between individuals and their political elites. The equalitarianism that democratic philosophies argue encourages democratic norms. Indeed, bureaucratic institutions themselves may serve to bring about acceptance of these norms and to strengthen democratic structures. Extremist politics may be expected in modern societies only as a response of those who are adversely affected by the changes toward a mass society and who are most insulated from mass institutions. Gusfield concludes:

> Mass conditions are thus likely to present many features which are not only consistent with a pluralistic theory of politics but even enhance such features. Rather than providing a source of extremist movements they are just as likely to mitigate the development of opposition and to increase the degree of toleration for dissent.[8]

In conclusion, we may point out that although theoreticians differ as to the degree of vulnerability of mass society to extremist, authoritarian politics, there is widespread agreement that mass society is vulnerable to *some* type of mass politics.

CROWDS

The crowd is a phenomenon of mass society, but not exclusive to it. We discuss it here because it plays such a significant role in mass behavior. It should be borne in mind, however, that the statements we are about to make apply to crowds in whatever type of society they may be found.

A French aristocrat, Gustav Le Bon, called attention to the crowd as a social phenomenon worthy of scientific scrutiny when he published his book *The Crowd* in 1896. Based largely upon his personal observation of street behavior during the French Revolution of 1871, it was limited in scope and consequently fell short of being a comprehensive study of all kinds of crowds. Moreover, it suffered from his bias, that of the aristocrat analyzing the behavior of the masses in revolt against these rulers. However, *The Crowd*, a classic of its kind, stimulated other scholars to study the phenomenon. Social psychologists and sociologists have progressively refined and reevaluated the concept of *crowd*.

A crowd is a temporary, largely unorganized group of individuals in physical proximity to one another and mutually influencing each other to a significant extent. The phrase "to a significant extent" is important to the definition. Twenty people idly watching a steam shovel scoop up soil are not a crowd. They do not have much intercommunication, and they influence each other only minimally, if at all. A group of individuals at a revival meeting may constitute a crowd. They are in physical proximity to each other, in a given place at a given time, and the religious fervor of one influences the others to a significant extent.

The interaction within a crowd does not require conversation, although there may be some. "Communication in the crowd is by means of natural signs rather than by means of significant symbols," notes Arnold M. Rose. ". . . the only thing that can be regarded as common to all members of the crowd is . . . 'feeling tone.' "[9] Evangelist Billy Graham's followers do not need to use language to communicate their fervor to each other. The "feeling tone" is generated by the proceedings. "Natural signs" influence the crowd—facial expressions, the swaying of bodies, and the like.

Rose classified crowds as expressive and acting.[10] We shall use that distinction here.

EXPRESSIVE CROWDS

Billy Graham's followers are an *expressive* crowd. Other terms that have been used to designate the same phenomenon are *orgiastic* crowd and *dancing* crowd. The terms derive from the rhythmic movements characteristic of such groups; these movements bear no direct relation to the fundamental purpose of the behavior. At revival meetings, worshipers often become excited by the proceedings. They chant, cry out "Amen," clap their hands in unison. Their bodies sway from side to side and backward and forward, rhythmically. This does not directly further the goals of the religious meeting, which has to do with developing a mystical feeling of awe of and reverence for God. However, the feeling tone generated within the crowd is augmented by the orgiastic or dancing behavior.

Rose remarked about such revival sessions that participants come expecting excitement, perhaps a feeling of "possession" by some sort of spirit. They refer to it as "a religious experience."

The rhythm of audience participation stimulates the circular process which is so necessary for crowd behavior. . . . As the stimuli come more and more from within the group relative to that from the preacher the [lay participants] gradually become transformed into a crowd. . . . As people participate collectively in the noisemaking they increase their sense of solidarity as a crowd. Since people are no longer exactly acting as they would in the privacy of their homes or on a public street, the bizarre element in behavior has become more acceptable. People begin to feel a sense of anonymity. "Everyone is doing something strange and therefore it is all right if I act a little odd, too."[11]

Another example of an expressive crowd is a group of persons intently concentrated upon performing a vigorous dance requiring skillful movements performed in unison. The couples respond to each other's movements; one couple stimulates another; all are engaged in rhythmic steps, twirls, twists, and gyrations. While performing these, they are also intent upon avoiding a collision with other dancers. The rhythmic movements are secondary to, although part of, the major objective, which is to achieve a sense of exhilaration in following the music.

ACTING CROWDS

An acting crowd is one that becomes organized around a particular purpose, its behavior directed toward the achievement of that objective. So defined, we might say that every expressive crowd is also an acting crowd, but that not every acting crowd is an expressive crowd. However, as we shall attempt to establish, there are acting crowds that do not manifest the expressive, or "dancing," behavior of a revival meeting or a dancing group.

A *mob* is one type of acting crowd. (It may be expressive, too. Some mobs chant, clap hands, perform other behaviors in unison, much as does a crowd of people at a revival service.) The Watts area of Los Angeles, a deteriorated section inhabited by poverty-stricken minority groups, furnishes an example of mob action:

It all started when two men—Joe Garcia, 26, a Mexican-American, and Dwayne Graves, 16, a Negro—bumped into each other outside a Watts liquor store. Between the Negro ghetto and the Mexican colony clustered in nearby East Los Angeles, there is a tradition of jealous rivalry, and tensions have been rising. Negroes, who resent the lightskinned Mexicans because they find it easier to get jobs, had stabbed several of their rivals in the previous riots.

Mexicans, for their part, regard themselves as better-educated and racially superior to their Negro neighbors, whom they accuse of monopolizing antipoverty funds.

After last week's sidewalk encounter, a scuffle ensued. Graves and a fellow Negro were subsequently wounded by shotgun blasts from a car; accused of the shooting were Garcia's brothers, Carlos and Robert, who were later charged with assault with intent to kill. Word swiftly spread through Watts. Next afternoon, Negro dropouts hanging around a high school began lobbing rocks at Mexicans and other Caucasians driving by. One stone hurled by a Negro struck a white . . . teacher in the head, and—said onlookers—when police dragged the suspect from a barbershop, he yelled, "Police brutality! Riot! Riot!" A crowd of Negro teen-agers took that as an order.

Swelling into the hundreds, a mob stormed through the twelve-block area . . . overturning vehicles, smashing store windows, pommeling and stabbing whites. A Mexican-American truck driver, Lawrence Gomez, 30, was surrounded, beaten, and shot to death. Negro Joe Crawford, 33, for no apparent reason was killed by a sniper. Molotov cocktails started a dozen fires while looters pillaged stores.[12]

When a mob erupts, as pictured in the foregoing news report in *Time*, it does not do so entirely on the spur of the moment, although this may seem to be the case. Mob formation and action are generally the outcome of a slow, gradual process. It is not true, as reported in the news story, that "it all started" when two men bumped into each other. This is an oversimplification. Mobs do not form and riots do not take place simply because two men bump into each other. But, given a gradual build-up of resentments, frustrations, and rivalries, a single incident, such as two men colliding, may trigger a riot. The seeds of warfare were already planted, so to speak. An incident triggered the war.

Let us examine the process of mob formation and action a little more closely.

1. One element of mob behavior, we have seen, is *tension*, a tension built up gradually. The Watts area of Los Angeles has come under considerable study recently, following a much more costly riot than the one we used as an illustration. An official report suggested that smouldering dissatisfaction of the residents with their impoverished, disprivileged condition was one factor leading to the rioting. The people were poor;

they blamed the white man for exploiting them; they objected to what they considered unfair, brutal treatment of Negroes by the police; Mexican Americans and Negroes resented each other. There was, according to the testimony of the report, widespread belief that something was radically out of joint in the community, and that traditional methods of solving the area's problems would not work. That is, as tension rose, the normative standards of behavior by which residents usually were guided seemed to some of them inadequate for the solution of their problems. These standards broke down as tension mounted. One person did something out of the ordinary, and this triggered the formation of a mob and the subsequent behavior of that mob.

But that one individual's act only *triggered* the process. Had there been no dissatisfactions, frustrations, or hostilities, this act would not have evoked the response it did. Long felt but pent-up feelings exploded. What happened was not a concerted attack, although it may appear to have been. *A group of individuals who felt the same way* about the situation reacted simultaneously. One influenced the other by a sort of contagion of emotion. One reinforced the other and the total reaction of the mob was consequently stronger than the reaction of any single individual, behaving unilaterally, would have been.

2. Another element of mob behavior is *explosiveness*. The behavior of the group is likely to be eruptive. A "lynch mob" is an example. Often an innocent scapegoat becomes the object of aggression. Thus, in the Watts riot described by *Time,* the Mexican American truckman, Lawrence Gomez, was the scapegoat. He happened to be in Watts, delivering bottled water, when the mob erupted. Its members had no specific grievance against him, and most of them had not seen him before, according to report. But as he entered the riot area, someone shouted, "Let's get the whitey!" He was immediately attacked and slain.

A mob is a vigilante group. It takes the law into its own hands, in violation of law. Frequently it does not bother to ascertain that the intended victim is guilty of anything. It does not await the evidence and conduct an orderly trial. It may lynch an innocent person. One study revealed that in 26 percent of the lynchings of Negroes in the South between 1889 and 1933, the person lynched was not even alleged to have committed a crime. He merely happened to be on the scene when the mob was prepared to erupt. It was incensed, not against the victim, but against local Negroes generally.[13]

3. *Leadership emerges spontaneously in mobs,* as a rule, although some studies of lynchings show that in a number of instances planned leadership existed. Suppose a leaderless group of people form outside a courthouse as a man accused of some particularly atrocious crime (as defined by the group) is led out after arraignment. Some onlookers mutter ominously; others glare at the suspect. Suddenly someone shouts, "Let's get him!" This someone has become the leader, if he succeeds in triggering the lynch behavior.

4. Another characteristic of mobs is that *the members act as if oblivious to the consequences of their behavior,* both to themselves and to others. Individually, in calmer moments, members of a lynch mob would realize that by taking the law into their own hands they are committing a crime, injuring others, and subjecting themselves to possible prosecution. At the moment, however, in the heat of the encounter, they do not act as if they are aware of this. They commit their crimes without regard to the consequences.

But, let us remember, not all mobs are lynch mobs. Not all are activated by hostile intentions. Some are friendly mobs, attempting to show their respect for or adulation of a person or persons. On occasion, an *acting crowd* gathers to see and cheer a movie idol, a popular singer, or a politician. It strains against police lines, screaming and applauding as the celebrity appears. Tension builds up as officers push the crowd back, prevent it from surging forward to touch or shake hands with the person. Suddenly, one man breaks the police cordon. Others pour through the breach. The crowd becomes a *mob,* pushing, elbowing, fighting its way forward. Yet it does so with the best intentions and with nothing but good wishes for the celebrity it is mobbing.

Considering all types of crowds, expressive and acting, hostile and friendly, we can discern certain common elements beyond those noted for mobs.

1. *A crowd is a temporary social group.* Figure 13.1 shows an attack on young men of South Boston who had symbolized their opposition to the nation's Vietnam policy in 1966 by burning their draft cards. When the affray was over, the crowd dispersed—a crowd no longer existed. The ongoing interaction of a crowd is not durable.

2. *Crowd formation is often spontaneous.* A basketball referee, officiating at a hotly contested game, angered a number of spectators by his decisions. As he left the court after the game, spectators hooted and jeered. Suddenly two men jumped him as he passed down their aisle. According to his statement, made later, some twenty to thirty men thereupon joined the two original aggressors and beat the referee so badly he required hospitalization. The attackers became a hostile crowd, of the mob variety, quite spontaneously.

3. *A crowd represents a casual kind of relationship.* The members, for the most part, are not intimately associated with one another. They come together casually, cease close interaction within a relatively brief time. Probably few, if any, of the men who attacked the basketball referee were intimate acquaintances. Most likely they ceased interaction immediately after the attack.

Figure 13.1
Hostile Mob
World Wide Photos.

4. *A crowd is largely unorganized.* Its objectives may not be deliberately planned. There is no stipulated division of functions among members. Although leadership may develop, there is no hierarchy of authority. There are no formalized rules by which members are to be guided. For the most part, each individual is on a par with every other individual. An example might be a crowd watching a football game. Each spectator is one social unit. There is no division of functions among the spectators. Any rules of behavior for the occasion that are recognized are likely to be informal, according to the folkways rather than according to law. About the only leadership that is likely to develop is in the event one or more persons stimulate others to race onto the field with them to carry off the goal posts.

5. *A crowd is characterized by loose internal controls.* As individuals, the football fans may follow the leader onto the field to remove the goal posts. As individuals, some may refrain from following the leader. Either way, they behave as they do voluntarily. Their behavior is not controlled by authority formally vested in certain members of the crowd. Nevertheless, group pressure, of itself, may be very powerful, despite the absence of formal controls. If you were in a crowd watching a football game and your team's cheerleader directed the crowd to give a certain yell, you might very well comply even if you did not feel like yelling at the particular moment. If you joined with the others in cheering the team, it would, in the given circumstances, be largely because the crowd itself, as a group, informally but definitely exerted pressure on you to conform.

6. *Membership in a crowd invests the individual with some degree of anonymity.* The football fan is one of thousands in the stadium. If he blows a whistle, honks a horn, shouts imprecations at the rival players, behaves as he would not behave at a small dinner party, he is scarcely noticed. His is fairly typical behavior for the setting, and there are many others acting much the same way. No one fan stands out.

AUDIENCES

Like crowds, audiences are found in mass societies, but not exclusively there.

You enter a theater, find every seat taken, people standing in back of the house. "What a crowd!" you say. The sociologist would correct you. This is an *audience*, not a crowd, in sociological analysis. What is the difference between an *audience* and a *crowd*? It is a rather subtle distinction sociologists draw, based mainly on the degree of intercommunication among members. Remember that we defined a crowd as a group of individuals in physical proximity to one another, and *mutually influencing each other to a significant extent*. The audience differs from the crowd in that its members do not usually influence each other to the same extent as do members of a crowd. For instance:

When playwright Arthur Miller was trying out *Death of a Salesman* in Boston prior to bringing it to New York for an official opening, he moved about in the theater, studying faces, listening for comment, laughter, applause. The audience sat in stony silence. There was the merest flutter of applause at the end of each act. Otherwise the audience remained undemonstrative. It did not laugh when it should, show surprise when it should, sorrow when it should. The unhappy playwright was certain he had a flop on his hands.

When the final curtain rang down, Mr. Miller stood in the lobby, intently watching the faces of departing patrons. They showed nothing. He listened for comment about the play. Nothing. But then, in the sea of impassive faces the stricken playwright spotted one man heading for the front exit whose face was streaked with tears. Miller pushed through, identified himself, exclaimed, "Tell me, sir! What did you think of it? Did you like the play?"

" 'Twasn't bad," was the calm reply.*

What Miller mistook for apathy was only the reserve of the "proper Bostonian." The audience enjoyed *Death of a Salesman,* one judges, but it gave little external evidence of this. Each person enjoyed it *to himself*. And therein lies a difference between an *audience* and a *crowd*. Members of a crowd influence each other mutually, to a significant extent. *An audience is a temporary group of individuals exposed to a common stimulus, each reacting to it unilaterally with a minimum of communication among the individuals concerned*. (The mass, you will note by comparing definitions, is a type of audience.) Miller's audience, a group of individuals, watched the same stimulus, *Death of a Salesman*, and did so with very little inter-

* Paraphrase of a conversation between Arthur Miller and the author, 1951.

communication. Each reacted to the drama *individually*. The focus of attention was from individual patron to the stage. "Communication in the audience," says Rose, ". . . tends to be one way rather than mutual. Members . . . may act in *similar* ways because of their common stimulation but they do not act together *cooperatively* because there are no bonds among them."[14]

Another difference between a crowd and an audience is that members of a crowd are in fairly close physical proximity to each other, whereas a hundred, or a million, individuals, separated by great distances, may constitute an audience. All the people watching a television show in their respective homes, throughout the nation or even the world, comprise the audience of that show.

You perhaps wonder why a group of theater patrons is considered an audience while a stadium full of baseball fans is termed a crowd. Although the factor of physical proximity is present in both groups, the baseball fans, much more than the theater patrons, feel a common tie. They are for one team, against another. Even when a Dodger fan sits alongside a Giant fan, there is the common interest in the outcome of the contest. There is also very definite intercommunication between the Dodger and the Giant adherent. The members of the crowd, too, influence each other, regardless of respective loyalties, into demonstrations of how they feel about their favorite team and its adversary. They are vociferous, ebullient, raucous, and sometime rowdy in expressing themselves. The theatergoer, by contrast, normally watches the onstage action with little or no consciousness of his neighbors. He reacts directly to the actors and the action on stage.

Note, however, that an audience may be transformed into a crowd. Suppose a theater is filled with young people come to listen to a singing group, let us say the Beatles, the talented long-haired entertainers from Great Britain. As the performance opens, those young people comprise an audience. But let us further suppose (without stretching the imagination) that with succeeding numbers from the singing-playing group, the young people become increasingly excited. They applaud, then squeal, then shout, and finally they are in the aisles, swaying to the rhythms onstage, moving toward the stage, attempting to reach, to touch the Beatles. Individual members of the audience have influenced each other significantly. They are now intercommunicating. The audience has become a crowd. If all goes reasonably well, it will not become a mob type of crowd.

MASS COMMUNICATION

A phenomenon characteristic of mass society is a system of *mass communication*. This is not to imply that every feature of the mass media we know today originated in contemporary mass society. By 105 A.D., the Chinese had learned to make paper and ink. Well before our own century, invention brought the printing press, the newspaper, telegraph, and telephone. The linotype, radio, and television were invented more recently.

Many people think of mass media as meaning communication for the "masses," the "common man." The concept has no such connotation for the sociologist. It does not refer to communication intended especially for, or understood mainly by, one class of people. The term mass media refers to *those instruments and techniques making possible the simultaneous presentation of identical messages to large numbers of people not in close physical proximity to one another*. Newspapers, magazines, films, radio, television are examples of mass media.

In this context, *mass* means that large numbers of people can receive the communications, although they will not necessarily interpret a message identically. The word *media* refers to the transmission devices or instruments utilized in making communications possible. A *medium* is something between. One medium by which we transmit voice is a radio mechanism that causes it to be heard simultaneously over a network of stations. The transmission media for the written word consists of such instruments as the telegraph, linotype, and the printing press. As transmission media for visual images, we use the camera, photoengraving, and television.

The United States leads the world in use of mass media of communication. In 1963, there were 1,754 daily newspapers in the country, with a paid circulation of 58,905,000.[15] We had 4,851 commercial radio broadcast stations on the air,[16] beaming programs at 180 million owners of receiving sets.[17] A total of 547 commercial television stations[18] broadcast to 61.5 million owners of television receiving sets.[19] Also in 1963, a total of 25,784 different titles were issued by book publishers.[20] Over

1 billion books—1,172,456,000—were sold that year.[21] Average weekly attendance at motion picture theaters in 1962 was 43 million.[22]

An indication of the impact of mass media on our culture is suggested by the speed with which television became an integral part of our daily lives. In California, television sets are essentials, by legal definition. They are on the list of household items deemed so necessary to life that they are exempt from attachment in the event of bankruptcy. In 1954, the master of ceremonies of a television show suggested that each member of his unseen audience send a nickel to a housewife he was interviewing. Two days later her mail was being delivered in sacks. Within two weeks the lady received 140,000 nickels as a result of the casual remark of an entertainer over a mass medium of communication.

Obviously, the process of mass communication involves (1) an audience, (2) a message, and (3) a communicator of the message. Let us consider each.

THE MASS AUDIENCE

In an interesting book on mass communication, Charles R. Wright discusses the nature of the mass-media audience.[23] *It is relatively large.* Wright defines as large ". . . any audience exposed during a short period of time and of such a size that the communicator could not interact with its members on a face-to-face basis."

It is heterogeneous, that is, it consists of persons from a wide variety of social backgrounds. Messages directed toward an exclusive or elite audience are not classifiable as mass communications. An example would be a closed-circuit television program that gets through only to the board of directors of a corporation, seated together in the board room.

Its individual members are anonymous, generally remaining personally unknown to the communicator. This does not signify they are socially isolated, however. Much of mass-communication exposure takes place within the setting of small social groups; and even a physically isolated audience member is likely to discuss the communication with friends and acquaintances, who may modify his reaction to the message. However, the mass communication is aimed at anonymous individuals in that the communicator in effect addresses himself "to whom it may concern," not to John Jones, Susan Smith, or Harry Doheny.

THE MESSAGE

Here again we follow Professor Wright.[24]

The message is public, addressed to anyone who will receive it.

It is rapid. The intention is that the message ". . . reach large audiences within a relatively short time, or even simultaneously—unlike works of fine art, which may be examined at leisure over centuries."

It is transient, usually intended for immediate consumption. The journalist's news story is rushed into print, appears for one day only, and sometimes only in one edition of the newspaper that day.

THE COMMUNICATOR

And what of the communicator? Wright points out[25] that he works through a complex organization, for mass communication is organized communication. Expense and division of labor are involved. Production of a motion picture may cost several million dollars. Expenditures for advertising alone, of cinematic productions by United States companies in 1961, was 100 million dollars.[26] A fifteen-minute network newscast reportedly cost the producers 3,400 dollars.[27]

Division of labor is illustrated by the process of preparing a movie for the market. Of the many activities involved, the following are best known. A producer, writers, directors, and secretaries have respective functions in preparing a script. Cameramen and other technicians shoot the picture. Actors and actresses play it. Musicians commit to sound track the music that a composer has written especially for the production. Film editors cut and tighten the action. Distributors get the cans of film off to movie outlets, as publicity, promotion, and advertising departments go into frenzied action.

RESEARCH ON MASS MEDIA

Research on the uses and influence of mass communication has been extensive, but much of it is inconclusive. We do, however, have some credible information on who relies on what medium to get which type of message.

1. The habit of relying on a given medium of communication remains relatively fixed. When a new communication technique is introduced, this does not significantly decrease use of older media. The advent of television has thus far done little to change our norms for reading books, magazines, and newspapers. Although the total *number* of newspapers has declined somewhat since 1948, due principally to consolidations of competing organs, readership does not seem to have decreased. Magazine readership has increased, while book buying, as differentiated from book reading, has decreased slightly, according to market surveys.

2. Audiences do not care particularly for new experiences via mass media. They prefer repetition and elaboration of earlier, familiar experiences. They want to project themselves into the particular situation, and this is more readily accomplished when they can identify with known features. Witness that: people tend to read only those newspapers that espouse their own political views; they read those sections of newspapers that report on their own political views; they read those sections of newspapers that report on their own hobbies most fully.

Newspaper executives, who formerly considered radio newscasts serious competition, have discovered that their fears were groundless. People hear the news on the air, then buy a paper.

Market research indicates that some persons listen to the news by car radio on the way home from work, settle down after dinner to read the daily newspaper, and catch a favorite television newscast covering the same events they heard on radio or read about in the paper.

3. Women show less interest than men in using mass media for informing themselves on public affairs. In their magazine reading they prefer fiction, while men favor nonfiction. (Convinced of this, the editors of a national magazine some years ago adopted a policy of running short stories of the sort that would appeal to women and not men, and fact articles beamed at men but not at women.)

4. Sex of the audience member plays a part in determining reaction to a communication. Asked to name their favorite movie stars, the majority of men mention actors, while women favor actresses. Men notice pictures of males in printed media

more often than do women, and women are more likely to look at pictures of females.

5. Heavy users of one medium are likely to make use of others as well. The newspaper reader probably also reads magazines, listens to radio, and watches television. Persons who avoid one medium tend to be somewhat resistant to exposure to other media. If an individual rarely reads a book, he may be uninterested in reading magazines and newspapers. He may also have little use for radio or television.

MASS MEDIA & PUBLIC OPINION

In order to discuss public opinion we should first have an understanding of the concept of *public*.

"The public is outraged by this offense against common decency!" cries a police chief.

"The public demands less government and more individual freedom!" asserts a politician.

"My public loves me!" says an actress.

"Public apathy is responsible for our underfinanced schools," avers an educator.

Who, or what, is *the public* in each of the above assertions? In the sociological sense, *a public is a human grouping, or collectivity, whose members take positions on a given issue.* A 1958 Roper poll found the majority of persons in the United States opposed to capital punishment. That majority was not the total public on the subject, although it did take a position —against the death penalty. All those who considered the question and took positions, on either side of the issue, comprised the public on that subject.

Some characteristics of publics are:

1. *There are a great many of them on a great many issues.* Should young people under twenty-one be allowed to vote? Should the People's Republic of China be admitted to the United Nations? Should dry martinis be stirred or shaken in the cocktail shaker? There are publics on these and on an incalculable number of additional subjects.

2. *An individual simultaneously belongs to a number of publics.* You agree with an editorial in your local paper advocating the reelection of the mayor. The same day, you take a stand with others for lower taxes. You are against professional boxing, in favor of pulling out of West Germany, and on the

side of those who argue that stricter controls should be placed on stock market speculation. You vote for John for class president, and you agree with those who urge that overpopulated countries be educated to the use of birth control. All in one day.

3. *Publics are voluntary groups, to be joined or left at the will of the individual concerned.* There is, in fact, no way of making membership compulsory, for one does not "enter" a public physically, but by reflection and by the mental attitude based upon it. Suppose there is debate in your community as to whether the oldest dwelling in town should be preserved as an historical monument or torn down to make way for a modern office building. You consider the pros and cons as you understand them and decide you are in favor of preserving the historic landmark. You may or may not make that conclusion known to others. They may or may not know where you stand on the issue. But you joined the public concerned with that issue, by thinking about it, and by deciding which side of the argument you espoused. Had you taken the opposed stand, you would still be a member of that public.

And having become part of a public on a particular question, you may leave your position on your own volition. Suppose you join with those who believe that the French Impressionist painters are the finest painters. Later you change your mind. Now you agree with people who hold that nonobjective art is the finest expression of the creative spirit. That is your option.

Can you not be forced to take a given side on an issue? Did not Hitler force Germans to hate Jews? No. There was a public on the question: Are Jews to be despised and hated? Some members of that public took one side, some the other. Some were forced into *behavior* suggesting they hated Jews when in fact they did not. The behavior was compulsory, but the mental attitude adopted could be concealed. There is reason to believe that many Germans did not agree with Hitler's policy for the extermination of Jews, even though very few did anything to circumvent that policy.

4. This points to another generalization: *Publics are rarely unanimous in their positions on respective issues.* Is there no question on which there is unanimity or very widespread consensus? Yes. In our culture, murder, incest, and treason are so antagonistic to our values that we may safely assert the public stands practically unanimous against them. But on literally millions of issues, great and small, there is no such con-

sensus. Hence, when the politician says, "The public demands
. . . ," we have a right to inquire, "What segment of it?" When
the actress declares, "My public loves me!" we may properly
ask, "All of it?"

There is widespread belief that mass communication results
in influencing a *public* to such an extent that it creates *public
opinion*. Stating the matter in terms of sociological concepts,
there is the belief that mass communication has the effect of
helping an audience form into a public that holds positions on
a particular issue. These positions, pro, con, and in between
collectively represent *public opinion* on that subject.

*Public opinion consists of the positions taken by members
of a public regarding a given issue.* Assume a city council is
considering a sales tax on cigarettes. It so states, and it calls
public hearings to allow for free discussion of the proposal.
Privately held opinion will develop as the matter is reported in
the mass media. As individuals follow the debate in the media
and discuss the issue among themselves, a public opinion on
the subject will emerge.

Public opinion is not unanimous opinion. The various shades
of opinion, taken together, constitute the public's opinion. If
that opinion should eventually be unanimous or close to it, it
would cease to be public opinion and would become what is
termed *consensus*.

Do the mass media create public opinion? That they transmit
messages to millions of people is clear. But to what extent does
a message create or mold public opinion? This is by no means
clear.

What about newspapers? The first publishers did not seek to
create public opinion. They were simply transmitting gossip.
Newspapers began as newsletters. In seventeenth-century England, country squires paid correspondents to write them letters
once a week, circulating the gossip of court and town. These
handwritten missives later became the printed newspapers we
know.

Although contemporary news organs carry weighty dis-
patches on all subjects, they still contain a fair amount of
gossip, on the assumption that readers also want reports on the
trivia of life. Journalists have learned that a local three-alarm
fire is of greater interest to many readers than the fact that a
foreign power demands the withdrawal of a United States am-
bassador. On November 15, 1944, when we were at war, a

newspaper carried as its banner headline: TWO WOMEN BRUTALLY SLAIN. The secondary front-page story was: PATTON'S TROOPS STORM METZ SUBURBS.

Some journalists assert the modern newspaper creates public opinion, and on subjects more weighty than village gossip. They cite the newspaper-sparked destruction of the Tweed Ring in New York. *The Kansas City Star*'s exposé of election frauds in that city in 1946 was followed by a cleanup. There are other examples in the history of journalism of newspaper crusades followed by what seemed consequential action. Despite such cases, probably a majority of newsmen reject the idea that newspapers create public opinion. They take the position that the fact that action followed an exposé does not establish that it was caused by it, or by it alone. Newspapers, according to persons of this persuasion, do not so much create public opinion as play upon existing stereotypes, thereby supporting, enhancing, or otherwise altering existing opinion. It has been averred that toward the close of the nineteenth century William Randolph Hearst, publisher of a chain of newspapers, wished the United States to fight Spain. He sent word to his news photographer in Cuba that he wanted photographs depicting serious trouble on the island and indicating a war was building up. The photographer assertedly cabled Hearst there was no war spirit or war in Cuba, upon which the press lord cabled back, "You furnish the pictures, I'll furnish the war." If this was Hearst's message, he was laboring under a misapprehension. He could not have delivered a war single-handed. Public opinion for war could not, in the opinion of students of the subject, have been created entirely by newspapers. There must be the mental and emotional readiness first; then a paper might build further upon it.

Apparently, too, newspapers are not as influential as some believe in helping elect political candidates. Two of the worst beatings ever taken by Presidential aspirants were those administered to "Alf" Landon, running against Franklin D. Roosevelt in 1936, and Thomas E. Dewey, competing against Harry S. Truman in 1948. In the respective campaigns the press overwhelmingly favored Landon and Dewey.

Do motion pictures affect public opinion? Probably even less than newspapers, for they are offered as entertainment. The producer is not selling a message but a movie. Far from trying to create a new taste or course of action, he hopes to satisfy existing taste, and the only action he wants is a stampede to the box office. But despite absence of intent, cinema influences the public in certain ways. It affects manufacturing, for example, and fashions in dress and hair style. All three were influenced after Rudolph Valentino became a sensation when he appeared in *The Four Horsemen of the Apocalypse* in 1921. Bell-bottomed trousers similar to those Valentino wore in the picture became a vogue. Men plastered their hair down and made it shiny, like Valentino's. Catering to demand, manufacturers turned out bell-bottomed trousers and hair pomades.

Many feminine motion picture stars have influenced women's fashions and coiffeurs. Not only was Marilyn Monroe's blonde hair style widely copied, but also her way of holding her mouth half open—supposedly it made a girl look sexy.

Motion pictures have shown millions of people how other people behave. From locales such as Monte Carlo to Chicago's gangland, from war stories to plots involving horse racing, cinema has provided visual images of behavior, some true to life, some not. Either way, this undoubtedly has had some effect upon already existing opinion.

Television has affected public opinion in much the same respects as motion pictures. Additionally, the television "commercial" disseminates advertising messages designed to influence viewers' buying habits.

PROPAGANDA & MASS MEDIA

Much of public opinion is fashioned from the give-and-take among members of the society, without any calculated, organized attempt to do so. On the other hand, a good deal of public opinion is the result of deliberate propaganda campaigns. Propagandists launch such campaigns in order to manipulate the attitudes of people. They hope to mobilize existing tendencies to act, and to mobilize them in the direction desired.

The organized attempt to convert a public into acceptance of an idea or course of action may be termed propaganda. Actually, true *conversions* seem rare, if we define the convert, in context, as an individual who does something as a result of propaganda that he had no inclination to do previously. Suppose, after watching a television commercial extolling Smoothy Greasy toothpaste, you go out and buy it for the first time. You are not thereby converted to using toothpaste. You already were preconditioned to want *some* tooth cleanser, because you learned that using it might retard tooth decay. You could have used salt or baking soda for this purpose, quite beneficially. You chose instead to use, let us say, Green Goose toothpaste. Then you switched to Smoothy Greasy. Already converted to toothpaste use, you simply switched brands.

How about the boy who has never smoked? He reads a magazine ad showing a rugged-faced man smoking a handsome pipe. The advertising message describes the alleged pleasures of smoking pipe tobacco. It suggests that all he-men smoke and that girls admire he-men. The boy buys his first pipe. But this is not a matter of conversion. The boy had already been preconditioned to the notion that rugged-faced men are he-men and to the desire to be admired by girls. The advertisement simply played on this preconditioning.

But this line of reasoning can go to extremes. We are not certain, from research findings, that absolutely no conversion ever takes place. There may be few or no conversions as a result of short-range propaganda campaigns, but the long-range effects of incessant, prolonged bombardment may be great. If advertisers did not believe they had some evidence to this effect, they would be less inclined to spend millions on communicating their propaganda messages. We may assume that the doctor shown in Figure 13.2 has some faith in propaganda as an influence for conversion.

Some analysts think of propaganda as a technique for shaping opinion through dishonest means toward an unworthy objective. Others use the term propaganda to refer to *any* attempt to convert others to *any* point of view. By the latter conception, the objective of propaganda may be quite worthy, entirely honorable. When a health department warns the public through mass media that children should be immunized against an epidemic disease, the department is utilizing propaganda methods, in a manner consistent with the second viewpoint.

Many volumes have been written on propaganda techniques. According to the experts, effective propaganda takes into account the following:

1. *Simplicity of language.* Gesture and speech need to be quickly and easily grasped.

2. *Use of "color words."* *Sweat* hits harder than *perspiration,* *stink* harder than *odor.*

Figure 13.2
Propaganda
Drawing by Stevenson;
© 1958 The New Yorker Magazine, Inc.

3. *Use of slogans.* Examples: Suppose Nobody Cared! Uncle Sam Needs YOU!

4. *Use of stereotypes.* When the recipient of propaganda is someone who has accepted a stereotype, he is likely to be receptive to the propaganda if it contains the stereotype. *Shylock* represents a stereotype of a greedy usurer. When Fascist countries wanted to create ill will against the mighty, wealthy United States, their propaganda referred to *Uncle Shylock.*

5. *Distortion.* By emphasizing some features of a situation and ignoring others, the propaganda agent distorts or fails to tell the entire truth, while at the same time seeming to be logical. A liquor ad will show a tall, frosted glass containing a cool Tom Collins. The message may proclaim the gin mixture a great refresher, cooling and relaxing, a drink that can only make one feel fine. It will not mention that the alcohol and sugar in the concoction will raise the drinker's temperature or that alcohol, far from refreshing, fatigues the human organism when intake exceeds a given quantity. In Figure 13.3, the man watching television is reacting against a distortion.

6. *Exaggeration.* Almost any advertisement contains some exaggeration, even if it is no more harmful than the one in the radio commercial for a supermarket; the singing refrain went: "Every day's a special day at _____." If that were so, no day would be special, for they would all be alike.

7. *Falsification.* Distortion and exaggeration alter truth only in part. Propaganda sometimes contains an out-and-out lie,

Figure 13.3
Propaganda
Drawing by P. Barlow; Copr.
© 1957 The New Yorker
Magazine, Inc.

"A quart is a quart, damn it!
How can it be a big, jumbo quart?"

"facts" made up of fiction. Hitler held that the monstrous lie would be accepted ahead of the little one. Its very boldness, he asserted, made it acceptable.

8. *Repetition.* In a radio or TV commercial the name of the product is repeated a number of times. The assumption is that repetition facilitates recall. If you want shoe laces, what brand do you ask for? Probably none. Why? You cannot remember the name of any. Why not? Shoe laces are not advertised by trade name. You have not heard the name over and over. What about toothpaste? You ask for it by name, because you have become familiar with it.

ADVERTISING AS PROPAGANDA · In long range terms, advertising probably disseminates more effective propaganda through mass media than any other enterprise. It is, therefore, worth study.

Advertising could not sell people the idea they should wear clothes if the mores were against it. But where people have been culturally conditioned to wear clothes, advertising can influence them into buying *certain* articles of apparel. In the nineteenth century no amount of advertising would convince a "respectable" American lady that she should appear in public dressed in slacks. Today she will wear them, as well as shorts, pedal pushers, or "stretch" pants, because they are acceptable, and advertising suggested their particular form. Advertising does not change people's characteristics, but it can give a characteristic a changed direction. When it does this, advertising depends in some measure on the power of suggestion. Figure 13.4 offers interpretation of this situation.

Some 200 years ago, Samuel Johnson pontificated: "The trade of advertising is now so near to perfection that it is not easy to propose any improvement." There have been many "improvements" since Johnson made this statement. Today, advertising uses the bludgeon approach and the subtler snob appeal. It bombards "prospects" in newspapers and magazines; on billboards; over radio, television, telephone, and telegraph. Planes puff out smoke messages urging people to buy borax or drink soda pop. Manufacturers spend millions to discover what "message" will encourage "impulse buying." Within the limits already suggested, advertising has changed the eating, drinking, smoking, playing, sleeping, dressing, love-making, and even burial habits of man. Much of this has been accomplished by propaganda based on emotional rather than on intellectual appeals. A direct quotation from the recorded deliberations of advertising men at a convention reads: "Appeal to reason in your advertising, and you appeal to about 4 per cent of the human race."[28] Nevertheless, even the most emotional appeal needs to be gaited to existing conditions and stereotypes in order to be effective.

WHO'S BOSS? · Students of propaganda investigate answers to a question that you might ask yourself: Who makes up your mind? You, or media of mass communication? Are you in charge of them or are they in charge of you? We have already suggested that the media's influence upon us is based in part upon our receptivity. This, in turn, depends on social conditions. There is a give-and-take involved. But you can help decide who is boss. You help create the need of and place for mass communication. Intelligent selection and analysis of messages received will determine to what extent you want to be guided by those messages, to what extent you will listen further and seek more data.

FADS & FASHION

Brief mention needs to be made of fads and fashion, phenomena characteristic of mass society. We discuss them jointly since fads are special cases of fashion.

Figure 13.4
Propaganda
Courtesy *True,*
The Man's Magazine

*"Now, podners, in case Mom isn't serving
Friskies for dinner tonight, let me
briefly explain to you just
what a hunger strike is . . ."*

FADS

A fad is a cultural pattern that appears suddenly and disappears as suddenly. Years ago, flagpole sitting was a fad. More recently it was a fad among college boys to see how many could be packed into a telephone booth. Possibly—and from the viewpoint of most older persons, hopefully—the current use of hallucinatory drugs by many young people is a fad.

In 1964, a curious fad arose in Italy. Individuals competed to see who could stay awake longest. A house painter in Modena claimed the record after 273.5 hours without sleep, thereby exceeding the record set by another Italian, 272 hours. The record smasher was quoted as saying: "I could stay awake a lot longer but I'm happy just to beat the record and show it's not so hard after all."[29]

Some fads become all-engrossing to the faddist, occupying much of his time and thoughts. In such cases we call them crazes. Land speculation sometime reaches craze dimensions. Pre-1929 stock market gambling reached proportions amounting to a craze; shoeblacks, housewives, and soda clerks joined financiers and corporation executives, investing in stocks that presumably were bound to increase in value steadily.

Kingsley Davis says fads and crazes are distinguished by ". . . the quickness with which they alternate, the utter superficiality of their content, and the irrationality and intensity of the temporary fascination for them."[30] How else might one describe the Davy Crockett craze among youngsters, following the showing of a movie about that frontiersman? Manufacturers could hardly keep up with the demand for frontier clothing and other paraphernalia. Small fry throughout the country sported costumes similar to that shown in Figure 13.5.

No satisfactory theory has been advanced to explain why fads and crazes "catch on." However, they usually must have at least one characteristic in order to capture popular imagination. A fad must be appropriate to its time. People would not be receptive if it completely violated their sense of propriety. The frug and certain other recent dance forms, which would have been shocking a few years ago, have become fads. But in the same period, attempts to popularize "mate swapping" have made little headway.

We said that *usually* a fad must be appropriate to its time if it is to "catch on." There have been apparent exceptions, the current "hippie" culture being one. It represents an extreme break with "middle-class" proprieties. However, it may not be as inappropriate to its time as it would seem upon casual consideration. The "Beats" preceded the hippies, and to some extent established a cultural climate favorable to hippies. Furthermore, both Beat and hippie behavior became fads in a period of great social unrest, which involved criticism of middle-class values among other things. Perhaps, as a contemporary "protest song" puts it, "the times they are a'changing," and hippie culture is closer to its time than many people believe.

FASHION

Fashion is a cultural pattern that endures for a short time. It has to do with styles of clothing, architecture, automobile designs, many other items in a culture. Like a fad, a fashion is widely accepted in a given society at a given time. But although continuous change is commonplace in the realm of fashion, it occurs more gradually than in the case of fads. A fad might be originated by anyone. Fashion innovations seem most likely to become popular if introduced by a person of prestige. When some highly prestigious female member of "society" appears in a new style of dress, other females are more likely to adopt her style than the style of an "unknown"

Figure 13.5
Fad
Ralph Morse,
Life Magazine © Time Inc.

person. When the former King of England, Edward Windsor, was still the Prince of Wales, he tied his cravat in a special way. It came to be called a Windsor knot, and a great many men use it even today. When General Dwight D. Eisenhower wore a uniform jacket especially designed for him, the Eisenhower jacket became popular in civilian life as well.

Fashions in other fields also "catch on" more readily if innovated by a person or a group of high prestige. Private dwellings and office buildings follow fashion trends. After Hollywood entertainers received publicity for their swimming pools, householders in various sections of the country installed their own pools.

But fashions in the United States may have their origin in

less prestigious groups, such as the working class. Dungarees, "work shirts," various kinds of jackets, and certain types of shoes were first worn by working people, after which a segment of the middle class (usually younger people) approved, and these items of wear became fashionable throughout the nation.

Extensive historical studies indicate that fashions do not follow predictable patterns, except in fluctuating. The evidence does not permit us to say whether women will wear their skirts shorter next year than this; about all we can safely predict is that they will continue to wear skirts.

Since this has been a lengthy chapter, we recapitulate: In mass society, as differentiated from nonmass society, the individual is relatively anonymous and psychologically isolated. Existing relationships are comparatively impersonal. Other conditions closely associated with mass society are functional interdependence, accelerated social change, exclusion of the mass from meaningful participation in certain aspects of culture, and vulnerability to mass politics. Mass media are largely phenomena of mass society and, among other things, are used to promote political ends, to create public opinion, and to propagandize.

We also discussed crowds, audiences, and fads and fashion, which are to be found in mass society although they are not restricted to it.

· NOTES

1. Herbert Blumer, "The Mass, the Public, and Public Opinion," in Alfred McClung Lee (ed.), *New Outline of the Principles of Sociology* (New York: Barnes & Noble, 1946), pp. 185–193.
2. Arnold M. Rose, *Sociology, the Study of Human Relations* (New York: Knopf, 1956), pp. 285–286.
3. *Ibid.*, p. 292.
4. William Kornhauser, *The Politics of Mass Society* (New York: Free Press, 1959), p. 227.
5. Joseph R. Gusfield, "Mass Societies and Extremist Politics," *American Sociological Review*, XXVII (February 1962), 19–30.
6. Kornhauser, *op. cit.*, pp. 36–37.
7. *Ibid.*, p. 41.
8. Gusfield, *op. cit.*
9. Rose, *op. cit.*, p. 268.
10. *Ibid.*, pp. 268–269.
11. *Ibid.*, pp. 273–274.

12. *Time*, LXXXVII, 12 (March 25, 1966), 19. Courtesy *Time;* © Time Inc., 1966.
13. Arthur Raper, *The Tragedy of Lynching* (Chapel Hill: University of North Carolina Press, 1933).
14. Rose, *op. cit.*, p. 280.
15. U. S. Bureau of the Census, *Statistical Abstract of the United States, 1964*, 85th annual ed. (Washington, D. C.: U. S. Government Printing Office, 1964), p. 523, Table No. 717.
16. *Ibid.*, p. 519, Table No. 710.
17. *The World Almanac, 1965* (New York: Newspaper Enterprise Assn., 1965), p. 768.
18. U. S. Bureau of the Census, *op. cit.*, p. 519, Table No. 710.
19. *The World Alamanac, 1965*, *op. cit.*, p. 768.
20. U. S. Bureau of the Census, *op. cit.*, p. 525, Table No. 719.
21. U. S. Bureau of the Census, *Statistical Abstract of the United States, 1966*, 87th annual ed. (Washington, D. C.: U. S. Government Printing Office, 1966), p. 524, Table No. 748.
22. U. S. Bureau of the Census, *Historical Statistics of the United States, Colonial Times to 1957, Continuation to 1962 and Revisions* (Washington, D. C.: U. S. Government Printing Office, 1965), p. 35, Table No. 1.
23. Charles R. Wright, *Mass Communication, A Sociological Perspective* (New York: Random House, 1964), pp. 13–14.
24. *Ibid.*, p. 14.
25. *Ibid.*, pp. 15–16.
26. U. S. Bureau of the Census, *Statistical Abstract, 1964*, *op. cit.*, p. 847, Table No. 1205.
27. *Variety*, November 12, 1952, cited in *Television, A World Survey* (Paris: United Nations Educational, Scientific and Cultural Organization, 1953), p. 68.
28. E. S. Turner, *The Shocking History of Advertising!* (New York: Dutton, 1953), p. 214.
29. Long Beach (California) *Press-Telegram*, February 5, 1964, p. A-12.
30. Kingsley Davis, *Human Society* (New York: Macmillan, 1949), p. 79.

· SUGGESTIONS FOR FURTHER READING

BERELSON, BERNARD, and GARY A. STEINER. *Human Behavior, An Inventory of Scientific Findings.* New York: Harcourt, Brace & World, 1964, Chapter 13, "Mass Communication."
A summary of research findings regarding mass communication.
CANTRIL, HADLEY. *The Psychology of Social Movements.* New York: Wiley, 1941, Chapter 4, "The Lynching Mob."
A graphic description of two lynchings.
DOOB, LEONARD W. "Goebbels' Principles of Propaganda." *Public Opinion Quarterly*, XIV (Fall 1950), 419–442.
Goebbels' principles of political propaganda, as deduced from the Nazi minister's war diaries, are discussed. Very enlightening on

the use of a propaganda machine to manipulate public opinion for political purposes.

GUNTHER, JOHN. *Taken at the Flood.* New York: Harper & Row, 1960.

A journalist reviews the career of Albert D. Lasker, creator of modern advertising.

JACOBS, NORMAN (ed.). *Culture for the Millions? Mass Media in Modern Society.* Boston: Beacon Press, 1964.

A collection of articles on mass culture in mass society, with some emphasis on the function of the mass media. Easy, pleasurable reading.

LANG, KURT, and GLADYS ENGEL LANG. *Collective Dynamics.* New York: Thomas Y. Crowell, 1961.

Of particular interest are the chapters dealing with crowd behavior, fashions, and public opinion.

LONG, HUEY P. *Every Man a King.* Chicago: Quadrangle Books, 1964.

This autobiography of Huey P. Long was originally published in 1933, when "The Kingfish" was a well-known, demagogic politician who held wide appeal for the masses.

LAZARSFIELD, PAUL F., BERNARD BERELSON, and HAZEL GAUDET. *The People's Choice.* New York: Duell, Sloan and Pearce, 1949.

A very enlightening study of the effects of political propaganda on people.

MEYERSOHN, ROLF, and ELIHU KATZ. "Notes on the Natural History of Fads." *American Journal of Sociology,* LXII (May 1957), 594–601.

A well written and interesting analysis of the origin and function of fads and fashions.

WERTHAM, FREDERIC. *Seduction of the Innocent.* New York: Holt, Rinehart and Winston, 1954.

A psychiatrist's own opinions about the influence of comic books on the behavior of young people.

WRIGHT, CHARLES R. *Mass Communication, A Sociological Perspective.* New York: Random House, 1964.

A sociological analysis of the manifest and latent functions of mass communication.

14 SOCIAL ROLES & STATUSES

In all human groupings, individuals are assigned social roles and statuses. We discuss group life from this perspective in the present chapter. What are social roles? What is status, from the sociological point of view?

Assume you are seeking a career and that all those listed below are equally available to you. Which would be your first choice? Your second? Select five choices in order of preference.

Physician	Blacksmith	Lawyer
Derelict	Nuclear physicist	United States Supreme Court Justice
Chemist	Police detective	Diplomat
Dentist	County judge	Governor of a state
Member of a United States President's Cabinet	Senator	Director of a large corporation
College professor	Scientist	Social worker
Airline pilot	Psychologist	Street vendor
Farm worker	Minister	Mayor of a large city
Civil engineer	Priest	Biologist
Banker	Coal miner	Department head in state government

Now pick the one occupation you would least want to make your career.

How did you arrive at your choices? Upon reflection you will probably conclude that a number of factors influenced you. Important, surely, was the income you would derive from a given occupation. You also no doubt considered whether you would find the work interesting. Perhaps your primary consideration was not income or the degree of interest you have in the work, but the prestige you would gain as a member of certain occupational groups. In effect, all these considerations had to do with your *position in society* should you select a given career. All of us are very much concerned with gaining a satisfying social position in life, and by "social position" we do not necessarily mean a niche in "high society."

The drive for social position exists among all peoples, everywhere. And occupation is but one of many factors determining what that position will be. Each person wants to be considered of some importance, some worth, as these qualities are defined in the particular society. Probably, in making your selections from the list, you followed pretty closely the conceptions in our society concerning what is a high- or a low-ranking career. Each society and subsociety has its own system of classification, varying to some extent from that of other societies and subsocieties, despite which there is surprising agreement among certain modern nations as to the ranking of occupational pursuits. Alex Inkeles and Peter H. Rossi[1] reported on the correlations between prestige scores (ranks) given to comparable occupations in six national studies. Some of the results are shown in Table 14.1. The authors concluded that they reveal "an extremely high level of agreement, going far beyond chance expectancy, as to the relative prestige of a wide range of specific occupations, despite the variety of sociocultural settings in which they are found."[2]

Let us return to your own choices. How closely do they agree with those of other people in the United States who established the ranking shown in Table 14.2, which is based on a study by the National Opinion Research Center of the University of Chicago?[3] Most, but not all of the occupations given above are listed in Table 14.2. Note that the 1963 ranking is different from the 1947 ranking. Obviously, our estimation of where a given occupation belongs in the ranking system is subject to change from time to time. Also to be noted is that a category is not always discrete (separate and distinct from all the others). A judge is also a lawyer. A nuclear physicist is also a scientist. It is therefore something of a problem to establish categories, then rank them.

But despite some ambiguities, *position in society* becomes fairly well established in the minds of its members. We all have certain roles to perform, and these play an essential part in establishing our social position.

TABLE 14.1 · *Correlations between Prestige Scores (or Ranks) Given to Comparable Occupations in Six National Studies**

	U.S.S.R.	Japan	Great Britain	New Zealand	United States	Germany
U.S.S.R.		.74	.83	.83	.90	.90
Japan			.92	.91	.93	.93
Great Britain				.97	.94	.97
New Zealand					.97	.96
United States						.96
Average correlations	.84	.89	.93	.93	.94	.94

* A *correlation* shows the degree of closeness of relationship or association between one variable and another. It is expressed above in terms of *coefficient of correlation,* a numerical index that represents this relationship or association. Thus, the correlation coefficient of the rankings in the U.S.S.R. and Japanese studies is .74. Correlation coefficients vary from .00 to 1.00. All of the correlations shown above are direct, or positive—that is, one variable tends to increase whenever the other increases. When the U.S.S.R. ranking of a given occupation is relatively high, the same is true of the Japanese ranking. A direct, or positive, correlation of 1.0 is "perfect." All of the correlations in the table are high, in a positive direction, although none is "perfect."

SOCIAL ROLES

To understand how we achieve status, or position, in society, we must comprehend the meaning and nature of social roles. *A social role consists of behavior an individual has learned to enact in responding to the expectations of particular groups in specific social situations.*

Why does a waiter give the restaurant check to the man and not the woman when a couple dine together? Because he normally expects the man to pay. Why do you ask your instructor to explain something he has not stated clearly enough for you? Because the instructor expects students to raise questions

TABLE 14.2 · *How Americans Rate the Prestige of Occupations, 1947 and 1963*

Occupation	1963	1947
U. S. Supreme Court Justice	1	1
Physician	2	2
Nuclear physicist	3	18
Scientist	3	7
State governor	5	2
Government scientist	5	10
Cabinet member	7	4
U. S. Congressman	7	7
College professor	7	7
Chemist	10	18
Lawyer	10	18
Diplomat	10	4
Dentist	13	18
Architect	13	18
County judge	13	13
Psychologist	16	28
Director, large corporation	16	18
Mayor, large city	16	6
Minister	16	13
Department head, state government	20	13
Airline pilot	20	24
Priest	20	18
Civil engineer	20	23
Banker	24	10
Biologist	24	28

under those circumstances and you, a student, expect the instructor to answer your questions.

A social role, it will be observed, is a culturally defined pattern of behavior. Every social situation in which human beings are involved is characterized by mutual expectations of the participants with respect to the appropriate response to the situation. These expectations are derived largely from what we have come to regard as the "proper," "normal," "right" ways of behaving in particular circumstances. Having learned these *norms of behavior,* we employ them in enacting social roles.

In *As You Like It*, Shakespeare has one of his characters say:

> All the world's a stage,
> And all the men and women merely players;
> They have their exits and their entrances;
> And one man in his time plays many parts.

The sociologist puts it in more prosaic language: *Each individual in a society enacts many roles.* In a single day you perform many roles. If you reside with your parents, you respond to them as a son or daughter. You behave toward a brother or sister pretty much as would be expected. On campus, you enact the role of male or female, of a student, of a casual acquaintance to certain individuals, of a close friend to certain others. In the cafeteria you perform the role of a consumer. On your way home you execute the role of a motorist, a bus passenger, or perhaps a pedestrian. If you go on a date tonight, you will enact the part expected in those circumstances. Over the years you will have enacted roles expected of an individual of a given age, sex, family background, occupaton, religion, city, state, nation, and political affiliation —not to mention many other classifications.

You will already have observed that *some social roles are shared by a great many people.* There are many adults, citizens, voters, outdoor men, executives, ministers, authors, and so on.

Some roles can be enacted by only one given individual or by comparatively few individuals at a particular time in a particular place. There is only one President of the United States at a time. There are relatively few persons performing the role of governor of a state, of Justice of the United States Supreme Court, or of conductor of a symphony orchestra.

Some social roles may be assumed voluntarily. The individual may enact certain roles or not, as he pleases. He may decide to compete in a bowling tournament or not. He may affiliate as a member of the Republican party or not. He may elect to be a city dweller or a suburbanite.

The assumption of certain roles is largely involuntary. The enactment of such roles cannot readily be held in abeyance, and the roles are to be enacted continuously. Very early in one's life the sex role must begin to be enacted, a female acting as a female is expected to behave, and a male as a male.

Age is a rough determinant of role performance, too. A child who cries for candy is behaving as children may be expected to behave, but an adult is not expected to stamp his feet, burst into tears, and scream that he will not get up and get dressed in the morning unless his wife first serves him coffee in bed. We expect the adult to "act his age."

Actually, it is unrealistic to hold that the enactment of *every* particular role is either compulsory or voluntary. Some do fall in one category or the other, but expectation regarding other role enactments lies along a continuum. Observe people at a formal church wedding, then at the gala party that follows. During the religious ceremony each participant punctiliously follows the culturally acceptable and relatively rigid pattern of behavior expected. At the party, the guests have much greater freedom of expression. Some will be sedate, others gay, still others perhaps rowdy.

We definitely expect a husband and father to support his dependents; within reason, we expect him to behave in certain other ways as a responsible husband and father; but sometimes, depending upon the circumstances, we place no sanction against him if he does not cohabit with his wife or is aloof with his children.

By and large, however, we take for granted that members of our society will conform to behavior norms for a given role, allowing for some leeway on the continuum. When an individual deviates too sharply or enacts the "wrong" role, this is generally called to his attention with some emphasis. What would happen if you blew a bugle in the school library? Someone would "put you in your place." The cartoon, Figure 14.1, provides an example of a boy enacting the "wrong" role. He has incorrectly defined the social situation. It would be appropriate for an adult to ask for "a small beer," but such behavior is unacceptable in a youngster.

REFERENCE GROUPS

How do we estimate whether we are performing our roles successfully? We compare our own role performances with those of other people, using these judgments as logical yardsticks to measure and explain our achievements and lack of achievement. The people with whom we compare or contrast ourselves in measuring our own success and failure are called reference groups. A reference group, which is actually a category of people and not necessarily a group, provides a behavioral frame of reference or a system of standards within which an individual can measure his own accomplishments.

An individual who has undertaken a legal career, for example, is apt to measure his success or failure by comparing his accomplishments with those of other attorneys. To the

Figure 14.1
"Wrong" Role
Drawing by Whitney Darrow, Jr.;
© 1958 The New Yorker Magazine, Inc.

"No, your father hasn't come in yet, and, no, you can't have a small beer while you're waiting."

extent that they measure achievement in terms of income, he will probably use the same criterion in judging his own success. If they think a lawyer earning 15,000 dollars a year after ten years of practice is a failure, and he earns less than that ten years after admission to the bar, chances are he will feel he has failed. But a college professor with a decade of teaching behind him, earning 15,000 dollars annually, might feel he has achieved economic success. Each of these comparative judgments would be based upon comparison with reference groups.

Here are some other examples of people utilizing reference groups to determine how they are performing in their own roles:

Mrs. Tally complains she seldom goes out, while her neighbor went to two shows last week.

Mr. Hawkins is unhappy when two Johnny-come-latelies at the firm are promoted over his head to positions he thinks he is better qualified to hold. He feels he has been most unfairly treated and that his services are not appreciated.

Studies conducted during World War II showed that soldiers serving overseas felt that fate and classification officers had been unjust. They were inclined to contrast their situation with that of friends in the states who, they imagined, were relaxing in comfortable USO lounges and dating "the girls we left behind."

The evangelist says, "I saved more souls than any other evangelist in this country."

Individuals have considerable choice in the reference groups they select against which to measure their own accomplishments. A lawyer may feel he has had little financial success when compared with other attorneys, but he may logically preserve self-esteem by shifting to another reference group, saying, "I put principle above wealth. I take only cases I believe in, even if they don't yield handsome fees." Or he might tell himself, "After all, I may not be worth millions, but I am a professional man, and most of the fellows I went to elementary school with are laborers." Reference groups, then, may be used flexibly. Generally, people choose the one that satisfies the purpose in the particular situation.

ROLE COMPLEX

The entire array of an individual's social roles may be considered his role complex. He is, let us say, a male, adult, single, a son, a soldier, a painter, a member of a wealthy family, a Presbyterian, a political liberal. All of his social roles combined constitute his role complex.

It goes without saying that an individual does not play all of his roles simultaneously. That is neither possible nor desirable. He is expected to enact only those roles appropriate to the particular situation. A soldier home on leave enacts the role of a son or a husband and father, as the case may be. He is not expected to perform the role of a fighting man, at least not to the extent of fighting. Attending a baseball game, the son holds in abeyance his role as a soldier. In church he worships according to his religion and does not enact the role either of a soldier or of a sports spectator.

An individual's role complex changes in some respects as he progresses from one stage of life to another. New roles are added to the complex, old ones discarded. The infant's ways of behaving are gradually replaced by those of the child, then the adolescent, then the adult. The role of single person is given up when the individual marries. The unskilled laborer may become a skilled technician.

Social roles function to standardize behavior. The individual becomes habituated to the requirements of a social role and acts accordingly. On the battlefield the soldier behaves in accordance with his role. In the classroom, the instructor acts as he has learned instructors are supposed to act. A judge on the bench enacts the role expected of a jurist appearing in public. In Figure 14.2, Worthal, a student and fraternity man, is informed he is expected to conform to standards of behavior set by the fraternity regarding the kind of vehicle that members may drive.

ROLES & PERSONALITY FORMATION

The positions people occupy in society (status) and the corresponding roles they enact have far-reaching consequences with regard to the development of individual personality. Recognition of the roles he is to perform leads an individual to perception of his *identity*. He is a boy, a man, a violinist, a scholar, a seaman. She is a girl, a daughter, a tennis champion, a fiancée. When we reach the point where we perceive our identity, which is based upon our role complex, we gain a *self-concept*. "I am such and such a person."

Our roles place demands upon us with regard to attitudes we are expected to assume and behavior we "ought" to enact. We want to fulfill these demands, and in attempting to do so we develop a disposition to behave in certain ways. This constitutes our personality.

What are bureaucrats' personalities like? They vary from individual to individual, of course, but the roles that bureaucrats play make an imprint on their tendency to behave. Here is Robert K. Merton's description:

The official is tacitly expected to and largely does adapt his thoughts, feelings and actions to the prospect of this career. But *these very devices* which increase the probability of conformance also lead to an over-concern with strict adherence to regulations which induces timidity, conservatism, and technicism.[4]

Here is another example of self-concept and personality related to social role. A man bearing the improbable name of George Washington Plunkitt was a Tammany district leader in the years when that New York political organization was

Figure 14.2
Standardization Demanded

Reprinted with permission from
Richard Bibler, *Little Man on
Campus*, Stanford, Calif:
Stanford University Press.

*"Sorry, Worthal, but our fraternity makes
certain requirements of its pledges."*

very powerful and very corrupt. A man of meager education
and personal attainments, Plunkitt died in 1924, at the age of
82, possessed of very considerable wealth, which was of du-
bitable origin. William L. Riordan, of the *New York Evening
Post*, interviewed him at length and published the Tammany-
ite's commentary in a volume titled *Plunkitt of Tammany
Hall*.[5] Discoursing on graft, the Tammany leader said:

Everybody is talkin' these days about Tammany men growin'
rich on graft, but nobody thinks of drawin' the distinction between
honest graft and dishonest graft. There's all the difference in the
world between the two. . . . I've made a big fortune out of the game
. . . but I've not gone in for dishonest graft—blackmailin' gamblers,
saloonkeepers, disorderly people, etc. . . .

Just let me explain. . . . My party's in power . . . and it's goin' to
undertake a lot of public improvements. Well, I'm tipped off, say,
that they're going to lay out a new park at a certain place.

I . . . buy up all the land I can in the neighborhood. Then the
board of this or that makes its plan public, and there is a rush to
get my land, which nobody cared particular for before.

Ain't it perfectly honest to charge a good price and make a profit
on my investment and foresight? Of course it is. Well, that's honest
graft.

I . . . don't own a dishonest dollar. If my worst enemy was given the job of writin' my epitaph when I'm gone, he couldn't do more than write:

"George W. Plunkitt. He Seen His Opportunities, and He Took 'Em."[6]

CONTRADICTORY & CONFLICTING ROLES

How would you respond to the following?

1. You are a cashier in the school cafeteria. Your best friend comes through the line with a tray of food priced at 97 cents. She murmurs, "I've only got 70 cents. Can't you charge me just that much?" What would you probably do, in view of your dual roles? On the one hand you are a cashier, who should collect the full amount owed. On the other, you are a good friend of the girl who has only 70 cents. Would you charge the full price? Or ring up a lesser amount, to help your friend?

2. Backing out of a parking space on campus you accidentally scrape the fender of the vehicle next to yours. No one has seen you. Your car insurance will not cover the damage, and you know your parents cannot easily afford to pay for the repairs. What would you probably do, in view of your role as a responsible, law-abiding individual and your role as a person who has deep affection for his parents? Leave a note on the damaged car, giving your name and address? Drive off without doing so?

3. You are president of an organization combating prejudice and discrimination against ethnic minorities. An ugly incident occurs. Your organization, along with others, calls a protest meeting to demonstrate against such practices. You are to be an important participant, essential to the success of the meeting. However, the date and hours set for the meeting are the same as those for commencement exercises, and you are due to receive your diploma. You love your parents but you are also deeply committed to the cause of fighting prejudice and discrimination. You are expected to enact separate, conflicting roles. What would you probably do? Please your parents and attend the graduation ceremony? Enact the role of president of your organization, passing up the commencement and attending the protest meeting instead?

In each of these instances you must choose between contradictory roles. Whatever your decision, you are involved in role conflict.

Individuals are frequently expected to enact roles that, at a given time, are incompatible with each other. The conflicting demands cannot be fully fulfilled.

The housewife in Figure 14.3 illustrates this. When her husband unexpectedly brings the boss home for dinner, she plays the role of amiable hostess as they come in, but when the employer's back is turned, she becomes the persecuted wife, glares and gestures hostilely at her inconsiderate spouse.

SOURCES OF ROLE CONFLICT

What are the sources of role conflict? We have already suggested some, inferentially, but let us consider the matter more systematically. Role strain may be a consequence of:

1. *Incompatibility between or among roles* that are required in the culture of the same individual. Mirra Komarovsky, an American sociologist, collected some interesting data concerning incompatible sex roles imposed in our society upon college women.[7] They are expected to play a "feminine" role, manifesting certain attitudes toward men, family, work, love. It is anticipated they will not be as dominant or aggressive as their male counterparts. They should be more emotional, sympathetic.

But a second, more recent role assigned the young college woman is in a sense not a sex role at all, according to Komarovsky, ". . . because it partly obliterates the differentiation in sex. It demands of the women much the same virtues, patterns of behavior, and attitude that it does of the men of a corresponding age." Komarovsky refers to this as the "modern" role.

The conflict between the "feminine" and the "modern" roles centers around academic achievement, social life, vocational plans, excellence in specific fields of endeavor. The young woman is to be feminine and not as aggressive as men. And she is also expected to pursue scholarship and a professional career, as do men.

The incompatibility of roles is reflected in the diverse goals set for the college girls by their families. Twenty-six percent of Komarovsky's study group complained that their families failed to confront them with clear-cut, consistent goals. One girl said that her uncle telephones every Sunday morning,

Figure 14.3
Conflicting Roles
Salo Roth,
The Saturday Evening Post.

inquires: "Did you go out last night?" He would consider her a "grind" if she stayed home Saturday night to finish a term paper. Yet her father expects her to get an A in every subject. Another respondent asserted that one of her two brothers told her, "Cover up that high forehead and act a little dumb once in a while." The other constantly urged upon her the importance of rigorous scholarship.

Forty percent of the students told Komarovsky they occasionally "played dumb" on dates, concealing some academic honor, pretending ignorance on a subject, or allowing the man the last word in intellectual discussions. Some girls "threw games," played down skills. Thus they were being "feminine," less "dominant" than the male sex. At the same time, Komarovsky comments, ". . . in other areas of life, social pressures were being exerted upon these women to 'play to win,' to compete to the utmost of their abilities for intellectual distinction and academic honors."

Criticizing Komarovsky, other sociologists point out that she used a biased sample for her study, consisting as it did of Barnard College girls, who are probably not representative of the total college girl population in the United States. However, it seems a fact that at least to some degree incompatible sex roles are imposed in our society upon female college students.

2. *Distaste for roles that are uncongenial with the individual's personality.* The late President John F. Kennedy, although in general relishing his role as a politician, had a definite distaste for kissing babies while electioneering. Some college professors prefer to teach and not write scholarly papers, others to write scholarly papers and not teach, yet to some extent both roles are expected of them.

3. *Ambiguity within the society concerning the require-*

ments of a given role. As an extension of Mirra Komarovsky's inquiry, let us ask: Should a young woman be a "homemaker" or follow a career outside her home? Up to about the turn of the century there was some consensus on the subject. Except where dire necessity precluded it, a woman's place was in the home and not in an office, factory, or shop. In our continuously changing culture, however, it is not clear whether there *is* a consensus. In 1890, of females fourteen years of age or older in the United States, 18.3 percent were in the labor force. By 1965, there were 37.5 percent working outside the home.[8] But there are still men and women who hold to the earlier notion that women's place is at her hearthside, while others insist there need be no incompatibility between being a wife and mother and at the same time following a career.

Is an adolescent youth a boy or a man? We are not entirely certain. We say he is a man and often treat him as a child. He likes being considered a man but sometimes prefers to be comforted by his parents as if he were a youngster. He is an adult when we send him to war and a minor on election day. He is mature enough to marry at sixteen or eighteen but not old enough to open his own charge account. In most states he is mature enough to have a license and drive a car several years before we deem him sufficiently "grown up" to decide for himself whether he shall buy a can of beer or a bottle of whiskey.

Faced by ambiguities such as these, can the adolescent fail to be somewhat confused as to the roles he is expected to enact? And are not adults likewise confused on this score?

Preliterate peoples make the transition from adolescence to adulthood easier and less ambiguous through the medium of puberty rites, which initiate youths into manhood. The rites may test the boy's endurance, cause him physical pain, but when they are completed he is no longer a youth. He has become a man, with all of the duties and privileges of that role.

Another kind of role ambiguity is revealed in Figure 14.4. The father understands his role, vis-à-vis his son, to involve one thing. His son has a different conception. Both conceptions are accepted to greater or less degree in our society.

4. *Conflicting role obligations resulting from occupancy by one individual of two or more social positions.* A very extreme but convincing illustration of role conflict is that of a type of man who in effect lives two separate lives. Most of those with

Figure 14.4
Role Ambiguity
Reprinted by permission of Henry
R. Martin and *Saturday Review*.

*"Gee, Dad, what I want is a father,
not another pal."*

whom he works and otherwise associates know him as a respectable, responsible citizen, husband, and father. These people—including even his immediate family—are unaware of his "other life," unaware that secretly but frequently he enacts the role of a male homosexual. He holds two positions in society. A journalist, William J. Helmer, has portrayed very graphically the dilemma of what he calls the respectable "middle-class homosexual":

The homosexual's position in society is often precarious. Discovery can cost him his reputation and perhaps his career. . . . He feels society hates him, and unjustly. Frequently he is guilt-ridden, aware or not, and lacks the self-acceptance he needs in order to live comfortably with his condition.[9]

5. *Discontinuity of role.* A person may move from one role to another during his lifetime. He may not have had an opportunity fully to learn the requirements of the newly assumed role. For a time, role strain results. Often it is not easy for the young, newly wed individual to understand the norms of behavior for a husband or wife. A prizefighter gives up ring competition and becomes a business executive. He may discover, after painful experience, that he has yet to learn the differences in language, etiquette, and ethics between one line of work and the other.

CONSEQUENCES OF ROLE CONFLICT

What are the consequences of role conflict? There is insufficient scientific evidence on this subject, although enough exists to give a basis for reasonable inferences.

The most important consideration is whether or not the role conflict has been internalized by the individual. If not, if he is unaware of role inconsistency or, being aware, is not disturbed by it, he does not feel role strain. Take a mother who considers it her duty to help her son "grow up" but who finds no inconsistency between this objective and her overprotective attitude, which actually retards his maturation. If she fails to comprehend this, she will not suffer role strain. If she is told she is enacting incompatible roles, understands this to be so, but still is not disturbed, again she will not suffer from role strain.

But suppose role conflict is internalized. Some consequences may be:

1. *Delinquency and crime.* Some criminologists hold that by violating the law the offender is aggressing symbolically against a society in which he has been unable to enact the roles expected of or desired by him. Other students of the subject take an environmental position. They point out that an individual is required in his society to take care of himself and his dependents along certain lines. But suppose that, for whatever reasons, he has been unable to enact this role, even though he wants to do so. He may decide to achieve legitimate ends by illegitimate means, stealing in order to get money and thus take care of his needs.

2. *Mental illness.* Confronted by what seem to them irreconcilable demands in role playing, some people break down mentally, escaping into neurosis or psychosis. Leo Rosten, a fine writer of fiction, has drawn a remarkably realistic picture of a man escaping the reality of sharply conflicting role demands. In his book *Captain Newman, M.D.,* the scene is the psychiatric ward of a fictional Air Force base. A patient is admitted. An intelligent, flamboyantly bearded man, he has been a highly successful officer, a colonel, but he insists on calling himself Mr. Future. Captain Newman, in charge of the unit, is convinced that Colonel Norval Algate Bliss, the patient, has used insanity as a means of escape from his real self, in order to make it inaccessible, both to himself and to others. He cannot stand the pain of attempting to fulfill two separate,

conflicting roles. He is and wants to remain a brilliant, sensitive man and leader of men. He is and wants to forget that he is also sexually deviated, a person whose compulsions horrify him and would horrify his associates. He became Mr. Future in order to escape from Mr. Past, and he now resists all of Newman's sympathetic efforts to bring him to confront Mr. Past so that he may somehow conquer him and be able to face Colonel Norval Algate Bliss. On one occasion, Newman tells him, "You are afraid."

Hate flared up in the blue eyes; then they widened in a parody of dismay. "Afraid? Bless my soul. O penetrating pharmacist of the psyche: of what?"

"Of what you may reveal."

"Careful!" Mr. Future whispered. "Do not overplay your hand."

When, much later in treatment, Dr. Newman presses Mr. Future, touches the real person beneath the disguise, gets at what has been occasioning such anguish, Mr. Future retreats still further, announces to the psychiatrist, "I am now entering a state of catatonia. These are the last words that shall ever pass my lips."

"Wait! What about Mr. Past?"

There was no answer.

"Don't do this to him!" exclaimed Newman. "He's part of you. Where can he go if you leave? Where? To whom?"

A shield, glazed and impenetrable, covered those blue, blue eyes.

"Think, Norval! Mr. Past—he has *no place to go*, no place on earth, except to you. He understands you. He needs you. You need him. Together you can be whole—"

Not even a tremor touched the lips or eyes or beard.

Mr. Future had entered the future and would not return.[10]

3. *Physical illness.* We have learned from psychosomatic medicine that mental strain can make one genuinely ill physically. Some types of ulcer are psychosomatically induced. Heart disease can result from mental-emotional distress. So can blindness, arthritis, and other ailments. If we accept the view that psychic strain can result in physical illness, the latter probably can be an outcome of role strain in given cases.

STATUS

Each role we enact is associated with a corresponding status. *Status is the social position identified in the society as associated with a role, a pattern of behavior expected or required, under given circumstances, of persons occupying the position.* Status is distinct from the individual who may occupy the particular social position. All who occupy that position have the same status. That is, they have a *collection of rights and duties* by virtue of occupying the position. Since, as anthropologist Ralph Linton pointed out, these rights and duties "can find expression only through the medium of individuals, it is extremely hard for us to maintain a distinction in our thinking between statuses and the people who hold them and exercise the rights and duties which constitute them."[11]

Consider the person who is exercising certain rights and duties as someone who is enacting his role. Linton, who has contributed heavily to the thinking in this area of human interaction, says that a role represents the dynamic aspect of a status. When an individual puts the rights and duties that constitute the status into effect, he is performing a role. "Role and status are quite inseparable, and the distinction between them is only of academic interest."[12]

To illustrate: You have the *status* of a student. It carries with it certain rights and duties assigned to all students in our society. You enact the *role* of a student, which entails such items as your right to attend class and your right to challenge something the instructor says with which you disagree. You have the right to be recognized and respected by fellow students and teachers. Your status also entails duties, or responsibilities. In enacting your role, you are expected to treat students and teachers with respect, to do a creditable job of learning, to behave properly on campus.

An important role is associated with correspondingly important status. The chief of a preliterate tribe has higher status than other tribesmen. In our society, a physician has higher status than a day laborer.

Every person has many statuses. In combination they represent the status of that person. Ralph Linton explains:

A *status*, in the abstract, is a position in a particular pattern. It is thus quite correct to speak of each individual as having many statuses, since each individual participates in the expression of a number of patterns. However, unless the term is qualified in some way, *the status* of any individual means the sum total of all the statuses which he occupies. It represents his position with relation to the total society. Thus the status of Mr. Jones as a member of his community derives from a combination of all the statuses which he holds as a citizen, as an attorney, as a Mason, as a Methodist, as Mrs. Jones' husband, and so on.[13]

This leads to the observation that *role and status facilitate social control.* It is through understanding of his role and status that an individual becomes informed on how he should behave in his society. Again we quote Linton:

Status and role serve to reduce the ideal patterns for social life to individual terms. They become models for organizing the attitudes and behavior of the individual so that these will be congruous with those of the other individuals participating in the expression of the pattern. Thus if we are studying football teams in the abstract, the position of quarter-back is meaningless except in relation to the other positions. From the point of view of the quarter-back himself it is a distinct and important entity. It determines where he shall take his place in the line-up and what he shall do in the various plays. His assignment to this position at once limits and defines his activities and establishes a minimum of things which he must learn.[14]

Linton further emphasizes the importance of role and status in society when he remarks that "so long as there is no interference from external sources, the more perfectly the members of any society are adjusted to their statuses and roles the more smoothly the society will function."[15] Thus, we might imagine a nonagricultural, preliterate tribe that subsists on hunting and fishing. It is isolated from any other society. Every member has his statuses and roles and is very well adjusted to them. The chief accepts his, and his tribesmen accept him as chief, with certain statuses and roles. Hunters and fishermen accept that they are hunters and fishermen, parents that they are parents, children that they are children. All behave according to what is expected of them. Inasmuch as they are adjusted to their statuses and roles, the tribal society functions smoothly, each category of human being accepting its position.

Now suppose that another tribe, forced out of its habitat for some reason, wanders about and eventually settles very near the first one. The newcomers till the soil, reap good harvests yearly, sufficient to live more comfortably than their hunting and fishing neighbors. The new arrivals urge members of the other tribe to cultivate the soil, too. Some of the nonagricultural tribesmen decide to learn the ways of their neighbors, to abandon hunting and fishing for farming. They want the entire tribe to do the same. The chief objects. So do traditional-minded tribesmen. A period of tension, of unadjustment, sets in. Those who advocate change are abetted by their agriculturist neighbors, who urge that the issue be brought to a head. The malcontents in the hunting-fishing tribe now demand that the two groups merge their lands, live jointly as an agricultural community, and be ruled by the two chiefs.

Thus, statuses and roles in the first tribe are threatened. The chief loses some of his influence. Tribesmen waver between remaining hunters and fishermen and becoming farmers. Some young men, wanting to farm, treat their more traditional parents in ways that show little respect for their traditional statuses and roles as parents. Another dimension of statuses and roles may emerge eventually, but not before there has been a struggle within the tribe. However that struggle between those who seek change and those who resist it may come out, it would not have reached the point of being a struggle had there been no external source of new ideas— the agricultural tribe.

ASCRIBED & ACHIEVED STATUS

In a rather broad sense, there are two types of status, *ascribed* and *achieved*. Linton described *ascribed statuses* as *"those which are assigned to individuals without reference to their innate differences or abilities. They can be predicted and trained for from the moment of birth."*[16] (Emphasis added.)

In all societies, ascribed statuses include age, sex, place of birth, kinship by birth relationship (mother-child, brother-sister, and so on), birth into a socially recognized group (religious faith, ethnic group, and so on). People say, "She is a child, a girl, a Kentuckian, the daughter of Jane and Hal Kenyon, a Presbyterian." She simply *is* all of these by ascription.

Some of these statuses, held by an individual, will change and others can change; some will not or cannot. Age will change. Sex ordinarily will not, nor will place of birth or kinship by birth relationship. Birth into a socially recognized group may change or may not. One may abandon a given religious faith, adopt another, or become an atheist. One may enter the world in the lower socioeconomic class, eventually qualify as a member of the middle class.

As a minimum, Linton observes, *the achieved statuses are those requiring special qualities, although they are not necessarily limited to these. Achieved statuses are not assigned to persons from birth. They are left open to be filled through competition and individual effort.*[17] Among the commonly recognized achieved statuses are: education, occupation, income, marital status, kinship in the family of procreation (husband-wife). Statuses that may be achieved in our society include, for example, college graduate, union organizer, police chief, mayor, gang leader, electrician, millionaire, pauper, married man, and a great many more.

Achieved statuses are obviously more attainable through voluntary effort than ascribed statuses. It is almost impossible in our society for a man to have the ascribed status of "woman." But a man *or* woman may achieve the status of school teacher, airplane pilot, scientist, doctor of philosophy.

What is an achieved status in one society, however, may be an ascribed status in another. For instance, in the United States, if a woman adopts a certain occupation or profession, we consider that this assigns to her an achieved status. In other lands, occupation may be an ascribed status, on the basis of sex. Linton points out that there are few societies in which every important activity has not been definitely assigned to men or to women. And, speaking of village life in contemporary Burma, anthropologist Manning Nash writes: "Women must feed, nurse, train each other's children as they would their own. They must cook for the common pot. Men . . . must share the economic tasks . . . and work cooperatively."[18] These are not voluntarily selected roles. They are not based on special talents. They are ascribed on the basis of sex.

· NOTES

1. Alex Inkeles and Peter H. Rossi, "National Comparisons of Occupational Prestige," *American Journal of Sociology,* LXI (January 1956), 329–339.
2. *Ibid.*
3. *National Observer,* May 18, 1964.
4. Robert K. Merton, "Bureaucratic Structure and Personality," *Social Forces,* XVIII (May 1940), 561–568.
5. *Plunkitt of Tammany Hall,* recorded by William L. Riordan, (New York: Dutton, 1963), paperback edition.

6. *Ibid.*, pp. 3–7. Reprinted by permission of E. P. Dutton & Co., Inc.

7. Mirra Komarovsky, "Cultural Contradictions and Sex Roles," *American Journal of Sociology*, LII (November 1946), 184–189.

8. U. S. Bureau of the Census, *Statistical Abstract of the United States, 1966*, 87th annual ed. (Washington, D. C.: U. S. Government Printing Office, 1966), p. 219, Table No. 309.

9. William J. Helmer, "New York's 'Middle-class' Homosexuals," *Harper's*, CCXXVI, 1354 (March 1963), pp. 85–92.

10. Leo Rosten, *Captain Newman, M.D.* (New York: Harper & Row, 1961), pp. 271–299.

11. Ralph Linton, *The Study of Man, An Introduction* (New York: Appleton-Century-Crofts, 1936), p. 113.

12. *Ibid.*, p. 114.

13. *Ibid.*, p. 113.

14. *Ibid.*, p. 114.

15. *Ibid.*, p. 114–115.

16. *Ibid.*, p. 115.

17. *Ibid.*

18. Manning Nash, *The Golden Road to Modernity, Village Life in Contemporary Burma* (New York: Wiley, 1965), p. 46.

· SUGGESTIONS FOR FURTHER READING

BECKER, HOWARD S. *Outsiders: Studies in the Sociology of Deviance.* New York: Free Press, 1963.
The author discusses, with particular emphasis on the jazz musician, deviant social roles and the processes by which individuals learn to play them.

BURCHARD, WALDO W. "Role Conflicts of Military Chaplains." *American Sociological Review*, XIX (October 1954), 528–535.
Chaplains and former chaplains in the armed forces are subjects of this examination of role conflict.

GOFFMAN, ERVING. *The Presentation of Self in Everyday Life.* New York: Anchor Books, 1959.
The author says we all play roles so that others may see us as we want to be seen.

HUGHES, EVERETT C. "Dilemmas and Contradictions of Status." *American Journal of Sociology*, L (March 1945), 353–359.
A discussion of the effects upon individuals placed in incompatible roles.

LINTON, RALPH. *The Study of Man.* New York: Appleton-Century-Crofts, 1936, Chapter 8, "Status and Role."
The scholar who introduced the concepts into anthropology and sociology discusses status and role. Linton is always easy, pleasurable, and very sound reading.

MEAD, MARGARET. *Sex and Temperament in Three Primitive Societies.* New York: Morrow, 1935.
An anthropolgist observes the function of culture in molding masculine and feminine behavior.

MITCHELL, WILLIAM C. "Occupational Role Strains: The American Elective Public Official." *Administrative Science Quarterly*, III (September 1958), 210–228.
A political scientist analyzes role strain as it applies to persons in politics.

STEINMANN, ANNE. "Lack of Communication between Men and Women." *Marriage and Family Living*, XX (November 1958), 350–352.
A role-focused analysis of communication difficulties between the sexes.

15 SOCIAL STRATIFICATION

In all human societies, we stated, persons have roles and are accorded differential prestige or status on the basis of those roles. This situation, we are about to point out, is directly related to *social stratification. Caste* and *class* are forms of social stratification.

LET'S BE BASIC

"Let's be basic," he said. "The fact is that, despite all the arguments against it, there will always be Society in any country. . . . If there are three people on an island, one will say he got there first—and so he is Society. Pretty soon another one will climb up a hill and build a big house and say *he* is Society. And finally, the third one will climb up a tree and corner all the coconuts and claim *he* is Society. Who is Society? Obviously all of them are: the first has family, the second has prominence, and the third has money."*

The speaker was giving his definition of "Society," which is only one segment of the *society* with which the sociologist deals. Nevertheless, the quotation is relevant here, since it takes cognizance of three facts: (1) individuals are accorded differential prestige or status in society, (2) through a system of *social stratification* (to be defined), (3) which accounts for

* Statement by a "Society" man, in Cleveland Amory, *Who Killed Society?* (New York: Pocket Books, 1962), p. 55.

the existence of *social classes*, and *castes* (also to be defined and discussed).

SOCIAL STRATIFICATION

Every society is characterized by a hierarchy of rank. In sociology this is referred to as social stratification. *Social stratification is a system for ranking individuals in different levels, or strata, of prestige or status.*

Although stratification is found in all societies, its particular form varies according to the society. And rarely does one criterion alone, such as wealth, education, or hunting prowess, determine what social position a given individual occupies. Rather, that position is determined on the basis of a complex of characteristics.

It may be helpful to think of social stratification as a ladder on the top rung of which are persons of highest status. From rung to rung, stratification establishes relative positions. When we get to the bottom, individuals on that rung are deemed most inferior in status.

The different levels of social differentiation always involve subjective values. Intrinsically, black skin is neither "better" nor "worse" than white, red, or brown. Hunting ability is neither "better" nor "worse" than proficiency in fishing. *The rank of individuals is determined by the value that members of the society normally place upon given social roles,* and this is a matter of subjective judgment.

However, that judgment, although subjective, may be founded upon objective considerations. For instance, assume a society that must depend upon wildlife for sustenance. If the members have no access to a body of water, but live in an area where animals and fowl are available, they will probably place high value on hunting prowess. But if they have access to water and not to land game, they are most likely to hold the fisherman in esteem. The objective fact is that the hunter or the fisherman, as the case may be, can provide food. The subjective fact is that persons who can provide food are deemed "better" or "worthier," in our hypothetical society, than those who cannot.

The social stratification system is a continuum on which every individual has a position, and the position, in turn, provides the basis for according certain rights and privileges. The hunter, for instance, may have the privilege of better housing than is available to a non-hunter. He may perhaps have the right to demand the choicest portion of the animal he has brought down.

FUNCTIONS OF SOCIAL STRATIFICATION

What are the functions of social stratification? Before considering this, let us introduce a concept: *functionalism*. We discuss it at greater length in Chapter 23, but it is necessary to touch on it here, at least briefly, so that you may better understand social stratification.

Society is characterized by a variety of activities that form a pattern, occurring over and over. *Functionalism,* as one sociologist defines it, *"is the doctrine which asserts that all recurrent social activities have the function of maintaining a social system."*[1] (Emphasis added.) Thus, our form of family life represents recurrent social activities, including as it does an approved pattern for getting married, rearing children, and conducting family life. These activities are seen as a means of maintaining our social system. The social life of the community is viewed as the functioning of the social structure. "The function of any recurrent activity, such as the punishment of a crime, or a funeral ceremony, is the part it plays in the social life as a whole, and therefore the contribution which it makes to the maintenance of structural continuity."[2]

The same activity patterns and social structures have multiple functions. Thus, a funeral ceremony may serve a religious purpose by satisfying the need of the bereaved to show love and respect for the deceased, and it may also be a public health measure for the disposal of dead bodies.

Some functions are *manifest,* some *latent*—that is, some are intended and recognized while others are unintended and may not be recognized. For instance, we establish criminal law, which has the manifest function of preserving public order. Among many latent functions of criminal law are the erection of edifices to house prisoners, the creation of a corps of prison personnel, and the forfeiture of certain civil rights of specified types of offenders. Obviously not all latent functions are viewed in the society as undesirable. However, they are not identical with the manifest functions; they are in a sense by-products of those functions.

The functions of given activities and social structures may be different for a society as a whole as distinguished from component segments of that society. For instance, the manifest function of our economic system is to provide wealth and stability for the nation, but it also results in an employer-employee differentiation; some segments of the population possess more wealth than others; and certain groups are more severely handicapped by economic depressions than are others.

The social consequences of societal patterns and structures are not always advantageous for the whole society or for certain of its component parts. There can be both positive and negative results from a single pattern or structure. Thus, the lumbering industry in the United States functions in a positive way to increase the gross national product and to provide housing and other necessities. It also functions in a negative way to destroy forest preserves, reduce available recreational space, and impede soil conservation. Negative results are said to be *dysfunctional*.

Now, in this frame of reference, what are the functions of social stratification? They are both manifest and latent. They affect the society as a whole; they affect groups within the society differentially. Some results of stratification are positive, and some are negative, or dysfunctional.

Stratification functions to maintain a social system. It is a mechanism whereby individuals in respective strata of society may understand their roles and the privileges and rights they may expect or demand as a consequence of enacting these roles. The stratification system spells out patterns of behavior for each role and status, these patterns being distinct from those shared by all participants in the general culture. All United States adults are expected to follow certain behavior norms, but only those with the status of citizen are expected to vote. And as citizens, they have rights and privileges accorded to persons in that category. They elect public officials; they may bring about the removal of public officials.

Some sociologists have viewed social stratification as a necessity in any social system. They argue that it is necessary if society is to be a functioning mechanism. Our society needs unskilled and skilled laborers, doctors, artists, teachers, scientists, farmers, and many others; otherwise our needs are not served. Therefore, the argument runs, members of the society must be distributed in social positions; individuals must be motivated to fill certain positions and to perform the duties connected with them. But not all of these duties are equally pleasant for individuals; not all are of equal importance to the survival of society; and some require more training or special talents than others. Therefore, it makes a difference who gets into what positions. We must encourage appropriate people to occupy particular positions.

How can this be accomplished? According to the line of reasoning we have been following, we must have a system of rewards to induce individuals to occupy the positions. And there must be a way of distributing the rewards differentially, according to positions. These rewards are comparatively scarce; they cannot be equally divided among all individuals. Consequently, the persons who are prepared for less important work should receive more modest rewards than those who made greater sacrifices, who prepared themselves for more vital positions in the society. The rewards, which include sustenance, comforts, self-respect, the respect of others, are built into respective positions. They consist of rights and perquisites associated with them. Since the rights and perquisites of different positions need to be unequal in order that appropriate people be attracted to them, society must be stratified, else it will not function effectively. By this argument, social stratification becomes a necessary form of social inequality, an inequality among different strata in the distribution of scarce and desired rewards. Viewed this way, social stratification is functional in a positive direction and inevitable in all societies.

Although such a formulation is provocative and helpful, it may mislead students. Society is referred to as a functioning mechanism, as if it were an entity in itself, with objectives, purposes, and survival needs of its own, apart from the values and objectives of its members. For instance, as previously noted, the argument holds that society must somehow instill in individuals the motivation to want to fill certain positions and to perform the duties connected with them. In other words, an *entity*, society, has a *purpose*: to instill motives in individuals. Society therefore transcends and is separate from the members of that society.

Actually, society does not exist as an entity separate from

the individuals comprising it. An *entity*, society, does not have a purpose. The individuals within that society do.

Other criticisms have been leveled at the formulation. Is stratification actually functional in a positive direction in every sense and in all ways? May it not be dysfunctional in some respects, impeding rather than enhancing effective societal functioning in certain regards? A stratified society provides unequal access to motivation to occupy certain positions. Stratification systems therefore serve to limit the possibility of discovering the full range of talent available in a society. A tenant farmer's son is unlikely to encounter people and ideas that will stimulate him to want to become a physicist, schoolteacher, or astronomer. The darker skinned boy in Figure 15.1, we may assume, conceives of his social position as one that offers practically no hope that he can become President of the United States.

Even should an individual develop the motivation to occupy certain positions, the channels of recruitment may be largely inaccessible to him. Where will the tenant farmer's son meet a physicist who might recruit him into the field of physics? But suppose he does meet one, who encourages him and explains how he can prepare himself to become a physicist. It is still quite possible that the young man will be financially unable to go to school to gain the required education. In thus limiting the range of talent available, stratification systems actually reduce rather than enhance the possibility of expanding the productive resources of the society. If this is a consequence of stratification, then to that extent it is dysfunctional rather than functional.

Currently there is a shortage of natural scientists, social workers, and engineers in the United States. Undoubtedly there are young people with potentialities for eventually filling such posts who have had no opportunity to test and develop their abilities in these directions. The productive capacity of our nation depends upon highly educated specialists, yet the U. S. Department of Labor estimated that of all young people entering the labor force during the 1960s, 2.5 million will have done so without having completed grade school.[3] Some of those who have left school early lack talents for the specialized fields where scarcities occur. A proportion of those who have the ability lack motivation. But various studies indicate that a significant percentage of intellectually superior young people

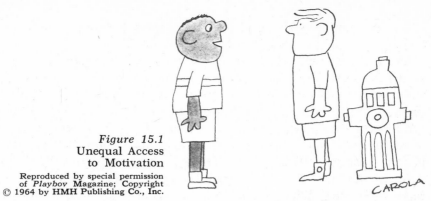

Figure 15.1
Unequal Access
to Motivation
Reproduced by special permission
of *Playboy* Magazine; Copyright
© 1964 by HMH Publishing Co., Inc.

"I'll sell you my chance to be President for a nickel."

who did have the motivation to attend college, and who did enter, dropped out before getting the desired degree, due, among other reasons, to insufficient financing.

Another commentary that has been advanced regarding the functional-dysfunctional character of social stratification is to the effect that it may be dysfunctional in providing the elite of a society with political power to gain the acceptance of their ideology. Since this situation generally argues perpetuation of the status quo as "logical," "natural," and "morally right," the stratification system functions as an essentially conservative influence. In a continuously changing society, conservatism that is directed at maintenance of the status quo may be dysfunctional (as well as functional) under given conditions. Property owners, unwilling to be taxed for public improvements, have successfully fought slum clearance and expansion of educational facilities. Caucasians have been largely successful in protecting the status quo with respect to Negro-white stratification.

CASTE & CLASS

Social stratification takes many forms, ranging from systems of caste, as in traditional India, to relatively "open class." The distinction between *open class* and *caste* is frequently used in sociological analysis. Actually, neither caste nor class exists in a "pure" state in any society. Instead, elements of both are found in all societies, although one form of stratification or the other usually predominates.

A closed caste system is an arrangement of status relation-ships that prevents people from achieving higher status, or social position, than was accorded them at birth. As we said, this is relative, but the caste system remains the most rigid form of social stratification in society.

Some characteristics of caste are:

1. It is the fixing or legitimation of social distance, considered within the society to be the dictates of nature and perhaps the prescription of a deity.

2. Membership in a caste is hereditary, ascribed and unalterable. Theoretically, it is fixed for life. By virtue of being born into a family of a given caste, the child gains membership, and for life.

3. But failure to abide by requirements may lead to expulsion from the caste. This is by action of its members, and the person so expelled is said to have "lost caste."

4. Relationships between members of one caste and those of another are very carefully defined and limited. Social intercourse between persons of different castes may or may not be entirely prohibited, but social intimacy between members of higher and lower castes usually is.

5. Rules in each caste within a society generally provide that marriage be confined within the caste.

6. A caste may move upward or downward on the stratification ladder, but this is unusual. If it does occur, it is not by sudden fiat, as a rule; and such mobility (except for those who lose caste) is generally a collective, not an individual, matter. The entire caste moves, not one individual from it.

Hindu castes are often used to illustrate this form of stratification. The people of India have traditionally accorded social position in terms of the caste of a family into which an individual is born. Wealth, privilege, and, to a great extent, even occupation were determined and set throughout life by the caste of an individual's family, according to strict interpretation and as supported by philosophical and religious doctrines. However, the caste system in India is undergoing large-scale changes, although many evidences of it still exist. Literally hundreds of castes remain in contemporary India, extending from the high aristocracy, the Brahmins, to a number of "untouchable" castes at the lowest extreme. The idea of moving from one social position to another is apt to have little meaning to people living in such a society.

We must not jump to the conclusion, however, that these people are frustrated or necessarily unhappy if their culture does not provide them with a "ladder of opportunity." There is reason to believe that, in this respect, persons in a closed caste society have less intense frustrations than those living in an open class society. Individuals in the United States, which has a basically class rather than caste orientation, may aspire to status levels beyond their reach. This may lead to dissatisfaction. Those living in a closed caste society are neither expected nor permitted to achieve a social position higher than that of their parents. They are probably more inclined than we are to accept and be reconciled to circumstances of their lives, to "cooperate with the inevitable." Persons everywhere become ethnocentric about their cultures, hence what looks to us like lack of opportunity may very well have seemed right and proper to the people of India. On the other hand, there have been instances in which members of a caste have been unhappy with their lot. Some have fought to alter their position on the stratification ladder.

Although the United States does not have a caste system in the strict sense of the term, there are caste-like features in the American Negro's position, despite some changes stimulated in recent years by the United States Supreme Court's decisions and despite the struggle of Negroes to gain social equality with whites and social change in general. The Negro remains socially ostracized in many sections of the country, isolated from Caucasians in subtle and not so subtle ways. De facto segregation exists in schools and churches. Certain employment avenues are virtually closed to Negroes by at least informal agreement among whites. Until a 1967 Supreme Court ruling, Negroes and whites were forbidden by law to intermarry in more than twenty-five states. The Supreme Court ruling has not as yet materially affected rigid custom by which such intermarriage is disapproved.

Nevertheless we do not have a true caste system. It is becoming more and more possible, however difficult, for Negroes to cross the figurative color line. Negroes and whites do intermarry. Segregation in schools and places of public accommodation is breaking down. "Restricted" neighborhoods have been breached by Negroes who have bought or rented homes there.

Employment barriers have been lowered, and Negroes have been elected to public office in a number of states.

CLASS

In a caste system, social position is established at birth, ascribed to people exclusively on the basis of the caste to which the parents belong. In a class system this is not the case. *A social class consists of a number of people who have approximately equal position in a society, which may be achieved rather than ascribed, with some opportunity for movement upward or downward to another class.* Max Weber writes that class consists of a category of persons having a "typical chance for a supply of goods, external living conditions, and personal life experiences, in so far as this chance is determined by the amount and kind of power . . . to dispose of goods or skills for the sake of income in a given economic order."[4] The contemporary sociologist, Ely Chinoy, centers his definition of class in the economic system when he says that class may be defined "as a *number of persons sharing a common position in the economic order.*" He adds that property ownership, usually a source of income and therefore of the things that money can buy, "also carries with it power or control over economic resources, and, therefore, to a considerable extent, over other persons." But, Chinoy points out, the validity of ownership of property as the central determinant of class structure has been diminished in Western society. Occupational distinctions, such as skilled, semiskilled, and unskilled workers; clerks; salespeople; independent entrepreneurs; officials; managers; and professionals, "now appear to be more significant criteria of class than mere ownership or nonownership of property."[5]

When we say that a social class consists of a number of people who have approximately equal status in a society, we tread on uncertain ground. The concept is generally used with the implication that people are divided into fairly distinct categories. Presumably there are upper classes of people who are accorded the highest status and privilege. These shade into the middle classes, which in turn shade into the lower classes, the members of which have the lowest status and fewest privileges.

But what factors delineate a class? What positions Joe in an upper and Susan in a lower class? Sociologists hold somewhat disparate views on this. They agree that the concept of class has to do with the stratification of a population, in figurative, roughly defined layers or strata. They disagree about the *basis* of these positions. Is it income? Accumulated wealth? Power? Occupation? The individual's conception of where he "belongs"? A combination of certain of these? Which? No substantial consensus exists.

There have been two main approaches in the analysis of the social strata in which people are placed: objective and subjective. In the objective approach, emphasis is placed on the income or possessions that an individual has, or on his education, or on the power he possesses. In the subjective approach, psychological factors are particularly important: (1) the feelings of individuals concerning their class affiliation, and (2) the opinions that other people hold as to where they would place a given person in the class hierarchy. But the two orientations are separable only for purposes of analysis. Actually, there are both objective and subjective determinants of social stratification. And in no society can any single factor, whether objective or subjective, be appropriately used as a sole criterion of class status.

An influential example of the objective approach is the Marxist. The German revolutionary Karl Marx insisted there was a clear-cut distinction between classes in Europe and in America. The upper class consisted of capitalist exploiters. The lower, exploited class were productive workers. The two classes, Marx held, were in a state of continuous conflict, which would be resolved only when the workers dispossessed the capitalists of their economic privileges and took possession of the tools and fruits of labor. However, inferentially and explicitly, Marx recognizes a subjective element in social stratification, since he holds that members of each class, exploiter and exploited, develop, at least in the long run, a class consciousness, an identification with others who hold the same class position.

In the subjective approach, class consciousness is viewed as an important criterion, as are attitudes regarding given social positions, as indicated above.

In either orientation, or both, sociologists have variously delineated four types of social class systems in the United States:

1 · *A three-class system,* consisting of an upper, lower (or working), and middle class.
2 · *A two-class system,* encompassing a working class and a business class, the latter including professional persons.
3 · *A multiple-class system,* as exemplified in the work of W. Lloyd Warner and his associates. They listed six classes in their research, from an upper-upper, an upper-middle, and so on to the lower-lower class.
4 · *A continuum of higher and lower status without any distinct lines of division.* This seems to the author the most plausible and realistic statement on the subject, as applied to the United States.

We have still not clearly specified what characteristics assign an individual to a class or to higher or lower status within a society. Let us turn to this consideration.

CRITERIA OF SOCIAL CLASS · Among factors that have been identified as contributing to the establishment of class position are:

1. *Family prestige.* This is one of the very most important factors contributing to the establishment of class position in the United States, as in most other societies. Prestige accorded a family tends to be culturally transferred to the children and the children's children. Members of old families, the traditional "400" and "bluebloods" of American cities, are usually considered to belong to the upper classes. (Actually, the "upper class" is almost nonexistent at the present time, as will become clear as we develop our discussion of social class.)

Professor E. Digby Baltzell, a native Philadelphian, described the "upper-class" social organization in his city. Certain members of what many consider the very uppermost class date their family and traditions back to colonial times. "This relatively small group of families forms a subculture at the top of the social class system which is, in turn, set apart from the rest of the community by various exclusive associations and neighborhoods and distinguished by symbolic behavior patterns, beliefs and artifacts."[6] These are "the Proper Philadelphians." In 1940, when Baltzell studied them, they were described as having the following attributes:

A · The Proper Philadelphian was usually of English or Welsh descent. His great-great-great grandfather was a prominent

Philadelphian in the first years of the new republic. Somewhere along the line an ancestor made or married into a good deal of money.

B · The family of the Proper Philadelphian was listed in the *Social Register* at the turn of the nineteenth century.

C · He was born on Walnut Street, facing Rittenhouse Square.

D · He was educated at the Episcopal Academy or another private school in the city, after which he attended one of the fashionable boarding schools in New England.

E · Unless his parents were unusually loyal to and proud of local institutions, he then went to Harvard, Yale, or Princeton, where he belonged to one of the most exclusive clubs.

F · After attending law school at the University of Pennsylvania, he entered a fashionable and powerful law firm in Philadelphia, eventually becoming a partner. Or he entered the field of banking or finance. He sat on the board of directors of several prestigious cultural and economic institutions.

G · At the proper time, he married, lived in Chestnut Hill or the Main Line, the two most exclusive neighborhoods of Philadelphia. He had three or four children. He walked either up or down Walnut Street to lunch with his peers at the Rittenhouse, or preferably at the Philadelphia Club.[7]

2. *Occupation or profession.* Along with family prestige, occupation is one of the salient criteria employed in the United States. What people do to gain their income has a great deal to do with their class position. This is distinct from *how much* a person earns. Although white-collar workers may earn less money than skilled workers of the blue-collar class, they are inclined to look down on them. The Prohibition era gang lord took in millions of dollars annually, but he was not accorded a high position in the class hierarchy.

Occupation may help to establish an individual's social position regardless of his family background. This applies (in our country) to persons holding high political office, diplomats, ecclesiastical dignitaries, corporation executives, lawyers, physicians, and so on. It may also apply to the country parson, whose parents had low status, and who is earning a pittance himself: he may yet occupy a higher social position than some of his wealthier parishioners.

The status accorded given occupational groups varies widely in accordance with the society. Throughout most of its modern history, Germany rated military officers higher than we have done in our country. Catholic clergymen have greater prestige and privilege in the United States than their counterparts in the Soviet Union. University professors are evaluated more highly in Sweden, France, and Germany than in the United States.

Status based on occupation also varies with the times within a given society. During and for some period after a war, a country's fighting men, and particularly the spectacularly successful officers, often enjoy high status. This diminishes with the passage of time. College and university professors have higher status in our country today than they were accorded two decades earlier.

3. *Possession of wealth.* Although not usually an overriding consideration (as indicated above), the amount of money controlled by an individual or a family is widely accepted in our society as evidence that people belong in a given class position. But there are no clearly defined boundaries indicating where one "class" ends and another begins. How much wealth entitles a person to a position in an "upper class"? A hundred thousand dollars? Then are we prepared to say that an individual or family controlling 99,999 dollars does not belong in that class? It would seem that with regard to this or any other criterion of class position, it is most useful to think of *higher* and *lower* status on a continuum, not of a precisely fixed point beyond which one class position ends and another begins.

4. *Possession of power.* Some sociologists, the late C. Wright Mills among them, believe individuals can be classified according to their position in the power structure. The "power elite" in the United States, according to these thinkers, give orders that are nationwide in scope; their decisions influence the behavior of people throughout the land. The middle class gives and takes orders; it transmits and enforces the decisions of the elite. Members of the lower class take orders; they are on the receiving end of the power decisions. Possession of wealth, of course, is closely related to possession of power, for wealth is a means to power.

5. *Possession of leisure.* In his classic work, *The Theory of the Leisure Class*, Thorstein Veblen wrote that the upper classes are comprised of those individuals who have sufficient leisure, supported by wealth, to follow their own inclinations to a considerable extent. Veblen's observation may be corroborated by the fact that people who can afford to enjoy a good deal of leisure do hold prestige in our country. In certain seg-

ments of "Society" a person who works, even in a high-ranking occupation and for a munificent financial return, does not belong in the "upper crust." To be accepted in "Society," according to some who are, it is even fatal to be of a family in which a member worked as far back as a century or more ago. Mrs. John King Van Rensselaer, a New York socialite in the 1920s, did not accept the contemporary Astors as legitimate members of "Society." "The first John Jacob Astor," she declared, "born in Walldorf, Germany, came to New York in 1783 as a piano merchant."[8] His descendants did not deserve to be numbered with the truly elite of "Society."

Veblen focused much of his attention on one end of the class continuum. A contemporary sociologist comments:

Parasites are prevalent on both ends of the class continuum, among the derelicts of the skid-row, as well as among the playboys of Nob Hill. A tramp, for example, considers any kind of productive labor disgraceful. Obviously, Veblen was not thinking about all those who live lives of leisure when he wrote of the leisure class.*

In the same commentary, Professor Korber points up the ambiguity of criteria of social class:

Apparently, too, times and fashions are changing. The Rockefellers and Lodges, true American Brahmins, are vigorous workers. Conspicuous leisure is stylish only for the ladies of the clans in our time.

Baltzell, referring to the Proper Philadelphians, also points out:

Although inherited wealth is almost an indispensable aspect of upper-class position, the gentleman of leisure, contrary to the stereotype popularized by Thorstein Veblen, is rare in Philadelphia. On the contrary, there is a traditional emphasis on the "Protestant ethic" of hard work and a mistrust, amounting almost to an incapacity, for leisure.[9]

6. *Educational background and achievement.* The level of formal education achieved is viewed by a great many people in the United States as at least a partial test of class distinction.

*Private undated communication from Professor George W. Korber to the writer.

The college graduate is often accorded higher status than the person who has not graduated from college. And the university attended is for some a more important factor than the number of degrees earned, the Ivy League colleges undoubtedly having top prestige value. Currently, however, the trend has been to encourage the idea of a college education for everyone who has the intellectual ability to go through college and a reasonable probability that he will be able to finance his education. It remains to be seen whether the fact that there are a great many more college graduates today than formerly will result in a downgrading of educational achievement as a factor in establishing class position.

The function of formal education in conferring status is not limited to highly complex, industrialized societies such as ours. In agricultural regions of Burma, for example, education brings prestige.[10] And Africans of the Rhodesian Copperbelt, which has become somewhat more industrialized than previously but is still not in a class with England or the United States in this respect, have accepted education as a status symbol:

Africans on the Copperbelt were quick to recognize this new stratification. Although there was no reason why they could not communicate with each other in their vernacular language, a man who did not speak English felt inferior when he was talking to an English-speaking African. This sentiment was . . . expressed by adult Africans attending English night classes.[11]

Formal education as a criterion of status has become increasingly significant in most "developing" societies, and for good reason. More and more the amount and quality of education are closely associated with occupational position, with income, and, to some extent, with power and influence.

7. *Location of residence and standard of living.* Living on the "right" or "wrong" side of the tracks is often used as a test of class difference, as for instance in Philadelphia, where, as we have learned, most Proper Philadelphians lived in neighborhoods generally defined as most exclusive, while persons of lower status dwelt in less prestigious areas. (The social importance of residence is discussed more fully in Chapter 16.)

Whether or not families include such cultural products as telephones, television sets, large homes, and extensive grounds has also been a basis for making class distinctions. In our society automobiles are important. The distinction between domestic and imported cars, for example, and between Rolls Royces and Volkswagens, if the imported varieties are preferred, provides one of the most tangible indicators of status.

8. *Taste preferences*. One's taste preferences are sometimes used, usually along with other criteria, to assign status. The distinctions are rather subtle as a rule, although nevertheless real when applied. The connoisseur of fine wines tends to rank above the beer drinker. The woman who wears only original Paris or Italian creations enjoys a special prestige. And male Proper Philadelphians

wear distinctive types of clothes, usually in the Brooks Brothers tradition . . . and various symbols of exclusive associational affiliation. The various totem symbols of class position—the club necktie and hatband, the little charm (Ivy League or Porcellian Pig) on the watch chain . . . are as much as to say, in Max Weber's words, "I am a gentleman patented after investigation and probation and guaranteed by my membership.[12]

9. *Identification and acceptance*. We said that class position is partly determined by subjective judgments in the society. The Proper Bostonian, like his Philadelphia counterpart, *knows* he belongs with Proper Bostonians. Other Boston residents who do not belong in that class know they do not and acknowledge that Proper Bostonians do. An individual's class position is established in part through the estimation of other people and his own appraisal of his appropriate position. He *identifies* with a class, is *accepted* by members of that class, and is *acknowledged to belong* to that class by persons from other classes.

Although many studies have been made, many tests applied, some sociologists do not believe that the evidence supports the thesis that there are distinct, tangible differences between social classes in our society. Family and possession of money undoubtedly have a great deal of status value in the United States, but they do not open all doors. Some self-styled members of "Society," we have seen, have contempt for the *nouveaux riches*. If money is a test of class status, then many professional criminals must be included in the upper classes. If power is a criterion, then "Boss" Tweed of Tammany Hall, a corrupt, uneducated man of crude manners and cruder methods of winning elections for his political puppets, was of the upper classes, for he wielded tremendous power in government. Nor does taste seem an adequate criterion. Some people with beer incomes have champagne tastes and vice versa. Standards of living as a test do not invariably apply, for some individuals of great wealth prefer to exist like beggars. Hetty Green, worth about 100 million dollars when she died, dressed like a pauper and lived like one. Increasing amounts of education and leisure are now almost considered rights rather than special privileges of many American people. As a result, education and leisure have become much less useful as measures of social class position.

Even if we should agree on one criterion, how can we apply it to show clear and obvious distinctions between social classes? Suppose we use the amount of money individuals earn or possess. Every adult citizen and family in the United States fits somewhere along the same continuum. Where do we draw the line separating upper, middle, and lower classes? The same difficulty inheres if we try to apply any other criterion. The problem is compounded when we attempt to use several criteria simultaneously.

And yet, whatever the problems of sociological analysis, social position is very real in the *minds* of many persons. A banker may "look down" on an unskilled worker as belonging to a class less fortunate, privileged, or ambitious than his own. If you were introduced to the President of the United States, you might "look up" to him, as someone who seems very high on the social ladder. Class distinctions, then, among other things, are mental markers on psychological yardsticks, enabling people to determine whether and when they have superior, equal, or inferior status to that of others.

Korber holds that American social classes are disappearing.

Today most Americans, the preponderant majority, think of themselves as members of the middle class. Furthermore they fit into most of the objective criteria of the middle class. The "upper class" is almost non-existent, this in part a product of graduated income taxes, and our good respectable workers have disappeared into the nebulous labyrinths of the mediocre classes. This compression of the classes seems to have resulted in a new three-class system: upper middle, middle middle, and lower middle, with the vestigial remains of the upper and lower classes gradually disappearing. Several studies show this trend.*

* Private, undated communication to the author.

We may generalize from the foregoing that *class systems are nonrational,* founded in part on feelings and attitudes rather than on strictly objective criteria. There is no intrinsic reason why white-collar workers should have a higher status than blue-collar workers, for instance. *Class systems tend to be relatively stable, but they are dynamic nevertheless and subject to change.* Russia's system endured for centuries, changing only slowly; eventually it underwent drastic and sudden change, with the establishment of the Soviet Union. *Some societies are more "open-class" than others.* Sociologists use the term "open-class" to denote a society in which individuals can move upward or downward in social position with relative ease. Such movement is referred to as *social mobility,* which is discussed later in this chapter.

CLASS AND SOCIAL LIFE: ATTITUDES AND VALUES · A large number of sociological studies in recent years have been devoted to the relation of social class to patterns of attitudes and values, informal modes of social behavior, political views, and so on. Here some of the findings of such studies are sketched, in the form of responses to the following questions:

1. *Do voluntary personal relations in this country, such as friendships, the formation of cliques and associations, and dating, cross class lines to a significant extent?* Research reveals that these relations are for the most part carried on within classes. And this is especially true at the extremes of the class order. There is more "crossing over" on the part of middle-class individuals, upward and downward, than on the part of the upper or lower classes. Middle-class youths may court girls from the lower or upper classes, while lower-class boys are less likely to pursue girls from the middle or upper echelons. Upper-class boys tend to pay court to girls of their own social position rather than to middle- or lower-class young women. Stated another way, upper-class girls are more apt to carry on a romance with upper- or middle-class boys than with members of the lower class; similarly lower-class girls are more likely to accept the attentions of lower-class youths than the attentions of either middle- or upper-class youths. And middle-class girls are most likely to be courted by middle-class boys, but may cross class lines and allow themselves to be courted by a lower- or an upper-class young man.[13]

2. *Are there class differences with regard to the value placed*

on formal education? In the United States and parts of Europe, the higher the class position, generally the more the value placed on formal education and the knowledge it is assumed to provide. (There are important exceptions to this generalization—for example, first and second generation Jewish Americans in the United States value education regardless of social class.) And in the higher classes, education tends to be regarded both as a means to attaining occupational objectives and as an end in itself, something to be desired without regard to what "use" is made of it. The lower classes place less value on formal education.[14]

3. *Assuming three social classes in this country—upper, middle, and lower—which tends to conform most strictly to the conventional value system and conduct norms?* Almost by definition, the answer is the middle class. The latter, for instance, is characterized by less alcoholism than the other two classes, more rigid observance (in the South) of anti-Negro taboos, and stricter observance of sex mores. However, Bernard Berelson and Gary A. Steiner point out, this "may be simply a statistical artifact: being middle, they are usually more numerous, and hence account for more of 'the society as a whole.' "[15]

Recently we have witnessed a repudiation by many middle-class youths of the values and conduct norms said to be identified with their class. The so-called hippies furnish one example. Additionally, a large number of middle-class young people who do not consider themselves hippies are nonconformist in dress, hair styles, political activity, and attitudes toward formal education. These nonconformists may fade from the scene, as have others before them, or they may in time bring about significant changes in our value system and conduct norms generally.

4. *Who are the most tolerant of political and religious deviation?* Substantial evidence suggests that persons in upper-class positions tend to be more tolerant than individuals in lower-class positions. This was the finding, for example, of the late Samuel A. Stouffer, in *Communism, Conformity and Civil Liberties,* a study conducted during the "McCarthy era" and published in 1955.[16] Stouffer used a national sample of almost 5,000 residents of the United States, testing them on a scale based on fifteen questions dealing with willingness to tolerate nonconformists who are admitted or alleged Communists, ad-

vocates of government ownership of industry, and atheists. He divided his respondents into three categories—"less tolerant," "in-between," and "more tolerant"—and found that the higher the rung on the stratification ladder, the greater the tolerance.

Another American sociologist, S. M. Lipset, who has done extensive work in the same area of investigation, and with similar results, speculates on why lower-class individuals tend to be more authoritarian than persons at other stratification levels. Authoritarian predispositions and ethnic prejudices, he believes, flow more readily from lower-class social circumstances than from those of the middle and upper classes. The lower-class way of life "produces individuals with rigid . . . approaches to politics." This is a consequence of the fact that:

> The social situation of the lower strata, particularly in poorer countries with low levels of education, predisposes them to view politics in . . . terms of black or white, good and evil. Consequently, other things being equal, they should be more likely than other strata to prefer extremist movements which suggest easy and quick solutions to social problems and have a rigid outlook rather than those which view the problem of reform or change in complex and gradualist terms and which support rational values of tolerance.[17]

Adopting a social-psychological frame of reference, Lipset further attempts to explain what there is about lower-class life that produces in individuals this rigidity and hostility toward more democratic ideas and attitudes: lower-class individuals, he notes, are more likely than others to have been exposed from early childhood to punishment, lack of love, and a general atmosphere of tension and aggression. These experiences often produce deep-rooted hostilities, the manifestations of which are likely to be prejudice against ethnic minorities, political authoritarianism, and religious fundamentalism. The lower-class person's educational attainment is less than that of men with higher socioeconomic status, and "his association as a child with others of similar background not only fails to stimulate his intellectual interests but also creates an atmosphere which prevents his educational experience from increasing his social sophistication and his understanding of different groups and ideas."[18]

Although people who see things as either black or white appear to come disproportionately from the lower-class positions, as Lipset holds, they have company—at least among some individuals of higher-class status. Robert Welch, to name an extreme case, is founder and authoritarian leader of the ultra-right-wing John Birch Society. By virtue of his wealth, education, lineage, and power position, he is "upper-class." And among John Birch Society members whose identities have become known, there are middle- and upper-class people from such fields as law, medicine, the teaching profession, business, banking, and manufacturing.

SOCIAL MOBILITY

We have already indicated that an individual's class position may change, that social mobility is possible in an open-class society. *Social mobility is the movement of individuals from one stratum of society to another*. It is distinguished from *physical mobility*, which refers to geographical movement. Social mobility is *vertical mobility*, movement upward and downward in the social scale. Physical mobility is "horizontal," but the latter term also refers to shifts in occupation without change of status. Social mobility is often associated with geographical movement, as when a family that has risen on the stratification scale moves into a high-prestige neighborhood. Physical mobility, of course, does not necessarily involve social mobility, although it may. Here we are concerned primarily with social, vertical mobility.

In our society an individual can move to a higher or lower status up or down the class continuum, under given conditions. A soldier is promoted or demoted. The son of a lower-class family studies law, eventually becoming a successful attorney. The heir apparent of a family in the very highest status position, himself well educated and a person of high-level taste preferences, becomes dissolute, abandons family, occupation, and the way of life of his class of social origin. These persons —the soldier, the lawyer, and the scion of a high-status family —all have experienced social mobility. They recognize this, and so do others in the society.

Social mobility involves the recognition, evaluation, and re-evaluation of classes through two factors: demonstrable differences among members of a society and a scale of values by which these differences are measured. Thus, you might note that Mary drives a tomato-red 1967 Mustang while Ida comes to school in a battered 1952 Ford. Here is a demonstrable difference between the two with regard to a criterion that often is applied in establishing social position. If possession of sufficient means to purchase a new Mustang is an important value to you, you may place Mary higher on the social scale than Ida, provided, of course, this is your only criterion.

But in an open-class system, in which social mobility is possible, Ida can reach that position in life where she, too, owns a Mustang. By using the same criterion used in ranking Mary, you would thereupon change your conception of Ida, moving her, mentally, into a class with Mary. Ida may accept this definition, as you do, of her social position.

How mobile is social mobility? That depends upon the society. In our own society, it is often said that ambition, courage, and perseverance—plus luck—will get a man almost anywhere and anything. A rail-splitter became President of the United States. The son of a garment worker can become a banker. The daughter of poverty-stricken, alcoholic parents can become head of a women's college.

Countering such optimistic views, some observers of the social scene believe that although social mobility is possible and does take place, the *rate* of movement has declined in our society over about the past century. However, we may safely assert that our society is still characterized by considerable social mobility, as it has been from generation to generation, although the trend has not been consistent in the past hundred years. A large minority (possibly even a majority) of Americans move a little upward or downward in the class hierarchy in each generation. The unskilled worker category has been decreasing proportionately since about 1920. Compare this decrease with the increase of higher occupational echelons. There is considerable upward mobility from the white-collar occupations. Since mobility does occur, we may continue to assert we have an open-class society.

W. Lloyd Warner and James C. Abegglen several years ago made a study of occupational mobility in American business and industry of members of the "business elite." They posed the question:

Are the top-status levels increasingly open and accessible to those born at lower levels, or less open, and accessible only to the sons of top-status fathers? . . . We wanted to know whether hereditary and aristocratic principles operate to hold families at the top or whether the competitive forces which emphasize individual achievement determine who will be a leader.[19]

The authors found not only that some persons from the working class gained opportunities at the top level of business and industry, but that they had been climbing the social ladder faster during the preceding quarter century. There had been

not only an increase in the proportion of the men who come from the lower ranks, but an accompanying decrease in the proportion of sons of highly placed men, particularly of businessmen. Certainly occupational succession (within the limits of this study) is more fluid, and more vertical mobility has been taking place.[20]

At the same time, however, the authors concluded: "There is not full freedom of competition; the system is still sufficiently status-bound to work to the considerable advantage of men born to higher position."[21]

FACTORS AFFECTING SOCIAL MOBILITY

Several studies made during the last two or three decades support the following generalizations:

1. *In general, a high rate of social change increases social mobility.* The Crusades occurred during a period of great social readjustment. Indirectly, they accelerated the demise of feudalism and the advent of the Industrial Revolution. Subsequently, a partially open-class society with a degree of social mobility emerged in England as the manors were abandoned and agricultural workers flocked to the cities, where they were in great demand for industrial labor.

Rapid social change is characteristic of wartime. Cornelius Vanderbilt gave the world an example of vertical mobility during two war periods. At seventeen, he borrowed a hundred dollars, bought a barge, and went into the ferrying business in New York harbor. When the War of 1812 broke out, a year later, he made a tidy sum transporting supplies to military posts. From then on, inside and outside the law, Vanderbilt carved himself a great fortune; by the end of the Civil War he was the only citizen of his country worth more than twenty million dollars.

2. *Barriers to communication between classes generally*

limit social mobility. When one class of people is insulated against others, class lines are established and made rigid within that group. When a class of people learns the ways of life of another class, the barriers tend to be lowered somewhat, permitting greater mobility. Years ago, people in isolated rural territory in the United States had relatively little interaction with people in urban areas. Their occupation was largely farming. The farmer in such remote areas was generally a man of modest means, living a rather simple, routinized existence. His son was likely to follow in his footsteps, becoming a farmer himself. The farmer's daughter had little choice but to marry another farmer's son. Few young people left home to attend college, and even high-school education was fairly rare. Insulated as they were against "the outside world," these people had limited opportunity for social mobility.

As time went on, however, the boundaries of cities expanded, reached into outlying, once-isolated sections. Good roads, easy transportation, motion pictures, and radio greatly helped to bring the city to the farm and the farm to the city. One population learned about the other, about its values, aspirations, and ways. Communication was established. Barriers were lowered, permitting greater social mobility. Today the farmer is often college-educated, well-to-do, and as sophisticated in the ways of the world as his urban counterpart. When he visits the city, he is undistinguishable from the urban dwellers with whom he rubs shoulders in restaurants, theaters, and department stores. His children attend schools in faraway places and frequently abandon agriculture for business and the professions. Many of them settle in urban areas.

3. *The more distinguishable the physical appearance of a class, the greater the likelihood that these characteristics will affect the mobility rate of its individual members.** Caucasoids in a predominantly Caucasian open-class society generally find upward social mobility easier than do Negroes in the same society. The mobility rate of each group is affected by its physical appearance. The black-skinned Rhodesian is strictly limited in social mobility. His visibility as a non-Caucasoid makes it the more certain he will not evade the limitations im-

* For the balance of this section, I lean heavily on, and am indebted to, Bernard Berelson and Gary A. Steiner, *Human Behavior, An Inventory of Scientific Findings* (New York: Harcourt, Brace & World, 1964), pp. 465–468.

posed upon him. The Caucasian in Rhodesia, by the same token, has greater freedom of upward mobility, and the visibility of his Caucasoid features gives him a distinct advantage over the Negroid Rhodesian. Early in this century, the white man in Haiti was unable to move upward *or* downward in social position—he was accepted by neither the black-skinned Haitian nor the brown-skinned Indian-French-Negro Haitian.

Note, however, that it is not visibility as such that affects mobility, but how the particular physical features are defined in the society. The black-skinned Rhodesian's color simply identifies him among Caucasoids who place all native Africans low on the status scale. The white man's physical characteristics merely identified him in Haiti in the years when black-skinned and brown-skinned Haitians considered "le blanc," or white man, of lesser status than themselves.

3. *Industrialized societies tend to be marked by upward and downward mobility.* The wealth produced by industrialization creates additional industrial and commercial development, which in turn results in an increasingly varied array of social positions to be filled. There are more opportunities than previously to occupy social positions, particularly as a scarcity of persons available to occupy them develops. Downward mobility may be a consequence of accelerated specialization and technological change. Persons competent to do certain work become "obsolete," like machines that are outmoded with changes in industrial techniques.

In a study of worldwide cultural and scientific developments during the twentieth century, the authors point out that wherever industrialization has occurred it has brought radical changes in the occupational structure of the industrial countries, and these changes, in turn, have resulted in still others.

Skilled craftsmen who had constituted the aristocracy of labour lost their position as their trades became obsolete; unskilled workers found themselves replaced by machines. In their places a new group of trained engineers and managers, technicians, salesmen, statisticians, office workers, advertisers, operatives and mechanics arose to plan, design, manage and carry on the processes of modern industry and distribute its products. New occupations developed in wholly new industries such as radio or aviation, motion pictures or plastics. With mounting requirements for scientific research and diversified education, with more wealth and greater leisure, professions and service occupations expanded and the numbers of scientists, teachers, doctors, nurses, entertainers, restaurant keepers and providers of holiday and travel facilities multiplied.[22]

The authors go on to report that the old class structure fell before the changes in occupations and sources of income. Men of industry replaced the landed aristocracy as the dominant group, leaving the aristocracy with "hollow titles and waning prestige." The old, small middle class of professional persons, tradesmen, and skilled craftsmen was overshadowed by a new army of industrial technicians, administrators, and white-collar workers. The bulk of the population was pushed toward the middle-class position. Although the social and economic distance between the richest and the poorest remained, modern industrialization steadily reduced the proportion that fell in these extremes. It tremendously expanded the great middle group.

Historically, industrialization in many parts of the world, though not all parts, has been closely associated with urbanization.

5. *Urbanized societies are more likely to show social mobility than rural societies.* There are more class strata in urban communities, as a rule; more differentiation in social positions to be occupied; greater impersonality, so that family background is not as important. In cities the caste element in social stratification is less likely to prevent mobility than in rural communities.

Both rapid industrialization and large-scale urbanization have marked the "modernization" of Russian society, especially since the early years of the Soviet regime. Thus the U.S.S.R. and the United States, notwithstanding their contrasting political institutions and systems of social control, provide the two largest examples of societies wherein industrialization and urbanization have strongly encouraged social mobility.*

6. *The greater the ethnic diversity and the in-migration, the more open the social system is likely to be.* As new ethnic groups arrive, and find a place on the stratification ladder, often at the bottom, an open-class system is facilitated. The United States, of course, is a major case in point:

* On social mobility in the Soviet Union, see, for example, Alex Inkeles and Raymond A. Bauer, *The Soviet Citizen* (Cambridge, Mass.: Harvard University Press, 1959), Chap. 4.

In the United States . . . almost every generation has had the benefit of rising on top of new groups coming in at the bottom of the system—European immigrants in several waves, urbanized Negroes, migrant farmers. As such groups, usually ethnic in character, themselves become assimilated, they begin moving up the class ladder.[23]

7. *An equalitarian social philosophy encourages an open system of stratification.* Under such a philosophy an hereditary aristocracy is not favored. Where all are presumed to have the same right to ascend the stratification ladder, in principle they may do so commensurate with available opportunities—and such principles often have objective consequences.

8. *A society with a widespread system of education is likely to be more open than one without such a system.* When a society emphasizes education and at the same time does not reserve the right to an education to any special group, it is likely that interchange of ranks can go on. Education is not inheritable.

9. *The greater the differential in fertility rates among classes in a society, the more open the system tends to be.* When the number of members of the upper classes decreases because the fertility rate is too low to maintain it, there is room for others.

IS A CLASSLESS SOCIETY POSSIBLE?

Social reformers and creators of fictional utopias often envision a society that is totally classless, with no differences in rank, no stratification whatever. Is this a possibility in a real as well as a philosophical sense? It is doubtful. Let us consider one type of contemporary community that was founded on the premise that it would remain classless.

The collective farm (kibbutz) system of Israel has been reported on by Eva Rosenfeld (among others).[24] At the time she made her observations, each kibbutz averaged about 200 inhabitants (there were a few exceptions)—small enough, one might assume, to make it possible to maintain an unstratified social system.

In the kibbutz system the means of production and all other property belong to the commune. Members who leave have no claim on it. An elected work committee assigns tasks to the kibbutz dwellers. Governance is provided by elected officials, who serve brief one- or two-year terms. The philosophical orientation of the kibbutz is: "From everyone according to his ability. To everyone according to his need." Accordingly, the manager of an important communal undertaking might live in smaller quarters and eat less well than some unskilled workers who need special food and housing. All commodities are distributed from a central point. Meals are taken in a common dining hall. Children are reared in communal children's homes.

Can such a system become stratified? It already has. Differentials in power and status exist. Managers have come to hold higher status than individuals whose work they direct. Persons with required skills or talents that are in short supply are at a premium, and this is apt to gain them high status. Additionally, the *vatikim*, kibbutz pioneers, constitute an aristocracy, by seniority alone. Certain terms in the language bespeak a status system: a *yish hashoov* is "an important personality," while a *stam pkak* is "just an unskilled, movable worker." The kibbutz, then, is not unstratified.

Moreover, the kibbutzim constitute a rather small part of the nation's total population. Much of Israel is urbanized, and large segments of its people occupy class positions similar to those found in many modern societies. It is unlikely, in fact, that the utopian goal of classlessness can be achieved in any society today, when a complex division of labor is required to meet the needs of modern life.

· NOTES

1. Ian Whitaker, "The Nature and Value of Functionalism in Society," in Don Martindale (ed.), *Functionalism in the Social Sciences* (Philadelphia: American Academy of Political and Social Science, 1965), pp. 127–162.
2. *Ibid.*
3. U. S. Department of Labor, *Manpower, Challenge of the 1960s* (Washington, D. C.: U. S. Government Printing Office, 1960), p. 16.
4. H. H. Gerth and C. Wright Mills (eds. and trans.) *From Max Weber: Essays in Sociology* (New York: Oxford University Press, 1946), p. 181.
5. Ely Chinoy, *Society: An Introduction to Sociology*, 2nd ed. (New York: Random House, 1967), p. 171.
6. E. Digby Baltzell, *An American Business Aristocracy* (New York: Collier Books, 1962), p. 70.
7. *Ibid.*, pp. 431–433.
8. Cleveland Amory, *Who Killed Society?* (New York: Pocket Books, 1962), p. 49.
9. Baltzell, *op. cit.*, pp. 75–76.

10. Manning Nash, *The Golden Road to Modernity, Village Life in Contemporary Burma* (New York: Wiley, 1965), p. 95.

11. Hortense Powdermaker, *Copper Town: Changing Africa, The Human Situation on the Rhodesian Copperbelt* (New York: Colophon Books, 1965), p. 274.

12. Baltzell, *op. cit.*, p. 74.

13. Bernard Berelson and Gary A. Steiner, *Human Behavior, An Inventory of Scientific Findings* (New York: Harcourt, Brace & World, 1964), p. 482.

14. *Ibid.*, p. 485.

15. *Ibid.*, pp. 486–487.

16. Samuel A. Stouffer, *Communism, Conformity and Civil Liberties* (New York: Doubleday, 1955).

17. Seymour M. Lipset, "Democracy and Working-Class Authoritarianism," *American Sociological Review*, XXIV (August 1959), pp. 482–501.

18. *Ibid.*

19. W. Lloyd Warner and James C. Abegglen, *Occupational Mobility in American Industry, 1928–1952* (Minneapolis: University of Minnesota Press, 1955), p. 3.

20. *Ibid.*, p. 33.

21. *Ibid.*, p. 36.

22. Caroline F. Ware, K. M. Panikkar, and J. M. Romein, *The Twentieth Century* (New York: Harper & Row, 1966), pp. 99–100. Volume VI of *History of Mankind: Cultural and Scientific Development.* Copyright 1966 by UNESCO.

23. Berelson and Steiner, *op. cit.*, pp. 466–467.

24. Eva Rosenfeld, "Social Stratification in a 'Classless' Society," *American Sociological Review*, XVI (December 1951), 766–774.

· SUGGESTIONS FOR FURTHER READING

American Journal of Sociology, LVIII (January 1953).
> *The entire issue deals with social stratification in the United States, Latin America, China, and France.*

AMORY, CLEVELAND. *Who Killed Society?* New York: Harper & Row, 1960.
> *An entertaining account, by a professional writer, of the rise and fall of American "Society."*

BALTZELL, E. DIGBY. *An American Business Aristocracy.* New York: Collier Books, 1962.
> *A highly enjoyable book, which deals with an elite subculture of Philadelphians.*

BALTZELL, E. DIGBY. *The Protestant Establishment: Aristocracy and Caste in America.* New York: Random House, 1964.
> *The author traces the growth and decay of American aristocracy. His thesis is that it has deteriorated from a ruling class into a mere caste, stubbornly concerned with protecting its privileges even though it is no longer capable of leadership.*

DUBE, S. C. *Indian Village*. London: Routledge, 1955.
A study of the operation of caste in a village in India.

KUPER, LEO. *An African Bourgeoisie*. New Haven, Conn.: Yale University Press, 1964.
An interesting analysis of an emerging African middle class.

LIPSET, SEYMOUR M. "Democracy and Working-Class Authoritarianism." *American Sociological Review*, XXIV (August 1959), 482–501.
The belief that lower-class status predisposes individuals to take extremist positions in politics and religion is supported by evidence from a number of societies.

LYND, ROBERT S., and HELEN M. LYND. *Middletown*. New York: Harcourt, Brace & World, 1929.
A classic inquiry into the stratified social class life in a Midwest community.

MILLS, C. WRIGHT. *White Collar*. New York: Oxford University Press, 1951.
A sociological evaluation of what Mills sees as America's new middle classes.

PAULUS, CALEB R. "A Study of the Social Stratification in Bangalore City." *Pacific Sociological Review*, II (Spring 1968), 49–56.
During the past two decades, industrialization and urbanization have changed the Indian social structure in urban centers. The author shows how, in the growing industrial city of Bangalore, caste occupations are being abandoned and the hereditary caste system is being replaced by class stratification.

SHOSTAK, ARTHUR, and WILLIAM GOMBERG (eds.). *Blue Collar World*. Englewood Cliffs, N. J.: Prentice-Hall, 1964.
This is a collection of articles on the blue-collar worker in the United States.

WARNER, W. LLOYD, and JAMES C. ABEGGLEN. *Occupational Mobility in American Industry, 1928–1952*. Minneapolis: University of Minnesota Press, 1955.
A study of occupational mobility, based on an analysis of the social origins and careers of some 8,000 major business executives.

WHITE, R. CLYDE. "Social Class Differences in the Uses of Leisure." *American Journal of Sociology*, LXI (September 1955), 145–150.
White finds that a person's use of leisure time depends partly upon his class position.

16 SPATIAL PATTERNS OF GROUPS

We live in groups. Groups of people also become arranged in characteristic spatial patterns. We discuss these patterns and the process by which they come into being. We are dealing with *community*, a concept we shall examine at some length.

THE MEANING OF COMMUNITY

Ask certain residents of New York City where they live and they will reply, "Harlem." Now, Harlem is on Manhattan Island and politically part of it. Harlem has no official boundaries separating it from other sections of the island. No resident can tell you where Harlem begins and ends, except in vague general terms. Yet when residents say, "I'm from Harlem," it means something specific to them.

Ask a Negro in certain cities of the Deep South where he lives and he may reply, "In the quarters." This is a term going back to the days before the Civil War, when it signified the slave quarters. When slavery was abolished, it became a euphemism for areas where Negroes may and must live.

Harlem's boundaries are only vaguely defined. The "quarters" have strict lines of demarcation. Nevertheless, to the Harlemite and the man from the quarters the respective domiciles are located in what each considers his community. He may or may not like living there, but he shares common interests with other residents, identifies himself as one who has certain rights and obligations as a member of that community.

The idea that "my community" is "the place where I live" is quite in accord with the sociological definition. From that point of view, *a community emerges when a number of people, living in the same general locality, realize they share common interests and have mutual needs as a consequence of the fact that they live near one another.* A community develops as the residents work together to satisfy their common needs with respect to the use of the available space.

Sociologists do not all agree on a definition of *community*, but consensus on certain of its elements does exist. Attempting to find areas of agreement, George A. Hillery, Jr., analyzed and compared ninety-four different definitions of community he found in sociological literature.[1] Seventy of the ninety-four indicated that *area* and *social interaction* were essential to the definition. We will begin with these in elaborating on what *community* means.

1. *A community has area. It occupies space.*

2. *A community is characterized by social interaction, involving the use of space the residents occupy.* This interaction may be direct or indirect. The inhabitants of a household almost certainly have developed a feeling of unity through direct association. The residents of a small village generally know one another personally and interact directly to a considerable extent. But in the larger and more complex levels of community it is impossible for individuals to associate directly and know personally more than a few of the people who share and participate in city, state, regional, national, or international levels of community. Inhabitants of these levels can and do interact indirectly with each other, through mutual acquaintances and mass media. Even in large cities, practically everyone knows someone who knows someone who knows the mayor. And many people not personally acquainted read the same newspapers, watch the same television programs. They tend to develop common sentiments and ideas about their communities. People develop a common understanding of the meaning and function of community on each of its respective levels through both direct and indirect associations.

3. *Members of a community feel that it exists.* There is a subjective sense of "belonging together." A man says, "I live in Flatbush." Flatbush is a subjectively recognized section of Brooklyn, New York, and the person who asserts he resides

there means that he belongs in the Flatbush community of residents and that it is vaguely but in fact differentiated from the rest of Brooklyn, even though no one can say precisely where the boundary lines are.

4. *A community is an area in which an individual could live his entire life.* Robert M. MacIver and Charles H. Page write: "One cannot live wholly within a business organization or a church; one can live wholly within a tribe or a city. The basic criterion of community, then, is that all of one's social relationships may be found within it."[2] An individual may have relationships outside the community, and generally does, but he *could* live his entire life in the community and have all of his social relationships there.

How do we apply the term *community*? "My home town," as I see that town, is a community in the sociological sense, since it refers to the geographical location where I live as well as to my understanding of the way in which I share the use of the available space with other residents of that locality. But the same definition applies equally well to "my house." It, too, incorporates my ideas of the particular place where I reside and (unless I am a hermit) the interests I have in common with other people as a result of sharing the space within that house. As a matter of fact, this definition of community is flexible enough to be applied to the spatial organization of residents of an area as small as a tiny room or as large as a number of nations. In Figure 16.1 the artist pokes wry fun at state boundaries, but his drawing also has its serious side. The householder obviously accepts the state of California as his community. His city of residence and his home would be communities, too.

You live in your home town, but you live in a number of other distinct communities at the same time. These vary considerably in the amount of space occupied, the number of residents involved, and the complexity of the organization needed to resolve problems related to the use of space. Moving from the small and simple to the large and complex levels of community, you live simultaneously in a household, neighborhood, town or city, county, state, and nation. Every level of community meets the specifications of our definition.

The United States is a useful locale for studying the emergence and development of communities, because its comparatively brief history provides many records of what actually

Figure 16.1
The Community
Feeling

From the book *What's
Funny About That?*
by The Editors of
This Week. Copyright,
1954, by E. P. Dutton
& Co., Inc. Reproduced
by permission of the
publishers.

"Welcome to California!"

occurred when people migrated to a new locality. Pioneer families, living on adjacent homesteads, repeatedly recognized their common need to share space and agreed to strive cooperatively for mutual fulfillment of their needs. Consider two settlers who live on adjoining farms in a narrow valley, their property so located that each farm blocks the other from access to needed objectives. Pete cannot get wood for fuel without going through Oscar's place. Oscar is unable to get water for his livestock without going through Pete's. The two talk things over and decide: "Both of us need a road running through each other's land. If we each donate some land and labor, we can build one. Let's do it."

This illustrates the genesis of a community. When an area becomes populated, paths, sidewalks, and roads needed by the residents are likely to be developed by negotiation among them. As population burgeons, still further agreements become necessary. Thus in our country, as we extended our borders from east to west, occupying more and more space on this continent, streets, sidewalks, boulevards, highways, and superhighways connecting and facilitating movement between houses, farms, villages, cities, and states were constructed, partly as a consequence of direct, face-to-face conference and agreement. However, because of the increased complexity of our society it became necessary to get much of the work done through representatives of the people rather than in the more direct, face-to-face manner possible in a pioneer society. Secondary agencies developed, with a mandate to advance certain common ends. Thus, public highway commissions, city and state planning boards, legislatures, and to some extent courts are included among the agencies now playing a role in determining whether and where a superhighway shall be built or a city street extended. But these agencies, under our theory of government, represent and act for the people and help develop communities for the people. To be sure, a home owner may object that he does not want a city planner to tell him he must sell his house so that it may be razed to make way for a freeway. The city planner, however, is charged with acting for the presumed welfare of the community as a whole, and the welfare of the many must take precedence over the wishes (and perhaps welfare) of one individual or family.

When official representatives of the United States meet with official representatives of Mexico, to agree on cooperative efforts to build bridges and highways connecting the two countries, this also represents the genesis of community. Whatever the level of community involved, people meet and agree upon objectives and plans.

Moving from one place to another is only one of the objectives satisfied through community relations. Others include shelter, relaxation, recreation, safety, order, cleanliness, sanitation, comfort, and peace within the space we occupy. We need clean water and unpolluted air. We need a constant supply of food, for which the economic community must make provision.

Latterly we have become aware, too, of a need for privacy. In our society, we are beleaguered from all sides by telephone solicitations, house-to-house salesmen, inquiring reporters, electronic listening devices, television commercials, advertising mail urging us to buy anything from a book to a tombstone. As cities become more crowded, dwelling units are pushed closer together, so that we hear a neighbor taking a shower. The separate dining room is disappearing; the kitchen merges with a "dinette," which is actually a corner of the living room. This is "open plan" domestic architecture, providing less and less privacy.

Privacy, according to *Time* magazine, "must be fought for resolutely step by step: the door closed, the questionnaire ignored, the mass resisted, the electronic eye outstared, the moment of silence stolen and cherished." That way is "the best, indeed the only way toward community. For only in the healing and sometimes illuminating moments of privacy can a man make himself truly fit to live with others."[3]

Each of our needs, whether for privacy, shelter, or something else is based on cultural values we have learned to consider desirable in our society. We try to assure ourselves of adequate room to satisfy these needs. Therefore we enter into reciprocal agreements to share the use of the available space in a way that will be beneficial to all involved. This is the function of community relations within each of the respective levels. Through community relations people provide themselves with space for homes, parks, playgrounds, public schools, churches, factories, markets, many other things. When the community is extended to mean the United States, we make spatial provision for highways girdling the nation; air, water, and railroad transportation; national parks; government buildings; military camps. When representatives of two nations enter into a pact permitting airliners from both countries to fly over their respective territories, they are transacting business on an international level of community relations.

As a result of cultural conditioning, inhabitants of every level of community reserve for themselves a certain amount of local autonomy and extend the same privilege to residents of adjacent communities. Members of one household may resent it when neighbors ask them to keep their lawn free of weeds. The people of Minneapolis do not want the people of St. Paul telling them where to locate a new industrial area inside Minneapolis. The inhabitants of the United States would resist strenuously if Soviet Russia's leaders interfered in any way with our country's use of space in Hawaii.

RURAL & URBAN COMMUNITIES

Sociologists have traditionally studied communities from several vantage points. Some have examined them from the perspective of history, noting that evolutionary processes were occurring among human societies and that civilizations were changing in nature from comparatively simple to increasingly complex social relationships. Thus, Ferdinand Tönnies, a German sociologist of the late nineteenth century, wrote that the processes of modern history have resulted in an atomization or mechanization of primary social relationships. As he viewed history, there has been a continuous weakening of the communal bonds of family, guild, and village, which he referred to as *Gemeinschaft* (community). There has been a constant maximizing of what he called *Gesellschaft* (society), with its more impersonal, mechanical relationships. Emile Durkheim also called attention to the weakening of common bonds in complex societies, attributing this to such phenomena as technology, the spread of individualism, and the division of labor. These societies, he asserted, were held together by *organic solidarity* rather than by *mechanical solidarity.*

In the United States, sociologists early differentiated between *urban* and *rural* community (other types being delineated a little later). They recognized that certain differences exist between the two types; these differences having to do with size, density of population, characteristic occupations of residents, and other features. However, although certain distinguishing features of rural and urban areas are apparent, similarities also exist. An entirely satisfactory definition of one type, clearly distinguishing it from the other, is not easy to devise. Do not make the mistake, for instance, of believing that rural territory is inhabited mainly by farmers. This was once the case, but no longer. Slightly over 30 percent of the total United States population lived in rural areas in 1960. Approximately 9 percent were rural-farm dwellers, while some 21 percent were rural nonfarm residents.

Some sociologists contend that rural and urban communities are fundamentally different in *nature,* that is, in very basic respects, as well as taken as a whole. Others hold they differ only in *degree,* that is, that both have the same basic characteristics, but these exist in different proportions in the two types of community. On the whole, we would seem on sounder ground if we say that rural and urban areas differ in degree only. Continuous social change in both types in the United States has progressively made them more and more alike in certain respects. Consider such facts as these:

1. Over a century ago, this country was largely rural and agricultural. In 1790, there was no city with a population as large as 50,000. By 1840, there were only 5 in this category. But a century after that, we had 199 cities of 50,000 and larger. And by 1960, the number had risen to 334.[4] Urbanization has been an outstanding feature of social change in this country.

2. In 1800, approximately 6 percent of the total United States population lived in urban areas, while 94 percent resided in rural sections. By 1950, some 64 percent lived in

urban areas, 36 percent in rural. In 1960, urban dwellers represented almost 70 percent of the nation's population, the balance, about 30 percent, living in rural districts.[5] Thus, our history is marked by an increasing urban and a decreasing rural population.

3. What has occured is a *redistribution* of population, to be discussed in more detail later in this chapter. First there was a steadily increasing concentration of population in urban centers. Following this centralization, a period of decentralization set in and continues to the present. It consists of a movement of a portion of the population out of the cities into the suburbs. Population growth in recent decades has not been in central cities as much as in surounding areas. Some cities, in fact, have lost population as surrounding suburbs gained residents.

Leo Schnore, an American sociologist, says that decentralization is "one of the most significant movements in the long history of urban communities."[6] In effect, what has happened over the years is a movement into, and then out of, the cities to an extent that has produced changes both in urban and rural territory and brought one closer to the other in some ways. The modern farmer, as was indicated in the preceeding chapter, is no longer an undereducated, frugal man who can afford few conveniences and pleasures. He is much like the city dweller. The way of life of the predominantly rural United States of 1800 was quite different from what it is now. In 1800, barter was common; for example, a farmer exchanged eggs for flour. There was only a primitive distribution system. Itinerant peddlers offered what could not be bought in the local "general store." Householders made their own clothing, churned butter, put up foods for the winter. The family doctor had not been nudged aside for the transmission-belt medical specialist. Apartment houses were unknown. A man knew his neighbor. A trip of a thousand miles, which we can make comfortably in a few hours, was a major undertaking requiring weeks, even months. Today, much of this is changed. There are still pockets of semi-isolated rural communities, some of them marked by extreme poverty and primitive living conditions, but viewed in the whole, it does not seem that urban and rural localities represent completely different types of community. In mass society, the smallest town is influenced in some measure by "outside" forces, even while retaining some features of traditional local community life.

An elderly man, looking back over the years, recalling his childhood in a rural area, may reflect: "I wish I were back home. It's wonderful there! Everybody is warm and friendly. Life is simple. No rush, no bustle. People help each other at harvest time. They're always ready to do a favor for a neighbor. Too bad city folk don't live like country people!"

If this man were to return to the scenes of his childhood, he would probably discover that many of the assumed differences between rural and urban life exist only in imagination. The small farm is disappearing and being replaced by great combines. In 1940, there were 506,000 farms in the United States with fewer than ten acres. By 1964, there were only 183,000. On the other hand, 101,000 farms had 1,000 acres or over in 1940, and the number had risen to 145,000 by 1964.[7] And just as the small farm is disappearing, so too are the tenant farmer and the sharecropper. Such agricultural workers still exist, but they are on the way out. Farming has become highly mechanized; the farmer can harvest and thresh his grain without help from neighbors. He has the same modern plumbing as his city cousin; his wife uses an electric clothes washer, and her kitchen is equipped with an electric dishwasher. The children do not attend the little red schoolhouse but a large, centrally located consolidated school. The family shops at a chain supermarket, not a "cracker-barrel" general store. It reads metropolitan newspapers, listens to the same television programs as do city dwellers. There is more rush and bustle than some decades ago. There are more cars, more places to go, and the young folks, like their city cousins, go to drive-in movies, which have helped to replace the lovers' lanes of fifty years ago. There is more business to seek and more competition to meet. Our nostalgic man, looking back, remembers that everybody used to be warm and friendly. Probably this was not entirely the case even then, but if he returned to his childhood home today he would find some of the hardness, the conflict, the cruelty that one can find in the city. To an extent, the city way of life has moved to the country.

And when farm people move to the city, they take their rural values and customs with them. The rural belief that every American boy needs a dog and that every household group needs some garden space persists in the minds of many urban residents, even though dogs and gardens have little economic value in the city.

To a significant extent, then, not only has the city moved to the country but the country has moved to the city. And while some differences between urban and rural communities still prevail, both have moved and are moving in the same direction along the same historical continuum. Partly as a consequence of the widespread acceptance and use throughout our society of automobiles, television sets, telephones, and many other technological innovations, differences between farm and city, rural and urban life, are disappearing.

DECENTRALIZATION IN URBAN AREAS

We have noted the increasing decentralization of cities in the twentieth century. Now let us consider some specific patterns of urbanized areas.

THE METROPOLITAN COMMUNITY · Largely a phenomenon of this century, *a metropolitan community consists of a central city or several cities, and surrounding suburbs, villages, and farm land economically dominated by the central city or cities.* Metropolitan development, Schnore observes,[8] is a new form of urban growth especially characteristic of twentieth-century America. For many years, this country received large numbers of European immigrants, who settled mainly in the cities, contributing to their growth. However, the first decade of the twentieth century saw a change, marking the end of one phase of urban development, in Schnore's view. In that decade, which included the World War I years, migration from overseas was greatly reduced, and overall urban growth in the United States was slowed down, although not stopped.

The in-migration rate did not rise to prewar levels after peace was declared, largely as a consequence of highly restrictive immigration laws enacted by our Congress, establishing rigid quotas for the admission of people from the very countries that before this had contributed most of the migrants. The national population continued to increase, nevertheless, and cities grew rapidly between 1920 and 1930, but now this was principally a consequence of internal migration, from rural to urban centers.

The growth of cities slowed down somewhat between 1930 and 1940, a consequence of the decline in migration from abroad, but also of a lessened flow of rural-to-urban migration, caused largely by the economic depression of that decade. Job opportunities in the cities had dwindled, hence there was less incentive than formerly for individuals from outlying areas to gravitate to urban centers.

During the early 1940s, employment opportunities multiplied, for the nation was girding for defense and war. Throughout World War II and for some years thereafter, as the nation returned to a peacetime economy, urban employment continued at fairly high levels. It was further stimulated by the Korean war. City population continued to increase in absolute numbers.

But despite this, the general, though erratic, tendency in the fifty years since 1900 has been for the *rate* of growth of metropolitan population to decline. This has been an outcome of decentralization. The American sociologist Amos H. Hawley, a contemporary student of human ecology, points out that, especially and most conspicuously since 1920, there has been "a shift of high growth rates from central cities to those parts of metropolitan areas not included in central cities, commonly referred to as satellite areas."[9] That is to say, rates of population growth in immediately outlying areas have reduced city rates proportionately, by comparison. The declining rates of increase in central cities have been "functions mainly of the slowing growth of central cities, for growth rates in satellite areas increased over the 50-year period."[10]

Schnore's investigations show that:

. . . the presently defined metropolitan areas have captured a disproportionately large share of the total national increase in population throughout the entire fifty-year period. Within metropolitan areas, however, central city growth has become progressively slower, while the ring [satellite area] has tended to grow more and more rapidly. It is this over-all pattern of differential growth in favor of the peripheral area that is usually labeled "decentralization."[11]

Schnore found that part of this slowed-down city growth stems from the failure or inability of cities to annex surrounding densely settled areas. Another factor has been a tendency for residents of the central city to move in increasing numbers to various parts of the adjacent ring area. A third factor is the tendency for migrants from outside the metropolitan area to move directly to the peripheral ring rather than to the city itself. "The total effect is a *relative* decentralization or net peripheral growth in excess of that of the center."[12]

For statistical purposes the Bureau of the Budget, in 1964, defined a "Standard Metropolitan Statistical Area" (SMSA) for the census as a county or group of contiguous counties (except in New England) containing at least one central city of 50,-000 inhabitants or more, or "twin cities" with a combined population of at least 50,000. In addition, other contiguous counties are included in an SMSA if, according to certain criteria, they are essentially metropolitan in character and are socially and economically integrated with the central city. In New England, towns and cities rather than counties are used in defining SMSAs. On the basis of this definition, there were 231 SMSAs in the United States as of July 1, 1967.[13] (Puerto Rico is not included in this figure.) About two-thirds of the population currently resides in SMSAs, there having been an increasing concentration of people in them in the past several decades.

However, the SMSA includes both urban and suburban territory, and the population shifts into metropolitan areas include movement into the suburbs of those areas. This "suburban sprawl," as it has been called, has pushed metropolitan-area boundaries farther and farther out into rural territory. Using census figures as a base, Ben J. Wattenberg and Richard M. Scammon have presented a rough statistical measure of this sprawl. For their purposes, they defined suburbanites as persons residing within an SMSA but outside of a central city in that SMSA. In 1940, they found, 51 percent of the United States population resided in SMSAs. Of these, 32 percent lived in central cities and 19 percent in suburbs. By 1960, SMSAs had 63 percent of the population within their boudaries. Thirty-two percent lived in central cities—the same proportion as in 1940. On the other hand, suburban dwellers represented 31 percent of the total in SMSAs, almost equal to the proportion who were central-city residents.[14]

THE CITY, THE SUBURBS, AND THE URBAN FRINGE · Assume a large city, or several cities, surrounded by less densely populated land. This urbanized area (it may or may not classify as a standard metropolitan statistical area) consists of three distinctive segments: (1) the central city or cities, (2) the suburbs, (3) the urban fringe.

The city is urban territory of comparatively dense population with a social organization and economy that affect life in the suburbs and urban fringe.

Suburbs have been defined by William M. Dobriner as *"those urbanized, residential communities which are outside the corporate limits of a large central city, but which are culturally and economically dependent upon the central city."*[15] However, Schnore adds something to this definition. All suburbs are not "bedroom cities," he points out. Some are primarily devoted to manufacturing, others to providing specialized services, such as education and recreation. Still others are primarily dependent upon extractive industries, such as mining and oil production. From an economics standpoint "it appears that the range of specialties found among suburbs approaches that discoverable in other cities." Schnore suggests that suburbs are of two types, "residential" and "employing." The basis of the distinction "is extremely simple: whether or not the suburb tends to attract more workers to its confines every day than the number of working people who sleep there every night."[16]

Elsewhere, Schnore refers to the "employing" suburban center as a "satellite."

We can say that *goods and services* tend to flow out of the *employing satellites* to other areas (both local and non-local), while *persons* are attracted into these areas for employment. On the other hand, *residential suburbs* send out *workers* and tend to receive an influx of *goods and services* for consumption by their inhabitants.[17]

The urban fringe is a land belt surrounding the central city containing both urban and rural characteristics and characterized by mixed urban and rural use of land. It lies at a point where full city facilities are no longer available and where agricultural use of land predominates. This is where urbanized territory begins to blend into rural territory.

CITY AND SUBURBS COMPARED · Sociologists have at times attempted to make out a case for distinctive urban and rural personality types. They have not been altogether convincing, as we would expect if rural and urban ways of life have become quite similar.

Since the advent of "suburban sprawl," social scientists,

fiction writers, and cartoonists have depicted what they believe to be the suburban type. More often than not he has been portrayed as a well-to-do individual, politically conservative, socially gregarious, prejudiced against Negroes and Jews, and a lover of green lawns, giddy house parties, and lethal martinis. No doubt such a "type" can be found in suburbia, but since it is also encountered inside the city, the delineation has little use, for we have not determined what is typical rather than exceptional about the respective populations. If we had evidence that, per capita, the delineated type is significantly more prevalent in the suburbs than in the city, we might accept the statement that there is a suburban type. But such evidence is not available.

However, certain research findings shed some light on the character of the suburban population, taken as a whole. Otis D. Duncan and Albert J. Reiss, Jr., for instance, published an interesting report in 1956, based on an analysis of 1950 national census statistics.[18] Below is a digest of part of the data, concerning characteristics of suburban populations of urbanized areas.

1. On the average, the suburban population is younger than the central city population. The median age of suburban residents was 30.9 in 1950, while in central cities of all urbanized areas combined it was 32.7.

2. Fertility rates of suburbanites are higher than those of city dwellers. In all central cities combined there were 452 children under the age of 5 per 1,000 women age 20–44. In the combined suburban population there were 534 children per 1,000 women in the indicated age bracket.

3. Proportionately, there are more native whites in suburbs than in cities (other categories are foreign-born white, Negro, and "other races"). The proportion of Negroes in central cities was nearly three times what it was in the suburbs—12.6 percent as compared to 4.5 percent. (Today, the proportion of Negroes in cities as compared to suburbs is even greater.) These differences reflect a typical pattern of migration of nonwhites to the central portions of urbanized areas; they also reflect a typical pattern of the residential segregation of nonwhites, and of socio-economic differences between central cities and suburbs.

4. There is a higher proportion of married persons in the suburbs. Of the population fourteen years of age and over, the figures for 1950 were:

a. For whites of both sexes the percentage married was greater in the suburbs. The percentage of single, widowed, and divorced was smaller than in cities.

b. For nonwhites, central cities had a somewhat higher proportion of widowed and divorced persons, for both male and female, than was the case with the suburban population.

c. Unlike whites, the percentage of nonwhite married *males* was greater in central cities, while the percentage who were single, for both nonwhite males and females, was greater in the suburbs.

5. A substantially larger proportion of married-but-separated individuals reside in cities as opposed to suburbs. This holds for whites, nonwhites, and the population as a whole.

6. The white suburban population is ahead of the white city population by a full year in educational attainment, as shown for 1950. The median for city residents was 10.3 years of schooling; for suburbanites, 11.3 years. For nonwhites the difference was in the reverse direction. The city median exceeded the suburban median by 0.2 of a year.

7. There is no marked difference in labor-participation rates for males, as between cities and suburbs. In the cities, in 1950, 80.2 percent of white males were in the labor force, as compared with 81.6 percent in the suburbs. For nonwhite males there was no difference at all between the two groups.

8. Median incomes were higher in the suburbs. In 1950, for all classes of income recipients, the median in the suburbs was 250 dollars above the median in the cities. However, city-suburb differences were more pronounced for whites than for nonwhites. And differences for females were in the opposite direction from that for males. Thus, for white males, the suburban median exceeded the city median by over 350 dollars, while for nonwhite males the difference was not quite 100 dollars. Among white females, the suburban median was 150 dollars less than the city median. A difference in the same direction of 65 dollars was observed for nonwhite females.

REGIONAL, NATIONAL, & WORLD COMMUNITIES

Having considered smaller communities, let us now turn our attention to the larger types.

With improved communication systems and increasingly

faster transportation, it becomes impossible in our mass society for a small town, a suburb, a city, a metropolitan community, or even a state within the United States to be altogether self-contained. Suburban dwellers rely on the city for goods, services, and employment. Residents of Florida depend upon seasonal visitors who will bring business to resort areas. Michigan industrialists manufacture automobiles, which they must sell in states throughout the Union. California officials cannot solve that state's water shortage problems unless they form a pact with neighboring states for diverting certain rivers and constructing dams.

REGIONS

We conceive of *regional* communities as well as those more local in character. Our nation, like others, is characterized by a series of regions, each with distinctive cultural elements. We think of a North and a South, a Midwest, a Southwest, even if we cannot precisely define the respective borders. "Dixie" is perhaps a region within a region. It is somewhere "down South," and where it begins and ends is less certain than that it is a community whose residents *feel* they belong there. When a Southerner tells you "Dixie is a state of mind," he speaks the truth.

Sociologists have suggested that regions may be classified according to certain types of characteristics:

1. *Natural regions* are geographically determined. They are large areas, separated from each other by geographical phenomena, such as a river, a mountain range, prevailing climate (tropical, subtropical, and so on), soil condition, or combinations of these factors. These natural phenomena are favorable to the emergence of distinctive communities—a dairy region, a corn belt, a cotton belt, cattle country, and others.

2. *Cultural regions* are distinguished by particular folkways, cultural pursuits, a regional literature, and the like. Mountaineers adhere to folkways and follow cultural pursuits quite different from those in lowlands and metropolitan cities. The New Orleans environs, for example, are noted for jazz and also for a population that, in many respects, is culturally distinct from the rest of our national population.

3. *Service regions* are established for various administrative purposes. Thus, the federal government subdivides the nation

into census tracts and does so in order to compile population and other statistics. The Automobile Association of America is a national organization; its affiliates serve given regions throughout the country.

Natural, cultural, and service region characteristics have been combined by social scientists and classified into *composite regions,* each roughly distinctive from the other in certain respects and degrees. The composite regions delineated by the Bureau of the Census are Northeast, North Central, South, and West. (See Figure 16.2.) You will observe that each of these composite regions has its subdivisions; the Middle Atlantic and the New England states, for instance, are subdivisions of the Northeast region. Each composite region is presumed to have its own quality and traditions, its economic emphases and social problems.

THE NATION AS A COMMUNITY

MacIver and Page have remarked that the wholly self-contained community "belongs to the primitive world" and that in the modern world "the nearest approach to it is found in the huge nation-community within the frontiers of a single state." And even nations are no longer self-sufficient. Political forces make it virtually impossible for the biggest or smallest nation to be absolutely self-contained. "We have been approaching a stage where no completely self-contained community can be found on any scale unless we extend the limits of community to include the whole earth."[19]

Industrialization, to cite one influential phenomenon, has had profound effects upon the territorial aspect of community. It has produced a community of *interests,* as differentiated from *territory,* which cuts across national lines. Manufacturers of the weaponry of war—in France, Germany, the United States —share common interests transcending national boundaries. So do international chemical and optical cartels. Aside from an international industrial community, we can conceive of a world-wide community of scientists, artists, or businessmen. There is certainly a world-wide community of believers for each of many religions. Thus, communities of *place,* such as nations, are cut across by a community of *shared institutions and values.*

Nevertheless, it is pertinent to think of the nation as a type

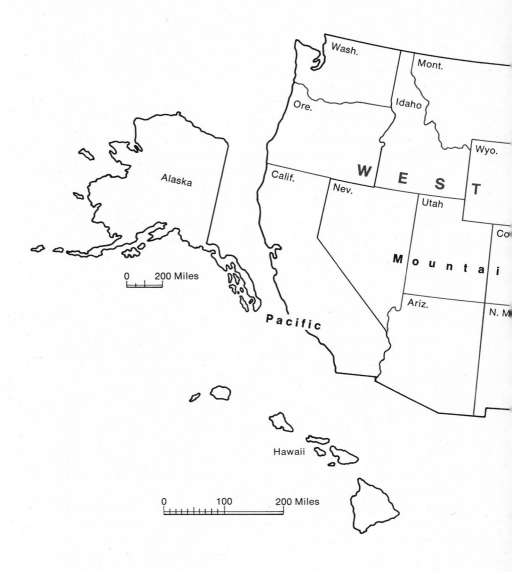

Figure 16.2
Regional Divisions in the United States (Alaska and Hawaii are drawn
at different scales from conterminous United States and are not shown
in their correct relative geographic positions).

Statistical Abstract of the United States, 1967 (Washington, D.C.: Department of Commerce, Bureau of the Census), p. xii.

0   100   200 Miles

of community. A man says, "I live in France," meaning, "I live in a geographical area known as France." Men are willing to fight and if necessary to die in order to keep their national boundaries intact. New nations, as in Africa and elsewhere in recent decades, emerge and are fiercely defended against encroachment by foreign armies or ideologies. In this sense a nation is a geographical place and also an idea and a point of identification for its individual residents. In effect, a person says: "This is my country, one whose values and territorial integrity we must jointly strive to preserve." This is the spirit of what is called nationalism. It is a frame of mind, an allegiance to a community of space.

THE WORLD AS A COMMUNITY

The world may be regarded as a great community spanning the entire earth. There is little to indicate that all peoples on earth have a common feeling of belonging to a world community. This generation has experienced international tensions, hot and cold wars, ideological battles. Nations of great power struggle with each other and tiny nations become pawns in the struggle. Nevertheless, it is proper enough to speak of a world community.

We indicated, at the beginning of this chapter, that a community emerges when a number of people, living in the same general locality, realize they share common interests and have mutual needs as a consequence of the fact they live near one another. If this definition makes you wonder how there can be a community consisting of people who live as far apart as New York and Singapore, bear in mind that we also said, earlier, that interaction within a community is both direct and indirect. Planes fly at incredible speeds. The sound of your voice can reach someone thousands of miles away almost instantly. Common interests and mutual needs do exist, among people as far from each other geographically as the inhabitants of Thailand and the United States. Certainly the housekeeping task of keeping the atmosphere clean is an international community problem, involving the use of space. The U.S.S.R. and the United States entered into agreements not to contaminate the atmosphere with atomic fallout. Recognizing that criminal operations are often world-wide in character, many nations banded together to establish Interpol, an international police organization designed to keep an eye on criminals and to clear information concerning their activities with the cooperating police systems. Thus, people separated by great distances may "live near each other" by virtue of the ease with which they can communicate with each other.

The world community, then, is not purely a figment of the imagination. Politically, the United Nations represents a step toward dealing with world problems on a community-of-nations basis. UNESCO, a world organization of the United Nations, deals with educational, social, and cultural matters around the world. Scientists have a world-as-community outlook, exchanging knowledge freely, whatever political differences may exist among the nations in which they dwell. And, in some measure, other scholars, as well as artists, share a similar international community outlook.

A UNIVERSE-COMMUNITY?

So great a change has there been in cultures around the world, so vast the accretion of scientific and technological knowledge during recent decades, that we may legitimately speculate whether the peoples of this world may not soon discover that even this planet on which they live is not self-contained or self-containable. We are already in contact with outer space. Artificial satellites circle the earth and "hardware" has landed on the moon. The conquest of outer space has already resulted in a great many social changes on our earth. It has necessitated codes defining who is responsible for civil damages when "hardware" falls from outer space onto the earth, creating death, injury, or destruction of property. And so real is the possibility that the entire universe may have to be considered one vast community that a new branch of legal study—metalaw—has emerged. Andrew G. Haley, writing for the *Harvard Law Record*,[20] defines it as the law of governing the rights of intelligent beings of different natures and existing in an indefinite number of frameworks of natural law. Suppose we find intelligent, sensate creatures on a planet other than our own. How can we protect them against harm we may unintentionally inflict upon them out of ignorance of their world and their nature? Such creatures, if found to exist, might be unlike human beings in constitution, reaction to germs carried by humans, and so on. They may be susceptible to phenomena to which we are immune, and vice versa. Our communications system may harm intelligent creatures in outer space. What will be the effects of our electromagnetic and pressure waves, propulsion, infrared rays from heat, radiation from the nuclear process? In what manner may our space exploration have an effect on outer-space life, by way of "para-psychological" or "telepathic" impacts? Body offenses? Germ dissemination? What may be the impact of the ideas and customs of man?

For the legal philosopher, a universe-wide problem of great

import has been created by space exploration, and metalaw is an attempt at bringing all intelligent creatures, anywhere, into beneficial rather than harmful association.

HUMAN ECOLOGY & COMMUNITY

A specialized branch of sociology, the study of *human ecology*, adds to our understanding of community life. The word *ecology* is borrowed from biology. Charles Darwin, influenced by Thomas Robert Malthus, called attention to the fact that all species of life were engaged in *competition* for the limited sustenance available in the natural environment. On your lawn or city street you will see birds of various species competing for the crumbs, worms, and insects necessary for the preservation of life. Moreover, that same food is sought by other animals.

Other biologists noted that while competition was present in all of life, mutually beneficial relationships analogous to human *cooperation* existed, too, in the struggle for existence. Many organisms of different species depend upon one another for survival. White ants live upon cellulose derived from wood, but they cannot digest it. They take into their bodies one-celled animals, protozoa, which provide this service by digesting the cellulose.[21] This interdependence the biologist calls *symbiosis*. *Symbiosis is the process of sustenance interrelationships in plant and animal communities.*

Cooperation, competition, and *symbiosis*, universal processes among plants and animals, are the focus of interest of ecologists. In the biological sense, *ecology is the study of the relationships between organisms and their environment.*

In the early 1920s, some sociologists thought the theoretical principles of ecology might be applied in studying the growth and development of human communities. Pioneers were Robert E. Park, Ernest W. Burgess, and Roderick D. McKenzie, all of the University of Chicago. They noted that competition and symbiotic relationships exist among human beings and between humans and their physical environment. Man competes with man for sustenance, but he also is dependent upon other men in a struggle to wrest from the physical environment the sustenance all require.

Thus began the study of *human ecology*. It was different in important respects from what the biologist studied. In the first place, biology is concerned mainly (but not exclusively) with *interspecies* symbiosis, as in the case of the white ant and the unicellular protozoa. The sociologist investigates *intraspecies symbiosis, the interdependence of human being with human being.*

Further, the biologist studies symbiotic relationships that are largely unaffected by human culture. The white ant acts as it does exclusively through biological influences. The sociologist studies symbiotic relationships that are affected by human culture. Two men may want the same piece of land because, biologically speaking, it furnishes sustenance for survival of the organism. The culture may be such that they will not kill each other for that land; they will agree to occupy it jointly, or one will move on to other land. Whatever decision is reached, it will be determined on the basis of what is defined as desirable in the culture.

The study of human ecology early led to a recognition that *man and the space he occupies are closely interrelated.* McKenzie declared that in human groups "social organization accommodates itself to the spatial and sustenance relationships existing among the occupants of any geographical area." Buildings, roads, shops, houses, people "tend to become spatially distributed in accordance with forces operating in a particular area at a particular level of culture."[22] For instance:

You would not expect to find a piano salesroom on a dirt road leading to a farm. People who want to sell pianos locate where they will be seen and easily reached by prospective piano buyers. Popcorn stands do well in movie theaters. Florist shops flourish near hospitals and funeral parlors. But a liquor store that opened across the street from a high school might very well be driven out of business.

Amos H. Hawley defined *human ecology* as *the study of* "*how men relate themselves to one another in order to live in their habitats.*"[23] McKenzie says essentially the same thing when he observes that human ecology "is fundamentally interested in the effect of *position,* in both time and space, upon human institutions and human behavior."[24]

Three *ecological processes* described by students of the subject deserve particular notice.

1. *Segregation.* Suppose a Ford showroom opens on Avenue A. A Chevrolet dealer might follow, feeling that the man looking for a car shops around, compares before purchasing. A

Buick agency comes in next. Soon we have an automobile row on Avenue A, every make of car being represented. The human ecologist calls this process *segregation*.

2. *Invasion*. Now, as population increases, business closer to the heart of the city pushes out from the center. Since this business consists of the largest and also highly successful enterprises, it can command space by force of dollars and zoning ordinances. Its great need, immediately around the retail district, is for office buildings. Entrepreneurs buy a lot occupied by a car dealer, in order to erect a skyscraper. The dealer must move. This illustrates the process of *invasion*.

3. *Succession*. More skyscrapers invade Avenue A, pushing the dealers out altogether, for they cannot afford to rent or buy in the section now, values having risen fantastically. Moreover, Avenue A is no longer the logical place for a car showroom. It is not a convenient location for prospective customers. No more automobile dealers remain. Avenue A has become exclusively a street of office buildings, by a process of succession.

These are examples of commercial segregation, invasion, and succession. There are other than commercial kinds of ecological processes. For instance: The wealthy residents of a small but growing community, who comprise its "aristocracy," build imposing homes in a secluded area just outside the corporate limits of the town. This is now the most fashionable and exclusive residential area of the environs. Segregation by social class has occurred.

Population booms; business and industry burgeon; commercial and industrial structures push onward, eventually to the very rim of the fashionable district. Moderate-priced housing is urgently needed for the growing population. Land developers acquire parcels of real estate, ring the fashionable homes with high-rise apartment buildings. The exclusive district is losing exclusivity. A few of the old residents give up, move away. Their homes are torn down and replaced by apartment houses renting to people of middle income, not members of the town's aristocracy. Invasion has set in.

Finally, all of the original homeowners have moved away. They are supplanted by apartment dwellers. Succession has occurred. Middle-class families have replaced those who rank in the upper classes.

In discussing developments of this sort, early human ecologists spoke of *natural processes* of symbiosis and competition. They thought of them as closely analogous to biological counterparts. A "natural process" inevitably ran its course despite human effort to change it or avoid its consequences.

Because of "natural processes," human ecologists believed, "natural areas" developed. Thus, potential juvenile delinquents were impelled into certain areas by "natural processes" and became delinquent by virtue of "natural processes" concentrated in "natural areas."

Criticism has been leveled against the concept of "natural areas" and "natural processes." Critics assert that early human ecologists did not make sufficient allowance for the force of human culture and rational behavior. Human competition, they say, is fundamentally different from biological competition. It is modified and controlled by cultural "rules of the game," which have no counterpart in the natural scheme of things. Human competition, they add, cannot be considered in the same category as natural symbiosis. It is culturally induced and can transcend natural obstacles of time and space.

Juvenile delinquency provides an example. Factors in the culture forced certain families into the depressed areas of a city. These factors included low educational attainment of the wage earner and meager income. The families went where the rent was cheap. It was cheap because the housing was dilapidated. Run-down, unsanitary housing breeds disease, which may affect the wage earner. Or poverty might lead to domestic discord, perhaps the desertion of the husband. As families become disorganized, parental controls weaken and some children may roam the streets, where they encounter other young people like themselves. One "infects" another with ideas that eventually lead to what society defines as delinquent behavior.

This chain of circumstances is given here only to make a point. Obviously, many families in the same area do *not* become disorganized; they do *not* lose control of children. And a great many factors influencing family life have been left unmentioned. However, critics of human ecology would point out that every step described, while partly produced by forces beyond the control of the individuals concerned, is mainly the result of human action. Low wages, desertion, delinquency, these are man-made and can be man-controlled. A spider is biologically set to behave in a certain way, but a human being's behavior can be changed through the influence of other human beings. Delinquency is a *social*, not a *natural* problem.

But while human ecology does not provide an entirely

rounded foundation for understanding human relations, it makes important contributions to sociological research. One of the most noteworthy is Ernest W. Burgess' *hypothesis of concentric circular zones.* Burgess studied a number of American cities and concluded that they tend to develop a pattern like that shown in Figure 16.3.

Zone 1 is the *central business district,* located in the heart of the city and containing large retail establishments, office buildings, financial houses, commercial hotels, restaurants, and theaters. It is densely populated during the day, but practically no one lives there, except for transients in hotels.

Zone 2, the *zone in transition,* immediately surrounds Zone 1. It was once the good residential district, but those old residents who could afford to do so gave up their homes and moved out. The area had depreciated as a place of residence as the business center of the city pushed outward. Here, now, are rooming houses, low-priced hotels, and "flophouses." Serving their occupants are cheap business establishments. In days of high in-migration, this was an area of first settlement for many foreign-born workers. The zone in transition has a high concentration, or segregation, of crime, delinquency, decrepit housing, diesase, poverty, broken homes, vice. "Skid row," the haven of derelicts, is located here.

Zone 3 is an *area of workingmen's homes.* Dwellings are somewhat better than in the zone in transition. Actually, there is no clear-cut line of demarcation between Zone 2 and 3. Rather, the second zone gradually blends into the third, the housing becoming a bit more improved the greater the distance from the center of Zone 2.

Zone 4 is the *area of better workingmen's homes.* Burgess originally called it the *residential zone.* As workers gain more security, they move farther out, where the housing is better. Zone 4 has local retail establishments for daily shopping—grocery stores, drug stores, cleaning and dyeing shops, beauty parlors, and barber shops. The area contains more space than Zone 3, housing is less crowded, there are fewer children, and there is a higher per-capita income.

Zone 5 was called the *commuter's zone.* It is the fashionable district, the suburbs. People who can afford expensive homes and the cost of commuting to and from work live here. It is the area for prosperous business and professional folk.

Burgess acknowledged that geographic barriers could and

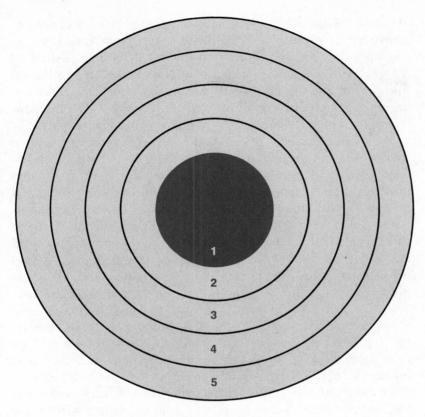

1 Central Business District
2 Zone in Transition
3 Area of Workingmen's Homes
4 Area of Better Workingmen's Homes
5 Commuters Zone

Figure 16.3
The Growth of the City

Robert E. Park, Ernest W. Burgess, and Roderick D. McKenzie, *The City* (Chicago: The University of Chicago Press, 1925), p. 51. Adapted by permission.

did prevent zones from approximating perfect circles. But on the whole, he felt, the pattern was typical. His theory seems realistic in describing the growth of many communities, but it does not hold up entirely. For instance, European cities do not seem to conform to the pattern. And there are exceptions within the United States. For example, in the past quarter of a century or so, Zone 5, the commuter's zone, is not always a fashionable suburb. Huge working-class suburbs have grown up in various parts of the country. New York City exemplifies another deviation from the zonal pattern posited by Burgess. In Long Island, which is in New York City, we should find part of Zone 5, and we do. But in the same zone there are segregations characteristic of Zones 2, 3, and 4. We find, for example, a high delinquency and crime rate in some parts.

What Burgess did not include in his hypothesis was a process that might help explain the Long Island situation. Recent years have seen the development of a pattern of city growth that has been called *rurbanization*. Beyond what would be Zone 5, additional areas have developed. They do not necessarily follow the logical progression noted in the Burgess theory, in which each succeeding zone contains a higher level of residential district. In rurban areas one may indeed find the country squire on a beautiful, expensive estate. But because home building outside cities is not rigidly controlled by law, and also for other reasons, some of these sections are conglomerate aggregations of the following: expensive, moderately priced, and low-priced housing; single dwellings and apartment houses; branches of fine department stores and branches of dollar-down-and-dollar-a-week establishments. There are airfields, night clubs, truck farms, and perhaps a hidden brothel. It is not surprising that in such a section we find some of the characteristics of a zone in transition.

Another development is the current decentralization of big cities, discussed earlier. As population increases and the boundaries of a municipality push very far out from the business center, decentralization takes place. Small communities have grown up, each with its own shopping center. Department stores and other types of stores have followed the trend and established branches where the customers live. In some areas there are even the beginnings of something like five concentric zones within the larger framework of the city.

The business heart of Los Angeles contracted; it did not grow with increased population. At peak periods, such as the Christmas shopping season, promotional schemes have had to be launched by centrally located merchants in Los Angeles in order to urge shoppers to travel inward for their needs instead of buying in their neighborhoods.

An even more recent development than decentralization has been what might be termed recentralization. The heart of downtown Los Angeles, to use this example again, "dried up" more and more as decentralization progressed. Businessmen, concerned over loss of trade, got together with representatives of city government and the Chamber of Commerce, made long-range plans for recentralization. Additional freeways were constructed, leading from outlying areas into the heart of the city. A music center, a theater for stage productions, and numerous public buildings were constructed. Good restaurants opened up, to take care of persons in town for an evening of entertainment. The department stores advertised that persons who were in downtown Los Angeles to attend a concert or stage production would find it convenient to arrive early, do some shopping. To a noticeable extent, the trend of past years has been reversed, and downtown Los Angeles has again become a business and cultural center.

Although Burgess nowhere specifically so stated, it would seem that he and the early human ecologists were thinking about *very large* cities with *mobile and growing populations* when they propounded their theories. The zonal pattern described by Burgess does not as commonly develop in smaller cities of stable population and slow growth.

Burgess' work stimulated subsequent research along similar lines. Homer Hoyt developed a *sector theory* of city expansion. (See Figure 16.4.) Land values, he found, were important considerations in determining where certain ecological units would locate. Cities, he held, tend to grow out along the main traffic arteries that converge at the center of the community, while the spaces between the arteries lag behind in development.

The *multiple nuclei theory* is still another attempt at explaining ecological processes within the city. According to this theory, a number of centers—business, shopping, manufacturing, residence—become established early in a city's history. Their location is partly based on historical accident, partly on the topography of the available land, on building costs, and on other considerations. Once established, these concentrations, or nuclei, tend to survive. It would be very costly, for instance, to remove a fifty-story hotel or to push an office building three feet back in order to widen the pavement. As a consequence, the original concentrations tend to fix the pattern of subsequent growth of the city. Figure 16.5 illustrates the multiple nuclei theory.

Clearly, studies in human ecology demonstrate the importance of the *spatial* component of social life. This com-

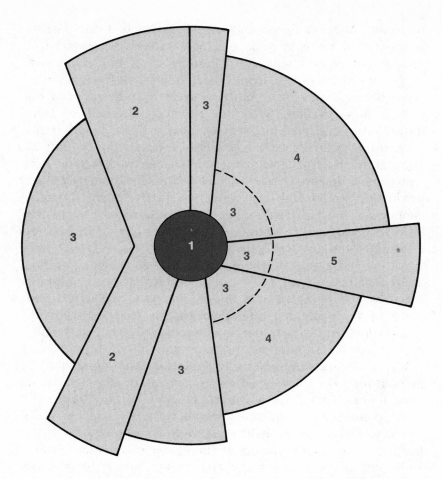

1 Central business district   3 Low-class residential
2 Wholesale light manufacturing   4 Medium-class residential
5 High-class residential

Figure 16.4
Sector Theory

Reproduced by permission, from C. D. Harris and E. L. Ullman, "The Nature of Cities,"
The Annals of the American Academy of Political and Social Science, CCXLII
(November 1945).

ponent is closely linked with such significant aspects of
community life as housing, commercial and recreational specialization, and class and ethnic living patterns. It is also linked
with such social problems as poverty, crime and delinquency,
and discrimination against ethnic minorities, which will be
discussed in Part V. The ecologists stress that spatial patterns
are directly related to certain social processes—for example,

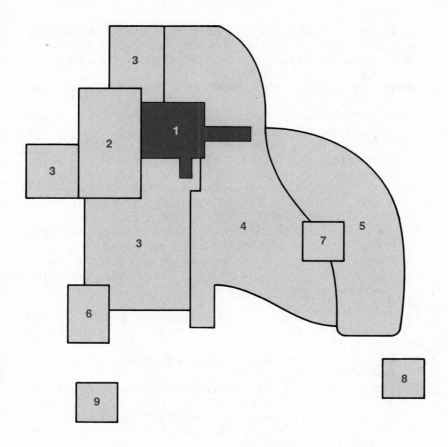

1 Central business district
2 Wholesale light manufacturing
3 Low-class residential
4 Medium-class residential
5 High-class residential
6 Heavy manufacturing
7 Outlying business district
8 Residential suburb
9 Industrial suburb

Figure 16.5
Multiple Nuclei Theory

Reproduced by permission, from C. D. Harris and E. L. Ullman, "The Nature of Cities," *The Annals of the American Academy of Political and Social Science,* CCXLII (November 1945).

conflict and cooperation, which are among the subjects discussed in the next chapter.

· *NOTES*

1. George A. Hillery, Jr., "Definitions of Community: Areas of Agreement," *Rural Sociology,* XX (June 1955), 111–123.

2. Robert M. MacIver and Charles H. Page, *Society: An Introductory Analysis* (New York: Rinehart, 1949), pp. 8–9.
3. "In Defense of Privacy," *Time*, LXXXVIII, 3 (July 15, 1966), 38–39.
4. Roland L. Warren, *The Community in America* (Chicago: Rand McNally, 1963), p. 75.
5. U. S. Bureau of the Census, *Statistical Abstract of the United States, 1964,* 85th annual ed. (Washington, D. C.: U. S. Government Printing Office, 1964), p. 16.
6. Leo Schnore, "The Growth of Metropolitan Suburbs," *American Sociological Review*, XXII (April 1957), 165–173.
7. U. S. Bureau of the Census, *Statistical Abstract of the United States, 1967,* 88th annual ed. (Washington, D. C.: U. S. Government Printing Office, 1967), p. 607, Table No. 895.
8. Leo F. Schnore, *The Urban Scene, Human Ecology and Demography* (New York: Free Press, 1965), pp. 80–94.
9. Amos H. Hawley, *The Changing Shape of Metropolitan America: Decentralization Since 1920* (New York: Free Press, 1956), p. 12.
10. *Ibid.*, p. 161.
11. Schnore, *The Urban Scene, Human Ecology and Demography, op. cit.*, pp. 81–82.
12. *Ibid.*, p. 82.
13. U. S. Bureau of the Census, *Statistical Abstract of the United States, 1967, op. cit.*, p. 897.
14. Ben J. Wattenberg, with Richard M. Scammon, *This U.S.A., An Unexpected Family Portrait of 194,067,296 Americans Drawn from the Census* (New York: Doubleday, 1965), p. 76.
15. William Dobriner (ed.), *The Suburban Community* (New York: Putnam, 1958), p. xvii.
16. Schnore, "The Growth of Metropolitan Suburbs," *op. cit.*
17. Leo Schnore, "Satellites and Suburbs," *Social Forces*, XXXVI (December 1957), 121–129.
18. Otis D. Duncan and Albert J. Reiss, Jr., *Social Characteristics of Urban and Rural Communities, 1950* (New York: Wiley, 1956), pp. 117–133.
19. MacIver and Page, *op. cit.*, pp. 10–11.
20. Andrew G. Haley, "Recent Developments in Space Law and Metalaw—Work of International Groups," *Harvard Law Record*, XXIV, 2 (February 7, 1957), 1–4.
21. L. R. Cleveland, "The Social Genius of White Ants," in Charles Neider (ed.), *The Fabulous Insects* (New York: Harper & Row, 1954), pp. 59–69.
22. R. D. McKenzie, "The Scope of Human Ecology," in Ernest W. Burgess (ed.), *The Urban Community* (Chicago: University of Chicago Press, 1926), pp. 167–182.
23. Amos H. Hawley, *Human Ecology, A Theory of Community Structure* (New York: Ronald Press, 1950), p. 74.
24. R. D. McKenzie, "The Ecological Approach to the Study of the Human Community," in Robert E. Park, Ernest W. Burgess,

and Roderick D. McKenzie (eds.), *The City* (Chicago: University of Chicago Press, 1925), pp. 63–79.

· SUGGESTIONS FOR FURTHER READING

BURGESS, ERNEST W. (ed.). *The Urban Community.* Chicago: University of Chicago Press, 1926.
This volume contains papers dealing with the urban community. Some of the earliest formulations on the ecology of the city will be found on pp. 167–229.

DOBRINER, WILLIAM (ed.). *The Suburban Community.* New York: Putnam, 1958.
A collection of articles dealing with the growth and social organization of the suburbs.

Editors of *Fortune. The Exploding Metropolis.* New York: Anchor Books, 1958.
Beautifully written material on the changing character of metropolitan areas in the United States.

FAVA, SYLVIA FEIS. "Suburbanism as a Way of Life." *American Sociological Review*, XXI (February 1956), 34–37.
The author sets out to determine whether people living in suburbs have different socio-psychological characteristics from those living in cities.

PARK, ROBERT E., ERNEST W. BURGESS, and RODERICK D. MCKENZIE. *The City.* Chicago: University of Chicago Press, 1925.
Leaders in the development of the study of human ecology present some of their earliest formulations on the subject. Read particularly Chapters 1, 2, 3.

SEXTON, PATRICIA CAYO. *Spanish Harlem.* New York: Harper & Row, Colophon Books, 1966.
A look at a poverty-stricken neighborhood in New York City.

WEST, JAMES (pseud.). *Plainville, U.S.A.* New York: Columbia University Press, 1945.
An examination of the culture and social structure of a rural community, somewhere in the United States.

17 PROCESSES OF GROUP INTERACTION

We have spent considerable time in preceding chapters discussing characteristic *patterns* of human groupings. We now inquire: How do members of human groupings *interact* with one another? What *processes* are involved? Clearly, these questions are of great concern in the study of group life.

As previously stated, human interaction occurs when two or more human beings influence one another in any way. Two men are loading a piano into a truck. One calls, "Yo-UP!" Both lift simultaneously. This constitutes simple interaction, the behavior of one man stimulating the other to respond. Interaction enables them to coordinate and synchronize their efforts, to do a job neither could accomplish alone or with the same amount of effort.

Here are some other examples of interactive behavior:

Two men with bayonets are engaged in a life-and-death struggle. One lunges at the other, is met by the counterthrust of his adversary's weapon.

Several young people are gliding, leaping, and gyrating. To an outsider this may seem meaningless and random movement, but it has a definite pattern in time and space. The individuals concerned are following the rhythm of a dance band.

A man in a tiny cell that has barred windows is writing an answer to his wife's letter.

A motorist approaching an intersection extends her hand. The driver behind her steps on the brake pedal of his car.

Each of these instances represents interactive behavior because the participating human beings stimulate and respond to one another.

An interactive situation commences whenever two or more people come under the influence of one another. It lasts as long as the participants continue to be influenced by one another without shift of interest away from the immediate contact. It is terminated when the contact is broken and the interest of those involved shifts to another situation. Thus, a man reading an editorial is momentarily participating in an interactive situation with its author. This situation is terminated when his wife distracts his interest from the editorial by exclaiming, "Herbert! Those eggs are getting cold!" Another interactive situation emerges as husband and wife discuss their son's difficulty with the new mathematics. This situation ends suddenly when the man glances at his watch, jumps up, kisses his wife, and rushes for the 8:15.

INTERACTION VIEWED IN SEVEN DIMENSIONS

For purposes of analysis, it will be helpful to think of interaction as having dimensions. We apply the term *dimensions* in a different sense than do mathematicians, to suggest the several criteria that may be used as a basis for studying interaction. From a theoretical point of view, of course, each of these dimensions represents a conception that has been employed many times by sociologists. We use them here to help you understand the many complex factors involved in human interaction.

There is the *functional* dimension. In analyzing it, sociologists ask: What motivates the participants to interact with one another? Do they get out of the situation what they anticipated? Motives for interaction vary in intensity and persistence—from the comparatively simple, momentary desire of one individual to greet another on the street, to the enduring, complex need of a mother to behave toward her daughter in a manner she has learned to consider appropriate.

There is the *behavioral* dimension. How do participants behave in their interaction with one another? Is their behavior characterized largely by words, actions, or both? Interaction may be conducted either through symbolic or nonsymbolic behavior. People engaged in "bull sessions," letter writing, sending semaphore signals from ship to ship are interacting symbolically. The interaction of persons rowing a boat together is characterized by nonsymbolic behavior.

Interaction may be said to have a *numerical* dimension. How many people are involved in the interactive situation? As few as two may interact. At the opposite extreme, it is theoretically possible for all the people in the world to be involved in the same interactive situation. The mass media have made it possible for most of the world's population to respond to a single stimulus, such as a declaration of war by leaders of one of the world powers.

Interaction has a *temporal* dimension. Is the interactive situation isolated in time? Or is it one of a continuing series of related situations? When complete strangers respond to one another in traffic, one yielding to the other at an intersection, that situation seldom has more than momentary significance. But the separate incidents of a long-standing family feud can be more realistically understood as links in a continuing chain of interlocking situations. "From birth to death," writes Wilbert E. Moore, "the human individual never quite escapes from the limits of time and its fleeting quality."[1]

Interactive situations are characterized by a *spatial* dimension. How much space separates the participants? Can they touch one another? Can they see and hear each other directly? Or are they far removed from one another? People engaged in interaction may be in direct physical contact, as in the case of lovers kissing or two men fighting. They may be as far apart as the circumference of the earth permits, as is sometimes true of the distance separating two radio "hams" conversing with one another. When, in 1966, astronauts John W. Young and Michael Collins, 474 miles up in space, received messages from and communicated with persons on this planet, by electronic devices, the spatial dimension of this interactive situation transcended even the bounds of the earth.

It is helpful, too, to analyze interaction in terms of the *familiarity* dimension. How intimately associated are the participants? Do they know each other well, casually, or only in passing? Obviously, the extent to which people are well acquainted and therefore able to anticipate one another's behavior has considerable bearing on how they conduct themselves during interaction. When you and your father see the image of the President of the United States on the television screen, you probably know what your father's response would be if you hissed. But if you should hiss in the company of someone you have just met, you could scarcely anticipate that individual's response.

There is a *status* dimension to social interaction. Who are the leaders, who the followers? In given situations some persons tend to become dominant, some subordinate. Sometimes the status of leader is alternated or rotated. In a family situation, the senior male of the house may be accorded the status of leader. In other interactive situations, one or another of the participants may achieve leadership status, as when a young woman is chosen to run for public office over many males and females older than she.

After a congenial discussion, someone remarks, "Mrs. Smith is such a valuable member of the club! She always dominates the conversation, but what she says is so helpful!" That suggests that Mrs. Smith gained the position of leader in that interactive situation. In friendly discussions of this nature, the status of leader is frequently shifted from one person to another.

PROCESSES OF INTERACTION

It is useful, too, to think of interaction in terms of the processes that occur. Is the behavior of participants harmonious? Do they mutually assist one another? Do they try to satisfy their own desires at the expense of others? Are they trying to harm or destroy one another? Answers to questions such as these will occupy our attention for the remainder of this chapter.

PRIMARY PROCESSES OF INTERACTION

There are three primary processes of interaction: *cooperation, competition,* and *conflict.* All other so-called processes of interaction are actually one of, or a combination of, these three.

When two or more human beings are working together to

achieve objectives that will be mutually beneficial to all concerned, they are engaged in cooperation. If the householders in a given locality compact among themselves not to buy from any house-to-house salesman in order to discourage this type of selling, they are engaged in cooperation. Cooperation with an ironic twist is shown in Figure 17.1, where two senators are pictured engaged in logrolling.

Peter Kropotkin and other social thinkers have advanced the theory that the most basic form of interaction is cooperation. They contend that the entire process of evolution emerged from the abilities of individual organisms of certain species to integrate their activities through mutual aid. Survival of the fittest, they said, is actually survival of the most cooperative types of organisms.

There is no doubt that cooperation, broadly defined, serves the ends of many organisms. But the cooperative attributes of human beings differ considerably from those of other animals. When you buy a carton of milk at the market, you are purchasing a product that required interlocking of human effort to make it available to you. There were the cattle raiser, the farm work involved, transportation, scientific methods of pasteurization, advertising, mathematics, your knowledge of the value of milk as a food, and hence your desire for it, business techniques, the wholesaler-retailer chain—these and many, many other factors made that carton of milk possible. This is a far more complex type of cooperation than one in which two coyotes cooperate in cornering a jack rabbit.

This complexity is made possible by the ability of human beings to identify with each other's attitudes and feelings much more than seems to be the case with other animals. We can put ourselves in the place of the other person, in imagination. Cooperation among individuals and groups is somewhat proportionate to their ability to understand each other, and such understanding depends upon the ability to identify with the feelings of others. When four firemen pick up a net, preparing to break the fall of a woman who must jump from the second floor of a burning building, they are cooperating, for they understand each other in this frame of reference. Without being instructed, each man takes firm hold of his corner of the net, steps back so that it opens to a certain point of tautness, and places his feet in a position to brace his body for the moment the woman lands in the net.

Figure 17.1
Cooperation

From *Collier's* and *Best Cartoons of the Year*, 1954, Lariar, Ed.

"Then it's agreed, Senator—I'll vote
for your economy measure
if you'll support my appropriation bill."

To be sure, there are exceptions to the generalization that understanding brings cooperation. A man and wife, living together for years, at times understand each other's moods, gestures, and facial expressions to an uncanny degree. They seem able to divine what the mate is thinking, "reading into" unvoiced cues quite accurately. This ability can lead to cooperation. It can also lead to the reverse, as when one member of the couple understands but does not symphathize with what the other is presumably thinking.

Another facet of cooperation should be pointed out. When two or more human beings work together to achieve an objective, they may benefit mutually but unequally from their efforts. The word "cooperation" should not be taken to imply equal distribution of the rewards. Management and labor cooperate in bringing coal out of a mine, but their respective rewards for such effort are not the same. And one miner earns more than another, because he produces more or because he holds a more responsible post than his associate.

When two or more individuals are trying to obtain possession of something that is not available in quantities sufficient to satisfy all of them, they are engaged in competition. Say two grocery stores open up in a neighborhood that cannot supply enough business to provide both store owners with the margin of profit that will make their labor worthwhile. The two shopkeepers are in competition. In Figure 17.2 we see another kind of competition, this in the field of professional baseball. Only one of the two competing teams can win the game.

Several social philosophers and other students of social life have argued that competition rather than cooperation is the most basic of social processes. They reason that every living organism must compete for materials indispensable to life but limited in availability. This was essentially the viewpoint of Charles Darwin, and it is unquestionably correct in a general sense. Plants compete for sunlight, water, and nourishment. Animals compete for sexual gratification and food. Competition, according to this thesis, is more than a process of human interaction; it is the natural condition of all existence.

It is quite possible for human beings to be involved in a situation where they must compete for something essential to life—food for instance. During this country's pioneering period, groups of men pushing westward were in competition for what fish and game there might be on the plains and in the forests. One group might not know that another was in the region, but the situation was competitive nonetheless, for there was not enough fish and game to feed all of the people who needed it.

But although the view that competition is the natural condition of all existence applies generally to human interaction, it fails to explain much of the competition in which individuals engage. People compete for objectives in no sense indispensable to life. The important distinction here is that these are things they learned to want as they internalized their culture. Two chess players would survive if they never competed in another game. Mrs. Smith will continue to live even if her dinner party is attended by fewer members of "society" than Mrs. Smythe's. We compete for trophies, grades, money, impressive automobiles and clothes, political office, favorable attention from the opposite sex. All these items satisfy culturally acquired needs, but none is imperative to life.

It may seem strange that people would compete to determine who will take the most pain without flinching, yet this occurs and is a culturally acquired need. Many boys will not cry when they are hurt; they do not want to be considered "chicken." One investigator tested the willingness of 12-to-14-year-old boys to withstand what he considered "intolerable pain." He subjected each boy to pain, with no one else present. Then, in another series of experiments, he inflicted the pain in the presence of others. Willingness to take pain without flinching was greatest when pairs of boys competed. Social pressures undoubtedly were a factor.[2]

When do we compete and when cooperate? No one generalization would hold for every possible interactive situation. However, an interesting proposition was tentatively advanced as an outcome of a study made some years ago.[3] In that study, Mark May and his associates suggested that three sets of conditions are influential in determining whether cooperation or competition is likely to characterize social interaction:

1. If the value for which people are striving is scarce, com-

Figure 17.2
Competition
The New York Times.

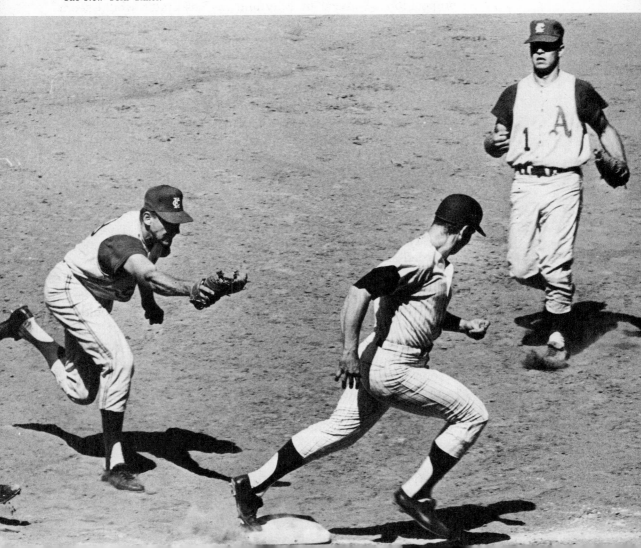

petitive behavior is likely to predominate; if abundant, cooperation is more probable. But there will be exceptions on the basis of the relationships among the individuals or groups. For instance, a mother in a famine area may give the little food she has to her child.

2. It may follow, then, that where such relationships as kinship or affection exist, the individuals or groups concerned are more likely to cooperate than if they did not know or like each other. In the latter instance, they would be more prone to competition. Interpersonal attitudes are effective determinants.

3. Whether people will cooperate rather than compete is in part determined by how much each would share in the rewards of the activity. The research cautiously suggests that if the rewards are to be equally shared, cooperation is probable; if they are to be unequally distributed, competition is more likely.

In the light of more recent sociological observations, the proposition advanced by May and his associates would seem to require some qualification and additions. Many of the objectives for which individuals and groups compete are based, not on sustenance needs alone, but on nonrational value patterns of the culture. Some competition is stimulated by the desire to attain intangible items of value, such as status in the society. The successful competitor for an item deemed worthy of eliciting rivalry is accorded superior status in the society, and it is this that the person or group seeks. Thus, the baseball team that wins its league's pennant holds higher status than the teams that lose out in the competition.

Further, as is implicit in the study by May and his research colleagues, the forms of competition are defined by the culture:

1. The culture determines which items of value are to be regarded as desirable. In our society, it is desirable to work so as to be able to support one's dependents, undesirable to live an idle existence if this renders the individual unable to support those who, according to the cultural definition, should be supported by him.

2. The culture defines which items of value may appropriately be attained by competitive effort and which may not. It is considered appropriate in our society to compete for profits from business enterprise, inappropriate for one man to compete for the affections of another man's wife.

3. The culture delineates who may and who may not com-

pete for a given item of value. Holders of the M.D. degree may compete for patients in our society. Persons who do not hold the degree are forbidden to practice medicine, hence to compete with medical doctors for patients.

4. Fairly well recognized rules for competition are defined by the culture. In the United States, the retail establishment may properly offer merchandise at a cost below that of its competitors. However, it is deemed contrary to the rules to make false and defamatory accusations concerning a competitor's merchandising practices.

Sociologists, and notably social psychologists, have contributed additional understanding concerning the roles of competition and cooperation. Their observations and empirical research have yielded such generalizations as the following:

1. Competition tends to shape the attitudes of the competitors. Rivals for a given item of value frequently develop unfriendly and unfavorable attitudes toward one another, as when two labor unions compete to recruit workers in a given industry. On the other hand, when individuals or groups pursue a common goal cooperatively, friendly attitudes are likely to be engendered. For instance, leaders of two unions engaged in a joint effort to further labor legislation will probably hold favorable attitudes toward each other in the course of their endeavors.

2. Competition often stimulates individuals and groups to their greatest achievements. Experiments have demonstrated that when employees in a manufacturing plant are placed in a situation in which they must compete for income and promotion, overall productivity is usually increased (although the quality of the product suffers at times). On the other hand, certain manufacturing operations are best handled by cooperation. On an assembly line it would not do for an employee to work at a faster pace than his fellow workers, for this would only upset the work rhythm and cut back on productivity.

3. Although the competitive spirit actuates much of our behavior, the stimulus to compete is limited by certain factors:

Some individuals and groups decline to enter a competitive situation, since one person or group will lose out to another or others. Competition creates anxieties; losing out brings unhappiness and perhaps feelings of insecurity. For example, a young man who enjoys football may not try out for the school team lest he suffer frustration and chagrin.

Some people withdraw from competition after having lost

out a number of times. Thus, the slow learner may eventually lose the incentive to compete for grades and may even drop out of school rather than pit himself against pupils who achieve more.

As we have indicated, in many instances cooperative effort encourages friendly attitudes among the participants. However, very rigorous rivalry may turn into downright conflict, and individuals and groups may withdraw from a situation involving such fierce competition in order to avoid a conflict situation. Thus, Negroes competing with whites for homes in a certain neighborhood, finding hostility building up as they bid against the whites, may withdraw from the competitive situation rather than risk being subjected to explosive conflict.

When two or more individuals are striving to thwart, harm, or destroy one another, they are engaged in conflict. Figure 17.3 shows a violent conflict situation in which, in 1965, sheriff's possemen and state troopers charged into a packed mass of civil rights demonstrators in Montgomery, Alabama.

Although Figure 17.4 pictures no active violence, it, too,

Figure 17.3
Conflict
Charles Moore, Black Star.

Figure 17.4
Conflict

John Dominis, *Life*
Magazine © Time Inc.

represents a conflict situation. According to the news story that accompanied this photograph in *Life*, the two individuals in the foreground are "company men," working for a town's only industry during a bitter union strike. Their truck has broken down; they are stranded in hostile territory. The pro-union garage that is repairing the truck will not allow them to hide out there. The "company men" watch fearfully, for if a striker discovers them there will be trouble.

Conflict, like competition, has been viewed as a natural and inevitable condition of life. The seventeenth-century English philosopher, Thomas Hobbes, expressed this belief. He contended that men are naturally destructive and vengeful. He considered it a redeeming characteristic of human beings that they had the ability to develop strong governments that prevented them from following their natural inclinations to indulge in perpetual conflict. Evidence collected since Hobbes does not support his theory as a universal principle. Some societies with comparatively few restraints on individual behavior are relatively peaceful. Others maintaining rigid control over individual behavior are strongly oriented toward conflict.

Conflict among human beings, where it does exist, has distinctively human characteristics that are culturally patterned to a substantial extent. When two nonhuman animals battle each other, the fight is characteristically noncomplex in nature: they strike with teeth, claws, horns, and the like. Conflict between scorpions and bees is somewhat more complex. The cornered bee flies about aimlessly, buzzing loudly, making sorties, until it is tired out. Then the scorpion whips his tail out laterally with incredible suddenness, seizes the bee, puts it in his pincers, paralyzes it with a sting, bites a hole in it, and injects digestive enzymes that turn all the bee except its shell to fluid. Then the scorpion pumps the insect dry.* But even such finesse in assassination is bested by the conflict practiced by humans. We learn to fight in many different ways. We can deliver death by air, land, or sea; fight an enemy thousands of miles away by hurling missiles that travel the distance without human pilots. We can gas or burn people to death, disintegrate them with nuclear bombs.

Nor is this complexity restricted to death-dealing conflict. We fight people with words that can ruin reputations and careers. We can even fight without uttering a word, as in Figure 17.5.

Conflict and competition tend to separate people and groups. However, this is not entirely so. Competition often involves some cooperation, as we shall see. And conflict tends to increase the internal unity of the contending groups. During World War II, we in the United States felt closer to the Soviet Union than we had before or have since—Russia was our ally against the common enemy, Nazi Germany.

Some writers have contended that a major source of conflict lies in inadequate communication. It has been argued, for example, that if all peoples of the earth spoke a common language, world-wide understanding might be increased to such an extent that international tension and conflict could be elimi-

* Some would contend that the interaction between the bee and the scorpion is not really conflict as we use the term in sociology, but rather the scorpion's way of obtaining his dinner. Viewed this way, the situation corresponds with the relationship between butchers and beef cattle in Chicago slaughterhouses.

Figure 17.5
Conflict
Reprinted by permission of
Charles Rodrigues and
Saturday Review.

"*You said you'd ruin me, Featherson.
How far do you intend to go?*"

nated. There may be a measure of truth in the proposition that
conflict decreases when communication is improved. But the
fact remains that people who speak the same language engage
in family feuds and civil wars. Some conflict is an outgrowth
of factors only indirectly related to communication. An individual or group may have needs they consider impelling and
may demand satisfaction even at the expense of others. Two
nations may aspire to own the same territory or natural resources. Union members and management, as has been noted,
may understand one another "only too well." Communication
alone will not solve these problems. In fact, increased contact
may accentuate the differences and the seemingly irreconcilable objectives, fears, and insecurities arising out of observation
of a potential rival.

So far we have discussed cooperation, competition, and conflict as if they were separate and distinct processes. Differences
among processes of interaction, however, are not always clear
and distinct. Take two hypothetical pharmacists in the same
neighborhood. Neither would survive if both kept a full line
of merchandise, one competing with the other for customers.
Suppose they made an agreement that both would continue
to fill prescriptions. One would not have a luncheonette
counter, the other would. One would not stock greeting cards,
stationery, or magazines, referring customers who wanted
these items to the other store. The druggist so favored would
not stock hairbrushes, cameras, or toys, referring customers
who wanted these to the other store. Now both pharmacists
can make a living. Are they cooperating or competing? Both, it
would seem. Although they cooperated in an agreement de-

termining who would sell what, the two stores remain in business competing with each other, to an extent. For instance, they still compete for the prescription trade.

What appears to be competition in business affairs may be cooperation. American business is less competitive today than it was a half century ago. Price-fixing by fair trade agreements and laws may not altogether eliminate competition, but it does cut it down. Cartels go even farther. They are associations of industrialists or business firms for establishing a national or international monopoly. Outwardly, the members of a cartel compete against each other. Actually, they cooperate, through interlocking directorates and agreements on prices. The result is that what is good for one firm is good for all, since they actually form one great organization. Norman Thomas, a Socialist, once remarked that the only free enterprise in America today consists of small boys shooting marbles for keeps. He was, of course, exaggerating, but business competition clearly is not unrestricted free enterprise in which each firm or plant competes with all others.

Clearly, too, cooperation, competition, and conflict may occur in a single interactive situation. In a high-school or college football game between two rival teams, the interactive struggle is competitive, but you will witness cooperation on the field among the members of each team during every play. Such cooperation is called teamwork. Conflict may occasionally flare up when players lose their tempers and fists fly. Then the competitive desire to win is momentarily forgotten, and cooperation no longer exists. Two or more players become intent on hurting or vanquishing one another.

SECONDARY PROCESSES OF INTERACTION

There are two secondary processes of interaction: *accommodation* and *assimilation*. Both are essentially related to *cooperation*.

When two or more people involved in conflict with one another agree to suspend or cease hostilities, this interaction between them is termed accommodation.

Accommodation is a state of cooperation emerging from a conflict situation. One example is an agreement between two individuals to postpone their struggle if only because they are physically exhausted; another example is a truce between groups that have been involved in a race riot; still another example is a "cold war" on the international level. *Accommodation* is also exemplified by relatively permanent adjustments, as when two nations that have been warring over their respective boundaries lay down their arms, sign a treaty delineating the agreed-upon borders of each country, and respect the agreement thereafter. The Jewish ghetto, a phenomenon of some European countries in the past, persisted for generations, an accommodation to situations of conflict and other circumstances. The ghetto emphasized the social distance between its residents and those outside the area, but accommodation existed in the fact that establishment of the ghetto and its acceptance by Jews and non-Jews alike represented a substitute for conflict.

For another example of accommodation, take a community in which two ethnic groups have been hostile toward each other for years, engaging in open conflict from time to time. Gradually, the members of one group come to know those of the other better and better. They vote on the same issues, fight common community perils, unite to make civic improvements. The children of one group find themselves playing with children of the other group. The parents work in the same establishments, shop in the same stores, attend P.T.A. gatherings in the same schools. Imperceptibly, individuals from one group decide those from the other are worthy of respect. Conflict diminishes, finally exists no longer. The two groups have accommodated, one to the other, more or less permanently.

When two or more cultural groups living in the same locality are in the process of uniting, becoming a single cultural group, the form of interaction taking place is termed assimilation. This process is marked by the gradual disappearance of some cultural differences distinguishing the groups and is a product of prolonged cooperation between or among them.

We in the United States are a people who have received and assimilated cultural elements from many lands. Our culture, which has its distinctive characteristics today, has borrowed from the cultures of both the American Indian and the immigrants from many lands who came and still come to our shores. A full measure of the cultures of incoming Poles, Russians, English, Italians, Germans, and many others, has been incorporated into our way of life. Negro Americans have contributed elements of their original African cultures. The progenitors of the American in Minnesota gave us elements of Swedish culture. The ancestors of the American in Pennsylvania contributed elements of Hungarian culture.

And just as we "Americans" have taken over many cultural elements from other groups, so have newer arrivals to this land borrowed aspects of the culture they found and find here. Assimilation is a two-way process.

But this does not mean that in that process one group exchanges all of its cultural characteristics for an entirely different set of cultural characteristics. Immigrants to America do not enter a figurative melting pot and then emerge "100 percent Americans," each exactly like every other individual in this country, in every respect culturally identical. Ours is not one culture, realistically considered, but a mosaic of a number of cultural patterns. There is indeed a recognizable, identifiable, overall culture that we may call "American." It is shared by most of the people who have lived here for some time. But there are other, subsidiary cultures, those of identifiable groups that, while sharing the overall culture, retain some aspects of life styles that are distinct from what we think of as "our own." Scandinavians, Chinese, Irish, English, French, Dutch, are among these groups. So are Negroes, Mexicans, and Puerto Ricans. All these have certain of their own ways of behaving, believing, thinking, even though they have assimilated the greater part of the "100 percent American" culture. There are, in fact, different American cultural identities: there is a Yankee type, there are "hillbillies," whose particular cultural traits are identifiable. Catholics, as a religious group, have their distinctive cultural characteristics, as have Jews and Moslems. American Indians, numerically a tiny minority in this country, cannot be considered fully assimilated into the culture of the land they once owned exclusively, for they maintain their cultural identity to a marked degree.

So it is that what we call an "American," meaning a native of the United States, is a product of assimilation, but of a partial assimilation only. Cultural persistencies have played and continue to play a strategic role in our way of life. Our modes of speech, recreation, eating, farming, manufacturing, burying our dead, singing, dancing—these and many more have been partly shaped by various class, ethnic, nationality, religious, and other groups.

The African continent offers contemporary examples of assimilation in progress. Where white men have come in and industrialized a region, they have assumed the dominant role, even when constituting a minority. They need cheap labor, hence they teach the black man to mine and tend machines. But the black African usually goes beyond that, incorporating other elements of the Caucasian culture into his own life-ways. He does this even though the white man offers resistance. Thus, on the Rhodesian Copperbelt, native black Africans leave their villages to take work in the cities. They join unions, participate in strikes—activities quite unknown to them before. Some attend the white man's school. Some read newspapers and books; they use radio and attend movies. Family life has undergone some change, influenced by the culture the white man brought with him. Some assimilation, then, has already occurred. And it is a two-way proposition. The white man is influenced by the black man, as the black man is influenced by the white man. The Caucasian learns to communicate with the black man, to use his labor effectively, to sell to him at retail. To date, however, the assimilation has been largely in one direction; the black African is borrowing more of the white man's culture than the white man is borrowing of his.

CULTURAL VARIATIONS IN NATURE & INTENSITY OF INTERACTION

People in all societies engage in cooperation, competition, and conflict, but there is a great deal of variation in the nature and intensity of these forms of interaction in different societies. Numerous anthropologists have conducted studies of these variations. They found that some societies place more stress on competition and conflict than others. Thus, the Zuni tribe of North American Indians deemphasizes the competitive spirit to such an extent that almost all originality and unusual ability is discouraged. By contrast, the Kwakiutl Indians are fiercely competitive, working hard to accumulate wealth, not so much for the material comfort it will provide as for what it will bring the owner and his family in prestige. The "potlatch," a ceremonial festival, serves this purpose. Ranking chiefs vie with each other to give away or even destroy their property. A chief may work a lifetime accumulating wealth, then dissipate it in one potlatch. His extravagance enhances his own status and establishes that of his children. The Quakers, a contemporary American subcultural group, emphasize cooperation more than competition in family and religious activities. They are quite effective in preventing conflict from being openly manifested among their own people.

The people of the United States are for the most part invested with the competitive spirit. One must "get ahead," "succeed," "make a good showing." We compete in business, politics, sports, even in church membership. Advertising employs such terms as "the greatest," "the most sensational," "the cheapest," "the most respected"—all suggesting competition. The aspiring actress wants to become a "star," not a bit player, and if she becomes one, engages in sometimes furious rivalry for "top billing" on a poster or theater marquee. Members of "society" compete in giving posh parties and hosting the "right" people.

And yet competition in the United States has its limits, often set by or on behalf of erstwhile or would-be competing parties. "Fair trade" laws establish the retail price of specified products, presumably as a means of reducing cutthroat competition in the market place. The National Labor Relations Act and subsequent legislation and court decisions mitigate the intensity of competition between management and labor. Minimum-wage laws hopefully will make it unnecessary for workers to scrabble, one against the other, for a bare existence. Medical associations establish codes forbidding physicians to compete against each other by advertising their names and services. Competition for occupancy of space is reduced, to an extent, by laws prohibiting discrimination on the basis of race, creed, or color in renting or selling housing.

When we consider the Zuni, the Kwakiutl, the Quakers, and the people of the United States as a whole, it should be obvious that in order to understand human interaction we must first understand the culturally induced motives of the people who are interacting.

SUMMING UP

What features and forms characterize the principal processes of group interaction we have been discussing?

Cooperation reflects the common interests of members of a group or of cooperating groups. They work together to attain desired objectives. *Competition* reflects like interests, but in this case the individual group members or groups engage in rivalry to attain certain objectives. Some of the competitors will win out, some will lose. *Conflict* reflects opposed interests. Individual members of a group, or several groups, have antithetical interests that they consider irreconcilable. They strive, by resistant or hostile action, to gain their ends over and against the ends desired by the opposition.

Cooperation is usually conceived of as a desirable state, leading to peace, tranquillity, and the achievement of ends by mutual aid and support. *Competition* is apt to be envisioned as a necessary state, even if less than desirable. There is a scarcity of a certain item of value that all of the competitors feel they must attain. *Conflict* is viewed as an undesirable, often intolerable state that works toward dissolution of the group or one or more of the hostile groups. Conflict among members of a small business group threatens to injure its morale and bring about its dissolution. War between one nation and another will harm both and may reduce one to a position subordinate to the other.

The group is the agent of cultural transmission, and there are close interconnections between processes of group interaction and group arrangements. These processes are operative in determining family, school, and work relationships. They are factors in determining governmental structure and international relations. Cooperation, competition, and conflict contribute to the fixing of role and status within a society. They serve to delineate and accent class differences. In a complex society, they have a bearing on the ecological structure of a community, bringing given individuals and groups into particular areas: rural, urban, and suburban areas, the inner city, the slum, the fashionable sections. In these and other respects the processes of group interaction play a part in the determination of how, and under what conditions, groups become arranged in society.

· *NOTES*

1. Wilbert E. Moore, *Man, Time, and Society* (New York: Wiley, 1963), p. 15.
2. As reported in Richard T. LaPiere and Paul R. Farnsworth, *Social Psychology* (New York: McGraw-Hill, 1949), p. 524.
3. M. A. May *et al., Memorandum on Research in Competition and*

Cooperation (Washington, D. C.: Social Science Research Council, 1937).

· SUGGESTIONS FOR FURTHER READING

BERNARD, JESSIE. *American Community Behavior.* New York: Dryden, 1949. Part II.
Part II of this readable textbook deals with competitive behavior in the community.

COSER, LEWIS A. *The Functions of Social Conflict.* New York: Free Press, 1956.
Coser points up some of the functionally useful consequences of conflict.

PARK, ROBERT E., and ERNEST W. BURGESS. *Introduction to the Science of Sociology.* 2nd ed. Chicago: University of Chicago Press, 1924, Chapters 4, 5, 6, 8, 9, 10, 11.
The classic explanation and discussion of the social processes of cooperation, competition, conflict, accommodation, and assimilation.

PARK, ROBERT E., and H. A. MILLER. *Old World Traits Transplanted.* New York: Harper & Row, 1921.
An engrossing treatment of the process of assimilation as it pertains to European immigrants in the United States.

YOUNG, PAULINE V. *The Pilgrims of Russian Town.* Chicago: University of Chicago Press, 1932.
A very readable description and analysis of the assimilation process undergone by a Russian sect after migrating to the Pacific Coast.

part five
social problems

18 SOCIAL PROBLEMS

In the preceding section of this volume (Part IV) we discussed the meaning of *group,* examining the kinds of social organization that involve relationships among people interacting directly and indirectly with one another. These relationships operate to fulfill human needs and contribute to the well-being of people. At times, however, they function to create problems for us. In this chapter we develop an understanding of the concept of social problems. The balance of Part V is is devoted to discussion of several specific social problems.

WHICH IS A SOCIAL PROBLEM?

In your opinion, which of the following statements refers to a social problem?

1 · Over 30 million Americans live in poverty.
2 · Half of the working-age population of the United States lacks a high school education.
3 · In Burma, a household *nat* named Min Mahagiri is an evil spirit that harms human beings who fail to tie a coconut to a *nat* post as a mark of respect for the spirit.
4 · The cost of health and medical care in the United States amounted to 3.6 billion dollars in 1940. It had increased to eight times this amount by 1963, to 28.6 billion dollars.
5 · Almost 60 percent of United States children ages 5 to 14,

in families with annual incomes of less than 2,000 dollars annually, have never been to a dentist.

6 · Lightning kills people every year.

7 · In 1920, about one-fifth of the women who worked were married. By 1962, over 60 percent of all working females were married women living with their husbands.

8 · Approximately 153 people of every 100,000 in our population entered a mental hospital in 1963, as compared to 92 of 100,000 in 1940.

9 · There are about 5 million alcoholics in this country.

10 · In Lebanon, some husbands beat their wives when the latter appear in public with their faces incompletely concealed behind veils.

In order to respond effectively to these items, you of course need to have a definition of *social problem* in mind. Go by your present conception of what the term signifies. It cannot be expected at this point that your definition will necessarily accord with a sociologist's. Have you decided which of the ten statements reflect a social problem? Then let us proceed to a sociological definition of the term.

WHAT IS A SOCIAL PROBLEM?

A social problem is a condition growing out of human interaction that is considered undesirable by a significant number of people who believe it can and must be resolved through preventive or remedial action.

The condition inferentially set forth in Figure 18.1 fits this definition. Most of us believe that good medical and hospital care should be within the means of all. Further, a good many people are concerned over rising medical and hospital costs. And they believe something can and should be done to bring them within the means of all.

Let us analyze our definition of *social problems*.

1. Why are they termed *social*? They are social in that they have to do with human relationships within society. They pertain to people, their moral values, their social institutions, their relations with one another.

They are social *problems* because they are regarded as involving undesirable dislocations in social patterns and relationships within the society. They represent what is "wrong" or "improper," violations of the "right" and "proper." "Social prob-

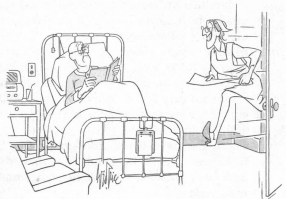

Figure 18.1
A Social Problem
Drawing by Geo. Price;
Copr. © 1955 The New
Yorker Magazine, Inc.

"Good news, Mr. Murdock!
You can go home as soon as you fork over $593.50."

lems," write sociologists Robert K. Merton and Robert A. Nisbet, "cannot be understood except in the light of what a society holds to be good or right."[1]

2. We indicated that in order for a condition to be defined as a social problem *it must be considered undesirable by a significant number of people.* What constitutes a "significant number"? We might say that a significant number, in the frame of reference, consists of any number from two to millions of individuals. Here, the reasoning would be that if even only two people agree that a social problem exists, it is a social problem—to *them,* by *their* definition. Assume that twenty persons, who comprise the total membership of a religious sect, feel very strongly that it is immoral and injurious to allow male school teachers to instruct female pupils. The members of the sect object to employing male teachers. Since they must send their female children to these schools, they are confronted by what they consider a serious social problem threatening their children's morals and the stability of family life. We might conclude that since twenty, representing 100 percent, of the sect members hold these views, they constitute a significant number, and the instruction of their children by male teachers does represent a social problem generally. But let us consider for a moment. There is no question that the practice concerned is a serious problem *to the members of the sect.* The problem is *social,* since it concerns a number of human beings in a society. But shall we call it a *social problem* when

only twenty individuals object to male teachers, while millions of other people do not? This would seem far-fetched.

Then shall we say that "a significant number" means a majority, or perhaps an overwhelming consensus of the persons who are affected by a given condition, and who define the condition as a social problem? That would certainly be a highly significant number, and when so many are concerned about a deviation from a norm that is commonly and widely cherished in the society or subsection of the society, a social problem does exist. Very likely, a majority opinion, or possibly a consensus, exists in the United States to the effect that drug addiction is a social problem. It is a social problem.

But at times, less than a majority can and do define certain conditions, circumstances, and behavior as social problems, and sociologists would agree. For some social situations and behavior, numerical criteria are inadequate to define what constitutes a social problem. In these circumstances it is not so much "a significant number" of people who arrive at the definition as "a significant number of significant people," who may represent nothing approximating a majority. Society, we learned, is characterized by a system of social roles and statuses. By the processes of social stratification, some individuals have more prestige and influence than others in connection with given matters.

There is not a merely numerical democracy of judgment in which every man's appraisal is assigned the same voting power in defining a condition as a social problem. It is a mistaken . . . notion that each member of society sets about to define social problems for himself and that it is the aggregate of these independent judgments that decides the array of problems in the society and the comparative importance of each in the array.[2]

Persons occupying strategic positions of power and authority carry more weight than others in establishing for the members of the society what are to be considered acceptable standards of behavior and which should be deemed significant departures from these standards. Ministers play an influential role in identifying what beliefs and behavior should be considered appropriate or inappropriate in a community. A President of the United States can report the existence of pockets of poverty in an otherwise affluent society and, by so identifying what he conceives of as a social problem, may influence millions of people to agree.

"A significant number," then, may mean a comparatively large number of people within a society or any number of individuals who are significant in that they occupy strategic positions of power and authority.

3. Our definition indicated that *for a condition to constitute a social problem the people who so define it must believe that something can and should be done about it.* We attack poverty in the belief we can ameliorate the condition by human effort of some sort. But consider a cyclone. It creates havoc, is indubitably a serious and undesirable condition. It is a problem to us. But not a social problem, since we have thus far found no way to prevent cyclones or to protect ourselves effectively against them. Human interaction cannot solve this problem. War, mental illness, alcoholism, traffic casualties, air pollution, venereal disease—these *may* be defined as social problems in some societies. Cyclones are not so defined.

OBJECTIVE & SUBJECTIVE ASPECTS OF SOCIAL PROBLEMS

A number of years ago, Richard C. Fuller and Richard R. Myers contributed a very helpful general analysis of social problems[3] in which they pointed out that every social problem involves an *objective condition* and a *subjective definition.* The objective condition is *a situation that can be verified by trained, impartial observers.* We can, for instance, assert, on the evidence, that over 30 million people in the United States live in poverty. The subjective definition involves *the awareness by certain people that the condition threatens certain of their cherished values.* In our country, many people feel that no one ought to live in poverty. The fact that there are millions of poverty-stricken families in our midst strikes a great many of us as a serious deviation from cherished values.

Although the objective condition is an element, it is not itself sufficient to constitute a social problem. It is additionally necessary that people define the problem as a problem. "Social problems are what people think they are," Fuller and Myers declare. Hence: ". . . if conditions are not defined as social problems by the people involved in them, they are not problems to those people."[4]

Most Americans probably hold that a husband should never beat his wife, and that if there are many wife beaters among us there is a social problem calling for amelioration. But what of many Lebanese, male and female alike, who agree that it is justifiable and perhaps even required that a husband strike his wife—if she fails to veil her face on certain occasions? In that case, wife beating, so provoked, is not a social problem in the view of those Lebanese. Whether wife beating is a duty or a social problem or, say, "just a natural part of life," depends on one's *subjective definition* of the condition. If a significant number of individuals in a given population define the condition as a social problem, it is one.

MANIFEST & LATENT
SOCIAL PROBLEMS

Subjective and objective aspects of social problems may be viewed in a related context. Sociologists distinguish between *manifest* and *latent* social problems.

Manifest social problems are those that are *subjectively* recognized by the group to *be* social problems. That is, group members perceive certain conditions as being at odds with their values, hence undesirable. There may, of course, be objective evidence supporting the view. Thus, venereal disease is a manifest social problem in the subjective judgment of many people and according to objective evidence.

Latent social problems are those *objectively* defined social conditions that are identified by the definers as being at odds with group values, although they are not recognized to be such by the group. Analysis based upon objective evidence presented by social scientists may indicate that population increase in a given area constitutes a social problem. The inhabitants of that area may not recognize this as being the case. A latent social problem nevertheless exists.

Is this not in opposition to what we said earlier to the effect that social problems "are what people think they are"? In one sense, no. It is still a fact, as Fuller and Myers explain, that if conditions are not defined as social problems by the people involved in them, they are not, subjectively, problems *to those people*. But in another sense, what we are now saying with regard to latent social problems does differ from the Fuller-Myers position. People may not recognize that a certain condition or circumstance constitutes a social problem in their community, despite which, if scientific evidence establishes that the condition is a threat to group values, it must be considered a social problem. As such, sociologists are concerned with it, even if the community is not. Merton and Nisbet adopt this position when they assert:

For a sociologist to confine himself only to the conditions in society which a majority of people regard as undesirable would be to exclude study of all manner of conditions that are in fact at odds with the declared values and purposes of those who accept or endorse these conditions. . . . [N]ot all conditions and processes inimical to the values of men are recognized as such by them. It is the function of the sociologist to discover and to report the human consequences of holding to certain values and practices just as it is his function to discover and to report the human consequences of departing from these values and practices.[5]

The sociologist is not imposing his values upon others when he points to latent social problems. He is merely presenting verifiable facts and their observed relation to the society. If the members of that society eventually recognize the existence of a social problem as a consequence of this, the latent social problem becomes manifest. Otherwise, it remains latent.

TWO CATEGORIES OF SOCIAL PROBLEMS

For purposes of analysis it is useful to classify social problems into two broad classes, according to whether they represent *social disorganization* or *deviant behavior*.

SOCIAL DISORGANIZATION

You will recall that in Chapter 14 we stated that *position in society* becomes fairly well established in the minds of its members. We said that all of us have certain *roles* to perform, culturally defined patterns of behavior to enact, in responding to the expectations of particular groups in specific social situations. Each role is associated with a corresponding *status*. Status is the social position identified in the society as associated with a role, a pattern of behavior expected or required under given circumstances of persons occupying the position.

When there are inadequacies or failures in the arrangement and operation of interrelated roles and statuses within a society, this indicates some degree of *social disorganization*. In other words, the social system of roles and statuses has broken down to some extent. Social disorganization is a matter of degree, but where it is a fact in any degree, the collective as well as individual objectives of the members of society are to an extent frustrated. They are not as effectively realized as they could be under an alternative arrangement and operation of roles and statuses. "When we say that a particular group or organization or community or society is disorganized in some degree, we mean that the structure of statuses and roles is not as effectively organized as it, then and there, might be."[6]

Among a number of factors contributing to social disorganization is the disparity of values and interests held by respective status groups within a society despite the fact that they also share common values and interests. In the United States, the upper and middle classes may oppose being taxed to support indigent members of the society. They may see no reason to underwrite slum clearance since, in their conception, the role of the indigent person includes residing in substandard housing. The slum dweller may have accepted this conception fatalistically, giving up any idea of improving his condition. Thus, both the wealthier and poorer classes would be enacting their respective, expected roles. Despite this, social disorganization would be a fact, for slum life is a social problem to the entire community, directly and indirectly. Slum dwellers and those more fortunately located must cope with the hazards and conditions of slum life—disease, juvenile delinquency, crime, and others—in one way or another.

We have just posited a situation in which disparate values and interests result in acceptance of a status quo representing a social problem. They may also lead to conflict. Prolonged battles between management and labor may upset the economy of a locality or nation. Incompatible views on the purposes and policies of a university may create a schism between faculty and administration that will disrupt the teaching process.

Roles go through evolutionary change. In the process, conflict may produce social disorganization. Negroes, gradually moving toward an improved status and reinterpretation of roles, were no longer willing to enact the role of second-class citizens. They demanded full constitutional rights. Powerful status groups resisted these demands. Civil disobedience was one outcome, viewed by many as a social problem. Riots and looting or retaliatory mob violence and killing by whites were another outcome, and these manifestations, like civil disobedience, were expressions of social disorganization.

Social disorganization may be based partially on defective socialization. Some of our residents, for a variety of reasons, are incompletely socialized, having failed to acquire values, attitudes, knowledge, or skills needed to fulfill their social roles. Some, lacking in education and vocational training, are unable to support their dependents. Others have not learned that they *should* do so. Poverty, dependency, and other problems constituting aspects of social disorganization are thus partially attributable to defects in the processes of socialization.

DEVIANT BEHAVIOR

Social disorganization refers to a breakdown in *the social system* of roles and statuses. Deviant behavior, as defined in Chapter 10, refers to *individuals* in a social system. Deviant behavior is conduct that varies significantly, in direction or degree, from the social norm for that behavior. The conduct, in other words, departs significantly from the norms set for individuals according to their social statuses. The same behavior may be defined as deviant when enacted by one individual, and as conforming behavior when enacted by another. The social status of the individual concerned will determine this. Thus, when a civilian dresses in an admiral's uniform and poses as a naval officer, he exhibits deviant behavior. When an admiral dons his uniform and enacts the role of a naval officer, he is exhibiting conforming behavior.

Merton and Nisbet distinguish between the type of social problem involved in social disorganization and the type involved in deviant behavior. In general terms, they write:

. . . the type of social problem involved in disorganization arises not from people failing to live up to the requirements of their social statuses, as is the case with deviant behavior, but from the faulty organization of these statuses into a reasonably coherent social system. Rather than role-conformity leading to people's realizing their several and collective purposes, it leads to their getting in one another's way.[7]

It should be pointed out that although deviant behavior is often defined as a social problem, it may have positive social functions. Emile Durkheim actually argued that crime is functional in that it serves to increase solidarity in the group against the common enemy, the criminal. Some criminologists, who might not like Durkheim's argument, would nevertheless hold that crime is functional in another sense: it solves a problem, serves a need felt by the perpetrator. He is hungry; stealing solves his problem. At the same time, stealing is a social problem. Thus, crime is both "adjustive behavior" and deviant behavior.

It cannot be gainsaid that certain problem situations constitute solutions to certain other problems. Organized crime must be regarded as a social problem in our society, but its entrepreneurs would not reap the huge rewards they do if they were not purveying something that a great many people want and find difficulty in getting through legal channels. From this viewpoint gambling, prostitution, and the sale of narcotics have a positive aspect.

WHICH *IS* A SOCIAL PROBLEM?

We now direct your attention once more to the ten statements at the beginning of this chapter. Which of them represent social problems? Which *may* represent social problems?

1. What we consider a decent standard of living is a cherished cultural value in our society; in addition, a significant number of Americans are concerned about the condition of poverty; moreover, we are of the understanding we can do something about this condition. For these reasons, the fact that over 30 million of our people live in poverty does reflect the existence of a social problem.

2. Evidence indicates that a higher level of educational attainment than ever before is required if individuals are to find means of livelihood in this era of scientific and technological development. The fact that half the working-age population of the United States lacks a high school education represents a social problem, according to the criteria applied in the preceding item.

3. The evil spells cast by a *nat* named Min Mahagiri are a social problem to the Burmese, who believe in the existence of *nats* and of this particular *nat*. *Nats* do not represent a

social problem to us; we do not believe in their existence or evil power. Min Mahagiri is a social problem to the Burmese in that (1) all *nats* are considered harmful, (2) Min Mahagiri especially is considered harmful because it is a household *nat*, capable of entering every home, (3) but its evil may be propitiated by a coconut affixed to a *nat* post; something can be done about the social problem created by Min Mahagiri, non-human spirit though it be.[8]

But if there were no means of appeasing *nats*, their existence and behavior would not represent a social problem, even in Burma, where the people believe in their existence. If human beings can do nothing to prevent Min Mahagiri from working his evil, then Min Mahagiri is a problem to the human beings he harms, but not a *social* problem.

4. The figures on costs of health and medical care indicate that their rise is due to more than an increase in total population. Costs in 1963 were eight times what they were in 1940. Population did not increase to that degree during the period. Steps can be taken to reduce costs to the consumer of health and medical care. We have a social problem here.

5. There is also a social problem in the fact that such a large proportion of children from low-income families have never been seen by a dentist. The reasoning should be clear by now.

6. What about lightning, which kills people? It is not of itself a social problem, since we cannot prevent lightning. We can minimize its detrimental consequences through taking certain precautions, however, such as teaching people what to do when they are outdoors during a lightning storm. A social problem occurs when some people jeopardize their welfare or the welfare of their families by refusing to act in a way that protects them.

7. Is the proportionate increase of married women (living with their husbands) who are in the labor market indicative of the existence of a social problem? In this instance, much depends upon which of several definitions of the situation you choose to accept. There is no unassailable evidence that indicates the effects of the entrance into the labor market of married women who live with their husbands. The *objective condition*, in other words, is not entirely clear. Some persons believe the evidence warrants classifying this condition as a social problem, pointing to what they assume to be the effects on home life, the rearing of children, and the like. Others are

not ready to say the condition constitutes a social problem. They await more evidence.

8. No doubt we all deem mental illness a serious social problem. But whether the increased hospital admissions reflect more mental breakdowns than heretofore is a matter of conjecture. Some of the increase undoubtedly is due to better means of identifying the mentally ill person. Any amount of mental illness concerns us, however, and we may answer this item in the affirmative: Mental illness, whether increasing or not, still constitutes a social problem in our society.

9. Alcoholism is viewed as a social problem in our society. It meets our criteria.

10. Finally, what about Lebanese husbands who beat their unveiled wives? Their behavior does not constitute a social problem to those Lebanese who consider it improper for women to appear in public unveiled. To them, the women in question create and are a social problem. However, the behavior of the husbands in beating their wives is viewed as a social problem in some Lebanese circles, for many of the women of that country have become "emancipated," abandoning the more traditional custom. And their husbands no longer regard the veil as an essential mark of the respectable woman. When Supreme Court Justice William Douglas visited Lebanon in 1951, he was astonished when he saw a husband beat and curse his wife because she allowed her veil to slip. The husband drove her out of sight, then, returning to Douglas, apologized for the shameful behavior of the wife. But the same Justice Douglas also attended mixed parties in Lebanon and found unveiled women presiding as hostesses. "The old and the new styles still jostle each other," writes Daniel Lerner.[9] Here we have a condition that would be defined by some Lebanese as a social problem. An appreciable number of others would feel differently about the matter.

SOCIAL PROBLEMS & VALUE CONFLICT

Two different kinds of value conflict are involved in social problems: (1) People disagree on whether a given condition threatens fundamental values, that is, whether a social problem actually exists in a given condition, (2) where there is agreement that a certain condition is a threat to those values, people disagree over proposed solutions of the problem in question. Some people believe the House Committee on Un-American Activities threatens constitutional liberties by its inquiries into what it considers subversive activities. Other individuals are convinced that the committee defends rather than threatens the fundamental values inherent in our Bill of Rights. This illustrates (1) above. An illustration of (2) is the fact that there is a widespread belief in this country that juvenile delinquency is a threat to our basic values, but much less agreement on how to prevent, control, or treat delinquency.

Having pointed out that social problems involve two different kinds of value conflict, let us now put things a little differently, in order to indicate the organization of succeeding chapters.

1 · All social problems are characterized by some degree of value conflict.
2 · The people concerned hold conflicting views on whether a social problem in fact exists.
3 · Where they agree that it does exist, the conflict revolves about the question of the precise nature and extent of the problem.
4 · A further source of conflict has to do with how best to attack the problem that those who are concerned agree exists.

Let us apply this reasoning to an emerging situation, the increased number of unmanned missiles and artificial satellites being lofted into space by the great powers. Some attempts at launchings have failed, the equipment being destroyed in the air electronically, by remote control. Some objects shot into space have dropped debris to earth, not according to plan. This "hardware" can cause considerable harm to persons, structures, and land. Increased traffic in outer space also raises the possibility of a collision between two vehicles or between one vehicle and a planet. Now then, does this state of affairs signify the existence of a social problem? Undoubtedly many people around the world would answer in the negative. They may have heard of no real damage resulting from the space flights. Or having heard, they do not believe the situation has reached a critical point, sufficient to warrant real concern.

Countering these are the many individuals known to be deeply concerned. They insist a social problem does exist, here and now. The United Nations organized committees to study the problem. The United States government published a symposium by leading scientists and lawyers throughout the world on what needs to be done to solve many specific problems conceived to be an outgrowth of the major social problem—the hazards of unrestricted and uncontrolled ventures into outer space. In the estimation of a significant number of individuals, then, the world is confronted by a social problem arising from the spectacular development of space exploration. In the estimation of a significant number of individuals, no such problem exists or is imminent. We are faced by conflicting views on the question.

If a problem does exist, what are its dimensions? What is the nature and extent of the problem? Again, views conflict. Even space scientists disagree on the exact nature of the hazards involved, the extent of the hazard, the degree to which damage to people, structures, and land may be anticipated from debris and other causes. There is disagreement on precisely how much damage has already occurred, and scientific organizations are currently conducting research on this phase of the matter. However, the fact that a number of international meetings have been held on the subject and that the United Nations has adopted certain safety rules for the exploration of outer space by member nations indicates that no matter how much disagreement there may be as to the precise nature and extent of the problem, space exploration does represent a social problem insofar as physical hazards to the earth are concerned.

How shall we resolve the problem? Once more we are confronted by conflicting points of view. Some of those who have expressed themselves would immediately set up a code by which all nations would be bound and which would establish traffic control in space. Others assert this would violate the principle of the sovereignty of nations. Some would follow maritime law in assessing damages, whereas others would call for entirely new, ground-breaking space law on the subject.

A report by one expert, I. H. Ph. de Rode-Verschoor, clearly indicates that different and to an extent contradictory solutions to the problem have been proposed. He refers to three influential proposals that have been advanced in international negotiations: (1) The state that launched a space vehicle could be held responsible for damages incurred. (2) The state might be held to account for such damages, but with the right to certain exclusions, as, for instance, in the event of an unforeseen collision with a meteor. (3) The state might be only secondarily deemed responsible. Prime sources of remedy would be an international fund, contributed to by all nations interested in astronautics, deposited in a central place, and administered by an international tribunal.[10]

SOCIOLOGICAL STUDIES OF SOCIAL PROBLEMS

In the following four chapters, we shall discuss certain social problems. We cannot of course consider all major social problems. With respect to those we do explore, to greater or less degree, the author strives to maintain an objective attitude. We are concerned with evidence, therefore we shall not characterize a given condition as good, bad, desirable, or undesirable, except as these judgments have been applied by others.

Beyond this, we will search for answers to such questions as:

1 · What are the several conflicting views on whether the condition under scrutiny constitutes a social problem?
2 · What conflicting views exist regarding proposed attacks on the problem?
3 · What conflicting views exist between beliefs, ideas, and proposed solutions to the problem, on the one hand, and available factual data concerning the problem, on the other?
4 · What are the discernible historical trends related to the problem? Have value conflicts with respect to the problem increased in intensity? Decreased? Shown comparatively little change over the years?
5 · What structural, institutional, and cultural circumstances give rise to the social problem? What is the comparative influence of each circumstance?
6 · What would be the expected outcome if given proposals for resolving the problem were carried out?

This, in general, is the format of the chapters immediately following.

· NOTES

1. Robert K. Merton and Robert A. Nisbet (eds.), *Contemporary Social Problems* (New York: Harcourt, Brace & World, 1961), p. 11.
2. *Ibid.*, p. 706.
3. Richard C. Fuller and Richard R. Myers, "The Natural History of a Social Problem," *American Sociological Review*, VI (June 1941), 320–329.
4. *Ibid.*

5. Merton and Nisbet, *op. cit.*, p. 708.
6. *Ibid.*, p. 720.
7. *Ibid.*, pp. 722–723.
8. Manning Nash, *The Golden Road to Modernity, Village Life in Contemporary Burma* (New York: Wiley, 1965), pp. 168–169.
9. Daniel Lerner, *The Passing of Traditional Society: Modernizing the Middle East* (New York: Free Press, 1958), p. 198.
10. I. H. Ph. de Rode-Verschoor, "The Responsibility of the States for the Damage Caused by the Launched Space-Bodies," in United States Senate, *Legal Problems of Space Exploration* (Washington, D. C.: U. S. Government Printing Office, Document 26, 1961), pp. 460–461.

· SUGGESTIONS FOR FURTHER READING

BERNARD, JESSIE. *Social Problems at Midcentury*. New York: Dryden, 1957, Chapter 5, "The Criteria of Social Problems."
An excellent statement on what constitutes a social problem.

FULLER, RICHARD C., and RICHARD R. MYERS. "The Natural History of a Social Problem." *American Sociological Review*, VI (June 1941), 320–329.
The authors present their analysis of the "natural history" of a social problem, as it passes through successive stages of awareness, policy determination, and reform.

MCGEE, REECE. *Social Disorganization in America:* San Francisco: Chandler, 1962.
A brief text on the disorganized person, group, organization, and society. Illustrates what the sociologist means by the term "social disorganization."

19 THE PROBLEM OF OVERPOPULATION

We are about to embark on an examination of specific social problems, beginning in this chapter with one that has world-wide import—expanding population in its relation to means of sustenance.

RABBIT ISLAND, SYMBOL OF A PROBLEM

This story may be apocryphal, or it may be basically true. Either way, it gets to the heart of what we shall be discussing in this chapter.

Rabbit Island is a speck of land about a mile square. You might locate it on a map of the Hawaiian Islands provided it were done to a scale permitting microscopic pinpointing. According to the story, a wayfaring seaman left a couple of rabbits there about a hundred years ago. Just two. It was lush country for the animals, containing plenty of sweet, nourishing grass. The rabbits ate well, were fructified, and multiplied, as rabbits do. In less than ten years, according to report, there were more than ten thousand rabbits on that island. But by that time there was not enough grass to go around, and times were bad. Hungry, enfeebled rabbits sat around on their haunches as if waiting for each new blade of grass to pop up out of the ground. Finally, they commenced gnawing the roots under the surface of the soil. Of course, that killed off a lot of grass for good. It also killed off rabbits. They starved to death by the hundreds and then the thousands. Finally only about a hundred were left.

The rainy season came on, and with only those few grass eaters around, the vegetation got a fresh start. Tropical grass grows rapidly. Soon it was as thick and lush as it had been when the first rabbits arrived. Their descendants ate well again. With nourishment, they gained strength and started increasing once more. As their number increased, the grass was eaten away again. As the grass was eaten away . . . so it went. The cycle started all over again.

DOES THE WORLD CONTAIN TOO MANY PEOPLE?

The story applies in considerable measure to people. In a manner of speaking, our planet is an expanded Rabbit Island. The number of people it can support is dependent upon the sustenance potential. William Vogt, in *Road to Survival,* and Fairfield Osborn, in *Our Plundered Planet,* vigorously express this view. They do not, of course, believe humans are as much at the mercy of natural forces as rabbits. They recognize that human beings have an adaptable culture that enables them to increase the productive capacity of the land they inhabit. But they do hold that food production can be stretched only so far and that while the earth has a limited capacity to provide men with their daily bread, the human race has an unlimited capacity to reproduce.

That peoples suffer hunger and starvation is well documented. Study the emaciated face of the woman in Figure 19.1. This photograph was taken in the Arctic in 1950. The woman is a member of the Paddlemiuts, an Eskimo tribe. She and her tribesmen had set out on their twice-yearly migration to hunt caribou, a mainstay of the Paddlemiut diet. Supplies dwindled, there were no caribou to be hunted, and starvation set in. The woman in the picture, gay and fat only a few months earlier, was one of several left behind to die as stronger tribesmen pushed forward in search of food. When the photographer came upon the abandoned people, they were rechewing old bones and caribou skins, stoically awaiting death in a land that could not feed them.

Most population experts, called *demographers*, would agree

Figure 19.1
When Food Gives Out
Richard Harrington.

with the basic premise of Vogt and Osborn that the number of people a locality can support is fundamentally dependent upon the sustenance potential. But there is disagreement on how many people can and should live on the earth at one time.

How many people are too many people?

Is it possible to improve technology to such an extent that the planet will sustain ten or twenty times as many persons as now exist? Can human beings deliberately plan and control their numbers on a world-wide basis? If so, are such planning and control desirable? If we do not regulate population, are we headed for catastrophe? These are questions bearing on the social problem of expanding population, questions that contemporary thinkers answer in different ways. Some, like Vogt and Osborn, view population trends with alarm. Others contend that the situation is not serious, or if it is, we cannot do anything about it by human planning. Even those who agree that population trends represent an urgent problem disagree on what should be done to recitfy the situation.

So that we can better understand the opposing points of view, let us first consider some of the data concerning population, as revealed in demographic studies.

FACTS ON HUMAN POPULATION

Statistics, and figures generally, frighten or overawe some individuals. Others are likely to consider them insufferably dull devices for telling a story. However, if you will give careful attention to the few statistics presented here, you may agree that the quantitative facts about population not only are not dull but are strikingly dramatic.

First, however, a precautionary word. When a great number of noses are counted, complete accuracy is virtually impossible. For one thing, while you were counting one million people, some of the first in the count would have died. But when an actual census count is made during a short period of time, we can be confident it is quite accurate. Figures based on estimates are much less so, and most population figures are approximations.

WORLD POPULATION

A little over 300 years ago, there were no more than 500 million persons in the world. Today, there are more than 3 billion. About three-fifths of them live in Asia.

And world population is increasing at a phenomenal rate. According to United Nations estimates, 8,000 persons are born every hour, somewhere on this planet. That amounts to more than 190,000 every day, for a total of approximately 70 million a year.[1] In one year, enough people are born to equal the combined populations of France, Belgium, and Holland.

If the current rate of increase continues, within about fifteen years one billion more people will populate the earth, and if one billion is difficult to comprehend, remember that it is one thousand million. That would be more than all of the people presently inhabiting the fifty-five countries of Europe, plus all of those in the entire Western Hemisphere.[2] At that rate, current trends indicate the population of the world will double by the end of this century.

It is important to understand that population has increased not only in absolute numbers but in *rate*. For thousands of years the rate of population increase was something below .02 percent per year. About 300 years ago, it began a slow ascent. Then the rate of increase accelerated. Between 1650 and 1930, world population rose at an average of 0.5 percent a year. Between 1930 and 1940 the increase averaged 1 percent annually, and since the end of World War II it has averaged 1.6 percent annually.[3] These percentages may not project the story of world population changes with sufficient impact. Let us consider the matter from a different perspective, noting the exceedingly slow increase in population for thousands of years, then the tremendous acceleration in the present century particularly.

When the Stone Age came to an end, there were probably no more than 10 million people in the world. During Christ's time, the population was somewhere between 200 and 300 million. In 1650, often considered the beginning of the "modern era," 500 million persons inhabited this earth.[4] World population did not reach a billion until about 1820. But after that it took only a little more than a century to reach the second billion. That was around 1930. Then, between 1930 and 1960, a period of only thirty years, one billion more people were added to the planet's population. Thus, it took many thousands of years to reach the first billion, a little more than a century to achieve the second, and a third billion was reached in a mere three decades.

And incredible as it may seem, it will take no more than fifteen years beyond 1960 to add the fourth billion, according to United Nations estimates. After 1975 the time span narrows still further in the forecasts. It will take only ten years, to 1985, to reach a population of 5 billion. By the close of this century, the world will have between 6 and 7 billion inhabitants if present rates of increase hold.[5]

Table 19.1 shows estimated world population, by continents, projected to 1975. Note that the estimate of total population for 1975 is 3,828,000,000, slightly below the 4 billion estimate given above. This is accounted for by somewhat differing bases for compiling the two estimates. The 3,828,000,000 figure is "medium expectation," that is, according to neither the highest nor lowest valid estimate, but one that is in between the two extremes.

Figure 19.2 shows the comparative population ranking of ten nations, as of 1960. At that time the United States, with 179 million, was the fourth most populous nation in the world. Since 1960, some 200 million more people have been added to world population, but the United States still ranks fourth. Mainland China is the most populous nation on earth. We have less than a third as many people as mainland China, less than half as many as India, and many millions fewer than Russia.[6]

TABLE 19.1 · *Estimates of World Population by Continents, 1650–1975*

| | *Millions of Persons* | | | | |
	1650	1750	1850	1950	1975
WORLD	470	694	1,094	2,497	3,828
Africa	100	100	100	199	303
America:	8	11	59	331	543
North[a]	(1)	(1)	(26)	(168)	(240)
Latin[b]	(7)	(10)	(33)	(163)	(303)
Asia[c]	257	437	656	1,380	2,210
Europe[d]	103	144	274	574	751
Oceania	2	2	2	13	21

[a] *America north of Mexico.*
[b] *America south of the United States.*
[c] *Excluding the Asiatic part of the U.S.S.R.*
[d] *Including the Asiatic part of the U.S.S.R.*

SOURCE: For 1650–1850, United Nations, *Proceedings of the World Population Conference, 1954,* Vol. 3, New York, 1955, "The Past and Future Population of the World and Its Continents," Table 1, p. 266. For 1950 and 1975, United Nations, *The Future Growth of World Population,* New York, 1958, Table 5, p. 23. Present author's source, Murray Gendell and Hans L. Zettterberg (eds.), *A Sociological Almanac of the United States,* 2nd ed. (New York: Scribner, 1964), Table 1.10, p. 39.

UNITED STATES POPULATION

Along with the rest of the world, the United States, you will have noted, has expanded its population, and at a rapid pace in recent decades. Nine million were added to our ranks between 1930 and 1940; in the decade following, we gained another 19 million; and between 1950 and 1960, our population jumped by 28 million, a still greater rate of increase.[7] The total population residing in the United States on July 1, 1964, was

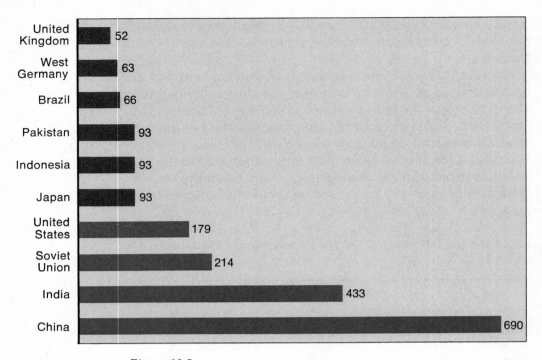

United Kingdom	52
West Germany	63
Brazil	66
Pakistan	93
Indonesia	93
Japan	93
United States	179
Soviet Union	214
India	433
China	690

Figure 19.2

Source: U.S. Bureau of the Census, *Our Growing Population,* Graphic Pamphlets, GP 60–1. Present author's source, U.S. Dept. of Health, Education, and Welfare Administration, *Converging Social Trends, Emerging Social Problems* (Washington, D.C.: U.S. Government Printing Office, 1964), p. 13, Chart 9.

about 191,334,000—an increment of 6.7 percent since April 1, 1960.[8]

Even if our growth rate is leveling off, and some evidence points in that direction, the United States population will continue to expand and will probably pass the 300 million mark before the year 2000.[9]

OUR NEIGHBORS' POPULATION

The population of nations in the environs of the United States is mounting at rates well above our own. Mexico's people increase at the rate of about 3 percent a year. This is the highest rate of increase of any large country today. Mexico's 1960 population, 36 million, is expected to expand to 123 million by the year 2000.[10]

After Mexico's, the most rapid population increases in the

world are taking place in the Caribbean and in Central America. The combined 1960 population in those two areas was 66 million. By the year 2000 it is likely to stand at 200 million,[11] a threefold increase in forty years.

In 1960, South America's population was 140 million. By the close of the century, it is estimated, this will have mounted to 394 million,[12] a rise to almost three times its population of forty years earlier. If these predictions hold, South America's population, which in 1960 was well below that of the United States, will be substantially larger than ours by 2000—394 million as against this country's 300 million.

MEASURING & COMPARING POPULATION TRENDS

Is the phenomenal expansion of world population too much growth? Have we too many people on earth now? Will we have too many a few years from now? And how is "too many" to be defined?

Demographers have developed two useful concepts for measuring and comparing population trends. One is the *birth rate*, the other the *death rate*. A birth rate of 20 means there were 20 births during a given year for every 1,000 individuals who lived in the population at the beginning of that year. A death rate of 10 means there were 10 deaths in a given twelve months for every 1,000 persons who lived in the population at the beginning of the year. Suppose we had a population showing a birth rate of 20 and a death rate of 10. That would mean a net increase of 10 persons per 1,000 during the year under consideration. If we had a population with a birth rate of 10 and a death rate of 20, this would signify a net loss of 10 persons per 1,000 during the year. In the first instance the population was more than holding its own; in the second it was losing ground.

Study the figures in Table 19.2. They show crude birth rates, crude death rates, and rate of natural increase for selected countries as of 1960. "Crude" rates indicate the number of births or deaths for every 1,000 persons of all ages. The rate of "natural increase" is the difference between the birth rate and the death rate. You can see how rapidly some of the world's national populations are increasing. Mexico's birth rate is almost four times its death rate; it would double its population in about thirty years if the rate continued. In the United States, the birth rate is a bit less than two and one-half times the death rate. The Soviet Union's birth rate is roughly three and one-half times its death rate.

But the important fact is that the world's long-range population gains have not occurred as a result of an increasing birth rate. Actually, birth rates have *dropped* sharply among certain populations that continue to *increase* rapidly. How can birth rates decline while the respective populations increase? This, of course, is the consequence of the fact that the death rate is decreasing more rapidly than the birth rate.

TABLE 19.2 · *Crude Birth and Death Rates,*[a] *and Rate of Natural Increase, for Selected Countries, 1960*[b]

	Birth Rates	Death Rates	Rates of Natural Increase[c]
United States	23.6[d]	9.5[d]	14.1[d]
Sweden	13.7	10.0	3.7
Japan	17.2[d]	7.6[d]	9.6[d]
Soviet Union	24.9	7.1	17.8
Puerto Rico	31.7[d]	6.7[d]	25.0[d]
Taiwan	39.5	6.9	32.6
Tunisia	43.7	10.8	32.9
Mexico	45.0	11.4	33.6

[a] *Crude rates indicate the number of births or deaths for every 1,000 persons of all ages.*
[b] *The selection of countries has been limited by the fact that many countries do not yet have reliable vital statistics.*
[c] *The rate of natural increase is merely the difference between the birth rate and the death rate.*
[d] *Provisional.*

SOURCE: United Nations, *Demographic Yearbook 1961* (New York, 1961). Copyright, United Nations, 1961. Reproduced by permission. Table 6, pp. 162ff., for birth rates and Table 14, pp. 264ff., for death rates. Rates of natural increase obtained by calculation. Present author's source, Murray Gendell and Hans L. Zetterberg (eds.), *A Sociological Almanac of the United States*, 2nd ed. (New York: Scribner, 1964), Table 1.21, p. 41.

BIRTH-DEATH RATES

Human beings have gained knowledge that enables more of them to live longer than did their ancestors. The Grim Reaper has had to make concessions to human culture. More accurately, we have slowed him down by devising ways of cutting the death rate. Thus, during the fourteenth century, 25 million persons died in Europe of bubonic plague; today the disease itself is practically dead as a result of scientific investigation and discovery. Typhoid fever killed millions in every part of the world until man discovered what caused and spread it and how it could be controlled. Not long ago men, women, and children perished by diphtheria, tuberculosis, anthrax, dysentery, each of which can now be so controlled that death is the exception rather than the rule. The new vaccines may eliminate polio entirely in a very few years.

Kingsley Davis reports[13] that the underdeveloped areas of the world, including many with a high ratio of population to resources, have had an unprecedented decline in death rates in the past several decades. Outstanding is the case of Ceylon, where the crude death rate fell by 34 percent in one year (from 1946 to 1947) and continued to decline thereafter. The main reason for this, Davis notes, was the use of DDT spray to control malaria, for centuries the major cause of death and illness on the island.

The discovery of sulfonamides, antibiotics, insecticides, and new immunization serums has been highly influential in reducing death rates in other underdeveloped areas. It was demonstrated in Bosnia, Yugoslavia, that endemic syphilis can be wiped out by the use of penicillin. In two years, Davis reports, a campaign, sponsored by WHO and UNICEF, eliminated the disease as a public health problem in areas containing approximately half a million people. Other programs involving other diseases have shown similar results in Haiti, Indonesia, Iraq, the Philippines, and Thailand.

In general, . . . the great reduction of mortality in underdeveloped areas since 1940 has been brought about mainly by the discovery of new methods of disease treatment . . . , by the diffusion of these new methods from the advanced countries to the unadvanced through international organizations and scientific communication, . . . and by the use of experts and medical personnel furnished primarily by the industrial countries.[14]

Particularly in the battle for the lives of infants and children has the world made great strides. The earlier very high mortality rate of newborn infants has decreased greatly in populations making use of scientific knowledge. Many infectious diseases, for example, measles, smallpox, and scarlet fever, have yielded to man's culture. Death rates have been reduced by increased knowledge of hygiene, sanitation, and diet.

Thousands of years ago, man's expectation of life at birth was somewhere between twenty and thirty years. Compare this with the fact that babies currently being born in the United States can expect to live to age seventy, on the average, if boys, and to seventy-three if girls.[15]

There have been spectacular gains in this respect in various countries. In Japan, expectation of life at birth was extended about five years in the single year 1948; the best record for any Western country was five years' extension in a ten-year period. In Ceylon, life expectancy was thirty-two years in 1921; it rose to forty-six in 1946, to fifty-six in 1950, and to sixty by 1954.[16]

We see, then, that the decreasing death rate is the prime factor in the explosive expansion of the world's population. By far the most significant factor involved is that fewer people die shortly after birth. And those who mature into adulthood live longer than their predecessors did, benefiting from improved sanitation, medical practice, public health measures, and other factors having to do with the prolongation of human life. The mean age of the population is increasing all over the world. Figure 19.3 presents longevity rates over the centuries. From the time of Neanderthal man to the fourteenth century A.D., the life span appears to have hovered around thirty-five years, an exception being thirteenth century England. The increase in longevity, partly accounting for the population increase, has been confined largely to the modern era. In the United States, you will note, longevity increased approximately ten years in the last half-century.

Let us oversimplify, in order to recapitulate the relationship among birth rates, death rates, and average length of life. Imagine a population of mice having a natural tendency to live an average of one year, cats permitting. Assume this particular rodent society has a stable population, held at 1,000, year in, year out. It is clear that for this population to remain constant, it must replace itself each year. One thousand mice will die; 1,000 mice must be born. Birth and death rates must balance at 1,000 in order that a stable population of mice whose average longevity is one year be maintained. In reality, of course, many unpredictable factors affect populations of both mice and men.

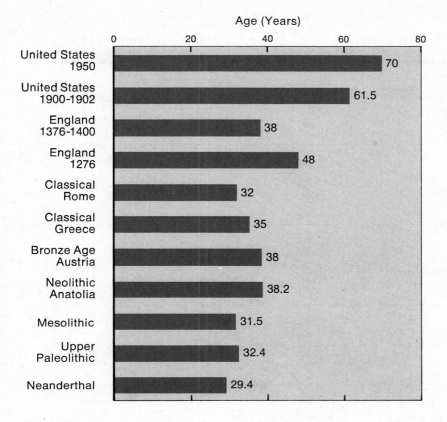

Age (Years)

United States 1950 — 70
United States 1900-1902 — 61.5
England 1376-1400 — 38
England 1276 — 48
Classical Rome — 32
Classical Greece — 35
Bronze Age Austria — 38
Neolithic Anatolia — 38.2
Mesolithic — 31.5
Upper Paleolithic — 32.4
Neanderthal — 29.4

Figure 19.3
Longevity in Ancient and Modern Times

From Edward S. Deevey, Jr., "The Human Population," *Scientific American,* Vol. 203, No. 3 (September 1960), p. 200. Copyright © 1960 by Scientific American, Inc. All rights reserved.

POPULATION DENSITY

Population densities are important in the social problem implications of expanding world population. Density is often measured in terms of the number of persons inhabiting each square mile. Figure 19.4 portrays the increasing density of the earth's surface since the Lower Paleolithic era.

In Table 19.3 you will find density used as a basis for comparing populations of the various continents and in a number of selected countries, the figures clearly indicating that some lands have much greater numbers of people than others. The population of Asia (exclusive of the U.S.S.R.) is more than one hundred times that of Australia and Oceania. But this in itself is not as significant as the relation between the amount

Years Ago	Cultural Stage	Area Populated	Assumed Density per Square Kilometer	Total Population (Millions)
1,000,000	Lower Paleolithic	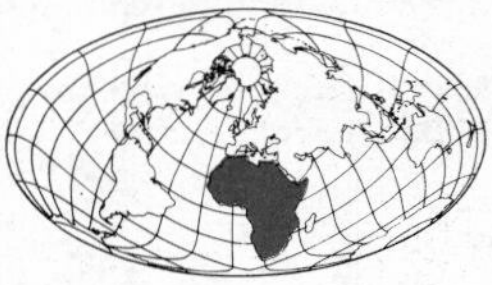	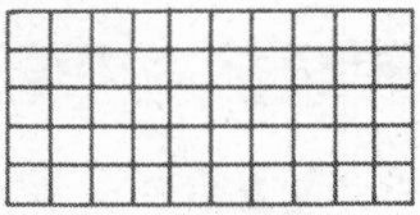 .00425	.125
300,000	Middle Paleolithic	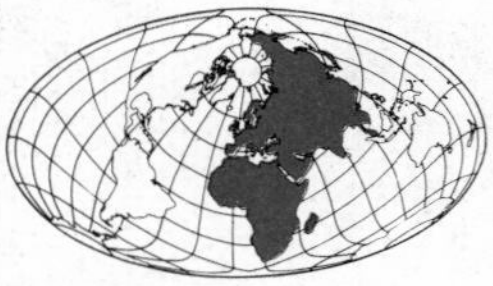	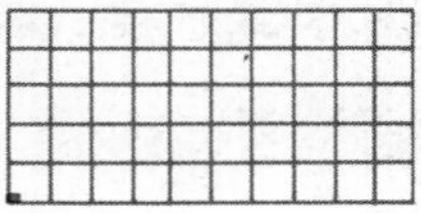 .012	1
25,000	Upper Paleolithic	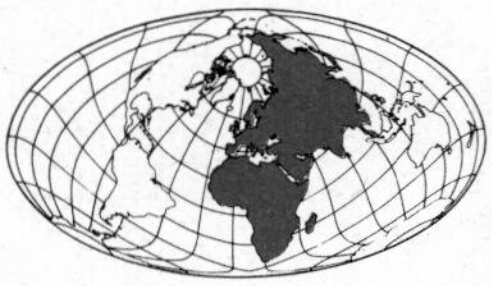	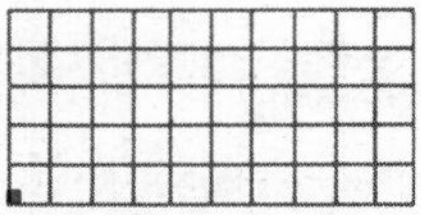 .04	3.34
10,000	Mesolithic	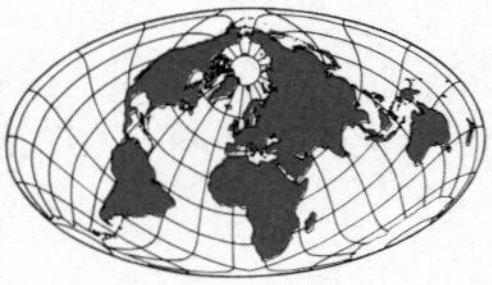	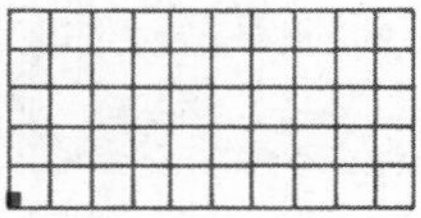 .04	5.32
6,000	Village Farming and Early Urban	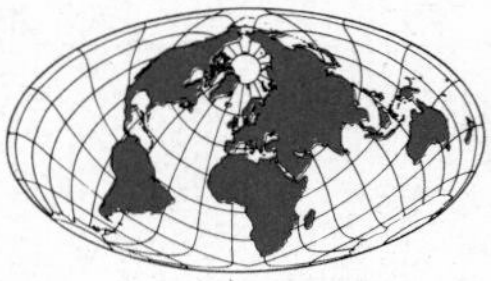	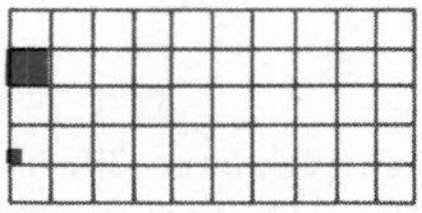 1.0 .04	86.5
2,000	Village Farming and Urban	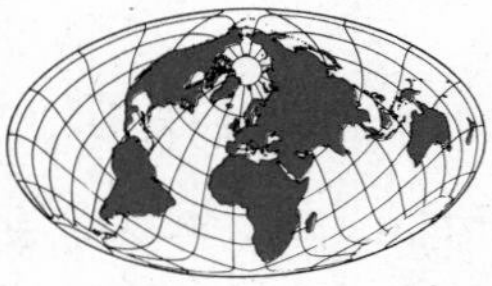	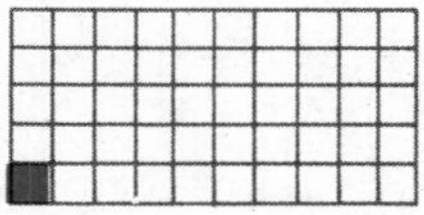 1.0	133

Figure 19.4
Population Density, From the Lower Paleolithic Age
to a Projected 2000 A.D.

From Edward S. Deevey, Jr., "The Human Population," *Scientific American,* Vol. 203, No. 3 (September 1960), p. 196. Copyright © 1960 by Scientific American, Inc. All rights reserved.

Years Ago	Cultural Stage	Area Populated	Assumed Density per Square Kilometer	Total Population (Millions)
310	Farming and Industrial		3.7	545
210	Farming and Industrial		4.9	728
160	Farming and Industrial		6.2	906
60	Farming and Industrial		11.0	1,610
10	Farming and Industrial		16.4	2,400
A.D. 2000	Farming and Industrial		46.0	6,270

of fertile agricultural land available and the total number of persons in the population. The latter gives some indication of the potentiality of the land for feeding the people on it. Density figures are suggestive in this regard, although they merely show number of persons per square mile without indicating how many of those sections are arable. Note that Australia had about 11½ million people and Belgium about 9½ million in

TABLE 19.3 · *Estimated Population and Density by Continents and Selected Countries, 1966*

	Population in 000	Persons per square mile
Continents		
Africa	312,065	26.8
Asia (exclusive of U.S.S.R.)	1,916,515	179.6
Australia and Oceania	17,695	5.4
Europe (exclusive of U.S.S.R.)	447,399	235.0
North America	296,092	31.6
South America	170,219	24.7
WORLD POPULATION	3,391,854	64.8*
Selected Countries		
Belgium	9,499	806.3
Japan	98,710	691.6
West Germany (including W. Berlin)	59,297	617.9
Italy	52,931	455.1
India (including Kashmir)	499,000	395.5
France	49,157	232.7
China, Communist	772,000	209.1
Spain	31,871	163.5
Indonesia	108,000	146.9
Ireland	2,881	106.2
United States	195,857	54.2
Mexico	42,231	55.4
Sweden	7,789	44.8
U.S.S.R.	231,869	26.8
Brazil	84,679	25.8
Argentina	22,691	21.2
Canada	19,919	5.2
Australia	11,545	3.9

* *In computing the world density the area of Antarctica is omitted.*

SOURCE: Adapted from *Britannica Book of the Year, 1967* p. 636, Table II. By permission of Encyclopaedia Britannica, Inc.

1966. But Australia had much more land for its inhabitants than Belgium: its density is slightly less than four persons per square mile, while that of Belgium is over 800 per square mile. The people of Belgium are 200 times more crowded on their available land than are the residents of Australia. If Australia were as crowded as Belgium, then it would have a population of approximately 2.5 billion people at the present time, roughly equivalent to three-fourths of the world's population.

Summarizing what we have presented to this point, and relying further on statistical information compiled by demographers in recent years, the following generalizations are warranted: The population of the entire world, and in almost every locality, is increasing rapidly. In almost all instances, prolonged population increases have appeared as a consequence of a decreasing death rate rather than an increasing birth rate. Among most nationalities for which information is available, both birth and death rates have decreased during the past three centuries, death rates more rapidly than birth rates, however. Increases in the average longevity of individuals is directly related to prolonged decreases in the death rate. As the former goes up, the latter goes down. Population densities vary considerably, but the fact remains that as population increases, people are becoming more crowded everywhere, except in Ireland and uninhabited Antarctica. This creates social problems, differing by area, according in part to the *rate* of population growth.

In areas of low density and moderate population growth (Anglo-America, Latin American countries with temperate climates, the Soviet Union, and Australia), certain problems develop despite the comparative absence of population pressures. There are geographic regroupings and concentrations in particular parts of a country as a result of migration, and this creates problems. The inhabitants of those regroupings and concentrations must be assimilated into the culture of the region. They must learn new customs and, perhaps, new ways of making a living.

Regions of low density and rapid growth (Africa, the Near East, and most of Latin America) contain surpluses of inhabitants whose economic needs, including jobs, must be met somehow. Further, in such regions, accelerated urbanization is usually a factor, and this tends to create economic and other dislocations and disorders.

Areas characterized by high density and moderate growth (nearly all of Europe) have quite different problems. The Industrial Revolution originated in Europe, and the population explosion began there. But mortality was reduced by the distribution of industrial goods to the masses of people, as well as by the introduction of public sanitation and modern medicine. Fertility was decreased through the availability of birth control devices. With its comparatively low birth rate, Europe must nevertheless strive to maintain adequate living levels by increasingly efficient utilization of existing resources.

Areas of high density and rapid growth (half of the world's

population) constitute a world problem of great magnitude. In most of Asia, poverty is at a very high level, presenting acute problems not only in connection with subsistence, but with regard to the health and education of the inhabitants.

Another demographic fact requiring notice is that the international migration of human beings from their native lands to less densely settled countries or to areas of greater economic opportunity has slowed down considerably during the past half century. The population in those countries of earlier great migrations becomes even more dense. Social and economic problems become more acute.

THE THEORY OF THOMAS ROBERT MALTHUS

To gain some insight into the nature of population problems, let us turn to the theoretical formulations of Thomas Robert Malthus (1766–1834), a British social philosopher and father of modern demography. Malthus held that human populations have a natural tendency to expand more rapidly than human beings can increase the life-sustaining capacity of the land they occupy. He put it this way: Food is essential for the existence of man and ". . . the passions between the sexes is necessary, and will remain nearly in its present state." Thus, man would continue to procreate and ". . . the power of population is infinitely greater than the power in the earth to produce subsistence for man."

According to Malthus, therefore, all human societies inevitably will be confronted by the problem of an ever increasing number of mouths to feed and a constantly decreasing amount of food for each. Malthus saw famine, disease, and war as natural checks that helped to maintain a balance between the human need for food and the capacity of land to supply that food. He viewed expanding populations as a *natural* rather than a *social* problem, in that he considered the developments he foresaw as inevitable, inexorable, and in the nature of things. They could not be changed much by human action. A certain amount of land would support a certain number of people, and that was that. And people were going to reproduce far beyond their ability to get additional sustenance from the land. Although Malthus was inclined to accept these premises with resignation, he did believe that human beings might partially solve their problem by deliberate control. His solution was to curb procreative rates through late marriages and sexual abstinence.

We know now that Malthus viewed history from a short-range perspective. He did not and could not foresee, for example, the development and extensive use of artificial techniques for birth control, nor did he anticipate discoveries and inventions in medical science that have served human beings in preventing and remedying many of the diseases that once decimated populations. Living during the earlier years of the Industrial Revolution, he could not know the extent to which people could extend their ability to exploit natural resources.

Despite Malthus' short-range perspective, however, his theories have not been entirely discredited. India and China currently reflect conditions similar to those Malthus deemed inevitable. The peoples of these countries are packed into a limited land space. They spend most of their energies in an endless quest for food and what they wrest from the land barely supplies subsistence. Even in prosperous years, the caloric content and quality of their available food is inadequate when compared with standards we take for granted in the United States. The people are regularly at the mercy of floods, drought, insects, plant diseases—which jeopardize their immediate food supply. Demographers apply the term *subsistence population* to people who live under these conditions. The natural checks that Malthus contended must inevitably apply to all human populations at least are applicable to subsistence populations.

And the subsistence population of the world is vast. Half the people on earth are insufficiently nourished in terms of both quantity and variety of food. Over half of the 130 million babies born this year, it is claimed, will not have enough to eat.[17] An average of about 2,500 calories a day is required to maintain good health. Daily intake in the United States and Western Europe is approximately 3,000 calories or more, whereas inhabitants of many African and Asian nations average fewer than 2,000 calories. Moreover, their diet is poor, lacking variety and balance. According to the U. S. Department of Agriculture, diet-deficiency areas include most of Central America and the Caribbean, the northern portion of South America, all of Africa except the southern tip, and all of Asia except Japan and Israel.

Malthus never understood a truth that has been demonstrated many times since his death—that a rise in population does not inevitably decrease the total amount of food available to that population. Contrast subsistence conditions, as in India, with the balance between people and available food characteristic of the United States. Our nation has had one of the world's most rapidly increasing populations during the past two centuries, yet our food supply has more than kept pace with population. Government warehouses have been packed with food surpluses in recent years. Even during the economic depression of the 1930s, the millions who suffered did not do so because there was not enough sustenance to go around. The United States had enormous surpluses of unconsumed food. What had gone askew was another aspect of our economy. The food was there, but several million workers were not earning enough to purchase the food their families required.

Actually, it seems likely that more people in the United States die prematurely from overeating than from undernourishment. Some demographers apply the term *surplus economy population* to people who live under conditions well above mere subsistence level. Evidently the Malthusian natural checks do not apply to such a population. Thus, we can find some evidence both in support of and in opposition to Malthusian views.

CONFLICTING VALUES ABOUT WORLD POPULATION

At present there are two principal opposing schools of thought concerning the implications of Malthusian doctrine. The more optimistic thinkers assert that human beings can solve the major problems associated with expanding populations if and when they are willing to face them realistically. Pessimistic observers of the social scene point out that a majority of the earth's people now exist on a subsistence level, yet have not demonstrated a readiness to attack this problem. Actually, this represents no head-on controversy, since the optimists refer to what they believe human beings are *capable of doing*, whereas the pessimists stress what most humans are *actually doing*. Exponents of the first viewpoint cite Ireland and Sweden as evidence of human ability to maintain populations on a fairly constant level while operating under a surplus economy. They contend that if these nations can do it, all can. The pessimists point to India, China, and Burma, where millions barely subsist but do not seem prepared rationally to attack the Malthusian problem. This school of thought holds that it is misleading to use as an example supposedly refuting Malthus those nations where births are limited by voluntary controls. Most of the world's people, they say, are not willing to adopt these voluntary techniques.

These proponents present some impressive arguments in support of their conclusions. William Vogt writes, "Every grain of wheat and rye, every spoonful of olive oil and glass of wine depends on an irreducible minimum of earth to produce it. The earth is not made of rubber; it cannot be stretched; the human race, every nation, is limited in the number of acres it possesses. And as the number of human beings *increases,* the relative amount of productive earth *decreases* by that amount."[18] Vogt estimates that there is only about one acre of productive farm land for each living person at the present time.[19] He points out that American nutritionists calculate that 2.5 acres are required for an adequate standard of living.[20] If this be so, the earth is approaching its saturation point for the capacity to sustain human life. Already, in fact, certain populations cannot be permanently sustained on what many Americans consider a "decent" standard of living.

In the meantime, world population continues to grow. One sociologist has estimated that if present trends were to continue (an impossibility, of course) 2,746,000,000 persons ultimately would have to occupy one square foot of land surface. We can understand, therefore, when biochemist Harrison Brown remarks, "A substantial fraction of humanity today is behaving as if . . . it would not rest content until the earth is covered completely and to a considerable depth with a writhing mass of human beings, much as a dead cow is covered with a pulsating mass of maggots."[21]

No doubt humanity would be doomed if population were actually to approach the density suggested. According to the optimists, however, there is no need to worry. There are many variables in the situation, numerous imponderables that may reverse population trends or enormously increase the production of food and other necessities or both. Until the rise of modern science, almost everybody lived under subsistence conditions. The very existence of prosperous surplus economy populations is encouraging evidence of human capabilities.

The world, some demographers and other scholars argue, is potentially able to sustain a population several times that of today. This point of view is supported, for example, by Kingsley Davis:

> The very fact that numbers are increasing indicates that the means to support them is increasing too. Otherwise mortality would have risen and the population would never have grown to its present size. To think of the world's population as "outrunning" its normal food supply is like thinking of the hind feet of a horse outrunning the front feet.[22]

The production of food is one major component of "the population problem"; the other is the acceptance of techniques for birth control. Widespread and large-scale development of the latter trend would play an important part in balancing people and food. There are current impediments to such programs, stemming in part from positions taken by representatives of organized religion and, especially in Asia and Africa, from the persistence of folk beliefs and practices. Despite these obstacles, inroads have been made, aided by the changing attitudes of religious groups and at least some of their leaders. In 1966, probably 5 million American women and 2 million women elsewhere (mostly in English-speaking countries and Scandinavia) used oral contraceptives. In the United States, sales of the pills totaled approximately 50 million dollars in 1965.[23] Despite the opposition of the Catholic Church to the use of contraceptive devices, 30 percent of the Catholics interviewed in a fertility survey in the United States reported using methods not approved by the church.[24] Other surveys have revealed that a majority of nonclerical Catholics would like to see their church remove the ban on the use of contraceptive devices.

Intra-Uterine Devices (IUD) were introduced in Taiwan recently. In less than two years, one in every twelve women was equipped with an IUD. India budgeted 200 million dollars in 1966 for a five-year plan calling for the distribution of 20 million IUDs within that period.[25]

Voluntary sterilization, another means of preventing conception without affecting sexual relations adversely, has met with limited success as a program, although about 100,000 persons in the United States are sterilized annually. The Indian government hopes to reach a point in its five-year family planning program where it will perform 2½ million vasectomies (sterilization operations) annually. This operation is performed without cost, in mobile vasectomy camps, where thousands of men are sterilized weekly.[26] In 1965, Turkey repealed its law forbidding sterilization.[27]

In Western societies, conflicting values regarding abortion exist. Some people favor it as a means of planned parenthood. Others, representing power and prestige groups, are opposed, on moral, religious, and to an extent medical-psychiatric grounds. Voluntary abortions for other than therapeutic medical reasons, consequently, have not met with much acceptance in the West. Japan, by contrast, legalized abortion and halved its annual birth rate in one decade, largely as a result of the legalization. In the period 1947–1958, legal abortions at times outnumbered live births in that country. Turkey, the Soviet Union, and mainland China have legalized abortions, not alone for therapeutic, medical reasons, but as a means of birth control.[28] It might be noted that illegal abortions almost equaled births in some European countries—Germany and France for example—in the years preceding World War II.

Birth control is not the only subject of controversy among those seeking solutions to population problems. Another controversy has developed in several surplus economy nations between those who favor a policy of national "isolation" and others who advocate international cooperation. The isolationist argument is: People of the "have" countries cannot possibly produce enough surplus food to provide adequate nourishment for all "have-not" countries. The former, therefore, should not concern themselves with the problems of subsistence populations, because they cannot solve them. William Vogt, for example, states that when American surplus food is sent to such countries, we only compound their problems. Adequately fed, they procreate more and in so doing re-create a gap between the number of mouths to feed and the amount of food available. Vogt sees no reason why the United States should "subsidize the unchecked spawning" of India and China.[29]

Many isolationists oppose immigration into the United States, holding that aliens coming to our shores are so many more mouths to feed. Adherents of this view believe that it would be catastrophic if we literally followed the words inscribed on the base of the Statue of Liberty:

> Give me your tired, your poor,
> Your huddled masses yearning to breathe free . . .

Unstinting generosity in following this creed, say isolationists, would make all of us part of the poor, huddled masses.

Internationalists counter with the argument that whether they want to or not, the "have" nations cannot divorce themselves from problems of the "have-nots." Due to tremendous changes in communication and transportation, the nations of the world have become vastly more interdependent. Every country is directly or indirectly affected by conditions existing anywhere on the face of the globe.

Moreover, according to some internationalists, we are morally obligated to do what we can to alleviate famine whenever and wherever it exists. This was the principle behind the United Nations Relief and Rehabilitation Administration (UNRRA). Founded in 1943 by 44 countries, it preceded the United Nations itself and offered food, medicine, raw materials, and the means of reconstruction to the war-shattered countries. It curbed devastating starvation and averted economic collapse in seventeen countries.

Some individuals with an internationalist point of view are not particularly concerned with the moral argument. We should send surplus food to hungry people, they say, but principally because this will promote our own national interest by winning us friends and allies in a hostile world. They also say that we should encourage immigration into the United States, since our land can support the newcomers, and it is economically and otherwise beneficial to have them settle here.

Adherents of the internationalist philosophy sometimes hold that wars are produced by the misery and frustration common when men are crowded into a limited area that cannot furnish them decent subsistence. They must expand their land holdings or perish. There is undoubtedly some merit in this argument, but some of the most crowded and hungry nations have been among the least warlike—India, for example. And certain sparsely settled lands have been comparatively aggressive, as in the case of most of Europe during the Middle Ages.

Isolationists and internationalists almost always agree on one point—the desirability of helping the depressed people of the world help themselves. The isolationists would not grant them goods directly. They have, however, on occasion, approved educating other populations in techniques calculated to increase their food production or decrease the production of infants. Even this proposal, however, is not fully accepted by all in the isolationist camp.

HOW SOCIOLOGISTS VIEW
THE PROBLEM

Sociologists and other social scientists do not necessarily agree or disagree with either the isolationist or internationalist point of view. They try to understand both and to formulate their own conclusions. They are, on the whole, neither optimistic nor pessimistic about what is happening. Short-range optimism seems as unwarranted and unrealistic as long-range pessimism. Their objective is to shed light on the problem so that a solution may be found.

In every social system there is a balance between those forces tending to increase the rates of birth and death and those tending to lower them. Phrased differently, some balance exists between population and subsistence. It may or may not permit an easy life, but the balance is determined not merely by biological but by social forces as well. At least in a measure, man orders his way of life and controls his numbers. When, by overuse, he destroys the yield of his soil, he develops ways to restore its fertility.

If he chooses, man also can substantially control biological processes. In every society reproduction is socially controlled, and procreation is almost never permitted to reach its maximum potential. Of fundamental importance in controlling fertility are social arrangements that govern such matters as who is eligible to marry, at what age, and what marital practices are to be considered normative and approved. The culture is highly influential in determining whether and when children shall be brought into the world. Anthropologists have found evidence that thousands of years ago man made crude contraceptives and sanctioned abortion and infanticide. Nevertheless, strictures against birth control still prevail and are related to the current problem of overpopulation.

Sociologists agree that a rapidly expanding world population constitutes a major social problem. The problem has many causes and will be extremely difficult to solve. It is oversimplifying, for instance, to assert that what we need to do is convince people they should accept proven techniques and utilize them to control the number of births in their societies. People cling tenaciously to cultural values and beliefs. And cultural resistance is never easily overcome. We cannot be certain that man will ever succeed in establishing a balance between his need to consume food and his ability to produce it. This is partly because we have no way of predetermining how vigorously a given people may resist a particular proposal to resolve the problem. We can, however, make some predictions on the basis of knowledge of the particular culture.

Based on existing evidence, it is most likely that populations will continue to expand rapidly. Many inhabitants of the earth will not know, throughout their lives, what it means to have enough food. They will continue to suffer from malnutrition, a polite word for slow starvation. This problem may be alleviated somewhat by changing technology. The oceans, for instance, might be further exploited as a possible source of food. We may learn the secret of photosynthesis, the process by which plants transform air and water into carbohydrates, our prime source of food.

But however valuable such innovations might prove to be, present indications are that they would at most provide but temporary respite. Human populations will continue to bear some resemblance to the nonhuman inhabitants of Rabbit Island unless and until human beings adopt a means of controlling their numbers. A thousand years from now, our descendants may well conclude, looking back on the era in which we live, that electronic devices and atomic power were relatively minor contributions compared to the birth control techniques first used extensively in France during the nineteenth century. On the other hand, a thousand years from now we may have no descendants. Thermonuclear bombs may furnish a definitive check to population.

HOW MANY ARE TOO MANY PEOPLE?

In all that we have discussed up to this point there has been an implicit question: How many people are too many people? The answer to this question depends on the cultural values people have learned to accept. These values relate, in part, to *the kind of technology* people use, *the standard of living* they consider desirable, and *their culturally acquired attitudes*.

Before Europeans began settling America, it is estimated that there were less than one million Indians living within the area that is now the United States. They gained their subsistence almost entirely by hunting and fishing. We do not know whether Indians were concerned about population problems, but we do know that their technologies could not support more than a fraction of the more than 200 million people presently living in the United States. By way of contrast, we could at this time support several times our present population if the inhabitants were willing to support a standard of living comparable to that now prevalent in some parts of Africa. If we could make such a choice, would we do so? Would it be worth the possible sacrifice of the comforts and luxuries we have learned to enjoy, even demand? That depends upon our culturally acquired attitudes.

On a different scale, this is the question facing young married people when they decide how many children they want. It is on this level, multiplied many times, that future population changes will be determined.

In the final analysis, then, the question of how many are too many people is intimately connected with *acquired values* derived from the culture. A Belgian may not feel overcrowded in a land with a density of more than 800 persons per square mile. By contrast, Daniel Boone, according to backwoods legend, pulled up stakes in Kentucky because a family had settled a hundred miles away.

· NOTES

1. *The Population Bomb*, 11th ed. (New York: Population Policy Panel of the Hugh Moore Fund, 1966), pp. 4, 17.
2. *Ibid.*, pp. 16–17.
3. Frederick Osborn, *This Crowded World* (New York: Public Affairs Committee, 1960), pp. 1–2.
4. *Ibid.*, p. 1.
5. *The Population Bomb, op. cit.*, p. 20.
6. U. S. Department of Health, Education, and Welfare, *Converging Social Trends, Emerging Social Problems* (Washington, D. C.: U. S. Government Printing Office, 1964), p. 13.
7. *Ibid.*, p. 7.
8. U. S. Bureau of the Census, *Population Estimates*, P-25, No. 293 (Washington, D. C.: U. S. Government Printing Office, October 21, 1964).
9. U. S. Department of Health, Education, and Welfare, *op. cit.*, p. 7.

10. Osborn, *op. cit.*, p. 13.
11. *Ibid.*
12. *Ibid.*
13. Kingsley Davis, "The Amazing Decline of Mortality in Underdeveloped Areas," *American Economic Review,* XLVI (May 1956), 305–318.
14. *Ibid.*
15. U. S. Department of Health, Education, and Welfare, *op. cit.*, p. 7.
16. Osborn, *op. cit.*, p. 11.
17. *The Population Bomb, op. cit.*, p. 5.
18. William Vogt, *Road to Survival* (New York: Sloane Associates, 1948), p. 194.
19. *Ibid.*, p. 27.
20. *Ibid.*, pp. 193–194.
21. Harrison Brown, *The Challenge of Man's Future* (New York: Viking, 1954), p. 221.
22. Kingsley Davis, *Human Society* (New York: Macmillan, 1949), p. 612.
23. Harry Nelson, "Life or Death Crusade—Man vs. Birth Rate," *Los Angeles Times,* March 6, 1966, p. C-1.
24. Ronald Freedman, Pascal K. Whelpton, and Arthur A. Campbell, *Family Planning, Sterility, and Population Growth* (New York: McGraw-Hill, 1959), pp. 181–182.
25. *The Population Bomb, op. cit.*, pp. 10–11.
26. Nelson, *op. cit.*, p. 1.
27. *Ibid.*
28. *The Population Bomb, op. cit.*, pp. 11–12.
29. William Vogt, *op. cit.*, p. 77.

· SUGGESTIONS FOR FURTHER READING

BROWN, HARRISON. *The Challenge of Man's Future.* New York: Viking, 1954.
A pessimistic view of what the future holds for us in the way of a balance between population and resources.

CHANDROSEKHOR, S. "Family Planning in Rural India." *Antioch Review,* XIX (Fall 1959), 399–410.
An interesting report on attempts to introduce the use of contraceptives in an Indian village.

DAY, LINCOLN, and ALICE DAY. *Too Many Americans.* Boston: Riverside, 1964.
An assessment of the problems surrounding the growth of American population.

OSBORN, FREDERICK. *This Crowded World.* Public Affairs Pamphlet No. 306. New York: Public Affairs Committee, 1960.
A brief pamphlet explaining lucidly and forcefully why we need to be concerned about population growth in the world.

SAX, KARL. *Standing Room Only*. Boston: Beacon Press, 1955.
A botanist discusses the dangers of overpopulation and presents a dismal forecast of the future.

STOCKWELL, EDWARD G. "The Relationship Between Population Growth and Economic Development." *American Sociological Review,* XXVII (April 1962), 250–252.
About two-thirds of the world's people are jammed into countries unable to support them.

THOMLINSON, RALPH. *Demographic Problems*. Belmont, Calif. Dickenson, 1967.
A concise yet comprehensive statement about the social problem of population growth and control.

20 PROBLEMS OF PREJUDICE & DISCRIMINATION

In this chapter we discuss prejudice and discrimination against minority groups as a social problem in societies of the world. We examine the nature and extent of the problem in the United States and consider conflicting values as to its causes and the means of resolving prejudice and discrimination.

SOME CONSIDERED OPINIONS

These white people have a right to defend themselves. They haven't did any part of what they ought to do. White America, all over, not just the South, ought to rise up and demand that these Niggers go home and stay home, or get 'em out of here and send 'em back to Africa and let their kinfolk eat 'em.

The Reverend Connie Lynch

You got your Nigger Jews, you got your Asiatic Jews and you got your white Jews. They're all Jews, and they're the offspring of the Devil.

Col. William P. Gale, U.S. Army, Retired

Those [Jews who migrated to Israel] from Morocco had no education. Their customs are those of the Arabs. . . . Maybe in the third generation something will appear from the Oriental Jew that is a little different. But I don't see it yet. The Moroccan Jew took a lot from the Moroccan Arab, and I don't see much we can learn from the Moroccan Arabs.

David Ben-Gurion, Former Prime Minister of Israel

CALIFORNIA, A LAND CONTROLLED BY CATHOLICS, JEWS,
NEGROES, AND LEFTISTS
Truth Seeker, XCII, 5 (May 1965), 67.

> Red, white and blue,
> Your father is a Jew,
> Your mother is a Japanese,
> And so are you.
>
> Rope-skipping rhyme.

SOME HISTORICAL BACKGROUND

We selected the above quotations in order to make a point:
A number of people in our own and other societies consider
it a social problem that Jews, Negroes, Catholics, Moroccans,
as the case may be, live in their midst. And other individuals
in the same societies consider it a social problem that fellow
inhabitants are prejudiced against certain categories of people
and frequently are willing to take discriminatory action against
them.

The roots of these attitudes lie deeply buried in the history
of culture. For centuries, ethnocentrism revolving around race
has been both a basis and a reflection of prejudicial attitudes
about people who are "different," although race is by no means
the sole factor involved in prejudice and discrimination, as
we shall see.

. . . the attempt to interpret history on a racial basis is as ancient as
history itself. Hebrews, Greeks, Romans, and Medieval man left
copious evidences of their conviction that their achievements were
attributable to the heroic stock from which they had sprung and to
the particularly gifted blood that flowed in their veins.[1]

And when a people view themselves as of heroic stock, it is
an easy next step to argue that anyone not of that stock is of
lesser worth.

We must go back to ancient times to trace the origin of the
notion that fair-haired, fair-skinned people represent a superior breed, a "master race," whose members have every right to
regard other groups with contempt. The Vikings of the North
Sea basin expressed what amounts to a theory about race in
the *Rigsthula*, a cultural poem believed to have been reduced
to writing in the last part of the tenth century, although it

existed for many generations before that, having been passed on by word of mouth.* The *Rigsthula* describes the racial constituency, functions, and relationships of social classes in Viking society, explaining the origins of classes and their functions on a mythological basis. According to the poem, the god Rig created the different classes of Viking society. One character in the poem, Thrael, is of the lowest class and is depicted as ugly, black-haired, with a twisted back, big heels, wrinkled skin, and rough hands. Thrael's wife fares no better. She has crooked legs and a flat nose. It is the lot of this couple to carry heavy loads, dig soil, spread dung, and tend swine and goats.

By contrast, Karl, a yeoman of the upper classes, is described as a strong, sturdy man with a ruddy face and flashing eyes. Karl manages the farm, builds houses, and fashions other artifacts. And Mothir, of noble birth and still higher social position, has bright brows, a shining breast, and a neck "whiter than the new fallen snow." Her son Jarl, sired by the god Rig, is blond, with bright cheeks and glowing eyes. He is a warrior and ruler.

The mythological Thraels, members of the lowest class, appear to be prototypes of the thralls, the short, brunet, round-headed people whom the tall, blond, long-headed Vikings conquered when they moved into Scandinavia at the opening of the Viking Age. The Vikings captured and enslaved other individuals when they raided England, Ireland, and continental Europe. Most of these captives were shorter and darker than their captors. Accordingly, certain supposed racial characteristics, such as short stature, dark hair and skin, and a flat nose came to be associated with inferior social status among the early Norsemen. The slaves were deemed in all ways inferior to the Vikings. And since the latter tended to be blond and light complexioned, these features became associated with superiority, resulting in an atmosphere in which what we today call "racism" might flourish.

The roots of prejudice and discrimination against "other" people can be further traced to the time when European explorers and traders began keeping written records of their contacts with the people of Africa, Asia, and North and South

* What follows is based on Christen T. Jonassen, "Some Historical and Theoretical Bases of Racism in Northwestern Europe," *Social Forces*, XXX (December 1951), 155–161.

America. The Europeans and the people they met in their travels sometimes regarded one another as nonhuman creatures. Social psychologists LaPiere and Farnsworth cite a passage in which sixteenth century Europeans appraised the Oriental as a ". . . strange and wondrous creature, undoubtedly possessed by many human attributes, but yet in no sense truly human."[2] The authors quote from a letter written by a Chinese observer, noting his impressions of Jesuit priests during the same century:

The most bestial of peasants are far more human, although these Ocean Men . . . are in some respects exceedingly clever. It is quite possible they are susceptible to training and could with patience be taught modes of conduct proper to a human being.[3]

When Europeans first established colonies in distant lands, they frequently regarded the natives as nonhumans or subhumans. This belief provided ethical grounds for exploiting, enslaving, and even exterminating native populations. Although most of these Europeans accepted some semblance of Christian ideology under which people are expected to treat others as "brothers," this moral principle was circumvented in the case of natives, who were not regarded as people. Thus, Christian doctrine was viewed as not incompatible with the institution of slavery; the Catholic Church itself owned slaves for several centuries. The enslavement of the Negro posed no more of an ethical problem for some Christian slave owners than the possession of horses. For comparable reasons the extermination policy that early American settlers applied to wolves was equally applicable, in the view of some individuals, to American Indians.

Gradually the prevailing beliefs that non-Europeans were nonhuman were found to be untenable. This was due in part to the efforts of the biological scientists, Linnaeus, Darwin, and others, who found convincing evidence to substantiate their theory that Europeans, Africans, Orientals, and American Indians all belonged to the same species. By this time, however, many European settlers had a strong vested interest in continuing to exploit non-Europeans. A new rationale was developed to justify the prevailing practices. It shifted toward the view that slavery and exploitation advanced the welfare of the exploited people. Non-Europeans were no longer excluded from the human species. They were now regarded as human beings of an inferior variety, simple and irresponsible, incapable of taking care of themselves without paternalistic supervision. This philosophy is implicit in the words of Kipling, who regarded non-Europeans as "the white man's burden." Such beliefs are still in evidence in the United States, South Africa, and a number of European colonies.

During the twentieth century, anthropological and psychological research has challenged the belief in racial superiority and inferiority. With each succeeding generation this evidence gains increasing acceptance in our society. Moreover, we seem to be gaining some understanding of the fact that the matter of "equality" or "inequality" among races is not germane to questions of policy and practice. The argument runs that we should advocate nondiscriminatory practices not because racial or ethnic groups are "equal" in ability, intelligence and other respects, but because racial differences (assuming they exist) are improper grounds for discrimination. Equalitarianism is a matter of social ethics. In the ethical view, if we hold that some groups of individuals are entitled to certain considerations—justice for all, equality before the law, the right to worship as they please, and so on—these same considerations should hold for all members of all groups, whatever differences there may or may not be among them.

The fact is, however, that the Jew has been persecuted and otherwise discriminated against for centuries in various parts of the globe. American Indians were deprived of their land, forced onto reservations, and subjected to discriminatory practices that worked to the benefit of their subjugators. Catholics have encountered persecution, and in certain countries Protestants are the disprivileged minority.

A case of great interest today is that of Israel. This small nation, a haven for persecuted Jews of the world, not only contains the dominant and minority groups of Jews and Arabs but has developed an important social cleavage among Jews themselves:

A nation created by anti-Semitic prejudice, its toughest internal problem today is how to absorb the great numbers of Jewish immigrants from the Arab-dominated countries of North Africa and from Asia who are lumped together under the label "Oriental Jews." These Oriental Jews look different, dress differently, worship differently and react differently to the goals of the industrializing Israeli society.[4]

Many of the Israeli who think of themselves as "European Jews" consider themselves superior to "Oriental Jews." The "European Jew" often shows hostility if an "Oriental Jew" wants to move next door or to marry his daughter.

PREJUDICE, DISCRIMINATION, & RELATED CONCEPTS

In the foregoing we used the terms "prejudice," "discrimination," "race," "ethnic groups," and "minority groups." It is time now to define and discuss these concepts.

Prejudice consists of stereotyped attitudes that people categorically feel toward certain other people. "Categorically" means that the feeling is directed primarily at an entire division of people rather than one individual. The Reverend Connie Lynch, quoted at the opening of this chapter, apparently dislikes Negroes categorically. Perhaps if he corresponded with one, not knowing he was Negro, Lynch might like him. But once it became established that the correspondent was a Negro, as Lynch would define the term, then he would probably dislike him. We say probably because, to give him the benefit of the doubt, Lynch might be like many prejudiced persons who dislike a category of people but presumably like one or more individuals within the category. For instance, although Colonel Gale, also quoted above, dislikes Jews as a group, he might be able to say, as do others in the same position, that some of his best friends are Jews.

Prejudice may be *positive,* as indicated when a man says: "My country is the greatest in the world, with absolutely nothing that can legitimately be said against it. I love my country." Prejudice may be *negative,* as represented in the statement: "All Mexicans are lazy. I don't like them."

In *Racial and Cultural Minorities*, George Eaton Simpson and J. Milton Yinger emphasize that, whether positive or negative, prejudice is ". . . an emotional, rigid attitude (a *predisposition* to respond to a certain stimulus in a certain way) toward a group of people."[5] The authors point out: "They may be a group only in the mind of the prejudiced person; that is, he categorizes them together, although they may have little similarity or interaction."[6] Thus, white Anglo-Saxon Protestants may be classed by some as one group, the members of which all possess such characteristics as honesty, love of country, and devotion to God and family. Yet we know this does not apply to *every* white Anglo-Saxon Protestant.

Simpson and Yinger further point out that prejudice ". . . involves not only prejudgment but . . . misjudgment as well. It is categorical thinking that systematically misinterprets the facts."[7] When you say, "All living human beings have a breathing apparatus," you are prejudging the next and the next human being you will encounter, but this is no misjudgment. On the other hand, if you say, "All Russians are drunks. They consume huge quantities of vodka daily," you are both prejudging and misjudging, for many Russians partake of no alcoholic beverages whatever.

We may expect to find prejudice against some group or groups in any society. "Inter-group prejudice is universal," observes Robert M. MacIver, "wherever groups are brought into contact as groups, and only a utopian can cherish the hope that any reform of society or re-education of man can wholly eradicate it." The basis, intensity, and form of prejudice are not immutable, however. ". . . prejudice of this kind is fluctuating, is intensified or modified by changes in the conditions or in the stimuli to which it is responsive, not infrequently takes new directions, and may find expression in relatively harmless or in quite destructive outlets."[8]

Being an attitude, prejudice is a *tendency* to behave. It may not yield overt action with regard to members of the groups concerned. An employer may hold prejudicial attitudes concerning Negroes yet, for a variety of reasons, not discriminate against them in recruiting personnel or in other respects. Thus, although prejudice may and often does lead to discrimination, it is not to be equated with it.

Discrimination consists of categorically treating other people in an unfair, inequitable manner. The Reverend Connie Lynch evinces *prejudice* when he speaks of Negroes as he does. If he succeeded in bringing about the expulsion of Negroes from this country *because* they are Negro, that would be an example of *discrimination*.

Like prejudice, discrimination may be positive or negative in character. If a police chief considers Irishmen the best possible material for recruitment, favoring any man of Irish birth or extraction over a candidate not of that category, regardless of their respective abilities, he is discriminating in a *positive* manner, favoring Irishmen unfairly and inequitably. If the members of a sorority, deeming Filipino students undesirable as friends and associates, rule Filipino girls ineligible for membership, they are discriminating in a *negative* manner, being unfair and inequitable in their treatment of Filipinos in this respect.

Prejudice is an internal attitude, a psychological attribute, whereas *discrimination is external behavior*, one form of social interaction. Both are based on generalizations of a categorical nature. When you judge other people and react to them in terms of what you know about them as individuals, there is no evidence of prejudice or discrimination in your behavior; these become evident only if you judge and react to others in terms of preconceived generalizations. If you believe that all red-headed people are fiery-tempered and disagreeable, then you have an attitude of *prejudice*. If you vote to keep an applicant out of your fraternity because of the color of that person's hair, you are *discriminating* against him.

Another distinction between prejudice and discrimination may be drawn. *Prejudice cannot be controlled by legal restraints alone, whereas discrimination, in its more public manifestations, can be.* No law will effectively prevent your continuing to believe that all long-haired young men are effeminate, if that is your attitude. But statutes do forbid you to assault any individual, regardless of his hair style, and you will probably obey the law rather than assault long-haired youths.

We suggested earlier that *prejudice and discrimination are not always directly associated*, that some people do not discriminate against those toward whom they feel prejudiced. Simpson and Yinger enlarge on this:[9]

1 · There can be prejudice without discrimination. ("I dislike right wing extremists, but I'll hire them if they have the talents I'm looking for.")
2 · There can be discrimination without prejudice. ("I have nothing whatever against Negroes, but if I invite them to my house for dinner, my neighbors will become unfriendly, so I'll play it safe, have no Negroes over.")
3 · Discrimination can be among the causes of prejudice. (Guided by the profit motive, farmers pay itinerant farm

hands a meager wage, less per hour than they would have to pay if they were hiring local help for longer periods. The itinerants are financially unable to provide their children with adequate formal education. The farmers think: "Those kids are an illiterate bunch, just like their parents! They're all alike!")

4 · Prejudice can be among the causes of discrimination. ("I don't like Catholics. Why should I vote one into our Yacht Club?")

5 · Probably most frequently, prejudice and discrimination are mutually reinforcing. Although this is not always the case, prejudice and discrimination are often directly associated. When you dislike someone, it is easy to mistreat him. When you mistreat him, it is easy to dislike him. Thus the two factors tend to reinforce one another.

This is well brought out in *An American Dilemma,* the famed study of the Negro in the United States, by Gunnar Myrdal and associates, which was first published in 1944. In it, reference is made to a "self-perpetuating color bar," based on the following: Prejudice yields discrimination. White prejudice and discrimination keep the Negro's standards of living, health, education, manners, and morals at a low level as compared with white contemporaries. This gives further support to white prejudice against Negroes. White prejudice and Negro standards thus "cause" each other. Discrimination breeds discrimination, in a "vicious circle" which MacIver diagrams: discrimination $\longrightarrow$ lower income level $\longrightarrow$ lower standards of living $\longrightarrow$ lower education $\longrightarrow$ lower earning capacity $\longrightarrow$ discrimination.[10]

It should be evident from the foregoing that prejudice and discrimination exist with regard to many subjects, persons, and things, but we are here concerned with these phenomena as manifested in relation to racial, ethnic, and other minorities. Let us therefore define and discuss certain other terms bearing on our subject.

A minority is a social group in some way or ways distinct from the dominant, more influential group of the society. Note we do not define it as a statistical category, although minority groups are in fact often numerically smaller than the dominant group. The numerical strength is not the criterion, but the fact that the members of a minority group have less power and authority and less influence than members of the dominant group in that society. Black men outnumber whites four to one in South Africa, but the whites, nevertheless, hold a position of dominance.

A given type of group may be dominant in one society and a minority in another. For instance, Arabs are dominant in Saudi Arabia, but those Arabs residing in France are a minority. Roman Catholics represent the dominant group in Spain, but not in the United States.

Ordinarily, membership in a minority group is ascribed, not achieved. An individual does not generally become a member by deliberate choice. The United States, of course, includes many minority groups set apart by national origin, ethnicity, race, religion, or combinations of these criteria—Negroes, Orientals, Mexicans, Jews, Roman Catholics, and so on. On the other hand, it is sometimes possible to achieve membership in certain minority groups. A United States resident born to a family espousing Protestantism, for example, may become converted to the Catholic faith, moving from a dominant to a minority position in this regard.

The attitude of prejudice or the willingness to act in a discriminatory manner against a minority group may be based on categorical distaste for the race, religion, or other distinguishing feature represented. However, in our further discussion we shall, for the most part, be considering prejudice and discrimination in general and not specifically as directed against members of a particular race, creed, nationality or ethnic group.

Some racial groups represent a minority in a given society. What do we mean by *race*?

Test yourself on these questions:

1 · Is there a European race?
2 · Are the Japanese people a separate race?
3 · Are Negroes innately lazy, irresponsible, happy-go-lucky?
4 · Is the capacity to build "great civilizations" concentrated largely among people of white racial extraction?
5 · Do American Indians have keener vision than white people?
6 · Can scientists determine the racial origins of a blood donor from his blood sample alone?
7 · Are Orientals naturally passive and unemotional?

Certain popular conceptions of race would support an affirmative answer to each of these questions. But on the basis of scientific evidence such answers in every case would be incorrect or misleading.

In common parlance, the term *race* has been applied to various categories of persons considered to be separate and distinct from others. A good many people, including certain writers, used to refer to the "German race." Here race is confused with *nationality*. Germans are German because they are members of a specific political entity. Others, including certain Jews, continue to speak or write about the "Jewish race." In this case, race is confused with *ethnic background*, to be defined and discussed below. Scientifically speaking, there is no Jewish race: the genetic background of Jews is enormously diversified, reflecting centuries of great mobility and intermixture with many groups.

Technically, race is a biological not a sociological concept, although popular uses of the term "race" clearly are of great interest to sociologists. Certain inherited physical characteristics are observed to be similar among particular people. Scientifically, then, *a race is a category of people with a common genetic heritage.* Many traits, however, which in the popular view are thought of as "racial" characteristics are culturally, not genetically, transmitted. Furthermore, there is no "pure race," although certain segments of the population are distinguished by visible biological differences.

Prolonged and intensive research has produced very little, if any, evidence that races differ in nonphysical characteristics, such as potential ability to learn human behavior or to develop complex cultures. A century of investigation has disclosed no inherent variations in temperament, motivation, or perceptive ability. (However, some differences, such as susceptibility to certain diseases, have been established, although not as yet explained.) Artistic, musical, athletic, and mechanical aptitudes, clearly, are not a matter of race but of culture. It is important to keep in mind, however, that when people *believe* that they—or others—"naturally" possess such attributes as, say, athletic ability or sexual prowess, these beliefs can have behavioral consequences; this is to say that cultural and psychological circumstances often tend to lead people to "live up to" their racial reputations—in athletic skill, musical ability, or sexual conduct, and so on.

As to observable physical distinctions, physical anthropologists often cite three broad classifications of race: *Negroid,*

Mongoloid, and *Caucasoid* (although other divisions are sometimes listed). The presumed racial constituency of the United States population for 1960, for instance, was as follows: Altogether, 88.6 percent of the population was Caucasoid; 10.5 percent Negro; and less than 1 percent belonged to other racial categories, as these are loosely defined by the Bureau of the Census.*

Actually, racial characteristics are only roughly discernible. Generally, Negroid people have dark, Mongoloids medium, and Caucasoids light skin pigmentation. But skin color is a very unreliable indicator of race. All shades of skin pigmentation are found among Negroids, Mongoloids, and Caucasoids, and there is a considerable amount of overlapping in different racial categories along a continuum. We are all to some degree Caucasoid, Negroid, *and* Mongoloid. All of the human beings on earth today are genetically related, for they are descendants, over the ages, of the same common ancestors, an original male and female. The living species, *homo sapiens,* represents the natural fruit of one genealogical tree.

Contrary to some popular notions, there are no distinctive differences among the several races in shape or size of head or of the genital organs. Body odor is no criterion of race. Where differences in odor develop, they have their sources in such environmental factors as diet, bathing facilities and customs, use of perfumes, occupational activity, and disease.

Size of the brain is not a criterion of race. The Pygmies are the only group with brains consistently smaller—as is their anatomy, generally—than those found in other populations. Nor has it been established that any one race is superior to another in innate intelligence.

But with respect to a few characteristics, some relative differences are found among the races. Caucasoids, considered collectively, have more body hair than do Negroid and Mongoloid peoples, although there are wide variations within each group. Mongoloid people tend to have an "epicanthic fold" of skin in the upper eyelid, giving the impression of "slanting eyes." The eye itself is the same in shape as it is in other racial groups. And some persons not generally classed as Mongoloids have epicanthic folds. Another example pertains to the four principal types of blood—O, A, B, and AB; these are found

* Indian, Japanese, Chinese, Filipino, "all other."

among all races, but are distributed in different proportions among them.

No scientific tests of blood samples make it possible to ascertain whether the donor is Negroid, Caucasoid, or Mongoloid. Therefore, the notion of white or Negro or Oriental "blood" is spurious. This is a lesson that a good many Americans, among both donors and recipients, have not yet learned.

In short, whatever sharp racial distinctions existed in earlier times among human beings, it now seems evident that the races have so intermingled and interbred that clear dividing lines no longer exist. The visible traits differentiating breeds of dairy cattle, such as Holsteins and Jerseys, are much more pronounced than the differences among human racial categories. From the contemporary scientific point of view, *the similarities among human racial categories are far more impressive than the differences.*

"Race" is not a synonym for "ethnicity." *An ethnic group is any social category of people who have a common culture that sets them apart from others in a society.* The distinguishing features may have to do with race, nationality background, religion, or other factors such as regional location. Ethnic differences may be of trivial or tremendous social significance and are especially important when they are associated with established patterns of prejudice and discrimination supported by strongly held *beliefs*—however erroneous—about the presumed "natural" attributes of this or that ethnic group.

Earlier, we defined a minority as a social group in some way or ways distinct from the dominant and more influential members of the society. We should point out here that *minority* and *ethnic group* are not synonyms. A minority and an ethnic group both are in some manner distinct, set apart from others in a society, but a minority is less influential than the dominant group, whereas an ethnic group may or may not be. Negroes are both a minority and an ethnic group in most of our states—an ethnic (and "racial") minority. White American-born Protestants are an ethnic group but not a minority in most parts of our country. They are the dominant group.

The concept of *ethnic group* is useful in our present discussion, partly because it is more flexible than such terms as *race* and *minority group*. Jews are not members of a race, but they do comprise an ethnic group. Negroes, roughly classifiable as a racial group, are at the same time an ethnic group, as we have defined the latter term. Germans and Italians are members of nationality groups, which are also ethnic groups.

PREJUDICE & DISCRIMINATION IN THE UNITED STATES: A SOCIAL PROBLEM

Prejudice and discrimination against minority groups constitute a social problem in the United States. There are no important conflicting judgments as to whether the problem exists, but there are important differences in interpreting it.

Many say, yes, we do have a problem here; the problem *is* Negroes—or Jews—or Catholics—or Mexican Americans—or Orientals. This view is reflected in the comment of a Georgia sheriff in 1962:

We are a little fed up with this voter registration business. . . We want our colored people to live like they've been living for the last hundred years—peaceful and happy. . . You know, . . . there's nothing like fear to keep the niggers in line.[11]

That is, the problem for such white persons is seen only as the fact that the Negro no longer is willing to live as he has in the past.

Countering this view is that of other individuals who assert that this important social problem is essentially the responsibility of the dominant group in our society. For example, Dr. Martin Luther King, Jr., referred to the ". . . slow fire of discontent, fed by the continuing indignities and inequities to which the Negroes were subjected."[12]

There are still others, certainly a diminishing number, who even insist that there is no problem at all, that all people are accepted everywhere so long as they behave according to established norms. There is no "Negro problem," said Mayor Allen Thompson, of Jackson, Mississippi. ". . . our colored citizens are happy and they are proud of Jackson. . . . There is no racial tension here. We are all living in harmony together."[13]

Opinions differ, then, about the nature and importance of the social problem of attitudes toward and the treatment of minorities. There are few persons today, however, who can dismiss the matter altogether, especially in view of the growing militancy of Negro Americans and the explosive conditions of Negro urban slums.

Opinions also differ, of course, about other minority groups in the United States, and these opinions have changed substantially over the years. The history of Jews in America provides a revealing case study in prejudice and discrimination. Some of the earliest settlers, quite naturally, brought their Old World prejudices with them. When the first 23 Dutch Jews arrived in New Amsterdam from Brazil, Governor Peter Stuyvesant asked his superiors, the Dutch East India Company, for permission to expel the "very repugnant . . . deceitful race . . . lest they infect and trouble this new colony with their customary usury and deceitful trading with the Christians." The Dutch East India Company turned down Stuyvesant's request.[14]

Stuyvesant's attitude was not characteristic of most colonists of the era. Jews generally enjoyed full civil and political rights as Dutch, and later as English, colonials. Severe prejudice and discrimination did not begin until shortly before the Civil War. Between 1841 and 1850, some 1,700,000 immigrants entered the United States, a small proportion of them Jewish, a considerable number Roman Catholic. The slavery issue had set "brother against brother," and in this embittered atmosphere religious minorities began to feel the sting of prejudice. The Know-Nothing party built its political platform on hatred of aliens in general, Catholics and Jews in particular. In December 1862, General Ulysses S. Grant issued General Order No. 11, expelling from the extended area under his direct command ". . . the Jews, as a class, within twenty-four hours." (President Lincoln revoked the order.)[15]

Jews, along with Catholics, were discriminated against after the Civil War ended. Another great wave of immigration began in 1880 and lasted for four decades. Over two and one-half million of the twenty-three and one-half million newcomers were Jewish.[16] They were different from most people already in the country in dress, education, cultural traditions, occupations, background, and because of their differences became the butt of jokes, vaudeville humor, and songs. They were ostracized, ridiculed, and discriminated against in numerous ways.

In the 1920s the Ku Klux Klan was revived, its members carrying on campaigns vilifying and threatening Jews, Catholics, and Negroes. Henry Ford's newspaper, the *Dearborn Independent,* launched a seven-year anti-Semitic assault.

The anti-Semitism of the 1920s was succeeded and exceeded by what took place in the 1930s after Hitler came to power in Germany. People in the United States began hearing from the German-American Bund, the Silver Shirts, and other native fascist, anti-Semitic organizations. With the entry of the United States into World War II, however, ". . . there came a national revulsion against totalitarianism and its concomitant of race hatred. Since then, a whole new American generation has grown up which can be regarded as generally sympathetic toward the fight against all forms of anti-Semitism . . . Anti-Semitism is alive and virulent, but at least, it has been reduced to manageable proportions."[17]

Jews, Roman Catholics, Italians, Slavs, and other minority groups have been the object of some degree of prejudice and discrimination in the course of our history, but probably persons with skin color other than "white" have most consistently been the victims of such attitudes and behavior. In 1948, MacIver found it pertinent to assert:

It is beyond contention that in the United States all "colored" people—and this designation must here be extended to include Chinese, Hindus, Japanese, Koreans, and Filipinos, as well as Negroes, and for fuller measure American Indians and Latin Americans—are commonly regarded as and commonly treated as constituting a lower caste.[18]

The situation is not markedly different today.

NATURE & EXTENT OF PREJUDICE & DISCRIMINATION IN THE UNITED STATES

In general, three processes of human interaction have been involved in the perpetuation of prejudice and discrimination against ethnic minorities in the United States: *competition, segregation,* and *conflict.*

COMPETITION · The dominant group in a society is in a favorable position to reduce or eliminate competition from the minority, whether it be in the economic or other fields. American Indians and people of Chinese, Japanese, and Mexican descent have suffered adversity in that competition. Catholics and, to a greater extent, Jews have suffered setbacks at one time and another, in one region or another, especially with regard to employment opportunities. Recent surveys by the Anti-Defamation League of the B'nai B'rith revealed that of 844 top officials in eight of New York City's large commercial banks, only 30, fewer than 4 percent, were Jews. In San Francisco, 75 of 340 private employers in major industry—22 percent—acknowledged a policy of discrimination against Jews.[19]

Negroes have been virtually excluded altogether from certain occupations. Although there has been some change in the situation in very recent years, they still find it extremely difficult, if not impossible, to obtain employment in managerial or sales capacities in companies owned by and catering largely to whites. There are few Negro foremen and skilled workmen in industrial plants in proportion to the black population in the respective areas. Prior to about 1965, there was not a single Negro newscaster on a major television network. The idea of a black man playing the romantic lead opposite a white woman in a motion picture was shocking. Judged by illustrated advertisements in newspapers and magazines, the products offered, from sable coats to deodorants, were for whites only; Negroes did not pose for such advertisements. In the economy generally, Negroes have found employment, if at all, mainly as domestics, unskilled laborers, and in other low-paying fields.

SEGREGATION · Physical segregation of minorities has for centuries been a device establishing social distance between dominant and minority groups. Ghettos are an outstanding example of such physical segregation. *A ghetto is a residential area completely or largely restricted to people of a particular ethnic group.* European Jews, for instance, were forced to live in ghettos. But ghettos in the United States—for Jews, Negroes, Mexicans, Chinese, Puerto Ricans—are the product of two forces. First is the internal social force. Individual members of a given ethnic group, feeling drawn to others of their kind, join them by voluntary attraction. Thus, as Puerto Ricans migrated to this country in increasing numbers in recent years, the newcomers took up residence in neighborhoods already settled by Puerto Ricans. Ghettos thus developed, partly by voluntary attraction.

But there are also external social forces representing compulsion, whereby persons of given ethnicity are compelled to live in ghettos. Probably the internal forces are a stronger factor among Jews than Negroes. The latter have, to a greater extent than Jews, been forced into segregated ghettos through external pressures.

But among every ethnic minority there is certain to be some voluntary attraction to the respective area, even if the segregation is imposed by compulsion. There is the attraction of being among one's "own people," for group solidarity is psychologically supportive.

No United States law has ever compelled Jews, Chinese, Japanese, Negroes, or Mexican Americans to reside in ghettos.* Pressures toward that form of segregation have been social rather than legal, but they have been as effective as if they were based on statutes. And ghettos are perpetuated by barriers set up against the removal of ghetto dwellers into certain other areas. Private agreements exist among realtors and property owners not to sell or rent to particular ethnic groups. Years ago, the United States Supreme Court ruled that such "restrictive covenants" were unenforceable, but the tribunal did not explicitly outlaw the covenants themselves. Thus it was that Negroes and Mexican Americans, for instance, found it very difficult, and often impossible, to get housing in areas other than those informally understood to be for Negroes or Mexican Americans.

In 1968, however, the Congress passed a new open-housing law, to become effective in 1969, providing penalties for discriminating in the sale of housing. The statute does not apply to individuals who sell their own property without the help of a realtor. Also excluded from application of the statute are persons who rent rooms in a boarding house that they own and live in.

An even more sweeping proscription against discrimination in housing was the decision handed down by the United States Supreme Court, also in 1968. It reached back to the first Civil Rights Act, which became effective in 1866. The Act had been ignored, the Court held. That statute stipulated that all citizens of the United States "shall have the same right, in every state and territory, . . . to inherit, purchase, lease, sell, hold and convey real and personal property." And when Congress passed

* However, after the United States entered World War II, Japanese and Japanese Americans residing in this country were forced, by legal decree, into internment camps. And other persons, classified as "enemy aliens," were confined in centers specifically established for this category.

that law, the Court asserted, it "meant exactly that." Discrimination in public and private housing was thus declared illegal.

The two legal steps taken in 1968 may become the instruments of radical change with respect to the problem of discrimination in housing. Until that change occurs, however, there will be no truly "open" cities in the United States where housing is as available to members of minority groups, in each and every part of the city, as it is to the dominant Caucasian population. This applies not only to those minority-group members who are most discriminated against, but to the somewhat more fortunately situated Jews. "American Jews," according to the Anti-Defamation League, "can find housing at every income level, but they cannot live in any neighborhood they wish."[20] During the first three decades of the twentieth century many resort hotels advertised, "No dogs. No Jews."

The events immediately following the United States Supreme Court desegregation decision, *Brown v. Board of Education*, in 1954, focused attention on conditions that had existed without much change since Civil War days. Legal and de facto segregation of Negroes and other minority people existed in public schools, not only in the South but in other parts of the United States. Until the late forties, for example, Mexican American children were segregated, by formal administrative action, in separate buildings or schools in Los Angeles.[21]

Public transportation facilities, parks, playgrounds, and swimming pools have been operated under the so-called "separate-but-equal" doctrine until very recently, largely in the South and mainly in an attempt to segregate Negroes.

Segregation was enforced also in personal, private areas through anti-miscegenation laws, prohibiting the marriage of Caucasians with members of other races, most particularly Negroes, until, in 1967, the United States Supreme Court struck down such statutes. Presumably, the states must now follow the court's dictate. No doubt social pressures against such marriages will continue, but legal penalties cannot be invoked.

CONFLICT · When competition and segregation fail to accomplish what members of the dominant group desire, or when the minority refuses to accept the conditions of competition or segregation, open conflict may result. It may take various forms.

It may be entirely within legal bounds, as when one group seeks, by legislation, to restrict or restrain the other. An example would be the attempt on behalf of one group to enact open housing legislation, while another group opposes it. In thus relying solely on legal means, neither group resorts to violence or other illegal acts.

Conflict may also revolve around what one group conceives of as legal conduct and another group as illegal, but which in any event is peaceable and nonviolent. Civil disobedience is the outstanding contemporary example. In such instances, an individual or group commits an offense against an ordinance or law that other individuals or groups hold to be sound. The offenders consider the legislation unconstitutional, or if constitutional, immoral or otherwise in violation of human rights and hence in need of change. Thus, on December 1, 1955, Mrs. Rosa Parks, a Negro, made history when she boarded a bus in downtown Montgomery, Alabama. She sat down in a section reserved for whites and refused to move when ordered to do so by the bus driver. Her arrest culminated in the boycott of all Montgomery buses by Negro residents, a movement organized by Dr. Martin Luther King, Jr. That boycott spearheaded the nonviolent civil disobedience movement, led by Dr. King until his assassination in 1968.

Conflict may be violent and for that reason illegal. The recent mass-scale riots in the Los Angeles community known as Watts and in Chicago, Newark, Detroit, and other cities were characterized by looting, the destruction of property and by the bludgeoning and shooting of residents by police and snipers. Lynching, which had been declining, took an upswing as a concomitant of the Negro struggle for civil rights. Both blacks and whites have been murdered in the course of this conflict. Other forms of conflict have included ejection of sit-down demonstrators from "white" premises, physical opposition to the admission of Negroes to polling stations and public schools, and street fighting between representatives of majority and minority groups.

CONFLICTING VALUES ON THE
CAUSES OF PREJUDICE & DISCRIMINATION

Why do we have an attitude of prejudice against minorities? Why do we practice discrimination against them? There is no common agreement on the answers to these questions, but much contradictory speculation. The various views on the subject may be summed up as follows:

1. *Minority people bring it on themselves. They are different, nonconformist.* High visibility is a factor here. Members of a minority group are identifiable; they are different from members of the dominant group in physical appearance, behavior, or in other respects. Dark-skinned Negroes and Orientals are distinguished from Caucasians by skin color and other physical features. Orthodox Jews wear distinctive costumes, follow "different" dietary laws, and attend synagogues, where they pray in the Hebrew language.

Such visible characteristics or customs do accentuate differences, but only in this sense can it be said that minority group members "bring it on themselves" if they are objects of prejudice or discrimination. We still must explain why these differences are held in low regard by members of the dominant group.

2. *Minority group members are clannish. They stick together. It is they who differentiate themselves from the dominant group. They hold themselves aloof. Naturally, this incurs resentment.* This is really a subordinate part of the first argument, that minority people are "different."

Again there is a foundation of fact in the argument. Minorities do tend to be self-conscious social units whose members have a consciousness-of-kind. But whether this is an *outcome* or a *cause* of dominant group attitudes toward them is not readily ascertained.

3. *Prejudice is instinctive. We are born with a dislike for people who are different from us.* Here incontrovertible evidence of a scientific nature is at hand. Prejudice is not instinctive. We are not born with it. Many studies support the fact that no one is born with an attitude of prejudice against any individual or group.

4. *Prejudice and discrimination are an outgrowth of personality factors that reside in given individuals.* According to this thesis, there is an intolerant type of personality. Evidence on this point is fragmentary and somewhat equivocal, but worth considering.

Sociologist Ely Chinoy writes:

The hostility that is usually characteristic of prejudice is also part of each affected individual's personality, and its origins and functions in the psychic economy of the prejudiced individual cannot be ignored. Much recent research has sought to uncover the psychological sources of prejudice, and there appears to be some evidence that those persons who conform rigidly to prevailing values, who are submissive to authority and critical of those who flout conventional norms, and who are preoccupied with problems of power and status are likely to be prejudiced.[22]

Psychologist G. W. Allport, who has done extensive research on the subject, upholds the proposition that there is an intolerant type of personality. He writes: ". . . one of the facts of which we are most certain is that people who reject one outgroup will tend to reject other out-groups. If a person is anti-Jewish, he is likely to be anti-Catholic, anti-Negro, anti any out-group."[23] This clearly suggests that prejudice is a personality attribute of some persons and that strongly prejudicial persons tend to dislike or hate those who are not in their own immediate in-groups. Prejudice tends to be general rather than specific in terms of its application to other people.

Several years ago, T. W. Adorno and several other scholars published a large-scale study, *The Authoritarian Personality,* that supports this view.[24] They constructed an ethnocentrism scale to measure attitudes regarding Negro-white relations; minority groups such as foreigners; political parties; religions; and patriotism. They found:

A. *A person who is ethnocentric in one test area tends to be so in others.* The individual who considers the white race superior to any others in all respects is also likely to be ethnocentric about his country and hostile toward minorities in this country.

B. *Persons with a high degree of ethnocentrism are found chiefly among certain "personality types."* They tend to be "projective" individuals who blame others for their difficulties and thus escape taking responsibility for their own attitudes and behavior.

C. *The most ethnocentric persons are authoritarian rather than democratic in their views,* as the terms "authoritarian" and "democratic" are commonly understood.

The Authoritarian Personality has come in for extensive criticism,* some of which needs to be considered here.

* See, for instance, Richard Christie and Marie Jahoda (eds.), *Studies in the Scope and Method of "The Authoritarian Personality"* (New York: Free Press, 1954).

A. It has been criticized for its methodology, the ethnocentrism scale employed being said to contain ambiguous items. It is also alleged that the sample studied was atypical of the general population. It was comprised largely of middle-class individuals and members of formal organizations, and these differ in various respects from other segments of the population.

B. The study, it was noted, found that a person who is ethnocentric in one test area tends to be so in others. Also, that the most ethnocentric persons are authoritarian rather than democratic in their views. Concerning these findings, the investigators suggested that the association between authoritarianism (as measured by the scale) and a number of other attitudes, including ethnocentric prejudice, indicated that there was a unified personality type, the authoritarian personality, incorporating these two tendencies.

Critics have attacked this hypothesis. They point out that authoritarianism, as an attitude, is related to certain factors that must be considered in any assessment of the attitude. It has been found that, for whatever reasons, persons of the lower intelligence brackets, who have a comparatively low level of educational attainment and a lower socioeconomic status, tend to be disproportionately represented among those holding authoritarian attitudes. That is, authoritarian attitudes are correlated in a positive direction with the three factors listed. The features that go to make up the "authoritarian person," therefore, are found in that individual, not because he represents a unified personality configuration, as such, but because these features are more normative for persons of the lower intelligence brackets, with comparatively lower educational attainment, and lower socioeconomic status than for others in the society.

Both authoritarian ideas and ethnocentric prejudices, the argument continues, are learned, partly through indoctrination. And economically and socially deprived persons are indoctrinated into these attitudes more often than are persons of more favored circumstances.

C. This leads into another criticism leveled at *The Authoritarian Personality*. It does not, according to some, place enough weight on the function of culture in the production of prejudice. Norms governing interracial behavior have evolved in our society; they are not identical for all regions; but whatever they are, applying to whichever region, they exercise very considerable pressure upon the residents of the respective areas, demanding conformity. The fact that an individual manifests prejudice does not, therefore, tell us very much about his distinctive personality modes—he is reacting to pressures in his immediate surroundings. Attitudes and behavior that in other parts of the country might be considered characteristic of an abnormal personality, may be considered quite characteristic of a normal personality in his community. As a businessman, for instance, he may refuse to sell to a Negro, even though he thereby loses that much business. This might make no sense in another section of the country, but it would be normal procedure in his community.

Research abundantly establishes that white Southerners, typically, are more intolerant of Negroes than are white Northerners, but this is primarily a consequence of cultural factors. It does not indicate that the South has more *basically* authoritarian, prejudiced persons than does the North. The South, for example, is much less anti-Semitic than most of the rest of the country, according to public opinion polls. Southerners, it would appear, are more intolerant of Negroes, as a class of people, than of Jews. Cultural orientations account for this in large measure.

D. Concerning the Adorno finding that the most ethnocentric persons are authoritarian rather than democratic, some writers hold that the study tends to equate authoritarian attitudes with those of the right wing only, and notably those of fascist orientation. What about left-wing Communist authoritarianism, these critics ask? Does it not exist? And, contradictory as it may seem, is it not possible even to hold authoritarian attitudes toward democracy? These critics are suggesting that what we are really studying may be a pattern of thought, a *generalized* dogmatism, rather than a set of beliefs concerning *particular* minorities—in other words, the closed-mind syndrome.

What can we conclude, finally, after balancing the assumptions of *The Authoritarian Personality* against the criticisms advanced against them? It is reasonable to hold that the attitude of authoritarianism, of the kind measured by the study, when present in a given person, does *tend* to increase the likelihood of ethnic prejudice in that individual. But there is nothing inevitable here. Neither the authoritarian attitude nor any other related personality tendencies must be present in order for prejudice or discriminatory behavior to exist. Prejudice and discrimination are come by in many ways, through various routes. If, as the Adorno study indicates, a person who is ethnocentric in one test area is likely to be ethnocentric in others, sociocultural factors play a predominant role in the development of such behavior.

5. *Economic and status needs are primarily responsible for prejudice and discrimination.* There is considerable support for this thesis. The argument runs: The more one individual gets of the nation's wealth, the less remains for others. Wealth brings prestige, status, power, luxury. The dominant group is strategically better prepared than the minority to attain wealth and its concomitants—it is an educated, trained group. But if it must discriminate against minorities in order to gain its ends, it has that power.

Sociologist Herbert Blumer sees prejudice and discrimination arising from what he terms *group position.* The dominant group comes to consider itself entitled to certain rights and privileges. Its members believe they should hold certain jobs, engage in certain occupations and professions. They feel they are entitled to choice property, to positions of power and prestige, to exclusive membership in given organizations, schools, and churches.

Race prejudice, according to Blumer, arises out of a fear on the part of the dominant group that the minority threatens or will threaten its more favorable position.

The source of race prejudice lies in a felt challenge to this sense of group position. . . . Race prejudice is a defensive reaction to such challenging of the sense of group position. It consists of the disturbed feelings, usually of marked hostility, that are thereby aroused. As such, race prejudice is a protective device. It functions, however short-sightedly, to preserve the integrity and the position of the dominant group.[25]

6. *Prejudice is learned.* Here we are on very solid ground. Abundant research testifies that prejudice is a social not a biological phenomenon. No one, we said earlier, is born with prejudices. The color, creed, or other prejudicial line is established sometime after the person is born through social inter-

action and the learning process. Prejudices are outcomes of social experience. The culture in which an individual is reared and in which he lives has a great deal to do with his attitudes. Consider the boy in Figure 20.1. He was not born with attitudes suporting the Ku Klux Klan. We may assume from the context of the photograph that he is learning or has learned—from others in his environment—to hold such attitudes.

7. *Prejudice is a product of the culture.* This follows from the immediately foregoing. Insofar as prejudice is learned in society, it is a cultural product, acquired by those who share the culture. People who hold attitudes of prejudice are ". . . conforming to the norms of their own groups and the expectations of their fellow members; expressions of prejudice reaffirm their membership and their unity with others. Failure to conform exposes them to criticism and social pressures . . ."[26]

8. *Prejudice and discrimination are abetted by hostile stereotypes held about minority people in the society.* There is evidence bearing out this assertion. If you were to read books, magazines, or newspapers published in the 1930s or earlier, you would encounter references to the "wily Oriental," "shiftless Negro," "frugal Scot," and the "stolid Swede," all stereotypes. You would read that when a prospective customer bargained with a shopkeeper he was attempting to "Jew him down," meaning to get him to lower his price, on the assumption that the shopkeeper had never expected to get the quoted price. If your grandfather served in World War I, he may have received basic training under a United States Army Manual that stated: "The foreign-born, and especially Jews, are more apt to malinger than the native-born."[27] (When President Wilson was informed about the statement, he ordered the entire edition of the manual destroyed.)

Through the promulgation of stereotypes in one form or another, millions of Americans have been exposed to the idea that Negroes, Mexicans, and American Indians represent inferior and to some extent subhuman branches of our species. Some prevailing cultural superstitions are expressed in these stereotypes, as for instance that Negroes are naturally lazy, dirty, malodorous, ignorant, and sexually aggressive as a group; that Orientals are naturally cunning, treacherous, deceitful, and

Figure 20.1
The Learning Process
United Press International Photo.

cold-blooded; that American Indians are naturally dirty, apathetic, vindictive, and deficient in intelligence. Scientific evidence shows that these beliefs are false, yet people continue to transmit them culturally to their children, thus maintaining systems of superiority-inferiority status from generation to generation.

Consider the stereotypes expressed in Figure 20.2—that Jews are too busy reading, "or whatever it is they do," to keep up with the times; that they are embarrassingly anxious to be liked; that they speak a different language. Where did these beliefs come from? Obviously they were transmitted in the culture, from parent to child, from peer group member to peer group member, from person to person.

In their musical, *South Pacific*, Richard Rodgers, Oscar Hammerstein II, and Joshua Logan effectively express the idea that prejudice is learned by cultural transmission:

Figure 20.2
Stereotype Talk
Copyright 1965 Jules Feiffer.

You've got to be taught before it's too late,
Before you are six or seven or eight,
To hate all of the people your relatives hate.
You've got to be carefully taught.[28]

CONFLICTING VALUES ON THE RESOLUTION OF THE PROBLEM OF PREJUDICE & DISCRIMINATION

Just as there are conflicting values on the causes of prejudice and discrimination in the United States, so there are disagreements on how best to resolve the problem. Such programs as have been advanced may be roughly classified into two categories, the *evolutionary* and the *revolutionary*.

THE EVOLUTIONARY APPROACH

Advocates of the evolutionary approach in effect call for a gradual, relatively painless transition, brought about through *legislation*, *education*, and *amelioration*.

LEGISLATION · Although agreeing that it is impossible to legislate human emotions, proponents of the evolutionary approach hold it is possible to legislate behavior. That is, although laws will not be likely to alter prejudices, they can be used to prevent discriminatory behavior. Thus, an employer may be prejudiced toward Puerto Ricans, but be forced to employ some in a state with a Fair Employment Practices law, or under the provisions of the federal Civil Rights Act of 1964.

EDUCATION · Formal and informal education are advanced as avenues for reducing, if not eliminating, prejudice. Since prejudice must be learned in the social environment, perhaps it can be forestalled or counteracted through the educative process. Given a reduction of prejudice, the tendency to discriminate against minorities will be lessened, it is argued. The informal education a child receives in his own home can be a telling factor, for children tend to adopt the attitudes of their parents. Formal education can play a vital role, too. MacIver points this out:

The school, if properly oriented, could no doubt become a powerful influence in counteracting the influences that work to canalize prejudice in the child, and thus might have some effect, through the child, on the grownup community.[29]

AMELIORATION · Amelioration refers to gradual, piecemeal improvement in the lot of those who are discriminated against. The gradual approach is advocated because, it is reasoned, it is less shocking to the majority and allows time for the acceptance of one palliative before another is introduced. Half a loaf is better than none, and to provide a whole loaf immediately would stir up resentments.

Those who favor the evolutionary viewpoint consider it more realistic than the revolutionary approach to the problem. They tend to disapprove of violence, the threat of violence, or even of nonviolent civil disobedience. They are committed to "the rule of law."

An example of the gradualist view is furnished in a study of Mexican American youths, themselves subject to prejudice and discrimination. Sociologist Celia Heller conducted depth interviews with a small number of Mexican American boys, residing in Los Angeles, who were mobility-oriented, that is, desirous of improving their position on the status ladder. Many of the youths favored extending opportunities for improvement to all—Caucasians, Negroes, Mexican Americans—but not one approved of the tactics Negroes were using in the civil rights struggle. The Mexican Americans expressed vehement disapproval of demonstrations and sit-ins and rejected the idea that their group should employ these means of fighting for their ends.[30] Since publication of the Heller study, however, Mexican Americans have taken a less gradualist view and have become more militant in some areas.

Apparently the "liberals," about whom the Negro in Figure 20.3 is speaking, are for integration, but only via an evolutionary process.

THE REVOLUTIONARY APPROACH

Advocates of the revolutionary approach seek the immediate elimination of discrimination. The approach is exemplified by Negroes and their white supporters who demand "freedom now" for the black population. They are unwilling to wait any longer. They propose to exercise the rights granted them in the Constitution but denied them in their communities. Both *nonviolent* and *violent* tactics have been employed.

NONVIOLENT TACTICS · Again using the Negro struggle for full citizenship rights as an example, the civil disobedience program originally launched by Dr. Martin Luther King, Jr., illustrates the nonviolent tactical approach. It depends upon sit-ins, sit-downs, and prayers and marches undertaken without violence on the part of the demonstrators. By peaceable means, demonstrators have dramatized their demand for integrated schools and housing, full voting rights, and equal employment opportunities. Violence has erupted in the course of many demonstrations, but most often it has been started by unsympathetic onlookers or police officers.

VIOLENT TACTICS · After a time, the Negro civil rights movement proliferated, and a group of militants abandoned the policy of peaceable tactics and embarked on campaigns in which force and violence were not to be eschewed. The Student Non-Violent Coordinating Committee (SNCC) reoriented under new leadership and no longer professed to be nonviolent. If attacked, blacks would fight back. SNCC came out for "black power," bluntly and boldly, and although the term was

variously interpreted, the implication generally accepted was that "black power" was to be achieved by a frontal attack on the white power structure. This interpretation was reinforced when Stokely Carmichael, a leading spokesman for the "black power" movement, explained, according to a press report: "When you talk of black power you talk of bringing this country to its knees. When you talk of black power, you talk of building a movement that will smash everything Western civilization has created."[31]

Other Negro spokesmen have asserted that "black power" is to be achieved, not by revolutionary means, but in the same way that whites have gained power in our society, that is, by political, economic, and educational means, all within the law and the Constitution.

The Muslims have demanded, not equality with the white man, but separation from him. For many years their leader, Elijah Muhammed, has preached Negro racial superiority. He once declared: ". . . by nature the black man was created good. By nature the white man was created evil."[32]

If unprovoked violence is eschewed by black militant *organizations*, the same cannot be said for particular Negroes, acting as *individuals*. Looting, unprovoked assaults, and even murders have occurred in the course of the riots of the past few years.

A SOCIOLOGIST'S PROPOSALS

In *The More Perfect Union*, published in 1948, Robert M. MacIver outlined what he deemed were the broad lines of strategy necessary to abate or eliminate discrimination against minority groups. Twenty years have elapsed since publication of the volume, but what MacIver has to say might have been written today in the light of contemporary developments.

The primary attack on discrimination, he suggests, *should not uphold the banner of particular groups but should emphasize what is needed to promote the national welfare and national unity.*

It follows that those who seek to educate our people should lay primary stress, not on the disadvantages and frustrations suffered by the disparaged groups or by any one of them in particular but on the common loss, injury, and discredit that the country as a whole, majorities as well as minorities, sustains from the cleavages, rifts, and tensions that ensue from the prejudicial and undemocratic treatment meted out to large portions of the citizen body. . .[33]

No one direction of attack on discrimination should be given preeminence or overall priority, he asserts. *All of the fronts are strategically important. An attack on several fronts at a time is more effective than an attack on one alone.*

There are those who say the only cure for discrimination is the economic one. . . There are those who . . . deprecate any action on the politico-legal front. Such claims needlessly divide the forces making against discrimination. . . . We should not minimize any agency of attack.[34]

Wherever a direct attack, that is to say, on discrimination, is feasible, MacIver continues, *it is more promising than the indirect attack on prejudice. It is more effective to challenge conditions than to challenge attitudes or feelings.*

It is better strategy to raise the economic level of the disprivileged, to remove the barriers to economic opportunity or to occupational status, to assure the right to vote, . . . than to refute directly the prejudices or myths that justify these handicaps. It is more expedient to strike at tangible than at intangible impediments.[35]

At another point in his outline, MacIver advises that *the primary business of strategy is to explore and attack the weaker points in the position of the discriminating forces.* These are the forward lines of least resistance, which are held less firmly than the back lines. For instance, on the economic front, the attempted entry of Negroes into positions of responsibility and authority in industry meets powerful resistance. The intermediate functions that lead up to these positions can be infiltrated and seized more readily. The focus of the attack should be there. Every advance will make the next one easier.[36]

Appropriate leadership must be developed if the forces of discrimination are to be effectively attacked. Those forces are organized. There are great potential forces that can be rallied to fight them.[37]

Strategy should be adapted to the prevailing mores. This does not mean that no action should ever be taken against discrimination until and unless the mores of the community support it. The mores are always changing, gradually and often imperceptibly. Good strategy calls for discerning trends of change and taking advantage of them. But the strategy must be so framed, nevertheless, as not to arouse, either then or later, latent antagonisms or to increase actual ones so as to endanger the objectives that the strategy is set up to accomplish. Radical demands, where the mores are strongly resistant to them, are often dangerous, particularly when advanced by the minority groups themselves. "They may serve sometimes to rouse the public to a consciousness of the problem, but if pushed too hard they may provoke a revulsion that will militate against progressive measures."[38]

SOCIAL CHANGE REGARDING PREJUDICE & DISCRIMINATION

Since World War II we have witnessed much change in the treatment of minorities in this country, most of it in the direction of removing discriminatory barriers. It has not been all in one direction, however. There has been an upsurge of activity by "hate" and native fascist groups, which have whipped up a certain amount of feeling against minorities. The resurgence of the Ku Klux Klan, for example, occurred during this period. The very rise of a strong civil rights movement has engendered a violent reaction in some quarters, resulting in assaults and even murders.

On the other side of the ledger, since the Supreme Court decision in *Brown v. Board of Education*, there has been a series of other court rulings reemphasizing and redefining civil rights beyond those having to do with public education. The first civil rights bill since the Reconstruction Era was enacted by the Congress in 1957, to be followed by additional enactments on the same subject. The Civil Rights Act of 1964 was unquestionably the most far-reaching law in this field since the Emancipation Proclamation and the Constitutional amendment supporting it. There are now adequate and sufficient laws to solve all of the problems of discrimination under consideration in this chapter—if they are enforced.

Less dramatic than the federal legislation has been the gradual decline of the maligning stereotype in the mass media. The word "darky" must now be deleted from old songs before they may be heard on the air. When Cole Porter composed the hit tune, "Let's Do It," the original version went: "Chinks do it, Japs do it, up in Lapland little Laps do it." It was later necessary to change the sheet music to read, "Birds do it, bees do it, even educated fleas do it."[39]

That attitudes concerning minorities have undergone some change is borne out by a National Opinion Research Center survey, reported by Bruno Bettelheim and Morris Janowitz.[40] At various times during 1942 and 1956, individuals were asked: "In general, do you think Negroes are as intelligent as white people—that is, can they learn things just as well if they are given the same education and training?" Although the proportion of affirmative responses was consistently lower for the Southern white population, compared with the Northern white, in both categories the percentages rose significantly each time a sampling was made, with one minor exception.

In 1966, *Newsweek* conducted a poll which revealed the extent to which whites have changed their views about Negroes. Taking all whites as a group, there was less opposition in 1966 than in 1963 with regard to each of the items listed. However, the degree of resistance varied by proposition in each year. Sitting next to a Negro in a restaurant or bus was unacceptable to 20 percent of whites in 1963 and to 16 percent in 1966. There was somewhat more resistance to the idea of sitting next to a Negro in a movie or using the same rest room as a Negro. Greatest opposition was expressed regarding the possibility of a teen-age child dating a Negro—90 percent of whites "would mind" this in 1963, and 88 percent would in 1966. Curiously, however, a lesser proportion "would mind" if a close friend or relative married a Negro—84 percent in 1963, and 79 percent in 1966.

The findings for Southern whites were somewhat different, but less opposition was expressed regarding six of the eight propositions in 1963 as compared with 1966. Southern whites "would mind" each of the suggested propositions in greater proportion than would all whites taken as a group. Their greatest objection would be to the idea of a teen-age child dating a Negro—97 percent in 1963, and 94 percent in 1966. And where 91 percent "would mind" in 1963 if a close relative married a Negro, the proportion actually rose in 1966, to 92 percent.

Attitudes, we know, predispose to behavior. Have there been behavior changes in the treatment of minorities?

Barriers against Negroes have come down in various sectors. They vote in areas where they could not vote before. Some attend desegregated schools. They ride buses, streetcars, and trains along with whites, where formerly they were relegated to Jim Crow sections of such vehicles. They take their recreation in desegregated public parks. Twenty states now have enforceable Fair Employment Practice laws; several more have investigating commissions; approximately forty cities have local ordinances against discrimination in employment. These, of course, apply to all people, not merely to Negroes.

In the late 1930s, according to surveys, employment agencies estimated that as many as 95 percent of their job orders specified "No Jews." By 1966, the figure had dropped to 25 percent, in states *without* FEP laws. (Where such laws do have force, no discriminatory job orders may be accepted by agencies.[41])

In 1948, the Supreme Court held that restrictive covenants were unenforceable. In 1968, as indicated earlier, a federal enactment and a Supreme Court decision called for housing open on equal terms to minority group members and members of the dominant group.

In 1957, a study of 1,065 resort hotels and motels in the United States, Canada, and the West Indies indicated that at least 22 percent discriminated against Jews. In 1963, this figure had dropped to about 9 percent.[42]

These and other changes were predicted by Gunnar Myrdal and associates in *An American Dilemma*. The Negro, according to this volume, occupies an inferior place in American society, not through any biological inadequacy of his own, but by virtue of imperfections in the society. Slavery cast him in an inferior role, and with emancipation he gained little in status. Various types of social discriminations have kept him subordinate, shut him off from access to the educational and occupational opportunities available to the dominant group. He must live in poverty in inferior, disease-breeding housing. His low position on the stratification ladder deprives him of political and legal equality. As whites, regarding the Negro's degraded position, gain in self-esteem, the Negro's estimation of his own comparative worthlessness is confirmed by the operation of "the self-fulfilling prophecy."

But, Myrdal holds, since the Negro's low status is socially derived, it can change. And it will, because people in this country become increasingly aware that they are faced by "an American dilemma."

That dilemma, according to Myrdal, stems from the fact that there is such a thing as an American creed, whether Americans are fully conscious of it or not. Americans have an historic sense of moral concern for others, a liberalism, and a dynamic belief in equality of opportunity and freedom.

Therein lies the dilemma. We are torn between commitment to the American creed on the one hand and social conditions that generate inequality on the other. And the power of the creed, Myrdal says, will before very long make itself felt so that, finally, Americans will not tolerate practical denials of human rights to any people.

Sociologist Robert K. Merton finds Myrdal's discussion of the gap between creed and behavior too simple.[43] Allegiance to the creed is highly variable, he points out, and depends upon relevant factors in the individual's social milieu. The creed does not exact the same degree of behavior at different times and places. It may be evaded when it is at odds with other beliefs and practices. It may be reinterpreted in a manner consistent with an individual's practice.

Actually, Merton says, Myrdal's variables—official creed and private practice—are not enough for effective analysis. There is a relation among three, not two, variables: the creed honored in cultural tradition and partly enacted in law; the beliefs and attitudes of individuals concerning the principles of the creed; and the actual practices of individuals with reference to the creed. When the third variable—beliefs and attitudes of the individual regarding the principles of the creed—is introduced, a new distinction becomes evident. Recognizing that the creed is an ingredient of the culture, an individual may yet have no personal conviction as to its moral validity and may feel he need not be bound by it. In terms of beliefs, two types can be identified: those who genuinely believe in the creed and those who do not. And with respect to actual practice, there are likewise two types: those individuals whose conduct does conform to the creed and those whose conduct does not.

Merton sets up a typology of ethnic prejudice and discrimination that takes into account variant attitudes and patterns of behavior. Each type, he asserts, can be found in every region of the United States and within every social class, although in varying numbers:

Type I. *The unprejudiced nondiscriminator or all-weather liberal.* These are racial and ethnic liberals who adhere to the creed in both belief and practice. They are not prejudiced, and they do not discriminate against minority group members. They occupy a strategic position in campaigns against prejudice and discrimination.

Type II. *The unprejudiced discriminator or fair-weather liberal.* He is a man of expediency. Although he himself is free of prejudice, he supports discriminatory practices when this is the easier or more profitable course. He may remain silent when others show prejudice or practice discrimination; thus he implicitly acquiesces in the attitude or practice. There is the expediency of the timid liberal who hesitates to speak up against discrimination lest he lose status or be otherwise penalized by his prejudiced associates. There is the expediency of the self-assertive person, who grasps at advantages in social and economic competition, as for instance in the case of the employer who, although not an anti-Semite or Negrophobe, will not hire Jewish or Negro workers because "it might hurt business."

Since the fair-weather liberal suffers from some degree of

guilt and shame for departing from his own beliefs in the American creed, he is vulnerable to the efforts of the all-weather liberal who would help him bring his conduct into reconciliation with his beliefs, thus removing the source of guilt. "He is the most amenable to cure, because basically he wants to be cured."

Type III. *The prejudiced nondiscriminator or fair-weather illiberal.* Here we have reluctant conformity by a prejudiced person who does not believe in the creed but conforms to it in practice through fear of sanctions that might otherwise be visited upon him. In this category is the prejudiced employer who discriminates against racial or ethnic groups until a Fair Employment Practices Commission threatens him with punishment. Here is the prejudiced trade union leader who does away with Jim Crow in his union because the rank-and-file demands that it be done away with. Here, too, is the businessman who forgoes his prejudices when he finds a profitable market among people he hates, fears, or despises and is willing to sell to them.

The fair-weather illiberal conforms to the creed only when there is danger or loss in deviating from it. He would not conform except for powerful institutional, legal and interpersonal pressures. He conforms because he feels he must; he will cease his conformity when the pressure is removed.

Type IV. *The prejudiced discriminator or the all-weather illiberal.* This is the confirmed bigot pure and unashamed, the man of prejudice who is consistent in his departure from the American creed. He is convinced that any white man is better than any "nigger." He looks upon differential treatment of Negro and white not as "discrimination," in the sense of unfair treatment, but as "discriminating," in the sense of showing keen discernment. One "ought" to accord a Negro and a white different treatment in a wide diversity of situations.

Merton points to the extreme importance of the social surroundings of the confirmed illiberal. As these surroundings vary, so does the problem of the consistent illiberal in some measure. In cultural regions where the American creed is widely repudiated, he is a social conformist. In areas dominated by a large measure of adherence to the creed, he is a social deviant. In the first cultural context, change in his ethnic behavior would involve alienating himself from people who are significant to him. In the second context, a change of personal outlook may mean fuller incorporation in groups meaningful to him. In the first situation, a modification of his views would require him to take the path of greatest resistance. In the second situation, a modification may require him to follow the path of least resistance. Clearly then, according to Merton, any social policy aimed at changing the behavior and perhaps the attitudes of the all-weather illiberal needs to take into account the cultural and social structure of the area in which he lives.*

Ambrose Bierce defined prejudice as "A vagrant opinion without visible means of support." If all-weather liberals are eventually successful in "selling" that definition to fair-weather liberals, fair-weather illiberals, and all-weather illiberals, the social problem of prejudice *and* discrimination against racial and ethnic minorities will be on the way to solution.

· NOTES

1. Christen T. Jonassen, "Some Historical and Theoretical Bases of Racism in Northwestern Europe," *Social Forces*, XXX (December 1951), 155–161.
2. Quoted in Richard T. LaPiere and Paul Farnsworth, *Social Psychology* (New York: McGraw-Hill, 1949), p. 228.
3. *Ibid.*
4. J. Robert Moskin, "Prejudice in Israel," *Look*, XXIX, 20 (October 5, 1965), 67, 70, 72.
5. George Eaton Simpson and J. Milton Yinger, *Racial and Cultural Minorities*, 3rd ed. (New York: Harper & Row, 1965), p. 10.
6. *Ibid.*
7. *Ibid.*
8. Robert M. MacIver, *The More Perfect Union* (New York: Macmillan, 1948), pp. 41–42.
9. Simpson and Yinger, *op. cit.*, p. 14.
10. MacIver, *op. cit.*, p. 64.
11. H. Frank Way, Jr., *Liberty in the Balance, Current Issues in Civil Liberties* (New York: McGraw-Hill, 1964), pp. 12–13.
12. Martin Luther King, Jr., *Stride Toward Freedom: The Montgomery Story* (New York: Ballantine, 1958), p. 31.
13. *Southern School News,* III (February 1957), 12.
14. Anti-Defamation League of B'nai B'rith, *Not the Work of a Day: The Story of the Anti-Defamation League of B'nai B'rith* (New York: Anti-Defamation League of B'nai B'rith, undated), unpaginated.

* All of the foregoing is paraphrased and quoted from Robert K. Merton, "Discrimination and the American Creed," in Robert M. MacIver (ed.), *Discrimination and National Welfare* (New York: Harper & Row, 1949), pp. 99–126.

15. *Ibid.*
16. *Ibid.*
17. *Ibid.*
18. MacIver, *op. cit.*, pp. 33–34.
19. Anti-Defamation League of B'nai B'rith, *op. cit.*
20. *Ibid.*
21. Celia Heller, *Mexican American Youth, Forgotten Youth at the Crossroads* (New York: Random House, 1966), pp. 46–47.
22. Ely Chinoy, *Society, An Introduction to Sociology* (New York: Random House, 1966), p. 234.
23. G. W. Allport, *The Nature of Prejudice* (New York: Anchor Books, 1958), p. 66.
24. T. W. Adorno, Else Frenkel-Brunswik, Daniel J. Levinson, and R. Nevitt Sanford, *The Authoritarian Personality* (New York: Harper & Row, 1950).
25. Herbert Blumer, "Race Prejudice as a Sense of Group Position," in Jitsuvichi Masuoka and Preston Valien (eds.), *Race Relations* (Chapel Hill: University of North Carolina Press, 1961), pp. 215–227.
26. Chinoy, *op. cit.*, p. 234.
27. Anti-Defamation League of B'nai B'rith, *op. cit.*
28. Richard Rodgers, Oscar Hammerstein 2nd, and Joshua Logan, *South Pacific*. Copyright © 1949 by Richard Rodgers and Oscar Hammerstein 2nd. Used by permission of the publisher, Williamson Music, Inc., New York and Williamson Music Ltd., London.
29. MacIver, *op. cit.*, p. 190.
30. Heller, *op. cit.*, p. 101.
31. UPI dispatch, *Los Angeles Times*, August 7, 1966, p. B-4.
32. Lee P. Brown, "Black Muslims and the Police," *Journal of Criminal Law, Criminology and Police Science*, LVI (March 1965), 119–126.
33. MacIver, *op. cit.*, pp. 245–246.
34. *Ibid.*, p. 247.
35. *Ibid.*
36. *Ibid.*, pp. 249–250.
37. *Ibid.*, pp. 250–251.
38. *Ibid.*, pp. 251–252.
39. Anti-Defamation League of B'nai B'rith, *op. cit.*
40. Bruno Bettelheim and Morris Janowitz, "Trends in Prejudice," in Bernard Berelson and Morris Janowitz (eds.), *Reader in Public Opinion and Communication*, 2nd ed. (New York: Free Press, 1966), pp. 91–109.
41. Anti-Defamation League of B'nai B'rith, *op. cit.*
42. *Ibid.*
43. Robert K. Merton, "Discrimination and the American Creed," in Robert M. MacIver (ed.), *Discrimination and National Welfare* (New York: Harper & Row, 1949), pp. 99–126.

ADORNO, T. W., ELSE FRENKEL-BRUNSWIK, DANIEL J. LEVINSON, and H. NEVITT SANFORD. *The Authoritarian Personality*. New York: Harper, 1950.
An important contribution toward an understanding of the "prejudiced personality."

ALLPORT, GORDON W. *The Nature of Prejudice*. Abridged. New York: Anchor Books, 1958.
A thoroughgoing examination of the nature of prejudice and the dynamics of its formation. Also, a discussion of methods, attempted and projected, for the reduction of group tensions.

CARMICHAEL, STOKELY, and CHARLES V. HAMILTON. *Black Power: The Politics of Liberation in America*. New York: Vintage Books, 1967.
An argument for Black Power, as advocated by the former chairman of SNCC.

COHEN, NATHAN E. "The Los Angeles Riot Study." *Social Work*, XII, 4 (October 1967), 14–22.
The man who coordinated the study of the Watts riot of 1965 summarizes the findings and reflects on the implications.

DOLLARD, JOHN. *Caste and Class in a Southern Town*. New Haven, Conn.: Yale University Press, 1937.
Old but still relevant. An analysis of the bases for the perpetuation of segregation and inequality in Southern communities.

HALBERSTAM, DAVID. "The White Citizens' Councils." *Commentary*, XXII (October 1956), 293–302.
An account of the movement that aims to preserve segregation in the South (and elsewhere).

KING, MARTIN LUTHER, JR. *Stride Toward Freedom: The Montgomery Story*. New York: Ballantine, 1958.
The leader of the nonviolent civil disobedience movement tells how he organized the Montgomery bus boycott, which marked the beginning of the civil rights struggle against segregation in the South.

MILLER, ARTHUR. *Focus*. New York: Reynal and Hitchcock, 1945.
A novel revealing the explosive power of prejudice, in this case based largely upon stereotypes concerning Jews.

ROSE, PETER I. *They and We: Racial and Ethnic Relations in the United States*. New York: Random House, 1964.
A brief treatment of the problem of prejudice and discrimination against minority groups in the United States.

21 POVERTY: A SOCIAL PROBLEM

The United States is the wealthiest land in the world. How can poverty be a social problem here? This question will be investigated in the present chapter.

CONFLICTING VIEWS ABOUT THE EXISTENCE OF POVERTY IN THE UNITED STATES

Ours has been called an "affluent society" because the United States has the highest per capita income in the world. Yet a substantial number of Americans, perhaps as many as thirty million, live below what has come to be known as the "poverty line." This fact receives a wide variety of interpretations.

A few still maintain that there is no poverty in the United States, except during severe economic depressions, and that we have not faced a real depression since before World War II. Others take the position that there are poor people, to be sure, but that their economic condition is their own fault. Such persons are viewed as lazy, shiftless, and unwilling to work, preferring to subsist on charity.

In contrast to those who hold either that poverty is non-existent, except during depressions, or that it is characteristic only of the shiftless, are individuals who adopt a somewhat fatalistic point of view. There is poverty in the United States, they concede, but it is inevitable. The poor shall always be with us, in good times and bad, for a variety of reasons. Some poverty-stricken people are social inadequates who, by personality and temperament, are unable to face up to the responsibilities of adulthood and will never be able to support families. Others are victims of their environment, unable to compete successfully for the good things of life because of their minority group status. Still others are biologically handicapped, intellectually unable to earn more than a meager income. In view of these circumstances, the fatalists say, a certain percentage of the population will always require economic support.

A good many persons who are representative of divergent political and social philosophies say that poverty is in fact a major social problem in the United States, but there are specific reasons for that poverty and something can therefore be done about it. Opinions differ, however, about appropriate remedies: proponents of this view range from the advocates of various brands of socialism, to those who would solve the problem by more and better social work.

However one regards the matter (and regardless of those diminishing few who deny the existence of poverty), a significant number of people, including most economists and other social scientists, believe that the problem of poverty can and should be solved. They also believe that this is a *social* problem: that there is a "culture of poverty," economically based but with many-sided implications for the way of life of millions of people in the United States.

WHAT IS POVERTY?

Curious as it may seem, in a very real sense poverty is a state of mind. Money income, for example, is no criterion unless it is considered in connection with a society's standard of living. Most of us would probably agree that if an individual has barely enough to eat to keep him alive and in reasonably good health, he is poor. By contrast, in many lands, the person who barely manages to survive may think of himself as fortunate.

Poverty is a culturally derived concept, measured in terms of cultural expectations. It is relative to the extent to which people believe they are deprived of the necessities of life. In societies where most of the people are hungry most of the time, a low level of living often is tolerated because it is expected. It is the "only" or the "natural" way to live. When a man suffers no more deprivation than his neighbors, he is apt to accept his lot as inevitable. Outsiders may think that he is miserable, but he may not feel that way. Only when he becomes aware that others fare better, that it is possible for people to live more comfortably, does he become dissatisfied with his own lot.

In an "affluent society" such as the United States, individuals deprived of goods and services enjoyed by most of the people around them are likely to consider themselves disprivileged. A better life is clearly attainable, but they have not attained it. Under these circumstances, individuals are poor if they have considerably less than their proportionate share of the available consumer goods and services.

In 1964, employing this orientation, the United States government was defining poverty in this country in terms of income. A family with an annual income of less than 3,000 dollars lived in poverty, according to this definition, as did unattached individuals with incomes below 1,500 dollars a year.[1] The U. S. Department of Health, Education, and Welfare commented about this standard:

. . . although the goods and services which families in the United States can purchase with incomes of under $3,000 would represent wealth in many places, such incomes represent poverty in the United States. To be acceptable in this country, a level of living must not merely provide some food, but sufficient food; not shelter only, but sound housing; as well as health care, educational opportunities, and other goods and services that are considered essential by the majority of citizens.[2]

Obviously, the 3,000 dollar mark does not always provide a clear-cut criterion for distinguishing poverty-stricken families from those that have relatively adequate incomes. Today, 3,000 dollars will buy little anywhere in the United States, but it comes closer to providing adequately for residents of rural neighborhoods in the Ozarks than it does for families that live in New York City. By 1968 a non-farm family of four earning less than 3,335 dollars annually was considered by the government to be living in poverty.

HOW MUCH POVERTY DO WE HAVE?

How much poverty, as officially defined, is there in the United States? Let us approach this question by first establishing some facts about this country's affluence.

One way of measuring a nation's wealth is according to its *gross national product*, that is, the sum total of all goods and services produced. In 1940, our gross national product stood at 242 billion dollars. By the end of 1966, according to preliminary computation, it had risen to more than 739 billion dollars.[3]

Personal wealth also increased. The median money income of male employed civilians in 1950 was 2,831 dollars annually; in 1965, it was 5,767 dollars. In 1950, female employee civilians had a median money income of 1,599 dollars a year, whereas, in 1965, the figure was 2,845 dollars.[4] In 1950, the median income per year of families with a male head was 3,435 dollars. By 1965, the median family income was 7,235 dollars, representing a very substantial rise.[5]

In the United States of the 1960s, the majority of people live well, enjoy luxuries, and maintain health. After paying for food, shelter, clothing and other essentials, most families have a little more money each year to spend for recreation. We paid out 9.2 billion dollars for recreation in 1947, as against 28.7 billion dollars in 1966.[6] A substantial majority of people have comforts that were not as widespread in earlier decades. In 1960, a total of 91.5 percent of households in the United States had radios; 78.5 percent had phones. In 1967, 93.4 percent of households had television sets, and 78.6 of the households owned one or more cars.[7]

And yet there is poverty in the midst of all this plenty. Statistics on personal income in the United States are often expressed in two kinds of averages, the *mean* and the *median*, but this can be deceptive. If, for example, the mean income of ten people is 10,000 dollars, representing a total of 100,000 dollars, it would be possible for one of them to receive 91,000 dollars and for the others to receive only 1,000 dollars each. Our concern here, of course, is the *distribution* of income, and both mean and median figures disguise the facts of income distribution. This is suggested by the figures for 1963, when the number of families living in poverty with annual incomes under 3,000 dollars was 8.9 million, or an estimated 29.2 million individuals. At the same time, the number of unattached individuals living in poverty, that is, with incomes under 1,500, was 5 million. Thus the total number of people living in poverty in 1963 came to 34.2 million, or between one-fifth and one-sixth of the nation.[8]

In some of its statistics, the United States government differentiates between *poverty* and *deprivation.* The latter is conceived of as a living standard above the poverty level but significantly below that of the majority of persons in the country. Those living in deprivation are considered as being denied that participation in the wealth and well-being of our economic system that they should enjoy. They are not "poor," but they are threatened with poverty in the event of any adverse turn.

Families with incomes below 5,000 dollars but above the 3,000 dollar poverty level and unattached individuals with incomes below 2,500 dollars but above the 1,500 dollar poverty level were by the 1963 definition living in deprivation.[9] In 1963, 8.6 million families in this country, an estimated 30 million individuals, and 1.9 million unattached persons lived in deprivation, a total of approximately 32 million people. Adding these to the number of people living in poverty in the United States in 1963, we have more than 66 million persons, or about 35.5 percent of our population, who lived in either poverty or deprivation in 1963.[10]

However, there has been some change over the years insofar as poverty is concerned. Between 1947 and 1963, the number of families in that category was reduced from 12 million to 8.9 million, but the average annual reduction was less than 0.2 million families, or only about 1.9 percent a year. If the same percentage rate should continue, it would require about forty-five more years beyond 1963 to liquidate family poverty in the United States.[11]

WHO ARE THE POOR?

Having defined poverty and indicated its nature and extent, we now ask: Who are the poor?

Michael Harrington, whose book, *The Other America,* made millions aware for the first time of the existence of persistent poverty in the country, wrote: "In a sense, one might define the contemporary poor . . . as those who, for reasons beyond their control, cannot help themselves. . . . They are born going downward, and most of them stay down."[12]

1. *They are a comparatively undereducated group.* In 1962, almost 52 percent of all the poor were in consumer units (families and unattached individuals) whose heads had eight years or less of education.[13]

2. *They are an underemployed group.* In 1962, about 40 percent were in consumer units whose heads suffered substantial unemployment during the year or were not in the civilian labor force because of inadequate job opportunity.[14]

3. *They live everywhere but are concentrated in certain sections of the country and in centers of big cities.* Almost 44 percent live in the South, which is predominantly rural. In Mississippi, poorest of all states, almost 40 percent of the population lives in poverty. About a third of the Arkansas population falls into that classification. In terms of sheer numbers, however, the poverty population is concentrated in the great cities. They must live near their work, if any, and, besides, color and income barriers make it impossible for them to move into the suburbs.[15]

"Pockets of poverty" exist in areas that have undergone radical economic change. In certain areas of West Virginia, for example, miners once were able to make some sort of a living to maintain their families. But after the veins of coal gave out, a high proportion of the erstwhile miners were thrown into chronic unemployment. Lacking occupational skills that might have enabled them to find work in other parts of the country, they settled down to a life of poverty in their home communities.

4. *Proportionately, more nonwhites than whites have incomes placing them in the poverty category.* In 1965, for instance, 14.4 percent of white families had incomes of less than 3,000 dollars a year. The rate for Negro families was more than twice as high—37.3 percent.[16]

5. *A large number of poor families depend upon a female head for income.* In 1962, almost 29 percent of the poverty-stricken individuals were in consumer units with female heads.[17] Generally, such units have low incomes.

Figure 21.1 summarizes data on the identity of the poor in the United States in 1962. The general pattern of poverty is about the same in 1968.

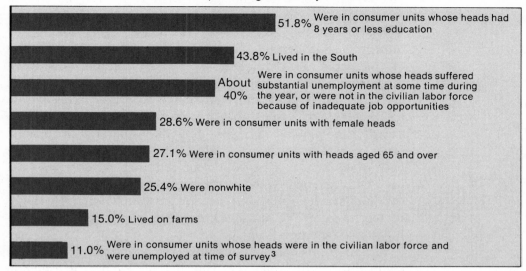

Of all People Living in Poverty[1] in 1962[2]

51.8% Were in consumer units whose heads had 8 years or less education

43.8% Lived in the South

About 40% Were in consumer units whose heads suffered substantial unemployment at some time during the year, or were not in the civilian labor force because of inadequate job opportunities

28.6% Were in consumer units with female heads

27.1% Were in consumer units with heads aged 65 and over

25.4% Were nonwhite

15.0% Lived on farms

11.0% Were in consumer units whose heads were in the civilian labor force and were unemployed at time of survey[3]

[1] All people living in families with incomes under $3,000, plus all unattached individuals with incomes under $1,500.

[2] 1962 used because 1963 data too fragmentary for these comparisons.

[3] This does not take account of those who suffered substantial unemployment at sometime during year, or were not in civilian labor force because of inadequate job opportunities and therefore underestimates connection between unemployment and poverty.

Figure 21.1
Who Live in Poverty in the United States?
Source: Leon H. Keyserling, *Progress or Poverty, The U.S. at the Crossroads* (Washington, D.C.: Conference on Economic Progress, 1964), p. 86.

CONFLICTING VIEWS ON CAUSAL FACTORS RELATED TO POVERTY

Why are people poor? There has been a wide range of views on this subject over the years.

Centuries ago, in Christian countries, it was believed that a man's inability to support himself was a consequence of his sinful behavior. His poverty was the punishment meted out to him by a righteous God.

When England passed from a feudal into an industrial society, it was generally assumed that anyone willing to work could find employment, and that the poor were in that condition because they were lazy and irresponsible. The reigning

Tudors first recognized that not all poor people were poverty-stricken because they preferred idleness to hard work. Although the English Poor Laws enacted in their reign were harsh and restrictive and were primarily intended to serve as standby legislation in the event of a threatened revolt among the hungry masses, certain of these laws, by setting up categories of "paupers," differentiated, at least by inference, between those who would not and those who could not work. Children and the "impotent poor" were to receive more considerate treatment than persons able to work. The impotent poor consisted of individuals who were physically impaired or in some other respect incapable of holding employment. Thus, for the first time, British statutes recognized that poverty was not invariably a consequence of laziness—it might result from conditions beyond the control of the given individual. He might be too immature to support himself or incapable of supporting himself whatever his age.

Although this conception gained force, and certainly by the eighteenth century had very considerable support in England and the United States, there nevertheless remained those who persisted in maintaining that poverty denoted personal shiftlessness and worthlessness.

Those who tended to emphasize the influence of the environment in producing poverty received powerful support from Karl Marx (1818–1883), the German founder of modern socialism and communism. He and his followers argued that poverty was a phenomenon of industrial society that resulted from the exploitation of the masses by the capitalist class, an exploitation that led to an unequal distribution of wealth. Because of this, a minority of individuals became vastly rich at the expense of the vast majority, who were miserably poor by comparison.

Although not a Marxist, Henry George, an American, published a widely read book, *Progress and Poverty*, in 1879, which in some ways was similar to Marxist thinking. Like Marx, George found a causal relationship between the amassing of wealth on the one hand and the creation of poverty on the other. According to his views, as the relatively few individuals gained great wealth, this generated and deepened the poverty of the many.

George's point of view was vigorously attacked. A counterargument was that the free capitalistic system was not entirely evil, even in the early days of the "robber barons." Ruthless though they were in exploiting human and natural resources, those early enterprisers brought economic gain to all, not to themselves alone. The rapid accumulation of private capital in the nineteenth century accelerated the economy, so that more goods and services became available to more people in less time than would have been the case otherwise. All in the society shared the good things of life, the reasoning went, even if they did not share it equally.

However one may evaluate broad, general explanations of poverty, certain direct causal factors seem to be well established insofar as our own contemporay society is concerned: *

1. Rapid changes in the techniques of production and in the kinds of goods and services needed have displaced many workers, producing some poverty.

2. Shifts in centers of production have created economic dislocations and unemployment. Since just prior to World War II, aircraft and other heavy industry plants have sprung up practically overnight in certain cities and regions. The exploration of outer space resulted in a still further concentration of industrial complexes in particular cities. Such concentrations bring a flood of employees from other parts of the nation. Then when such a complex shuts down or moves to another location, employees are left stranded. They must depart the area if they can, accept other types of work if it is available, or remain unemployed.

3. This country has seen a marked decline in the amount of employment available in farming, mining, and lumbering since the turn of the century. As a consequence, depressed areas have developed. After a mine shuts down or a lumbering region is exhausted, a great many of the persons dependent upon those occupations have no other place to turn. As a rule, there is not enough mining or lumbering elsewhere to justify migration. The people remain in "poverty pockets"—poor, frustrated, discouraged.

4. Automation is a phenomenon of our generation, one that demands highly specialized skills. This has meant that persons lacking those skills become progressively unable to find em-

* Part of what follows is adapted from the U. S. Department of Health, Education, and Welfare, *Converging Social Trends, Emerging Social Problems* (Washington, D. C.: U. S. Government Printing Office, 1964), pp. 1–3.

ployment as automation spreads. They become unemployable unless they learn new skills.

5. Automation and other new technologies have been introduced into farming. As a result, a proportion of rural manual laborers are displaced by machinery and by persons who are qualified to work under the automated, highly mechanized methods of agronomy.

6. The shift from a rural to an urban society has brought temporary and in some instances long-standing periods of dislocation for many people. When they migrate to cities, they must learn new ways of responding to others around them in competing for a livelihood. They do not always make the transition successfully, however, and often remain unhappy ruralists in an urban society to which they have failed to adjust.

7. When American Negroes were slaves, they worked mainly at agricultural hand labor in a predominantly agrarian South. After the emancipation, many of the cultural patterns of the slavery era persisted. One result was that the bulk of Negroes, in the South particularly, continued at an economic disadvantage. They lacked equal opportunity with whites to prepare themselves effectively for the then contemporary labor market. This situation persists to this day, although not to the same degree as formerly. The South is becoming, as the North is already, urbanized and industrialized. But, by and large, Negroes are unprepared for urban technological employment. And rural hand labor, as has been noted, is no longer in much demand in the remaining agricultural regions. The manual laborer has been largely replaced by farm machinery.

8. Ability to compete successfully in the labor market is to an important extent dependent upon the educational preparation of prospective employees. In 1963, about 44 percent of the more than 7 million families whose heads had less than eight years of elementary education lived in poverty. This contrasts with the less than 5 percent of the 5.3 million families whose heads had four or more years of college education. Even among the almost 13.5 million families whose heads had four years of high school education, a full 10 percent lived in poverty.[18]

It is legitimate to think of a culture of poverty in this country. Many of our poor are born into it, grow up in it, and become reconciled to it. They think in terms of their day-to-day lives, talk the language of the poor, feel removed from the more affluent population by a wide expanse of social distance. Their scrabble for existence effectively precludes their becoming interested in national or international affairs. They do not think of sending their children to college. True, some do, and these children become educated, break through the barriers, become more or less comfortably situated. But other children grow up expecting little and become resigned to having little as they enter adulthood.

Their lot is aggravated by the fact that they possess little political power in a nation where the majority rules and can bring about social change. Harrington comments:

. . . the poor are politically invisible. It is one of the cruelest ironies of social life in advanced countries that the dispossessed at the bottom of society are unable to speak for themselves. The people of the other America do not, by far and large, belong to unions, to fraternal organizations, or to political parties. They are without lobbies of their own; they put forward no legislative program. As a group, they are atomized. They have no face; they have no voice.[19]

CONFLICTING VIEWS ON SOLUTIONS TO THE PROBLEM OF POVERTY IN THE UNITED STATES

How may we solve the social problem we have been discussing in this chapter? Some commonly held views are:

1. Forget about poverty. If the poor receive no help, they will buckle down, go to work, and support themselves and their dependents.

This view presupposes that all or most poor people are shiftless, are able to earn a livelihood but prefer not to do so. The evidence points the other way. Studies have indicated that the great majority of indigent persons in the United States subscribe to the conception of the ideal American as an individual who can and should be self-supporting. Most of them, if receiving public assistance, go off such relief when circumstances permit, as for instance when an unemployed wage earner finds employment.

2. Destroy the capitalistic system. Establish a socialist state. The resultant redistribution of weath will eliminate poverty.

Aside from the fact that there is no indication that more than a tiny fraction of our population would willingly exchange the present political-economic system for a socialist state, there is the further consideration that poverty has not been eliminated in certain of the countries that have long lived under one or another variant of Marxism.

3. Redistribute wealth to some extent by social legislation. Tax the rich to help the poor. Furnish free education and medical care for those who cannot pay for it. Broaden the base of public assistance programs. Cushion unemployment by benefits to workers who lose their jobs through no fault of their own. Provide for the elderly when they cannot provide for themselves. Since some men have more money than they will ever use, and others need money, the wealth should be shared more equitably.

Particularly since the New Deal era, something has been done—gradually to be sure—along the lines suggested by this argument. The tax structure has been so revised as to place a greater proportion of corporation money than formerly into public coffers for the support of government; hence some of it is being used for aid to indigents who become recipients of public assistance. The income of wealthy individuals is also taxed proportionately higher than in the years prior to the New Deal. Although we have long had free public education, federal and local funds are now being used to furnish free lunches to school children and to transport them to and from school.

Since the inception of the Social Security program in 1935, great numbers of people have been aided. Approximately 19 million receive social insurance benefits to which they are entitled because they or a member of the family contributed to the Old Age, Survivors and Disabilty Insurance (OASDI) fund during their working years. About 7 million individuals receive their main, and often only, income from one of the public assistance categories under the Social Security Act.[20] That enactment also provides unemployment insurance benefits for eligible workers, and over 5 million persons a year have been receiving such benefits.[21] In addition, city and county funds, usually augmented by state monies, are employed to aid persons ineligible for public assistance under Social Security.

During the administration of President Lyndon B. Johnson a War on Poverty program was launched, to get at "hard-core" poverty areas and persons. Medicare, which defrays some of the medical-hospital-nursing expense of the aging population, was finally enacted into law in 1965 after several years of acrimonious debate.

Something has been accomplished, but poverty still exists. What we have done to date has been to alleviate, not eliminate, poverty. The most enthusiastic administrators of the Social Security program have freely admitted that the money granted to families has been meager and insufficient to meet more than the barest essentials of subsistence. People receiving public assistance, whether from federal or local funds or both, continue to live in poverty. Unemployment benefits do not equal what the worker was getting paid. Retired workers or their survivors receive insufficient Social Security payments to bring them above the poverty level if that is their only means of subsistence.

4. Let the nation's poor organize, gain political power. In this manner they can make their voices heard and secure the help they require.

In effect, such a program of action has been in progress for more than a decade. Leaders of the civil rights movement demand not only social and economic opportunities for members of minority groups equal to those available to the dominant majority but a fair share of political power as well. They argue that minority individuals need political muscle for reasons beyond the democratic principle of giving all people a voice in their governance. Political power can serve as a weapon for getting at the underlying bases of discrimination and disprivilege, which in considerable measure are the root sources of poverty.

Hardheaded realists point out that even in a democracy power tends to be manipulated to achieve the aims of the majority, not a minority. If the members of the dominant group are unaware of the existence of poverty, or do not choose to recognize its existence, it is questionable whether even a highly organized and vocal minority can force them to acknowledge that there are poor people in their midst or, if this is the case, that something must be done about the situation. In effect, that is what concerns Michael Harrington, author of *The Other America*. He pleads that all of the inhabitants of this country, not merely the minority, become conscious of and concerned about "the invisible poor." Up to now, says Harrington, ours are the strangest poor in the history of mankind:

They exist within the most powerful and rich society the world has ever known. Their misery has continued while the majority of the nation talked of itself as being "affluent" and worried about neuroses in the suburbs. In this way tens of millions of human beings became invisible. They dropped out of sight and out of mind; they were without their political voice.

Yet this need not be. The means are at hand to fulfill the age-old dream: poverty can now be abolished. How long should we ignore this underdeveloped nation in our midst? How long shall we look the other way while our fellow human beings suffer? How long?[22]

Gunnar Myrdal described the American dilemma, you will recall, as consisting of a belief, on the one hand, in the American creed that all of our people should have equal opportunity to enjoy the fruits of the earth and the practice, on the other hand, of discrimination and inequitable treatment that prevented many of our people from realizing any such opportunity. In time the creed would win out, he held. This generalization may be applied to the social problem of poverty in the United States. If Myrdal is prophetic, the American creed will lead Americans to solve the dilemma by which they are faced. A people who believe in democratic values will not permit part of the people to remain mired in destitution.

· NOTES

1. Leon H. Keyserling, *Progress or Poverty, The U.S. at the Crossroads* (Washington, D. C.: Conference on Economic Progress, 1964), p. 16.
2. U. S. Department of Health, Education, and Welfare, *Converging Social Trends, Emerging Social Problems* (Washington, D. C.: U. S. Government Printing Office, 1964), p. 1.
3. U. S. Bureau of the Census, *Statistical Abstract of the United States, 1967*, 88th annual ed. (Washington, D. C.: U. S. Government Printing Office, 1967), p. 319, Table No. 452.

4. *Ibid.*, p. 337, Table No. 480.
5. *Ibid.*, p. 336, Table No. 478.
6. U. S. Bureau of the Census, *200 Million Americans* (Washington, D. C.: U. S. Government Printing Office, 1967), p. 51.
7. *Ibid.*, p. 38.
8. Keyserling, *op. cit.*, p. 17.
9. *Ibid.*, p. 22.
10. *Ibid.*, pp. 22–23.
11. *Ibid.*, p. 17.
12. Michael Harrington, *The Other America: Poverty in the United States* (Baltimore: Penguin Books, 1963), p. 22.
13. Keyserling, *op. cit.*, p. 83.
14. *Ibid.*
15. U. S. Department of Health, Education, and Welfare, *op. cit.*, pp. 20–22.
16. U. S. Bureau of the Census, *Statistical Abstract of the United States, 1967, op. cit.*, p. 335, Table No. 476.
17. Keyserling, *op. cit.*, pp. 83–84.
18. *Ibid.*, p. 40.
19. Harrington, *op. cit.*, p. 13.
20. U. S. Department of Health, Education, and Welfare, *op. cit.*, p. 25.
21. U. S. Department of Health, Education, and Welfare, *Social Security Programs in the United States* (Washington, D. C.: U. S. Government Printing Office, 1966), p. 61, Table 9.
22. Harrington, *op. cit.*, p. 170.

· SUGGESTIONS FOR FURTHER READING

COLES, ROBERT. "Life in Appalachia—the Case of Hugh McCaslin." *Trans-action*, V, 7 (June 1968), 23–33.
A graphic description of living conditions in one of the most economically depressed areas of the nation.

GLAZER, NONA Y., and CAROL F. CREEDON (eds.). *Children and Poverty, Some Sociological and Psychological Perspectives.* Chicago: Rand McNally, 1968.
The focus is on the impact of poverty on children. See especially Part II, "They Speak for Themselves."

HARRINGTON, MICHAEL. *The Other America: Poverty in the United States.* Baltimore: Penguin Books, 1963.
This book is a powerful exposition of the plight of the poverty-stricken in the United States. Its eloquence and compassion are said to have excited President John F. Kennedy into setting up plans for what later, under the Johnson Administration, became known as the War on Poverty.

HARRIS, T. GEORGE. "Do We Owe People a Living?" *Look*, XXXII, 9 (April 30, 1968), 25–27.
A journalist states the arguments for and against a guaranteed annual income for persons earning below a stipulated sum.

KEYSERLING, LEON H. *Progress or Poverty, The U.S. at the Cross-roads.* Washington, D. C.: Conference on Economic Progress, 1964.

How much poverty is there in the United States? Who are the poor? What shall be done to alleviate poverty in this country? These questions are answered statistically and otherwise in this study backed by the United Auto Workers.

MEISSNER, HANNA H. (ed.). *Poverty in the Affluent Society.* New York: Harper & Row, 1966.

A selection of items on the subject of poverty in this affluent country of ours, from the nineteenth century to the present time.

WADE, ALAN D. "The Guaranteed Minimum Income: Social Work's Challenge and Opportunity." *Social Work,* XII, 1 (January 1967), 94–101.

A social work educator proposes that social workers attack poverty by bringing about the "constructive destruction" of the public assistance program and advocating an action program for a guaranteed minimum income for every family in the United States.

22 OTHER SOCIAL PROBLEMS

We conclude this section of the text with a brief discussion of several additional social problems current in the United States: crime and delinquency, alcoholism and narcotics addiction, the increase in the number of elderly people in our country, and mental illness. There are, of course, many other social problems that concern us, but we cannot discuss all of these.

CRIME & DELINQUENCY AS SOCIAL PROBLEMS

No one will deny that crime and delinquency constitute serious social problems in our society. However, there are differences of opinion as to the number of crimes and delinquencies with which we must cope annually, the causal factors functioning to produce them, and how we may most efficiently prevent, control, and treat crime and delinquency.

THE EXTENT OF CRIME & DELINQUENCY

There is good reason to believe that the United States is one of the most criminal nations in the Western world and that crime in our country has risen fairly steadily, per capita, throughout this century. Uniform Crime Reports, published annually by the United States Department of Justice, shows that during 1966 almost 3¼ million crimes of a nature classified as "serious" by the Federal Bureau of Investigation were known to police of the nation. This represents an 11 percent increase over 1965.[1] On a per capita basis, crime has risen consistently in the past few years, from 1,115.8 per 100,000 residents in 1960, to 1,656.0 per 100,000 in 1966.[2] A breakdown of these data, according to types of crime, appears in Table 22.1.

Official though these statistics are, they are accepted with skepticism in many quarters. It is pointed out that not all police units report crimes in their areas to Washington. Furthermore, law enforcement standards affect a department's statistics. Vigorous enforcement of all laws results in high

TABLE 22.1 · *Serious Crimes Known to Police, 1966*

Offense	Number	Rate per 100,000 inhabitants
Total	3,243,400	1,656.0
Murder	10,920	5.6
Forcible rape	25,330	12.9
Robbery	153,420	78.3
Aggravated assault	231,800	118.4
Burglary	1,370,300	699.6
Larceny $50 and over	894,600	456.8
Auto theft	557,000	284.4

SOURCE: Adapted from *Uniform Crime Reports,* 1966, p. 4.

figures on crimes known to police. If vigilance and enforcement are relaxed, the figures decline, although crime may not. Finally, a great many crimes go unreported, for a variety of reasons unrelated to the efficiency of the police department concerned. Victims of blackmail, for instance, often do not notify police they have been "shaken down." Many individuals are unaware that they have been victimized by crime, as for instance when their property is stolen but they do not miss it. Thousands of items are purloined (or at least they disappear) annually from department stores. Unless there is a likely suspect, management is unlikely to report the disappearance as a theft, particularly if the item concerned is of modest value. There have even been verified instances of murders undetected and unreported for years, with the facts coming out, often by chance, long afterward. How many more remain undetected and unreported forever is speculative.

For these and other reasons it is clear that published, official crime statistics are, at best, conservative estimates of how much crime actually occurs. The question remains of how much there is in addition to what the figures indicate, and here opinion varies widely. Some of it is based upon guesswork and wishful thinking, some on reasonably adequate research. Several studies suggest that the actual number of crimes committed in any year is several times that published in Uniform Crime Reports.

The situation with regard to juvenile delinquency is no more certain. Every indication is that it has increased in the past two decades; that it about doubled between 1948 and 1958; and that the rise continues. It is an increase in rate as well as an absolute increase, that is, the rise in delinquencies is exceeding the increase in child population. Official records indicate that in 1965, as in preceding years, a majority of all arrests for so-called major crimes against property were of persons under 21, as were a substantial minority of arrests for major crimes against the person.[3] We know that over a half million juvenile delinquency cases (excluding traffic offenses) are handled in juvenile courts annually. But, as critics of statistics on this subject point out, we do not really know how many juveniles are adjudicated delinquents in any one year. Again, indications are that the official records are no more than conservative estimates and that a great many delinquencies and delinquents go undetected and unreported. This assumption is reinforced by studies revealing that perhaps 90 percent of all young people have committed at least one act for which they could have been brought into juvenile court. The great majority of these were not so cited.

Another basis for difference of opinion concerning the incidence of delinquency is that the legal definition of delinquent behavior varies by jurisdiction. Moreover, in all states, juvenile court law is so vaguely worded on this score as to allow very wide discretion to a judge in deciding whether a particular child's behavior does or does not constitute delinquency. In most states, a person of juvenile court age is delinquent if he is "incorrigible," or "ungovernable." But what constitutes incorrigibility? What are the specific elements that must be

Figure 22.1
Delinquency or Ingenuity?
Reprinted by permission of Charles
Skiles and *McCall's*.

*"It's a get-the-kids-off-the-street
drive, sir. A quarter will seat some
deserving lad at a soda fountain!"*

present in order that a child be deemed ungovernable? According to one state's law or judicial opinion, the boy shown in Figure 22.1 may be adjudged delinquent for illegal street solicitation. In another jurisdiction he might be considered not delinquent, but an ambitious young man with a salesman's personality. There is a saying in juvenile court circles that "delinquency is what the judge says it is," and this is true to a considerable extent.

As with adult criminality, official policy may produce startling increases or declines in a jurisdiction's juvenile delinquency rate. For instance: Upon assuming office, the mayor of a large city instructed his police chief to abandon the policy whereby all juveniles coming to the attention of law-enforcement officers were routinely scheduled for juvenile court appearances. Every effort was first to be directed to enlisting the services of a social agency willing to help the youngster. Only those who were definitely dangerous or who were unacceptable for social agency care were to be routed to juvenile court. Only this group, then, became "statistics." Within a year, the delinquency rate in that city had fallen by almost 50 percent—on the record.

There is, then, good reason for the existence of conflicting views regarding how much crime and delinquency we have in this country. But we do know that the problem exists, that it is serious, and that it requires remedial action.

"CAUSES" OF CRIME & DELINQUENCY

If you accept the statements of those who claim to know, crime and delinquency are "caused" by:

1 · Too much parental affection during the individual's childhood.
2 · Not enough parental affection during the individual's childhood.
3 · Too much corporal punishment in the home.
4 · Not enough corporal punishment in the home.
5 · Inconsistent corporal punishment in the home.
6 · Underprivileged childhood.
7 · Overprivileged childhood.
8 · Too much education.
9 · Insufficient education.
10 · Absence of religious training.
11 · Overstringent religious training.
12 · Broken homes.
13 · Unbroken homes when they would have been more wholesome if broken by divorce.
14 · Poverty.
15 · Affluence.
16 · Tough police.
17 · Overpermissive police.
18 · Feeblemindedness.
19 · Intellectual brilliance.
20 · Comic books.
21 · Depiction of violence in movies and on TV.

Every one of these "causes" has been advanced at one time or another, by a supposed "expert" before an official body investigating crime and delinquency. Obviously, the persons testifying cannot all have been correct, since so much of the testimony is contradictory. What can we believe?

In the first place, we *know* we have found no cause of crime or delinquency if by cause is meant an *invariant relationship*. A factor, let us say broken homes, would have to be present, without any exception, in every instance where an individual is found to have committed an illegal act. And not a single instance of a broken home must be found among those who have not committed illegal acts. Only then could we properly claim to have a cause of crime or delinquency. We have none.

According to reasonably scientific data we do have some *causal* or *etiological* factors that seem to be *correlated* with crime and delinquency. That is, they appear more frequently, per capita, among the non-law-abiding than in the general population. The inference is that they play some part in producing illegal behavior. Among these are personality disturbances and certain family conditions, neighborhood influences, peer group associations, and economic circumstances.

There is no evidence, by the way, that reading comic books or viewing depictions of violence will *create* a desire to commit crime or a delinquent act. It may *trigger* such an act in a person already predisposed to the behavior in question. The lady who makes the comment in Figure 22.2 seems to place more importance on the reading of comic books than do most criminologists.

Several sociologists have attempted to formulate theories that would explain all illegal behavior. They have not fully succeeded, but some of their conceptions are provocative and warrant comment.

One influential formulation is sociologist Edwin H. Sutherland's *theory of differential association,* the substance of which is that criminal behavior, like all behavior, is learned in association with people and that a person becomes delinquent because, in his social environment, there is an excess of definitions favorable to violation of law over definitions unfavorable to violation of law. The youngster who associates more frequently with persons who are law-abiding than those who are not learns behavior favorable to observance of law, all else being equal. Sutherland himself recognized the shortcomings of his theory and hoped others would improve upon it. As it stands, it fails to explain all illegal behavior, as for example compulsive crimes such as kleptomania (stealing out of a compulsion to steal, rather than a need for the object stolen). But it does take a realistic view of how many, if not most, criminal patterns are formed.

Another interesting development in criminological theory has to do with social class and delinquency. Albert K. Cohen, James F. Short, Jr., and others have postulated that lower-class

Figure 22.2
The Comics
Bugaboo

Reprinted by permission
of Stan Hunt and
Saturday Review.

"Well, at least they aren't reading comic books!"

boys join gangs and commit delinquent acts as a consequence
of frustration when they attempt to meet the standard set by
middle-class values. The working-class boy grows up in a
middle-class society and is evaluated by a middle-class measuring rod in school and elsewhere. To an extent, he shares in
the evaluation of himself as below standard, since he has
internalized some of the middle-class culture to which he is
exposed. He wants to achieve, to be a "success" in middle-class
terms. But he is unable to achieve these ends by legitimate
means. He becomes hostile, joins a gang of working-class boys,
and aggressively violates middle-class standards in peer associations constituting a "delinquent subculture."

The "delinquent subculture," according to Cohen and Short,
is largely nonutilitarian, that is, the boys do not behave as
they do in order to get something tangible they feel they need,
such as property. They act out of situational frustration. This
joint action provides an alternative status system. Unable to
achieve status in the middle class, the boys form their own
value system and gain status in their subculture by attacking
middle-class values, the source of their status frustration.

Walter B. Miller presents another social class theory on this
subject in disagreement with the one just discussed. Working-
class boys in gangs are not acting symbolically out of hostility

toward the middle class. They do not behave as they do from frustration over being unable to achieve status by middle-class standards. They are actually behaving in accordance with the value system of the working class. Focal concerns of this class, says Miller, are *trouble, toughness, smartness, excitement, fate,* and *autonomy.* Trouble is what life gets one into. Toughness refers to physical prowess. Smartness means the ability to outwit and manipulate people. Excitement is engaging in activities that help one forget the dullness of most of one's waking hours. Fate refers to the conviction that one's life is determined by factors beyond his control, hence why worry or be inordinately cautious? Gamble, drink, have fun when you can. Things either will or will not break right for you, no matter what you do or do not do. Autonomy is concern over the amount, source, and severity of control by others.

SOLUTIONS OF THE PROBLEM OF CRIME & DELINQUENCY

If we know little about causal factors related to crime and delinquency, we know still less about methods of preventing, controlling, and treating these phenomena. And, of course, there are widely divergent views on the subject.

Agencies established to attack the problem include police, courts, prisons, reformatories, and, to a lesser extent, private social work organizations and institutions.

Many laymen as well as penologists hold that the police are all too often corrupt or incompetent. Others insist that the police forces of the United States, taken as a group, rank with the best in the Western world.

Courts are praised by some for their dispassionate adherence to "the rule of law," criticized by others as unscientific, inhumane, and failing to match dispositions to the needs of the community and the individual defendant.

A great many people, including wardens and superintendents themselves, declare that prisons and reformatories are abysmal failures, that they turn prisoners back into the community worse than they were when they came in. Countering this view is one that argues that places of incarceration *need* to be unpleasant, or the prisoner will not repent his past life. In the interest of public safety, this argument runs, the thing to do with offenders is to "lock them up, throw the key away if you can, and in any event treat them rough, so they will learn to behave."

Private social work agencies and institutions are highly regarded by some observers, considered far superior to their public counterparts in the areas of prevention and treatment. Investigators have pointed out, on the other hand, that although some benefits do derive from these sources, such results as are measurable and have been measured indicate that we do not know enough as yet to be able to bring about basic changes in personality, attitudes, and behavior with any degree of consistency.

Programs include psychological-psychiatric care, social work, probation, parole, and community delinquency prevention activity. Here, too, opinion runs the gamut, some claiming great accomplishments, some modest achievements, some no results.

It is a fact that our knowledge and professional skills have been inadequate to the task, at least to a degree. Police do a fairly effective job of controlling crime and delinquency. They do solve cases and make arrests. But in 1966, only 24.3 percent of serious crimes known to police were solved by an arrest, which does not necessarily mean subsequent conviction.[4] Despite spectacular advances in criminalistics and other laboratory techniques for detection and apprehension, crime continues to increase.

Courts do a reasonably efficient job of convicting the guilty and freeing the innocent, but mistakes are made, the guilty sometime go free, and the innocent, on comparatively rare occasions, go to prison or are executed. The conviction of defendants, however, does not sufficiently deter other people from committing like crimes. Sentences are fixed by law, and although judges are allowed some discretion within established maximum and minimum limits, the sentence in a given case is likely to be based more on what is prescribed for the crime committed than on considerations of public safety and the needs of the individual offender if he is to become rehabilitated.

Most peno-correctional institutions are indeed of a very low order; they do turn many offenders back to society unimproved and indeed more thoroughly schooled in crime itself. But some institutions are better conducted than others. And the personnel in some probably does help a few inmates reach the conclusion that they would like to remain law-abiding when they come out.

The evidence is that, on the whole, private agencies and institutions accomplish more in the area of prevention and treatment than do those in the public realm, but results thus far have not been outstanding.

All of the prevention and treatment programs have proven only modestly effective, at best. Psychological and psychiatric treatment of the offender group is generally acknowledged to have had discouraging results. Although about 70 percent of individuals on probation and parole do not revert to crime or delinquency and do not violate the conditions of their supervision in other serious respects while under care, there has been very little scientific evidence indicating that it is the treatment accorded the probationers and parolees that accounts for this. It may or may not be. In the field of prevention, community approaches of many kinds have been launched; most have accomplished but little; and it becomes more evident every year that we know less about prevention than we do about control or treatment, even though our knowledge in those areas leaves much to be desired.

Thus we have barely scratched the surface in the prevention, control, and treatment of crime and delinquency. We must confess that up to now we have not solved this social problem.

ALCOHOLISM

A completely satisfactory definition of the alcoholic person has not yet been formulated. Some people drink every day, yet are not alcoholics. Some who go on two- or three-day binges now and then are not necessarily alcoholics or on the way to becoming alcoholics. There is a blurred, intermediate stage somewhere along the way between the "social drinker" and the alcoholic. In that stage certain individuals may be classified as "problem drinkers." Their consumption of alcoholic beverages is too much for their own good. They create problems for themselves and others. Just when a problem drinker crosses the brink and becomes an alcoholic is difficult to determine and define.

We do know this: An alcoholic, when he reaches that stage, is an individual who has lost control over the use of alcohol;

it controls him. He must have it in order to feel comfortable, and after he has had it he loses the ability to comprehend whether he is comfortable or miserable. A drink becomes an overriding necessity, and he will do just about anything to get it when he feels he needs it. When he has had his first drink, his will power diminishes: he often continues to drink until he is comatose.

We do not know exactly how many alcoholics there are in the United States, but it has been estimated that approximately 70 million Americans drink and that about 4.7 million of these are alcoholics.

We know little about causal factors connected with alcoholism. The alcoholic has been termed an "escapist," a psychopath, and an emotionally immature person by various investigators. More recently, the conviction has emerged that there is no one alcoholic personality type and no one set of circumstances that establishes the alcoholic pattern of behavior. However, we do know of some personality and environmental features associated, to some degree at least, with alcoholism.

Seldon D. Bacon[5] classified four-fifths of some 1,200 alcoholics he studied as maladjusted in marriage. Albert D. Ullman[6] compared the first drinking experiences of addictive drinkers with those of so-called normal drinkers. He found that the confirmed alcoholic began drinking later in life; more often became intoxicated from the very beginning of his drinking habit; drank away from home; and had parents who were in disagreement over whether one should or should not use alcohol.

Investigators have noted that alcoholism rates vary by ethnic groups. Why should this be? In a study of the initial drinking experiences of college students, Ullman[7] found evidence supporting the hypothesis that the variations in alcoholism rates are associated with differential amounts of ambivalence in particular settings toward drinking. In ethnic groups in which drinking is generally considered immoral, the parents tend to discourage children from partaking of alcoholic beverages. In such groups, as for instance among Irish and English Americans, the children have relatively high rates of alcoholism. In other ethnic groups the consumption of alcohol is scarcely a moral issue and may in fact be a part of daily social life and of religious and cultural ceremonials.

Thus, adult Italian Americans allow their children to drink moderate amounts at meals at an early age. Jews, parents and offspring alike, partake lightly of wine as part of religious ceremonials on certain occasions. Children from these ethnic backgrounds exhibit relatively low alcoholism rates.

Some psychologists interpret findings such as Ullman's as meaning that where drinking is frowned upon by the parent generation, the children have guilt feelings when they do drink, and this, for reasons not fully clarified, leads to a loss of control over alcoholic intake. A more sociological interpretation, with which Ullman seems to agree, is that the very fact that alcoholic intake is forbidden, as "wicked," makes it a fascinating prospect for young people. Moreover, drinking becomes identified with a shift in status. By partaking, the adolescent becomes a "man" in the eyes of his peers.

Both of these formulations merit consideration, but neither explains why, in any one ethnic group, some drinkers do and some do not become alcoholic.

In another of Bacon's contributions to this field of inquiry,[8] he relates alcoholism to the complexity of society. In such an environment, he says, social adjustment is comparatively difficult to achieve, creating a need to escape reality.

. . . stratification, individualism, ignorance, intergroup and internal competition, all engendered by the complexity of society, enhance the function of alcohol. Complexity results in need for greater integrative functioning; relaxation of tension, uncertainty, and suspicion is necessary for this function; alcohol has been found useful in its accomplishment.[9]

This characteristic of our culture, Bacon asserts, creates numerous personal problems of adjustment, involving tensions, insecurity, anxiety, and guilt. The feelings are present because the individual wants to have a favorable conception of himself, despite the difficulties he encounters in competing with and relating to others. He wants to feel secure, and to achieve his goals in life, despite the roadblocks in his way. He wants to gain and hold the respect and affection of others. In all of these areas, alcohol reduces inhibitions and anxiety. It allows the person to relax. "It has taken away the power from agencies of control which could once be efficiently used."[10]

An investigation undertaken by the Research Council on

Problems of Alcohol at Yale University[11] deals with the process of becoming an alcoholic. It was discovered that the future alcoholic tended to pass through a series of phases.

About 90 percent of the 98 subjects interviewed began their drinking with others; solitary drinking was uncommon at this stage, with only 10 percent engaging in it. At about age 25, the subjects began to have blackouts. They would awaken the morning after a "party" and have no recollection of what took place the night before. A little later, they might begin showing dependence on drink by sneaking it. As host, a subject might toss one off in the kitchen as he prepared highballs for guests, making himself another to imbibe publicly. Perhaps two years later, the alcoholics began losing control—they drank heavily, beyond their capacity to maintain sobriety. About two years beyond that, they began rationalizing their excessive drinking. The excuses were unreal. Approximately a year later, further evidence of loss of control appeared. The drinker began tossing off "a quick one," first thing in the morning, in order to "get going." This was a sign that drinking was becoming a compulsion.

After a few years, the drinker began going on "benders," being absent from home and work for days at a time. His irresponsible behavior evoked rebuffs and eventually rejection by his group, and he was driven into isolation. (This is when solitary drinking is apt to become a fixed habit.) The drinker brooded, created pseudo-problems, and centered all his thoughts on himself. Antisocial acts were likely to develop in close connection with solitary drinking. The alcoholic visualized his aggressive behavior as in part a compensation for the humiliations he had suffered or imagined he had suffered. Periodically, remorse set in and he decided to "go on the wagon." When he did so, he "fell off."

About two years after the beginning of the "benders," the alcoholic developed unreasonable resentments and an exaggerated sense of self-importance. Remorse was rejected. What he did was right, as he saw it. He hid bottles of liquor in the most unlikely places, so that he would always have a drink, even should someone find and destroy the bottle he had been working on. Tremors and indefinable fears developed. But intoxication had become a goal in itself and not a means to a good time. The alcoholic's egocentrism had become dominant.

After three years of excessive drinking, physical disease

might result. The alcoholic would perhaps seek medical aid or the consolation of religion.

It usually took five years for him to admit he was defeated by alcohol, and two more years to bring him to what he considered his "lowest point." Then he might seek help in an organization such as Alcoholics Anonymous. On the average, it took from twelve to eighteen years to pass from the beginning of "the benders" to "the lowest point."

The alcoholic is a problem in society, costing others much time, worry, misery, and money. What can be done for and about him? Diverse answers to the question have been advanced.

Jailing the alcoholic is the most common "treatment" program available to him. But it does practically no good. Chronic drunks go in and out of jails regularly and repetitively. Two million arrests in 1965—one of every three arrests in the United States—were for the offense of public drunkenness.[12] (Not all of these, of course, involved alcoholics.) A study of six chronic offenders, conducted in 1957, found that they had been arrested for drunkenness a total of 1,409 times and had served a total of 125 years in penal institutions.[13]

Prohibition, the drying up of the liquor supply, produces equivocal results, even assuming the law is fully enforced. During the years the United States was "dry," there was a significant decrease in alcohol consumption. The reduction was chiefly in beer drinking, however. Although there was a very considerable drop in arrests for drunkenness, deaths from acute alcoholism rose nearly fourfold.[14]

Psychiatric help has proven of little practical value, often because it is too expensive for the alcoholic or because he does not make himself accessible to treatment. He fights it. The attitude of the alcoholic is the all-important consideration. He must want to be helped, else he cannot be helped.

The Antibuse, conditioned-reflex treatment has been disappointing on the whole. Along with an alcoholic drink, the patient is given a drug that will cause violent nausea and vomiting. He has his drink, and immediately begins to retch and vomit. Theoretically, after a series of treatments he will avoid alcohol because the very thought of it evokes unpleasant sensations. And some therapists claim the treatment produces just such effects, and that up to 50 percent of patients have been cured of drinking. Skeptics question the figure and doubt that the asserted recoveries are permanent, since the treatment does not get at the causes of the drinking.

There have been encouraging reports on another "aversion" drug, tetraethylthiuram disulfide, that works much the way Antibuse does. However, some investigators believe that as many as 70 percent of those who have the treatment eventually go back to drinking.

A concerted attack on alcoholism has been conducted by the Yale Plan Clinics, the first of which was established in New Haven in 1944. The clinics are public, open to all, and staffed by psychiatrists, psychologists, physicians, and psychiatric social workers. The team method prevails, and the treatment includes attempting to get at and eliminate the causes of a patient's alcoholism. Not much that is conclusive can be reported on the program.

Probably no attack on the problem has been as effective as the program of Alcoholics Anonymous, founded in 1934 by two alcoholics who wanted to break themselves of the drinking habit. A nonprofit organization, entirely devoid of any professional leadership, AA depends upon what is actually group therapy conducted by alcoholics for the mutual benefit of alcoholics. They meet regularly and discuss their problem but do not seek to discover the underlying causes of their difficulty. All they must do is stop drinking for a minute, then an hour, then a day at a time. Once they have regained enough sobriety to understand what is going on, they work on their Twelve-Step Program, which begins with the admission that the particular individual is powerless over alcohol and ends with the willingness to help any and all alcoholics who seek help. The theory is that an alcoholic is never cured, that he can only stop drinking. Should he ever take another drink, he would immediately revert to the condition he was in before "going on the program."

Alcoholics Anonymous is a primary group for the alcoholic who stays with it. In it, he cannot rationalize his drinking, lie about it, alibi out of it, because the others will not permit it. They have "been there," too, and they know all the evasions, the self-deceptions, and the self-justifications common to the alcoholic.

AA believes that about 75 percent of its members stop drinking permanently. To reach that figure, they deduct the 90 percent who come once or twice then drop out. Three-fourths of the remainder do "dry out," according to the estimates. Some do so immediately and permanently, others after a slip or two. Some members of AA have been "on the program" and sober since joining the organization when it was founded in 1934, a period of more than thirty years.

This program has earned the respect of professional therapists throughout the world. AA groups have been formed in many countries. Psychiatrists very often urge alcoholic patients whom they are treating to attend AA meetings at the same time.

DRUG USE

Certain drugs have serious adverse social and physical effects on human beings. On this score there is little difference of opinion in this country. Some of the drugs are *addictive*, with the user developing a bodily need for them and experiencing discomfort and pain if the drug is not available. Other drugs are *habituating*. Although no organic body need develops with continued use, there is a psychological attraction toward the drug and a tendency to keep using it for that reason. Still other drugs are *not addictive and rarely habituating* but can result in serious and sometime permanent harm to the user nevertheless.

ADDICTIVE DRUGS

The continued use of certain narcotic drugs leads to addiction, a state in which the individual concerned has lost the power to control his intake of that narcotic and uses it to his own and society's detriment. Drug addiction is widely defined as a social problem in the United States, very few persons having publicly expressed themselves to the contrary. In addition to the effects upon users, addiction involves other problems: an illicit drug traffic of international proportions; an organized criminal underworld that carries on the traffic; the cost of law enforcement in combating it; the expenditure of millions of dollars a year for the treatment of addicts. Users often become narcotics peddlers as a means of supporting their own habit. They steal in order to buy drugs, and some burglarize or rob pharmacies as a means of obtaining narcotics. Moreover, a number of physicians have become criminal, by definition, as a consequence of writing illegal prescriptions for narcotics. Thousands of families of addicts are forced to apply for public assistance when former wage earners within the group become addicted. Public officials have been corrupted by the racket underworld, bribed to close their eyes to the drug traffic. These are a few of the serious concomitants of the illegal use of addictive drugs.

Heroin is the most commonly used addictive narcotic drug in this country. We can only guess at the number of users. Estimates of the U. S. Bureau of Narcotics would indicate that there are approximately 45,000 to 50,000 active narcotics addicts in the country at any one time. This number is disputed by some, who allege that the Bureau of Narcotics consistently exaggerates the size of the problem. We do know that in any year there are over 30,000 arrests for violation of narcotic drug laws recorded in Uniform Crime Reports (excluding arrests under federal law). Even if the Bureau of Narcotics estimates are exaggerated, the fact remains that an undetermined number of drug addicts go undetected in a given year, and that there are an equally undetermined number of violations of narcotic drug laws, over and above the 30,000 a year officially recorded. Addictive drugs have the following effects on repeated users:

1. *Tolerance for the drug develops.* The user gets less and less of a "jolt" from a given dosage, so he must take progressively larger amounts in order to meet his compelling psychological need.

2. *Physical dependence develops.* Unless the addict gets his "fix" (drug dose), he becomes physically ill and in great pain. When the effects of his last fix begin to diminish, he goes into panic and tries desperately to obtain the narcotic before the pain becomes unbearable.

Why do some people turn to addictive drugs? Some develop the need after morphine has been administered to them for medical or surgical reasons. About 5 percent of addicts admitted to the federal hospital at Lexington, Kentucky, are believed to have formed their habit in this manner. But in the majority of cases addiction is not a consequence of medical administration of drugs. We are not sure why these people become addicts. We can say about them what we say about alcoholics—that they are not all of one personality type, that some may be neurotic, some psychopathic, but that the use of these terms with respect to addicts explains little.

Like alcoholics, drug addicts have been termed "escapists," individuals running away from reality and the troublesome problems of everyday life. But we are all escapists in some measure. We all need, and find, some form of escape at times, whether it be socially acceptable or not. One man overeats, another is a heavy drinker. One person finds his escape in fishing, another in dancing, still another in suicide. We understand some of the conditions that lead human beings to want to escape, physically or otherwise, but we do not know why Bill escapes by attending a movie while Jim does so by injecting heroin into his vein.

As to what to do about the drug traffic and its consequences for the addict, we again are not entirely certain, nor are we in complete agreement. There is pretty general consensus, it would seem, that we must have more effective law enforcement to curb the traffic in narcotic drugs. For the addict, psychological-psychiatric therapy has been largely disappointing, but it remains one treatment approach. When experimental clinics have been opened to issue restricted doses of drugs to certified addicts, in order to keep them going and able to maintain themselves while at the same time holding their required dosage steady, the program has been unsuccessful, according to most informed observers. The users did not avail themselves of the psychiatric therapy that was offered along with the drugs, and very often they went into the black market for additional supplies of narcotics to supplement what they received in the clinic. In England, where private physicians are authorized by law to prescribe narcotics for therapeutic and sustaining reasons, the results have been discouraging, according to a government report made in 1966. Physicians were found to be either careless or avaricious, writing prescriptions for fees even when the narcotic appeared to be contraindicated. Addiction increased, as did the sale of narcotics on the black market.

Narcotics Anonymous, which is patterned on Alcoholics Anonymous, appears to have been comparatively successful, although far from showing the results that AA claims for its alcoholics. Synanon, also based in considerable degree on the AA program, additionally provides that the addict live in a therapeutic community with other addicts, some no longer using drugs, some still fighting the temptation to use them. Synanon has been in operation for too short a period to allow for a definitive evaluation of results.

HABITUATING DRUGS

In terms of dollar value, there is a lesser market for habituating than for addicting drugs, but what market there is is substantial and growing, the trade running into millions of dollars annually. Although the traffic in habituating drugs is not as global as the traffic in heroin and its derivatives, it brings in its wake many of the same social problems.

Marijuana is an habituating drug that is very popular in the United States and is becoming so in many other countries in the West. Every indication up to now has been that smoking the weed does not set up a constitutional body demand for more. However, very recently some tentative research findings have suggested that possibly very heavy and long-term use of marijuana may eventually result in a physical craving for the drug. Whether this eventually proves true or not, marijuana does establish a psychological dependence in many of those who smoke it. They believe that they enjoy being under its influence and return to it for that reason.

In the light of what we do and do not currently know about the properties of marijuana, it must be considered at least potentially dangerous in the individual user's instance, both for its direct and indirect effects. We may before long confirm that it does lead to addiction in some people. There is also some reason to believe that it produces certain effects in constant users, such as memory loss, an inability to concentrate, and tremors. There is also the fact that many heroin addicts have testified that they started "chippying around" on marijuana, only to "move up to" heroin, since this was expected in their circles, the marijuana user being considered "sissy."

On this last score, it has recently begun to appear that the pattern of moving from marijuana to heroin use is not as common as formerly, at least in some groups. There remain those who conform to this pattern, but additionally, a new marijuana subculture has emerged. Young, often well-educated individuals of the middle classes are being introduced to marijuana by their peers. Thereafter they partake of it for pleasure and sociability, usually in the company of friends. There is reason to believe that this type of marijuana user is not made to feel that he must "move up to" heroin and that he does not commonly make the transition. Within his subculture it is not deemed "sissy" to stay with marijuana, and it may be considered dangerous and foolish to go on a heroin regimen.

NONADDICTIVE, RARELY HABITUATING DRUGS

Most recently, young people, in particular, have been experimenting with such drugs as mescaline, peyote, and LSD, which are nonaddictive and are said to be not commonly habituating (although there are some indications that a proportion of users do become habituated to the extent of trying a given drug more than once). These are so-called consciousness-expanding or psychedelic (mind-manifesting) chemical agents, and they can be extremely dangerous when administered under other than carefully controlled medical auspices. They belong with the hallucinogens, being powerful alkaloids that show promise of becoming useful in the investigation and treatment of mental illness. The danger lies in their administration for other than medical purposes by other than medical practitioners or scientific research teams. For example, a patient must be prepared for LSD in advance; must take it under carefully planned environmental conditions in exactly the proper dosage. The drug produces harmful effects in certain types of patient, even when medically administered. Neurotics, for instance, seem to react adversely. So do near-psychotics and the emotionally immature who are under stress.

When self-administered, the drug may kill or cause permanent brain damage. It has, for example, sent a number of young people to mental hospitals.

Although in the past the main emphasis has been on curbing the sale and use of the addicting narcotics, law enforcement agencies are more recently becoming concerned over the illicit market in other types as well. Here, opinion differs as to whether law enforcement in and of itself is a realistic response to the social problem in question. Critics point out that past experience suggests that writing laws and punishing violators will not go far toward solving the problem of harmful drug use. Critics of the critics respond that tough laws and severe penalties for their violation are deterrents to continued manufacture, sale, and use of drugs. Whichever argument deserves greater credence, there is still another to which most people would probably subscribe. A basic approach to the solution of the problem would call for learning more than we now know about what draws people to drugs; what family and other social conditions are conducive to the development of a pattern of drug use; and what can be done to strengthen people psychologically so that they will not feel they want to resort to the intake of drugs.

PROBLEMS CONNECTED WITH THE ELDERLY

Thoughtful observers agree that aging has become a social problem in our society, where once this was not the case. Older people present certain characteristic problems, and there are more elderly persons in our midst today, proportionate to the overall population, than there were a half-century ago. This is largely a consequence of improved medicine, sanitation, and nutrition. There are fewer deaths shortly after birth, and those who survive the first year live longer than people did formerly.

Consider these impressive figures: At birth, white males born in 1900 had a life expectancy of 48 years. White males born in 1965 could expect to reach the age of 67.6 years. White females born in 1900 had a life expectancy of 51 years, whereas those born in 1965 could be expected to reach the age of 74.7 years. The trend among Negroes is even more marked. Male Negroes born in 1900 had a life expectancy of only 32.5 years. The life expectancy of those born in 1965 was almost twice that—61 years. Negro females born in 1900 had a life expectancy of 35 years. Those born in 1965 could expect to live to age 67.[15]

The fact that we live longer than in earlier years results in figures such as these: In 1900, the United States had approximately 3 million people, 4.1 percent of the population, who were 65 years of age or older. In 1966, the over-65 population numbered 18½ million,[16] representing some 9 percent of the total population, more than double the proportion in 1900.

To the degree that elderly people present special problems in our society, those problems are likely to become accentuated with the passage of more time. During the next twenty years our older population is expected to increase almost 40 percent, to 25 million. It will grow to over 2 million in each of two states, California and New York, if present trends continue. Five states—Florida, Illinois, Ohio, Pennsylvania, and Texas—will have one million each by the end of the next twenty years.[17]

Problems result from another characteristic of the elderly population. Women tend to outlive men, as the figures cited above indicate. There are about 129 older women for every 100 older men in the country.[18] Most of the elderly men are married, but most of the elderly women are widows. There are almost four times as many widows as widowers.[19] Remarriage among older persons is not uncommon, hence the disproportion between widows and widowers is significant. There are at least 35,000 marriages a year in which the bride, the groom, or both are 65 or over, and this number is increasing, whereas the number of all marriages has shown a downward trend.[20]

We have spoken of "elderly," "aging," and "older" people. When does a person begin to age? Aging commences immediately after conception and continues throughout the life of the individual. At what point, then, is it proper to say a person is "old" or "aged"? There is no precise formula for computing this. There is no fixed age at which we can say, in every instance, "This person is old." In certain respects, an individual is as old as he feels. At 70, some men and women are more active physically and mentally than others at 40. The ages, 60 and 65, so often associated in our minds with the concept of *aged,* took on that meaning principally because these were compulsory retirement ages in many industrial pension plans.

But if in some respects a man is only as old as he feels psychologically, the fact remains that, physically, aging is an inevitable, irreversible process, although the rate of that process varies by individual to some extent. On this basis we can roughly delineate the aging person as one who is considered in his society to be past his physical prime.

HEALTH PROBLEMS OF THE AGING POPULATION

This brings us to a consideration of the health problems of the aging population. As we indicated, although physical changes take place progressively as one gets older, the rate of these changes varies widely by individual. Some physical degeneration is, however, inevitable if a person lives long enough.

Among biological changes that accompany aging are:

1 · The lenses of the eye begin to lose elasticity sometime before age 15.
2 · Hearing begins to decline at about age 20.
3 · Muscular strength tends to weaken after age 25; bones become brittle and cartilage hardens sometime after age 30.
4 · The sense of taste begins to weaken at about age 50, and the sense of smell begins failing somewhere around age 60.
5 · As a person enters and proceeds through what is roughly defined as middle age, the body begins to take on an increased amount of fat and there is a decrease in oxygen utilization. The excretion of hormones, especially by sex and adrenal glands, is lower.

However, certain abilities continue unimpaired to advanced ages, and many even increase with age, as for instance, judgment and accuracy of comprehension; endurance (which increases through about age 45); and wisdom in general. Samuel Johnson once said: "As a man advances in life he gets what is better than admiration—judgment to estimate things at their own value."

Contrary to what many believe, serious mental impairment is not an inevitable accompaniment of aging. Many of history's foremost thinkers, artists, composers, scientists, and statesmen made their major contributions after they were 60 and even 70.

Living to a ripe old age does increase the statistical chance that one will contract a chronic illness. Almost four-fifths of our population age 65 and over are afflicted with one or more chronic ailments, as compared with less than two-fifths of persons under 65.[21] Persons 65 and over averaged 6.8 visits to doctors annually, compared with 4.8 for those under 65, according to a recent National Health Survey.[22] One out of six older persons enters a hospital each year, and the average hospital stay is two weeks, twice as long as the average stay for younger persons. The hospital bill of older individuals runs about twice as large as the bill of younger people.[23]

Approximately 1 percent of people 65 and over are in mental hospitals. Although older persons constitute a little over 9 percent of the total population, they constitute 27 percent of first admissions to public mental hospitals. This rate is more than 2½ times the rate for younger people.[24]

INCOME & EMPLOYMENT
PROBLEMS OF THE ELDERLY

A major problem of the older person is loss of income. Many employers prefer younger workers, and some will not hire a person above a given age, even though they have long-time employees who are older. The unhappy scene in Figure 22.3 is a fair depiction of the business-industrial climate today.

In those occupations where age is a factor in hiring, the most common upper limit for men is 45. In some occupations, such as police, probation, and parole work, the maximum age may be as low as 30 or 35. A major airline ran an advertisement for flight officers in which the maximum age for applicants was set at 29, although it did add that "exceptionally well qualified applicants through age 35 may be considered."[25]

James R. Morris sent questionnaires to 300 of the largest firms in the United States, inquiring about their employment practices.[26] Fifty-one percent responded, and 14 percent of the firms reported that they did not generally hire male hourly workers past the age of 45 (or lower in some instances); 22 percent applied these limits to male salaried workers. The crucial barrier seemed to be age 50—37 percent of the employers did not hire male hourly workers beyond that age, and 40 percent did not hire salaried male workers beyond age 50. Only 6 percent of the firms had attempted any study of the relation of age at hiring to subsequent job performance.

How do employers explain age discrimination policies in taking on employees? The U.S. Bureau of Employment Security explored this question,[27] and received the following explanations:

1 · Older workers are not as efficient as younger workers. They are unable to maintain production standards.
2 · Older workers cannot meet the physical requirements set by the firm. They lack strength, stamina, endurance.
3 · Older workers are set in their ways. They cannot make necessary adjustments to a new work situation.
4 · Older persons in a work force increase insurance and pension costs.
5 · Older workers are above the compulsory retirement age set by the firm or too close to it to justify taking them on.
6 · Company policy is to hire younger persons, and there is a reluctance to mix age groups.

Figure 22.3
A "Social Problem"
Reprinted by permission of Mrs.
H. T. Webster.

7 · Older workers are too difficult to train for new jobs. They do not catch on fast enough.

8 · The absentee rate due to illness and accident is higher for older than for younger workers.

9 · The policy is to promote from the ranks, within the firm— older workers would not fit in with this policy. It would be unfair to those already on jobs to bring older employees in at a high level, because of their long experience. It would be equally unfair to experienced older applicants to bring them in at the lower levels.

Some of these arguments cannot be gainsaid, as for instance item 4 above. As to some of the others, investigation discloses there is much misconception regarding what older persons can and cannot do. Let us examine the evidence.

1. Regarding maintenance of production standards, these differ according to job. And the elderly are a heterogeneous group insofar as their individual capacities are concerned. If we considered all workers over 50, we would find them as variable in productive capacity as workers under 50.

2. Concerning physical strength, stamina and endurance, the demands of different jobs are so varied that it is untenable to make general statements in this connection. Ability to per-

form heavy labor does decline with advancing age, but the decline tends to be gradual. In jobs demanding less in the way of physical labor, older employees frequently perform as well as, or better than, younger workers.

3. Older workers show up very well indeed in statistics on absenteeism. Employees 45 years of age and over have better safety records than younger workers, according to a study by the U.S. Bureau of Labor Statistics.[28] The highest rate of non-disabling injuries was found to be not among older workers but in the 25 to 29 year category. Rates *decreased* with age, reaching the lowest point in the age 70 to 74 category.

In absenteeism for all reasons, older workers have a better record than younger employees. However, a selective factor operates to an extent. The elderly person who is in poor health frequently drops out of the labor force entirely, leaving the more vigorous individuals still in employment. Those older folk who do continue to work have very good attendance records.

4. There is some truth to the assertion that older workers tend to be set in their ways. They *tend* to be. Again, there is considerable variation with regard to this.

5. No acceptable evidence sustains the belief that intermingling older and younger workers decreases efficiency. If each employee has the ability to perform his particular function, the age factor probably affects efficiency very little, if at all.

6. To some extent older workers find it difficult to learn new, complex jobs. Again, there are individual differences, and any broad generalization applied to all workers above a given age would be untenable.

Although there has been a trend toward dropping older persons from the labor force, they still comprise a sizable portion of it. Of all males employed in September 1965, 37 percent were 45 or above. Of all females then employed, 39 percent were 45 or over.[29] But not every older person who wants to work can find employment. Unemployment records for recent years have shown that one out of every thirty persons 65 and above who is in the labor force is unemployed. And large proportions are in low-paid employment.[30]

Through unemployment and other sources, about 350,000 couples, where the head of the family was 65 or over, had incomes of 10,000 dollars or more in 1963, according to a report published in 1966. Close to 940,000 couples received between

5,000 dollars and 10,000 dollars in income. But, on the bleaker side, approximately 2.6 million couples—more than half in that age bracket—had incomes under 3,000 dollars. Almost 2.7 million—three out of five—persons 65 and above living alone or with nonrelatives received incomes under 1,500 dollars in 1963.[31]

Among couples in this age group, more than one-sixth had no assets of any kind, or at most assets of less than 1,000 dollars. Almost another quarter had no assets or less than 1,000 dollars except for equity in their home. More than a quarter of the nonmarried older persons had no assets at all, and another tenth had no assets except for equity in a home.[32]

We know, then, that a considerable proportion of our elderly live marginally, insofar as their own resources are concerned. On the other hand, the *aggregate* income for the entire 65-and-over population is estimated at about 40 billion dollars a year or more,[33] and this makes our older residents a very significant factor in the economy as consumers of goods and services.

SOCIAL PROBLEMS OF THE ELDERLY

There is a psychological hazard in growing older, and people react to the inexorable passage of time quite differently as they are confronted with problems of adjustment in their modes of living and interactions with others.

Widowhood requires changes in interpersonal relations. A man and wife, let us say, have a circle of friends, most of whom are married and living with their respective mates. Then the husband dies. The widow will then have to make some adjustments since widowed individuals often do not fit in socially with the married couples with whom they associated prior to the demise of their spouses.

Another problem is that as children grow up, marry, and establish their own households, their parents feel less needed or not needed at all. Many of them, not wanting to be "in the way," will not live with their married children, even when they would be welcome. More and more they associate with persons their own age, to the exclusion of younger people, and this can become depressing and injurious to the morale.

What often happens is that the self-concept of the older person undergoes change, and not for the better. In our society the elderly tend to be considered members of a fading, useless generation, to be housed, fed, and treated with consideration up to a point, but not to be respected or turned to for advice and counsel. Yet in many Asian and African societies the older people are the most respected; they carry authority and are regarded with deference. Family life in traditional China is a case in point. Another example is Turkey, where the old men always sit in a place of honor at the table, and male diners are served in order of age. Within their own ranks, women give respectful attention to the elderly. Social classes exist in Turkey, but, writes anthropologist Joe E. Pierce: "Within each class, if you are older than someone else, you outrank him."[34] Our own society places such value on youth and vigor that it could almost be said the younger person always outranks the older one.

An individual's self-concept is an important determinant of how he conducts his interpersonal relations. Some refuse to accept that they are "old" and interact with others accordingly. Others decide that they are indeed "old" and withdraw into that portion of our society's social world where they think they belong.

Many persons conclude that they are "old" at the point when they retire from employment. For this reason, the idea is growing that it is unrealistic to establish a compulsory retirement age affecting all employees in a given enterprise. One person is ready and even eager to retire at 50, whereas another is reluctant to do so at 80.

Zena Blau found that retirement produced alterations in self-concept among the 468 men and women 60 years of age and above whom she studied. She asked whether the people who were important to them thought of them as being old and whether they thought of themselves that way. A high percentage of the subjects who considered themselves old believed that others who were important to them thought of them that way, too. More retired than employed persons classified themselves as old. Among individuals under 70, one-third of the retired persons, as compared to less than one-fifth of the employed, considered themselves old. For those over 70, two-thirds of the retired considered they were old, as compared with two-fifths of the employed.[35]

Among studies of the aging process, some of the most interesting deal with the matter of adjustment in relation to self-concept. Two theories in particular, both concerned with the individual's role complex and the changes taking place as he ages, are worth mention.

One is the _disengagement theory,_ outlined by Elaine Cumming and William Henry in _Growing Old._[36] As a person ages, he gives up certain of his social roles in the normal course of events. He ceases being the father of young children. If he loses his wife, he no longer enacts the role of husband. He gives up a leadership role in business or in his fraternal organization. As his health declines, as he becomes less able to move about nimbly, he begins to face up to the fact that he must some day die. With greater or less courage he prepares for his ultimate demise by gradually withdrawing from active societal roles. This is the process of disengagement.

Sometime this process is initiated by the individual himself, sometime by members of the society, sometimes by both.

If both the individual and society are prepared for the disengagement at the same time, the outcome will very likely be successful. For example: People in the community are of the opinion that John has reached that stage in life when he ought to retire from work; John feels the same way; in that case, successful disengagement ensues. John retires and is content in retirement.

If neither members of the society nor the individual himself is ready for his disengagement, he remains engaged. Say John's role is viewed in his community as that of an active participant; he feels the same way; he does not disengage himself from society.

If the individual is prepared to disengage himself before members of the society expect him to, engagement is likely to continue. John has prepared himself, in his own mind, to retire from work, but he is convinced, by listening to the counsel of meaningful members of the society, that it is his duty to remain at work. He does not become disengaged.

If the individual is not ready for disengagement, but in his society the feeling is he should be, disengagement is likely to result. John does not want to retire. He learns he is expected to retire. He becomes disengaged.

The same process, of course, would occur with women, except that their original roles are different from a man's in many respects.

If societal forces function to disengage an individual from his central life role—work in the case of men, family functions for women—before the person is prepared for it, that individual will very likely experience a decline in morale. He may nevertheless adjust successfully to his disengagement. A great deal will depend upon whether he is able to find substitute roles that satisfy him.

The second formulation concerning the aging process is called *role flexibility theory.* Robert J. Havighurst and Ruth Albrecht outline it in *Older People.*[37]

According to this theory, the key to successful adjustment to aging is role flexibility. The authors of the study found that those persons who were active in a wide variety of social roles or who were very active in one given social role were more likely to be happy and to have made a satisfactory social adjustment to aging than those who were less active.

TOWARD SOLUTIONS OF PROBLEMS OF THE ELDERLY

An entire branch of medicine has developed in the past three decades, dealing with the diseases and hygiene of the aging. It is called *geriatrics,* and its practitioners concern themselves with retarding the degenerative processes in the aging, improving their mental health, and making them feel they are useful and needed people. It is believed that life can be prolonged if the individual concerned is convinced that he has significant roles to perform in society.

Many elderly folk are in mental hospitals, not because they are psychotic, but because they are too old to take care of themselves. It is estimated that over half of the patients 60 and over in public mental hospitals could be cared for outside. Foster home placement is being substituted for stultifying institutionalization.

Recreational and cultural activities for "Senior Citizens" are being provided in many cities.

For a time there was a trend toward building tract homes and apartments exclusively for the aging, with ramps instead of stairs, windows that could be opened by pressing a button, and other conveniences. More recently, however, it has been recognized that communities for older people do not appeal to those who refuse to surrender to the self-concept of the aging person as one who should be completely disengaged. Now, a trend has begun toward building special units for older folk in complexes of housing for all age groups.

The 1961 White House Conference on Aging gave especial attention to employment of the aging. It reported that the increasing tempo of industrial advance and the rapidly growing complexity of technological innovations have produced a labor market in which older workers find themselves on the bare fringes. It was recommended that basic economic and other policies be established in order to create a healthy economy while at the same time making place for all persons in the labor market, older persons included.[38]

What can be done for the physical well-being of the elderly has its limits, in the final analysis. The human organism at last runs down. There is, however, a huge area of endeavor yet to be exploited in the interest of the older population. It relates to status and roles, and the feeling that one is wanted, needed, respected, and loved. We have barely scratched the surface in this respect, despite the impressive gains otherwise achieved through the practice of geriatrics. What remains to be done is more than a matter of medical practice. It is a task within the total society, to be performed by many disciplines and groups.

MENTAL HEALTH PROBLEMS

Nearly one out of every four adults in the United States has felt the need for psychological-psychiatric help at some time in the course of his life. One in seven has actively sought it. Almost a million people attend mental health clinics in the country each year. Approximately 300,000 persons visit psychiatrists in a nonclinical setting. About a quarter of a million individuals are admitted to public mental hospitals annually. In any one day, more than 500,000 patients reside in public mental hospitals.

Most patients admitted to state hospitals for the mentally ill remain a relatively short time. As many as 80 percent of first admissions are discharged within the initial year of hospitalization. But those who are not released early tend to become custodial cases, remaining in the hospital for a long time, perhaps until they die. Seventy-five percent of the mental patient population has been in the hospital for more than two years; 55 percent for more than five years.[39]

As these figures indicate, mental illness must be deemed a serious social problem in the United States even if we consider only the number of people who succumb to such ailments. Beyond that, there is the fact that mental illness is, at least in part, a socially rooted phenomenon susceptible to social remedies.

We have not attacked the problem with marked success even to this day, although we have made improvements in that direction. Throughout most of our history, in common with that of many other societies, we understood so little about mental states that we were able to identify only the most extreme breakdowns, that is, the psychoses. We hospitalized psychotics, kept them under some restraints in order to protect them and others, but knowing very little about treatment methods, we made mere custodial cases of them for the most part.

In 1909, however, the year the National Committee for Mental Hygiene was founded, a new era dawned in the treatment of the mentally ill. At first the committee devoted its efforts solely to providing humane care and scientific treatment to hospitalized patients, which meant that only psychotics were served. In time, however, the committee promoted programs out of the hospital for the maintenance of mental health. This meant we were beginning to take an interest in ambulatory cases such as neurotics, as well as other emotionally disturbed persons who needed professional help but did not require hospitalization. The committee not only educated the public to modern concepts of what constitutes mental health but established programs calculated to prevent mental breakdown. It furthered, and furthers, research into methods of treatment. Increasingly the emphasis has been on the prevention of mental illness, the development of a healthy personality, and the maintenance of all-around mental health.

Although psychologists, psychiatrists, and social workers have made the major contributions to this field, sociologists have also been concerned with the phenomenon of mental illness. Behavioral scientists believe that most mental illness is precipitated by emotional conflicts, especially those provoked by anxiety, frustration, and guilt feeling. The sociologist is particularly interested in the role of culture in the production of emotional conflict in members of the society.

The evidence is tentative, and partly equivocal, but it suggests that individuals in complex societies, particularly in those undergoing relatively rapid cultural change, are more subject to emotional conflict than those residing in more simple, well-integrated societies. Consider the prevalence of schizophrenia, which is the most common form of psychosis treated in our country. The disease is uncommon in more primitive societies. According to one report, no field investigator has found a high rate of schizophrenia in a stable, primitive society, which is isolated from Caucasian influence, and, "wherever schizophrenia is recorded, the society is in the process of change."[40]

In attempting to explain the relatively high rate of mental illness in our society, sociologists point to a number of hypothetical factors—and they are hypothetical only, not established scientifically.

There is the strain resulting from certain role transitions, which may create emotional conflict. The transition from childhood to adolescence seems to be more stressful in our culture than in some less complex and well-integrated societies. Similarly, moving from youth to the responsibilities of adulthood and from active adulthood into retirement may set up strains that eventually play their part in the development of mental illness in given individuals.

The drive for status can create emotional conflict and ultimately mental illness. Men are taught to admire, hence they seek to emulate, the "dynamic" individual who fought his way up from the bottom to the very top of a giant corporation, despite fierce competition. He is a "success." We want to be rated one, but the competition is often very keen. As soon as we can afford to do so—and sometimes before then—we move into the fashionable part of town. That "proves" we are successful. The drive for status, in the case of many individuals, is beset by anxieties and frustrations in our competitive society.

In a related area of investigation, a team of sociologists and psychologists, getting their data from hospitals, clinics and private psychiatrists, pursued the question whether there were significant differences in the incidence and prevalence of mental illness among social classes in the United States.[41] They found the rate of persons under care on a given date who were diagnosed as schizophrenic to be eight times as high in the lowest of five class strata as it was in the top two strata. However, most of this difference in rates is a consequence of the fact that lower-status patients had much longer hospital stays than did those in other categories. Once they were identified as mentally ill and placed under care they were more likely than higher-status patients to remain hospitalized. Thus, more of the former were found in a hospital on a given day. The statistical figure for this would represent *prevalence* of treated schizophrenia. When statistics were compiled on *incidence* of schizophrenia, that is, the frequency with which patients initially became ill, the 8-to-1 ratio no longer held. The rate for lower-status patients was only slightly greater than that for higher-status individuals.

Although acknowledging the rather inconclusive nature of these findings, Merton and Nisbet point out that other research on social class differences in family relationships and on the process of personality formation ". . . increases the plausibility of the hypothesis that in the United States and Great Britain, at least, schizophrenia is more likely to occur in lower-status families than in those higher in the social structure."[42] They base their assertion on sociological observations that have been made concerning patterns of parental dominance in relation to the incidence of schizophrenia:

Lower-status families are more often characterized by the pattern of maternal dominance together with a weak or even absent father figure that so often is found in the families of schizophrenics. For the male child especially, it appears that the environment of the lower-class family less often affords adequate opportunity for the achievement of self-confidence and success in terms valued by the community at large. . . . Most of these children will not, of course, be . . . severely mentally ill . . . , but it does appear that personality development of children drawn from the lowest socioeconomic fifth of the population is fraught with many more hazards than is the development of more favored children.[43]

Schizophrenia, although the mental ailment most commonly under treatment in this country, is of course not the only psychosis, and sociologists have barely scratched the surface in their research on the psychoses as a whole in relation to the culture. The neuroses, probably more prevalent than the psychoses, will very likely also come under intensified sociological scrutiny in the years ahead.

Meantime, we may regard with some satisfaction these developments in the mental health area over the past half century, developments that were generated by thinkers and workers in a number of fields:

1 · The establishment of child guidance clinics in the early 1920s as a means of preventing mental illness and identifying and

treating individuals at the earliest possible time, if they should require treatment.

2 · Establishment of mental health clinics for outpatient treatment.

3 · Development of the private practice of psychiatry, psychology, and psychiatric social work.

4 · Improved hospital care. There is room for further improvement, but patients do not inevitably become custodial cases. Efforts are made to get them back to normal life in the community.

5 · Introduction of new treatment approaches: individual and group psychotherapy; vocational training and rehabilitation; "milieu therapy," which is treatment in a "therapeutic community," in which patient helps patient; and chemotherapy, the utilization of chemicals in treatment.

6 · Introduction of mental health services into schools.

7 · Improved treatment of the mentally retarded. Revived interest in this long-neglected field was sparked by the personal interest and leadership of the late President John F. Kennedy.

8 · Intensified efforts to promote the mental health of the aging and of alcoholics and drug addicts.

9 · Improved techniques of dealing with juvenile and adult offenders, mainly through the agency of social work and psychiatry.

10 · Introduction of professional training of personnel for the mental health field.

Although much has been done to cope with the problem of mental illness, a great deal remains to be done. We still have no certain means of curing the ill; we still have an accretion of patients in mental hospitals who will probably remain until their demise; we still seek answers to the riddle of the neurotic, the psychopath, the psychoneurotic. We have not yet found effective enough ways to "minister to a mind diseased."

Social problems, the subject matter of this section of the text, are closely related to institutional arrangements. In the section that follows, we turn to the consideration of social institutions.

· NOTES

1. U. S. Department of Justice, Federal Bureau of Investigation, *Uniform Crime Reports for the United States, 1966* (Washington, D. C.: U. S. Government Printing Office, 1967), p. 1.

2. *Ibid.*, p. 59, Table 2.
3. The President's Commission on Law Enforcement and Administration of Justice, *The Challenge of Crime in a Free Society* (Washington, D. C.: U. S. Government Printing Office, 1967), p. 55.
4. U. S. Department of Justice, Federal Bureau of Investigation, *op. cit.*, p. 27.
5. Seldon D. Bacon, "Inebriety, Social Integration, and Marriage," *Memoirs of the Section on Alcohol, Laboratory of Applied Physiology, Yale University,* No. 2, 1945.
6. Albert D. Ullman, "First Drinking Experiences of Addictive and 'Normal' Drinkers," *Quarterly Journal of Studies on Alcohol,* XIV (June 1953), 181–191.
7. Albert D. Ullman, "Ethnic Differences in the First Drinking Experience," *Social Problems,* VIII (Summer 1960), 45–56.
8. Seldon D. Bacon, "Alcohol and Complex Society," *Alcohol Science and Society, Journal of Studies on Alcohol* (1945), pp. 179–200.
9. *Ibid.*
10. *Ibid.*
11. E. M. Jellinek, "Phases in the Drinking History of Alcoholics," *Memoirs of the Section on Alcohol, Laboratory of Applied Physiology, Yale University,* No. 5, 1948.
12. The President's Commission on Law Enforcement and the Administration of Justice, *Task Force Report: Drunkenness* (Washington, D. C.: U. S. Government Printing Office, 1967), p. 1.
13. *Ibid.*
14. Clarence Darrow and Victor S. Yarros, *The Prohibition Mania* (New York: Boni and Liveright, 1927), p. 231; Herman Feldman, *Prohibition: Its Economic and Industrial Aspects* (New York: Appleton, 1927), p. 397.
15. U. S. Bureau of the Census, *Statistical Abstract of the United States, 1967,* 88th annual ed. (Washington, D. C.: U. S. Government Printing Office, 1967), p. 55, Table No. 63.
16. U. S. Department of Health, Education, and Welfare, *Facts About Older Americans* (Washington, D. C.: U. S. Government Printing Office, 1966), unpaginated.
17. *Ibid.*
18. *Ibid.*
19. *Ibid.*
20. *Ibid.*
21. U. S. Department of Health, Education, and Welfare, *The Health Care of the Aged* (Washington, D. C.: U. S. Government Printing Office, 1962), p. 17.
22. *Ibid.*, p. 23.
23. President's Council on Aging, *The Older American* (Washington, D. C.: U. S. Government Printing Office, 1963), p. 14.
24. President's Council on Aging, *On Growing Older* (Washington, D. C.: U. S. Government Printing Office, 1964), pp. 59–60.

25. *Los Angeles Times*, December 9, 1965.
26. James R. Morris, *Employment Opportunities in Later Years* (Burlingame, Calif.: Foundation for Voluntary Welfare, 1960).
27. Reported in Governor's Commission on the Employment and Retirement Problems of Older Workers, *Employment and Retirement of Older Workers* (Sacramento, Calif.: State Printing Office, 1960), p. 31ff.
28. *Ibid.*, p. 37.
29. U. S. Department of Labor, *Monthly Report of the Labor Force: September 1965*, p. 21, Table A-10.
30. U. S. Department of Health, Education, and Welfare, *Facts About Older Americans, op. cit.*
31. *Ibid.*
32. *Ibid.*
33. *Ibid.*
34. Joe E. Pierce, *Life in a Turkish Village* (New York: Holt, Rinehart and Winston, 1964), p. 83.
35. Zena Smith Blau, "Changes in Status and Age Identification," *American Sociological Review*, XXI (April 1956), 198–203.
36. Elaine Cumming and William Henry, *Growing Old* (New York: Basic Books, 1961).
37. Robert J. Havighurst and Ruth Albrecht, *Older People* (New York: Longmans, Green, 1953), Chaps. III, VI, XVII.
38. U. S. Department of Health, Education, and Welfare, Special Staff on Aging, *The Nation and Its Older People: Report of the White House Conference on Aging, January 9–12, 1961* (Washington, D. C.: U. S. Government Printing Office, 1961), p. 142.
39. Ruth I. Knee and Warren C. Lamson, "Mental Health and Mental Illness," in Harry L. Lurie (ed.), *Encyclopedia of Social Work* (New York: National Association of Social Workers, 1965), p. 489.
40. Daniel C. Miller, Guy E. Swanson, *et. al.*, *Inner Conflict and Defense* (New York: Holt, Rinehart and Winston, 1960), p. 45.
41. A. B. Hollingshead and F. Redlich, *Social Class and Mental Illness* (New York: Wiley, 1958).
42. Robert K. Merton and Robert A. Nisbet (eds.), *Contemporary Social Problems* (New York: Harcourt, Brace & World, 1961), p. 165.
43. *Ibid.*

· SUGGESTIONS FOR FURTHER READING

Anonymous. *Alcoholics Anonymous*. New York: Alcoholics Anonymous Publishing, 1955.
Members of Alcoholics Anonymous refer to this volume simply as "The Book." It is the official publication of Alcoholics Anonymous, setting forth its program, and telling how and why it works. There are many interesting first person recitals by alcoholics who quit drinking after going "on the program."

Anonymous. "Drug Addict—Inactive," in David Dressler (ed.), *Readings in Criminology and Penology.* New York: Columbia University Press, 1964, pp. 116–126.

This is a transcript of a tape recording in which the subject reveals that he is both an alcoholic and a drug addict. He describes how he became that way, his life as a person with the double problem, and finally, under what conditions he stopped using both alcohol and narcotics.

BORDUA, DAVID J. "Delinquent Subcultures: Sociological Interpretations of Gang Delinquency." *Annals of the American Academy of Political and Social Science,* CCCXXXVIII (November 1961), 120–136.

Reviews and analyzes the existing theories concerning why boys engage in gang activities.

HORNEY, KAREN. *The Neurotic Personality of Our Time.* New York: Norton, 1937.

An excellent and readable discussion of the hazards of contracting mental illness in our stressful, highly competitive society.

LOETHER, HERMAN J. *Problems of Aging: Sociological and Social Psychological Perspectives.* Belmont, Calif.: Dickenson, 1967.

A great deal of information is in this small volume about the aging process and problems associated with it.

O'DONNELL, JOHN A. "The Lexington Program for Narcotic Addicts." *Federal Probation,* XXVI (March 1962), 56–60.

A description of the treatment of narcotics addicts in the best known federal narcotic hospital.

SUTHERLAND, EDWIN H. *Principles of Criminology,* 4th ed. Philadelphia: Lippincott, 1947, pp. 3–9.

Sutherland's theory of differential association: an attempt at explaining the etiology of crime and delinquency.

The President's Commission on Law Enforcement and Administration of Justice. *The Challenge of Crime in a Free Society.* Washington, D. C.: U. S. Government Printing Office, 1967.

A far-ranging report on the extent, cost, control, prevention, and treatment of crime and delinquency in the United States.

YABLONSKY, LEWIS. *The Tunnel Back: Synanon.* New York: Macmillan, 1965.

An interestingly written account of Synanon, a therapeutic community in which drug addict helps drug addict in a program of recovery.

part six
social
institutions

23 THE CONCEPT OF SOCIAL INSTITUTIONS

When we considered the meaning of *group*, we were examining the kinds of social organization that involved relationships among people interacting directly with one another. Now we shall view social organization in broader perspective. Consider, for example, a plane pilot at the airport who sees in minute detail the people, buildings, and trees about him but does not see much beyond the immediate vicinity. Then he takes his ship aloft, and as it goes higher and higher, the details on the ground recede and finally disappear. Instead, he sees entire villages, farmland, interconnecting roads, and rivers. He has gained an enlarged perspective. Figuratively, this is what we do in the present chapter with regard to social organization as we study the meaning of *institutions*.

INSTITUTIONS & "INSTITUTIONS"

George and Cathy are en route to a football game between Midvale College and a visiting team. George, who is driving, keeps his eyes on the road ahead but his ears attuned to what his girl friend is saying.

"I'm so excited!" she cries. "I know I'll just scream my head off!" She looks at George. "What's the matter? Aren't you excited? You don't look excited."

George shrugs. "Frankly, when it's football, I can take it or leave it alone. My game's baseball. *There's* a great American institution!"

As they drive past the local orphanage, Cathy remarks, "Ugh! I hate seeing that place! Poor kids! Growing up in an institution!"

"Speaking of institutions," George remarks, "I hear Professor Grimm is retiring, after 25 years on the job."

"How is that speaking of institutions?"

"Well, old Grimm's been around so long he *is* an institution at Midvale. Place won't be the same without him."

"This is a most stimulating conversation," Cathy declares, "but may I remind you, sir, that unless *you* want to wind up in a certain institution known as the pokey you'd better slow down, even if you *are* late and going to a football game just to please me."

THE CONCEPT *INSTITUTION*

George and Cathy employed the term *institution* to denote several ideas (or concepts) that seem to be quite dissimilar. Although they were not consciously trying to use the term in its sociological meaning, there is nevertheless some relationship between the meanings of the word as they used it and the sociological concept. Certain common factors were present in each of the "institutions" to which they referred, factors basic to the sociological concept. We shall return to George and Cathy, but first let us repeat something we said in an earlier portion of this volume. We discussed social institutions in preliminary fashion in the chapter dealing with folkways and law, you will remember. That was necessary since, as we pointed out, an institution is *a system of interrelated folkways and laws, organized around a given function of society.* We spoke of an institution as *an established, organized mode of performing a function in society.* And we attempted to make clear that this "organized mode" consists of *rules of conformity concerning what we consider the most basic human needs.*

Now we deal with the concept of *social institutions* in greater detail. Let us first propose still another definition. It in no way conflicts with what has already been given, but it will better enable us to focus on several salient features of institutions.

An institution is a durable organization of forms of procedure enabling people in a society to satisfy one or more of their long-range essential needs. Considered collectively, institutions are the relatively permanent framework of culture and society. The organized systems of family, education, religion, economic order, and government exemplify social institutions.

The concept of social institutions is very important in the study of sociology. Through examination of institutional ideology and organization we can gain a basic understanding of the forces that effectively integrate and, at times, strain and bring conflict to society.

Human beings, we said earlier, base their behavior largely on the required and preferred norms they have learned. An institution is a system of such norms built around certain societal functions. Norms concerning family life, for instance, are interwoven into the other elements that constitute the institution of family. MacIver and Page put it this way: "When we speak of institutions we think . . . of the system of controls that extends beyond personal relations. This system of controls is the bond between the past and the present and between the present and the future, linking men to their ancestors, their gods, and their descendants."[1]

A social institution is *a system of control, an approved form of procedure*, characteristic of group activity; but the term *institution* is not synonymous with *group*, as such. "If we are considering something as an organized *group*, it is an association; if as a form of procedure, it is an institution. Association denotes membership; institution denotes a mode or means of service."[2] You belong to a group or association. You do not belong to an institution.

The term *institution* is an abstraction. You cannot see the institution of family, although you can see members of a family. You are unable to see religious institutions, but you can see a place of religious worship. *Institution*, in each instance, refers to *the form of procedure* characteristic of the respective group activity.

The observable group activity or physical structure connected with it is symbolic evidence of the abstraction *institution*. The assembly of worshipers, on the one hand, and the cross on a church, on the other, symbolically express the value system of the religious institution of Christianity.

Society is preserved and maintained through institutional controls. Consider a few of the many functions our governmental institution fulfills for us. We depend upon it to protect us from disease, contaminated food, theft, bank deposit losses, military aggression, and the deprivation of our civil rights.

Every institution has the same basic function, that of enabling people to satisfy their needs. Through institutional activities group members plan their lives, worship their deities, earn their daily bread, gain acceptance from others, and socialize their children.

Now let us return to George and Cathy. To what extent have they grasped the meaning of *institution* in the sociological sense?

George referred to baseball as "a great American institution." The game does represent *a durable organization of forms of procedure* whereby a great many of us satisfy a need for recreation. For many years players and spectators alike have accepted the game as a national sport. Its procedures are meticulously spelled out, so far as rules of the game are concerned. And the spectator's role is well systematized by custom. He may come to the game dressed as he pleases so long as it is not in violation of law. He has the right, established in tradition, to applaud, scream, stamp his feet, or hurl imprecations at the umpires. It is his prerogative to shout instructions to the players, although the players have the prerogative of ignoring such advice. The spectator may munch frankfurters or drink beverages as he watches the game, and he may drop peanut shells on the ground.

Professor Grimm, who assertedly is retiring, is not an institution in himself, although George called him that because the professor has been around a long time. From George's point of view, Grimm seems permanent. Actually, he is not permanent, but a more or less durable individual who enacts his role as part of the institution of higher learning, an institution that *enables people to satisfy certain long-range needs.*

Neither the orphanage nor the "pokey," referred to by Cathy, are institutions merely by virtue of being buildings. What makes them institutions in the sociological sense is the fulfillment of human needs through the continuing social interaction that occurs within the buildings. That interaction *is part of the relatively permanent framework of the culture and society.*

Going back to our definition of institutions, let us review their principal features.

Institutions are durable. The Milwaukee Braves went out of existence as a baseball team, but the institution of baseball persists. Professor Grimm may retire, but the institution of education will continue. When the British people cry, "The king is dead; long live the king!" they mean that the British monarchy goes on although individual monarchs come and go.

Like other elements of culture, institutions do change gradually, but people tend to be strongly resistant to change in their institutional activities, having been indoctrinated with the idea that these activities are "right." For example, we may be disturbed that new methods of teaching mathematics to children are being used in the primary grades. Members of family groups often oppose change in their traditional familial activities. Thus, in Figure 23.1, we may assume the homecoming husband adopts the view that, incapacitated or not, his wife (and any wife) must have supper ready when her spouse returns from work.

The fact that institutions are considered indispensable explains their durability. If you feel your family is essential to your welfare, you will do what you can to preserve it. Such sentiments, multiplied in the minds of millions of individuals, perpetuate the family as an institutional system. Whatever jeopardizes the tried and tested ways we have learned to use in order to satisfy our fundamental needs constitutes a threat to our personal and mutual security. Columnists inveigh against alleged encroachments on "the American way of life." When Russian Jews were subject to pogroms during the czarist regime and forbidden to worship as they considered necessary, they prayed behind locked doors, risking detection and death.

Institutions consist of organized forms of procedure. Inside the building Cathy saw, she could have observed the organized human activities of the orphanage. Members of the group there enacted their respective roles. The matron managed the budget, hired and fired the staff, and supervised employees. The staff dressed and fed the small children and got the older ones off to school. Some administered psychological tests. Others stoked the furnace, washed laundry, or kept up the grounds. The children did some things at specified hours; other times they were free to do as they pleased. They accepted certain instructions, asked particular staff members for guidance, formed affectional ties for others, and played with children their own age.

The organized forms of procedure that comprise institutions enable people throughout a society to satisfy their long-range, essential needs. Different societies institutionalize different

Figure 23.1
The Durable
Institution of Family
Reprinted by permission
of Brad Anderson.

"What's for supper?"

procedures, but the functions of all institutions are of long-range and collective interest. Education, religion, the police system, industry, government, all satisfy needs. In each instance, the institution has an assigned function considered essential to human welfare.

INSTITUTIONAL SYSTEMS & UNITS

Before proceeding further it is necessary to make an analytical distinction between general institutional *systems* and specific institutional *units*. When we think in a general way of government, education, religion, commerce, or the family, we are thinking of *institutional systems*. But when we direct our attention to our own city government, the church we attend, our alma mater, the market in which we purchase our food, or the Smith family down the street, we are concerned with *institutional units*. We will refer to both the systems and the units as institutions in the discussion to follow.

A COLLEGE AS AN INSTITUTIONAL UNIT

A college is a specific unit in the general institutional system of formal education. The activities of individuals within this institution follow patterns established over a long period of time. The historical antecedents of lectures, laboratory demonstrations, libraries, and seminars can be traced back many centuries through the cultures of Western Europe to ancient Rome and Greece. The college carries out functions that are considered essential to the welfare of individuals in our society. We believe, generally, that it is necessary to train young people for such specialized professional careers as the practice of medicine, law, and engineering. We also deem it essential that students have a general understanding of the world in which they live. The college has other functions, of course. For some students it is a marriage mart, for others a recreational center, for still others a place to mark time before accepting adult responsibilities. But these are secondary, not basic, functions. The college can be considered part of the institution of education only if some *essential* objective is assigned to it. That objective is the furnishing of higher education. Unless it does that, it is not a college, an institutional unit of the institutional system of education.

From a student's particular point of view, his college is what it does for him (his rights) and what he is expected to do in return (his responsibilities). He may think of his college as a number of separate groups of individuals with whom he identifies and where he is accepted as a member. These include classes, fraternities or sororities, recreational clubs, discussion groups, and dates. Since these group activities are attached in some way to his college, he thinks of them when he thinks of the college. He is also aware that when he associates with any of these groups, he is expected to enact certain roles in response to other participants. He has learned to adjust his behavior to a score of instructors, some seemingly reasonable, others unpredictably eccentric. He must do a considerable amount of work, attend classes, use the library, and get along with his colleagues. But the college is more than what it means to this student, what it does for him, and what it requires of him. It is more than a number of groups in which he participates and a series of roles that he enacts. The college is an institution. From his own subjective point of view the student sees only a few groups attached to the institution—he may view the college only in a fragmentary and disconnected way, as if it consisted of a few pieces from a jigsaw puzzle.

So, the problem confronting us, as we move from an understanding of groups toward understanding institutions, is one of expanding our perspective or, in technical terms, of moving from the concrete—readily perceived groups—to a level of analysis requiring such abstract concepts as institution. How can you achieve the frame of reference sociologists use in studying institutions?

To begin with, you have some very real impressions of your school, fragmentary though they may be. They can be used as a starting point. You know what your school means to you. To increase your understanding, it is necessary to find out what it means to others—students, faculty, administrators, parents of students, alumni, secretaries, janitors, campus police, and residents of the locality served by the school. You must see the school from all the viewpoints of those who serve and are served by it before you can visualize it as an institution. As you collect and synthesize many such impressions, the composite picture of the institution will finally begin to emerge.

Studying this or any other institutional unit, you would raise questions about its *functions, organizational structure, social problems*, and *historical trends*.

As to *functions*, you would want to know what most people who participate in it expect of it. Are they getting what they want? Are some people satisfied, some dissatisfied, others indifferent to the services rendered by the school? Is its work in accord with the objectives of the entire educational system, from kindergarten through the graduate schools of universities? Does it satisfy the needs of most of the residents of the locality? Does the school perform unintended or latent functions that are inconsistent with or even detrimental to its stated objectives as well as manifest functions? The last question is of major importance in realistic sociological analysis. An important contribution of sociology has been its identification and examination of both latent functions and dysfunctions of various social arrangements.

Regarding the *organizational structure* of the college, you would find out how students, faculty, and administrators are expected to behave in response to one another on the campus. You would try to discover how many campus groups are linked into the composite entity of the school. You would investigate the hierarchy of status used to measure the comparative importance of specific persons and groups. You would want to know who has final responsibility for the maintenance and operation of the school and what circumstances lead people to communicate formally and informally with one another. You might investigate the extent to which the power structure of the school is authoritarian (that is, arbitrarily controlled by administrative directives from the top) or democratic (that is, controlled through a continuing search for mutually desirable means and ends among all participants).

Questions of function and structure of an institution carry implications of possible *social problems*. Students and instructors may have different ideas about the functions of a college. There may be conflicting opinions between faculty and administration on how a school can most effectively accomplish its objectives. In both instances, conflict produces problems. A question constantly plaguing colleges, for instance, is whether football is—or should be—of major importance. Another is whether drinking and unrestricted contact between the sexes should be suppressed, ignored, or encouraged. Again, should hazing or religious and racial discrimination among fraternities and sororities be a matter of official concern?

Questions concerning *historical trends* relate to changes that have occurred and are constantly occurring in an institution. In what respect are the functions, structure, values, and problems of the college changing in time? Are any trends marked and persistent enough to provide valid bases for predicting what is likely to occur in the future? To what extent are old customs and traditions being preserved or displaced? In long-range terms, do certain institutional practices have functional or dysfunctional consequences with respect to professed objectives?

Since the questions proposed are aids toward understanding all institutional systems, we shall bear them in mind in ensuing chapters, when we discuss certain social institutions, such as the family and educational and religious systems in our society.

SOME MISCONCEPTIONS ABOUT INSTITUTIONS

Perhaps you still find it difficult to understand what the sociologist means when he uses the concept *institution*. It may be helpful, therefore, to go over the ground in a different way, by considering some of the erroneous ideas people have about institutions.

In remarking that Professor Grimm was an institution, George expressed one of the common misconceptions. Grimm, an individual, is not an institution. Neither is the queen of

England. Sometimes individuals *seem like* institutions, either because they are comparatively durable in time, or the roles they enact are closely associated with institutions. Such persons are sometimes referred to as *institutional functionaries*.

Some people are confused as to the distinction between the concept *group* and the concept *institution*. A group refers to something relatively specific and concrete in the minds of those who consider themselves members. The meaning of institution is much more general and abstract.

Consider the hypothetical Smith family. They are a group, and their activities as a group are organized in substantial measure to follow the institutional pattern of the family in our society. In their relationships with one another, therefore, they constitute an institutional group, but not an institution. The institution of the family has its existence in the generally accepted meaning and purpose associated with the family, as conceived by the people who are involved in family life in the society. Each individual sees the family as an organized system of behavior enacted for the purpose of satisfying specific goals. The Smith family was launched with an institutionally prescribed wedding and will be terminated by funerals conducted according to institutional tradition. But the *institutional system* of the family will continue long after this particular family has disappeared.

Another misconception regarding institutions stems from the erroneous idea that buildings and physical equipment are institutions, or at least essential parts of institutions. If you have gone on conducted field trips through industrial plants or mental hospitals, you may have left with the false impression that you had "been through the institution." You did not actually "see" the institution. You saw buildings and perhaps some people enacting institutional behavior. As has been emphasized, institutions have their existence in human minds—they are mental constructs. The physical equipment in an institutional system is a useful adjunct to, but not the essential part of, an institution. Machinery is not the institution of industry, any more than hospital beds are the institution of hospital care. Physical equipment suggests an institution in a symbolic sense, but it is not a real or essential part of an institution, any more than a wedding ring is a marriage or a flag is the government.

Still another misconception about institutions is that they

press all persons in a common mold, so that all come to behave in the same way. You have heard the expression, "Oh, he's institutionalized!" an assertion generally intended to convey the idea that an individual has been subjected to certain institutional influences to the point where his behavior is completely standardized and conforming. We hear that prisoners become "institutionalized." Or that children raised under communism have been "sovietized" and presumably are as alike as peas in a pod. Institutions are highly influential in patterning the behavior of people, to be sure, but individual differences in behavior exist nevertheless. Even the Prussian generals who attempted to develop armies that would operate like clockwork had to allow for these differences. Institutional behavior must be standardized to an extent, but no two human beings perform their institutional roles in precisely the same manner. If all persons enacted such roles exactly alike, every priest, minister, army officer, judge, and mother would be a carbon copy of all other persons in the same category. We know they are not. Social institutions are not like machines, turning out millions of identical products, although a considerable amount of conformity is associated with institutional behavior.

SOCIAL INSTITUTIONS VIEWED FUNCTIONALLY

In Chapter 19 we introduced the concept of *functionalism,* an orientation that emphasizes that a major function of recurrent social activities is to maintain social systems. A social institution is a recurrent social activity having this function. As we have pointed out, it is an established, organized mode of performing specific functions in society, consisting of rules of conformity concerning what in that society are considered basic human needs. In order to discuss social institutions in functional terms, we now recapitulate and enlarge upon points presented in Chapter 19, applying them specifically to the subject under discussion.

1. *Society is characterized by a variety of social activities that form patterns, recurring over and over.* Our economic system, which is an institutional system, exemplifies this. Its pattern of activities includes, for example, banking, mining, lumbering, and fishing; management-labor-governmental rela-

tions; the manufacture, transportation, and sale of goods; and the education of the young so they may understand and respect the "free enterprise" way of conducting business.

2. *A main function of these recurrent social activities is to help maintain the social system.* Thus, our economic system is intended to help maintain the larger social system.

3. *The social life of the community is viewed as the functioning of the social structure.* An important function of any recurrent activity, such as banking, is the part it plays in social life as a whole, that is, the contribution it makes to the maintenance of the social structure.

4. *The same activity patterns and social structures have multiple functions.* The manufacture of goods, for instance, serves to stabilize the national economy, bring entrepreneurs a profit, and supply a livelihood to employees. It functions to establish and codify employee-employer relations, to increase the revenues of advertising companies, and to contribute to the support of government through payment of taxes based on manufacturing income.

5. *Some functions are manifest, others latent.* Society may be viewed as an operating system, a functioning whole. Some of the consequences of given recurrent activities associated with institutions are desired and intended, while others are unintended and may be unknown to the individuals directly involved. Therefore, in examining the functions of a particular social institution, as we suggested earlier in the discussion of the college, we must distinguish between the purposes and objectives that the institution is supposed to achieve and the actual consequences of the activities involved. The expected may not be the actual outcomes. What is intended may be wholly or partially achieved, or not achieved at all. For this reason, sociologists distinguish between *manifest* and *latent* functions.

Manifest functions are those consequences for a society or any of its segments that are "intended and recognized by participants in the system" (the material in quotation marks being the phraseology of sociologist Robert K. Merton).[3] A manifest function of laws prescribing what shall constitute a legal marriage in the United States is the establishment of an approved, stable family structure. That is what is intended, and members of the society recognize this.

Latent functions are those consequences for a society or

any of its segments that are neither intended nor recognized.
Legal regulation of marriage, placing responsibility on the
husband for support of the wife and children, sometimes results in desertion of his family by a husband seeking to evade
that responsibility. This consequence is not intended, and the
members of the society do not view the legal regulation as
having that objective.

6. *The social consequences of given institutional activity
patterns and social structures may be different for the society
as a whole as distinguished from component segments of that
society.* Thus, the function of our economic system is to provide wealth and stability to the nation. However, it also functions to create wide differences in personal incomes, the
indirect result of which is poverty and dependency for a substantial part of the population.

7. *The social consequences of a single institutional pattern
and social structure may be both positive and negative within
the same society.* For instance, in a country that officially
recognizes and sanctions only one religion, governmental
power is likely to be in the hands of followers of the faith,
through whom the religion can be supported and maintained.
These are positive consequences, as viewed by adherents of
the dominant religion. However, such a system may create
difficulties for those who do not espouse the religion. They
may be disfranchised, or discriminated against in other ways,
to their own disadvantage and to the ultimate disadvantage of
the society as a whole. These are negative consequences.

*Positive consequences are those that make possible or sus-
tain other patterned activities that function to maintain the
social system.* In our illustration, an official state religion
makes possible the assumption of governmental power by the
faithful. It will very likely contribute to the further maintenance of the religious institution by way of financial and other
support.

*Negative consequences are those that tend to decrease the
stability of the social system or any of its component parts.*
Such consequences are said to be *dysfunctional*. Discrimination against those who do not espouse an officially sanctioned
state religion is dysfunctional when it creates social disprivilege, internal dissension, economic deprivation, and the like.

8. *All institutions have interlocking social functions.* The
family cares for children and regulates sexual behavior, but

it also provides support to each of the other social institutions of the society. When young people learn the value of money in their families, this reinforces the economic institution. As children acquire respect for law and order through their parents, governmental institutions are sustained. Children who accept the religious beliefs of their parents or who get from them an appreciation of higher education generally support the institutions of church or college.

Just as many functions of the family support other institutions, so these institutions reinforce the family, as well as each other. We might consider the college as one example of this. Some of its complementary functions are more apparent than others. It is evident that classes in political science provide knowledge of governmental institutions and support for as well as criticism of these institutions. One must probe deeper to see that competitive examinations associated with these courses induce a kind of learning that students can later transform into useful roles in competitive economic institutions. The *manifest function* of political science courses is to provide knowledge of, support to, and criticism of governmental institutions. A *latent function* is to enable students to perform successfully in competitive economic institutions.

Colleges *manifestly* support the family through special classes relating directly to that subject. They give it *latent* support in providing young men and women with opportunities to get acquainted, perhaps to date and eventually marry. The cartoon, Figure 23.2, facetiously suggests that college grading may have latent functions complementing the military services.

Most people readily understand how institutions directly complement one another through manifest functions. It is more difficult to comprehend the extent to which they indirectly reinforce one another through latent functions.

When we understand the mutually reinforcing functions of institutions, manifest and latent, we begin to see society in broad perspective. Figuratively, institutions might be thought of as the supporting columns of a building. The complementary functions they render one to the other are like the cross beams that hold the columns together. In such a figurative conception, the building in its entirety is a society. But this is figurative thinking only. We must not lose sight of the fact that social institutions are abstract concepts. The essence

Figure 23.2
Latent Function?

Reprinted with permission from
Richard Bibler, *Little Man on
Campus*, Stanford, Calif.: Stanford
University Press, 1952.

*"What are we going to do with you, Worthal?
This report shows you're flunking
half your courses."*

of an institution, we repeat, is what it signifies to those who
participate and mutually share what they accomplish through
their own efforts. In the final analysis, *all institutional activity
consists of the behavior of individuals following procedures
established in their society for the satisfaction of mutually
felt needs.*

In the chapters that follow in this section of the book, we
will consider in some detail several social institutions: the
family and the religious, educational, economic, political, and
social welfare systems.

· NOTES

1. Robert M. MacIver and Charles H. Page, *Society: An Introductory Analysis* (New York: Rinehart, 1949), pp. 18–19.
2. *Ibid.*, p. 15.
3. Robert K. Merton, *Social Theory and Social Structure*, rev. ed.
   (New York: Free Press, 1957), p. 51.

· SUGGESTIONS FOR FURTHER READING

CUBER, JOHN F. *Sociology, A Synopsis of Principles.* 5th ed. New
   York: Appleton-Century-Crofts, 1963, Chapter 24, "The Study
   of Social Institutions in Process."

A good statement on the nature of social institutions; theories of institutional change; analytical concepts for studying institutions.

HORTON, PAUL B., and CHESTER L. HUNT. *Sociology.* New York: McGraw-Hill, 1964, Chapter 9, "Social Institutions."

A very well written chapter dealing with the concept "social institution;" the development of institutions; institutional traits, structures and functions.

MERTON, ROBERT K. "Manifest and Latent Function: Toward the Codification of Functional Analysis in Sociology," in *Social Theory and Social Structure.* New York: Free Press, 1957, pp. 19–84.

Deals with manifest and latent functions; both are important considerations in the study of social institutions.

24 THE FAMILY AS AN INSTITUTIONAL SYSTEM

We shall now discuss the family, the most basic of institutional systems. We shall examine its functions, organizational structure, the social problems connected with it, and the principal historical trends in family life in the United States.

In anthropologist Ralph Linton's *The Study of Man,* he reported on the family pattern then current among the Nayar of India.[1] When a girl reached puberty, she went through the marriage ritual with an obliging stranger of at least equal caste. After three days of married life, she divorced him. From then on, it was required that he stay away from his ex-wife. She engaged in informal, socially sanctioned love affairs and bore children by her lovers. It was her privilege to enter into relations with several men simultaneously, and they, for their part, were not expected to restrict their cohabitation exclusively to her. A love affair did not lead to a permanent bond between woman and man, and no male lover was considered related in any way to his offspring.

The woman and her children lived in a household, or *taraved,* consisting of a group of related women and their brothers. Neither the original, ceremonial husband nor the informal lovers had a place there.

If a woman and her lover found themselves very compatible, they might continue their relationship for years. If not, one or the other could break it off without advance notice.

This system has changed somewhat since Linton reported on it. Currently, although males frequently have several mates simultaneously, plural relationships entered into by women have all but disappeared, the female tending to restrict herself to one lover at a time.

Martin Yang, a Chinese social scientist, described family life in a farm village of Shantung Province as it was in 1945.[2] Marriages were arranged by the parents, and the young people had no romantic relations before, usually not even having met. They first met at the wedding ceremony and took up residence with the husband's people thereafter.

After his marriage the husband maintained closer relations with his own family than he did with his wife. He showed her no affection in public and greeted his parents, brothers, and sisters before acknowledging his spouse's presence. A good mate understood that she should not demand attention to the point where her husband neglected his duty to his own family. At social gatherings she sat removed from her spouse, scarcely acknowledging she knew him. At home she waited until all family members had retired before she joined her husband in their room.

As the couple had progeny, they established residence in a home of their own or took over the abode of the husband's people. They exercised authority over their offspring. The wife, no longer under the rule of her in-laws, became undisputed head of her household, and the husband now had a less dominant position. He managed the farm and the business connected with it, leaving management of the home to his mate.

In this phase, the two might sit together publicly and talk with each other at family gatherings. There was more give and take in daily relations.

Perhaps, when they were about fifty, they would have several daughters-in-law living with them as they themselves had lived with the husband's family. As the respected grandmother of a long line of children and the overseer of a large household, the wife would become still more dominant. Her middle-aged sons would have developed strong attachment to her rather than to their father. The latter, no longer working in the fields, would have lost much of his original authority and would no longer have much control over family business transactions. He would, however, retain the privilege of venting his anger upon any of its members except his daughters-in-law.

After the married sons and families departed to set up their own homes, relations between the old couple would probably undergo still another change. The wife would lose her authority and be on equal terms with her husband. They might have a common feeling of being neglected by their children and share a need for mutual sympathy and understanding. Thus the earlier companionship would become reestablished.

Since the Communist takeover of mainland China, the government has attempted to break down the traditional form of family life. The marriage law promulgated in 1950 established equality between the sexes, making man and wife equal in their economic and social rights. Choice of mate is in the hands of each individual, and parents no longer have a legal right to control the lives of their married children.

Among the Cuna Indians, a monogamous people living on a string of islands along the eastern coast of Panama, marriages are parent-arranged. When an agreement is reached, the fathers notify the marriage maker, who, with his assistants, picks the prospective groom up bodily and carries him to the girl's house, calling out as they go, "Husband! Husband!" The two young people are placed in one hammock. The man, in accordance with prescribed ritual, bounces out and runs away, but the marriage maker recaptures him. If at that point he refuses to return to the hammock, the marriage is off. Otherwise, he returns, runs away four times in all, and is brought back. On his fifth visit to the hammock, he stays all night, but no intimacies occur. The two remain awake all night, for it is a bad omen to fall asleep. Next morning, the young man accompanies his future father-in-law to the mainland and helps him to fetch firewood. This act seals the marriage. That night it is consummated.

The husband moves in with his wife's family, where several generations dwell. The household is united through the female line, but the oldest male is its head, and all other residents acknowledge his authority.[3]

These are three illustrations of family. They are different in certain respects, but all have certain features in common. Families everywhere are expected to fulfill two general, primary functions.

First, the procreative and mating behavior of individuals is regulated largely through the institutional system of the family. Biological reproduction is essential for human survival, yet the foundation of the human family is social, not biological. The biological factor is directed and controlled by social norms. Biologically, most human beings can procreate, but the particular conditions under which they do so are socially determined.

Since norms differ by society, we find varying forms of family in different societies. The Nayar and the Chinese have dissimilar mores and family forms. But since the family functions to control reproduction, the institutional system is limited by the biological nature of humanity. No amount of social pressure can make a man bear children or a woman produce a child every week. The biological nature of the human organism thus limits the possible variations of family forms.

The second general and primary function of families is the care, protection, and early socialization of children. The infant's first and most intimate contact is with its family, and it is through this group that it survives its helpless years. The family is closely and persistently connected with almost everything the child does in this early formative period. The socialization of children within the family is an important factor in personality formation.

All human families are alike with respect to these general functions, and these only. Functionally, then, *the institutional system of the family is that form of social organization which is universally used to regulate the mating behavior of adults and to provide for the rearing of children.* Within this system, specific family units consist of institutionalized social groups whose members are related by descent, marriage, or adoption.

While families everywhere have the same primary functions, they have secondary functions that differ considerably according to the society. In some, *economic activities* are concentrated almost entirely within the family group. In others, such as our own, this function is widely distributed and carried on through the agency of business, industrial, and agricultural systems, although the family remains a consuming unit of products and services.

In some societies the family assumes responsibility for the *health and protection of its members*. In our own, these functions have been largely transferred to public health agencies, hospitals, and fire and police departments.

Among some people the family is assigned almost complete responsibility for the *education,* or socialization, of children, but we expect the school system to share this task with the family to an increasing extent.

Families also vary with regard to their expected responsibility for the *care and welfare of elderly persons*. Among some people parents have an unquestioned right to depend on adult offspring during their declining years. But in the United States, this job gradually is being transferred to public and private agencies established for that purpose.

STRUCTURAL ORGANIZATION OF THE FAMILY

CLASSIFICATIONS OF FAMILY ORGANIZATION

The family is a durable but not a permanent group, for the members are not immortal. But there is continuity from family to family over the generations, adults transmitting to offspring elements of culture that were transmitted to them. In this manner human beings everywhere develop social norms determining the composition, size, and living arrangements of their family units. They establish rules for entering and leaving family groups. The status and role of each member within the family group are culturally determined.

The structural form of the family may be analyzed from several vantage points. It can be conceived of, for example, in terms of *conjugal* and *consanguine* units.

A *conjugal unit consists of husband, wife, and children*. When Victor marries Ruth, they make up a conjugal unit, and when they have childen, these become part of the conjugal unit. A *consanguine unit, on the other hand, is composed of persons related by common descent.* Victor, his parents, sister, grandparents, aunts, uncles, and cousins form a consanguine family unit. (See Figure 24.1.) A conjugal family unit generally lives together, but a consanguine unit may or may not occupy one household.

Figure 24.1
Consanguine Family Unit
Carl Mydans, *Life* Magazine © Time Inc.

The conjugal family is often referred to as a *nuclear* family
and the consanguine family as an *extended* family. Where the
conjugal family is concerned, the alternate term is appropriate
when we are referring to a family *unit,* but not when we have
in mind a family *system.* There is no known nuclear family
system, if by that we mean one in which, normally, families of
a given society maintain few if any relations with their more
extended kin.

Every society recognizes both a conjugal and a consanguine
family unit, but there is variance in the degree to which each
is a functioning organization. In the United States we consider the conjugal unit the more significant. Our daily lives
revolve around it, and we feel closest to its members. Grandma

and Aunt Sally do not usually live with us, and if they do, they probably have little authority.

Elsewhere the consanguine family functions as a unit, an example being the "great family" in traditional Chinese society described by Yang. A variant of this system, the bilateral extended family, is found in such countries as France, Belgium, Spain, Italy, and Portugal.* It typically includes parents, their children, and both the maternal and paternal grandparents, aunts, uncles and cousins. Thus, instead of only the husband's *or* wife's kinfolk being integrated into the consanguine unit, the families of *both* are so integrated.

Another difference between the "great family" such as that found in older China and the bilateral extended family in certain European countries is that, in the former, the entire family dwells in one household, whereas, in the latter, the extended family comprises a number of nuclear units, most of them occupying separate establishments. Collectively, these nuclear units form a family hierarchy in which the members have differential status, generally associated with age, wealth, and potential utility. Certain kinds of decisions are arrived at within this hierarchy in an informal family council. According to sociologist Dorothy R. Blitsten, this council ". . . can bring important pressures to bear on each nuclear unit to conform to family standards and contribute to family enterprises and welfare."[4]

The extended family of the bilateral type usually spans three generations, the members of which honor obligations to each other.

The bonds of mutual responsibility . . . are permanent, whether they are reinforced by affection or not. Whatever their internal tensions, these families usually present a united front to outsiders. Furthermore, they are closed circles. The introduction of strangers is rare and not lightly undertaken. Children do not bring playmates or companions into their homes indiscriminately; men do not bring home their colleagues or business associates; neighbors do not drop in to introduce themselves. . .

These extended families constitute a private world which is a center of dependable relationships for life. . .[5]

* For an interesting, detailed description of the bilateral extended family in Latin Catholic Europe, see Dorothy R. Blitsten, *The World of the Family* (New York: Random House, 1963), pp. 132–165.

Actually, the "great" and the bilateral extended family households have been relatively rare. They are restricted mostly to wealthy families. A distinction must therefore be borne in mind, between the *real* and the *ideal* family forms in traditional China and elsewhere.

Another way of classifying family units is in terms of the *type of marriage sanctioned*. Throughout the world there are two fundamental forms of marriage: *monogamous* and *polygamous*.

Monogamy is the union of one man with one woman.
Polygamy is plural mating.

Plural mating may be subdivided into three categories:

Polyandry: One woman mates with two or more men.
Polygyny: One man mates with two or more women.
Cenogamy: Two or more men mate with two or more women in group marriage.

The most prevalent form of marriage is monogamy, as in our country. In all societies, whatever other forms are recognized, monogamy is a legitimate type of marriage, often desirable for economic, if for no other, reasons.

Among polygamous forms, polyandry is relatively uncommon. Anthropologists suggest that this mating pattern is correlated with economic hardships and the necessity for limiting family size. In Tibet, when Linton wrote *The Study of Man*, all arable land had passed into family holdings, many so small they could scarcely support a conjugal group, and certainly not if they were further subdivided as each son married and set up an independent household. It had become customary, among those of low economic status, for sons jointly to marry one wife and work the family holding together.[6]

Not all polyandrous marriages are of the fraternal type, in which brothers form a union with one woman. In some societies the female marries several men not related to each other.

Polygyny is much more prevalent than polyandry. It exists among the Eskimo hunters and pastoral peoples in Asia, Africa, and America. In Moslem societies, four wives at one time are allowed by the Koran, the sacred book of Mohammedans. Polygyny is also sanctioned in Java, but, generally speaking, only the wealthier men can afford plural wives. Among the nonliterate Tiwi of North Australia, it was not uncommon for a half dozen wives to live with one husband, and there are cases on record of Tiwi men having taken as many as twenty or more wives.[7] Since the introduction of Catholicism, however, polygyny has been discouraged.

Cenogamy is very rare. Where practiced, it does not amount to promiscuity, for such matings are regulated according to established custom. Cenogamy is usually approved only among "age mates." In a New Guinea group, for instance, all males born within a given period of time have certain duties and privileges in common, including the sharing of individual wives.

Family may further be classified by the manner in which descent is recorded, thus:

> *Patrilineal:* Descent comes down through the male line.
> *Matrilineal:* Descent is recorded in the female line.
> *Bilineal:* Descent is recorded in both male and female lines, as in the United States.

Family may also be categorized according to the residence of the married pair. A *patrilocal* family is one in which husband and wife take up residence with the parents of the man, as in the traditional ideal Chinese system described at the beginning of this chapter. In a *matrilocal* scheme, residence is with the wife's parents, as in the case of the Cuna Indians.

As we have noted, in some societies the conjugal family does not dwell with a consanguine unit at all. This is the case in the United States, where the conjugal family is relatively self-sufficient and tends to be independent of other relatives.

We have also seen in the case of the Nayar that if the reports are correct—and some controversy on this score has arisen—there is a family plan fitting none of the above categories. The family consists of the mother and her offspring by several lovers. Neither the original husband nor the later lovers form part of a conjugal or consanguine family with the woman and children.

Still another vantage point for viewing the family is in terms of the *dominance factor,* that is, who is for the most part considered its head. There are *patriarchal, matriarchal,* and *equalitarian* patterns.

In the *patriarchal* form, a male plays the dominant role. Many societies have family systems approaching this type (an "ideal type," for there are no pure cases), including, for example, ancient Rome and, more recently, Old World Jews of the Orthodox persuasion. In the latter, the father is head of the household; theoretically he is the final arbiter, the seat of authority in all matters. Should he decide to divorce his mate, he simply states his reasons to the rabbi, and if they are accepted, the divorce is granted. The wife has no right to be heard in the matter. Should she want to divorce her husband, she could not do so without his consent, and then it would be he who would take the action in severing the relationship.

In the *matriarchal* family, the woman plays a dominant role. Note we do not say *the* dominant role. Matriarchy is relatively a very rare type of family and, again, never found in what might be thought of as a pure form, if by that we mean a society actually ruled by women. No such society is known to exist. We use the term "matriarchal family" in a relative sense, to refer to a pattern in which women play a very important, perhaps a major, role. Among the Navaho, for example, descent is in the wife's line (matrilineal), and women play a major part in the social and economic life of the community. They have a voice in all family affairs and often their decisions are final.

In the *equalitarian* family, husband and wife share responsibilities and authority about equally. The United States offers as close an example as can be found, although at most it is an emerging rather than an established pattern. The United States family is still basically patriarchal, although women are becoming more and more influential in many family activities and, of course, frequently play the dominant role in child rearing.

Obviously, individual exceptions will be found no matter what the basic form of family within the culture. There are dominant males in what, by broad definition, we designate as matriarchal family societies. There are dominant females in patriarchal groups. In the so-called equalitarian family, a husband or wife may exercise more authority than his or her spouse. Or one member of the couple may rule in some matters, bow to the superior influence of the mate in others. (And many American parents ruefully assert that neither father nor mother is the authority, that the children dominate both.)

DATING, COURTSHIP, & MATE SELECTION

Dating, courtship, and mate selection are discussed here in connection with the structural organization of the family, since they play an important part in the founding of specific families.

DATING · *A date is a casual social undertaking for mutual pleasure, a means by which individuals test themselves in relations with persons of the opposite sex.* Dating, as we understand the concept, is most common in societies following the conjugal family pattern. In other family systems, dating is unnecessary or prohibited, since marriages are arranged by adult members of the family. Among Moslems, for example, family interests are the primary considerations involved, not the feelings of the boy and girl. Often, a contract between two families is sealed when the children concerned are very young, with the marriage taking place later.[8] Among the Tiwi, prior to the introduction of Christian ideology, infants were betrothed at birth.[9] In some societies, not only are marriages prearranged, but the prospective bride and groom do not see each other until the day of the ceremony. In others, they are permitted to meet and become acquainted prior to marriage but only after a betrothal has been arranged by representatives of the two families.

Despite the tradition of arranged marriages, however, in some societies the boy and girl see each other at family and ceremonial gatherings, although they may exchange little conversation. If, let us say, the girl develops a romantic interest in the young man, and he is eligible by family and other status, she may prevail upon her parents to initiate proceedings for a marriage agreement.

In the United States, marriages are not ordinarily arranged by adult members of the families concerned. Traditionally, they are based on personal choice and "romantic" love. Young people, therefore, must have an opportunity to meet and become acquainted. Dating serves this function. In our society, a date does not indicate that a couple is in love. The date has no meaning beyond that indicated in our definition: It is a casual social undertaking for mutual pleasure, a means by which individuals test themselves in relations with persons of the opposite sex. Nevertheless, some of its aspects may not be considered casual by outside observers. Scenes such as those in Figures 24.2 and 24.3 do not represent casual boy-girl relations to many concerned parents.

COURTSHIP · When dating leads to "going steady," the courtship period may begin, although "going steady" need not have that connotation. In recent years, junior high school and even elementary school children in the United States have been "going steady." We may assume, however, that most of their parents would consider them too young to engage in courtship. *Courtship is behavior by which an individual attempts to bring about consent to marriage by a person of the opposite sex whom he or she wants to marry.*

Just as dating is not a universal practice, so not all societies practice courtship as a prelude to marriage. It would not be permitted in the Chinese village described by Yang, where arranged marriages are the rule. On the other hand, in Burma, where marriage by arrangement is a current practice, there is also marriage by choice, with courtship preceding the wedding. In our own society, of course, where selection of a mate

Figure 24.2
Dating Behavior
Ralph Crane, Black Star.

Figure 24.3
Dating Behavior
W. C. Rauhauser.

is by personal consent, courtship is possible and even necessary.

MATE SELECTION · Between courtship (or some other preliminary pattern) and marriage there is the intermediate step of mate selection, that is, the formal recognition that two people undertake to be wed. In our society, as in certain others, this intermediate step may take the form of *engagement*, which is *a formal announcement by two people of their intention to be married*. Engagement is quite prevalent in England, France, Spain, Germany, and other European countries. And it is not unheard of in Asia. In Burma, after a period of court-ship, if a young man and the girl he has been seeing agree they want to be wed, he tells his parents, who then call upon the girl's parents. This formal visit is called *hyaung hlande*, which means "opening the road." If the visit is well received, the couple is considered engaged, or ready to marry.[10]

In the United States, engagements are agreed upon first and primarily by the two people concerned. Only after they have agreed they *are* engaged is it likely that the respective parents will be informed. The latter may or may not thereafter an-nounce the engagement publicly. Sometimes, a couple become secretly engaged, not informing the parents at all. Custom in our country is less rigid with respect to engagement than it is in many others.

MARRIAGE

Marriage is a formal, usually durable, and socially recog-nized union between persons of opposite sex. A majority of adults in all societies are married, as marriage is here defined.

According to estimates of the Bureau of the Census published in November 1967, some 91 million individuals were married, among the 200 million of all ages in our population.[11] Ap-proximately two-thirds of all women and over one-third of all men in the United States are married by the time they reach the age of 21. In the past several years there have been about 1.5 million marriages annually.[12] We are indeed a marrying people, as witnessed by the fact that 95 percent of persons between the ages of 45 and 54 are, or have been, married at some time.[13]

Marriage is socially defined. In no society may an individual decide for himself what constitutes a valid marriage. Every-where, the way to enter a marriage is prescribed in the culture.

In the United States, a legal marriage is a civil contract entered into with the consent of both parties, each capable in law of contracting, that is, by age and mental status being deemed legally competent to contract. Monogamy is the sole form of mating permitted by custom and law, and personal consent is a requirement, legally and socially. In our culture, marriage places a man and woman under certain legal obli-gations to each other. Every state has laws prescribing how the members of the couple shall behave toward each other with regard to such matters as establishment of common domicile, financial support, and responsibility for debts incurred by a member of the couple. Laws also define parental responsibility for the care, custody, and education of their children. Other statutes spell out children's obligations toward their parents. In addition, there are legally established procedures for modifying the civil contract of marriage by separation and divorce. Penalties are assessed for family desertion.

SOCIAL PROBLEMS RELATING TO THE FAMILY

Let us consider some of the social problems related to the institution of family in the United States.

FAMILY BREAKUP

Perhaps the most frequently mentioned is family breakup by separation, desertion, or divorce. One of the reasons for the conflict of values on this subject is that many people consider marriage a sacred state, ordained in heaven, to be dissolved only by death. All major religious groups in this country frown on family breakup. The Roman Catholic Church forbids divorce in all cases where it considers that a valid marriage exists, although one may be granted by special papal dispensation in specific cases.

No accurate figures are available on the extent of desertion or of legal separation of husbands and wives by means other than divorce. Statistics on legal divorce are somewhat more reliable. In 1965, an estimated 481,000 divorces were granted in the United States. The rate was 2.5 per 1,000 population.[14] In the past fifty years our divorce rate per 1,000 population appears to have doubled,[15] despite some year-to-year fluctuations.

Roman Catholics have a lower divorce rate than Protestants or Jews, but Catholic couples seem to be involved in desertion cases to a greater degree than is to be expected from their proportion in the population.

Contrary to some opinion, the United States does not lead the world in divorces. A majority of primitive societies have higher rates of marital dissolution than we have.[16] Divorce rates fluctuate everywhere from year to year. Japan's rate exceeded ours in the 1880s, and Egypt had a slightly higher rate than the United States in 1955. In Great Britain, Belgium, Holland, Sweden, and New Zealand the per capita rate of *increase* is higher than ours. But the fact remains that although the United States does not always stand at the very top in divorce rate, it does rank among the highest consistently, if we exclude marital dissolution in primitive societies.

Economic conditions seem to be a factor in divorce in the United States. Generally, when the economy is sound and there is little unemployment, the number of divorces increases; during economic recessions and depressions, divorce declines. One explanation may be that when incomes are relatively high, people are able to pay the lawyers' fees, court costs, and alimony involved in such litigation, as a consequence of which the tendency to break up an unhappy marriage by legal divorce increases. In hard times, evidence suggests, unhappily married people are more likely to be involved in family desertion and separation without legal sanction.

A major concern regarding divorce in the United States is over the future of the children involved. In a large consanguine family such as prevails elsewhere, close relatives in the household care for a child of divorced parents. Because in our small conjugal American family a child may be left stranded, courts demand assurance that offspring will be properly cared for before they grant divorces.

Another problem centering around family breakup is the law itself. Divorce is a litigious action in this country, that is, one party must be shown to be "at fault." The other member of the couple must establish in court that a legal cause exists, in that the mate has been guilty of adultery, cruelty, or other statutory basis for granting a divorce. Curiously, if *both* parties have been guilty of behavior constituting grounds for action, in legal principle, a divorce will *not* be granted. Yet, many critics of our divorce laws assert, in the vast majority of cases both parties are to some extent at fault when a marriage founders.

It has been suggested by some (against the vehement opposition of others) that a divorce should cease being a matter for litigation. The two persons concerned, it is posited, should be able to come into court and, without acrimony or recrimination, obtain a divorce simply on the contention that they find themselves incompatible. Yet mutual incompatibility, perhaps the *actual* reason for most divorces, is accepted as a legal ground in only a small proportion of United States jurisdictions. Hence subterfuges are often used by divorcing couples and their attorneys.

Since there is no federal law on divorce, each state writes its own. As a result, there is a considerable variety of acceptable grounds for action, and it is harder to obtain a divorce in one jurisdiction than another. For instance, there are ten acceptable grounds in Kansas. In New York there was only one—adultery—until 1966, when the grounds were widened by the legislature to include a total of five. Experience reveals that, in "tough divorce" states, annulment and family desertion are resorted to in many instances in lieu of legal divorce.

It should not be assumed that sociologists are categorically opposed to divorce and family breakup. Much depends upon the particular circumstances and the values the couple hold. For many, family breakup offers the only way to rectify an intolerable condition. Others, adhering to the religious tenet that "What God hath joined together, let no man put asunder," regard divorce or separation as more intolerable than continuing to endure a disappointing marriage. Parents may stick to marriages only because they believe that maintaining the family intact will serve the best interests of the children. Other parents feel it will be better for the offspring if the incompatible adults separate. As sociologists, we strive to understand all points of view.

COUNTERING FAMILY BREAKUP · In the face of a rising divorce rate, countermoves have been directed at sustaining family life. One of the primary sources of unhappy marriages and family breakups in our society seems to be the inability of young people to determine before marriage whether they can live together harmoniously. Often a boy and girl, meeting for the first time, feel an almost spontaneous mutual attraction. This is sometimes called "love at first sight." Such superficial impressions have about the same predictive utility for selecting a life partner as would be the case if someone picked a name from a hat and married that person. The cartoon, Figure 24.4, suggests that some criteria young people use in choosing husbands and wives are not even remotely related to the personal attributes they will later learn to consider desirable in their spouses.

Studies have been undertaken to determine what conditions

Figure 24.4
In the Romantic
Marriage Tradition
Drawing by Geo. Price;
Copr. © 1953 The New
Yorker Magazine, Inc.

*"When I think of some of the men I might
be married to now if it hadn't been
for you and that damn ukulele!"*

generally lead to successful marriage. Prediction scales have been worked out in attempts to foretell marital outcome, although they are highly experimental and limited in value at present. But some of the research findings upon which they are based are worth considering.

1. Indications are that chances for happiness are decreased when males marry before age twenty and females before they are eighteen. The optimum (most favorable) age seems to be somewhere between twenty-one and twenty-five for women, somewhat higher for men.

2. Persons engaged less than six months have the highest failure rate.

3. Some evidence, not altogether conclusive, indicates that persons of different religious faith, each sticking to his or her religion, have a higher breakup rate than individuals of like religion, other things being equal.

4. Individuals from families in which the parents were happily mated, gave children affection and moderate and consistent discipline, and encouraged a healthy attitude toward sex are more favorable matrimonial risks than those from backgrounds not meeting these specifications.

5. The sociable, conventional person who is somewhat of a joiner and a church and Sunday school attender is said to

have a better than average chance for successful—or at least permanent—marriage. But the couple needs to have traits in common, similar tastes and views. A sociable husband and an introverted wife might not make a good combination.

6. A moderate income at marriage, rather than a low or high one, is associated with marital felicity, as are a regular work record on the part of the wage earner and the habit of consistent saving.

7. Romantic marriages "for love" that disregard practical factors entirely tend to turn out unsatisfactorily, as do elopements and whirlwind marriages of the love-at-first-sight and let's-get-this-settled-for-keeps type.

8. Compatibility of the couple during courtship is a plus factor. With exceptions, of course, persons who were, on the whole, mutually compatible and who had relatively few violent quarrels during courtship have a better chance of being happily wedded than individuals who were comparatively incompatible during the courtship period.

9. Adaptability is a factor in marital adjustment. Individuals who are slow to anger and quick to get over it, who can compromise in arguments, and who do not feel a strong need to dominate others do best in the married state.

10. All else being equal, the higher the educational level of the partners and the closer they are in educational achievement, the greater the chance of successful adjustment in marriage. Although the more highly educated tend to be slower to marry than is the case with persons of less education, it seems they are more likely to "make a go of it" once they take the vows. In 1960, for instance, some 86 percent of married professionals and technicians in the middle ages of 45 to 54 were living with their first wives, as against 72 percent of farm laborers.[17]

Marriage prediction studies, like insurance actuarial tables, are an exercise in probability. Generalizations about *groups* are arrived at on the basis of experience with *individual* cases. Actuarial statistics show, let us say, that of 1,000 persons of a certain background, 900 will live beyond age sixty. Similarly, a marriage prediction scale may lead to the expectation that of 1,000 individuals of a particular background, 900 will have successful, or at least permanent, marriages when they do wed. That is a probability and a generalization with respect to the entire group. The question remains: *Which* 900 will "succeed," and which 100 "fail"? If you were to rate yourself and a person in whom you have a romantic interest according to the scale, to determine whether you are "well matched," you might be misled. You would have 900 chances of eventually "succeeding" in marriage, but you might be one of the 100 in that 1,000 who would "fail" if you married the particular individual with whom you matched yourself.

The prediction of marriage outcome may be rendered more effective by current computer research, and this may prevent some unions that have little statistical chance of turning out well, but the comment made above holds here, too. The predictions are generalizations about groups; they do not "guarantee" a like outcome in the individual case.

Another approach to maintenance of family life consists of services for alleviating tensions in already existing families. The case study and other methods of investigation have pinpointed elements of family life particularly productive of friction. High on the list is the economic condition of the household. When the wage-earning husband becomes unemployed or unemployable, he tends to lose status in some families and in the community. Even if the other members of the family do not remind him of his inability to support his dependents, his own feelings may bring him to abdicate his headship, symbolically, in favor of his wife. At the same time, his altered status may render him unhappy or resentful over the situation. Tensions and discord could be a consequence.

Other factors that appear to have some bearing on family tensions include sexual incompatibility of husband and wife; religious differences over the rearing of children; emotional instability of one or both spouses; parent-child friction; chronic illness; and, especially among upwardly mobile families, disparities between husband and wife in adaptability to changing styles of life.

PLANNED PARENTHOOD

Historically, the size and quality of the family, as well as of the general population, have been controlled for centuries in various parts of the world. Sexual taboos and the cultural regulation of marriage have had the effect of limiting the size of the family. Measures like infanticide, abortion, sexual abstinence, and castration have been used in a deliberate attempt to achieve this end. But often population control has been the accidental result of external events like famine, pestilence, and war. Among planned institutional methods have been restrictive marriage laws, eugenics, sex education, and sterilization.

In its wider connotation *birth control is the regulation, by any means, of births within a family or society.* However, in this country we generally apply the term only to *those practices consciously designed to prevent conception* at a particular time. This differentiates it from attempts to *interrupt a pregnancy* after conception. In the sense in which we use the term, birth control may be accomplished by mechanical or chemical contraception, sexual abstinence, and other means. It is not practiced solely to keep a couple childless, but to give the husband and wife some choice as to the number of children they will have and the chronological spacing between them. Voluntary regulation of family size is a subject on which members of our society evidence conflicting values, of course, but, as many recent studies demonstrate, there is a growing acceptance (in all major religious groups) of deliberate contraceptive controls.

Mechanical and chemical contraceptive methods were known as far back as the fourth century B.C. The American Medical Association officially recognized this area as an integral part of medical practice and education in 1937.

The Roman Catholic Church has, with great consistency, ruled the utilization of mechanical and chemical contraceptives to be immoral. It does sanction regulation of births under certain circumstances through the limitation of sexual intercourse to the so-called safe period, although in 1951, Pope Pius XII warned that this practice should not be abused by overuse. Very recently, some members of the Roman Catholic hierarchy have suggested the advisability of restudying the entire matter of contraception in the light of a changed and changing culture and the accretion of scientific data on the subject—and the use of birth control techniques by Catholics has increased substantially.

Protestants are not united in their position. The Federal Council of Churches of Christ in America as far back as 1938 held, through its Commission on Marriage and the Home, that the careful and restrained use of contraceptives by married people was valid and moral. However, a few Protestant denominations still oppose this view.

Orthodox Judaism, in religious principle, is opposed to the use of chemical-mechanical contraceptive devices under all circumstances. Reformed Jewry, through the Central Conference of American Rabbis, wrote into its 1929 social justice program the recognition that "intelligent birth regulation" was a legitimate method for coping with certain social problems. And Conservative Jewry passed a resolution in 1934 through the Rabbinical Assembly of America, urging Congress and the states to enact legislation to permit the dissemination of contraceptive information by responsible medical agencies. The official positions of these three branches of American Judaism, as reflected above, remain basically unaltered to this time.

While some individuals still regard the very subject of birth control as abhorrent, such pioneers as Margaret Sanger and leaders of the Planned Parenthood Foundation have convinced a great many other people that contraceptives can be utilized to improve and strengthen family life in the United States. Agencies furnishing birth control information have increased; physicians and social workers generally advise in the matter; state laws have been liberalized.

THE DISPARATE SEX RATIO

A social problem of limited magnitude exists in the fact that for some years now, more girls than boys have been born in this country. In 1967, for every 100 girls aged 18 to 22, there were only 91 boys of ages 20 to 24.[18] This means that there are not enough males to mate with all of the available females. This creates a competition of sorts for husbands, but the situation is not alarming at the present time. A better male-female balance may come about in the near future. And if it does not, and the disparate sex ratio remains about what it is, this will scarcely create a crucial problem bearing on the institution of the family in the United States.

TRENDS IN AMERICAN FAMILY LIFE

Let us turn to a consideration of some of the changes in American family life over the years.

CHANGING ATTITUDES TOWARD SEXUAL BEHAVIOR

Although the culture of a people changes continuously, the change is not always in one direction. We have more sexual freedom today than did our fathers and grandfathers in 1900. On the other hand, there were periods prior to 1900 when greater freedom was permitted than is the case today. Sex mores follow one direction, then another, and in any one period both conservative and liberalizing influences are at work.

In the third and second centuries B.C., sexual freedom in Greek culture was far greater than in twentieth century America. By present standards, English and French court life of several centuries ago was licentious in the extreme. We think of Victorian England as the epitome of sexual inhibition, and in certain respects it was, yet as Steven Marcus makes clear in *The Other Victorians*,[19] this same mid-nineteenth century England was characterized by great licentiousness and a flood of pornographic writing.

Early in our history, a girl who "walked out" with a young man made sure to be very circumspect. She insisted upon observance of the properties. So much so that she shocked the French novelist-essayist Marie Henri Beyle (1783–1842), better known by his pen name, Stendhal. He was shocked, not by what the dating couple did, but by what they did not do. In his book *On Love,* he wrote: "American girls are so saturated and fortified with reasonable ideas that in that country love, the flower of life, has deserted youth. At Boston a girl can be left perfectly safely alone with a handsome stranger—in all probability she is thinking of nothing but her marriage settlement." Young people, he wonderingly reported, went sleighing together, yet "no inconveniences ever result." The Frenchman wryly asserted: "I admire such happiness, but I do not envy it. It is like the happiness of human beings of a different and lower species."

Of course Stendhal spoke from limited observation. The proprieties were indeed carefully observed for the most part— in public. But from the earliest days of settlement, in New England and elsewhere, sexual behavior in individual cases was of a sort that the French writer would apparently have found more to his liking had he been aware of it. Other visitors, including the Frenchman, Alexis de Tocqueville, did observe and report on it.

Dating and courtship now begin earlier than at the time of Stendhal's or Tocqueville's observations, and it is not unusual for a junior high school or even an elementary school girl and boy to go out together. Abigail Van Buren, a columnist specializing in "heart and home" problems, published the following exchange:

DEAR ABBY: Even though I am only 13, I know I am in love. Don't tell me I don't know what love is because for the last week all I have done is cried over him. Loving him is no problem, but him loving me is the problem.

Not long ago I thought I had a chance, but now there is no hope because of an 11-year-old girl who is throwing herself at him. Please tell me how to get him back, Abby. I will do anything.

BROKEN-HEARTED IN FLORENCE, S.C.

DEAR B.H.: It is difficult to compete with a "younger woman." But dry your tears, honey, and pretend you don't care. It may not win him back but at least you will show courage and good sportsmanship.

And if you're still crying by your 14th birthday, write again and we'll try something else.[20]

The liberalization of attitudes toward sexual behavior began on a large scale shortly after World War I and has, with some fluctuations, extended into the present time. Nevertheless, premarital chastity is still highly regarded in some social circles, although, as with respect to many modes of behavior, there is a difference between real and ideal norms in this area. Alfred Kinsey and his associates, in their studies conducted some years ago, found that more than half the women they interviewed had engaged in premarital intercourse. Of these, 53 percent confined it to the men they eventually married. An even higher rate of premarital intercourse characterizes the male population.

Nonvirgin girls are not considered "ruined" for life nowadays, and they are able to marry. Moreover, unwed mothers are regarded with greater tolerance and understanding than in the days of *The Scarlet Letter*.

The extent to which sexual *behavior* has changed in the past half century is often surmised but not really known. What is clear is that general *attitudes* on the subject have undergone a very marked change, and this has brought information about sexual behavior out in the open. It may be that this behavior has not changed a great deal in the past fifty years, but that we simply know more about contemporary patterns than was known earlier.

CHANGING PATTERNS OF AGE AT FIRST MARRIAGE

In 1890, the average age of men entering their first marriage was 26.1. For women it was 22.0. In 1920, the median age of males at first marriage was 24.6, and, in 1966, it was 22.8. The median age of females undertaking marriage for the first time in 1920 was 21.2; in 1966, it was 20.5.[21] Clearly, the trend is toward earlier marriage. Various circumstances account for the fact, an important one being that engagements tend to be of shorter duration than was characteristic prior to the present century. It was not uncommon in the nineteenth century for a couple to be engaged for three, four, or five years prior to marriage. Today, a year is a "long" engagement, and many young people are wed after a brief courtship, without an intervening formal engagement.

This trend is partly a consequence of an emerging pattern in which there is an overlap between schooling and the assumption of marital and even family responsibilities by young people. Often now—but rarely in earlier decades—two persons meet while attending college, are wed, and continue their schooling. Deferring marriage until after graduation is no longer considered desirable by some young people, hence long engagements are unnecessary.

CHANGING ROLES OF HUSBAND & WIFE

Since about the termination of World War I, the wife-mother has been freer to engage in pursuits of her own choosing than was her counterpart prior to that. She has a social life outside the family. She may undertake a career in business or industry. Many have entered professions, such as medicine, law, teaching, and social work. This is not to suggest that women never worked outside the home prior to World War I. Throughout our history, in fact, some women have performed work other than homemaking. Their labor was necessary in colonial America, and after the republic was founded, if community activities were to be maintained. For example, a granddaughter of Oliver Cromwell was the director of a salt works on this continent. Women have served as pawnbrokers, shopkeepers, shipowners, butchers, bakers, brewers, and innkeepers. With the advent of industrialization, they worked in factories and as bookkeepers, clerks, and stenographers. But to assert that women have always worked outside the home does not deny that important changes have taken place, particularly during the twentieth century.

Proportionately more *married* women are now in the labor market, as compared with earlier times. They enter more fields than previously, and they have become increasingly important to the economy of their households, contributing significantly to the family budget.

Some facts and figures:[22]

1 · One worker in three is a woman.
2 · In any average month in 1962, there were some 23 million women at work; by 1970, it is estimated approximately 30 million will be employed outside the home.
3 · Approximately three out of every five working women are married.
4 · Among married women, one in three is working.
5 · About one-third of these are employed only part time. Three-fifths of all part-time work is done by married women.

These trends do not signify that our culture places less value than formerly on family life. The latter still holds a paramount position in our value system. And it should also be noted that although one-third of married women are employed outside the home, part- or full-time, two-thirds are not.

There is even reason to believe that women are becoming more, not less, significant in the overall activities of family life. Some sociologists believe a *matricentric* family pattern is emerging in the United States, with the wife-mother assuming increasing authority. According to these social scientists, as cities push their boundaries outward and suburban life becomes a familiar pattern, father is more and more likely to be a commuter, gulping his breakfast coffee and dashing for his train to the city and returning at night, tired and anxious to relax. In between, mother handles the daily problems of household management. She is in charge of the family budget; she represents the family at the PTA. She makes many decisions that father formerly made, and the children look to her for guidance. It is she who is asked to aid in the Red Cross drive and the community chest campaign. She belongs to social clubs, engages in civic activity, and often has to explain to her husband what *is* going on in town. Cartoonists recognize the existence of the matricentric family, as in Figure 24.5.

Figure 24.5
Matricentric Family

Grin and Bear It by George Lichty courtesy Publishers-Hall Syndicate.

"Since the wife became active in her club committee work,
I feel painfully unimportant,
frittering away my time earning a living. . . ."

It is possible, however, that as the mother gains and the father gives up some authority, a greater balance of power will develop in the direction of a truly equalitarian family.

CHANGES IN SIZE OF FAMILY UNIT

Although young people are marrying earlier than in previous periods, family units are becoming smaller—that is, despite the fact that there are, on the average, more reproductive years for the conception of children, fewer have been born per family in recent years as compared with earlier periods. In 1790, the average family consisted of 5.7 persons, according to estimate. By 1900, the number had declined to 4.7. In 1954, it was 3.6. The size of the average United States family in 1964 was between 3 and 4, or about 3.5. Between 1954 and 1964, then, the size of the family unit has not changed appreciably.[23]

One factor in the seeming inconsistency between lower age at marriage and smaller family unit is that married persons have gained greater freedom to decide whether they want children at all and if so at what intervals and how many.

Close to 15 percent of married women never bear children. (However, the proportion of childless couples has declined during the past generation.[24]) College-educated parents have fewer children than those without higher education, and there are proportionately more married people with college educations than formerly.

Another important factor plays a part in the declining size of the American family. A great variety of attractive job opportunities have opened up for young women in the past several decades. Being married is no impediment where many of these are concerned, nor is motherhood. Married women, some with children, enter careers, perhaps when in their late twenties or early thirties, which are normally child-bearing years. For many, this puts an end to further procreation. Pregnancy, confinement, and the care of a newborn infant would interfere with a career, as some women view the matter.

Another factor tending to explain the smaller family unit is that the urban birth rate—for whatever reason—is lower than the rural, and we have become increasingly urbanized in the past century.

CHANGING FUNCTIONS OF THE AMERICAN FAMILY

In the past century, the American family has lost some of the functions once invested in it. It is not as self-sufficient an economic and production unit as formerly. It has given up some of its educative function to outside agencies. Government and other organizations have taken over some protective functions that were once the obligation of parents. Juvenile courts operate on the principle of *parens patriae*, meaning the state is the ultimate parent of minor children, responsible for their welfare. Government agencies have been established to furnish health protection, police and fire service, financial aid, unemployment insurance, stipends to the aging.

But if the American family has given up some of its functions, it is still not functionless. Rather it has become more *functionally specific*, concentrating upon certain remaining items of family life. It is no longer necessary for every member of every family to spend many hours either in outside employment or at household chores. The great majority of families have more leisure time nowadays. Husband and wife, parents and children can do things together. We place high value on the family that "plays together and stays together." Parents consider it their function to provide as good a home and schooling for their children as possible, in order that the entire family may have suitable status in the community.

CHANGING ATTITUDES TOWARD DIVORCE

As was pointed out earlier, our divorce rate is one of the highest in the world. With minor fluctuations, it has been rising since 1867. It declined during the depression of the 1930s, but at the lowest point in this decline, in 1932, the rate was still twice as high as the figure for 1890. An alltime peak was reached in 1946. There has been a modest decline since, but we are still far above the rate at the turn of the century.

We cannot say to what extent a changing culture has yielded tensions conducive to family dissolution. Nor do we know to what degree there were unofficial, unrecorded breakups in prior decades, when legal divorce was frowned upon more than today.

In the nineteenth century, a divorced woman was apt to be a social pariah, regardless of the circumstances leading to her status, and it was not easy for her to find another man willing to take a chance on her. A divorced man was likely to be categorized as a roué, a bounder, or at the very least a person who must be impossible to live with. Marriage was "for keeps," particularly in the eyes of churchmen, and divorce was consequently viewed with alarm and abhorrence. As late as 1926, a Bishop Charles Fiske characterized the then trend in marriage, as he discerned it, as "a tide of consecutive polygamy."[25] He meant that couples were too prone to take to the divorce courts, and he deplored this.

Today, divorce is still regarded by many as an undesirable device for terminating what should be a permanent relationship. Others, however, consider it a necessary and desirable legal procedure whereby marriages that never should have occurred may be dissolved. But whichever view may be the more prevalent, today divorced people are no longer pariahs. They need no longer feel ostracized. They are socially acceptable. And a divorce does not necessarily mean an end to living in the marital state: more than half the divorced persons remarry.[26]

CHANGING RELATIONS WITH CHILDREN

As we have gained more knowledge in the behavioral sciences, parents have been increasingly advised by psychologists and others on how to help their children become mature, wholesome personalities. The advice has not been consistent, as between one presumed authority and another. Child psychologists have run the gamut from one extreme to the other, some arguing that a youngster should never be pampered, while others have urged, "Never frustrate a youngster." During the 1920s, John B. Watson, following his own behaviorist thinking, insisted that it crippled children emotionally if they were shown much affection. Other psychologists, taking vigorous exception to this viewpoint, declared that a demonstration of affection is absolutely essential if a child is to achieve emotional maturity. The resulting controversy led some parents to become skeptical of the value of child psychology in general. Many others were simply confused, not knowing which side of the argument to espouse.

Neither of the extreme positions is currently in vogue. In recent years, parents have been influenced by the thinking of Benjamin Spock, Arnold Gesell, and others, whose books have become best sellers. We tend to be neither entirely permissive nor entirely authoritarian in rearing children. The preponderance of present-day opinion perhaps is that children should be helped to face life situations realistically; that some amount of frustration is inevitable and even desirable; that demonstration of parental love is a necessity if children are to achieve the emotional security that is a bulwark against the shock of overmuch frustration.

Young people are no longer to be seen and not heard. Their questions are answered without condescension. They are encouraged to develop their talents, to be individualistic to a degree, so long as they do not become antisocial.

Our present day thinking is grounded in the belief that one of the most important functions of individual family units is to foster a sense of emotional security in children, a feeling of belonging, a desire to perpetuate the institution of family and to keep it strong. The American poet, Robert Frost, expressed this for the millions when he wrote: "Home is the place where, when you have to go there/They have to take you in." The mother in particular in the American family is seen

as the fountainhead of love and understanding. The photograph in Figure 24.6 suggests this. It appeared over the caption, quoting Proverbs 3:18: "She is a tree of life to them . . ."

Having devoted a chapter to the family as an institutional system, we proceed, in the next, to discuss the institutional system of religion. We remind the reader, however, that all institutional systems of a society are interrelated. The separate discussion of each is only for the purpose of analysis.

· *NOTES*

1. Ralph Linton, *The Study of Man, An Introduction* (New York: Appleton-Century-Crofts, 1936), pp. 154–155.
2. Martin Yang, *A Chinese Village* (New York: Columbia University Press, 1945), pp. 54–67.
3. John Biesanz and Mavis Biesanz, *Modern Society, An Introduction to Social Science,* 2nd ed. (Englewood Cliffs, N. J.: Prentice-Hall, 1959), p. 25.
4. Dorothy R. Blitsten, *The World of the Family, A Comparative Study of Family Organizations in Their Social and Cultural Settings* (New York: Random House, 1963), p. 145.
5. *Ibid.,* p. 146.
6. Ralph Linton, *op. cit.,* p. 183.
7. C. W. M. Hart and Arnold R. Pilling, *The Tiwi of North Australia* (New York: Holt, Rinehart and Winston, 1960), pp. 16–17.
8. Blitsten, *op. cit.,* p. 201.
9. Hart and Pilling, *op. cit.,* p. 14.
10. Manning Nash, *The Golden Road to Modernity, Village Life in Contemporary Burma* (New York: Wiley, 1965), p. 250.
11. U. S. Bureau of the Census, *200 Million Americans* (Washington, D. C.: U. S. Government Printing Office, 1967), p. 7.
12. U. S. Department of Health, Education, and Welfare, *Converging Social Trends, Emerging Social Problems* (Washington, D. C.: U. S. Government Printing Office, 1964), p. 12.
13. U. S. Bureau of the Census, *op. cit.,* p. 19.
14. U. S. Bureau of the Census, *Statistical Abstract of the United States, 1967,* 88th annual ed. (Washington, D. C.: U. S. Government Printing Office, 1967), p. 47, Table No. 48.
15. U. S. Bureau of the Census, *200 Million Americans, op. cit.,* p. 20.
16. William J. Goode, *The Family* (Englewood Cliffs, N. J.: Prentice-Hall, 1964), p. 3.
17. U. S. Bureau of the Census, *200 Million Americans, op. cit.,* p. 20.
18. *Ibid.,* p. 19.
19. Steven Marcus, *The Other Victorians* (New York: Basic Books, 1966).

Figure 24.6
"She Is a Tree of Life to Them"
Consuela Kanaga.

20. "Dear Abby," in *Los Angeles Times*, September 2, 1966, Part IV, p. 5. Copyright 1966, Chicago Tribune-New York News Syndicate, Inc.

21. 1966 figures from U. S. Bureau of the Census, *200 Million Americans, op. cit.*, p. 23. All others from Ben Wattenberg with Richard M. Scammon, *This U.S.A., An Unexpected Family Portrait of 194,067,296 Americans Drawn From the Census* (New York: Doubleday, 1965), p. 35.

22. President's Commission on the Status of Women, *American Women* (Washington, D. C.: U. S. Government Printing Office, 1963), p. 27.

23. U. S. Department of Health, Education, and Welfare, *op. cit.*, p. 12.

24. *Ibid.*

25. Quoted in V. F. Calverton, *The Bankruptcy of Marriage* (New York: Macauley, 1928), p. 70.

26. U. S. Bureau of the Census, *200 Million Americans, op. cit.*, p. 23.

· SUGGESTIONS FOR FURTHER READING

BLITSTEN, DOROTHY R. *The World of the Family*. New York: Random House, 1963.
A comparative study of family organization in various parts of the world.

CUBER, JOHN F., with PEGGY B. HARROFF. *The Significant Americans, A Study of Sexual Behavior Among the Affluent.* New York: Appleton-Century-Crofts, 1965.
An intriguing inquiry into the sexual behavior of a group of people in the upper income brackets—their reasons for marrying, their conduct as married folk, patterns of infidelity, divorce.

EHRMANN, WINSTON W. *Premarital Dating Behavior*. New York: Holt, Rinehart and Winston, 1959.
A study of the dating and courtship practices of college students in the United States.

GOODE, WILLIAM J. *After Divorce*. New York: Free Press, 1956.
An investigation of the after-effects of divorce.

LINTON, RALPH. *The Study of Man*. New York: Appleton-Century-Crofts, 1936, Chapter 10, "The Family," Chapter 11, "Marriage," and Chapter 12, "Social Units Determined by Blood."
An interesting description of various forms of marriage and family life.

RODMAN, HYMAN (ed.). *Marriage, Family and Society*. New York: Random House, 1966.
This is a reader containing useful and interesting articles on dating relations and sex roles; mate selection; husband-wife relations; parent-child relations; adolescence; siblings and peers; extended kinship relationships; social class and family relations; and the changing American family. Among the inclusions are

some of the most significant sociological contributions to the study of the family as an institutional system.

THOMLINSON, RALPH. *Demographic Problems: Controversy Over Population Control*. Belmont, Calif.: Dickenson, 1967. Chapter 5, "Birth Control: Background," and Chapter 6, "Birth Control: Arguments."
The social and historical background of the birth control movement, with arguments that have been advanced for and against planned parenthood.

WARE, CAROLINE F., K. M. PANIKKAR, and J. M. ROMEIN. *The Twentieth Century*. Volume VI of *History of Mankind, Cultural and Scientific Development*. New York: Harper & Row, 1966, pp. 742–758.
Examines, historically and as social institutions, the urban family in the West, the joint family in the East, and the tribal family in Africa.

YANG, C. K. *The Chinese Family in the Communist Revolution*. Cambridge, Mass.: M.I.T. Press, 1959.
Describes changes in the Chinese family occurring as a consequence of the Communist revolution.

25 RELIGION AS AN INSTITUTIONAL SYSTEM

In this chapter we study the institution of religion, first as a universal phenomenon that is part of every culture. Then we address ourselves to religion as a social institution in the United States.

Not long ago a Christian church owned by Negroes was dynamited by white Christians. The same day, a Negro Christian minister's home was blasted by white Christians. They also blew up the house of a white Christian minister, pastor of a Christian church of Negro parishioners. White Christians of the town expressed horror and said they were revolted by the un-Christian violence of a handful of Christians.

Christianity preaches the brotherhood of man. The dynamiters called themselves Christians. The dynamited called themselves Christians. The whites opposed to the dynamiting called themselves Christians. Question: What is Christianity?

The Kaoka Speakers, who live on Guadalcanal, worship the spirits of certain warriors, sharks, and snakes. These spirits are said to possess *nanama*, a special power that can be exerted for the benefit of the living. Missionaries who came to Guadalcanal to convert the natives to Christianity considered the religious practices of the Kaoka Speakers a form of paganism, therefore to be condemned. Some Kaoka Speakers became Christians, others remained "pagans." Neither the "pagans" nor the Christianized natives are prone to be religiously orthodox today, tending to regard both religious systems—"pagan" and Christian—as valid. A common saying is that if a man remains faithful to the spirits and is prepared to make sacrifices to them, he can depend upon the help of ghostly *nanama*. If he turns to the Christian God and attends church regularly, he can expect to receive the benefit of divine *nanama*. The two forms of otherworldly power are seen as working in the same manner and achieving identical results.[1]

The missionaries insisted that Christianity was the only true religion, and the "pagans" insisted that spirit worship epitomized the only true religion. Many contemporary Kaoka Speakers believe that both spirit worship and Christianity are true religions. Question: What is *the* "true" religion? Which is the one and only "right" religion? Or may there be more than one? What, in fact, is *religion*, to begin with?

THE FUNCTIONAL MEANING OF RELIGION

Man wants to know about himself and his relation to the universe. When verifiable observations do not give him the answers, he sometimes falls back upon belief, accepting ideas on faith alone. *Every culture includes an institutional system of religious beliefs that provides an explanation of things that cannot be directly verified or explained otherwise.*

Although religion is found in every society, its beliefs and forms vary widely. In some societies people venerate their ancestors, in others they worship cows. Some believe in a single supernatural god, others in many. Most religions contain a promise of life after death, but some do not. Christianity discourages indulgence in "things of the flesh" except under carefully prescribed conditions. In ancient Paphos in Cyprus, women were required to prostitute themselves in the sanctuary of Aphrodite as a religious duty before marriage.

Earlier in this text, in discussing the scientific method, we differentiated between *knowledge* and *belief*. Let us now add that even under the most rigorous scientific observation, knowledge *is* belief in a sense. We *believe* a certain observed phenomenon represents *fact* because *we have learned in our culture to accept it as such.*

You hear a phonograph record. The voice is a *natural phenomenon* in your culture. Your study of science enables you to understand how sound is recorded on wax. You can test the theory of sound transmission, cut a record for yourself, prove that it works.

Now suppose you take the phonograph and the record into some remote part of the world, inhabited by a people who know nothing about modern science or technology. They are astounded, awed, terrified, by the unseen something making sounds. They cannot explain this by evidence from direct observation. They conclude, perhaps, that an invisible spirit is spinning about on the turntable, bringing them portentous word of something beyond their ability to comprehend but nevertheless requiring explanation. They attribute the circumstances to *sacred phenomena,* which are derived from a logic not based on objective observation and verification.

Either the natural or the sacred explanation is fact to those who believe it. In that sense both natural and sacred phenomena are such by *cultural definition.*

How does this situation relate to religion? Religious belief is based on what the persons concerned *consider* fact. For those who believe in a sacred phenomenon, it represents actual truth and has the force and effect of fact.

Man wonders about his origins. The scientist might trace life back to the amoeba. He cannot explain how that first amoeba began its existence but insists it must have been produced by a natural process that human minds are capable of comprehending. Another man within the same society declares that since we cannot explain the first breath of life on the basis of natural phenomena, there must be a sacred explanation. He concludes that God created life.

Thus, what we call religion is in part born of faith and accepted on faith. It is a powerful force in our society, as is science, and influential in determining the behavior of man and the course of his life.

We are now ready for a definition: *Institutional religion is a system that functions to maintain and perpetuate cultural beliefs about forces considered to be supernatural and sacred. This system provides guides for moral conduct and prescribes symbolic practices that are considered to be in harmony with beliefs about the supernatural.*

Varied as religious beliefs and practices are, they have at least one thing in common. Like all institutions, religion functions to serve the needs of a particular people. No social institution survives unless it does.

THE FUNCTION OF
INSTITUTIONALIZED RELIGION

What is the major social function of institutionalized religion? One of the best statements on the subject is contributed by Thomas F. O'Dea in *The Sociology of Religion*.² The central characteristic of religion, he says, is that it transcends everyday experience in the natural environment. And why should men require something that transcends experience? The need arises out of three fundamental characteristics of human existence: *contingency, powerlessness,* and *scarcity.*

Contingency. Man lives under conditions of uncertainty. Events of crucial significance to his safety and welfare are beyond his ability to foresee. (If you are single, for example, how efficiently can you predict whom you will marry or how that marriage will turn out?)

Powerlessness. Man's capacity to control and affect the conditions of his life is limited. (You can do something to assure yourself of a college education, but can you live forever merely by making up your mind to do so?)

Scarcity. This is a condition of all societies. Human beings everywhere are confronted by an insufficient supply of the things required to sustain life and to satisfy psychological and economic needs. (In our society there is a scarcity of fresh air and sweet water as well as of employment and educational opportunities.)

As a consequence of contingency, powerlessness, and scarcity, *frustration* and *deprivation* occur. *The major role of religion is to assist men to adjust to contingency, powerlessness, and scarcity, and thus to frustration and deprivation.*

This broad generalization on the functional meaning of religion may be reduced to some specifics. Religion has both *personal* and *social* functions for its participants. Some of the personal functions include the following:

1. *Religion provides a feeling of security.* "God is my Protector. I need not fear."

2. *It offers certainties in place of mysteries.* "Faith will be rewarded. There is an eternal life. I know I will share in it."

3. *It provides solace.* "The beloved dead are not really dead, but in The Promised Land. I will be reunited with them eventually."

4. *It gives believers a sense of power.* "A supernatural Power

is on the side of the believer. That Power will answer my prayers, punish my enemies, make it possible for me to achieve my goals."

The social, or interactive, functions of institutionalized religion include the following:

1. *Religion serves as a socializing force, a means of social control.* Possessors of the sacred knowledge, be they priests, ministers, or medicine men, tell the people what the deity wants, how he expects them to behave. Thus, the carriers of the word help build a moral order. In a sense they create good and evil, for they define morality and immorality. (See Figure 25.1.) Every society must have a devil of some sort. To accent the good way of life and its rewards, there is an evil way of life with its punishment. "A man never appreciates heaven until he has been to hell," comments an essayist.[3]

2. *The religious system supports other social institutions of a society, largely by providing guides for appropriate behavior.* It influences the form and behavior of families. It affects the institution of education. It sets some of the "rules" of economic practice. Religion and government are closely interrelated—in fact, in some societies religious law and the leaders of the religion *are* the government. While this is not so in the United States, there can be no question that religious attitudes play a part in government here. A President of the United States takes the oath of office by placing his hand upon the Bible. The oath of allegiance to the flag has children in the school system pledging loyalty to one nation, "under God."

3. *Increasingly, many religious organizations are becoming more involved in trying to improve the conditions of contemporary human life.* Instead of advocating reconciliation to undesirable conditions, some churches are now striving to resolve social problems and to control the direction of social change. Their leaders have interested themselves in such matters as equal justice for all the people, world peace, and the elimination of poverty.

Our previous discussion of manifest and latent functions of institutions in general can be applied to certain religious practices and customs. The ancient Chinese boiled their drinking water to drive out demons. This manifest function was purely religious in nature, but the latent function of this custom was to prevent the spread of cholera and other diseases. Similarly, the Jewish people traditionally considered it morally

Figure 25.1
Some Good in Evil?
Drawing by Alain; Copr. © 1943 The
New Yorker Magazine, Inc.

"Still, did you ever stop to think
where you and I would be if it weren't for evil?"

intolerable to eat the flesh of swine, and thus inadvertently they avoided contracting trichinosis, a disease that plagued their gentile neighbors.

4. *The religious system functions to promote social change,* as is implicit in the foregoing. For many years, Protestant churchmen furthered the conception that a man's condition on earth was preordained by God, hence no purpose was served by objecting to one's lot. With the advent of capitalism in the Western world, Protestant clergymen took a different view of the matter. They found religious justification for abandoning traditional norms that impeded the spread of the capitalist spirit. They approved the behavior of the new entrepreneurs, the businessmen. They encouraged people to forge ahead, rise above their immediate condition, and become "successful."

Religious injunctions stressing certain virtues and ways of life, such as love for one's fellowman, generated social change of another kind. The humanitarianism of the nineteenth century stemmed largely from Protestant teachings in England and the United States. These teachings fostered attitudes that led to the abolition of slavery, better treatment of the indigent, prison reform, the introduction of probation and parole, factory legislation, the growth of the charities movement, and other programs for human welfare.

In our own time, some religious groups have come out forcefully for social justice, equality of all men before God and in law, civil rights, amendment of abortion and birth control laws —all requiring social change.

5. *The religious system functions to retard social change.* There is no contradiction in saying it promotes both social change and social continuity. Both processes are continuously at work in society, we have learned.

When the institutionalized system of religion reinforces other social institutions of a society by providing guides for suitable behavior in the secular sphere, it promotes and helps perpetuate the existing social order. Confucianism, a philosophical-religious system, advocated the faithful performance of one's traditional duties and respect for traditional authority. This helped maintain the social status quo in mainland China for centuries.

Today, in our country, churchmen of various denominations urge their followers to maintain certain social norms unchanged. Christian fundamentalists insist on the maintenance of particular modes of behavior that presumably are approved by God. The "Protestant ethic," now that capitalism is well entrenched in Western countries, calls for the retention of given norms that will support a bourgeois capitalist economy: thrift, sobriety, hard work, and self-discipline. An employee should not watch the clock. He should give more of himself than is called for by the terms of his employment. If he abides by the morality of the Protestant ethic, he is the more likely to become a wealthy man himself, for the moral man is rewarded here on earth.

6. *The institutionalized system of religion may function both to promote and to diminish conflict.* Religious teachings and exhortations have brought the faithful to conquer and enslave nonbelievers and to slay them. Roman Catholics and Protestants have engaged in verbal and physical battles with each other on religious grounds. One Protestant denomination may attack another through its respective churchmen.

In recent years conflict has developed within the Roman Catholic Church over such matters as the manner of celebrating mass and whether priests should be permitted to marry or nuns allowed to modernize their garb. The orthodox Roman Catholic position on divorce has also been challenged from inside the fold. A Catholic priest has charged his cardinal with prejudice against Negroes. Another has written a book entitled *A Modern Priest Looks at His Outdated Church.*[4]

Although they have been a source of conflict at certain times and with regard to certain subjects, institutionalized religious systems have also functioned to diminish dissension and verbal or physical conflict. The injunction, "Peace on earth, good will to men," conveys the cooperative rather than the combative ideal. So do emphases on the brotherhood of man and on loving one's neighbor as one's self. The Quakers, for example, advocate peace and nonviolence at all times. Leaders of Eastern philosophical-religious systems urge an inner search for serenity, peace, and an understanding of self and the universe. Thus, Buddha

does not tell *why* we live, but *how* to live. He teaches a way of life, a way to rise above the troubles of life, and finally a way to achieve the ultimate happiness of Nirvana, in which state of blissful non-being untroubled peace is combined with the complete opening-up of understanding.[5]

STRUCTURAL ORGANIZATION OF RELIGION

FEATURES OF INSTITUTIONALIZED RELIGION

Religions are usually characterized by the following features:

1. *Beliefs.* Religious beliefs are expressed in the form of doctrines, articles of faith, and the like. Christian belief is incorporated in the Bible. Mohammedans have their Koran, Mormons the Book of Mormon. Much religious belief, however, is not committed to written form but is transmitted by word of mouth. This is obviously the case in nonliterate societies, where myths relayed from generation to generation by storytellers communicate religious beliefs. The snake spirits of the Kaoka Speakers of Guadalcanal, to which reference was made above, are the subject of myth. All of the spirits are said to be female. According to one myth, a snake spirit called Watumbala of Lasi clan had a human daughter who married a human being and conceived a human child. One day the mother left the baby in the care of its snake-spirit grandmother. When the husband came home, he was horrified to find his child in the coils of a serpent, not realizing that it was really a spirit. Seiz-

ing a stick, he tried to kill the serpent, but it escaped into the sea and swam to Guadalcanal. There it wandered about in search of a home and finally settled down in Moli village. That is why certain shrines were erected on Guadalcanal, for each represents a place where Watumbala stopped during its period of wandering. And Moli village, of course, remains its permanent home.[6]

2. *Hierarchy.* Many, but not all, religions are characterized by an hierarchical arrangement of personnel. Roman Catholic clergymen, for instance, perform the functions and have the status, respectively, of priest, bishop, archbishop, and pope. In addition to their purely ecclesiastical functions, many clergymen perform administrative duties within the church.

3. *Symbols.* The principal function of religious symbols is to emphasize the character and meaning of the supernatural force. The cross, for example, is a Christian symbol. A Judaic symbol is the phylactery, a small leather case containing slips inscribed with scriptural passages. One phylactery is fastened with leather thongs to the forehead of Orthodox Jewish males during morning prayer, another to the left arm.

4. *Rituals.* Numerous ritualistic activities are prescribed for believers. They have included the offering up of human and nonhuman sacrifices, feasts and fasts, dances and processionals, chanting, and birth and death rites. Kneeling is a ritual. So is prayer.

Anthropologist Manning Nash has described a Buddhist ritual, the taking of the five precepts, as practiced in Yadaw, Burma. The taking of the precepts is the act of making a promise or a vow to oneself. Upon arising in the morning, or before retiring at night, the individual stands before the Buddhist altar and recites aloud the five precepts, representing the moral code of the faith. Unless he goes through this ritual of taking the precepts at least once a day, he is not considered a Buddhist in fact.[7]

5. *Propitiation.* Ritual is intimately connected with the idea of propitiation, which refers to behavior deemed pleasing to the deity. Propitiation may be positive or negative. The first consists of things that should be done, the second of things that should not be done, if the deity is to be pleased.

Positive propitiatory customs with which you are probably familiar are the rituals of baptism, prayer, and confession of sin. Church attendance is a positive propitiatory procedure, too. In other societies, positive propitiation includes participation in what Christians would call sexual orgies, the slaying of Christians, and the performance of ceremonial dances. In Figure 25.2, a youth of a tribe of aborigines in the Australian bush is shown being initiated into adulthood. As he kneels, his totemic sponsor opens a vein in his own arm, lets the blood gush over the boy. In its meaning and purpose this ceremony is somewhat comparable to baptism among Christians.

Negative propitiatory customs are sometimes called *taboos.* Thus Christians must not commit adultery. Hindus must not eat the flesh of the cow.

In the broadest sense, propitiation defines what is acceptable behavior not only toward a deity but toward man. The injunction, "Honor thy father and mother," is in this category, as is the Christian doctrine, "Love thy neighbor as thyself." Persons following such teachings are presumed to please both man and God.

6. *Magic.* Many forms of institutionalized religion provide for the employment of magic to attain certain ends. In the religions that do not employ magic, ritual is presumed to place an individual in some sort of contact with the supernatural force and, hopefully, to elicit a favorable response from that force; thus the Christian prays to and hopes to be favored by his God, but he does not believe he can force God into doing anything by offering up his prayers. Magic ritual, on the other hand, is activity whereby the supernatural force may be manipulated to bring about the desired consequences in the empirical world. A causal relation is believed to exist between the magic ritual and control and manipulation of the particular supernatural force.

Thus, in Burma, the magician writes an *in,* a cabalistic charm, on a piece of paper, to prevent a specific kind of occurrence, such as illness or death from bullets.[8] Among the Burmese, magic may be *white* or *black*. White magic is beneficent in its effects, whereas black magic harms people. Burmese villagers practice a white magic in which they tattoo a blue band on their ankles or wrists to the accompaniment of incantations. This is supposed to repel snakes and prevent snake bite.[9] Black magic includes the kind worked by *sonma,* or witches. These malevolent creatures supposedly can manipulate a supernatural power, causing a mortal to fall ill. *Sonmas* can turn themselves into vultures, snakes, dogs, and horses,

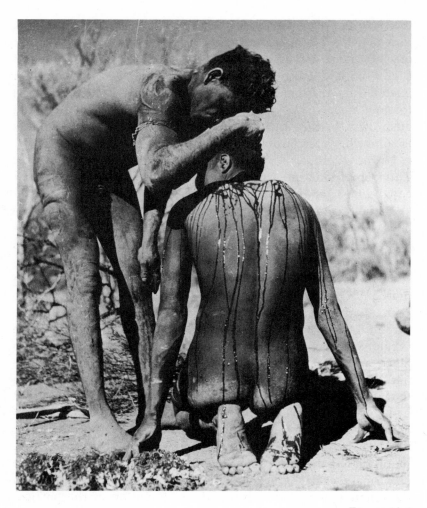

Figure 25.2
Propitiatory Behavior
Jens Bjerre.

and can work their evil from great distances. There is Daw Ni, for instance, a famous witch on the Mu river, in Nondwin, who caused so much trouble a great many years ago, according to the myth, that a band of men set out to call upon her and challenge her power. Her occult sense informed her of their approach, whereupon she worked her magic and caused their testicles to be removed. Horrified, the men continued their march and entered Daw Ni's presence, no longer to challenge her but to beg pardon for having thought of doing so. She pointed to a basket in which they found their testicles. Each took his own and returned to the village, never again to contest Daw Ni's power.[10]

SUBDIVISIONS OF INSTITUTIONALIZED RELIGION

The structural organization of religion takes many forms, differing by society. The present discussion is confined largely to certain structures characteristic mainly of Christianity and Judaism, since the bulk of our population claims membership in one or the other of these faiths.

1. *A sect is a relatively small group of religious separatists.* They consider themselves a select group who alone understand what the deity requires of mortals. They try to live, in all ways, according to the dictates of divine law as they understand it. Religious doctrine is strictly interpreted, and other interpretations are rejected as false. Heresy may be punished by expulsion from the sect. Membership in sects is voluntary. Jehovah's Witnesses is an example of a sect. Seventh Day Adventists is another.

All Protestant denominations began as sects and eventually reached the more advanced state of development.

2. *A cult is an aggregation bound together by acceptance of certain leadership, beliefs, and practices. Although relation to a supernatural force is part of its focus, a cult may be additionally oriented to a purely secular program.* No one is "born into" a cult. He joins of his own choice. Cults are usually loosely organized and formed around a leader whose personality attracts membership. Whereas sects have a comprehensive religious rationale establishing the relation between man and his deity, this is not necessarily true of cults. There have, for instance, been some with little or no religious doctrine other than a requirement that adherents engage in communal sexual life or turn their worldly goods over to the cult. As a rule, sects are not active in secular affairs, rarely joining with other groups in social action. By contrast, some cults make specific social action an integral part of their philosophy and program.

William R. Catton, Jr. describes a cult led by one Krishna Venta.[11] In one public appearance, this man, wearing a beard and long robe, perhaps in order to resemble traditional depictions of Jesus, declared: "I am Christ, the son of the living God." He reprimanded another audience for having paid him so little heed 1,900 years ago when, presumably, he walked the earth. His small band of followers believed he was indeed Christ returned.

3. *A denomination is a subcategory of a numerically larger religious organization, the latter being in a comparatively advanced state of development.* Children are considered "born into" their parents' denomination. Sometimes, however, additional formal steps need to be taken to establish membership, baptism being an example. Religious services are highly ritualized and generally conducted with less evangelical fervor than in the case of sects and cults. Whereas sect members subordinate all secular activities to their religious commitments, members of a denomination divorce religious considerations from most of their daily activities, engaging in formal religious procedures only a few hours a week.

Protestant denominations in the United States include the Baptists, Methodists, Unitarians, Presbyterians, and many more. Judaism is denominationalized into Orthodox, Conservative, and Reformed divisions. The Roman Catholic Church is not denominationalized.

A person may move from one Protestant denomination to another with relative ease. The same is true with respect to members of Judaic denominations.

We said earlier that every Protestant denomination was once a sect. Let us note additionally that it is not always a simple matter to decide whether a particular religious group represents a sect or a denomination. The dividing line is rather difficult to establish. Sect membership is voluntary, whereas one is "born into" a denomination; therefore the sect member may be more conversant than the denominationalist with the doctrines of his group. He may show more religious fervor and a firmer commitment to his form of worship. But knowledge of and commitment to doctrine and religious practice are not of themselves the most telling criteria differentiating sect members from denomination members. Formalization and secularization of religious groups are.

As a sect becomes more highly organized, and as it defines the qualifications required of its ministry more precisely, it moves toward denominationalism. It moves still further in that direction when, in order to survive in the society, or perhaps to influence and even dominate it, it comes to terms with certain secular aspects of that society. In a sense, a denomination is a sect that has become more highly organized, more formal in its rituals and procedures, more fully accommodated to the culture and the social organization of the society in which it functions.

RELIGIONS OF THE WORLD

Somewhat ethnocentrically, we may tend to think that this is a Christian world. It is not. Nor is it a Judaic-Christian world. Even if we combined what we call the "major" religions —Protestant, Catholic, Jewish—the number of adherents would be outnumbered by the sum total of others in world population. Although statistics are not entirely reliable, and the very definition of a religious person is subject to dispute, the best indications are that Christians numbered about 950 million in 1964. Add some 13 million of Jewish faith, and the total is 963 million. By contrast, there were almost 2¼ billion people in 1964 who were neither Christian nor Jewish. Roman Catholics constitute the largest single religious organization in the world, but all Christians combined are much fewer than all non-Christians taken together.[12]

In the United States, according to the best available statistics, there were almost 67 million Protestant church members, almost 45 million Roman Catholic church members, and about 5½ million members of Jewish congregations in 1965. Something over 3½ million persons were affiliated with other churches.[13] Combining Protestants, Roman Catholics, and Jews, there are over 117 million people in the "major" religions, as against 3½ million espousing other faiths. Therefore we can say that the United States currently is a predominantly Christian-Judaic country. Still further, we are a "Christian" country, if our criterion is the number of Protestants and Roman Catholic Church members in the population as compared with the number who attend other churches.

A word of caution: All of the statistical data cited here do no more than indicate the denominational affiliation that people claim for themselves. Church membership provides no understanding of the extent to which members participate actively in the affairs of the church of their affiliation; and there is reason to believe that the majority are passive or inactive members. Furthermore, many who claim membership do not accept the basic tenets of their churches nor follow all modes of behavior prescribed in their churches.

SOCIAL PROBLEMS RELATED TO RELIGION IN THE UNITED STATES

DIVERSITY OF FAITHS

There are approximately 250 different religious groups in the United States. This diversity, in itself, is the source of numerous value conflicts in our society. Christians are split into two major segments, Roman Catholic and Protestant. Jews are divided into Orthodox, Conservative, and Reformed persuasions. Protestants are themselves divided into more than 200 denominations. Roman Catholics are the most united of the three faiths, and where there is disagreement in Catholic circles, it usually relates more to secular than sacred phenomena. A particular priest may be criticized, as when one was recently removed from his parish after chiding his superior for his alleged unwillingness to support racial integration. Such internal disagreement does arise from time to time, but no faithful Catholic, be he priest or layman, questions the ultimate authority of the papacy in matters pertaining to church doctrine.

STRATIFICATION & DISCRIMINATION IN RELIGION

Conflicting values are evident, among and within religious groups, regarding class and status, ethnic divisions, and race. Many communities have "fashionable" churches for the elite and others for lower socioeconomic echelons. Christian churches often discriminate, subtly or openly, against Negro Americans, while Jews in the United States, overwhelmingly Caucasian, very rarely, if ever, show dissatisfaction over the presence in temples or synagogues of Oriental or Negro Jews.

Church membership reflects in substantial measure the social stratification pattern of the community. Small sects and cults attract many members of the lower strata, although the middle class is represented in several of these groups. Protestantism cuts across all class levels but is predominantly middle class, the upper socioeconomic strata being represented in the

Presbyterian, Episcopalian, Congregational, and Unitarian denominations in greater proportion than elsewhere—but with distinctive regional differences in this respect.

There being only one form of Roman Catholicism, all social classes are represented in its congregations. However, the location of individual Catholic churches tends to reflect the social stratification pattern of the community. Most Catholics attend services in their respective neighborhoods. As a consequence, some churches are largely of upper-class membership, while others are predominantly middle- or lower-class.

Roman Catholic congregations also tend to be organized along ethnic lines, resulting from the formation of neighborhoods housing people of the same ethnic origin. In some of the larger communities respective congregations become recognized as "Irish" Catholic, "Italian" Catholic, "Polish" Catholic, or "French" Catholic, and one city may have several such congregations, each attracting a different ethnic group.

Historically, the membership of the Orthodox Jewish denomination came from the lower-middle and lower-class levels, in the main, although this situation has changed considerably in recent years. With the upward social mobility of Jews in this country members of the upper-middle class are found in Orthodox ranks. Conservative and Reformed wings of Judaism have appealed especially to members of middle and upper strata, with the latter concentrated for some time in the Reformed congregations. These traditional patterns are now undergoing fairly substantial changes.

In the stratification along class and ethnic lines lies a partial explanation of differences in position on social issues taken by respective religious organizations. Numerous problems arise from the conflict over whether or not the church should encourage or resist social change. Some people believe that religious organizations have no business in social action, that their role lies exclusively in the spiritual realm, and that they should not take positions on secular issues. Others insist that the religious leader has a moral obligation to use the prestige and power of his church to smite not only Satan but social evils. These divergent value judgments, influenced by the class membership of parishioners, are reflected in the official policy positions of respective religious groups. The status level of denominational members, however, is not always an accurate indicator of their degree of "social activism," for there are conservative "lower-class" churches as well as socially prestigious denominations whose leaders at least espouse reform or even radical social programs.

When we read of Negro Christians being turned away from "white" Christian churches, we may wonder what this signifies as to basic religious tenets. Is it Christian to refuse Christians the right to pray in a Christian church? The answer depends upon one's definition of Christianity, a definition derived from more than religious doctrine. Social stratification yields a variety of definitions of the concept *Christianity*. Some whites who sincerely consider themselves Christians place no impediments in the way of Negroes who wish to join with them in prayer, while others, with equal sincerity, believe that they are not violating Christian doctrine when they turn Negroes away.

Many, but by no means all, clergymen hold that the churches have not presented Christians with a dynamic interpretation of Christian doctrine, realistic for its time. Thus, Robert W. Spike, former Director of the National Council of Churches Commission on Religion and Race, wrote:

> For years, most of our churches have aided and abetted the Anglo-Saxon white conspiracy. . . .
> The Christian churches have not influenced their adherents to practice racial justice in housing, education, job opportunity and public accommodations.
> The Christian churches, in their own internal life, have practiced discrimination and built barriers to prevent open membership in the very household of faith.
> . . . all in all, the churches in this country have been dominated by our society's equivocation and, sometimes, outright evil in the matter of discrimination.[14]

Spike did not indict all churches, nor did he claim a complete absence of personal leadership within them. "I realize," he said, "there are some shining exceptions to my general indictment of the churches," and he pointed to religous leaders who have followed their conscience even against local consensus.

THE REAL & THE IDEAL IN RELIGIOUS PRACTICE

We are told that a Judaic-Christian God commands: "Thou shalt not kill." Yet Christians and Jews commit murder every year. The Judaic-Christian God also is said to command: "Thou shalt not commit adultery." Yet our divorce court records—as well as other evidence—testify to thousands of instances of adultery by both Christians and Jews. There is no commandment that is not violated with persistent regularity. Are Christians and Jews hypocrites, pretending to a faith that they do not have?

Some are, of course. But hypocrisy does not explain why a great many people believe themselves to be true Christians or Jews yet act in a way that seems to others of their faith to violate basic religious precepts. We must probe a little for understanding of the seeming contradiction between religious precept and personal practice.

In the first place, as we have already pointed out, many who call themselves Christian or Jew do not understand the full meaning of the terms. They are Christian or Jew by social inheritance (ascription) and self-pronouncement alone. Further, adherents of a religious faith who do in fact have some understanding of its doctrines, being members of a society, have real and ideal patterns of behavior. Some go through the rituals of religious observance, while contradicting the meaning of those ceremonies in daily behavior. Church attendance in itself does not make a person religious. It may even not indicate a desire for religious inspiration. Churchgoing may be for mere conformity, or for the purpose of being seen, of showing off clothes, exchanging gossip, or even escaping the cold.

Christians, for example, are taught to follow the golden rule, to be honorable in their dealings, to love their fellowmen. But no one travels through life without a little deviation from the ideal in religious—or any other form of—conduct; there is always some discrepancy between ideal norms and actual behavior and some conformity to the demands of expediency. This is suggested by such a folk saying as "Be good; if you can't be good, be careful."

SEPARATION OF CHURCH & STATE

Our Constitution requires that church and state functions be kept separate. The Congress may take no action to establish any form of religion. Government may not interfere with religious practices, and religious organizations may not encroach upon government functions. Nevertheless, dispute arises over what constitutes separateness. May a religious organization engage in political activity? May it campaign for or against a candidate? May it lobby to bring about social legislation? May the state force school children to salute the flag even though this is contrary to their religious convictions? May it force a youth to bear arms when his religion prohibits this? May the state help finance the education of parochial school children?

Many Roman Catholics believe that children attending parochial schools should receive the same financial and other aid that government provides for pupils in public schools. Failure to do so is undemocratic, they hold, for parochial schools meet legal requirements set up for educational systems, adding only religious instruction. Many non-Catholics, on the other hand, have insisted that such aid would break down the separation of church and state, amounting to government subsidization of religion.

Protestants led the way in proposing a so-called released-time educational plan. It would permit students to leave public school before the end of the day to attend religious-educational classes elsewhere. For the most part, Catholics and Jews have been opposed to this principle. Jewish authorities base their position on the premise that religious instruction is a private concern of parents and churches and should not encroach upon secular education.

Protestants were instrumental in introducing the daily reading of the Lord's Prayer or a passage of the Bible in public schools. Opposition crystallized against this practice, on the contention that such procedures violated constitutional guarantees of freedom of religion. When Catholics and Jews protested that they did not want their children to be forced to listen to the King James version of the Bible, so-called nonsectarian biblical passages were substituted. Non-Protestants thereupon pointed out that there is no such thing as a nonsectarian Bible. The United States Supreme Court ultimately issued several opinions placing serious restrictions on prayer in public schools. These decisions have produced violent objections from people in public and private life who insisted that the Supreme Court itself was violating the constitutional provision against governmental interference in the religious sphere. The issue remains in the area of unsolved social problems.

WHEN RELIGION CLASHES WITH LAW

Some religious groups hold beliefs calling for behavior that is not in accord with the laws. We have made a number of effective adjustments to this circumstance. Conscientious objectors, subjected to harsh punishment during World War I, received more understanding treatment in World War II. Still further adjustments have been made during the war in Vietnam to cope with this problem.

On the other hand, the government has refused to yield to the original religious beliefs of the Mormons. According to their doctrine, it was right in the eyes of God for men to take several wives. But the great majority of non-Mormons in the country were culturally indisposed to polygyny, and it was prohibited under laws defining the crime of bigamy, despite the fact that nothing in the United States Constitution provides that the only form of married life shall be monogamy.

What shall be done about individuals whose religion forbids them to accept medical treatment? Should their children be permitted to die because the parents refuse to allow them the benefit of medicine? What about religious groups that do not want their children to attend public schools, believing such education is contrary to religious teaching? Should they be allowed to disregard compulsory education laws? These and other issues representing clashes of values have not been settled within the framework of our culture and Constitution.

HISTORICAL TRENDS IN RELIGION IN THE UNITED STATES

On the record, church membership in the United States is increasing. The proportion of the total population appearing on a church roster was about 20 percent in 1880; 33 percent by 1890; 47 percent in 1926; and 53 percent in 1948. By the 1960s, approximately 60 percent of the population were on church rolls. We have been, as you see, progressively more and more a church-joining population.

Why this is so is anybody's guess, because only conjecture and no real evidence is available. There are observers who say that the uncertainties of industrialized society cause man to look to a god for security. Others attribute the proportionate rise in church membership to wars and cynical diplomacy—fearing destruction of our mortal bodies, we need to believe in an immortal soul. Still others relate increased church membership to the modernization of religious doctrine and church practice. According to this thesis, as churches have reconciled religious precepts with the realities of contemporary existence, many who had not been attracted previously became church-affiliated.

Granted that we are church joiners, do we, individually, know much about our religious faiths? The following data strongly suggest that we do not:

Who delivered the sermon on the mount? Do you know? Two-thirds of respondents, asked that question in a Gallup poll, could not give the correct answer.

What is the Holy Trinity? If you know, you are better informed than the 60 percent who were unable to give Gallup pollsters a reasonably accurate definition.

How many of the prophets mentioned in the Old Testament can you name? Seventy-nine percent of Gallup interviewees could not list even one.

Judged by this sampling, we are quite uninformed on the fundamentals of the major religions in the United States.

And yet, whatever their background, people do claim they hold to the basic teachings of their religion. In another Gallup poll, 96 percent said they believed in God, 72 percent that they believed in an afterlife. (But only 35 percent could name four gospels, and 54 percent admitted that religion did not affect the way they conducted their business pursuits.)

TRENDS TOWARD UNIFICATION

Particularly in the past half century, attempts have been made to create greater unity among religious groups. The National Conference of Christians and Jews has worked to bring those two religious bodies closer together in promoting respect for all creeds. The National Council of Churches has striven to unify policy and social action among Protestant denominations. There has, however, been no real consolidation of the more than 200 Protestant denominations into one body.

The Ecumenical Council, convened under Pope John XXIII and continued under Pope Paul VI, has resulted in some change in age-old doctrine. Its membership urged unification of all Christians into one church.

MODERNIZATION OF RELIGIOUS
GROUPS & IDEAS

RELIGION AND SCIENCE · No religious organization in the country has remained completely unchanged as the culture itself underwent change. For centuries, Christians and Jews had held that Jehovah created man and the earth he inhabits. Then scientists raised questions about the basic assumption of the existence of a supernatural God. The Bible did not explain the origin of man, they suggested. And Darwin's theory of evolution, propounded in the nineteenth century, advanced what purported to be a scientific explanation of man's origins.

Religious folk sprang to the defense of biblical, as opposed to scientific, explanations. Science and religion were viewed as irreconcilable and scientific theory as dangerous. The Tennessee legislature enacted a statute providing, ". . . it shall be unlawful for any teacher in any of the universities, normals and all other public schools of the state . . . to teach any theory that denies the story of the Divine creation of man as taught in the Bible, and to teach instead that man has descended from a lower order of animals."

The assumed conflict between science and religion had its most dramatic test of the century in 1925, when John Thomas Scopes, a high school teacher of Dayton, Tennessee, was tried for instructing students in the theory of the origin of species. The famous attorney, agnostic Clarence Darrow, defended him. Acting as prosecutor was William Jennings Bryan, a politician who several times sought the presidency of the United States and who was a fundamentalist in religion. This champion of religion took the stand himself and attested to his belief that the world was created by God precisely as explained in the Bible. He was positive Eve was made from Adam's rib, and that a "big fish" swallowed Jonah. At one point the enraged Bryan shook his fist at Darrow, declaring that he had undertaken to serve as prosecutor in order ". . . to protect the word of God against the greatest atheist and agnostic in the United States!" To this, Darrow retorted that *his* aim in coming to Dayton was ". . . to prevent bigots and ignoramuses from controlling the educational system of the United States." Scopes, all but forgotten in the battle of the titans, was convicted.

Today, there is no such heated difference of opinion on the respective roles of religion and science. Most people find no conflict with religious teachings in the bulk of scientific findings, although as recently as 1966 a school teacher found herself in trouble for discussing the theory of evolution in class. Many accept the explanation of the movement of the solar system and do not believe that this conflicts with their conception of an all-powerful God who created it.

The belief systems of some religious organizations are basically in accord with the discoveries of science. Many Christians, for example, maintain that a deity potent enough to create the universe was certainly capable of generating such processes as biological evolution. Other religious thinkers, however, adhere to the idea of an immutable, unchanging deity who has established universal, absolute, and eternal laws.

THEOLOGICAL EDUCATION · Theological seminaries have broadened and enriched their curricula during this century. There has been a marked increase in the demand for professionally educated clergymen with a firm foundation in the liberal arts and humanities. Many contemporary men of the cloth hold doctorates. The clergy increasingly enters its calling with a broad view of the world and of the meaning of life and with an understanding of social issues. Narrow parochialism is declining.

NEWER CHURCH FUNCTIONS · Theological students going through school these days are very likely to take courses in the behavioral sciences and to receive special instruction in family counseling. A number of pastors now consider it within their function and competence to counsel parishioners with marital and parent-child relationship problems.

Church edifices have become social as well as religious centers in the community, with recreational and cultural activity an integral part of church function. Summer and day camps, health centers, and employment bureaus are frequently found in association with religious centers.

CONTEMPORARY CATHOLIC POSITIONS · Some observers believe that the Roman Catholic Church in the United States has undergone more change in the past thirty years or so than in the past several centuries. Whether this be so or not, there is no question that a good deal of change has occurred with respect to certain of the functions of the church and the activities of its leaders. This has been accomplished, be it said, without any noticeable alteration in basic Catholic doctrine.

Catholic institutions of higher education have invited non-Catholics to join their faculties and have introduced secular viewpoints into course offerings along with the religious Catholic orientation.

In many sectors, priests and nuns have been encouraged to broaden their educational backgrounds. Attendance at non-Catholic colleges and universities, once viewed with some concern, is now increasingly acceptable within the hierarchy.

Life in religious orders seems due for some change. In 1964, a member of an order wrote an article about convent life in which she described the wide variety of meticulous rules that prescribed the behavior of nuns in different holy orders. What would happen, she asked, if Mrs. X invited a group of sisters from different orders for an afternoon outing?

Sister A may go for the ride, but she can't get out of the car or eat an ice-cream cone on the way. Sister B may go for the ride and get out of the car, but refreshments are taboo. Sister C may go for the ride and have her ice cream, but all within the sanctuary of the car. Sister D may go for the ride, get out of the car, and eat the ice-cream cone. She may even name her own flavor if Mrs. X isn't a dictator. Sister E? She may come out to the car and wave goodbye to the others.[15]

The picture, as drawn by the nun, of rigidly prescribed behavior within holy orders is no doubt accurate. However, the situation is changing to a degree. Some orders have established more flexible rules. More individual choice in selecting activities is permitted. The cumbersome habit of nuns, unchanged for centuries in some instances, has been modified in several orders into a comfortable, practical, attractive garb.

It is not true, as some believe, that nuns all live in cloistered enclosures, completely out of touch with the outside world. They have long served in hospitals and schools. Members of certain orders go among the poor to render aid and comfort. Members of holy orders are currently performing community service as scientists, college teachers, and administrators. A nun has been admitted to practice before the United States Supreme Court. Sisters have marched in civil rights demonstrations and have expressed their convictions on contemporary issues in writing and orally.

True, only a small proportion of the approximately 180,000 women in 480 orders in the United States[16] have to date assumed new roles in society, but a trend seems to be emerging, and quite possibly the psychological and physical gap between religious orders and the outside world will be further narrowed in ensuing years.

SOCIOLOGISTS & RELIGION

Students often ask, "Aren't sociologists opposed to religion?" The answer is, "No." They are neither "for" nor "against" it in their professional thinking. Individually, some sociologists are religious, whereas others are agnostic or atheist. But, as sociologists, in their professional activities they all recognize that religion is within the area of interest of sociology, for it is a vital part of life in society. Religious beliefs are a force exerting a continuous influence on human behavior and human interaction, and the sociologist who studies these phenomena must include the institution of religion in that study. Like other social institutions, the religious system is social in source and consequence, and therefore of direct concern to sociologists.

· NOTES

1. Ian Hogbin, *A Guadalcanal Society, The Kaoka Speakers* (New York: Holt, Rinehart and Winston, 1964), pp. 72–79, 90–91.
2. Thomas F. O'Dea, *The Sociology of Religion* (Englewood Cliffs, N. J.: Prentice-Hall, 1966), pp. 4–5.
3. Don Marquis, *The Almost Perfect State* (New York: Doubleday, Page, 1927), p. 169.
4. Father James Kavanaugh, *A Modern Priest Looks at His Outdated Church* (New York: Trident, 1967).
5. *Sayings of Buddha* (Mt. Vernon, N. Y.: Peter Pauper Press, 1957), Foreword, unpaginated.
6. Hogbin, *op. cit.,* pp. 78–79.
7. Manning Nash, *The Golden Road to Modernity, Village Life in Contemporary Burma* (New York: Wiley, 1965), pp. 296–297.
8. *Ibid.,* p. 177.
9. *Ibid.,* p. 180.
10. *Ibid.,* p. 179.
11. William R. Catton, Jr., "What Kind of People Does a Religious Cult Attract?," *American Sociological Review,* XXII (October 1957), 561–566.
12. Based on *Encyclopedia Britannica 1966 Book of the Year,* p. 663.
13. Based on *Yearbook of American Churches for 1965,* p. 253.
14. Robert W. Spike, "Our Churches' Sin Against the Negro," *Look,* XXIX, 10 (May 18, 1965), 29–37. Adapted from a book by the same author, *The Freedom Revolution and the Churches* (New York: Association Press). Copyright 1965 by the National Board of Young Men's Christian Association.
15. Sister Mary Gilbert, S.N.J.M., in Joan M. Lexau (ed.), *Convent Life* (New York: Dial, 1964), quoted in Edward Waikin and Fr. Joseph F. Scheuer, "The American Nun," *Harper's,* CCXXXI, 1383 (August 1965), 35–40.

16. Waikin and Scheuer, *op. cit.*, 35–40.

· SUGGESTIONS FOR FURTHER READING

DYNES, RUSSELL R. "Church-Sect Typology and Socio-Economic Status." *American Sociological Review*, XX (October 1955), 555–560.
A study of the relation between social class position and church or sect membership and participation.

FAUSET, ARTHUR. *Black Gods of the Metropolis.* Philadelphia: University of Pennsylvania Press, 1944. Volume III of Publications of the Philadelphia Anthropological Society.
Negro religious cults in urban areas are examined in this interesting volume.

GLAZER, NATHAN, *American Judaism.* Chicago: University of Chicago Press, 1957.
This is a sociologically oriented history of Judaism in the United States.

HOSHOR, JOHN. *God in a Rolls Royce.* New York: Hillman-Curl, 1936.
A popularly written volume on the career of Father Divine, flamboyant leader of a most unusual religious group.

KAVANAUGH, FATHER JAMES. *A Modern Priest Looks at His Outdated Church.* New York: Trident Press, 1967.
This Roman Catholic priest's critique of his church suggests that change is taking place in world Catholicism, and that more will occur.

LENSKI, GERHARD E. "Social Correlates of Religious Interest." *American Sociological Review*, XVIII (October 1953), 533–543.
The author investigates differences in participation in religious practices of male and female, parents and nonparents, and various occupational groups.
———. *The Religious Factor.* New York: Anchor Books, 1963.
An inquiry into the influence of religion on the daily activities of Protestants, Catholics, and Jews.

NASH, MANNING. *The Golden Road to Modernity, Village Life in Contemporary Burma.* New York: Wiley, 1965. Chapter 4, "Buddhism, The Meaning and Organization of Religious Life," and Chapter 5, "Nats, Spirits, Predictive, Divinatory, and Curing Systems."
The two chapters give a fascinating view of the function of religion in a relatively noncomplex society.

O'DEA, THOMAS F. *The Sociology of Religion.* Englewood Cliffs, N. J.: Prentice-Hall, 1966, Chapter 3, "The Institutionalization of Religion."
A statement on the conditions under which religion becomes institutionalized in a society.

WEBER, MAX. *The Protestant Ethic and the Spirit of Capitalism.* New York: Scribner, 1930.
The interrelatedness of Protestantism and capitalism is the focus of this volume.

26 EDUCATION AS AN INSTITUTIONAL SYSTEM

All societies educate their members by formal and informal methods. In this chapter we discuss education as a major social institution.

Which of the pictures in Figure 26.1 represents an educational experience?

The answer is: All of them. The boy doing arithmetic (A) is learning in a school. The tot looking at the animal (B) is gaining knowledge on a farm. The musicians (C) are having an educational experience in a musical group.

THE FUNCTIONAL MEANING OF EDUCATION

Education, then, takes place both in and outside of schools. It functions to preserve and transmit the culture. It is, Durkheim writes, "the means by which society perpetually recreates the conditions of its very existence."[1] Defined in the most general sense, education can occur anywhere, in any setting, through any experience. Thus broadly conceived, education has the same meaning as *socialization*, the *internalization of culture*, and *learning human behavior*, all of them more or less interchangeable concepts.

All peoples have some system for transmitting the culture to the young, for guiding them into socially approved behavior.

A

Figure 26.1
Which Represents an Educational Experience?
(A) Nina Leen, *Life* Magazine © Time Inc.
(B) Ian Smith, *Life* Magazine © Time Inc.
(C) Photo by V. Kapustin. Fotokhronika *Tass*.

B

C

In small, stable societies, socialization takes place through training by adults with whom the child is in daily contact, and much learning takes place through imitation. In large, rapidly changing societies such as our own, it is impossible for parents and immediate associates to accomplish the full task of socialization, since the cultural heritage is so complex and extensive, and specialized occupations require intensive technical training. As a result, a large measure of the overall educational function is assigned to a separate agency—the school. In this manner the process of socialization is adapted to the needs of a society that emphasizes achieved status more than does a smaller, less complex society. In the latter, ascribed status is the more important.

At the same time as the manifest function of education in our society is advanced by sending children to school, a latent function is operative. Children have increasingly turned to their age peers for approval as well as for an evaluation of societal norms. This is particularly true of the adolescent, who in other ways normally tends to be somewhat independent of parents. In a study of that age group, James S. Coleman[2] suggests that our setting children apart in schools for longer periods of training than heretofore has had a particularly strong impact on the high school youth. Since he is cut off from the larger society for a good many hours of each school day, the teenager has been forced to turn to his own age group for certain knowledge and the satisfaction of particular needs. Although he is still aware of the larger society and by and large wants to fulfill his parents' expectations and desires, he also looks to a considerable extent to his peers for his values and for approval. Thus, if Coleman's thesis is sound, and it seems to be, we may expect the "generation gap" between parent and child to be widened by what adolescent learns from adolescent. Parents may maintain that "nice" boys and girls do not indulge in heavy petting; the boys and girls concerned may hold otherwise. Parents may favor government by "experienced," conservative leaders of mature years; young people may demand that the reins of government be placed in the hands of "vigorous," youthful, liberal, or radical leaders.

Another unanticipated (and often unwanted) function of education has been the creation of independent and even revolutionary patterns of thought among the educated. This evidences itself in various aspects of a community's life, but let us consider the political as an example. In colonial territories, when illiterate, "ignorant" natives have been provided an education, leadership has frequently emerged for revolutionary movements designed to oust colonial rule and establish independence. This was true of India. In noncolonial Haiti, which has one of the highest illiteracy rates in the world, it is the educated minority that has furnished the leadership in numerous attempts at overthrowing the iron-fisted dictatorship that has characterized that island "republic" for many years.

Not all revolutionaries have been highly educated, of course. We are merely saying that one latent function of the institutional system of education has been to provide some societies with some such leadership.

On the whole, however, since the educational system is vital for the transmission of the cultural heritage, it tends to be a conservative force—a bulwark against change and a champion of the status quo.

FORMAL & INFORMAL EDUCATION

Whether it takes place in or outside of a school system, education is of two kinds, formal and informal. *Formal education is imparted by direct instruction. Informal education comes about indirectly, the learner often being unaware that he is having an educative experience.* When parents are consistently courteous at home, the children are likely to be the same, even if they have received no instruction on the subject. It is not necessary for parents to preach in order to teach. Their remarks, expressed attitudes, and facial expressions at particular moments do the job. In similar manner, children are informally taught by playmates, teachers, casual acquaintances, even strangers.

In most settings, education is by both formal and informal means. The Kaoka Speakers of Guadalcanal may serve as an example. As soon as a child can walk, at about the eighteenth month, generosity and respect for property are inculcated informally. Without explaining why, the child is told that food must be shared with any playmate who happens to be around and that goods belonging to others must be left undisturbed.

A toddler presented with a piece of fruit is told to give half to "So-and-so," and should the order be resisted, the adult ignores all protests and breaks a piece off to hand to the child's companion. Similarly, although sometimes callers are cautioned to put their baskets on a shelf out of reach, any meddling brings forth the rebuke, "That belongs to your uncle. Put it down." Disobedience is followed by snatching away the item in question from the child and returning it to the owner.[3]

When the child is four or five, parents begin explaining why he should behave as he is told to behave. Disobedience is punished by a light slap or by ignoring the child for an hour or two, the parent pretending a withdrawal of affection.

When little girls reach an appropriate age, formal instruction begins. They are taught to mind a baby, fill the water bottles, and fetch a hot coal to kindle a fire. Formal instruction of a boy begins by his accompanying his father and uncles when they set out to catch fish. They make a small rod for him, teach him how to bait his hooks, tell him about the different species of fish and which are edible and which inedible.[4]

A boy is instructed in other tasks:

Most fathers have allocated at least one pig to the son by the time he is about eight; moreover, they insist that he accept the full obligation to gather and husk coconuts each day so that the animal can be fed in the evening. . . . The father kills the animal . . . when the need arises, but always makes a great show of consulting the boy first and explaining the circumstances of the decision.[5]

By informal, then formal, means, children are taught the kinship system and how to relate to it. They learn what is expected of a mature adult and grow into adulthood accepting the values they have been taught.

What a person learns in the family, play group, or other non-school setting influences his behavior, but he learns it from individuals whose principal function is not education.

Institutional education, on the other hand, is specifically charged with the function of transferring to its recipients the values, arts, skills, and knowledge that are deemed necessary or desirable for living in a given society. Institutional education generally refers to formal training, but informal learning is an incidental and very important by-product.

ORGANIZATION OF EDUCATION IN THE UNITED STATES

Both public and private education, at all levels, is available in the United States. A school system is a bureaucracy, with functionally interrelated positions. Typically, there is a *policy-making body* at the top, such as a board of education or a board of trustees. Its policies are carried out by an *administrative staff*, as for example, a superintendent of education and his subordinate executives. The administrators direct and supervise the *teaching staff*.

Unofficial but important adjuncts of the bureaucracy are the *professional organizations* of educational administrators and teachers respectively. These associations are clearing houses of information and research. To a degree, they establish professional standards for the field. Some organizations, such as teachers' unions, are concerned with salaries and working conditions of the members.

All of our educational organization is, of course, directed at serving the *student body*. Sociologists and others have contributed some interesting observations on this group.

All of the pupils of elementary and high schools, as well as students at colleges and universities, are presumably in attendance in order that they may be educated. However, precisely what this means is not agreed upon by all concerned.

In this connection, scholars have found distinctive subcultures within given student bodies. Suppose we develop this line of thought by asking you first to take a self-test. Assuming you are a college or university student, check those items below which, in your judgment, apply to you.

1 · I admire our school's athletic stars, and I want my school to be a champion at sports._____ *no*

2 · I enjoy popularity contests on campus, as for instance to select a beauty or homecoming queen._____ *No*

3 · Those who want to are welcome to be "independents," but I think fraternities and sororities are important features of campus life._____ *yes*

4 · Dating and having fun generally are important functions of campus life where I am concerned._____ *yes*

5 · I think students should show school spirit at athletic events and in all other respects. Loyalty to one's school is very important._____ *yes*

6 · I am satisfied to study just enough to get a passing grade. Why be a greasy grind?_____ *no*

7 · I am in school primarily to prepare for a job or a profession. _____ *yes basically*

8 · I can't get very excited about the need for school spirit, nor

do I think it is important to feel strong loyalty for my college or university._____

9. · I am willing to study hard at something that will advance my future career, but I don't see much sense in boning up on a lot of theoretical, intellectual stuff that will have no practical value for me after I graduate._____

10 · I don't care much for social or athletic activities connected with the school._____

11 · A college or university offers intellectual excitement, which is what I especially want as I go through the process of getting an education._____

12 · At school, I want to get involved in the world of ideas, of major intellectual issues._____

13 · For me, it is vitally important that I work hard, meet course requirements fully, and receive excellent grades._____

14 · I enjoy certain school activities, such as debating and listening to lectures by visiting scholars and other significant figures. On the other hand, I am relatively uninterested in purely social affairs, such as dances and fraternity-sorority functions._____

15 · I would rather have the faculty recognize me as an outstanding student and scholar than be admired by or popular with students as a "good guy" or a Joe College type._____

16 · I don't think I need to pay any particular attention to the ideas or wishes of "the establishment," on or off campus.

_____

17 · I am deeply concerned over political, economic, sexual, aesthetic, and other important ideas and intellectual issues of our time, particularly those that concern the larger, off-campus society._____

18 · I intend to follow my own rules of dress, of sexual and other behavior, the establishment notwithstanding._____

19 · Education is worthwhile only if it helps me and other students discover our personal identity._____

The above items, phrased by this author, are based on characteristics cited by observers as tending to indicate the subcultural affiliation of college or university students as members of a student body. If you understand yourself thoroughly and were entirely honest in your responses, you probably checked items representing affiliation with more than one student subculture. That would be typical. However, you perhaps placed greatest emphasis on items in just one classification. Thus, if you checked most of those numbered 1 through 6, you are, according to some students of the subject, principally of the "collegiate" subculture. If your heaviest emphasis was on items 7 through 10, you belong mainly in the "vocational" category of students. If you checked primarily items 11 through 15, you are oriented to the "academic" subculture. And if your responses are concentrated at numbers 16 through 19, you are close to being, or are, a member of the "nonconformist" student body classification.

Burton R. Clark and Martin Trow[6] find that college and university students fall primarily into one of the subculture classifications noted above.

The collegiate subculture is the world of "Joe College," of sports, dates, and fun generally. It is symbolized by the idolized star athlete, the homecoming queen, and the fraternity dance. The "collegiate" wants a lot of school spirit and unquestioning loyalty to that institution. Participants in the collegiate subculture tend to be resistant to intellectual demands and course requirements, being content to "get by," earning a grade point average just sufficient to gain them a diploma eventually. Largely from upper- and upper-middle-class homes, these students tend to have the money and leisure that enable them to participate in social life on the campus. On the whole, they have a light-hearted regard for higher education. They flourish in particularly large numbers on the campuses of large state universities.

The vocational subculture regards higher education as being primarily for the purpose of preparing students for a job or a profession. Consequently, members of this category tend to be only minimally interested in intellectualization, in ideas, or scholarship for the sake of scholarship. Coming largely from the lower-middle and working classes, many are working their way through school. They have neither the leisure nor the funds that would enable them to participate in those activities that are especially favored by the collegiate subculture. Since they do not participate very much in extracurricular life, they lack a strong sense of school loyalty. Like the "collegiates," they tend to resist intellectual demands beyond those required for them to pass courses preparing them for a career. Almost every college and university has members of the vocational subculture on campus.

The academic subculture emphasizes hard work and the attainment of that sort of excellence that will bring good grades. Members of the category are concerned with, and involved in, the world of ideas, of knowledge, of intellectual issues. These are the serious students, who identify with the intellectual concerns of the faculty. They are in the library and laboratory a great deal. They populate the seminars. Professors like and respect them, but "collegiates" call them "greasy grinds."

The nonconformist subculture, as the term implies, appeals to students who are unconventional and nonconforming in significant respects. Like the "academics," they tend to be intellectuals, but where the "academic" is oriented toward the ideas and intellectual pursuits that are the concerns of academia, the nonconformist feels detached from the campus and more directly identified with the world outside the academy. His concerns are what he thinks of as the burning issues of the day, not for students alone, but for the society at large. An activist, he debates issues, demonstrates for and against given causes. He has little respect for "the establishment" and often is hostile toward that one represented by the school's administrators. He scoffs at certain conventions, as a result of which he may affect highly distinctive dress and express very individualistic attitudes. In order to facilitate his pursuit of personal identity, he rejects convention and tradition. Whereas he may regard conforming classmates as unenlightened tools of the establishment, they are likely to look upon him as an "oddball," a member of the "great unwashed." The nonconformist is found primarily in small liberal arts colleges of high academic standards and also at large universities, according to Clark and Trow. However, since their work was published, nonconformity has become a phenomenon on practically all campuses, to a greater or lesser degree. Further, nonconformity has reached the stage where it has become conformist behavior, in a sense. Certain attitudes, habits of dress, and other-than-academic pursuits have taken on a *de rigueur* quality. The nonconformist must conform to the norms of nonconformity if he is to be accepted as a member of the category.

In another work, Burton Clark delineates three high school subcultures that differ in the attitudes their participants manifest toward education, how seriously it should be pursued, and which school activities are most important.[7]

A "fun" subculture is concerned with sociability, extracurricular activities, the world of clothes, movies, cars, dates, "hanging out in the right places," and having a "good personality." Good looks, personal popularity, and athletic prowess are more to be desired than academic achievement.

An "academic" subculture emphasizes the value of brain power and getting good grades. Its participants respect the hard-working, successful student. Extracurricular activities are not to be neglected, but preferred are those that bear some relation to academic matters. Debating is one example, working on the student newspaper another.

A "delinquent" subculture stresses defiance of authority and, sometimes, downright rebellion. Unlike the "fun" and "academic" subcultures, participants of this one reject the school altogether, its practices and objectives. Education is not for the "delinquent." He considers schooling of little or no value to him. He violates school rules and disregards course requirements repeatedly. He would like to escape from school entirely, and he does this by quitting at the earliest opportunity.

SOCIAL PROBLEMS CONNECTED WITH INSTITUTIONAL EDUCATION

Ask almost anybody whether there are social problems connected with education in the United States, and the answer will be affirmative. There will be less agreement on what the problems are, still less on how to attack them. But it is fairly evident that members of our society hold conflicting values concerning *administrative and fiscal policies of school systems;* the *method and content of institutional education; who should be educated;* and *extracurricular activities of students.*

ADMINISTRATIVE & FISCAL POLICIES

In the field of public education in elementary and high schools, considerable difference of opinion is expressed concerning such matters as appropriate teacher-pupil ratios, acceptable per capita cost of education, how much financial support schools need, and where the money should come from. These issues have come to the forefront in the past two decades because of the tremendous growth of school population and the still greater growth that is anticipated. Taxpayers want to know how much more they will have to contribute for public education. Individuals of one political orientation or another wonder what the implications of increased federal aid to the states for education will be. Others are concerned because their states do not support education adequately.

As will be documented later in this chapter, school enrollments have increased significantly in the 1960s. A population increase was one reason, demands of the labor market for specialized personnel another. High school and college enrollments, which had risen during the 1950s, rose still further in the 1960s. This rise in the educational level of the population is generally seen as desirable, but it has created some problems —not enough classrooms, not enough teachers, increased taxation for the support of public education.

Educators and others have pointed to the wide variations in the states in expenditures for public education, the inference being that some jurisdictions are not spending enough to ensure a satisfactory system. In 1959–60, the median expenditure per classroom in Alaska was 12,542 dollars. In New York, it was 12,215 dollars. These two states ranked at the top, spending more than three times the amount spent in Mississippi (3,756 dollars) and Arkansas (3,645 dollars). Whereas the average salary of teachers in 1959–60 was 6,136 dollars in Alaska, 5,608 dollars in New York, and 5,520 dollars in California, it was 2,851 dollars in Kentucky and 2,705 dollars in South Dakota. In some sparsely settled states there was a ratio of 11 pupils per teacher. Elsewhere the ratio was as high as 28 to 1.[8]

Commenting on these disparities, representatives of the United States Department of Health, Education, and Welfare point out that there is a definite correlation between low educational expenditures per classroom in a school district and a high "mental rejection" rate in the Armed Forces Qualification Test. The persistent correlation ". . . indicates the price that the Nation as a whole pays for neglect of pupils."[9]

METHOD & CONTENT

Method of teaching and curricular content must be considered together, since one inevitably is involved with the other.

SHOULD TEACHERS INDOCTRINATE? · Societies differ in the degree to which they allow young people to accumulate knowledge and experience of their own choosing. Since it is the elders who control the institutional system, they are in a position to prescribe the content of education. Their own well-rationalized values are the products of indoctrination, and they expect to have those same values indoctrinated in their children. The schools, of course, must carry out their assigned functions. Teachers in our country may claim that they do not indoctrinate, but indoctrination in some degree is an inevitable part of the teaching function.

In their volume, *Problems of American Society: Values in Conflict*, sociologists John F. Cuber, Robert A. Harper, and William F. Kenkel express the belief that our value judgments embody three distinct conceptions about institutional education:

1. That it should concern itself solely with *indoctrinating the young into the culture of the group that controls the educational system*. Each new generation would thus be taught to preserve the status quo and be as much a counterpart of the preceding generation as possible.

2. That its function is not merely to perpetuate the existing culture but to *evaluate it, analyze it, raise questions, and examine many proposals for the perpetuation or modification* of the society.

3. That the function of education includes *directing social change* along lines that seem desirable and in the public interest. By this conception, the school would facilitate the refashioning of society by shaping the attitudes and skills of children. This, too, the authors declare, is indoctrination, but of a dynamic rather than a static sort. "It warrants the term indoctrination . . . because the emphasis is placed upon teaching people what they ought to think, rather than simply training them to be critical, analytical, and open-minded about social issues."[10]

Cuber and his associates consider each of these approaches desirable for certain phases of education, but they seem to favor the second when a choice has to be made. Educators and laymen as a whole are nowhere near agreement, however, and some assert that the question is largely academic, inasmuch as indoctrination inevitably occurs in the teaching situation. Their major question is what to indoctrinate.

In a very real sense, an instructor indoctrinates when he assures pupils two plus two are four. But, many educators insist, he has a further obligation. Laying a million facts end to end serves little purpose. Facts do not speak for themselves. They must be related to each other. It is not enough to say two and two are four. The student must be guided into an understanding that the principle by which one reaches this conclusion can be applied in any addition (including the seemingly remarkable operations of most computers). Unlike the oracle of Delphi, the teacher is not a compendium of unrelated information. He is a systematizer, helping students see the relation between one fact and another. He is a teacher, not a computer.

This situation raises another question on which there has been much difference of opinion.

SHOULD STUDENTS BE EXPOSED TO ALL POINTS OF VIEW ON SOCIAL ISSUES? · David Riesman calls attention to the newer patterns of pressure to which public school teachers are currently exposed. In the past, he writes, in *Constraint and Variety in American Education,* harassment of the teacher was traditional in smaller American communities,

. . . but this used to take the form (particularly if the teacher was a woman) of policing her private life, her smoking and gallivanting and church-going, without much direct interference in her conduct of the classroom. Today, especially in the larger places, the teacher is much freer to lead her own private life, but what we might term her academic freedom is under a great deal of pressure.[11]

High schools, Reisman points out, are expected to teach the social studies. In many places they are also under pressure to teach a kind of all-embracing neutral religion, as well as "tolerance, democracy and citizenship, and all other good things." This is a precarious task, for in meeting this instructional obligation, teachers can be labeled by their students as controversial when any discussion in the social area becomes at all heated or close to home. "And while the kindergarten teacher gains admiration because she can control several dozen preliterates whose mothers cannot always manage even one, the high school social studies teacher has a harder time being one-up on American-born parents who can claim to know as much as she about civics or UNESCO."[12]

There is no doubt that there exists strong sentiment for carefully controlling educational content and method so that young people will not be indoctrinated in ideas deemed subversive of "our way of life." Not only have teachers been harassed because of what and how they taught in "sensitive" subject areas but textbooks have been attacked as well. They have been banned because they explained socialism or the communist system of government; because they gave Negroes too generous or not a generous enough place in our history; and because the United Nations was treated in a manner deemed inappropriate by the critics. Objections have been raised to history books that mention human weaknesses of American heroes and to social studies tests discussing unions.

Opposed to the would-be censors stand those who insist that it is the obligation of schools to present alternative points of view fairly in order to help students reach their own interpretations. Sometimes proponents of this viewpoint have been attacked by special interest groups. The cartoon, Figure 26.2, while an exaggeration, symbolizes a very real and crucial problem in the United States—the assault upon the principle of academic freedom, without which education would be greatly weakened. Champions of academic freedom fight for the principle expressed by Tom Paine, that "such is the irresistible nature of truth, that all it asks, and all it wants, is the liberty of appearing." The college professor, say advocates of academic freedom, is obligated to give truth as he understands it the liberty of appearing. If he is not permitted to do so, then it seems likely that Robert M. Hutchins was correct when he remarked that the college graduate ". . . is presented with a sheepskin to cover his intellectual nakedness."

IS THE COMPETITIVE ELEMENT IN SCHOOLS HELPFUL OR HARMFUL TO STUDENTS? · Is the emphasis on grades "good" or "bad"? The answer to this question depends in large part upon an individual's definition of "good" and "bad."

Our society stresses individual achievement. Young people sometimes are told that anyone can become President of the United States if he possesses sufficient ambition and ability. We make heroes of those who "achieve," artists, titans of industry, scientists, athletes. In thus minimizing ascribed status and emphasizing achieved status, we place a premium upon competition. And on this subject there is a difference of opinion insofar as education is concerned.

One viewpoint might be paraphrased as follows: Ours is a competitive society. Competition in school helps children adjust to that reality and stimulates them to work hard so as to reap the maximum benefits. Emphasis upon grades therefore is "good."

An opposing judgment could be expressed this way: The pursuit of education should be "an intoxicating delight," as an

Figure 26.2
All Truth Asks Is
the Liberty of Appearing
Reprinted by permission
of Frank Interlandi.

*"Oh Boy—the prof is going to give his opinions
on some major issue!"*

essayist once put it. The acquisition of knowledge is rewarding in itself. Concentration upon grades encourages rote memorization and a parroting of the teacher. It is not a *grade* the student should seek, but *understanding*. With the latter, he will be the better able to compete with his peers in adulthood.

Between these two extremes of value judgment lie numerous modifications along a continuum. Responsive to public opinion, some schools have deemphasized the competitive race for grades. In a few private schools, students are evaluated several times a year in conference with their parents; they do not receive letter grades at all. Which of the various systems "works" best? To date, the answer to this question is largely a matter of personal opinion, for objective research on the subject is scarce.

There is ample evidence, however, that the need to compete sometimes has disastrous effects upon individual pupils. Psychiatric clinics are familiar with the child who desires the status that comes with achievement but cannot stand the strain of struggling for it. The urge to compete is, within limits, conducive to achievement, but beyond a given point in certain cases frustration sets in and the individual may find unacceptable ways of escaping from competitive situations. Many school authorities now realize the need to balance the competitive motivations of students with their abilities to compete, so as to further the maintenance of mental health.

HOW AUTHORITARIAN SHOULD TEACHING BE? · Should a teacher's word ever be questioned? There are those who sincerely believe that the educational process is impaired if students are permitted to challenge a teacher's assertions. Others aver that teachers are human, hence fallible, and an admission of fallibility can be an aid in teaching and in freeing the student to examine, challenge, criticize, and think for himself.

An interesting observation related to the matter of authoritarian teaching is offered by the late Nathaniel Cantor, an American anthropologist and sociologist. Students come to school already conditioned by home training to bow to authority, he says. Their parents have met many frustrations of various sorts in the course of their lives. But, "There is one area . . . where every parent can play God and be supreme. In the home the parent is king. Children . . . represent a terrible temptation. They are one's private possession. Here one can dominate and be in absolute control."[13] And all parents do dominate their children to a greater or lesser degree, Cantor asserts. They impose a more or less blind authority. And the child, accustomed to being dominated at home, arrives at school prepared and even willing to be dominated there. The teacher becomes a parent symbol, the insigne of authority. The student is all too prone to sit back and say, in effect, "Here I am, come to be educated. You're the authority. You have the knowledge. Pour it in!" He accepts what is handed out uncritically. He is unhappy if things are not spelled out so that he may take neat notes with general headings, subdivisions, and subsubdivisions. Here is truth, logical and precise. Teacher says so.

Cantor deplored such educational methods. He insisted that students should not be permitted to take the easy road. Teachers should resist the temptation to "pour it in." Those who seek knowledge should be made to struggle and sweat for it, dig it out.[14]

ARE BASIC SKILLS BEING SUCCESSFULLY TAUGHT? · Here is an excerpt from an essay examination:

The main reasons for juvile delinquecy is parents not controling, religion, comics, not attention in the home, so they commit robbery, arson, bugler and rape. The solution of the crime problem is strike at the root, the family head, so the whole family is all togeather.

The writer was a college senior. There are others equally deficient in grammar, spelling, and composition. Although this particular student was unquestionably far below the general average in writing ability, the question remains why so many students arrive at college so ill equipped with basic skills.

Methods of teaching reading, writing, spelling, and arithmetic have come in for serious criticism. Many parents insist there must be something wrong with present-day pedagogy, that children are not acquiring the skills their parents did. College and university instructors shudder at the written work of some students, all graduates of high schools.

Rudolf Flesch created a storm of controversy with his *Why Johnny Can't Read*, published several years ago. Other educators maintain that Flesch's major premise is fallacious, that most Johnnies *can* read, and those who cannot should not be charged to the educational system. Why is it, these critics demand, that of students graduated from the same elementary school, some are practically illiterate whereas others read, write, and spell fluently? Does not this suggest that other factors are at work?

It is charged not only that Johnny too often can't read but also that he can't count. A recent study undertaken by the International Project for the Evaluation of Educational Achievement (IEA) offers data on this subject.[15] The IEA first compared the mathematics achievement of thirteen-year-olds in twelve countries and then compared the achievement of final year secondary students in the same countries. Participating in the study were 133,000 students from Australia, Belgium, England, Finland, France, Israel, Japan, Netherlands, Scotland, Sweden, the United States and West Germany. Japan scored highest in the tests given to thirteen-year-olds. The United States finished slightly behind Scotland, England, and France and slightly ahead of Sweden and Finland. At the end of the secondary school level, England rated high, whereas the United States was one of the three lowest countries.

Native ability in mathematics would not seem to be an important differential in the comparative ratings. The IEA investigators concluded that the amount of mathematics talent is much the same in all of the countries studied and that the differences in achievement are due to differences in the way talent is developed. *Class size* was not conclusively a factor in this connection. However, *teaching method* and *teachers' educational preparation* did seem, at least tentatively, to be related to the development of mathematics talent in pupils.

One radical change in *teaching method* has been the introduction of the "new mathematics," which is a way of learning and doing mathematics quite different from those that were normally used until recently. The IEA study found that pupils working with the new ways perform better than those using traditional mathematics. However, because of the relatively small percentage of students taking the new mathematics anywhere in the world up to now, this finding was considered in need of further investigation. Meantime, in the United States, a number of school systems have introduced the new mathematics at the elementary and secondary levels.

Concerning *teachers' educational preparation,* the IEA study found that the longer the teacher's total education, the better were the test scores of his or her pupils. This is an interesting finding, throwing some light on a situation that has been pointed out by educators in the United States. Some of them have suggested that individuals who are improperly or insufficiently prepared to teach mathematics are insecure when instructing it. This communicates itself to the children, it is said. Youngsters who are by native ability capable of understanding mathematics become frightened of the subject as a consequence of inept pedagogy. They are led to believe they cannot grasp mathematics. It has been estimated that fewer than 20 percent of prospective elementary school teachers understand simple arithmetic themselves. In response to what appears to be a need, schools of education are seeking better ways of teaching future teachers how to "count."

SHALL WE GIVE ACADEMIC CREDIT FOR NONTRADITIONAL SUBJECTS? · Yes, argues one camp. Driver education, for instance, prepares students for practical life situations. No, cries another group. Teach such "practical" subjects, but do not call them part of the academic program.

The complexity of our modern society is such that the school, through its experts, will probably need to continue teaching certain nontraditional subjects if students are to survive and be available for academic education. Parents can no longer be considered the most authoritative instructors in sex hygiene, driving, and proper diet. Whether such instruction should yield academic credit would seem a lesser issue than whether children should receive training in the preservation of health and life in a highly complex environment.

HOW MUCH "PRACTICAL" EDUCATION SHOULD BE OFFERED FOR ACADEMIC CREDIT AT THE COLLEGE AND UNIVERSITY LEVEL? · The question relates to a broader issue. The content of our culture has increased greatly. The amount of training necessary to adjust to life in this society has increased correspondingly. A person needs much more formal training, general knowledge, and specific skills than was the case fifty years ago. There has been a great increase in the number of occupational positions a person may seek to achieve. Individuals entering college today cannot be sure of their vocational aspirations; in fact a major function of college education is to provide options on this score. Therefore, colleges have attempted to lay out a scheme of broad general education in cultural skills and knowledge that will serve every student and be adaptable to a number of life situations and future careers.

But, at the same time, schools are expected to offer the specific occupational training that will make it possible for graduates to earn a living and establish families. Certain of these occupations, such as medicine and law, have long been acknowledged to be within the province of higher education. Others, however, have given rise to controversy when introduced into the curricula of colleges and universities. Is business a subject that should properly be taught at that level? Nursing? Police work? Some say no.

Why even raise such questions, proponents of another point of view ask. They argue that schools should provide as much as necessary to prepare people for all vocations requiring more than high school training. Following this line of reasoning, some colleges and junior colleges offer courses of study in police science, bookkeeping, business management, cashiering in supermarkets, and so on.

WHAT ABOUT PROGRESSIVE EDUCATION? · A good deal of the conflict over the content and method of teaching stems from an older controversy over *progressive education,* a movement that arose out of a conviction of educators that traditional school systems were outmoded in certain respects. It was contended that curricula were cluttered with academic subjects of no use to students after they graduated. For some of these, it was proposed to substitute studies that would help them solve the problems they would encounter in later life.

Teaching methods were criticized as not affording young people a rich enough learning experience. The progressive education leaders demanded greater individualization of pupils. They should be allowed to express themselves freely and learn by doing, it was argued. Some proponents of progressive education argued that the curriculum should be enriched for bright students, permitting them to advance at their own pace.

Progressive education has influenced some school systems and left others unaffected. Criticism has been leveled at its basic principles. The charge has been made that progressive education lowers academic standards; that it is too permissive; that it neglects essential drill in the basic skills; and that it graduates "educated illiterates."

Critics sometimes exaggerate, drawing mental images of children permitted to hammer teachers on the head and do anything they want with impunity, because if they were frustrated, they would become neurotic.

Laymen, and some educators, have held that progressive educational methods are responsible for the fact that some Johns can't read and some Marys do not know what to do with a divisor and a dividend in order to get a quotient. On the other hand, there is evidence suggesting that progressive education has proven itself in these and other respects. In *Did They Succeed in College?*[16] the authors compared records of high school graduates from progressive schools with those of students from more traditional institutions. They concluded that opponents of progressive education had a weak case and that young people trained in progressive schools were not at a disadvantage when they entered colleges and universities.

CLASS BIAS IN EDUCATION · Difference of opinion exists with respect to who shall do the educating in our elementary and high schools. These institutions are largely financed and controlled by the middle class. The teachers, themselves largely from the same social class, are likely to hold middle-class biases and, consciously as well as unconsciously, to communicate those values to their pupils. Yet many of these pupils come from lower-class families, and lower-class values are not in all respects identical with those of the middle classes. When the teacher places emphasis upon thrift, punctuality, or "conventional" sex behavior, the lower-class child may or may not be prepared to respond as expected. When she takes for granted that every pupil wants to attend college, she runs athwart of the fact that not all of her pupils' parents feel that way or stress higher education as a goal for their children.

As a consequence of this disparity between middle-class and lower-class values, pupils from low-status families may become alienated. Unable to respond "appropriately," frustrated by rebuffs and criticism, a number drop out of school. This is not the only reason they do so, and, moreover, middle-class children also drop out, but class bias does appear to play some part in terminating the educational careers of a number of lower-class children.

An answer to this problem may lie partly in the fact that since we have had several decades of relative affluence in our society, a larger number of young people from lower-class families than formerly are becoming teachers. In time we may find them represented to a significant degree in our public schools. If so, we may anticipate that they will have their own distinct impact upon the elementary and secondary school population, an impact that cannot be entirely predicted at this early stage.

PROBLEMS OF RURAL EDUCATION · The National Committee for Children and Youth points out that ". . . a large segment of our total school age population lives in our rural areas and . . . many of these children and youth attend schools offering little more than a low quality program."[17] The rural population is not as well schooled as the urban, a matter of concern to educators and others who work in the interest of the public welfare. According to the 1960 census, the median years of school completed by the population twenty-five years of age and above in the United States was 11.1 in urban areas, as against 9.5 in rural nonfarm and 8.8 in rural farm areas.[18] Although steps are being taken to improve the quality of rural education, partly through the infusion of federal monies and the consolidation and consequent improvement of schools, many of the local communities themselves have been comparatively apathetic, the residents being content to have their children educated by methods in use when they themselves went to school. However, rural education is gradually improving. And more and more rural youth are getting to college, even when they propose to return to their homes after graduation to operate farms or other nonurban enterprises.

WHO SHOULD BE EDUCATED?

The existence of compulsory education laws in each of our states indicates that the enactors of those statutes took the position that all residents above a specified minimum and below a certain maximum age not only should, but must, attend school, regardless of their sex, race, or economic condition. Theoretically, we are further committed to the proposition that at least elementary and high school education should be available to all at public expense. We know that in actuality not everybody wants that much schooling. We are also aware that many who do want it are unable to get it for a number of reasons. But in theory every child in the nation is entitled to elementary and high school education at public expense and for the most part he can get it.

The situation is somewhat different in higher education, which was originally privately financed in this country and available almost exclusively to males of some means. A college education was the prerogative of a "gentleman," as well as of the individual seeking a career in one of the approved professions. As the culture changed, however, so did the requirements of community living. Many new vocations opened up, creating a need for trained personnel to fill jobs. In an era of scientific and technological development, thousands of specialists were required; a high school education no longer sufficed as preparation for such positions. Women were taking their place along with men in business, industry, and the professions, and colleges and universities were opened to them. Finally, people simply needed to know more and more merely to understand the world about them and how to attempt to solve the social problems of their highly complex society. Thus it became evident to many educators and social thinkers that young men and women must be better educated now than ever before and that to make that possible for the greatest number, higher education, once a "class" privilege, must be opened to the masses.

Many privately endowed colleges and universities continue

to exist, of course, but the United States now has, in addition, a highly developed system of publicly financed institutions of higher learning. A substantial difference of opinion exists, however, regarding the appropriate functions of such schools. Is higher education everybody's right? Some say yes, that every legal resident of the area where an institution of higher learning is situated has a right to enter and take courses leading to the bachelor degree: graduation from a college has become every citizen's right. Countering this point of view is the opinion expressed by many educators and others that the only legitimate educational privilege of citizens in a democracy is the right to be admitted to a college, provided they have the demonstrated capacity to do college work. To admit any and all who wish to enter college, regardless of their abilities, would, according to this view, seriously deteriorate academic standards.

The latter view would appear to be the more realistic, and a majority of academicians would very likely adopt that position. Even with some restrictions on entrance, based upon the capacity to do college work satisfactorily, getting a higher education is no longer an elitist undertaking. College graduation is becoming a norm in our society, where earlier a high school diploma was something rather special. Indeed, what with the increasing demand for specialists of all types, graduate training is becoming a requisite for many vocations.

EXTRACURRICULAR ACTIVITIES

Particularly in recent years considerable controversy has developed around the matter of extracurricular activity, mainly, but not exclusively, in colleges and universities.

There is general agreement that athletic sports are beneficial to students. But there is disagreement on how far a school should go in furthering an extracurricular sports program. Some would set few limits; others believe that a very extended program encourages participating students to neglect their studies, the end result being a lowering of academic standards.

There is evidence that on many occasions the education of "amateur" football and basketball players has been subsidized by certain schools in violation of interscholastic agreements.

Advocates of extensive athletic programs argue that they foster good sportsmanship, build character, promote health, and "put the college (or university or high school) on the map." Those who would delimit the role of athletic sports argue that overemphasis on winning games engenders a system that harms students, faculty, and school. The athlete who is of average capacity scholastically may seek "fish courses." These might get him through school, but frequently he emerges unprepared for a vocation. One might suspect that would be the fate of the young man shown in Figure 26.3 should he accept the offer of the dean and seek a "helluva swell education" at that particular state university.

Not only are students harmed by an overenthusiastic athletic recruitment program, some argue, but the school is also hurt. It loses status in the world of scholarship; teachers who take their educational functions seriously are dissatisfied, and the best of them leave. The student body as a whole suffers when great status value is placed upon the athlete, the argument continues. If the football hero receives adulation, why not the brilliant student with an original mind? Why does he not receive a school letter? May not young people gain value judgments that will be harmful to them later if brawn and field generalship are exalted while brain and mastery of ideas are classed as third-rate commodities?

Another area of dispute regarding extracurricular activities has to do with fraternities and sororities. These societies have a special appeal to members of the middle classes. Sororities are often regarded as having an important marital function. Sociologist John Finley Scott explains the situation this way:[19]

Many simple societies have institutionalized ways of putting marriageable girls in touch with prospective husbands. The Bontok people of the Philippines keep their girls in an *olag*, a special house where lovers call, sex play is free, and marriage is supposed to result. The Ekoi of Nigeria, who admire fat women, send girls away to be especially fattened for marriage. The Yao of central Africa and the aborigines of the Canary Islands send their daughters to "convents" where old women teach them the special skills and mysteries that a young wife needs to know. But parents in all societies have more in mind than just getting their daughters married. They want them married to the *right* man of their own class or higher.

Figure 26.3
Yayyy! State!
Reproduced by permission of
Esquire Magazine © 1964 by
Esquire, Inc.

"State University can also provide your kid, here,
with a helluva swell education.
I'm speaking not just as a loyal alumnus,
but as the Dean of the Graduate School."

Americans, like the Bontok people, the Ekoi, and the Yao, also desire to control the marriages of their daughters.

The American middle class has a particular place where it sends its daughters so they will be easily accessible to the boys—the college campus. . . . American middle-class society has created an institution on the campus that, like the fatting house, makes the girls more attractive; like the Canary Island convent, teaches skills that middle-class wives need to know; . . . and without going so far as to buy husbands of high rank, manages to dissuade the girls from making alliances with lower-class boys. That institution is the college sorority.[20]

Professor Scott may have written his article tongue-in-cheek. In any event, he has overstated the case. Many girls who do not join sororities also consider a campus a hunting ground for eligible males. When first-semester freshmen women at a major Midwestern university were asked, "What do you hope to get out of college?" 70 percent hoped, among other things, for a happy encounter with "*the* man for me."[21]

The fact that sororities and, to a lesser extent, fraternities are breeding grounds for romance does not, in itself, create much controversy. Indeed, "proper" marriages resulting from such associations are generally regarded with approval. Fraternities and sororities have been criticized on a different score. It is well known that they often discriminate in selection on the basis of race, religion, nationality, and "social standing." These practices are, defended by a great many students and some educators. They are also condemned by many members of both groups.

In *Fraternities Without Brotherhood*,[22] Alfred McClung Lee, himself a "brother" in Sigma Chi as an undergraduate, charges fraternities and sororities with undemocratic practices. He tells of a sorority of white gentile girls at the University of Missouri that excluded a student from the Greek-letter organization because she was of Greek background. He cites other instances of discrimination but observes that a ferment is going on among the brothers and sisters. The present generation of college students, he believes, are increasingly opposed to discrimination clauses in their fraternity and sorority charters. It is the older alumni, and some college faculty and administrators, who seem to be trying to hold the line, according to Lee.

In the past decade or two (Lee's study was published in 1955), fraternities and sororities have moved in the direction of eliminating restrictive clauses in their charters. "White" sorority chapters have pledged American Indian and Negro sisters. Some fraternity chapters have defied their national constitution and violated segregation mandates. The State University of New York forbade racial and religious discrimination among fraternities. The "locals" (fraternities not affiliated with national societies) complied. Chapters of national fraternities fought the order, but in 1954 the United States Supreme Court sustained the university's action and gave chapters until 1958 to disaffiliate with nationals or go out of existence on the campuses of the university. Since then, a number of national constitutions have been revised to accord with the implications of the court ruling. Some national societies, however, have refused to follow suit.

Lee points out that not only have some charters been liberalized but certain organizations never did follow discriminatory practices. He mentions The American Association of

Common Clubs in the latter connection and also Beta Sigma Tau. The first is a national American-letter fraternity which declares its objective to be to make democracy a living reality on campus. It has no barriers on the basis of race, creed, or nationality that would prevent any worthy student from being invited to membership. Beta Sigma Tau operates on similar principles.

"STUDENT POWER"

A dramatic manifestation of the latter part of the turbulent 1960s has been the emergence of what has been referred to as a "student power" movement, particularly on college and university campuses. Those associated with it have demanded a part in governing every aspect of campus life. Many people, academic as well as nonacademic, regard this as a serious social problem, threatening the very existence of colleges and universities, at least as these have been administered traditionally. Others, also in both academic and nonacademic circles, view the movement as an altogether healthy and desirable manifestation, a step toward the ultimate development of an academia for contemporary times. If there have been some excesses on the part of the students, it is argued, this is because they are mounting a revolution of sorts. Once they have gained some authority and experience in governing, they will become more stable and responsible.

Students uninterested in race relations, politics, and international affairs have been replaced by a new generation that demands to be heard on these and other scores. They want a greater role not only in student government but in setting policy and orienting curricula along with the faculty. They publish ratings of their instructors and expect the faculty to teach for the times and not from the clouds. To be sure, by no means all students of higher education share these ideas and enthusiasms, but the trend amounts to more than a ripple and may become a tidal wave.

EDUCATION & SOCIAL CLASS

Anthropologists and sociologists have contributed a number of studies revealing that to a significant extent social class is a determinant in who receives formal education, how much, and of what type and quality. Summing up these investigations, sociologist Neal Gross observes:

> . . . nearly every phase of school functioning is influenced by the phenomenon of social class. Academic achievement, level of aspiration, participation in extracurricular activities, and the drop-out rate, for example, all tend to be positively related to the social class placement of the child.[23]

More specifically, findings on the subject include the following:

1. The desire to attain a higher education and its actual attainment depend on social class to a significant extent. Persons from the middle and upper social classes are more likely than those of the lower classes to want to attend college and to graduate when they do.

2. Lower-class boys who do go to college or a university are more likely to have parents who are dissatisfied with their own class position than is the case among boys from middle- and upper-class families.

3. Measures of class standing, such as occupation, income, and education, are fair indicators not only of whether children will go to college but of what sort they will attend if they do go—a liberal arts institution, a technical school, or a teachers' college; a private or a public institution. Children whose fathers are farmers or blue-collar workers, as contrasted with students whose fathers are in other occupations, are disproportionately attracted to teaching. Those whose fathers are in professional pursuits study law, medicine, dentistry, and music in disproportionate numbers.*

4. The higher the social class, the greater the value that is likely to be placed on formal education, both as an end in itself and as a means to an end, such as a life vocation.

5. The social class factor may become of lesser importance in determining educational aspiration, given the existence of certain other influencing conditions. For instance, the particular school an individual attends may modify his attitudes. Thus, when Alan Wilson studied the relationship between the academic setting and students' aspirations, he found that working-class boys attending predominantly middle-class

* See, for instance, R. A. Mulligan, "Socio-Economic Background and College Enrollment," *American Sociological Review*, XVI, 2 (April 1951), 188–196.

schools were more likely to want to go on to college than were working-class boys in schools populated mostly by pupils of working-class status. And when middle-class boys attended schools where they were outnumbered by working-class pupils, they were less likely to consider going to college than were middle-class boys in predominantly middle-class schools.[24]

TRENDS IN INSTITUTIONAL EDUCATION IN THE UNITED STATES

SCHOOL ENROLLMENT

By law, as noted above, education is compulsory for children between certain specified ages (which vary from state to state) in the United States. A consequence of this regulation, when related to the increase in population, is that school enrollment, at every level, has been on the increase for some time. In 1950, over 30 million persons were in school, elementary through college and university; in 1960, there were over 46 million. By 1980, according to projections, there could be anywhere from 62 million to 75 million persons enrolled in schools, depending upon certain variables.[25]

Figures indicate something more than merely an increase in school population based upon a population rise. Proportionately more children than formerly have been sent to school in recent decades. In 1920, of persons five to twenty years old, 64.3 percent were enrolled in schools. In 1930, the percentage was 69.9; in 1940, it rose to 70.8; in 1950, it stood at 75.2 percent; and in 1960, a total of 81.8 percent were enrolled.[26]

Analyzing projections according to level of education, the total enrollment growth in elementary schools, which leveled off somewhat late in the 1960s, is expected to remain stable until 1975, after which it will rise another 10 percent. High school enrollment will increase about 25 percent by 1975, while college matriculation will rise by a whopping 40 percent.[27]

The educational level attained by individuals attending school is rising. There was a marked increase in the 1960s, as compared with the 1950s, in the number who finished high school as well as in the number who went on to college. Currently, out of every ten students who enter high school, about seven will graduate, and three of these will enter college. By

1970, almost three-fourths of our young people will have at least a high school education before they terminate school for jobs.[28]

How do we compare with other nations in the degree to which our children receive a formal education? Quite favorably, despite the fact that the number of persons attending school, at all levels, including higher education, has increased substantially in most countries since World War II. This is so both as to absolute figures and to proportions of the total population of the respective nations. Among those showing marked increases are Egypt, France, Japan, Great Britain, and Russia.

A world survey of education undertaken by UNESCO reveals that, in the early 1960s, more than 25 percent of the total population of the United States was attending school. This compares with about 20 percent in England, France, Germany, and Russia. In the United States, almost 75 percent of the persons between five and twenty-four years of age were enrolled. We may compare this with the 67 percent of the five to twenty-year bracket attending school in Belgium and the 60 percent of the same age classification enrolled in Japan. Enrollment in Asian lands falls well below the European figures. Only 12.5 percent of the total Asian population was attending school in 1962. A little less than 10 percent of the African population was enrolled. However, Asian and African enrollments represent a very considerable expansion for those areas as compared with their enrollments in earlier decades.[29]

The emphasis upon higher education intensifies in the United States as elsewhere. Every indication is that the young people of our country will be subjected to increased pressures to attain higher levels of education in this age of scientific and technological development, when specialists are in unprecedented demand.

ILLITERACY

One outcome of our compulsory education laws is the low illiteracy rate in the United States. A literate person, in the context of this discussion, is one who can read and write in at least one language. Conversely, a person who cannot both read and write in some one language is defined as illiterate. In 1959, of individuals in the United States fourteen years of age and over, 97.8 percent were literate, 2.2 percent illiterate.

When these figures are broken down by color, 98.4 percent of the white and 92.5 percent of the nonwhite population were literate, which means 1.6 percent of the white and 7.5 percent of the nonwhite were illiterate.[30]

We may look at these figures another way. In 1959, when the overall 2.2 percent illiteracy rate prevailed, most persons in that category were older people. If we limit the analysis to individuals of ages fourteen to twenty-four, the illiterates number less than 1 percent. Even among the younger ages, the percentage of illiterates among the nonwhites is twice that of the whites, but formerly it was five times as much.[31] Our young people, both nonwhite and white, are thus receiving more education than did their parents.

The literacy record of the United States was achieved in a comparatively short period, historically speaking. Before the era of free public education began, about a century ago, the literacy rate was low. Today, the United States contains one of the most (but not *the* most) literate populations in the world. The highest literacy levels, almost 100 percent, are found in western and central Europe, northern America, Oceania, and the U.S.S.R. In Asia, Japan and Israel have literacy rates of almost 100 percent. Lowest literacy levels are found in Africa.[32]

TEACHERS

Increased school enrollments have brought certain problems. Schools are crowded beyond the staff's capacity to teach effectively in many jurisdictions, and the load will increase, as the projections indicate. Classroom shortages will become more acute and recruitment of sufficient teachers more difficult.

The teacher shortage is especially acute in the fields of mathematics and science. Persons who graduate with a thorough grounding in these subjects are in great demand in industry and other nonteaching occupations, where they earn considerably more than they can at teaching. Consequently there will continue to be a serious shortage of graduates trained in mathematics and science who are willing to enter the teaching profession. Furthermore, we may expect a "vicious circle" effect. When there is a shortage of competent teachers in any discipline, the number of students who can be trained in it must be curtailed correspondingly, with little chance to remedy the condition. Thus we may enter a period when mathematicians and scientists are in short supply outside the teaching profession.

On the plus side of teacher education is the fact that in the past half century there have been marked improvements in methods of training teachers in the elementary and high school fields. Standards of admission to schools of education have risen, and curricula have been broadened.

FEDERAL-STATE RELATIONSHIPS

With increased enrollments, the need for more school buildings, and a general rise in the cost of materials and other items related to teaching, indications are that local communities in some sections of the country, even when receiving state aid, will be unable to carry the financial burden unless they receive some form of federal assistance. There has, however, been opposition in some quarters to federal subsidization of education. The latter almost certainly will continue to be a political and ideological issue for some time, despite the fact that federal aid to education, involving millions of dollars annually, is an established fact. Federal funds go to the states for school lunches, scholarships, vocational rehabilitation, and many other purposes. Nevertheless, many educators and people in political life fear that federal control of local education will result from any marked increase in subsidization. Others who favor federal aid argue that the sparsely populated states in particular, with relatively little tax support, cannot operate reasonably adequate educational systems without help from the federal government.

DROPOUTS

Widely publicized is the fact that about a million young people leave school every year while still in the elementary grades or before completing high school.[33] Actually, there have always been pupils who dropped out of school when their capacities indicated they could and should go on. If we hear more about this problem than ever before, it is partly a consequence of the fact that, increasingly, a relatively high level of educational attainment becomes necessary if the individual is to make a satisfactory vocational adjustment in our complex, highly industrialized society.

Currently, half of the working-age population lacks a high school education. The highest educational level is attained by white women in the urban areas, who in 1964 had a median of 11.6 years of schooling. White men in these areas had a median of 11.3 years. In rural areas, white women were also more highly educated than their male counterparts, but the median for both men and women was one to two years lower than for urban and suburban dwellers.[34]

Educational patterns of the nonwhite population were similar, but at a lower level. Nonwhite men in urban areas showed a median of 8.5 years of schooling. For nonwhite, urban women, the median was 8.9 years. Medians in rural areas were 2 to 3 years lower for both sexes.[35]

The eighth grade has been the danger point for school dropouts. Pupils who quit school at the point did not often return for more education. Those who entered high school were likely to remain at least two years.[36]

The federal government predicts that altogether about 7.5 million pupils will have dropped out of school between 1962 and 1970.[37] Actually, the dropout *rate* is decreasing slowly. It was 44.7 percent in 1954 but only 36.4 percent in 1962. Increased enrollment, however, pushed the total figure on dropouts upward, from 1,031,000 in 1954 to an estimated 1,200,000 in 1965.[38]

When young people drop out of school prematurely, they are unprepared to find or hold a job that will offer them security and satisfaction for very long. This creates a serious economic problem in society. If the number of dropouts continues to rise, we shall be spending more each year on public assistance to indigent families.

It has been suggested that dropouts become delinquents, then adult criminals. There is no real evidence to support this contention. In any large group of young people, a certain percentage will become delinquent, whether they dropped out of school or not. According to some evidence, the majority of dropouts who have delinquency records had their first brushes with the law *prior* to quitting school.

A second look at the dropout problem may suggest that: (1) In some cases, no effort should be made to keep the youth in school. He will do better to learn a skill outside the school environment. (2) Other young people should be helped, financially and psychologically, to stay in school, since they have the intellectual equipment to do so. (3) Where academic education does not hold the interest of a youth, and if it appears early in his school career that he will not reach or graduate from high school, vocational education may serve him better.

The dropout problem is not confined to elementary and high schools. A relatively small but probably increasing number of college students, including some of established intellectual prowess, curtail their formal schooling in favor of "freer," less "artificial," less "bureaucratized," and more "meaningful" modes of life. They are apt to regard colleges and universities as part of the alienating "establishment." Some leave school to join youth colonies, many of which have been formed in both large cities and rural areas in recent years. These young people, clearly, are not the college equivalents of high school dropouts, but their disenchantment with modern society, including its educational institutions, is a problem of social and sociological significance.

· NOTES

1. Emile Durkheim, *Education and Sociology* (New York: Free Press, 1956), p. 123.
2. James S. Coleman, *The Adolescent Society* (New York: Free Press, 1961).
3. Ian Hogbin, *A Guadalcanal Society, The Kaoka Speakers* (New York: Holt, Rinehart and Winston, 1965), p. 33.
4. *Ibid.*, pp. 33–39.
5. *Ibid.*, p. 39.
6. Burton R. Clark and Martin A. Trow, "College Subcultures," in Leonard Broom and Philip Selznick, *Sociology,* 3rd ed. (New York: Harper & Row, 1963), pp. 453–456. This is an abridged, adapted version of an article by the authors titled "Determinants of College Student Subculture."
7. Burton R. Clark, *Educating the Expert Society* (San Francisco, Calif.: Chandler, 1962), Chap. VII.
8. Eugene P. McLoone and Forrest W. Harrison, "State Variations in Support of Public Schools," *Health, Education and Welfare Indicators* (May 1955), pp. 1–16.
9. *Ibid.*
10. John F. Cuber, Robert A. Harper, and William F. Kenkel, *Problems of American Society: Values in Conflict,* 3rd ed. (New York: Holt, Rinehart and Winston, 1956), pp. 306–307.
11. David Riesman, *Constraint and Variety in American Education* (New York: Anchor Books, 1958), p. 125.
12. *Ibid.*, pp. 125–126.

13. Nathaniel Cantor, *Learning Through Discussion* (Buffalo, N. Y.: Human Relations for Industry, 1951), p. 17.

14. *Ibid.*, p. 47.

15. Thorsten Husen (ed.), *International Study of Achievement in Mathematics* (New York: Wiley, 1967). A greatly condensed report on the subject appears under the title, "Why Johnny Can't Count," in *The University of Chicago Magazine*, LX, 2 (November 1967), 18–19.

16. C. P. Chamberlain *et al., Did They Succeed in College?* (New York: Harper, 1942).

17. Robert M. Isenberg, "Rural Education," Chapter 5 in Lee G. Burchinal (ed.), *Rural Youth in Crisis: Facts, Myths, and Social Change* (Washington, D. C.: U. S. Department of Health, Education, and Welfare, 1965), pp. 65–76.

18. Charles B. Nam and Mary G. Powers, "Educational Status of Rural Youth," Chapter 8 in Burchinal, *op. cit.*, pp. 113–129.

19. John Finley Scott, "Sororities and the Husband Game," *Transaction*, II, 6 (September-October 1965), 10–14.

20. *Ibid.*

21. Elizabeth Douvan and Carol Kaye, "Motivational Factors in College Entrance," in Nevitt Sanford (ed.), *The American College, A Psychological and Social Interpretation of the Higher Learning* (New York: Wiley, 1962), pp. 199–224.

22. Alfred McClung Lee, *Fraternity Without Brotherhood* (Boston: Beacon Press, 1955).

23. Neal Gross, "The Sociology of Education," in Robert K. Merton *et al.* (eds.), *Sociology Today: Problems and Prospects* (New York: Basic Books, 1959), pp. 128–152.

24. Alan B. Wilson, "Residential Segregation of Social Classes and Aspirations of High School Boys," *American Sociological Review*, XXIV (December 1959), 836–845.

25. Based on U. S. Bureau of the Census, *Statistical Abstract of the United States, 1964*, 85th annual ed. (Washington, D. C.: U. S. Government Printing Office, 1964), p. 111, Table No. 143.

26. Based on *ibid.*, p. 110, Table No. 140.

27. U. S. Bureau of the Census, *200 Million Americans* (Washington, D. C.: U. S. Government Printing Office, 1967), p. 56.

28. U. S. Department of Health, Education, and Welfare, *Converging Social Trends, Emerging Social Problems* (Washington, D. C.: U. S. Government Printing Office, 1964), p. 43.

29. UNESCO, *World Survey of Education, IV: Higher Education* (New York: UNESCO, 1966), Chap. 2.

30. Based on U. S. Bureau of the Census, *Statistical Abstract of the United States, 1964, op. cit.*, p. 117, Table No. 154.

31. U. S. Bureau of the Census, *200 Million Americans, op. cit.*, p. 56.

32. *Population Bulletin*, XIX, 6 (October 1963), pp. 150–151.

33. U. S. Department of Health, Education, and Welfare, *Converging Social Trends, Emerging Social Problems, op. cit.*, p. 43.

34. *Ibid.*, p. 39.
35. *Ibid.*, p. 42.
36. *Ibid.*
37. *Ibid.*
38. Barbara H. Kemp, *The Youth We Haven't Served, A Challenge to Vocational Education* (Washington, D. C.: U. S. Department of Health, Education, and Welfare, 1966), p. 20.

· SUGGESTIONS FOR FURTHER READING

Editors of *Ramparts,* with the assistance of staff reporters from Liberation News Service in New York City. "The Siege of Columbia." *Ramparts,* VI, 11 (June 15, 1968), 27–39.
An anti-Establishment report concerning a student revolt at Columbia University.

JEWETT, ROBERT E. "Why the Able Public School Teacher Is Dissatisfied." *Educational Research Bulletin,* XXXVI (October 1957), 223–234.
A report on an inquiry about better teachers deserting the profession.

KEMP, BARBARA H. *The Youth We Haven't Served.* Washington, D. C.: U. S. Department of Health, Education, and Welfare, 1966.
The youth we haven't served are the socioeconomically handicapped, who grow up without an adequate education, in a hostile and squalid environment. They will be trapped in a life of poverty, unless they receive appropriate vocational education.

LEE, ALFRED MC CLUNG. *Fraternity Without Brotherhood.* Boston: Beacon Press, 1955.
A readable, grim report on the racial and religious discrimination practiced by college fraternities.

LIPSET, SEYMOUR M., and SHELDON S. WOLIN (eds.). *The Berkeley Student Revolt.* New York: Anchor Books, 1965.
A documented appraisal of the conflict between student groups and the administration at the University of California. Provides some insights into the so-called Free Speech and Student Power movements.

RIESMAN, DAVID. *Constraint and Variety in American Education.* New York: Anchor Books, 1958.
A provocative critique of secondary and higher education in the United States.

ROSE, ARNOLD. *De Facto School Segregation.* New York: National Conference of Christians and Jews, 1964.
Various dimensions of de facto school segregation are revealed and programs for combatting it are explored.

27 OTHER INSTITUTIONAL SYSTEMS

We now deal briefly with several more social institutions: the economic, political, scientific, and social welfare systems. There are, of course, still others worth study, but we cannot devote space to them within the confines of a general textbook in sociology.

THE ECONOMIC INSTITUTION

Sociologists are not economists. They analyze the economic system as a social institution of society but claim no special competence in evaluating the effectiveness of any one economic system.

From a sociological point of view, *the economic institution is the cultural system of society directly concerned with the production, distribution, and consumption of goods and services.*

FUNCTION

The economic institution's principal function is to provide means whereby members of a society may survive and maintain themselves. Some relatively undeveloped societies achieve no more than a bare subsistence economy for most of their members. In those that are highly developed, goods and services beyond the requirements for survival and bare subsistence are available, not only to "elites," but to many, though not necessarily all, members of the society.

STRUCTURE

The structure of an economic system is based on the functions of *production, distribution,* and *consumption.*

PRODUCTION · Production requires *land, capital,* and *labor.*

Land consists not only of the physical territory, but the resources it contains, including fish, forests, minerals, and water power.

Capital consists of the means of production. Depending upon the society, it may include finances, buildings, tools, machinery, and other equipment. In an industrial society the capital of one entrepreneur may run into millions of dollars and thousands of pieces of machinery. In other societies, a man's capital may consist of a canoe, a spear, and a fish net.

Labor refers to the physical and mental manpower required to produce goods and services. Although we are accustomed to the terms "skilled" and "unskilled" labor, all workers must have some skills. The day laborer who scoops, lifts, and deposits a shovelful of dirt is using skills for the operation.

DISTRIBUTION · A distribution system is necessary if goods and services are to reach the consumer. Magazines of national interest published in New York must be distributed throughout the country if they are to reach ultimate consumers. Cattle raised in Nebraska must be shipped as beef to strategic markets.

Distribution involves a means of exchange. A farmer raises sugar beets and exchanges his crop for something else. In our country it would generally be money. But money is not the only means of exchange. Years ago, in our country, a man might trade a deer he shot for a barrel of flour at the general store. This is the barter system, in use in many relatively simple societies that have no currency. Some such groups have a form of money, however. Thus, the Kapauku Papuans of West New Guinea do little bartering. In buying and selling they use cowrie shell and two types of necklaces as the medium of exchange and the common measure of value.[1]

CONSUMPTION · For a healthy economy, there must be relative balance between the production and consumption of goods and services. Although in a highly developed society some accumulation of goods and capital is inevitable and desirable, a serious glut upsets the economy, forces prices down, and may create unemployment and economic recession.

SOME FORMS OF ECONOMIC SYSTEMS

The several economic systems characteristic of complex contemporary societies have their respective patterns, although there is some overlap between one and another. Each is associated with an economic philosophy.

CAPITALISM · Essentially a product of the eighteenth century, the economic philosophy of capitalism holds that wealth is primarily the private property of an individual and not the property of the state or of the people as a whole. In principle, the individual is the capitalist who has invested his property in expectation of gaining more property by his own enterprise, initiative, and ability.

In its fully developed state, capitalism is characterized by a *high degree of specialization*, a *division of labor*, and *extensive use of money*.

Theoretically, capitalism thrives on *competition*. The contention has been made, for instance, that when two manufacturers are permitted to compete for markets with no restriction on what they may pay for labor or ask for their products, the consumer benefits along with the entrepreneur. The consumer gets the best possible product for the lowest possible price, since each manufacturer strives to produce as cheaply as possible in order to sell the same product for less than his competitor.

Actually, capitalistic societies have not been altogether competitive, nor do consumers necessarily benefit from the "free enterprise" system. Mergers and monopolies have been established in certain industries, and these have called for cooperation rather than competition. The gains for consumers are, to say the least, questionable.

Capitalism is not the only economic system providing for private ownership of property. Socialism does too, as we shall see. Where the two systems differ is with regard to how much property may be held, what kind, and how absolute the individual's control over it may be.

Under an unalloyed capitalistic system, there would be no restriction on the amount or kind of property that could be held, and the holder would be in absolute control of it, with no interference from the government or any other source. However, there is no altogether *uncontrolled capitalism* in the large societies. Instead, there is *regulated capitalism,* the assumption being that the public interest demands some regulation, so that capitalists are not absolutely free to hold and dispose of property without restriction. Moreover, the theory has evolved that certain property should never be alienated from the state, hence should not be privately owned. Our postal system is an example, as is public ownership of highways and harbors.

One must look to an underdeveloped society for an example of out-and-out uncontrolled capitalism. We find it among the Kapauku Papuans of West New Guinea, mentioned above.* Until they were "pacified," these people were headhunters and cannibals. They are strict "rugged individualists" in economic enterprise. They not only have a true money (the relatively scarce cowrie shell) and savings but also a system of speculation and a market regulated by supply and demand. There is a system of sales and lease contracts, of the use of paid labor, and of absolute and unrestricted private ownership.

The cowrie shell money comes in various denominations and is used as the basis of exchange. Long practice has established a scale of customary prices for commodities, but this is adjustable to supply and demand, and prices go up and down from the customary base accordingly. Buying, selling, and contracting are strictly profit motivated. Long-term investments of money are made in pigs, chickens, bailer shell, inner bark, or animal teeth. These are speculative buys. The animals will be fattened, eventually sold for profit. The bailer shell and animal teeth are purchased for possible resale when the value goes up or for making artifacts to be sold at a profit.

Everything is for sale, at a profit. The Kapauku not only must pay for land, labor, manufactured products, animals, but also for surgery, curing, and midwifery. They

* What follows is from a lengthier description in Leopold Pospisil, *The Kapauku Papuans of West New Guinea* (New York: Holt, Rinehart and Winston, 1963), pp. 5–31, well worth reading in its entirety.

. . . have to pay for favors and acts for which even in our capitalistic society there is no charge. For example, one pays a bride price for a wife, the services of a foster father have to be paid for by the grown boy, a grief expressed by strangers of distantly related people over the death of a close relative has to be recompensed in money, and almost all crimes can be settled through a proper transfer of shell currency.[2]

The Kapauku know the institution of lease, rent, and loan. The credit system

. . . has greater importance in this society than in western capitalism. Among the Kapauku the role of credit is not limited to the economic sphere only. Through a proper allocation of credit, . . . a rich man assumes political leadership and also becomes a legal authority and judge in his group.[3]

A man may own whatever he wishes, as much as he wishes, and what he owns is absolutely his.

Every material item . . . is owned individually, a common ownership being simply inconceivable. They claim that two men cannot own a plot of land together because they would try to exploit each other by stealing from each other's crops and by avoiding work as much as possible. Thus money, movables, canoes, houses, and land have always only one owner. Even tracts of virgin forest belong to individual Kapauku.[4]

Unlike our form of regulated capitalism in the United States, the Kapauku exempt nothing whatever from private ownership. A main drainage ditch or a fence protecting an area consisting of gardens of numerous owners is considered composed of many segments, each owned by a given individual who is concerned only for the upkeep of his particular property. Even a bridge does not belong to a village as a whole. If it collapses, those who built it come to claim the logs and poles they contributed to its construction.

We have gone to this length to describe the Kapauku economy in order to indicate how different the capitalism we know is from Kapauku capitalism. The modern state in a highly developed society is premised on the right of that state to regulate capitalistic enterprise, to some extent, for the general welfare. The Kapauku do not have this conception of *state*.

SOCIALISM · Socialism, like *modern* capitalism, is a theoretical economic system. There is no known contemporary example of a society operating under pure socialism. As theoreticians have severally described and discussed socialism, it comes in many varieties. However, certain common characteristics can be singled out in the socialist model generally advocated.

1. *Private ownership would be permitted.* Entrepreneurs would be permitted to amass wealth, own private property, and sell for profit, provided that this does not work against the general welfare.

2. *The government, representing the society, would own the state's productive resources,* including key industries, such as railroads, coal, and steel, which would be classed as public utilities. It would be possible for private capital to be invested in them, for a time, and they might be operated by private entrepreneurs, but these utilities would be regulated by the government in the interest of all the people. Gradually, public utilities would be nationalized entirely; private capital would no longer be invested in them; and the government would eventually both control and operate them.

3. *Coordinated planning would eventually replace the free play of profit motives and a laissez-faire market economy.* This change would entail government regulation of industry, agriculture, commerce, and the professions. Production for use rather than for profit has generally been advocated by socialistic thinkers. Under this conception, workers and professional people would be guided by a desire for craftsmanship and service to the society rather than by purely acquisitive motives.

4. *Redistribution of income is an explicit objective.* The government, at the appropriate time in the evolution of the socialist state, would use its taxing power to reduce inherited wealth and great incomes. Social security benefits and welfare services, financed by taxation, would redistribute the national wealth and increase the well-being of the less privileged.

5. *Peaceful revolution is advocated by some socialists.* They mean by this the gradual extension of government ownership of all productive resources, but through the democratic process, when the people vote for it.

Socialism would not allow unrestricted private ownership of property. It would regulate private enterprise much more than under any capitalistic philosophy. It would oppose the accumulation of great wealth, where this is not opposed under capitalism. Socialists would seek to achieve their objective by gradual, peaceful revolution, whereas communism (actually a variant of socialism) advocates immediate, forcible revolution.

England's Labour government, in power several times during this century, exemplifies something very close to socialism in the modern state. Sweden has a socialistic cast to its economy. Various aspects of our own government and economic structure are also in the socialist pattern.

COMMUNISM · In 1848, Karl Marx and Friedrich Engels issued their *Communist Manifesto,* crying: "Workers of the world, unite! You have nothing to lose but your chains." Communism, as they envisaged it, was a "scientifically" based program, arguing that workers should—and would—destroy capitalism by revolution, seize control of the tools of industry, and build an economic system based on the proposition that the wealth belongs to all the people. There would be no gradual move toward the abolition of private property as under socialism. There would be no private property whatever, as under capitalism and socialism. The government, on behalf of the people, would own and control all property and determine how best to distribute income for the welfare of all. There would be but one class, not an exploiting and exploited class.

There is no pure communist economy by this definition, unless it be in some relatively primitive, simple society. The Soviet Union's system is called communistic, but it is far from what Marx and Engels envisioned. Russia's economy has elements of communism, socialism, and capitalism, and the same is true of other so-called communist nations, such as mainland China, Yugoslavia, Hungary, and Poland.

ECONOMIC TRENDS IN THE UNITED STATES

The successful private entrepreneur is still highly regarded in our society. In some measure, such men as Andrew Carnegie and Henry Ford continue to be folk heroes, examples of the American Dream, according to which every person can get where he wants, economically, provided he has the patience, courage, and fortitude. The adolescent's aspiration is sometimes like that of the boy in Figure 27.1, and those to whom he reveals it may assume that the dream can be translated into reality. Actually, "from rags to riches" was never an easy accomplishment in American society, and the spectacular "up-from-the-bottom" careers may have been as exceptional in the past as they are today. Nevertheless, there is still some verity in the dream of unlimited promise in an economy of great abundance. Fortunes are still made, by the few, on an investment of a shoestring, some effort and imagination, and perhaps luck. The national wealth increases steadily, despite large pockets of poverty and individual suffering by the poverty-stricken.

INDUSTRIALISM · Not every human society places as much emphasis as we do on an industrial economy. There have been and are nations showing greater interest in military expansion, or religious practice, or commerce, or other activity. The United States, on the other hand, embarked on a vast program of industrialization during the nineteenth century, culminating in mass production, elaborate occupational specializations, and automation. Social thinkers have offered various speculative reasons why we in the United States should have given rational economic activity the particular bent it has taken. Whether or not one accepts the hypotheses, the fact remains that our values made it possible for industrialism to play the highly important role it does in our society. Wilbert E. Moore observes: "For the world to beat a path to the door of the inventor of a superior mousetrap, it must first be interested in catching mice."[5] Millions of our residents feel they must have superior mousetraps, because in their value system mice must go. Millions of our people consider it desirable, if not essential, that they have available to them a vast array of particular goods and services. It would be an oversimplification to say that industrialization takes place solely because people feel they must have goods and services, but such cultural values do stimulate, and then function to maintain, our industrial society.

SPECIALIZATION · What are some of the effects of industrialism upon our society? For one thing, the division of labor required has resulted in a high degree of occupational specialization. In 1960, the Bureau of the Census guide to occupational coding listed some 30,000 different job titles. Among the

Figure 27.1
The Economy of
Abundance
Drawing by Saxon; © 1959 The
New Yorker Magazine, Inc.

"After you make a million dollars, what then?"

better known were: farmer, accountant, actor, architect, author, chemist, professor, doctor, engineer, social worker, lawyer, sawyer, manufacturer, sailor, mail carrier, politician, salesman, baker, bartender, carpenter, mason, toolmaker, meat cutter, miner. Some of the more picturesque jobs reported to the 1960 census included bum-boater (ice cream peddler), tombstone polisher, thumb cutter (operator of a glove-making process), and screen-ape (laborer in coal mining). Consider such highly specialized operations as tea bag stringer (he ties tags to individual tea bags, then packs the bags in cartons), Easter bunny (impersonator of the furry animal at children's entertainments during Easter season), jaw skinner (a specialist who trims meat only from the lower jawbone of the hog), and chicken sexer (who examines the genital organs of baby chicks, determines their sex, and places them in boxes according to whether they are male or female).

This highly diversified complex of occupations has brought consequences that are of interest to sociologists and other students of the social scene. It has been suggested that as men follow different occupational pursuits they develop disparate social values and interests. The ties that once bound the entire membership of the society together are no longer as binding as occupational groups develop subcultures of their own.

That such subcultures exist is indicated by the strong feelings of loyalty exhibited by members of occupational groups for other members of the same group. A physician may be convinced that a surgeon—whom he does not know personally—followed an improper and harmful surgical procedure when operating on the first doctor's patient. The physician is not likely to inform his patient of that. Policemen protect each other against charges of brutality brought by civilians. There is a camaraderie among long-distance truckmen that excludes people in other walks of life.

As occupational subcultures develop their own values and customs, they are very likely to create their own special languages, making for easy communication among members of the group while tending to exclude those who do not follow the given occupational pursuit. This exclusion may not be intentional, however. Speaking of the language of certain professional groups, Dressler observes that it is precise and that those who use it are not interested in making it intelligible to the general, lay public.

The purpose of a special language is economy. Everyone in the group thereby knows at once, in the briefest time, what is meant. When the mathematician says *hypotenuse* every other mathematician knows at once what is meant; he does not need a preliminary discourse on the concept of the hypotenuse.[6]

Similarly, persons in other occupations have their language, often incomprehensible to "outsiders." For example, how many of the following terms do you understand?

TERM	OCCUPATION
1 · Frogger	Logging
2 · Wiggle-tail	Mining
3 · Hole in the book	Magazine publishing
4 · Pork-chopper	Labor organizing
5 · Butcher	Show business
6 · Bird dog	Auto sales
7 · Technical market	Stock marketing
8 · Double truck	Advertising
9 · Heeling	Boxing
10 · Grass cutting	Aviation

Here are the explanations:

1 · A member of a skidding crew who follows the logs in case they become fouled on the way.
2 · An excavating drill.
3 · A condition produced by the nonarrival or nonacceptability of a story or article that has been scheduled for an issue about to go to press.
4 · An official who is considered to be in the union out of self-interest rather than to help workers.
5 · Vendor of candy or other items in a theatre.
6 · A person who steers a likely customer to a car dealer, for a fee.
7 · The condition of the market in which an unnatural level of price is maintained by manipulation or speculation.
8 · An advertisement set across two full pages.
9 · A maneuver in which a fighter, during clinches, runs the laced part of his glove over an opponent's face wound, so as to exacerbate it.
10 · Excessive taxiing at takeoff on the flying field.

The existence of occupational subcultures does not necessarily or significantly loosen the ties that bind people together in the society as a whole. Emile Durkheim[7] points out that the division of labor may actually be a source of solidarity. When people enter respective occupations, they must increasingly depend upon each other for many things. A primitive society is characterized by "mechanical" solidarity, founded largely upon similarities among the members. In a complex society, asserts Durkheim, there is an "organic" solidarity, based upon mutual need. No one occupation can supply all of the needs within the society; workers in one walk of life must depend upon workers in other occupations to a greater or lesser degree; the farmer needs the manufacturer, the manufacturer needs the farmer, and both need scientists, laborers, professional men, and others if their common needs are to be met. Each makes his contribution to the collective life of the group. In this respect, the interdependence produced by the division of labor enhances the solidarity of the society.

But, of itself, interdependence may not be sufficient to hold a society together, Durkheim observes. He points to conditions in the Western world prior to the end of the nineteenth century, when the extreme individualism and impersonality of industrial society threatened its unity. There need to be *shared*

understandings and *common* values, in addition to an awareness of interdependence, if there is to be consensus and solidarity. Men need a moral unity, Durkheim says, and that is not
furnished by individuals as individuals. Such unity can be
supplied by the state, or by occupational groups so organized
that they create a moral power that members of the society
will respect.[8]

AN EMPLOYEE SOCIETY · During the last fifty years or so we
have changed from an employer to an employee society. Peter
J. Drucker[9] develops this theme in an article in which he points
out that the great majority of people in the United States are
employees today. They expect to spend most, perhaps all, of
their working lives in that status rather than as employers. The
employer is disappearing, if by the designation we mean
someone who owns and directly operates an establishment
where employees are at work. A half century ago, a majority
of employees worked for employers of this type. Currently, in
the large as well as many of the smaller organizations, people
work for a "boss" but not for an "employer."

The boss is himself an employee who in turn works for a boss—
and so does the next boss and the next and the next. In the entire
organization there is nobody who is not himself an employee working for a boss.[10]

This change in the industrial system has great significance.
"Employeeship," to use Drucker's term, ". . . colors the social
values, the social mores, and the folklore of our society. It
increasingly determines and sets the ethos of American society."[11] The change

. . . means, in the first place, that this employee society is a hierarchical system—a system in which everybody is related to people
through his relationship to a strictly impersonal, strictly objective,
strictly abstract thing, the "organization," the "corporation," the
"government agency," etc. It means, second, that this is a society
which is based on, and ruled by, status.[12]

Elucidating, Drucker says that formerly a personal relationship existed between employer and employee, that is, personalities were involved. A contract obligated the employee to
further the employer's goal, which was defined primarily in

terms of property interest. In the employee society of today, personalities do not "count." The relationship of individuals to one another ". . . is defined by their relative status in respect to a goal and purpose which lies entirely outside all of them, though they are all subordinated to it and cooperate toward its fulfillment."[13]

That goal and purpose has resulted in the emergence of a new ruling group—management. It ". . . derives its authority and its responsibilities squarely from function, that is, from its status relationship to the organization, and not from anything it possesses such as property, birth, inherited magical power, or military force. . . . Its position, its power, and its responsibilities rest solely on indispensable function."[14]

In addition to management there is, of course, a worker group and often its union, the latter an outgrowth of the emergence of management.

Thus we operate our economic system under a hierarchical arrangement in which relationships are defined in terms of statuses—those of management and workers, for instance—rather than of personalities. Relationships within an organization are based on status, which rules and governs the contemporary employee society, according to Drucker. Some would question whether *all* relationships are based *exclusively* on status rather than on the personalities involved. There is evidence that the boundaries separating one status group from another are on occasion brushed aside, that personalities play a part in even the most impersonal of giant corporations. However, much of what Drucker has to say is corroborated by direct observation of our industrial complex. We are, largely, an employee society.

ORGANIZATION MEN? · In 1956, William H. Whyte, Jr., an American journalist, wrote *The Organization Man*, a volume that became a best seller, perhaps because so many of us see ourselves as one of those portrayed by the author:

They are not the workers nor are they the white-collar people in the usual, clerk sense of the word. These people only work for The Organization. The ones I am talking about *belong* to it as well. They are the ones of our middle class who have left home, spiritually as well as physically, to take the vows of organization life, and it is they who are the mind and soul of our great self-perpetuating institutions. Only a few are top managers or ever will be. In a system that makes such hazy terminology as "junior executive" psychologically necessary, they are of the staff as much as the line, and most are destined to live poised in the middle area that still awaits a satisfactory euphemism. But they are the dominant members of our society nonetheless. . . . and it is their values which will set the American temper.[15]

The organization man, according to Whyte's conception, is a product of our economic system, which is no longer dominated by an older-line culture of capitalism. Today's capitalistic enterprise deemphasizes raw individualism, the dictum of "the survival of the fittest," which is part of the Protestant ethic. Contemporary economic endeavor is motivated by a "social ethic," Whyte declares. It demands group effort, "belongingness," and the organization man is consequently obsessed by the desire to belong. At work and at home, he "plays it safe" as a team member. He minimizes competition and cultivates smooth human relations as a means of gaining security. He avoids making independent decisions when he can, getting his work done, his decisions made, as far as possible in committee. He hopes for collective solutions to problems, which will spare him the necessity of adopting an outspoken, individual stand. The solutions arrived at in committee will probably be pedestrian and conformist, but that is comforting, too.

In a magazine article,[16] Whyte describes the community life of the young, middle-class, college-educated organization man. "On the make," he lives in the suburbs, but he puts down only shallow roots, for he expects to move upward quickly, then on to a more prestigious residential area. Meantime, he engages almost frantically in a great many neighborhood and community affairs with local residents close to himself in age, income, and occupation. Social activity becomes the basis of local prestige.

At work and in his home community, then, the organization man envisaged by Whyte participates vigorously and conforms compulsively. Guided by the "social ethic," he looks to the group as the source of creativity, to "belongingness" as the ultimate need of every individual.[17]

Much of Whyte's thesis is convincing. There is, indeed, a trend toward "togetherness," or "belongingness," to cooperation in business, industry, and community life. But the culture of older-line capitalism is by no means dead. Fierce competition and individualism are still factors even along with the cooperation and group endeavor. The Protestant ethic still exerts its influence. What Whyte calls the "social ethic" is emerging, but slowly.

OTHER SIGNIFICANT TRENDS · 1. Occupation and family roles have become more and more separated. Most work undertaken for income is done outside the home. Family businesses and farms still exist, but are rapidly declining. The "ma and pa" grocery store has been displaced by the supermarket of absentee ownership.

2. As already suggested, ownership is increasingly divorced from management. Management people—executives and adminstrators—are hired by owners and stockholders to operate businesses and corporations. Management has become a professional undertaking for persons especially trained for the field.

3. Government regulation of business, industry, and labor is steadily increasing. Business and industrial firms must abide by laws regulating wages and hours of employment, health and safety measures, and many other matters. They must furnish certain data on employees in connection with the Social Security system. By law, management must recognize and deal with employee groups under specified conditions. Workers must meet their obligations under employment contracts, if the latter were legally negotiated and consummated.

4. The labor force has grown from some 22 million persons in 1890 to over 70 million in 1960. The proportion of the population represented in the labor force has remained at about 40 percent during the past several decades, however.

The increase in the number of workers during the 1960s in absolute figures will be by far the largest for any ten-year period in our history—50 percent greater than during the 1950s. By 1970, it is expected, 13.5 million more workers will be in the labor force.[18]

5. Women are entering the labor market in increasing numbers. By 1970, about 30 million will be working away from home, 6 million more than in 1960. One out of every three workers will be a woman.[19]

6. There has been a significant realignment in the distribution of the labor force since the opening of this century. The proportion of farm workers has dropped sharply. There has been a slight increase in manual laborers and persons engaged

in service occupations. The most marked rise has been in the proportion of white-collar workers, who now constitute about 40 percent of the total labor force. In 1960, the production industries (manufacturing, agriculture, construction, mining) employed 26 million workers. The same year, service industries (trade, government services, transportation and public utilities, finance, insurance, real estate, and other services) accounted for the employment of 32.5 million. Service workers had outstripped those in production.[20]

Proportionately, the number of service workers will rise, while production workers will decline in number, as our technology advances. Because of automation, fewer employees will be required to produce the same amount of goods. On the other hand, we shall require more workers to provide the increasing services that will be available and sought after if the living standard continues to rise.

7. The largest increases in employment in coming decades will occur in occupations requiring the higher levels of education and training. This is an outcome of such factors as the continuing shift from an agricultural economy to one that is predominantly industrial, the rapid expansion in research and development activity, the increasing size and complexity of business organization, and the growing need for educational and medical services.

8. Labor has been effectively organized since enactment of the National Labor Relations Act under the New Deal in the 1930s. Unions are much more powerful than at the turn of the century. In all likelihood, history will not reverse itself in this respect.

Economic and political institutions are increasingly intermeshed in our society. Indeed, government is a major part of the economy. It furnishes employment to millions of workers, subsidizes many private business, industrial, and agricultural operations, and finances other undertakings in the interest of a sound economy. The interrelatedness of the economic and political institutions needs to be remembered as we discuss the latter.

THE POLITICAL INSTITUTION

As in the case of the economic system, sociologists, not being political scientists, do not claim any special competence in evaluating the effectiveness of any one political system. They do, however, analyze the political system as a social institution of society.

The political institution is a cultural system of society, establishing relatively formal methods for acquiring and exercising power within a given jurisdiction through agencies deemed to have ultimate authority.

FUNCTIONS

A reasonable degree of order must be maintained if members of society are to be secure in their persons. Custom, expressed in the folkways and mores, and their (partial) internalization in the individual, assure a certain degree of order, but some behavior must be regulated by more formal means. The political institution functions to accomplish this in the following directions:

1. *Enforcement of behavior norms considered vital to the welfare of society.* Sorcery is prohibited by customary law among Eskimo people. Our own political institution includes, for example, laws prohibiting murder and assault and others commanding observance of motor vehicle regulations and the building of safety features into elevators.

Maintenance of law and order involves the settlement of disputes. Among certain African tribes, as reported by anthropologist Ralph Linton some years ago, courts presided over by the headman were convened for such settlement. The entire community acted as an informal jury. Accusations were made, witnesses examined, and the principals or their advocates pleaded the case. The headman then handed down the decision he believed in accord with the will of the spectators, about whom Linton comments:

Although these have no official place in the trial, they guarantee fair play, and it is a bold judge who dares to go against them. Such trials break the monotony of village life and are enjoyed by all. A dispute between two old women over a hen may provide amusement for half a day, while the wisdom of the head man's discussion will be discussed long afterward.[21]

In our own civil courts, judges act as arbitrators in litigation between private parties, as for instance when one man sues another for damages incurred in an automobile accident. In criminal courts, where the defendants are alleged to have aggressed against the dignity and welfare of the state itself, courts adjudicate cases in the interest of protecting society against future criminal activity by the instant defendant and of serving as a deterrent to others who might otherwise be tempted to violate the law.

2. *Planning, coordinating, and financing activities deemed for the joint welfare of members of the society.* For example, in the United States, government regulation is invoked to prevent the overproduction of agricultural products. Projects beyond the capacity of one individual or small group of individuals to accomplish are launched by government, as in the building of harbors and freeways, the prevention of water and air pollution, and the construction of dams.

Under the village adminstration plan of Nondwin, Burma, the headman promulgates decrees and collects taxes. All households are responsible for keeping up a section of the village palisade. These family units form the political community of the village. Those family members who are of proper age are entitled to vote for the village headman, such voting being the expression of membership in the political community.[22]

3. *Protection against outside enemies.* Centralized control and direction of men and weapons is necessary if a society is to be protected against an enemy. Our federal and state units furnish this. In other societies as well it is clearly understood who controls the fighting force and under what authority it shall be called to combat.

MacIver and Page suggest the following classification of governmental functions:

1 · Those functions *peculiar to the state*—maintenance of order, the attainment of justice, and the protection of property under the particular property rights system in existence.
2 · Those functions for which the state is *well adapted,* including conservation of natural resources, control of monopoly, and maintenance of such public facilities as parks and playgrounds, museums, and schools.
3 · Those functions for which the state is *ill adapted.* These vary according to conditions. In general they are functions that do not serve the needs of the entire community. In this cate-

gory are religion, literary and artistic production, and evaluation of cultural products.

4   Those functions that the state is *incapable* of performing, such as controlling people's opinions and regulating morality.[23]

STRUCTURE

The political institution defines who shall be accorded what power in government and when and how it shall be accorded. The persons so designated *are* the government, and as such, agents for the entire society. This is so, regardless of the specific form of the political system—monarchy, democracy, or dictatorship.

By the concept of "the divine right of kings," the absolute monarch ascends to power under a prescription that might be stated as follows: (1) *Who* gains power? The lineal descendant of the last ruler. (2) *What* power? Absolute, beyond veto by any means. (3) *When?* Upon the death of the incumbent monarch. (4) *How gained?* By divine right, by lineal descent, and after certain ceremonials.

The conditions would be different in the case of a democracy or dictatorship, but the formula would be the same, setting forth *who* shall gain *what* power, *when*, and *how*.

Coercion is a prerogative of the political institution. Inherent in governmental structure is the authority to command certain behavior and to punish those who do not abide by government commands. If order is to be maintained, government must have authority to enforce law-abiding behavior and therefore, in principle though never entirely in fact, exercises a monopoly over the use of *force*.

Government is limited by geographical boundaries. Jurisdiction extends only within these boundaries. In the United States, for example, jurisdiction is largely according to municipal, county, state, or national boundaries.

Territorial jurisdiction has been a major problem in world affairs for centuries. Often it is a source of conflict between nations, whether this be fought out over the conference table or on the battlefield. For example, Germany and France have shed blood over the issue of their respective boundaries. The diplomatic and military postures of Israel vis-à-vis the Arab nations is another case in point.

There are many different generic forms of government, including the three familiar systems of *monarchy, democracy,* and *dictatorship.* Each of these has several variants, and the form of government may be less significant than the specific political institutions that support it.

Thus *monarchy* may be absolute or constitutional. The absolute monarch *is* the law in its totality, and examples of this system are to be found almost entirely in the past. The constitutional monarch rules by virtue of authority vested in him by a legal document and may be as limited in power by parliamentary constraints as the cases of Britain and the Netherlands testify.

Democracy is a political institution providing government by will of the people. Many types of democratic governments exist. In small tribal societies, it is possible for all members to convene and pass jointly on matters at issue. In a society as complex as our own, government must be administered, not by the direct vote of the people on each and every issue, but through representation. Our elected representatives are authorized to act for us.

Dictatorship is a political system whereby one person, or a small group of persons, exercises all the powers of government. Like an absolute monarchy, a dictatorship, in principle, does not need to be responsive to public consensus. Unlike an absolute or a constitutional monarchy, accession to a dictatorship is not usually on a kinship basis. Rarely does a dictator receive his authority by delegation from the people. More often than not he seizes power and destroys whatever democratic institutions may have existed.

Since we live under a democratic form of government, let us consider some of the principal features of its structure:

All forms of government, the democratic included, are founded on power. What is our power base in the United States? Our society is so complex that it is not easy to answer this question. Do business and financial interests wield the power? Religious organizations? Working men? Is there one mighty power group or a number of groups, each exercising some influence?

Political scientists have differed as to the last question and so have sociologists. The late C. Wright Mills, a sociologist, concluded that the United States is ruled by one central "power elite," a unified group at the very apex of the power structure.[24] Nelson W. Polsby counters this with a "pluralistic" interpretation of community power.[25] There is not just one group of "influentials," he holds, but a number of groups, oriented to specific "issue-areas," such as housing, schools, political nominations, and others. This point of view receives support from Robert A. Dahl, whose study of New Haven found no one dominant group in that city, but several. Each was concerned with specific problems and issues, each able to exert considerable influence in determining public policy in that area.[26]

David Riesman and his associates offer a variant of the Polsby thesis of pluralistic community power.[27] There are indeed diversified power groups representing different interests, but they should be regarded as "veto groups." Each group is primarily devoted to protecting its jurisdiction; it attempts to accomplish this by blocking the efforts of other groups that appear to threaten that jurisdiction; there is no one decisive ruling group but rather a number of interacting groups. This tends to maintain a balance of authority in the community, one group being checked by another or others.

Mills notwithstanding, there does not appear to be one all-powerful group of elites who rule this country. That might have been possible many years ago but scarcely in this stage of our political and economic development. There undoubtedly are a number of different groups that exercise power, however, and on occasion some of these act in concert to attain an objective, whereas at other times one group tends to checkmate the other. In a modern, democratic, industrial society such as ours, where there are substantial differences in background and outlook among the citizenry, political parties have found it essential to appeal not to one, but to a variety, of power groups, if they are to win a majority.

For democratic government to operate effectively, it is necessary to have political competition and cleavage, and this calls for some diversity of power groups rather than only one group exercising control. Our party system expresses this point of view, in effect. A one-party system lends itself to ideological ossification, in which the will of only one segment of the citizenry has expression. At any one time, Britain, a monarchy operating under a democratic constitution, has a party in power and a "loyal opposition." Our essentially two-party system works somewhat the same way. When Democrats are in power, they justify their policies before the people, and Republicans criticize them. This airing of issues keeps voters informed and sharpens their ability to evaluate problems of government.

In theory we have "government by representation," and in certain respects we do in fact—congressmen, mayors, city councilmen, and others are elected by constituencies, and supposedly they act as their constituents would have them act. However, representation breaks down in at least three respects.

1. No elected official ever represents all of the voters and viewpoints in his territorial jurisdiction. The official, at best, can hope to represent the consensus. And sometimes he does not attempt to do even this, believing that he should exercise his judgment even though it may run counter to the consensus. Thus, a member of the United States Congress may be quite certain that most of his constituents are opposed to a pending tax law, yet vote for it. He may be criticized or praised for his individualism and perhaps risk his political future, but he does not represent his constituents by his vote.

2. We do not always, as individual citizens, directly decide who will represent us. Our elected officials appoint subordinates—police chiefs, judges, department heads—whose acts affect the citizenry.

And often we do not directly decide who will run for public office as elective officials. We are given only a choice of several preselected candidates. In New York State, for instance, each political party selects its candidate for governor, and New Yorkers are then presented with a slate. They may vote for the Democratic, Republican, or Liberal party candidate (or one running on a minor party ticket), but they had no real part in determining who would run.

A national convention is held by each major party to select presidential candidates. The general public has very little to say about the outcome, for primary elections by no means determine the outcome of national conventions. Moreover, professional politicians make deals and counterdeals behind the scenes before announcing their support of "that gr-reat American—" (see Figure 27.2).

3. The graft system weakens and sometimes nullifies representative government. When action by public officials can be bought, the people lose their voice as citizens. It is not what they want that is accomplished, but what a few people paid for. Perhaps the most infamous case of the graft system was

Figure 27.2
The Democratic Process?
Drawing by Leonard Dove; Copr.
© 1956 The New Yorker
Magazine, Inc.

*"Don't worry. We'll go along
with you fellows, all right, but first
we've got to get rid of our goddam favorite son."*

when the city of Chicago was in the grip of the Capone gang during the 1920s and most of the decade following. Aspirants for public office, from mayor to judge to prosecutor, had to get the nod from Capone (and after his death, from his henchmen) in order to be elected. Vice and crime flourished. "Justice" was bought and sold.

That kind of government scarcely represents the will of the electorate, and although corruption in high places still exists from time to time and in particular localities, the graft system seems to be less flagrant and widespread than it was in earlier decades.

POLITICAL TRENDS IN THE UNITED STATES

Among the major trends in government and politics in the United States during the past quarter century or so are the following:

1. The political affiliation of members of ethnic and religious groups has undergone substantial change. Negroes were once

pretty solidly Republican, where they were permitted to vote. Since the 1930s and 1940s, however, they have tended to vote Democratic. As more Southern Negroes go to the ballot box, present indications are that, at least in national elections, they will favor the Democratic party.

Class position plays some part in determining political preferences of ethnic, nationality, and religious groups. When, for instance, Irish Americans of Catholic persuasion were largely of the working class and heavily concentrated in urban areas, principally in the East, they were quite solidly Democratic. As their economic lot improved, and they moved upward from working-class status and outward from working-class neighborhoods, their voting record underwent some change. In 1952 and 1956, many of them voted Republican, especially in national elections. Currently, political analysts no longer think of Irish Catholics as a solid voting block. They are virtually unpredictable, neither confirmed Democrats nor confirmed Republicans. A similar development has taken place among other ethnic and nationality groups: as many of their members ascend the social class ladder, their political loyalties tend to change, from Democratic to Republican. They no longer form a "dependable" voting block for the Democratic party. Jewish Americans are something of an exception: Although upwardly mobile and widely dispersed residentially, they have voted heavily Democratic, about 4 to 1, since the Franklin D. Roosevelt administration.

But although class position is a factor in political party preference, it is not the only one. For instance, Protestants are more likely to vote Republican than are Roman Catholics or Jews, even when their respective class positions are alike.

2. Somewhat in disregard of class position and other factors, women tend to support the conservative parties more frequently than do men in local as well as national elections in this country (and in Europe). Seymour Lipset suggests this is a consequence of the fact that the female's role in societies such as ours brings her to place high value on stability and tradition.[28]

3. Many studies show that urban residents are somewhat more active in political affairs than rural residents. The massive urbanization of American society, resulting in a continuously shrinking rural population, should therefore result in increased participation by the electorate in political matters.

4. Special-interest lobbies exert an increasing influence on legislation. They spend millions of dollars annually, promoting or attacking proposed enactments in fields as varied as medicine, labor, sugar, wine, control of gun sales, planned parenthood, peno-correctional treatment of offenders, veterans' affairs, disarmament, and armament.

5. Government has assumed progressively more authority in regulating numerous activities that were once viewed as "private." Power has been increasingly centralized in Washington since the New Deal era. State governments also exercise more regulatory functions than formerly. Laws and administrative boards regulate, in some degree, stock market operations, medical practice, social work, hunting and fishing, public and private education, garbage disposal, the movement of aliens, maritime affairs, aviation, labor relations, and small business practices.

6. The expansion of government has resulted in the recruitment of a huge staff of public employees. In 1920, there were approximately 2,603,000 full-time and part-time nonmilitary government employees at federal, state, and local levels. By 1966, the number had grown to 11,479,000, more than four times the figure in 1920.[29]

7. A distinct trend toward what some call "the welfare state" is apparent, if by that term is meant an acceptance by government of an obligation to work for the health and welfare of all citizens. The Social Security Act, Medicare, and the Economic Opportunity Act of 1964 are examples, at the federal level, of enactments in the health and welfare areas. The several Civil Rights Acts of the decade also exemplify a concern for the general welfare.

8. Since the 1930s, more and more professionally trained persons, including lawyers, doctors, academicians, social workers, and scientists have become employees of the municipal, state, and federal governments. This is largely a reflection of the increasing number and complexity of governmental functions and responsibilities and the resulting need for trained specialists in many fields, including economics, sociology, psychology, and the natural sciences. In recent years scientists, partly but by no means entirely because of the development of modern weaponry, have come to play a major role in governmental activities including, significantly, policy-making itself.

How high is the moon?

Why does a stone fall when dropped from a height?

Does a tree have feeling?

Can dolphins understand the English language?

Why do you want to know these things?

Because, as Isaac Asimov says, in his *Intelligent Man's Guide to Science,* ". . . almost in the beginning was curiosity."[30] Man has an insatiable curiosity, and it has played an essential role in the development of science.

But curiosity can be led into one channel or another. Why into science? A number of reasons may be advanced.

Although the foundations of the rational and empirical methods had been laid earlier, the development of modern science began in the sixteenth and seventeenth centuries. This was an era of commercial expansion, and the needs of the economy called for increased knowledge in certain fields. Scientific interest turned to those fields. The scientist's pursuit, then, had a practical purpose. Merton points out that every English scientist of that period of sufficient importance to be mentioned in general histories of science thereafter ". . . at one point or other explicitly related at least some of his scientific research to immediate practical problems."[31] In the years 1661–1662, and 1686–1687, Merton found, 30 to 60 percent of the problems studied by members of the Royal Society in England were directly or indirectly related to military needs, navigation, or to the requirements of industry, notably mining.[32]

But economic need is not enough, of itself, to explain the extraordinary development of science in the sixteenth and seventeenth centuries. Since some of the practical problems that scientists attacked at that time had existed long before, why the increased *interest* in solving them by scientific means? Some social thinkers have suggested that in seventeenth century England, at least, a vital factor was Puritanism. It emphasized rationalism and encouraged men to strive to master the world in which they lived and to explore nature's mysteries. This would not only improve man's condition on earth but testify to the glory of the Lord by revealing the wonders of His handiwork.

The eighteenth century brought the Enlightenment, with

its emphasis upon the use of reason and upon freedom and humanitarianism. This further justified scientific inquiry. At midcentury England entered a period of accelerating industrialism that spread to Western Europe. As industrialism flourished and spread with increasing speed, there arose a great demand for research in a variety of subjects: chemistry, thermodynamics, metallurgy, hydraulics, and others. Military and political interests had their needs, too, calling for greater efforts to extend man's scientific knowledge.

Academia began to make its contribution. As scientific knowledge accumulated, as its usefulness was increasingly recognized, some universities undertook the teaching of science, but others were reluctant to do so. Where universities encouraged scientific inquiry, science flourished. Where they did not, science developed more slowly. Joseph Ben-David has shown that there was a close relationship between the "productivity" of medical science in various countries in the nineteenth century and the degree to which scientific research was encouraged and sponsored by the universities.[33]

By the nineteenth and especially the twentieth centuries, science had become an essential element of the culture of a great many nations throughout the world. So much so that although until recently the fact has been largely overlooked in the sociological literature, science has become institutionalized.

FUNCTION

In Chapter 1 we defined *science* as *a collection of knowledge and a deliberate search for additional knowledge through the use of a given method.* Gerard DeGré emphasizes its function as a social institution when he says: ". . . science is a social activity through which a society interprets the cultural and natural world."[34]

Science functions:

1 · To search out knowledge about the cultural and natural worlds.
2 · To accumulate a body of verifiable knowledge about those worlds.
3 · To develop verifiable theory about them.
4 · To interpret the cultural and natural worlds, explaining *how* events happen and *why* they happen.

5 · To apply theory and knowledge about the cultural and natural worlds toward serving the needs and solving the social problems of the society.

To paraphrase DeGré's *Science as a Social Institution,* the scientist:

1 · Discovers new facts about the natural world and the biological and social environments.
2 · Systematizes knowledge into a coherent theoretical system.
3 · Applies that knowledge to the solution of practical problems with which men living in social groups within specific environments and possessing certain life goals are faced.[35]

The scientist, like anyone else, is a product of his culture, hence he has internalized a good deal of the value system of his society. As he responds to the problems that arise in the culture, often investigating matters relevant to its value system, he strives to keep his own value judgments out of his scientific work. He does make value judgments, nevertheless: He concludes that since he injected a white rat with a particular drug, the animal has become sick, where it had been well. He decides the scientific method is a better way of determining this than any other method. Both of these conclusions are value judgments. But the scientist does his best to keep previously internalized value judgments from interfering with the strict objectivity of his observations during investigations. He wants to be sure his observations are verifiable by other objective observers.

STRUCTURE

We discussed science and the scientific method in the first section of this text. Science incorporates a set of values and attitudes concerning the nature of truth and its attainment. It is also a body of principles and methods of scientific procedure, as well as the body of knowledge derived from that procedure.

Without scientists there would be no science. DeGré points out[36] that the individual who meets the requirements, professional and otherwise, of his social circle enjoys a definite social status. His circle grants him certain status-conferring rights.

He may carry on specific activities as a member of his profession, such as the practice of medicine or research in atomic physics. He has the right to certain material values considered necessary for his subsistence on a level thought to be consistent with his role—housing, salaries, fees, royalties, and payment in kind, with which the scientist is rewarded for carrying on his activities. There are also ". . . some of the more ornamental attributes" of the scientist's social status, such as titles, orders, decorations, insignia, the privilege of certain forms of dress—the cap and gown of the professor, for example. Professional social status, finally, carries with it prestige, authority, and recognition. Some scientists occupy commanding positions in the organization of contemporary American society, including, as we have noted above, governmental activities for war, peace, public health, and the general welfare.

SCIENTIFIC TRENDS

It was in the sixteenth and seventeenth centuries that much of the equipment necessary for scientific work became available: machinery for lens grinding, which made the microscope and telescope possible; the thermometer, barometer, hand pump; Galileo's telescope (1609); and other specialized instruments. But these technological developments were undergirded by nonmaterial factors, as DeGré notes:

The most important events leading to the transformation of science during the seventeenth century . . . were not exclusively the creation of the instruments for scientific observation. Coupled with the development of these material culture traits, a transformation of the subjective, psychological approach of the scientist to his subject matter was taking place. This new orientation was based on two significant changes: first, the belief that mathematics could provide the instrument to make the natural world completely intelligible, and second, the growing conviction that observation and experiment are the most dependable methods for the acquisition of scientific knowledge.[37]

This orientation is implicit in the scientist's procedures today. His observations have extended into physical and biological phenomena, and his findings have penetrated every aspect of human life. We differentiate between *science* and *technology,* but the two are inextricable in one respect. To a large extent, especially in modern times, technology depends upon scientific knowledge for its development, and science upon technology for the furtherance of scientific investigation. The relationship is reciprocal. Figure 27.3 makes good-natured fun of the plumber, a technician, for thinking of his procedures as scientific. Actually, they are based on many scientific principles and facts, for scientific investigation determined the properties of water, what metals could contain it, how to create pressure to bring it through pipes, and so on. The steam engine, the submarine, the Erie Canal, the textile mill, the microphone, the steel bridge, structural steel, the telephone, radio, the camera, listening devices, radar, automobiles, jet planes, the electron microscope, nuclear fission—all make use of basic scientific discoveries and theories. Engineering, architecture, mining, electronics, and many other fields and practices are indebted to science.

But scientists often must await technological advances in order that they may proceed with their investigations. Machinery for lens grinding, we pointed out above, made the microscope possible. Without the microscope much scientific inquiry in the physical and natural sciences would have been impossible. Although scientists found out a great deal about outer space by means then at their command, technologists had to devise the "hardware" and other necessaries before scientists could actually probe outer space. In devising those necessaries, technologists made use of scientific knowledge. Thus the reciprocal relationship between science and technology was exemplified. The exploration of outer space, the most dramatic development of the 1960s, is *basically* a scientific rather than a technological undertaking, but technology facilitates and implements it immeasurably. So breathtaking have been the developments that the scene depicted in Figure 27.4 may be reproducible in fact in the near future.

Science has established an imposing and exciting record. It has brought enormous benefits to mankind—in medicine and public health, transportation and communication, manufacturing, leisure time activities, and many other fields. Grave concern has been expressed, however, about certain scientific discoveries, and especially their application.

1. The fact that science made possible the construction of fantastically devastating weaponry is regarded by many persons as a tragic and disastrous event in world history. Man has

Figure 27.3
Science and Technology
Drawing by Steig; © 1958 The
New Yorker Magazine, Inc.

"Science!"

learned to destroy the world before discovering how to make peace with his fellow man.

2. The concentration on science, in terms of governmental, educational, and financial resources, may weaken the humanities and social sciences. Yet unless science is harnessed to the peaceful purposes of man, as incorporated in the ideas and principles of the humanistic disciplines, it may destroy man rather than bring him comfort.

3. The greatly increased demand for scientists, in industry primarily, siphons off some of the finest scientific manpower in the world. In the long run this may serve as a boomerang for science itself. If too many scientists go "where the money is," if institutions of higher learning fail to retain them because they can or will not pay competitive salaries, who will train tomorrow's scientists?

THE INSTITUTIONAL SYSTEM OF SOCIAL WELFARE

Social welfare is another major social and cultural system that has been rather neglected by sociologists, although it has been strongly institutionalized in our society. Social welfare activities cost between 25 billion dollars and 60 billion dollars annually, depending upon the basis of computation. This in-

Figure 27.4
Tomorrow
Drawing by Robt. Day; © 1958
The New Yorker Magazine, Inc.

*"I'll have the orange juice,
scrambled eggs and bacon,
toast, marmalade, and coffee, please."*

stitution affects every member of our society in one fashion
or another.

FUNCTION

*Social welfare is a system of cultural patterns designed to
help individuals and groups attain maximum satisfactions in
harmony with community standards.* Its functions may be
more explicitly depicted as follows:

1. Institutionalized social welfare, as it has developed in
the United States (and other countries in Western society),
does not function as a system of mutual aid. Small tribal and
traditional rural societies often practice the sharing of food
and other necessaries in short supply. This is mutual aid,
based on kinship or close tribal relationships. In contrast, the
modern social welfare system is, in principle, designed for the
aid of any and all persons in need, regardless of family or
friendship ties. "Modern social welfare has really to be thought
of as help given to the stranger, not to the person who by

reason of personal bond commands it without asking. It assumes a degree of social distance between helped and helper."[38]

2. The objective of social welfare is to help people solve their more serious problems and, more importantly, to develop the ability to solve their problems efficiently in future. The social welfare system aims at promoting personal well-being and helping people realize their capacities to the fullest, so that they may live reasonably satisfying lives, comfortable within themselves and in society. This help, rendered by specialists, is offered in a variety of forms: family counseling, public health services, public assistance, unemployment insurance, parks and playgrounds, child guidance, medical clinics, and many others.

STRUCTURE

Social welfare activities are conducted by two types of agencies: *public* and *private*. The first is tax-financed and carried on by federal, state, or local government personnel. The second is supported by private contributions and administered by specialists who are not paid out of tax funds. A public hospital that does not charge patients for care is an example of a public social welfare service. Family counseling services are usually conducted under private auspices, as are settlement house programs.

What is the difference between medical aid rendered by a public hospital and the services of a private physician in his office? Are they not both "social welfare" services? Of course, both presumably are in the public interest. And a private physician who gives some of his time to working without fee in a hospital is at that time engaging in a social welfare service. But the greater part of the professional activities of most physicians is conducted on an individual basis for profit, not as part of a formal and privately or publicly funded organization.

Among the distinguishing characteristics of the social welfare structure are the following:

1. Social welfare is formally organized into agencies, services, and programs. To illustrate this divisional structure, we will describe one type of social welfare service, *social work*, as differentiated from health services such as medicine, psychiatry, mental health, and public health. (Social work is often

carried on within a health service agency, however, as one part of the total program.)

Public social work agencies are organized at federal, state, and local levels. Law prescribes who shall exercise what authority, and levels of authority are specified. Hundreds of thousands of employees conduct the affairs of public agencies. In 1966, almost 7 billion dollars was expended on public assistance alone.[39] There were over 7½ million recipients of such aid in December 1966.[40]

Private agencies are also highly organized, with volunteer boards of directors responsible for policy, executives responsible for administration, and supervisory staffs in charge of field workers. Funds are usually raised jointly, on behalf of the private agencies in a given locality, by an organization such as the United Fund, which in 1966 allocated an estimated 625,549,000 dollars to agencies in the United States.[41]

Education for social work is professionalized. A master's degree from an accredited graduate school of social work is the optimum background for entrance to the field. In 1963, however, there were only fifty-eight such accredited schools in the United States, and they had a full-time student enrollment of less than 7,000 persons.[42] In the academic year 1962–1963, only 2,678 master's degrees were awarded by these schools.[43] This number represents only a fraction of the social workers needed for replacements alone, without regard to an expansion of services. Consequently, some agencies, especially in the public sector, are forced to employ persons who hold only a bachelor's degree.

Except for persons "blanketed in" before the present standard was established, individuals must have completed at least one year of graduate work in order to be eligible for membership in the professional organization, the National Association of Social Workers. In December 1964 this organization had an estimated 42,000 members,[44] and in 1965 there were approximately 125,000 social workers. Thus only about one-fifth of the members of this occupational group had the basic education that would qualify them as professional social workers.[45]

The social work field is subdivided into several specialties, including the following:

Child welfare services: Adoptions, foster home care, day care, and related activities.

Family social work: Counseling of families and individual members, homemaker services, and the like.

Protective and correctional services: Especially probation, parole, and institutional programs.

Group services: Particularly community centers and settlement houses and work with youth gangs.

Medical social work: Serving patients in medical hospitals in a team effort with doctor-nurse staff.

Psychiatric social work: In settings such as psychiatric clinics and hospitals for the mentally ill.

Public assistance: Financial aid to the indigent.

School social work: In the interest of pupils with education-related personal and family problems.

Military social work: Treatment of problems of servicemen.

Community planning and development: Securing, supporting, and coordinating community social services.

Within these several types of services three principal social work *methods* are employed, as outlined below. Some graduate centers, such as at the Smith College School for Social Work, emphasize training in a single method, whereas others, for example Columbia University's School of Social Work, provide "generic" training in all three methods, although most students concentrate in one of them. Social work agencies require personnel trained in one or more of the following methods:

Social casework: Essentially a one-to-one relationship between worker and client. Training in this area necessarily includes means of manipulating the environment in the client's interest. Principles and methods of modern psychiatry also make up part of the training program.

Social group work: A one-to-group relationship, the worker in relation with a group of individuals, such as a boys' club or patients in group therapy. Training in group work is apt to include the sociological and psychological aspects of "small groups" and their "dynamics."

Community organization: A one-to-community relationship in which the worker mobilizes support for needed social services and for their proper functioning and coordination. Here, training requires study of the economic, political, and social structure of the modern local community.

2. Social welfare services are undertaken in the public interest and are sanctioned within the society. The purposes

of the social services, and the methods employed, are generally approved, but as we shall see below, approval is not unanimous.

3. The profit motive is absent from social welfare undertakings. Some private agencies do charge modest fees for counseling, but this is largely for therapeutic purposes, on the theory that if a person pays for treatment he wants his money's worth and will be more apt to cooperate in the treatment process. No social agency takes in more than it spends, whether or not it charges fees.

4. All social welfare programs are oriented to human needs and bettering the human condition. Subsistence, health, safety, personality growth and development, enjoyment of cultural and recreational activities—these represent major goals of social welfare services.

HISTORY & TRENDS OF SOCIAL WELFARE

In historical perspective, the institutionalization of social welfare is a fairly recent development. The orientation of the evolving institution has gone through three stages since about 1850.

The first period was heavily influenced by Social Darwinism. Private philanthropists saw fit, in their benevolence, to pay for the support of indigent persons, who in their opinion were of two types. One was the individual who was unemployed because of physical or mental incapacity beyond his power of control. This view held that he should receive help—but sparingly, lest he learn to prefer a handout to a job. A second type of individual could support himself but did not—the drunkard, the lazy, vice-ridden fellow. He was considered to be a social inadequate, one of the most unfit in the struggle for existence. According to this view, society would be better off if he were not around to procreate and increase the generations of unfit, but humanity required that he be kept alive. Let him be fed, but sparingly, and at the same time let him be reminded that he is a lesser member of society.

Both types of indigency were ministered to by volunteers, "friendly visitors" with no special training, who often delivered moral lectures along with a Thanksgiving turkey and adjured the poor never to forget to be grateful to their benefactors.

The second stage in the evolution of social welfare began to emerge toward the very end of the nineteenth century, with the beginnings of the professionalization of social work. Private agencies were the dominant force, and public social services, established under the Poor Laws, were regarded with contempt by the new professionals, who looked upon public workers (not altogether without reason) as political hacks and incompetents. In the second stage, Social Darwinism declined (although it has not disappeared entirely even today), and greater emphasis was placed upon the humanitarian aspects of social work. There was greater recognition that most indigents would prefer to be self-supporting and that with few exceptions their indigence resulted from conditions beyond the power of any one individual to control.

Emphasis began being placed on the *prevention* of poverty and the *treatment* of personal problems of individuals. Handouts, such as a week's relief or a ton of coal, were necessary, but these were seen as stopgap means whereby life was sustained. The long-term aims of professional social workers came to be the improvement of societal conditions and the treatment of individuals so that they might thereafter be able to solve their own problems. During this period, private donors were as important as in the Social Darwinism era, but they were no longer viewed as philanthropists whose gifts were prompted by generosity alone, by religious morality, or similar reasons. Instead, they were regarded as fortunate individuals, blessed with wealth, who owed it to the less fortunate to contribute to their rehabilitation. It must have been this vintage of philanthropist whom Ambrose Bierce defined as "A rich (and usually bald) old gentleman who has trained himself to grin while his conscience is picking his pocket."

Social work was not the only facet of social welfare undergoing change. Government was assuming more responsibility for the health and general welfare of the citizens, entering such fields as public health and primitive forms of social insurance. Throughout the nineteenth century, this responsibility lay largely with local, not federal, government and was carried out through the establishment of almshouses, the indenture of orphans, and other means. The first state law authorizing pensions for the blind was adopted in 1898, the first statewide mother's pension law in 1911.

During the first quarter of the twentieth century, social welfare, in such areas as relief and income maintenance, remained overwhelmingly an undertaking of private agencies. When public funds were brought to bear on social problems, usually they were locally raised and administered. Except for a few efforts—in the Bureau of Indian Affairs and some services for seamen, for example—the United States government stayed out of the social welfare field. It adhered to the theory of President Franklin Pierce who, in vetoing a bill in 1854 that would have given federal land to the states for the erection of hospitals for the insane, expressed the conviction that federal aid to states would be a violation of the Constitution and state sovereignty. The Pierce veto remained the controlling doctrine in American social welfare until the dawn of the third historical period.

The latter did not, of course, emerge on a given day, and the earlier orientation was not entirely abandoned when the third phase was under way. The enactment of the institutionalization of social welfare in the United States took place in 1933, under President Franklin D. Roosevelt and his New Deal.

At this time, the nation was in its worst economic depression. Roosevelt's predecessor, Herbert Hoover, had staunchly supported the Pierce principle of no federal aid to the states. Unemployment stood at almost 13 million, a quarter of the civilian labor force. Banks were failing, agriculture was withering, and private social agencies had run out of money. Roosevelt set in motion a two-pronged program: emergency aid to the needy financed by federal aid to the states for unemployment relief; and long-term social security legislation to protect individuals and families against unemployment, decreased income upon retirement of the wage earner, and economic deprivation on the part of dependents of a deceased wage earner.

This program produced several highly significant changes in the social welfare system: (1) It established the principle of "universal provision," that government is responsible for the general welfare of all and must take necessary steps to provide a reasonable minimum of goods and services for every person in the land. (2) It led to the recruitment of thousands of public welfare workers and placed the heaviest share of the welfare load on their shoulders. (3) This development removed from private agencies the greater part of the responsibility for relief and income maintenance, which in turn reoriented private social services to a heightened interest in the psychological sphere and therefore in casework counseling and guidance.

By the end of the 1930s, social welfare was an established

institution, which would undergo many detailed changes in the years ahead but which would continue to evolve within the general orientation that had been enacted by the New Deal. Social welfare has become an undertaking by many for all members of society. It strengthens the institution of the family, contributes to the stability of the political and economic institutions, and therefore is now an important part of the larger social system.

Major trends in social welfare since the inception of the New Deal include the following:

1. Perhaps the most meaningful of all is the emphasis in social work thinking now placed upon the dignity of man, the uniqueness of human personality, and the need to respect every human being, whatever his station in life may be. The indigent are no longer considered social inadequates by the very fact of indigence, except by a minority who still attack Social Security and other welfare programs and are certain that they are bankrupting the nation and creating millions of "relief chiselers" and malingerers.

2. The so-called War on Poverty, originally projected by President Kennedy and enacted into law during the administration of President Johnson, is a logical extension of the philosophy of the New Deal and a further implementation of the objectives of the institution of social welfare.

3. Public expenditures for social welfare programs have mounted in the past half century, and not only because of the increased population and the devaluation of the dollar. The greater acceptance of the thesis that reasonable health and comfort must be provided for all supports such increased expenditures as the following: In 1913 we were spending only 15 *million* dollars on social insurances, such as widows' pensions; by 1963, we were spending over 25 *billion* dollars. In 1913, health and medical programs cost 150 *million* dollars; in 1963, we spent 5½ *billion* dollars for this purpose.[46] Medicare, a government program for defraying the costs of medical, hospital, and nursing care among the elderly, is a recent addition to the public social welfare services, its ultimate cost as yet undetermined.

4. Throughout its history, professional social work has had a comparatively "poor press," in very considerable measure because social work treatment is very difficult to explain in lay terms. Another important reason is that social workers have

for the most part and until most recently been as inept as school teachers (to say nothing of psychiatrists and sociologists) in educating the public to their aims and procedures. Partly because the public is uninformed or misinformed, partly because it is true to a considerable degree, laymen have criticized what they consider to be the overbureaucratization of welfare activities. Other criticism has been to the effect that social workers attempt to inculcate middle-class values in clients who are largely not of the middle class. This is undoubtedly the case, if for no other reason than that the bulk of practicing social workers are themselves members of the middle class and therefore to a degree "captives" of that culture.

A serious allegation made about social workers has been that they lack regard for clients' privacy and individual rights. This charge is unjustified with regard to most sectors of practice, notably casework counseling in private social agencies and in psychiatric and medical settings, where the individual's right to discuss or to decline to discuss personal matters is considered virtually absolute. However, the criticism is often warranted where public assistance as well as protective and correctional agencies are concerned. In some areas, for instance, public assistance workers are instructed to gain entrance to clients' homes late at night or just before dawn in order to determine whether a widow, deserted wife, or unwed mother has a "man assuming role of spouse" living on the premises. But this policy, enunciated by local officials, often under pressure from the community to "get rid of relief chiselers," is almost without exception condemned by professional social workers.

5. The climate of the times, with its often militant emphasis on abolishing poverty and gaining for every individual his full measure of civil rights, has had much to do with the emergence of a new trend in social welfare—the welfare rights movement. In various sections of the country, poor people of all ethnic backgrounds have banded together to inform themselves on their legal right to public assistance. They have mobilized themselves to fight for those rights on the premise that Social Security enactments have defined eligibility for assistance. A person eligible for aid by law has a *right* to it, according to the argument. It is not a *privilege*, to be extended or not at the will of a bureaucrat.

This movement, still in its formative stage, meets with ambivalent reactions in the social welfare field, although indications (gained from official social work publications) are that professional social workers regard it as a healthy program on the whole, promising benefits to clients and the general public alike.

6. An even more recent development than the welfare rights movement has been the proposal, originally advanced from outside the social work field, that government replace public assistance and some facets of the social insurance program (such as unemployment benefits) by a national plan providing a guaranteed annual income to every family in the United States. Presumably, the plan would call for making up the difference, where one existed, between what members of the family earned and the minimum annual income provided in law. Advocates of the program argue that this would eliminate poverty, encourage people to work rather than depend upon public assistance, and eventually wipe out "relief," which many people persist in thinking of as a "dole" that encourages idleness.

The benefits of such a program might prove to be great, but there are hazards, too, unless preventive measures are built into a guaranteed annual income system. Over a century ago, England instituted an "allowance system" whereby Poor Law monies made up the difference between what a family needed for bare subsistence and what it earned in private employment. The system was abandoned because it virtually wrecked wage scales. Employers hired indigents at wages far below what they had been offering, on the argument: "What do you care? You'll get additional money from the government."

But the United States now has minimum wage standards established by law. It is probably possible to enforce a guaranteed annual income law that will provide against lowering wages generally. In this belief the official position taken by organizations representing social workers has been highly favorable to the idea of a stipulated guaranteed annual income.

In 1925, the president of the National Association of Manufacturers was able to tell a presumably approving audience that government intervention in the affairs of private individuals was evil. "Listen," he said, "to the strange philosophies of the living wage, the check-off system, the minimum wage, government controlled children, the closed union shop, and the socialistic redistribution of wealth."[47] Attack such satanic ideas, he advised. Such views are still held today by a proportion of the citizenry, but the institutionalization of social welfare in the United States is attested to by the fact that only occasionally will an advocate of such ideas speak out publicly, and then the consensus is usually against him.

· NOTES

1. Leopold Pospisil, *The Kapakau Papuans of West New Guinea* (New York: Holt, Rinehart and Winston, 1963), p. 18.
2. *Ibid.*, p. 22.
3. *Ibid.*, p. 26.
4. *Ibid.*, p. 29.
5. Wilbert E. Moore, *Industrialization and Labor: Social Aspects of Economic Development* (Ithaca, N. Y.: Cornell University Press, 1951), p. 182.
6. David Dressler, "The Semantics of Social Work," in Marjorie Bell (ed.), *Social Correctives for Delinquency*, Yearbook, National Probation Association, 1945 (New York: National Probation Association, 1946), pp. 217–235.
7. Emile Durkheim, *The Division of Labor in Society* (New York: Free Press, 1947).
8. *Ibid.*, preface to second edition.
9. Peter J. Drucker, "The Employee Society," *American Journal of Sociology*, LVIII (January 1953), 358–363.
10. *Ibid.*
11. *Ibid.*
12. *Ibid.*
13. *Ibid.*
14. *Ibid.*
15. William H. Whyte, Jr., *The Organization Man* (New York: Anchor Books, 1956), p. 3.
16. William H. Whyte, Jr., "The Outgoing Life," *Fortune*, XLVIII, 1 (July 1953), 84–88, 156–160.
17. Whyte, *The Organization Man, op. cit.*
18. U. S. Department of Labor, *Manpower, Challenge of the 1960s* (Washington, D. C.: U. S. Government Printing Office, 1960), p. 5.
19. *Ibid.*, p. 7.
20. *Ibid.*, p. 8.
21. Ralph Linton, *The Study of Man* (New York: Appleton-Century-Crofts, 1936), p. 227.
22. Manning Nash, *The Golden Road to Modernity, Village Life in Contemporary Burma* (New York: Wiley, 1965), p. 74.
23. Robert M. MacIver and Charles H. Page, *Society: An Introductory Analysis* (New York: Rinehart, 1949), pp. 458–463.
24. C. Wright Mills, *The Power Elite* (New York: Oxford University Press, 1956).
25. Nelson W. Polsby, *Community Power and Political Theory* (New Haven: Yale University Press, 1963).

26. Robert A. Dahl, *Who Governs?* (New Haven: Yale University Press, 1961).

27. David Riesman, with Nathan Glazer and Reuel Denny, *The Lonely Crowd* (New York: Anchor Books, 1955).

28. Seymour M. Lipset, *Political Man* (New York: Doubleday, 1959), p. 221.

29. U. S. Bureau of the Census, *Statistical Abstract of the United States, 1967*, 88th annual ed. (Washington, D. C.: U. S. Government Printing Office, 1967), p. 439, Table No. 606.

30. Isaac Asimov, *The Intelligent Man's Guide to Science*, Vol. I (New York: Basic Books, 1960), p. 3.

31. Robert K. Merton, *Social Theory and Social Structure*, rev. ed. (New York: Free Press, 1957), pp. 608–609.

32. *Ibid.*, p. 626.

33. Joseph Ben-David, "Scientific Productivity and Academic Organization in Nineteenth Century Medicine," *American Sociological Review*, XXV (December 1960), 828–843.

34. Gerard DeGré, *Science as a Social Institution* (New York: Random House, 1955), p. 3.

35. *Ibid.*, p. 22.

36. *Ibid.*, pp. 30–31.

37. *Ibid.*, p. 12.

38. Harold L. Wilensky and Charles N. Lebeaux, *Industrial Society and Social Welfare* (New York: Russell Sage Foundation, 1958), p. 141.

39. U. S. Bureau of the Census, *Statistical Abstract of the United States, 1967*, 88th annual ed. (Washington, D. C.: U. S. Government Printing Office, 1967), p. 283, Table No. 401.

40. *Ibid.*, p. 305, Table No. 434.

41. *Ibid.*, p. 311, Table No. 445.

42. Harry L. Lurie (ed.), *Encyclopedia of Social Work* (New York: National Association of Social Workers, 1965), p. 898, Table 42.

43. *Ibid.*, p. 898, Table 43.

44. *Ibid.*, p. 899, Table 45.

45. *Ibid.*, p. 532.

46. *Ibid.*, p. 873, adapted from Table 16.

47. Arthur M. Schlesinger, Jr., *The Age of Roosevelt*, Vol. I, *The Crisis of the Old Order, 1919–1933* (Boston: Houghton Mifflin, 1957), p. 72.

· SUGGESTIONS FOR FURTHER READING

American Association for the Advancement of Science Committee on Science in the Promotion of Human Welfare, "Science and Human Welfare." *Science*, CXXXII (July 8, 1960), 68–73.
A group of scientists discuss problems resulting from the recent radical changes in their field. Implications for the social role of the scientist are also considered.

BELL, DANIEL (ed.). *The Radical Right*. New York: Anchor Books, 1964.

A collection of articles on ultra-conservative movements in the United States.

GALBRAITH, JOHN KENNETH. *The Affluent Society*. Boston: Houghton Mifflin, 1958.

A provocative examination of economic and other social problems in a society of abundance.

KORNHAUSER, ARTHUR. "Public Opinion and Social Class." *American Journal of Sociology*, LV (January 1950), 333–345.

A study of the relation of a person's class position to his political opinion.

LAZARSFELD, PAUL F., BERNARD BERELSON, and HAZEL GAUDET. *The People's Choice*. New York: Duell, Sloan and Pearce, 1949.

This is one of the best known studies of voting behavior, especially of conditions under which people change their political opinions.

LUBOVE, ROY. *The Professional Altruist*. Cambridge, Mass.: Harvard University Press, 1965.

A history of the emergence of social work as a profession.

LUNDBERG, GEORGE A. *Can Science Save Us?* New York: Longmans, Green, 1947.

Addresses itself to the question whether the scientific method, applied to all social problems, represents our greatest hope of achieving a better society.

MACIVER, ROBERT M. *The Web of Government*. New York: Macmillan, 1947.

A distinguished sociologist discusses the theoretical bases of modern government.

MILLER, WALTER B. "Implications of Urban Lower-class Cultures for Social Work." *Social Service Review*, XXXIII (September 1959), 219–237.

An examination of the problems faced by middle class social workers who undertake to serve lower class clients.

WALTER, CHARLES H. *Toward the Automatic Factory*. New Haven, Conn.: Yale University Press, 1957.

This is a case study of what happens to steel mill workers when automation is introduced.

part seven
a final word

28 WHAT HAS THE STUDY OF SOCIOLOGY DONE FOR YOU?

Let us take a final look at the mythical Professor Grimm, whom you met quite some time back. Completing the semester's work, he devotes the final class session to review and discussion of questions raised by students.

Mary Holden asks timorously: "Do you expect us to remember all those population statistics in the book?"

"Of course not!" Grimm replies, in an even tone of voice. "I thought I'd make it clear that I hope you learn a *point of view* in this class, not an assortment of undigested facts. Do you know what I mean by a point of view, Miss Holden?"

"Well, I suppose you mean. . . . That is, I guess. . . ."

John Smith raises his hand.

"Ah! Mr. Smith? All right! What is a point of view?"

John says earnestly. "Now me, when I first came into this class, I had a lot of silly notions."

"Notions?" Grimm inquires.

"Yes, sir. Prejudices, dizzy ideas, unreal notions. I . . . before I started thinking about these things I was pretty mixed up, you know? About things like right and wrong, reasonable and unreasonable. I think I even had a little prejudice against Jews, until I came into this class."

"Until you started studying sociology, or until you met a certain young lady?"

"Well-l-l. Anyhow . . . ," John stammers. The other students roar.

"And now you don't have any value judgments?" Grimm asks.

"No, sir!" John says.

"Then I'm sincerely sorry for you. It must be most unrewarding to live and die like a vegetable."

"Oh, I didn't mean it like that . . . quite."

"What I've been trying to say all semester is this: Enter into any study with an open mind. Form whatever value judgments you please, but *know why*. I hope you will take vigorous stands on some of the issues of your time. I am passionately devoted to some causes. I hate certain conditions. But I try to form my value judgments with understanding and with as much objectivity as the human animal is capable of bringing to bear on a subject. So your first comment was appropriate, Mr. Smith. You developed a more consistent point of view, you imply. It is my hope each of you leaves this class with an objective *point of view*, an open, receptive inquisitive mind. Values are arrived at objectively and subjectively. But *truth* must be objectively derived. Of course we can never learn more than a fragment of the truth. I am forced to be objectively candid and confess I have not yet met the omniscient, intellectual giant who knows what truth is in a final and absolute sense, and I fervently hope I never shall."

Ronnie Palmer, known as a "brain" and something of an iconoclast among his colleagues, breaks in: "That's all well and good, Professor Grimm, but I had an open, receptive mind when I came into this class. I was eager to learn something of practical value. But now that I've been exposed to the principles of sociology, my question is—*so what?* What does sociology have to do with the real world I'm going to live in?"

Silence pervades the room.

"So what?" Grimm repeats, deliberately. "It's a good question, Mr. Palmer, but one that no teacher can answer directly. You live and work, you struggle and strive, you marry and raise children. *So what?* The answer depends on your values, Mr. Palmer. What do you want from life?"

"Well, I'll tell you what's really bothering me, sir," Ronnie responds. "Most of my study has been in literature. I enrolled in this class expecting to learn what sociologists propose to do about war and peace, crime and punishment, and my own social adjustment. But you never answer the important questions directly. You always say 'it depends upon' or 'it is relative to' or 'we don't have any conclusive studies, we only know that there are many factors involved and we haven't been able to measure their relative influence.' If that's all sociology has to offer, what's it good for?"

Grimm runs a hand over his face, smiles gently. "I really didn't intend to lecture today," he begins. "But Mr. Palmer inspires me. Let's consider his question in long-range perspective. Four hundred years ago the pioneer astronomers were contemptuously dubbed 'star-gazers.' Their work was regarded as the most futile of human endeavors. Yet the technology of navigation was immeasurably improved by the science of 'stargazing.' No one can even begin to estimate how many thousands of sailors have avoided watery graves as a consequence of the efforts of astronomers.

"Today sociology has arrived at about the same stage of development as that which the infant science of astronomy reached four centuries ago. People ask: 'What value does it have?' I'm tempted to counter with another question: What is the value of a baby? Sociology is just getting out of infancy. Those of us involved in sociological research believe that people will eventually be able to navigate the seas of social interaction with greater assurance as a result of the scientific study of human behavior. This is the long-range objective of sociology."

"So where will you and I be four hundred years from now?" Ronnie asks. "We're living now. I'd like to know how sociology is useful to me, *here* and *now*."

"Don't be impatient, Mr. Palmer. I'm coming to that. I firmly believe that what you learned *can* and *will* be valuable to you, *here* and *now*. Whether you realize it or not, your brief excursion into sociology enables you to get along more effectively with other people. Already you should have greater tolerance for the beliefs and behavior of others, if you recognize that everyone is what he has learned to be in his society. That is a basic principle of sociology. I think you've learned it well.

"In this same train of thought, you probably realize now the fallacy of thinking that your world is categorically inhabited by good and bad people, with a broad expanse of no-man's land separating the virtuous from the vicious. You should now see that your own judgments about right and wrong were learned from others, and that the behavior you judge as right or wrong was also produced by social forces.

"Furthermore, I think this course will have immediate value if it has introduced into your thinking some measure of caution about the cure-all panaceas that are continuously being proposed to settle the world's problems. I thought that you had all learned there are no easy, simple solutions for any of our problems, but you, Mr. Palmer, still seem to be involved in that search.

"Finally, since you live in a world where science is almost a religious cult, I think it will be most useful to you to be able to make some distinctions between your beliefs, which are based on faith, and your knowledge, which is founded on fact —at least fact as we understand it as of this minute. Please don't misconstrue that statement. I don't want anyone to leave here thinking, 'That old codger, Grimm, is trying to wean me away from my beliefs.' I believe you have a sacred right to your beliefs, but you should be able to distinguish between them and factual knowledge. If you have learned to make this distinction, you will be able to think, talk, and act more effectively in meeting the problems of your lives.

"If you have acquired these ideas from your study of sociology, you can and will apply them in a useful way here and now. That includes you too, Mr. Palmer.

"Well, I see we've exhausted our time, so from this moment on we go our separate ways and cease to be a group. But this shouldn't finish your work in sociology. Even though you may not enroll in another class, it's my sincere hope that all of you think of this course as the beginning rather than the end of your study of human interaction."

INDEX

Crowds
  acting, 326–31
  audiences distinguished from, 331–4
  casual relationships in, 330
  dancing, 325–6
  defined, 324–5
  expressive, 325–6
  individual anonymity in, 331
  interaction within, 325
  loose internal controls of, 331
  orgiastic, 325–6
  spontaneous leadership of, 330
  temporary nature of, 329
  unorganized nature of, 331
  see also Mobs
CUBER, JOHN F., 693
Cults, 667–8
Cultural borrowing, 57–8, 149–152
  defined, 149
  examples of, 149–52
  selectivity in, 152
Cultural change, 56–7, 139–58
  consequences of, 155–8
  crisis produces, 148
  cultural continuity and, 128
  cumulative effect of, 148
  defined, 141
  discontinuance of culture patterns and, 155
  discovery and, 154–5
  ethnocentrism inhibits, 134–8
  examples of, 139–40
  forced, 147–8
  homogeneity in, 142
  invention and, 152–4
  processes of, 148–55
  relativity of, 144–6
  resistance to, reasons for, 129, 132–8
  retention of traditional culture in, 142–3
  selectivity in, 141–2
  self-generating nature of, 148
  socially acquired needs produce, 146–7
  social values threatened by, 134
  special interest groups oppose, 134
  superimposed on existing culture, 144
  survival dictates, 146–7
  see also Cultural continuity
Cultural conservation
  see Cultural change; Cultural continuity
Cultural continuity, 56, 127–39
  and cultural change, 128
  defined, 128, 129
  examples of, 127–32
  readaptation promotes, 133–4
  reasons for, 129, 132–8
  see also Cultural change
Cultural diffusion, see Cultural borrowing

Cultural lag, 138–9
Cultural patterns, discontinuance of, 154
Cultural persistence, see Cultural continuity
Cultural regions, 422
Cultural values and attitudes, see Values and attitudes
Culture
  characteristics of, 54–60
  components of, 61–3
  defined, 44–6
  differentiated from society, 46–7, 64–5
  functions of, 60–1
  ideological system, 61–3
  individual differences within, 58–9
  inescapability from, 59–60
  material, 55–6
  mental health problems and, 596–9
  nonmaterial, 55–6
  objective view of, 47
  organizational system, 61–3
  personality and, 207–8
  power over individual of, 83–88
  as regulator of behavior, 87–88
  relativity of, 63–4
  subculture, 59
  technological system, 61–3
  as unique to man, 55
  variability of, 56
Culture, internalization of, see Socialization
Culture bound, 87–8
CUMMING, ELAINE, 593
Custom
  degree of freeedom permitted by, 121
  imprecision of, 121–2
  law distinguished from, 119–124
  static nature of, 120–1

DAHL, ROBERT A., 738
DARROW, CLARENCE, 677
DARWIN, CHARLES, 51, 428, 446, 677
Dating, 632–3
DA VINCI, LEONARDO, 197
DAVIS, KINGSLEY, 55, 169, 170, 186, 347–8, 489, 500
Death rates, 487–91, figure, 491, table, 488
  crude, 487–8
Decentralization in urban areas, 414–21, 434
  cities and, 418–21
  metropolitan communities and, 416–18
  suburbs and, 418–21
  urban fringe and, 418–19
DEGRE, GERARD, 744–6
Democracy, 737–40

Demographer, defined, 481
Dependent variables, 33–4
  defined, 29–30
DERODE-VERSCHOOR, I. H. PH., 477
Design, experimental, 29–30
Deviance, 238–42, 472–3
  alienation, 248–50
  anomie, 250–1
  approved forms of, 244–5
  by choice, 244
  classification of, 244–6
  and contradictory norms, 246–8
  defined, 240
  degree of, 240–2
  direction of, 240
  disapproved forms of, 244–245
  group, 244–6
  individual-centered, 246
  maladjustment distinguished from, 238–40
  patterns of, 252
  tolerance of, 242–4
  uncontrollable, 244
  see also Nonconformity
Dictatorship, 737
Diesel engine, economic effects of, 157–8
Differential association, theory of (Sutherland), 570
Discovery, process of, 154–5
Discrimination
  defined, 514–16
  see also Prejudice and discrimination
Dissociation, 231–2
Distribution, 719
Divine right of kings, concept of, 736
Divorce, 636–41
  changing attitudes toward, 650
DOBRINER, WILLIAM M., 419
DOUGLAS, WILLIAM, 475
DRESSLER, DAVID, 727
Dropouts, 713–15
DRUCKER, PETER J., 729–30
Drug use, 580–5
  addictive, 580–3
    effects of, 581
    extent of, 581
    motives for, 581–2
    treatment for, 582–3
    society affected by, 580–1
  habituating, 503–4
  legal solutions for, 584–5
  nonaddictive, 584
DUNCAN, OTIS D., 420
DURKHEIM, EMILE, 413, 473, 682, 728–9
Dysfunction, defined, 379

Ecology
  defined, 428
  see also Human ecology

Institutions (*Contd.*)
    long-range needs satisfied by,
        610–11
    misconceptions about, 614–16
    organizational structure of,
        613–14
    as organized forms of pro-
        cedure, 608–10
    physical equipment distin-
        guished from, 615
    social problems and, 614
    institutional systems, institu-
        tional units distinguished
        from, 611
    see also Economic institution;
        Education; Family; Po-
        litical institutions; Re-
        ligion; Science
Intelligence
    defined, 212
    personality and, 212–14
    tests, 213–14
Interaction, 7–8
    accommodation process, 454–
        455
    assimilation process, 455–7
    behavioral dimension of,
        441–2
    competition process, 445–50,
        453–4, 459
    conflict process, 450–4, 459
    cooperation process, 443–5,
        453–4, 458–9
    defined, 441
    examples of, 440–1
    familiarity dimension of,
        442–3
    functional dimension of, 441
    intensity of, cultural varia-
        tions in, 457–8
    nature of, cultural variations
        in, 457–8
    numerical dimension of, 442
    primary processes of, 443–54
    secondary processes of, 454–7
    spatial dimension of, 442
    status dimension of, 443
    temporal dimension of, 442
Internationalism, 501–2
Intra-Uterine Devices (IUD),
    500
Invention, 152–4
Isolationism, 501–3
Israel, 512–13

JAHODA, MARIE, 529
JANOWITZ, MORRIS, 541
Jews, 455
    see also Prejudice and dis-
        crimination
John Birch Society, 397
JOHNSON, HUGH, 323
JOHNSON, LYNDON BAINES, 561
JOHNSON, SAMUEL, 346, 587
JONASSEN, CHRISTEN T., 510
Judaism, birth control and,
    642–3

Juvenile delinquency, 245–6,
    431, 565–74
    agencies dealing with, 572
    causes of, 569–72
    comic books and, 570
    courts and, 572–3
    differential association, theory
        of, and, 570
    extent of, 565–9
    police forces and, 572, 573
    programs for combating, 573,
        574
    reformatories and, 572–4
    role conflict as cause of,
        368
    social class and, 570–2
    social work and, 573, 574
    solutions for, 572–4

KAPLAN, ABRAHAM, 288
KENKEL, WILLIAM F., 693
KENNEDY, JOHN F., 268, 365,
    599
Kibbutz, 403–4
KING, MARTIN LUTHER, JR., 521,
    527, 537
KINSEY, ALFRED CHARLES, 11,
    98, 645
KIPLING, RUDYARD, 512
KLUCKHOHN, CLYDE, 64, 133
Know-Nothing party, 522
KOLB, WILSON L., 65
KOMAROVSKY, MIRRA, 364–5
KORBER, GEORGE W., 47, 390, 393
KORNHAUSER, WILLIAM, 318–23
KROPOTKIN, PETER, 444
Ku Klux Klan, 522, 541

Labor, defined, 719
Land, defined, 719
LANG, GLADYS ENGEL, 315
LANGAN, KURT, 315
Language
    and cultural transmissions,
        178
    defined, 172
    and recording of human ex-
        perience, 177
    social control exercised
        through, 178–9
    as social phenomenon, 177
    symbols as reflection of at-
        titudes, 178
    and thinking, 177
    as unique to humans, 168
LAPIERE, RICHARD T., 61–2, 69,
    173, 511
Large-scale organizations
    bureaucracy and, 296–301
    nature of, 295–6
    see also Bureaucracy
LASSWELL, HAROLD D., 288
Law, 119–24
    changeability of, 120–1
    coercive authority of, 121
    common, 123–4

Law (*Contd.*)
    custom distinguished from,
        119–24
    defined, 27
    and emotions, regulation of,
        122–3
    folkways in conflict with, 123
    in effective areas of, 122–3
    precision of, 121–2
    private settlement of disputes
        prohibited by, 120
    religion, clashes with, 674–5
    universal applicability of, 121
Learning
    individual variations in, 183–
        185
    nature of, 179–83
    of social behavior, 179–83
    obstacles to, 185–7
    socialization and, 187–90
LE BON, GUSTAV, 324
LEE, ALFRED MC CLUNG, 707
LERNER, DANIEL, 475
Life expectancy, 488–91, 585,
    figure, 491
LINCOLN, ABRAHAM, 522
LINNAEUS, 511
LINTON, RALPH, 46–7, 62, 149–
    150, 154–5, 370–3, 622–
    623, 629, 734
LIPSET, S. M., 396–7
Logic, scientific method and,
    8–15
LONG, HUEY, 322–3
LSD, 584
LYNCH, CONNIE, 508, 513, 514
Lynching, 328–9, 527
LYND, ROBERT S., and HELEN
    M., 139

MAC IVER, ROBERT M., 69, 94,
    97, 111, 119, 187, 250,
    275, 279, 295, 409, 423,
    514, 516, 523, 536, 539–
    540, 608, 735, 761
MC KELLAR, KENNETH, 322
MC KENZIE, RODERICK D., 428,
    429
Maladjustment
    case study, 221–3
    deviance distinguished from,
        238–40
    as socially defined, 226–8
    see also Adjustment; Unad-
        justment
MALTHUS, THOMAS ROBERT, 428,
    456–8
MARCUS, STEVEN, 644
"Marginal man," 104
Marijuana, 583–4
Marriage, 635–6
    changing role of, 646–8
    earlier, trend toward, 646
    husband, changing role of,
        646–8
    successful, conditions for,
        638–41
    see also Family

MARX, KARL, 556, 560, 724
Mass media
  audience, 335–8
  communicator, 336
  defined, 334
  extent of, 334–5
  fixed nature of, 337
  impact of, 335
  message, nature of, 336
  new experiences via, 337
  propaganda and, 342–6
  public opinion and, 338–42
  research on, 336–8
  sex factor in use of, 337–8
  use of, degree of, 338
  see also Propaganda; Public opinion
Mass politics, 318–24
  see also Political institutions
Mass society
  audiences, 331–4
  authoritarianism and, 321–4
  conditions of, 315–18
  crowds, 324-31
  defined, 312
  emergence of, 314–15
  fads and, 346–8
  fashion and, 348–50
  functional interdependence in, 315–17
  intermediate social relations in, 320
  mass
    anonymity of, 311
    characteristics of, 310–12
    disunited nature of, 311–12
    individual needs determine behavior in, 311
    influence of, 312
    mass behavior, defined, 311
    nonrestricted membership in, 311
    physical proximity, lack of, 311
    unorganized nature of, 310–11
  mass media, 334–46
  nature of, 312–14
  negative features of, 317–18
  participation, lack of, 317–18
  positive features of, 318
  social change and, 317
  totalitarianism and, 320–4
  see also Crowds; Mass media
Mate selection, 634–5
Matrilineal descent, 630
Matrilocal family, 630
MATZA, DAVID, 246
MAY, MARK, 447–8
MEAD, GEORGE HERBERT, 174, 200–3, 204, 219
Medicare, 561
Men, changing role of, 646–8
Mental conflict, concept of, 217–18
Mental illness, 595–6
  aging and, 587, 594
  defined, 236

Mental illness (Contd.)
  extent of, 595–6
  historical background, 596
  role conflict causes, 368–9
  role transitions and, 597
  schizophrenia, 596–8
  social class and, 597–8
  social complexity and, 596–7
  solutions for, 598–9
  status, drive for, and, 597
  see also Psychiatry
MERTON, ROBERT K., 247–8, 303, 361, 470, 472, 543–6, 598, 617, 743
Metalaw, 427–8
Metropolitan communities, decentralization and, 416–418
  defined, 416
MILLER, ARTHUR, 332
MILLER, WALTER B., 571–2
MILLS, C. WRIGHT, 389, 737, 738
MINNEGERODE, MEADE, 92
Minority, defined, 516–17
Mobility, see Social mobility
Mobs, 326–9
  consequences of behavior disregarded by, 329
  explosiveness of, 328–9
  leadership, spontaneous emergence of, 329
  tension and, 327–8
Monarchy, 737
Monogamy, 629–30
MONTAIGNE, MICHEL DE, 86
MOORE, WILBERT E., 442, 725
Morality, relativity of, 63–4
Mores, see Folkways and mores
MORRIS, JAMES R., 588
Movies, public opinion and, 341–2
MULLIGAN, R. A., 709
Multiple nuclei theory, 435, figure, 437
Muslims, 538
MYERS, RICHARD R., 468, 469
MYRDAL, GUNNAR, 516, 542–4, 562

Narcotics, see Drug use
Narcotics Anonymous, 582–3
NASH, MANNING, 373, 664
National Committee for Mental Hygiene, 596
National communities, 423–6
Nationality, race distinguished from, 518
Natural regions, 422
Negroes, 226–7, 384–5, 400–1, 420–1, 450, 471–2, 554, 558, 585, 656, 672, 740–1
  see also Prejudice and discrimination
New Deal, 755–6
Newspapers, public opinion and, 340–1
NIMKOFF, M. F., 154

NI NI GYI, 144–6
NISBET, ROBERT A., 318, 470, 472, 598
Nonconformity, 189–90, 690, 715
  approval of, 105
  function of, 107–9
  see also Conformity; Deviance; Normative controls, resistance to
Nonelites, 319-24
Nonviolence, 537
Normality, deviance from, 239–240
Normative controls, resistance to, 98–105
  conflicting norms cause, 103–104
  cultural hybridization causes, 104
  lack of internalization causes, 101–3
  nonconformity, limits of, 99–100
  norm confusion causes, 104–105
  organic drives create, 101
  rejection of norms, 101–3
  subcultures, 101
  under pressure, 100
Normative system of society, defined, 93
Normlessness, 250
Norms, see Social norms
Nudism, 141

Objectivity, subjectivity and, 5–6
Occupational prestige
  international correlations, table, 355
  national correlations, table, 356
O'DEA, THOMAS F., 659
OGBURN, WILLIAM F., 138–9, 153–4, 155
"Open-class" societies, 394, 397–8
Organization of groups, 273–4
Organizations, see Formal organizations; Large-scale organizations
OSBORN, FAIRFIELD, 481–3
Outer space, exploration of, 427–8, 476–8
Out-groups, 136, 267–70
Overpopulation
  abortion and, 501
  acquired values and, 505
  birth control and, 500–1
  defining, 481–3, 504–5
  isolationist vs. internationalist policy and, 501–3
  Malthus, Thomas Robert, on, 496–8
  Mexico, 486–7
  optimistic views on, 499–501

Overpopulation (*Contd.*)
pessimistic views on, 498–9
Rabbit Island as example of, 480–1
sociologists' view of, 503–4
South America, 486–7
statistics, accuracy of, 483
United States, 485–6, *figure,* 486
voluntary sterilization, 500–1

PAGE, CHARLES H., 69, 94, 97, 111, 119, 187, 275, 279, 295, 304, 305–6, 409, 423, 608, 735
PAINE, TOM, 695
PARK, ROBERT E., 104, 428
PARKS, ROSA, 527
Patrilineal descent, 630
Patrilocal family, 630
PAVLOV, IVAN PETROVICH, 179–180
Permitted behavior, 117–19
Personality
adjustment and, 234–5
anatomical structure and, 211–12
biogenic factors and, 208–214
bureaucracy and, 361
culture and, 207–8
genetic theory of, 219
instincts and, 209
intelligence and, 212–14
nature of, 206–8
physiological structure and, 210–11
psychogenic factors and, 214–19
reflexes and, 209–10
social roles and, 361–3
society and, 208
sociogenic factors and, 219
see also Learning; Self
Philadelphia, social class in, 387–8
Physical mobility, 397
PIERCE, FRANKLIN, 755
PIERCE, JOE E., 66, 592
Planned parenthood, *see* Birth control
PLUNKITT, GEORGE WASHINGTON, 361–3
Political institutions, 733–42
behavior norms enforced by, 734–5
class voting trends, 741
coercion as prerogative of, 736
democracy, 737–40
dictatorship, 737
elitist power structure, 737–8
ethnic votes, trends in, 740–1
female vote, trends in, 741
functions of, 734–6
geographical boundaries limit, 736

Political institutions (*Contd.*)
government regulation, 742
graft, 739–40
law and order and, 734–5
lobbies, 742
monarchy, 737
pluralistic power structure, 737–8
professionals in, 742
protective function of, 735
public employees, number of, 742
representation, government by, 739–40
structure of, 736–40
trends in, 740–2
two-party system, 738–40
urbanization, participation and, 741
welfare of society and, 735
welfare state, trend toward, 742
see also Mass politics
POLSBY, NELSON W., 737–8
Polyandry, 629
Polygamy, 629–30
Polygyny, 629–30
Population
birth rates, crude, 487–8, *table,* 488
death rates, crude, 487–8, *table,* 488
defined, 35
density, 491–6, *figure,* 492–3, *table,* 494
world population, 483–5, *table,* 485
see also Overpopulation
PORTER, COLE, 541
PORTERFIELD, AUSTIN, 239
Position in society, 354–5
see also Status
POSPISIL, LEOPOLD, 721
Poverty
automation produces, 557–8
capitalism and, 556–7
causes of, 554–8
culture of, 559
defined, 550
deprivation distinguished from, 553
education and, 554, 558
existence of, 549–50
extent of, 552–3
female family head and, 554
historical background of, 555–6
legislative solutions for, 560–562
Marxist solution for, 560
nature of, 550–1
pockets of, 554
political organization as solution for, 561–2
poor, identity of, 553–5, *figure,* 555
redistribution of wealth and, 560–1

Poverty (*Contd.*)
shifting centers of population produce, 557
shiftlessness and, 555–6, 559–60
shutdowns produce, 557
skin color and, 554
solutions for, 559–62
technical innovations produce, 557
underemployment and, 554
urbanization produces, 558
POWDERMAKER, HORTENSE, 131, 141
Preferred behavior, 117–19
Prejudice and discrimination, 80
amelioration and, 535–6
causes of, 527–35
competition and, 523–4
conflict and, 526–7
as cultural product, 533
defined, 513–16
economic needs and, 532
educational solutions for, 536
ethnic group, defined, 520–1
evolutionary solution for, 535–7
examples of, 508–9
extent of, 523–7
historical background of, 509–13, 522–3
housing and, 524–6
legislative solutions for, 535–536
minority, defined, 516–17
nature of, 523–7
nonviolent tactics as solution for, 537
opinion differences about, 521–2
personality factors and, 529–532
race, defined, 517–18
racial differences, 518–20
revolutionary solutions for, 537–40
segregation, 524–6
social changes regarding, 540–6
as social phenomenon, 532–533
sociologist's proposals for, 539–40
solutions for, 535–9
status needs and, 532
stereotypes abet, 533–5
typology of, 544–6
in United States, 521–46
Viking *Rigsthula* as example of, 509–10
violence as solution for, 537–539
white superiority, origins of, 509–12
Prestige of occupations
international correlations, *table,* 355

776 · INDEX

about the author

DAVID DRESSLER is Professor of Sociology and Social Welfare at California State College at Long Beach, where he has taught since 1953. He received his bachelor's degree from the University of Chicago, the master's degree from Columbia University, and the doctor's degree from New York University. In a distinguished and varied career, Dr. Dressler has also worked in the fields of social work and corrections. He was Executive Director of the New York State Division of Parole and has been a consultant on corrections to many states and foreign countries.

Among Professor Dressler's published books are *Probation and Parole* (1951), *Parole Chief* (1951), *Practice and Theory of Probation and Parole* (1959), and *Readings in Criminology and Penology* (1964). He has also published approximately two hundred articles in both professional and popular journals.

In SOCIOLOGY: THE STUDY OF HUMAN INTERACTION Dr. Dressler combines his scholarship in sociology with his talent as a writer.